CATCHING UP WITH THE COMPUTER REVOLUTION

HARVARD BUSINESS REVIEW EXECUTIVE BOOK SERIES

Executive Success: Making It in Management

Survival Strategies for American Industry

Managing Effectively in the World Marketplace

Strategic Management

Financial Management

Catching Up with the Computer Revolution

Marketing Management

Using Logical Techniques for Making Better Decisions

CATCHING UP WITH THE COMPUTER REVOLUTION

LYNN M. SALERNO
Editor

116839

JOHN WILEY & SONS INC.

New York • Chichester • Brisbane • Toronto • Singapore

Library of Congress Cataloging in Publication Data:

Main entry under Title:

Catching up with the computer revolution.

  (Harvard Business Review Executive Book Series)
  Includes indexes.
  1. Business—Data processing—Addresses, essays,
lectures. 2. Information storage and retrieval systems
—Business—Addresses, essays, lectures. 3. Manage-
ment information systems—Addresses, essays, lectures.
I. Salerno, Lynn M.   II. Series.
HF5548.2.C37   1983   658'.054   82-21899
ISBN 0-471-87594-5

Printed in the United States of America

10 9 8 7 6 5 4 3 2 1

Foreword

For sixty years the *Harvard Business Review* has been the farthest reaching executive program of the Harvard Business School. It is devoted to the continuing education of executives and aspiring managers primarily in business organizations, but also in not-for-profit institutions, in government, and in the professions. Through its publishing partners, reprints, and translation programs, it finds an audience in many languages in most countries in the world, occasionally penetrating even the barrier between East and West.

The *Harvard Business Review* draws on the talents of the most creative people in modern business and in management education. About half its content comes from practicing managers, the rest from professional people and university researchers. Everything *HBR* publishes has something to do with the skills, attitudes, and knowledge essential to the competent and ethical practice of management.

This book consists of 29 articles dealing with the problems and opportunities managers face in keeping pace with developments in computer technology and its application to the organization. Neither abstruse nor superficial, the articles chosen for this volume are intended to be usefully analytical, challenging, and carefully prescriptive. Every well-informed businessperson can follow the exposition in its path away from the obvious and into the territory of independent thought. I hope that readers can adapt these ideas to their own unique situations and thus make their professional careers more productive.

Kenneth R. Andrews, Editor
Harvard Business Review

Contents

CATCHING UP WITH THE COMPUTER REVOLUTION

Introduction

LYNN M. SALERNO

It is by now a commonplace that computers are becoming cheaper, smaller, and more powerful every year. Also familiar to many readers are the grand, if not grandiose, promises of the futurists and others who have foreseen, from a 10- or 20-year advance view, the marvels that would come to us all from computers.

Some prognosticators had it right; some had part of it right but had the timing wrong. This book begins with two of these: Harold J. Leavitt and Thomas L. Whisler, who, writing in 1958, envisioned top managers of the future sitting at their desk terminals playing games, "trying to simulate (their) own behavior in hypothetical future environments." Though many executives today may be more familiar with the popular video space war games than computer-generated corporate strategy, we see the beginning of the scenario described by Leavitt and Whisler in Rockart and Treacy's article written in 1982, "The CEO Goes On-Line."

As Leavitt and Whisler saw it in 1956, future top executives, using their own computers, would be less dependent on subordinates for information and would have better control over decisions made at lower levels. More than 25 years ago, they predicted that, with the new information technology, there would be "fewer experience and judgment areas in which junior men have more working knowledge" than top managers.

In this new corporation, run with the aid of precise and accurate information, middle managers would be largely phased out, programmers and other "technocrats" would move to the top, and "groupthink" would characterize the decisions of the tight oligarchy at the top.

The 1982 article by Brandt Allen, "Technology Is Not Enough," might have been written in answer to Leavitt and Whisler's optimistic forecast. As Allen points out, the economics of computers have turned around. Though technological improvements still lower costs by almost 25% per year, staffing costs are rising steadily. According to Allen, the very programmers who would be so central to the new technologically managed corporation of Whisler and Leavitt have put the brake on the advance of computer technology. Furthermore, far from rising to the top to be admitted to the inner

1

councils of management, most programmers find themselves not only stuck at a lower level but distrusted and ignored by senior managers.

Role of Top Managers

Allen's is not the first, and it surely won't be the last, plea for top management involvement in corporate information systems. Richard Nolan and Cyrus Gibson, writing about 10 years before Allen, had already proposed that the MIS manager, as they called the information systems executive, report close to the top.

By 1974, when these authors were writing, corporate EDP had become complex and the gap between the data processing manager and others, especially senior managers, had widened considerably. Nolan and Gibson wanted top management not only to become involved but to understand what was happening as computers became entrenched in the corporate structure. Thus they explained the four stages of evolution of computer systems in a corporation, a concept they and others would later build on to help managers broaden their understanding and thus overcome their fear of the computer and the new technology that it has brought with it.

But even as some managers became more comfortable with computer technology, they saw their problems compounded when minicomputers and microcomputers became cheap enough to allow their spread throughout the organization. Today the economies of scale that ied companies to use one large computer in a central data processing center no longer apply. In addition, new technology makes linking up these smaller computers both practical and sensible.

With increasing use of computer networks come changes in responsibility. Authority tends to be withdrawn from the DP manager as users gain familiarity with and control of their own machines.

In "Understanding Distributed Data Processing," Jack Buchanan and Richard Linowes point out that the new complexities of computer systems require more than ever that managers change their simplistic view of data processing as a collection of machines and technical issues. The most important assumptions that managers should make, say these authors, are that information systems should match a company's strategy and that various individuals can execute or control these systems.

Need for Planning

Besides a broader view of computer-based information systems, most HBR authors have advocated a strong commitment to planning for these systems. More than 10 years ago, Warren McFarlan, after examining some companies with a reputation for effective use of computers, concluded that such organizations usually had a comprehensive written plan for their IS activities that spanned several years (Chapter 3). Elsewhere, however, he discusses the desirability of a "planned clutter" in information systems.

Has the passage of 10 years removed the need for careful planning? Probably not, since the number and variety of computer-based systems has increased over that period. What seems to argue for the more flexible approach is that diversity of systems and the fact that many companies today have a mix of the various technologies.

They may have several years' experience with some, such as batch processing, while their familiarity with others, such as word processing and office automation, may be slight.

The broader array of computer technology that many organizations now deal with may explain why, after business's more than 20 years' experience with computers, information systems projects sometimes still end as fiascoes. The authors in this book have developed various approaches to address these new situations. In his "Portfolio Approach to Information Systems," Warren McFarlan suggests that no one right way of managing a project exists; rather, a company should adopt a "contingency" approach that takes into account the risk of a project and its technological complexity.

Thus, as *HBR* authors recognize the need for continual planning in the management of information systems, they recognize too that the new approaches have to be more sophisticated. These two concerns—for planning and for increased sophistication—show up in an area that has grown in importance as computer-based technology has spread in the organization: financial control.

A Broader View

In "Managing the Costs of Information," Paul Strassmann emphasizes that management of information systems now goes far beyond just dealing with computers. He divides information processing into three parts; (1) data processing, (2) what he calls administrative processing, which covers type writers, word processors, various copiers and duplicators, and all the other equipment and processes for handling information, including mail and office supplies; and (3) nonmanagerial and nonprofessional office labor. I mention this detail to suggest a view held more and more by thinkers at the leading edge of information technology management—The manager's job now is one of data or information management rather than simply computer management. Richard Nolan reiterates this notion in "Controlling the Costs of Data Services," pointing out that seeing where computer-based technology is located in the total organization structure versus where it should be placed is one of the prerequisites to establishing adequate cost control.

In this piece we encounter again the sharp distinction between the jobs appropriate for the DP department and those that should be handled elsewhere. Nolan thinks control of expenditures for data processing belongs with the accounting department, not with technical personnel. This is a good idea, but one that some managers will readily accept for the wrong reasons. Because they will not, or cannot, adopt the broader view of information technology and services that we have been discussing, which sees computer-based technology as an integral part of the whole organization, or perhaps just because they still fear and fail to understand what's going on in those areas of the corporation, such managers use cost control as their chief means of keeping the upper hand.

This narrow viewpoint, instead of ensuring an orderly growth and development, can lead to sudden dislocations in service and eventually to catastrophic system breakdowns. Martin Buss, in his very pratical article "Penny-Wise Approach to Data Processing," points out that rigid cost control can lead to underinvestment in that area so that vital software becomes outdated and has to be replaced at high cost over a short time span.

The IS Manager

Following short-term goals with a bias toward financial benefits can also have poor results when managers set their priorities for computer projects. Martin Buss addresses this problem in "Squaring the Circle—A structured Approach to Setting Project Priorities." He thinks the information systems manager has to take the most active role in deciding which projects a company should pursue—at last a significant mission for the experienced DP professional!

Since such persons are in increasingly short supply and the outlook for improvement in their numbers is not favorable, authors are beginning to give some attention to their plight. Writing about executive steering committees, Richard Nolan notes that the number of DP managers chairing such committees has declined noticeably in the companies he has studied while the number of CEOs who are chairmen has increased (Chapter 11). The good news is that more top managers apparently now recognize the importance of their involvement in planning for information systems. But the bad news is that DP professionals are losing the voice they once had. In addition, Nolan's survey showed that the steering committee usually did not concern itself with staffing problems, such as the choice of top computer managers, and when they did they ranked this task as lowest in importance and least effective of their functions.

Brandt Allen would see a lesson in all of this. In "Technology Is Not Enough" (Chapter 6) he says that senior managers don't have confidence in their ability to manage information resources and they don't have confidence in DP management either. He concludes that top managers will have to educate themselves about computers and the new information technologies and that most companies should bring to executive rank persons with substantial experience in information systems. If companies heed this advice, the IS function and especially the IS professional may finally gain the benefit of informed attention from above. In addition, DP personnel may feel less stuck in dead-end positions if some of their colleagues make it to the top and the games of musical chairs for more desirable positions on the outside may slow down.

Executives and the Computer

If chief executives have ignored the needs of the information managers below them, the IS staff and others have not, perhaps understandably, neglected their superiors' wants. In this information era, when data are more readily obtainable then ever, most executives find themselves with a surfeit of reports and other material sent on by their subordinates. But in this, as in other ways, computers have failed to live up to their promise, at least in the eyes of many executives. Far from producing meaningful data for their use, computers have simply multiplied the paper output and added to the mass of information they must sift through. In two pieces concerning executive information (Chapters 27 and 28), we learn how so-called critical success factors can determine what data managers really need to help them fulfill organizational goals and how a few executives are obtaining their own information by going on-line at personal terminals. To be sure, some executives have taken to the computer in self-defense, to free themselves from the frustrating information gaps I've just described, but there are equally compelling reasons to explain this phenomenon. First, minicomputers have become less expensive so that it is now easier to justify their purchase at various levels in the organization. Second, and perhaps more important, the development of so-called user-friendly machines, which are interactive, that is, which can carry on a "conversation" in ordinary English with the user, make the learning period minimal. For these reasons some CEOs have overcome their fears or their ignorance of computers, perhaps to become the vanguard of the new computer-literate managers.

Moving Toward the User

Executive use of computers may be a special case of a trend most experts believe is beneficial—moving control of computers out into the organization and closer to the users of information services. As Richard Nolan says, "The heart of the matter is when and how to decentralize, not whether to do so." As computers have spread willy nilly throughout most organizations, DP departments have found it impractical if not impossible to maintain effective control. Thus arises one of the most critical problems in IS management today: where to place responsibility for the various aspects of a company's information resources.

Frederic G. Withington finds that the answer lies partly in distributing the company's experts along with its computers.[1] Although he, like Richard Nolan, advocates an executive steering committee for project review, Withington sees many advantages for an arrangement under which users, with help from DP professionals, take responsibility for their own systems.

The spread of computers both horizontally and vertically throughout the organization has brought new problems along with many new opportunities. I have already mentioned one of the most obvious of the difficulties that many machines in many hands can produce: lack of control and suitable placement of responsibility. First to be noticed are usually the headaches of ballooning expense. In the short history of corporate computers, stories of near-skulduggery in the acquisition of machines are fast becoming legend.

Despite fiats from on high aimed at limiting untramelled growth, determined and creative prospective users have managed to obtain and set up closet computers, some of which were described as "clerical enhancements," "data sorters," and the like on requisition requests. And even though minicomputer costs have come down, overall costs of information services, including staff salaries, have risen almost as much as the others have fallen, so companies must make choices among the competing bids for IS budget money.

As machines proliferate, so naturally do the data they produce. And many companies watch with growing alarm and frustration the multiplication of data files, some usable only by one department and some accessible only to one person who has developed the programming to handle a particular application. Though the problem of redundancy of data has troubled corporations for some time, the growing number and broader use of computers has made the potential loss of productivity that can result from the uncontrolled spread of information more obvious.

HBR authors have consistently pointed to the advantages of data-base systems for the orderly management of a company's information. Richard Nolan, writing 10 years ago, wanted companies to adopt what he called a data-base approach. Using this concept, they would consider data as a corporate resource to be managed systematically, and the definition of data would include all the information significant to the company, not just data that are computer readable. Following a structured approach, managers could begin to eliminate some of the redundant data as they prepared to convert appropriate data to data-base form.

In the years since Nolan alerted managers to the need for data-base planning, as many companies have adopted data-base systems, the problems as well as the benefits have become clearer. Though both hardware and software to support such systems have become increasingly sophisticated, many corporations now see that this is an area of computer management where planning must be paramount. Though few companies would be likely to rue the day they decided to convert to a data-base management system (DBMS) some say they would give their plans more careful thought if they had it to do over again. A step-by-step scenario for analyzing the costs and benefits of a DBMS can be found in a piece by McFadden and Suver, who emphasize that installing such a system is a major undertaking.

From the time computers first came into the corporation, some persons have been troubled by the possible problems of maintaining privacy for the data these machines would handle. For them, especially if they knew little about data processing, the stacks of key-punched cards being read by the computer contained information for the company was locking up and it was, in effect, throwing away the key. There is no question that the computer does raise questions about an individual's right to privacy. And the company has increasing concerns in this area as well. Now that anybody and everybody in the corporation can use the minicomputer, at least to call up data, the need to "lock up" some files becomes clear.

In some companies, such as retail chains that have large credit operations, the personal data can be extremely sensitive, but even smaller companies maintain personnel files that may be computerized and thus unprotected. In addition, as has always been the case, companies maintain many files containing information that would be useful to competitors and thus should be considered sensitive.

Fortunately, some help has come from the computer itself. By use of a data-base management system, a company not only gains control over the data it needs to protect but also limits access to those with a "need to know." In addition, the computer can have a steady eye out for those who do view the restricted files, noting who saw what and when. But readers should not become overconfident—on the contrary. A few years ago, to shake them up a bit, HBR published an "Embezzler's Guide to the Computer" to show companies that the job of overcoming computer security was all too easy. For by then even the average newspaper reader had heard of another way to use computers—to steal not information but money. This most modern of crimes now takes place not just in banks, an obvious target, but in companies with every kind of product, just as long as the important records are automated. Though computer fraud may be one of the hottest games in town, the "Embezzler's Guide" will tell you how to beat the thief by understanding the rules he plays by.

Office of the Future

If computers are growing like rank weeds, causing privacy problems and even sometimes a leakage of funds, we might by now expect to see businesses turning away from automation or at least limiting its spread. This has not happened, however. Despite the very real difficulties that have surfaced, many if not most companies are exploring new ways to use computers because of the possible enhancements they expect, especially in efficiency and productivity. One of the areas that has most needed the benefits of automation—the office—has been the last to receive them.

   While CAD/CAM and robots have come into the factory, the most modern equipment in many offices is a high-speed photocopier. Since businesses spend more each year for salaries and benefits for white-collar workers, the fastest growing segment of the labor force, they should welcome the automated office. So far, however, the office of the future is just that, except in some banks, which were among the first to automate many of their functions. At Citibank in New York and Continental Illinois of Chicago, computers have moved beyond the routine banking functions to the back office.

   At Continental Illinois, Louis Mertes, author of "Doing Your Office Over—Electronically," greets the visitor in an office that looks more like a living room than a place to do business in. No paper is in sight and no computer or other electronic gadgetry, yet his could be the prototype of the automated office. Seated on one of the couches that surround the central "coffee table," he flicks a switch and a terminal rises from the surface in front of him. When he is not in his office, he and other bank executives can dictate to the bank's word processing machines from airports, hotel rooms, or wherever a telephone is available. These and other features have made Continental Illinois probably the best known and most successful pioneer in the electronic office.

   Meanwhile, back at the ordinary office, the paper shufflers are still awaiting the new age. To try to determine why electronic marvels are gathering dust on suppliers' shelves while managers remain frustrated with the lack of productivity both in their own and their staff's jobs, Harvey Poppel undertook a major study of white-collar working habits. He discovered that more than half of the time of the professionals he studied was spent in what they described as "less productive" activities. Matching the tasks of these workers to a computer solution, be concluded that office automation was a financially sound answer to their productivity problems.

Lessons for Managers

What conclusions can managers draw from the authors of this book? Despite the variety of their subjects and their approaches, they sound some recurring themes. One of the most striking is that there is a disturbing gap between promise and reality where the performance of computers is concerned. After the first much heralded management information systems (MIS) a decade ago failed to live up to anybody's expectations, many executives became wary about new computer-based solutions to their problems. The experts discovered many reasons for the downfall of MIS, but beyond the fact that they were certainly oversold from the beginning was the rapid pace of the development of technology, which made it difficult for any but those trained in electronic data processing to keep up with the ever-changing assortment of hardware and software that became available for business use. To compound the problem, communications between DP professionals and the rest of the organization have never been especially good, so few companies had regular channels through which promising developments could come to top managers' attention, and requests from other departments for information on the state of the art were probably even less likely to find their way into the DP bastion.

In recent years, however, the situation of the beleaguered DP department—for this is how many computer professionals have seen it—has begun to change. Again, technology has been the driving force. With smaller, cheaper, and more powerful machines making their way into many departments that formerly depended on the central DP department for their data processing, managers are beginning to take care of their own information needs with their own small computers.

Though, as many of the authors of this book point out, this situation can cause problems for the organization, the broadening base of computer power may serve to narrow the gap between the expectations and the reality of computer solutions. Most important in this connection is the prospect of shortening the waiting time for development of computer applications, which recently has often reached several worker years. In addition, this user involvement with computers should bring about a wider understanding and appreciation of the potential of the computer for solving business problems.

With the smaller size and lower price tag of computers have also come, most fortuitously, new languages that are easier to learn and to use. Such "user friendliness" has also contributed to the number of eager applicants for a personal, desk-top machine. Thus we move closer and closer to the new office where a computer sits on every desk alongside the telephone. If this is to be the real office of the future, it makes sense for managers to pay heed to another admonition from these authors: plan your information services. As the IS budget grows, especially in businesses that are highly dependent on the computer, no one can afford to learn the hard way, when the system grinds to a halt, how crucial it is for companies to have written short- and long-term agendas for their computer projects.

We appear to be at the start of a new phase in the computer age— what might be called the communications era. As technology now permits easy linkage of computers into networks, a new dimension of opportunities and problems confront us. Now the data bases and their management systems, which several authors of this book see as both necessary and desirable in the evolution of computer systems, can easily be linked inside the company and across divisions, at home and abroad.

But this added layer of complexity also increases the need for planning and for technical staff. In the last few years, *HBR* authors have warned that data processing professionals are dwindling in number, with little hope of any significant increase in the next decade. Thus management may have to consider opening up for them better career opportunities at the top as well as more generally satisfying work situations.

Underlying most of the pieces in this book is the message to top executives that they must get involved with computers, if not yet personally at the keyboard, at least in informing themselves—in becoming computer-literate. And the corollary to that proposition is that information systems and services must fit in with an organization's goals and strategy. Thus managers, and especially top executives, will need to be familiar with both aspects.

The reader can draw another lesson from the writers represented here: computer-based technology seems to bring as many problems as benefits at every stage. But if computer management often appears to be just one more burden for the already overloaded executive, encouraging signs point to the possibility that the gains are beginning to be significant enough to outweigh the frustrations involved. In any case, there seems little doubt that, despite many disappointments, computers are in business to stay.

Notes

1.   Managing Information Systems by Committee," *HBR*, July–August 1982.

PART ONE

SIZING UP
THE PROBLEM

AN OVERVIEW

This section begins with a piece that is both prophetic and cautionary—
Leavitt and Whisler's 1958 view of management in the present decade. It is
prophetic because parts of it now ring true, such as the prediction of the
rise of professional managers trained in business schools and the growing
importance of technically trained staff to manage information systems. In
other ways, however, the piece is cautionary, though only in retrospect. The
authors obviously had high hopes for information technology. They thought
it would make management truly scientific as computers removed the guess-
work from executives' decision making, and they believed top managers
would become both more powerful and more creative with the help of these
new machines.

Few would argue that most companies today fall far short of this forecast, but we can learn from it. Leavitt and Whisler did have some prescrip-
tions for the managers of their day. They suggested that they search their
organizations for "lost information technologists," especially in the "organizationally fuzzy" departments of the company. These persons, they
thought, could help plan for "the inroads of information technology."

In these very perceptive passages, these authors suggested that the
technology they extolled could bring with it challenges that managers should
not shirk and that, in order to profit from its benefits, they would have to
adjust many of their long-established attitudes. Probably most important,
they wanted managers to pay attention to this relatively new phenomenon
of computer science. The real misreading of Leavitt and Whisler, one feels,
is that they saw the top managers of the eighties swept up in, and very much
a part of, the new information technology. The other authors in this section
show clearly that present-day executives, far from being enamored of their

11

new machines, tend rather to neglect them, partly from ignorance and partly from fear of their technological base.

In an effort to help top managers of today who may be lost in a forest of technology, the authors in this section show them the bigger picture of an organization's computer systems so that they can find the smoothest path through the thorns and thickets of managing them. Here we find the first description of Cyrus Gibson's and Richard Nolan's now classic four stages of electronic data processing growth, plus the two stages Nolan added later as more companies had years of experience with DP systems. Gibson and Nolan believe that these stages provide useful benchmarks against which a company can measure its handling of its information systems.

Also basing his conclusions on the experience of actual companies, Warren McFarlan gives executives another way of looking at their management of IS. Though he studied companies that were known for their effective management of computer systems, McFarlan thinks even they could improve their performances, for example, by ensuring more top management involvement than is likely with the bottom-up approach most of them adopt. In a piece that catalogs the many ills of today's information systems, Brandt Allen echoes McFarlan's concern when he says: "If ever there was a time for senior executives to be involved with information systems, this is it.. . .'' According to him, even when top executives do become involved with IS, they tend to occupy themselves with matters of secondary importance, such as approving new projects and selecting vendors. These are not part of the bigger issues they ought to be concerned with, such as the where and how of organization, development, and control of information resources, Allen says.

The picture Allen paints of what he calls the computer crisis is a grim one. Keeping up with the demand for computer applications is a race few companies are winning, and signs of any improvement in programming productivity are hard to find. The number of applications and systems programmers, already at very low levels, may be declining, and here also the prospects for future relief are not good. As if all this were not enough, says Allen, a great many companies now find that their most fundamental applications need replacing—a further strain on harried staff. To remedy these many ills, managers will have to do a balancing act. They will have to integrate the various parts of their computer-driven information systems and then decide on the degree of centralization of resources, all the while considering the costs in flexibility, money, and time. Like other authors here, Allen sees further decentralization as a necessary move for most companies. Like others also, he urges managers to strengthen their own understanding of computers and the new information technologies.

The last piece in this group aims to help managers do just that. It was written for managers who have lacked the time to keep pace with developments in computer technology, not only in its applications to business but also in its broader social and economic effects, which will inevitably influence how we work as well as how we manage.

1
Management in the 1980s
A View from 1958

HAROLD J. LEAVITT and THOMAS L. WHISLER

The authors, writing twenty-five years ago, predicted extensive use of the new computer technology by top executives of the future. With senior people having better control over information, middle managers would be phased out and technicians would take their place. How these predictions turned out and whether they will come to fruition in the future is the subject of many of the other articles in this book

Over the last decade a new technology has begun to take hold in American business, one so new that its significance is still difficult to evaluate. While many aspects of this technology are uncertain, it seems clear that it will move into the managerial scene rapidly, with definite and far-reaching impact on managerial organization. In this article we would like to speculate about these effects, especially as they apply to medium-size and large business firms of the future.

The new technology does not yet have a single established name. We shall call it *information technology*. It is composed of several related parts. One includes techniques for processing large amounts of information rapidly, and it is epitomized by the high-speed computer. A second part centers around the application of statistical and mathematical methods to decision-making problems; it is represented by techniques like mathematical programming, and by methodologies like operations research. A third part is in the offing, though its applications have not yet emerged very clearly; it consists of the simulation of higher-order thinking through computer programs.

Information technology is likely to have its greatest impact on middle and top management. In many instances it will lead to opposite conclusions from those dictated by the currently popular philosophy of "participative" management. Broadly, our prognostications are along the following lines:

13

1.   Information technology should move the boundary between planning and performance upward. Just as planning was taken from the hourly
worker and given to the industrial engineer, we now expect it to be taken
from a number of middle managers and given to as yet largely nonexistent
specialists: "operations researchers," perhaps, or "organizational analysts." Jobs at today's middle-management level will become highly structured. Much more of the work will be programmed, that is, covered by sets
of operating rules governing the day-to-day decisions that are made.

2.   Correlatively, we predict that large industrial organizations will
recentralize, that top managers will take on an even larger proportion of the
innovating, planning, and other "creative" functions than they have now.

3.   A radical reorganization of middle-management levels should occur, with *certain classes* of middle-management jobs moving downward in
status and compensation (because they will require less autonomy and skill),
and other classes moving upward into the top-management group.

4.   We suggest, too, that the line separating the top from the middle
of the organization will be drawn more clearly and impenetrably than ever,
much like the line drawn in the last few decades between hourly workers
and first-line supervisors.

The New Technology

Information technology has diverse roots—with contributions from such
disparate groups as sociologists and electrical engineers. Working independently, people from many disciplines have been worrying about problems
that have turned out to be closely related and cross-fertilizing. Cases in point
are the engineers' development of servomechanisms and the related developments of general cybernetics and information theory. These ideas from
the "hard" sciences all had a direct bearing on problems of processing
information—in particular, the development of techniques for conceptualizing and measuring information.

Related ideas have also emerged from other disciplines. The mathematical economist came along with game theory, a means of ordering and
permitting analysis of strategies and tactics in purely competitive "think-"
type games. Operations research fits in here, too; OR people made use of
evolving mathematical concepts, or devised their own, for solving multi-
variate problems without necessarily worrying about the particular context
of the variables. And from social psychology ideas about communication
structures in groups began to emerge, followed by ideas about thinking and
general problem-solving processes.

All of these developments, and many others from even more diverse
sources, have in common a concern about the systematic manipulation of
information in individuals, groups, or machines. The relationships among
the ideas are not yet clear, nor has the wheat been adequately separated
from the chaff. It is hard to tell who started what, what preceded what, and

which is method and which theory. But, characteristically, application has not, and probably will not in the future, wait on completion of basic research.

Distinctive Features

We call information technology "new" because one did not see much use of it until World War II, and it did not become clearly visible in industry until a decade later. It is new, also, in that it can be differentiated from at least two earlier industrial technologies:

1.   In the first two decades of this century, Frederick W. Taylor's *scientific management* constituted a new and influential technology—one that took a large part in shaping the design of industrial organizations.

2.   Largely after World War II a second distinct technology, *participative management,* seriously overtook—and even partially displaced—scientific management. Notions about decentralization, morale, and human relations modified and sometimes reversed earlier applications of scientific management. Individual incentives, for example, were treated first as simple applications of Taylorism, but they have more recently been revised in the light of "participative" ideas.

The scientific and participative varieties both survived. One reason is that scientific management concentrated on the hourly worker, while participative management has generally aimed one level higher, at middle managers, so they have not conflicted. But what will happen now? The new information technology has direct implications for middle management as well as top management.

Current Picture

The inroads made by this technology are already apparent, so that our predictions are more extrapolations than derivations.[1] But the significance of the new trends has been obscured by the wave of interest in participative management and decentralization. Information technology seems now to show itself mostly in the periphery of management. Its applications appear to be independent of central organizational issues like communication and creativity. We have tended until now to use little pieces of the new technology to generate information, or to lay down limits for subtasks that can then be used within the old structural framework.

Some of this sparing use of information technology may be due to the fact that those of us with a large commitment to participative management have cause to resist the central implications of the new techniques. But the implications are becoming harder to deny. Many business decisions once made judgmentally now can be made better by following some simple routines devised by a staff man whose company experience is slight, whose position on the organization chart is still unclear, and whose skill (if any) in human relations was picked up on the playground. For example:

We have heard recently of an electric utility which is considering a move to take away from generating-station managers virtually all responsibility for deciding when to use standby generating capacity. A typical decision facing such managers develops on hot summer afternoons. In anticipation of heavy home air-conditioning demand at the close of working hours, the manager may put on extra capacity in late afternoon. This results in additional costs, such as overtime premiums. In this particular geographical area, rapidly moving cold fronts are frequent. Should such a front arrive after the commitment to added capacity is made, losses are substantial. If the front fails to arrive and capacity has not been added, power must be purchased from an adjacent system at penalty rates—again resulting in losses.

Such decisions may soon be made centrally by individuals whose technical skills are in mathematics and computer programming, with absolutely no experience in generating stations.

Rapid Spread

We believe that information technology will spread rapidly. One important reason for expecting fast changes in current practices is that information technology will make centralization much easier. By permitting more information to be organized more simply and processed more rapidly it will, in effect, extend the thinking range of individuals. It will allow the top level of management intelligently to categorize, digest, and act on a wider range of problems. Moreover, by quantifying more information it will extend top management's control over the decision processes of subordinates.

If centralization becomes easier to implement, managers will probably revert to it. Decentralization has, after all, been largely negatively motivated. Top managers have backed into it because they have been unable to keep up with size and technology. They could not design and maintain the huge and complex communication systems that their large, centralized organizations needed. Information technology should make recentralization possible. It may also obviate other major reasons for decentralization. For example, speed and flexibility will be possible despite large size, and top executives will be less dependent on subordinates because there will be fewer "experience" and "judgment" areas in which the junior men have more working knowledge. In addition, more efficient information-processing techniques can be expected to shorten radically the feedback loop that tests the accuracy of original observations and decisions.

Some of the psychological reasons for decentralization may remain as compelling as ever. For instance, decentralized organizations probably provide a good training ground for the top manager. They make better use of the whole man; they encourage more active cooperation. But though interest in these advantages should be very great indeed, it will be counterbalanced by interest in the possibilities of effective top-management control over the work done by the middle echelons. Here an analogy to Taylorism seems appropriate:

In perspective, and discounting the countertrends instigated by participative management, the upshot of Taylorism seems to have been the
separating of the hourly worker from the rest of the organization, and
the acceptance by both management and the worker of the idea that the
worker need not plan and create. Whether it is psychologically or socially
justifiable or not, his creativity and ingenuity are left largely to be acted
out off the job in his home or his community. One reason, then, that we
expect top acceptance of information technology is its implicit promise
to allow the top to control the middle just as Taylorism allowed the
middle to control the bottom.

There are other reasons for expecting fast changes. Information technology promises to allow fewer people to do more work. The more it can
reduce the number of middle managers, the more top managers will be willing
to try it.

We have not yet mentioned what may well be the most compelling
reason of all: the pressure on management to cope with increasingly complicated engineering, logistics, and marketing problems. The temporal distance between the discovery of new knowledge and its practical application
has been shrinking rapidly, perhaps at a geometric rate. The pressure to
reorganize in order to deal with the complicating, speeding world should
become very great in the next decade. Improvisations and "adjustments"
within present organizational frameworks are likely to prove quite inadequate; radical rethinking of organizational ideas is to be expected.

Revolutionary Effects

Speculating a little more, one can imagine some radical effects of an accelerating development of information technology—effects warranting the ad-
jective "revolutionary."

Within the organization, for example, many middle-management jobs
may change in a manner reminiscent of (but faster than) the transition from
shoemaker to stitcher, from old-time craftsman to today's hourly worker.
As we have drawn an organizational class line between the hourly worker
and the foreman, we may expect a new line to be drawn heavily, though
jaggedly, between "top management" and "middle management," with some
vice presidents and many ambitious suburban junior executives falling on
the lower side.

In one respect, the picture we might paint for the 1980s bears a strong
resemblance to the organizations of certain other societies—for example, to
the family-dominated organizations of Italy and other parts of Europe, and
even to a small number of such firms in our own country. There will be
many fewer middle managers, and most of those who remain are likely to
be routine technicians rather than thinkers. This similarity will be superficial,
of course, for the changes we forecast here will be generated from quite
different origins.

What organizational and social problems are likely to come up as by-products of such changes? One can imagine major psychological problems arising from the depersonalization of relationships within management and the greater distance between people at different levels. Major resistances should be expected in the process of converting relatively autonomous and unprogramed middle-management jobs to highly routinized programs.

These problems may be of the same order as some of those that were influential in the development of American unions and in focusing middle management's interest on techniques for overcoming the hourly workers' resistance to change. This time it will be the top executive who is directly concerned, and the problems of resistance to change will occur among those middle managers who are programmed out of their autonomy, perhaps out of their current status in the company, and possibly even out of their jobs.

On a broader social scale one can conceive of large problems outside the firm, that affect many institutions ancillary to industry. Thus:

☐   What about education for management? How do we educate people for routinized middle-management jobs, especially if the path from those jobs up to top management gets much rockier?

☐   To what extent do business schools stop training specialists and start training generalists to move directly into top management?

☐   To what extent do schools start training new kinds of specialists?

☐   What happens to the traditional apprentice system of training within managerial ranks?

☐   What will happen to American class structure? Do we end up with a new kind of managerial elite? Will technical knowledge be the major criterion for membership?

☐   Will technical knowledge become obsolete so fast that managers themselves will become obsolete within the time span of their industrial careers?

Middle-Management Changes

Some jobs in industrial organizations are more programmed than others. The job that has been subjected to micromotion analysis, for instance, has been highly programmed; rules about what is to be done, in what order, and by what processes, are all specified.

Characteristically, the jobs of today's hourly workers tend to be highly programmed—an effect of Taylorism. Conversely, the jobs shown at the tops of organization charts are often largely unprogrammed. They are "think" jobs—hard to define and describe operationally. Jobs that appear in the big middle area of the organization chart tend to be programmed in part, with some specific rules to be followed, but with varying amounts of room for judgment and autonomy.[2] One major effect of information technology is likely to be intensive programming of many jobs now held by middle managers and the concomitant "deprogramming" of others.

As organizations have proliferated in size and specialization, the problem of control and integration of supervisory and staff levels has become increasingly worrisome. The best answer until now has been participative management. But information technology promises better answers. It promises to eliminate the risk of less than adequate decisions arising from garbled communications, from misconceptions of goals, and from unsatisfactory measurement of partial contributions on the part of dozens of line and staff specialists.

Good illustrations of this programming process are not common in middle management, but they do exist, mostly on the production side of the business. For example, the programmers have had some successes in displacing the judgment and experience of production schedulers (although the scheduler is still likely to be there to act out the routines) and in displacing the weekly scheduling meetings of production, sales, and supply people. Programs are also being worked out in increasing numbers to yield decisions about product mixes, warehousing, capital budgeting, and so forth.[3]

Predicting the Impact

We have noted that not all middle-management jobs will be affected alike by the new technology. What kinds of jobs will become more routinized, and what kinds less? What factors will make the difference?

The impact of change is likely to be determined by three criteria:

1. *Ease of measurement.* It is easier, at this stage, to apply the new techniques to jobs in and around production than in, say, labor relations, one reason being that quantitative measurement is easier in the former realms.

2. *Economic pressure.* Jobs that call for big money decisions will tend to get earlier investments in exploratory programming than others.

3. *The acceptability of programming by the present jobholder.* For some classes of jobs and of people, the advent of impersonal rules may offer protection or relief from frustration. We recently heard, for example, of efforts to program a maintenance foreman's decisions by providing rules for allocating priorities in maintenance and emergency repairs. The foreman supported this fully. He was a harried and much blamed man, and programming promised relief.

Such factors should accelerate the use of programming in certain areas. So should the great interest and activity in the new techniques now apparent in academic and research settings. New journals are appearing, and new societies are springing up, like the Operations Research Society of America (established in 1946), and the Institute of Management Sciences (established in 1954), both of which publish journals.

The number of mathematicians and economic analysts who are being taken into industry is impressive, as is the development within industry, often on the personal staffs of top management, of individuals or groups with new labels like "operations researchers," "organization analysts," or simply "special assistants for planning." These new people are a cue to the emergence of information technology. Just as programming the operations of hourly workers created the industrial engineer, so should information technology, as planning is withdrawn from middle levels, create new planners with new names at the top level.

So much for work becoming more routinized. At least two classes of middle jobs should move *upward* toward *de*programmedness:

1. The programmers themselves, the new information engineers, should move up. They should appear increasingly in staff roles close to the top.

2. We would also expect jobs in research and development to go in that direction, for innovation and creativity will become increasingly important to top management as the rate of obsolescence of things and of information increases. Application of new techniques to scanning and analyzing the business environment is bound to increase the range and number of possibilities for profitable production. Competition between firms should center more and more around their capacities to innovate.

Thus, in effect, we think that the horizontal slice of the current organization chart that we call middle management will break in two, with the larger portion shrinking and sinking into a more highly programmed state and the smaller portion proliferating and rising to a level where more creative thinking is needed. There seem to be signs that such a split is already occurring. The growth of literature on the organization of research activities in industry is one indication.[4] Many social scientists and industrial research managers, as well as some general managers, are worrying more and more about problems of creativity and authority in industrial research organizations. Even some highly conservative company presidents have been forced to break time-honored policies (such as the one relating salary and status to organizational rank) in dealing with their researchers.

Individual Problems

As the programming idea grows, some old human relations problems may be redefined. Redefinition will not necessarily solve the problems, but it may obviate some and give new priorities to others.

Thus, the issue of morale versus productivity that now worries us may pale as programming moves in. The morale of programmed personnel may be of less central concern because less (or at least a different sort of) productivity will be demanded of them. The execution of controllable routine acts does not require great enthusiasm by the actors.

Another current issue may also take a new form: the debate about the social advantages or disadvantages of "conformity." The stereotype of the conforming junior executive, more interested in being well liked than in working, should become far less significant in a highly depersonalized, highly programmed, and more machine-like middle-management world. Of course, the pressures to conform will in one sense become more intense, for the individual will be required to stay within the limits of the routines that are set for him. But the constant behavioral pressure to be a "good guy," to get along, will have less reason for existence.

As for individualism, our suspicion is that the average middle manager will have to satisfy his personal needs and aspirations off the job, largely as we have forced the hourly worker to do. In this case, the Park Forest of the future may be an even more interesting phenomenon than it is now.

Changes at the Top

If the new technology tends to split middle management—thin it, simplify it, program it, and separate a large part of it more rigorously from the top—what compensatory changes might one expect within the top group?

This is a much harder question to answer. We can guess that the top will focus even more intensively on "horizon" problems, on problems of innovation and change. We can forecast, too, that in dealing with such problems the top will continue for a while to fly by the seat of its pants, that it will remain largely unprogrammed.

But even this is quite uncertain. Current research on the machine simulation of higher mental processes suggests that we will be able to program much of the top job before too many decades have passed. There is good authority for the prediction that within ten years a digital computer will be the world's chess champion, and that another will discover and prove an important new mathematical theorem; and that in the somewhat more distant future "the way is open to deal scientifically with ill-structured problems—to make the computer coextensive with the human mind."[5]

Meanwhile, we expect top management to become more abstract, more search-and-research-oriented and correspondingly less directly involved in the making of routine decisions. Allen Newell recently suggested to one of the authors that the wave of top-management game playing may be one manifestation of such change. Top management of the 1980s may indeed spend a good deal of money and time playing games, trying to simulate its own behavior in hypothetical future environments.

Room for Innovators

As the work of the middle manager is programmed, the top manager should be freed more than ever from internal detail. But the top will not only be released to think; it will be *forced* to think. We doubt that many large companies in the 1980s will be able to survive for even a decade without major changes in products, methods, or internal organization. The rate of obsolescence and the atmosphere of continuous change which now characterize industries like chemicals and pharmaceuticals should spread rapidly to other industries, pressuring them toward rapid technical and organizational change.

These ideas lead one to expect that researchers, or people like researchers, will sit closer to the top floor of American companies in larger numbers; and that highly creative people will be more sought after and more highly valued than at present. But since researchers may be as interested in technical problems and professional affiliations as in progress up the organizational ladder, we might expect more impersonal, problem-oriented behavior at the top, with less emphasis on loyalty to the firm and more on relatively rational concern with solving difficult problems.

Again, top staff people may follow their problems from firm to firm much more closely than they do now, so that ideas about executive turnover and compensation may change along with ideas about tying people down with pension plans. Higher turnover at this level may prove advantageous to companies, for innovators can burn out fast. We may see more brain picking of the kind which is now supposedly characteristic of Madison Avenue. At this creating and innovating level, all the current work on organization and communication in research groups may find its payoff.

Besides innovators and creators, new top-management bodies will need programmers who will focus on the internal organization itself. These will be the operations researchers, mathematical programmers, computer experts, and the like. It is not clear where these kinds of people are being located on organization charts today, but our guess is that the programmer will find a place close to the top. He will probably remain relatively free to innovate and to carry out his own applied research on what and how to program (although he may eventually settle into using some stable repertory of techniques as has the industrial engineer).

Innovators and programmers will need to be supplemented by "committors." Committors are people who take on the role of approving or vetoing decisions. They will commit the organization's resources to a particular course of action—the course chosen from some alternatives provided by innovators and programmers. The current notion that managers ought to be "coordinators" should flower in the 1980s, but at the top rather than the middle; and the people to be coordinated will be top staff groups.

Tight Little Oligarchy

We surmise that the "groupthink" which is frightening some people today will be a commonplace in top management of the future. For while the innovators and the programmers may maintain or even increase their autonomy, and while the committor may be more independent than ever of lower-line levels, the interdependence of the top-staff oligarchy should increase with the increasing complexity of their tasks. The committor may be forced increasingly to have the top men operate as a committee, which would mean that the precise individual locus of decision may become even more obscure than it is today. The small-group psychologists, the researchers on creativity, the clinicians—all should find a surfeit of work at that level.

Our references to a small oligarchy at the top may be misleading. There is no reason to believe that the absolute numbers of creative research people or programmers will shrink; if anything, the reverse will be true. It is the *head men* in these areas who will probably operate as a little oligarchy, with subgroups and sub-subgroups of researchers and programmers reporting to them. But the optimal structural shape of these unprogrammed groups will not necessarily be pyramidal. It is more likely to be shifting and somewhat amorphous, while the operating, programmed portions of the structure ought to be more clearly pyramidal than ever.

The organization chart of the future may look something like a football balanced upon the point of a church bell. Within the football (the top staff organization), problems of coordination, individual autonomy, group decision making, and so on should arise more intensely than ever. We expect they will be dealt with quite independently of the bell portion of the company, with distinctly different methods of remuneration, control, and communication.

Changes in Practices

With the emergence of information technology, radical changes in certain administrative practices may also be expected. Without attempting to present the logic for the statements, we list a few changes that we foresee:

☐ With the organization of management into corps (supervisors, programmers, creators, commitors), multiple entry points into the organization will become increasingly common.

☐ Multiple sources of potential managers will develop, with training institutions outside the firm specializing along the lines of the new organizational structure.

☐ Apprenticeship as a basis for training managers will be used less and less since movement up through the line will become increasingly unlikely.

☐ Top-management training will be taken over increasingly by universities, with on-the-job training done through jobs like that of assistant to a senior executive.

☐ Appraisal of higher management performance will be handled through some devices little used at present, such as evaluation by peers.

☐ Appraisal of the new middle managers will become much more precise than present rating techniques make possible, with the development of new methods attaching specific values to input-output parameters.

☐ Individual compensation for top staff groups will be more strongly influenced by market forces than ever before, given the increased mobility of all kinds of managers.

☐ With the new organizational structure new kinds of compensation practices—such as team bonuses—will appear.

Immediate Measures

If the probability seems high that some of our predictions are correct, what can businessmen do to prepare for them? A number of steps are inexpensive and relatively easy. Managers can, for example, explore these areas:

1.   They can locate and work up closer liaison with appropriate research organizations, academic and otherwise, just as many companies have profited from similar relationships in connection with the physical sciences.

2.   They can re-examine their own organizations for lost information technologists. Many companies undoubtedly have such people, but not all of the top executives seem to know it.

3.   They can make an early study and reassessment of some of the organizationally fuzzy groups in their own companies. Operations research departments, departments of organization, statistical analysis section, perhaps even personnel departments, and other "odd-ball" staff groups often contain people whose knowledge and ideas in this realm have not been recognized. Such people provide a potential nucleus for serious major efforts to plan for the inroads of information technology.

Perhaps the biggest step managers need to take is an internal, psychological one. In view of the fact that information technology will challenge many long-established practices and doctrines, we will need to rethink some of the attitudes and values which we have taken for granted. In particular, we may have to reappraise our traditional notions about the worth of the individual as opposed to the organization, and about the mobility rights of young men and women on the way up. This kind of inquiry may be painfully difficult, but will be increasingly necessary.

Notes

1.   Two examples of current developments are discussed in "Putting Arma Back on Its Feet," *Business Week*, February 1, 1958, p. 84; and "Two-Way Overhaul Rebuilds Raytheon," *Business Week*, February 22, 1958, p. 91.

2.   Robert N. McMurry, "The Case for Benevolent Autocracy," *HBR*, January–February 1958, p. 82.

3.   See the journals *Operations Research* and *Management Science*.

4.   Much of the work in this area is (in 1959) still unpublished. However, for some examples, see Herbert A. Shepard, "Superiors and Subordinates in Research," *Journal of Business of the University of Chicago*, October 1956, p. 261; and also Donald C. Pelz, "Some Social Factors Related to Performance in a Research Organization," *Administrative Science Quarterly*, December 1956, p. 310.

5.   Herbert A. Simon and Allen Newell, "Heuristic Problem Solving: The Next Advance in Operations Research," *Operations Research*, January–February 1958, p. 9.

2
Managing the Four Stages of EDP Growth

CYRUS F. GIBSON and RICHARD L. NOLAN

In all that has been said about the computer in business, there are few clues as to how the EDP department ought to grow or what management ought to be doing about the department at each stage of its growth. Here is a convenient categorization for placing the life crises of the EDP department in perspective, for developing the management techniques necessary or useful at various points, and for managing the human issues involved. These human issues, as a matter of fact, complicate the problems of growth at least as much as the hardware and software questions, which have been so well massaged in the literature; the authors show how these issues change shape as a company moves through the four stages of development. This article will be particularly helpful to the new business that is about to buy its first computer. For the company in the throes of later-stage development, it offers a framework useful for identifying issues and evaluating and controlling the growth of EDP.

From the viewpoint of the executive vice president, "The EDP manager always waffles around when he has to explain his budget." From the viewpoint of the EDP manager, "The executive vice president never seems to understand why this department needs a lot of money."

The reason for this kind of impasse is clear enough: EDP, as corporations use it today, is so complex that controlling it, or even understanding it, is almost too difficult for words. However, through our work with a number of companies, we have reached certain conclusions about how EDP departments grow and how they should fit into the company's organization. These conclusions offer a framework for communication for both EDP managers and senior managers to whom they report.

There are four distinct stages in the growth of all EDP facilities, each with its distinctive applications, its rewards and its traumata, and its managerial problems. By breaking the evolution of the EDP department into four easy stages, it is possible to sort out the affairs of the department, if not into four neat, sequential packages, at least into four relatively small, sequential cans of worms.

The basis for this framework of stages is the recent discovery that the EDP budget for a number of companies, when plotted over time from initial investment to mature operation, forms an S-shaped curve.[1] This is the curve that appears in the exhibits accompanying this article. The turnings of this curve correspond to the main events—often crises—in the life of the EDP function that signal important shifts in the way the computer resource is used and managed. There are three such turnings, and, consequently, four stages.

In the companies we know, there are remarkable similarities in the problems that arise and the management techniques applied to solve them at a given stage, despite variations among industries and companies, and despite ways in which EDP installations are used. Moreover, associated with each stage is a distinctive, informal organizational process. Each of these seems to play an important role in giving rise to the issues which need to be resolved if the stage is to be passed without a crisis and if the growth of the resource is to be managed to yield maximum benefit to the company.

Our purpose here is to describe the four stages in turn, listing the key characteristics of each and explaining the underlying organizational forces at work in each.

In the space of an article we can touch only on the main problems of EDP management at the different stages. Hence the view we present is bound to be somewhat simplified. Caution is advisable in another respect, too: history has not yet come to an end, and we are sure that the S-curve we describe and the stages it seems to follow do not represent the whole story. At the end of the S-curve of contemporary experience there will doubtless be more S-curves, as new EDP technologies emerge, and as companies become more ambitious in their use of EDP techniques and more sophisticated in systems analysis. However, we hope that the dynamics of later cost escalations will be clearer after the reader has finished with our description— clearer, and perhaps even predictable and controllable.

Four Stages of Growth

Three types of growth must be dealt with as an EDP department matures:

☐ A growth in computer applications—see Exhibit 1.
☐ A growth in the specialization of EDP personnel—see Exhibit 2.
☐ A growth in formal management techniques and organization— see Exhibit 3.

The S-curve that overlies these three kinds of growth breaks conveniently into four segments, which represent the four stages of EDP growth: initiation,

Exhibit 1. Growth of Applications

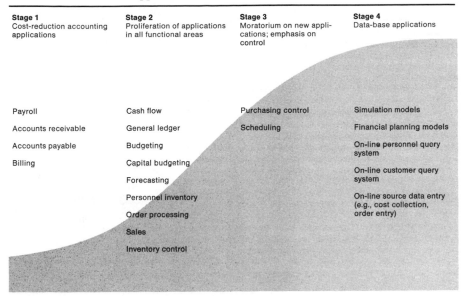

Stage 1	Stage 2	Stage 3	Stage 4
Cost-reduction accounting applications	Proliferation of applications in all functional areas	Moratorium on new applications; emphasis on control	Data-base applications
Payroll	Cash flow	Purchasing control	Simulation models
Accounts receivable	General ledger	Scheduling	Financial planning models
Accounts payable	Budgeting		On-line personnel query system
Billing	Capital budgeting		On-line customer query system
	Forecasting		
	Personnel inventory		On-line source data entry (e.g., cost collection, order entry)
	Order processing		
	Sales		
	Inventory control		

Exhibit 2. Growth of Personnel Specialization

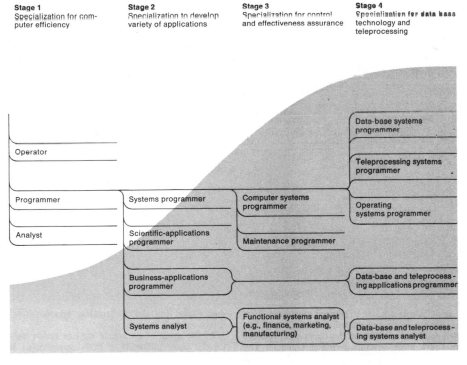

Stage 1	Stage 2	Stage 3	Stage 4
Specialization for computer efficiency	Specialization to develop variety of applications	Specialization for control and effectiveness assurance	Specialization for data base technology and teleprocessing

Operator

Programmer

Analyst

Systems programmer

Scientific-applications programmer

Business-applications programmer

Systems analyst

Computer systems programmer

Maintenance programmer

Functional systems analyst (e.g., finance, marketing, manufacturing)

Data-base systems programmer

Teleprocessing systems programmer

Operating systems programmer

Data-base and teleprocessing applications programmer

Data-base and teleprocessing systems analyst

27

Exhibit 3. Management Techniques Customarily Applied in Each of the Four Stages

	Stage 1 Lax management	Stage 2 Sales-oriented management	Stage 3 Control-oriented management	Stage 4 Resource-oriented planning and control
Organization	EDP is organized under the department of first-applications justification; it is generally a small department.	The EDP manager is moved up in the organization; systems analysts and programmers are assigned to work in the various functional areas.	EDP moves out of the functional area of first applications; a steering committee is set up; control is exerted through centralization; maintenance programming and systems programming become dominant activities.	EDP is set up as a separate functional area, the EDP manager taking on a higher-level position; some systems analysts and sometimes programmers are decentralized to user areas; high specialization appears in computer configuration and operation; systems design and programming take on a consulting role.
Control	Controls notably lacking; priorities assigned by FIFO; no chargeout.	Lax controls, intended to engender applications development; few standards, informal project control.	Proliferation of controls to contain a runaway budget; formal priority setting; budget justification. Programming controls: documentation, standards. Project management initiated; management reporting system introduced: project plan, project performance, customer service, personnel resources, equipment resources, budget performance. Chargeout introduced; postsystem audits. Quality control policies for computer system, systems design, programming, operations.	Refinement of management control system – elimination of ineffective control techniques and further development of others; introduction of data-base policies and standards; focus on pricing of computer services for engendering effective use of the computer.
Planning	Loose budget	Loose budget	Strong budgetary planning for hardware facilities and new applications.	Multiple 3-5 year plans for hardware, facilities, personnel, and new applications.

expansion, formalization, and maturity. Most notable are the proliferation of applications in Stage 2 (as reflected in Exhibit 1) that causes the budget to increase exponentially, and the proliferation of controls in Stage 3 designed to curb this increase (as reflected in Exhibit 3).

This sequence of stages is a useful framework for placing a company's current problems vis-à-vis EDP in perspective and helping its management understand the problems it will face as it moves forward. It is especially helpful for discussing ways to smooth out the chaotic conditions of change that have caused so many derailments in Stages 2 and 3. Even in our work with small companies, we have found the framework helpful—in obviating crises before they arise and in suggesting the kinds of planning that will induce smooth growth.

Thus one virtue of this framework is that it lays out for the company as a whole the nature of its task at each stage—whether it is a new company planning to buy its first computer, or a company in the throes of developing advanced applications, or a company with a steady, mature EDP facility.

Stage 1: Initiation

When the first computer is implanted in the organization, the move is normally justified in terms of cost savings. Rarely, at this point, does senior management assess the long-term impact of the computer on personnel, or on the organization, or on its strategy. Thus management can easily ignore a couple of crucial issues.

The Location Question

In Stage 1, the priority management issue is to fix departmental responsibility for the computer:

□ Initially it makes economic sense to locate the computer in the department where it is first applied—very frequently, in accounting— and to hold that department responsible for a smooth introduction and a sound control of costs and benefits. The costs and benefits can be clearly stated and rigidly controlled under this approach—and they usually are.

□ However, the department where the computer will first be used— accounting, say—may not be the best location for the EDP facility later on. The later and more complex applications, such as inventory control and simulation modeling, should ideally be located in an autonomous department of computer services or management information systems which reports through a high-level manager.

But granted this longer perspective, management may decide on a less rigorous application of payback criteria for judging the performance of the initial application. Costs for "future development" may not be scrutinized too closely at this stage, and budgets may expand very early under this arrangement.

Many companies resolve this issue in obvious fashion. Management simply locates the facility within the department of first application for an initial period; then, when its viability has been proved and other applications develop, management creates the autonomous EDP unit.

In practice, however, this seemingly simple resolution conceals a serious trap. The department that controls the resource becomes strongly protective of it, often because a manager or a group within it wants to build up power and influence. When the time comes for computing to assume a broader role, real conflict arises—conflict that can be costly in terms of management turnover and in terms of lingering hostilities that inhibit the provision of computer services and applications across functional areas.

Fear of the Computer

Another priority issue is to minimize the disruption that results when high technology is injected into an organization. Job-displacement anxieties appear; some people become concerned over doing old jobs in new ways; and others fear a loss of personal identity with their work. These fears may lead to open employee resistance. While reactions of this kind may occur at any of the stages, they can be particularly destructive in Stage 1, where the very survival of the EDP concept is at stake.

In plain fact some of these fears are probably justified. For example, some employees (although usually relatively few) may indeed lose their jobs when the computer is first installed.

On the other hand, the concerns that develop from rumor or false information are usually overblown, and they are readily transformed and generalized into negative sentiments and attitudes toward management, as well as the computer itself. The wise course for management is to spike rumors with the most honest information it has, however the chips may fall. Such openness will at worst localize fears and resistances that must be dealt with sooner or later anyway.

Unless management is willing to recognize the seriousness of this anxiety, it risks a more generalized reaction in the form of unresponsive and uncreative work behavior, a broader and higher level of uncertainty and anxiety, and even sabotage, as a surprising number of cases have demonstrated.

Management can make no bigger mistake than to falsely reassure all concerned that the computer will not change their work or that it will mean no less work for everyone. Such comfort blankets lead to credibility gaps that are notoriously hard to close.

Thus the key to managing this process of initiation to the computer is to accept the fact that people's perceptions of reality and their views of the situation are what have to be understood and dealt with, rather than some "objective" reality.[2] These perceptions will be diverse; management cannot assume that all organizational members are equally enthusiastic about introducing efficiency and reducing costs. Where you stand depends on where you sit and on who you are. In communicating its intention to introduce EDP, management should remember this and tailor its communications accordingly.

There will be variations from one situation and company to another in the manner and detail in which management releases information about future location and about the impact of the computer. Depending on circumstance, management directives may best be communicated downward by an outsider, by a department head, or by the new EDP manager. In settings where employees are rarely informed of management planning, it may even be wise to explain to the echelons why they are being given the explanation; again, in settings where the echelons have participated in planning, a formal presentation may be less effective than open group discussion.[3]

Stage 2: Expansion

The excess computing capacity usually acquired when a company first initiates an EDP facility, combined with the lure of broader and more advanced applications, triggers a period of rapid expansion. The EDP area "takes off" into new projects that, when listed, often seem to have been selected at random. As Exhibits 1–3 show, Stage 2 represents a steady and steep rise in expenditures for hardware, software, and personnel. It is a period of contagious, unplanned growth, characterized by growing responsibilities for the EDP director, loose (usually decentralized) organization of the EDP facility, and few explicit means of setting project priorities or crystallizing plans.

It is a period, further, in which the chaotic effects of rapid development are moderated (if they are moderated at all) only by the quality and judgment of the personnel directly involved in the process. While top management may be sensitive to some of the ill effects of the computer, it tends to be attracted to and carried along with the mystique of EDP as well.

This stage often ends in crisis when top management becomes aware of the explosive growth of the activity, and its budget, and decides to rationalize and coordinate the entire organization's EDP effort. The dynamic force of expansion makes this a fairly difficult thing to do, however.

Dynamics of Early Success

Once Stage 1 has passed, and the management and personnel of the computer area have justified and assured their permanent places in the organization, a new psychological atmosphere appears as the users from other departments (the customers) grow in number and begin to interact with the technical EDP staff. Although some users stick to economic value in judging the utility of computer applications to their particular problems and functions, other users develop a fascination with the computer and its applications as a symbol of progressive management techniques or as a status symbol for a department or individual. This fascination breeds an enthusiasm not moderated by judgment.

For their part, the technically oriented systems analysts tend to overgeneralize from the successes they have achieved with transaction-oriented computer-based systems (for example, order processing, payroll, accounts receivable) in Stage 2. They often feel that "now we can do anything"—in other words, that they have mastered problems of communication with users, that their expertise is solid, and that they are ready to select and deal with projects primarily on the basis of their technical and professional interest. In this heady atmosphere, criteria of economic justification and effective project implementation take a back seat.

When the users' exploding demands meet the technicians' euphoric urge to supply, in the absence of management constraint, exponential budget growth results. Overoptimism and overconfidence lead to cost overruns. And once this sharp growth has begun, rationales created in the mood of reinforced enthusiasm are used to justify the installation of additional capacity; this in turn provides the need for larger numbers of personnel and for more rationales for applying the now expanded resource to whatever new projects seem attractive to the crowd. So the spiral begins.

The spiral is fed by the fact that as the resource increases in size and ambition, it must have more specialists.[4] Indeed, even without this capacity expansion, the continuing pace of technological development in the computer industry creates a constant need for new specialist talent, especially in Stage 2 and beyond. This "technological imperative" is a driving force that has caused the growth of numerous and quite diverse professional groups of computer personnel in the industrial environment. (The reader might find it helpful to review Exhibit 2 at this point.)

Many of these personnel come into the company with a primarily professional orientation, rather than an understanding of or sympathy for the long-term needs of an organization. Like the EDP specialists already employed by the company, these people will be far more interested in tackling technically challenging problems than in worrying about computer payback. If they are allowed to pursue their interests at will, the projects potentially most valuable from the company's viewpoint may never be worked on. Moreover, the chores of program maintenance and data-base development may be neglected, sowing the seeds of costly future problems.[5]

All these factors together lead to the evolution of an informal structure among computer personnel and between computer personnel and users. The lack of clear management guidelines for project priorities, for example, often results in sympathetic wheeling and dealing between EDP systems analysts and the user groups with a preference for those projects which offer the greatest professional challenge. Without specific directives for project developments or new hardware acquisition, too, computer personnel develop expectations of a loose work environment. Some of the users, at the other end of the string, are easily enmeshed in impractical, pie-in-the-sky projects.

For short periods such an environment may be highly motivating for some, but, as we need hardly point out again, the other side of the coin is a rapidly growing budget—and a number of vocal and dissatisfied users.

In view of these informal dynamics and structures, what can management do to make this period one of controlled growth? How can control be introduced that will head off the impending crisis and dramatic cutbacks characteristic of such situations but at the same time not choke off experimentation with the resource and not turn off the motivation of specialists?

Here it is useful to compare the lists of management techniques shown for Stages 2 and 3 in Exhibit 3. For the most part, the problems that arise toward the end of Stage 2 can be greatly alleviated by introducing right at the start of Stage 2 the techniques that companies ordinarily use in Stage

3.[6] Before carrying out this step, however, attention should be given to two other important strategies: acquiring necessary middle-management skills and improving the company's procedures for hiring computer personnel.

Acquiring Managers

The main key to successful management in this stage is acquiring or developing middle managers for EDP who recognize the need for priorities and criteria in project selection and who have strong administrative skills: the ability to prepare plans and stick to budgets, the ability to seek out significant projects from users who may not be demanding attention, and, generally, the ability to manage projects.

Finding such managers more often than not means going outside the company, especially since most potential middle managers among systems analysts are usually caught up in the computer growth spiral. However, where it is possible, selection from within, particularly from the ranks of systems analysts, can serve the important function of indicating that career paths exist to management ranks. This can show computer technicians and technical experts that there are career rewards for those who balance organizational needs with professional interests.

Once those at the general-management level have determined that the time has come to institute such "human controls," the EDP manager must be brought to recognize the need for them (if, indeed, he does not recognize that need already) and the fact that he has the countenance and support of top management.

For his part, the EDP manager himself must resist the tempting pressures to see his resource grow faster than is reasonable. He has a delicate and important selling job to do in communicating this to other department managers who want his services. Once he is shored up with competent subordinate managers he will be free to carry out this role.

Finally, in addition to applying administrative controls, management needs to assess continually the climiate of the informal forces at work and plan growth with that assessment in mind. The formal organization of middle managers in the EDP department makes such planning, and its implementation, viable.

Acquiring Diverse Personnel

Senior management must also recognize the increasing specialization of personnel within the computer department:

> ☐   At one extreme are the highly skilled and creative professionals, such as computer systems programmers. Their motivation and interest are oriented to the technology with which they work; they have relatively little interest in organizational rewards. Their satisfaction and best performance may be assured by isolating them organizationally, to some degree.

☐   At the other extreme are the analysts who work closely with functional departments of the company. These people may be expert in particular fields relevant to only a few industries or companies, performing tasks that require close interaction with both users and programmers. Their interests and value to the company can coincide when they perceive that career-path opportunities into general management are open to them.

☐   There are also the operators with important but relatively low-level skills and training, with some capabilities for organizational advancement, and with relatively little direct interdependence with others.

To organize and control these diverse specialists requires decisions based on one basic trade-off: *balancing professional advancement of specialists against the need for organizational performance.*

To cater to specialist professionals, for example, a company might isolate them in a separate department, imposing few organizational checks and gearing quality control to individual judgment or peer review. Such an arrangement might motivate a systems analyst to become the world's best systems analyst.

Emphasis on organizational values, in contrast, suggests that the company locate and control the specialists in such a way as to increase the chances that short-run goals will actually be achieved on schedule. This strategy risks obsolescence or turnover among specialists, but it successfully conveys the important message that some specialists' skills can advance a management career.

However, in the early stages management is well advised to avoid the issue entirely: the highly sophisticated professional should not be hired until his expertise is clearly required. Moreover, at the time of hiring, the specialist's expectations for freedom and professional development should be explicitly discussed in the context of organizational structure and controls (these controls include those administered by the middle level of EDP management), as part of the "psychological contract."[7]

Such discussion can go a long way toward avoiding misunderstanding during the period of rapid growth of computer applications. In effect, making clear the terms of the psychological contract is an example of the management of expectations. In this instance, it is one of the means that can be employed to introduce the organization, controls, and planning procedures that are needed to head off the crisis atmosphere of Stage 3.

Stage 3: Formalization

Let us assume that Stages 1 and 2 have run their bumpy courses without too much direct attention from top management. More likely than not, top management becomes aware of the runaway computer budget suddenly, and it begins a crash effort to find out what is going on. Its typical question at this point is, "How can we be sure that we can afford this EDP effort?"

Top management frequently concludes that the only way to get control of the resource is through drastic measures, even if this means replacing many systems analysts and other valuable technical personnel who will choose to leave rather than work under the stringent controls that are imposed during the stage. Firing the old EDP manager is by no means an unusual step.[8]

From the perspective of computer personnel who have lived through the periods of initial acceptance and growth, but who have not developed a sense of the fit of the computer resource within company functions and objectives, the changes top management introduces at this time may seem radical indeed. Often what was a decentralized function and facility is rather suddenly centralized for better control. Often informal planning suddenly gives way to formal planning, perhaps arbitrarily. This stage frequently includes the first formalization of management reporting systems for computer operation, a new charge-out system, and the establishment of elaborate and cumbrous quality-control measures (again, see Exhibit 3).

In short, action taken to deal with the crisis often goes beyond what is needed, and the pendulum may swing too far. In response, some computer personnel may leave. What may be worse, most will "hunker down"—withdrawing from innovative applications work, attending to short-term goals, and following the new control systems and plans to the letter. All of this can occur at the expense of full resource utilization in the long run.

In addition, there is a parallel development that dovetails with the budget crisis to reinforce the overcontrol syndrome. Studies of computer usage show that the machines are first applied to projects that reduce general and administrative expenses—typically, replacement of clerical personnel in such tasks as accounting. Next come projects that reduce cost of goods, such as inventory control systems. The crisis atmosphere of Stage 3 roughly coincides with completion of these first two types of applications.

At this juncture the applications that have real potential for increasing revenues and profits and facilitating managerial decision making are still untouched. Financial-planning models and on line customer service systems are two examples of such applications.

As senior management ponders the problems of Stage 3, it tends to associate the applications of the earlier stages with preexisting manual systems and straightforward cost justification and control. In contrast, it finds projected applications for revenue-producing and decision-making projects hard to envision and define. The natural tendency is to assume that these projects will call for a faster, higher spiral of risk and cost. Thus senior management tends to introduce inappropriately strong controls that are designed, consciously or unconsciously, to put a stop to growth. This clearly may be too strong a reaction for the company's good.

Three Sound Steps

In general, three control steps that are appropriate and not unduly restrictive are available for most large EDP facilities in Stage 3. First, certain of the more established and less complex operations and hardware can be centralized. Second, the increasing impacts of computer applications can be flagged and defined for the top by introducing overseer and resource-allocation mechanisms at the general-management level. Third, some parts of the systems analysis function can be decentralized and other parts centralized, depending on where the systems work can best be done (we shall say more about this shortly).[9] Of course, this final step requires that the decentralized systems work be coordinated through a formal integrative mechanism.

But the real problem in Stage 3 is not what steps to take; it is how to take them. Management here is introducing change into a web of informal relationships and expectations. *How* the changes are managed is as important as *what* the changes should be, but more difficult to define.

That is, although there are few formal controls in the first two stages, the *informal* social structures and norms that have grown up by Stage 3 are very much a reality to the personnel involved. While it may appear that systems are replacing no systems, this will not be true:

☐ Lacking guidelines for project selection, systems analysts will have projected their own sets of priorities, either individually, as a group within the company, or as members of their profession.

☐ They will have created criteria and standards, although these will not ordinarily have been written down or otherwise articulated for higher levels of management.

☐ Without project management guidelines, systems analysts and users will have developed their own rules and procedures for dealing with each other.

On the whole, the stronger these informal controls and structures are (and the weaker the formal controls and structures are, the stronger they will be), the more resistant the personnel will be to change and the more chaotic and traumatic the introduction of formal systems will be.

In managing changes as pervasive as these there is probably nothing worse than doing the job halfway. Doing nothing at all is disaster, of course; but management action that is undertaken on a crash basis—without enough attention to execution and second- and third-order consequences—will sharpen, not resolve, the crisis.

For example, management cannot afford to be either squeamish or precipitous in making personnel changes. Trying to introduce needed formalization of controls with the same personnel and the same organizational structure more often than not encourages conflict and the reinforcement of resistance rather than a resolution of the crisis; by refusing to fire or to enforce layoffs, senior management may simply prolong the crisis, create further dissension, and further demoralize personnel. On the other hand, management must be sure that it retains the experienced personnel who have the potential to function well in the mature stages of the operation—it may not always be obvious who these people are or what their future roles will be.

Thus, although the crisis of Stage 3 calls for action, it first calls for analysis and planning—planning that sets forth clear and explicit objectives for exploitation of the computer resource vis-à-vis the user departments.[10] Such a plan, once it is developed and understood, can turn anarchy back into evolution, while at the same time avoiding the kind of overkill control that results in underutilization and underrealization of the potential of the resource. Here are our suggestions for general plan direction.

1. *Reposition the established components of the resource.* Whether or not EDP has been carefully managed in the past, most companies need to centralize some parts and decentralize other parts of the computer resource at about this point.

The issue arises here because the company reaches a turning point in the way it uses the resource. As the EDP function evolves from the early cost-reduction applications of initiation and early growth toward projects aimed at improving operations, revenues, and the quality of unprogrammed and strategic decisions, the influence of the computer will begin to move up and spread out through the organization. The function may truly be called "MIS" instead of "EDP" from this stage forward.

We have already discussed the need for middle managers' involvement in this stage or an earlier stage. The internal structure they represent reinforces the desirability of making the MIS department autonomous and having it report to a senior level of management. At this point, also, it becomes imperative to reexamine and make explicit the rationales for existing applications that have proved beneficial and to routinize them, so that expensive specialist skills can be turned to new applications.

The pressures of new applications ventures, maturing management, specialist personnel, and increasing routine make centralization of the company's core hardware resources just about mandatory at this stage. Too, the centralization eases the tasks of maintenance of data and programs, database development, and some of the applications that will be coming up in Stage 4.

The very creation of a central "MIS division," however, creates additional problems.

2. *Provide for top-management direction.* While centralization goes a long way toward placing the longer lead times, the greater complexity, and the higher development costs of new applications in perspective, it does not automatically help senior management to control the direction the resource takes.

Effective control derives from understanding, and some device is needed to educate senior management so that it can track and evaluate the department's progress sensibly. The device must also let the resource know what senior management's policies are and what is expected of it operationally and strategically.

This communications device becomes vital in Stage 3 because the resource has grown to a size and a power whereby its applications can affect the strategy and structure of the company as a whole. In a company where a working data base can be used to back up the corporate planning process, for example, corporate planning assumes a somewhat different shape from what it does in a company that has no such data base available. This is clearly a point at which a person at the vice-presidential level (or even the presidential level) must accept responsibility for directing the evolution of the resource.

An active, high-level steering committee is one such device.[11] It provides a means for setting project priorities. It not only brings together those who should be concerned with overall management and planning for the company; it also provides a vehicle for confronting and resolving the political problems that inevitably arise with the computer's more direct impact on managers' roles, organizational structure, and resource allocation in Stage 3.

For, from a behavioral perspective, political issues dominate at this time as never before. Managers throughout the company now see that the applications coming through the pipeline may affect their own roles directly. In the past it was their subordinates who were most affected, and it was largely their own decision to approve or not approve a project; but now a given application may be supported from above and may impinge on their established patterns of work, their decision making, and even their ideas about what it is they do for a living.

Moreover, the prospect of applications that hint at long-term changes in organizational structures and formal departmental roles raises concern within both formal and informal groups of managers—concern about the impacts these changes will have on the strengths of their positions relative to other groups.

Such political issues can only be debated fruitfully before top management, and an expert, informed steering committee provides a convenient forum for this debate.

For his part, as a member of this committee as well as the head of his own department, the MIS manager should expect to assume a stronger role in general management councils. He should not, of course, expect to be exclusively responsible for setting priorities among projects that would benefit different groups, or for implementing significant changes completely under his own initiative.

3. *Reorganize the systems analysis function.* Centralization, and tight guidelines and arbitration from a steering committee, however, can create a distance between the resource and its customers throughout the company. As Stage 3 draws to a close, the company will be planning its most important, most ambitious MIS applications to date. This is hardly a point at which to

divorce the users from the resource by erecting an impenetrable divisional barrier. Complete centralization of the systems analysis function would constitute such a barrier.

In fact, gearing up for this new era of applications and controlling their impacts requires that the company revise the Stage 3 concept, staffing, and organization of the systems analysis function. The concept should change from systems analysts as developers of *products for* users to systems analysts as developers of *processes affecting* users. The distinction between product and process means, among other things, that the new applications should rarely be considered bounded projects; they will require continual modification as they are integrated into user decision making.

Therefore, systems analysts themselves will necessarily become more and more a constant element in the functioning of the users' areas. As a corollary, they will act as communications conduits between the users, on the one hand, and the computer resource and its programmers, on the other.

Organizationally, this suggests that some systems analysts should be decentralized to user locations while others are retained at the core to build a research and testing facility for the company and its planners. Thus the problem boils down to a trade-off between centralization and decentralization of systems analysts.

These, then, are our best suggestions for minimizing the strains of Stage 3: centralize certain components of the resource, install a steering committee or some equivalent thereof, and spread enough of the systems analysts through the company to ensure that users' needs are met adequately. For the company wise enough to employ these suggestions at the outset of Stage 2, the trauma of Stage 3 may be almost entirely avoidable.

Stage 4: Maturity

When the dust has settled over the changes of Stage 3, the computer resource will have reached maturity in the organization, and it will have the potential to return continuing economic benefits. The applications listed for Stage 4 in Exhibit 1 suggest how very significant the contributions of the resource can be, if only they can be achieved.

The Manager's Dilemma

At this point the MIS manager has broken into the ranks of senior management, having risen to the level of vice president or equivalent thereof. In some instances he may even enjoy more than proportional support from the president for his view of his own function within the company. He faces this integrative dilemma:

☐   On the one hand, he is under pressure to maintain a steady work environment within his own unit. His line managers and specialists are now familiar with relatively formal structure and procedures; they are presumably satisfied with their career prospects, either within their professions or within the company. Thus they may well constitute a force resisting dramatic change, reorganization, or innovation. Similarly, at this point, senior management and the users probably have a general grasp of the existing technology and existing applications of the resource, and they are reluctant to see major changes.

☐   On the other hand, the MIS manager, if he is doing his job well, will be heavily involved in planning for the future. He will be aware that computer technology and modes of application and organization are continuing to change.

Thus, if he chooses to maintain stability, he knowingly runs the risk that his resource will become outdated and inefficient. If he chooses to keep up with technology, he knowingly runs the risk that he will lose the integrative fabric that makes his function applicable to the user groups and the company as a whole.

The MIS manager must strike a balance between protecting an organizational entity and keeping that entity up to date in its technical environment. He has power and credibility, but he sees that these can be threatened either by too little change or by too much change.

There are no hard and fast rules for resolving this trade-off. The key, however, lies in the quality of communications between the MIS manager and top management, and between the MIS department and users.

Communications with the Boss

By definition, the mature Stage 4 function is one which is being applied to the key tasks of the organization. This may well mean that most of the funding for MIS development is devoted to applications touching directly on critical business operations. This is the case of a large petrochemical firm with which we are familiar, where new applications focus on synthetic-fiber production activities.

But whether applications are for line operations or for management decision making, the computer manager in Stage 4 is, perhaps for the first time, in a position to communicate with top management in terms of meaningful, detailed plans.[12]

Because of the nature of his dilemma, he is bound to come under fire from the users—either for allowing parts of his department to obsolesce, in the name of stability, or for introducing change, in the name of progress and the state of the art. His relationship and communications with the top must be sound enough to allow him to weather the inevitable storms—given, of course, that the balance he strikes between stability and change is indeed reasonable in broad outline.

The experience of many suggests that the MIS manager and senior management think in terms of a three-year contract for the position, with explicit recognition that there will be organizational pressures to push out the MIS manager.

With long-term support from the top founded in such a basis, the MIS manager is in a position to legislate policies internally that will exploit the computer as fully as possible.

For his part, the senior line manager to whom a mature EDP department reports can little afford not to know the language of the computer personnel— at least to the extent necessary to evaluate project proposals.

Relations with Users

In Stage 4, the MIS manager must also move to strengthen the bridges that have developed between the users and computer personnel. Assuming that it is well managed internally, the computer resource still has a continuing extensive interdependence with departments it serves.

The first difficulty here is that the users are many and the MIS manager only one. He cannot hope for identical relationships with all departments.

Secondly, users naturally tend to co-opt computer personnel into their organizational spheres. If this occurs to any significant extent, user parochialisms will erode the potential for the computer unit to act as an agent for innovation and change.

However, the bridges can be strengthened and the innovative capability of the unit can be increased simultaneously through a policy of "buffering" the different subunits from user influence. Specifically, performance standards and short-term control devices should be formalized for the more routine tasks (such as all machine operations and some programming) and the MIS personnel involved with these should be removed from frequent interaction with the users. A system of project management, too, serves much the same function.

Finally, the systems analysis function at the core should by this time have taken on the character of an influential research unit, controlled primarily through checks on the progress of its projects. These projects will probably not be within the direct purview of the user groups; in a mature department, they are usually focused on long-term applications not likely to be demanded spontaneously by user groups or by the systems analysts decentralized into those groups (for example, corporate inventory control). The weight of this core group of analysts can be used to counterbalance undue user influence.

For example, when a user needs a new application, the core group might rough it out and approve the final, detailed design; but the final, detailed design itself should be the work of the systems analysts located in the user department. The decentralized analysts will be most familiar with the user's needs and best able to produce a working system for him; for their part, the systems analysts at the core can ensure that the system that is finally designed will mesh efficiently with the company's MIS efforts as a whole, to whatever extent this is possible.

The picture of EDP-user relationships that emerges here is one of considerable complexity and subtlety. Correspondingly, integrating this more specialized and internally differentiated EDP resource into the company as a whole becomes more difficult.[13] This integration requires that the MIS manager take steps to achieve common understanding of his objectives, not only with senior management but with all other functional managers at the vice-presidential level as well. The steering committee will be important as never before, not only as a committee for determining project priorities, but also as a sounding board for new techniques, policies, and changes within the MIS department itself.

Beyond Stage 4

Currently some large companies have reached the tail end of the S-shaped EDP budget curve: their departments are mature, in the sense defined by the exhibits. But has EDP evolution really come to an end for these companies? What can they expect in the future?

In retrospect, the curve seems to have been primarily driven by developments in hardware technology in the second- and third-generation computer systems. One thing certain is that computer technology advancements are continuing at an unrelenting pace. More S-shaped curves are inevitable.

Now, however, the advancements seem to be taking place more in software than in hardware; and at present the breakthrough most likely to start off another S-shaped EDP budget curve is the development of database technology. This development is providing a way to make the data collected and retained by the organization a companywide resource; and scores of middle management applications, such as computer modeling, appear to be on the way.

In the blush of enthusiasm for this newest advancement in computer technology, however, it is important to remember the painful lessons of the past. To efficiently exploit the newest technology, it must be managed. It must be reconciled with the capacity of the organization to assimilate new ways of doing business better. It is our belief that the forces underlying the crises and problems of the four stages we have described will also underlie future S-curves, such as one created by the emerging data-base technology. Consequently, management may be able to anticipate the problems and resolve them before they begin. A sign of success would be a dampening of the S-curve, with budgets rising more smoothly as future needs demand continuing investments and increasing budgets.

Notes

1. Richard L. Nolan, "Managing the Computer Resource: A Stage Hypothesis," *Communications of the ACM*, July 1973, p. 399.

2. For a related argument, see James G. March and Herbert A. Simon, *Organizations* (New York, John Wiley, 1958), Chapter 6.

3. For further discussion of this point, see Paul R. Lawrence, "How to Deal With Resistance to Change," *HBR*, January–February 1969, p. 4.

4. John Dearden, "MIS Is a Mirage," *HBR*, January–February 1972, p. 90.

5. Richard L. Nolan, "Computer Data Bases: The Future Is Now," *HBR*, September–October 1973, p. 98.

6. For an approach to introducing these steps in either Stage 2 or Stage 3, see F. Warren McFarlan, "Management Audit of the EDP Department," *HBR*, May–June 1973, p. 131.

7. Harry Levinson et al., *Men, Management and Mental Health* (Cambridge, Harvard University Press, 1962).

8. See Richard L. Nolan, "Plight of the EDP Manager," *HBR*, May–June 1973, p. 143.

9. See the section which discusses the McKinsey study on effective users, in F. Warren McFarlan, "Problems in Planning the Information System," *HBR*, March–April 1971, p. 78.

10. For mechanisms for improving the interface between EDP and users, see John Dearden and Richard L. Nolan, "How to Control the Computer Resource," *HBR*, November–December 1973, p. 68.

11. F. Warren McFarlan, "Problems in Planning the Information System," *HBR*, March–April 1971, p. 75.

12. Ibid.

13. Paul R. Lawrence and Jay W. Lorsch, *Organization and Environment* (Boston, Division of Research, Harvard Business School, 1967).

3

Problems in Planning the Information System

F. WARREN MCFARLAN

Putting flesh on the concepts of planning is always a difficult thing to do, especially in a new and fast-moving area of activity like computer-based information systems. The author makes planning in this area more manageable by outlining the factors that a company must consider in developing its strategies. He also defines some administrative structures that have worked out well in practice—structures for developing the plans themselves and structures for planning control. Much of the information that is presented in this article has been gathered in studies of companies that have been effective in planning their systems.

As computer applications have multiplied in size and complexity over the past decade, the task of managing a company's computer-based resources has become tough and intricate. To maintain good managerial control over this activity, companies are beginning to develop formal plans and formal planning methods for their computer-based information systems (CBISs).

This development is well justified. Recent field work shows that companies that formally plan their CBISs have more *effective* CBISs than companies that do not. A recent study by McKinsey and Company demonstrates this; the pertinent data are given in Appendix A.

Also, a study of my own fully corroborates this finding. My associates and I visted 15 companies that use CBISs extensively and have a reputation for using them effectively. We interviewed key executives, other users, and EDP personnel in these companies (a) to determine firsthand how effective their systems are, and (b) to analyze the planning processes behind the systems. (See Exhibit 1 and Appendix B.)

By comparing each company's approach to CBIS planning with its effectiveness as a user of CBISs, we have reached certain hard conclusions on what constitutes good planning practice in this area today. In this article

Exhibit 1.   Profile of Companies Studied

	Number of Companies
Sales volume	
Under $200 million	2
$200 million to $499 million	1
$500 million to $999 million	1
$1 billion to $1.9 billion	9
$2 billion and over	2
Number of EDP personnel	
Under 100	3
100–499	3
500–999	3
1,000 and over	6
Industry	
Government agency	3
Aerospace	2
Electronics	3
Paper	2
Insurance	1
Oil	2
Railroads	1
Utilities	1

I should like to sketch this kernel of good practice step by step. To do this, I shall proceed as follows:

☐   Discuss the pressures, both external and internal, that induce a company to plan formally. (These pressures define the parameters of the planning process and of the formal, or written, plan itself.)

☐   Exhibit the elements of the planning process in a diagram showing how they ought to interact.

☐   Summarize my conclusions on the relations that ought to exist between a company's CBIS planning effort and its corporate planning.

☐   Next, briefly analyze the critical issue of centralization versus decentralization of divisional CBIS facilities within a company. (This issue bears heavily on organization and corporate planning.)

☐   Finally, present two examples of effective CBIS planning which, although they are widely different, serve to illustrate basic principles by both their strengths and weaknesses. (In a sense, these two examples define the range of possibilities of contemporary information systems planning.)

Of course, the *full* range of planning possibilities is still undefined because this field is very new and evolving fast. Only one company of those we examined had been planning its CBIS systematically for as long as four years.

In general, CBIS planning today is at roughly the same stage of development as corporate planning was in 1960. As a refinement and elaboration, CBIS has naturally lagged behind. The same interest and enthusiasm that attended corporate planning a decade ago attends CBIS planning now, as well as a parallel confusion about how to approach the task.

Every company we visited had sweated with this confusion, and each had experienced enormous changes in its planning processes over the past three or four years. For example:

Three years ago, one multibillion-dollar company completely exhausted its thoughts about the future of its EDP activities in three pages of project names and weak documentations of schedules and costs.

Currently its formal plan is 150 pages long, and is substantively and qualitatively superior to the earlier one in every critical dimension. Its statements of goals and estimates of manpower and facilities needed two years hence are the result of intensive, detailed analysis, and, as such, are worthy of considerable attention.

This company has gone through a learning process that is paying off today in the remarkable effectiveness of its information systems.

Pressures to Plan

Learning to plan is never easy, but the general conclusions we have drawn from the experience of the pioneering companies in our sample may make it easier to understand how to structure the CBIS planning process and to define the senior manager's role in it.

Let us first look at the pressures that make it so attractive—indeed, necessary—for a company to plan in this area.

Technical Improvements

Because technological change in hardware and software occurs so rapidly, both company staff and consulting groups should hold regular, coordinated reviews of replacement and improvement options to identify significant shifts in cost/performance relationships and develop contingency plans to handle them. A planning system provides a focus for ensuring that this is done.

Also, the lead time for acquiring new equipment is often long, and, once acquired, a new piece of equipment must be thoroughly integrated with a company's existing configuration. This integration task is frequently so complex that integration procedures dictate the timing and sequence of acquisitions.

Together, lead time and integration considerations demand that a company plan with an extended time horizon—four years, in one company studied.

At the present time, this particular company has seven decentralized, "stand alone" computer installations, all within a 100-mile radius. They are all medium-sized, and the company is using equipment from two computer vendors.

The company plans first to phase out the equipment of one vendor and then to install two large central processing units (CPUs) at existing locations 15 miles apart. The medium-sized equipment at the other five locations will be converted to remote terminals for batch processing. Once installed, the two new CPUs will be connected for multiprocessing, and, finally, a third large CPU will be added to the network within 50 miles of the other two.

Company management states that laying out this particular technical plan has dramatically increased the effectiveness of its developing applications and its short-term decisions on hardware acquisitions.

Volatile environment: As new products appear, as the laws change, as mergers and spinoffs take place, the priorities a company assigns to its various applications are likely to change as well. Some low-priority or new applications may become critically important, while others previously thought vital may diminish in significance.

This volatility places a real premium on building a flexible framework within which such change can be managed in an orderly and consistent fashion. Hence recognizing it is vital to planning an effective CBIS.

In a similar vein, every information systems plan is built around very specific assumptions about the nature and rate of technological evolution. If this evolution occurs at a different rate from the one forecasted (as is often the case), then major segments of the plan may have to be reworked.

For example, if the present speed of access to a 10-million-character file were suddenly increased by one order of magnitude with no change in cost, most of the plans we have seen in use would have to be seriously revised, with dramatic reshufflings of priorities and applications structures. And such an increase is by no means farfetched.

Some executives choose to interpret this volatility as a pressure *against* planning. One installation manager stated that while his superiors required him to plan three years ahead, this single factor of technological uncertainty made it impossible for him to estimate realistically more than one year in advance. He said he goes through the long-range planning process as an elegant ritual that makes his superiors happy, without any personal conviction that his output is meaningful.

However, this narrow view of the effective time horizon for CBIS planning was certainly not common among the companies studied. The great majority of those interviewed feel that in this area it is now more effective to work from plans with multiple-year horizons, even though these plans must be revised unexpectedly from time to time, than to try to manage without them. They perceive a difference between revising from an established base and constantly improvising from scratch.

Personnel Scarcity

The scarcity of trained, perceptive analysts and programmers, coupled with the long training cycles needed to make them fully effective, has been the chief factor restraining CBIS development in the companies we studied. To circumvent this restraint, planning is definitely necessary.

An excellent illustration of this appeared in a company whose main business is information systems of a specialized kind—its major product is financial services. The company's primary EDP applications, on which its whole product structure is highly dependent, are intricate financial programs requiring the largest available computers.

When I visited this company, a new, sophisticated set of financial services, deemed significant and potentially very profitable by the executive vice president, had recently been developed in rough outline form. Bringing these services on-stream meant extensive systems design and programming—so extensive that, after a careful review of existing EDP operations, management concluded that this new product could not be operational for 4½ years. Independent consultants subsequently confirmed this estimate.

This estimate assumed that the company would devote four of its best analyst-programmers to the job, plus 10 assistants. Assistants could not be spared from regular operations, however, and hence would have to be recruited from outside.

The main reason for such a long preparation was this: the complexity of creating the new service package and the difficulty of consolidating it with existing applications was so great that a new assistant, even one with a strong financial background, would need to pass through a two-year training cycle before she or he could be fully effective on the project.

Management considered that even this relatively modest rate of recruitment would reduce departmental efficiency on necessary maintenance and developmental work, since senior analysts would have to spend more time than formerly on training and less on developmental work.

The company decided to proceed with the introduction of the new services, but, because of the hiring and training problem, the process is proving very painful and difficult. Planning it earlier would have made it easier. Planning it now, step by step, to make every move count, is smoothing the process somewhat. In general, the scarcity of critical personnel and the length of training cycles make formal planning in this field a virtual necessity.

Scarcity of Corporate Resources

Another critical factor that induces companies to plan is the limited availability of precious company resources, both financial and managerial.

CBIS development is merely one of many strategic investment opportunities for a company, and cash invested in it is often obtained only at the expense of other areas. In most of the companies surveyed the EDP budget is charged directly against earnings. Hence this is a matter of intense interest and a critical limiting factor for new projects in companies under profit or cost pressure.

One must also mention the scarcity of EDP managers available within any given company. Companies' inability to train sufficient project leaders and supervisors has significantly restrained CBIS development. As a result, companies have delayed implementing various valuable applications.

In one case, a company needed to install new systems for message switching, sales reporting, and production scheduling, all at the same time, while maintaining satisfactory service levels on other existing applications. This simply could not be managed with the company's thin group of skilled project leaders.

Together with the difficulty of hiring qualified people "off the street," the problem of juggling these resource restrictions has stretched the necessary CBIS planning horizon to three or even five years in the companies studied.

Planning as resource drain: Even within the EDP area, of course, assigning a person to planning diverts dollars away from system and program development. The extent to which financial resources can be effectively and profitably diverted to planning is still very much a question.

For example, of the companies studied, the one with the heaviest commitment to planning has assigned only 1.5% to 2.0% of its total information service group to planning as a full-time activity. This may not be a sound yardstick, however, because a major part of its planning task is done by executives, project leaders, and analysts as part of their own general responsibilities; the company has made no attempt to estimate the total size of its aggregate planning effort.

Four organizations studied are quite concerned about the wisdom of establishing a planning group as such, regardless of the contribution it could make. As a highly visible overhead item, the group would be vulnerable to sharp budget cutbacks during periods of economic stress, and these companies realize that this effect would seriously compromise the quality of their CBIS planning. They feel the better strategy is to needle planning in as a component of many people's jobs, thus ensuring the continuity of the effort, albeit at some cost in reduced effectiveness.

Legitimate competitor for funds: In general, therefore, these companies are aware of the connection between formal CBIS planning and CBIS effectiveness, and such planning certainly is becoming a serious, legitimate competitor for budgeting funds and managerial personnel.

One company that has chosen to set up an independent planning department has recognized the difficulty and complexity of the task of managing CBIS planning by pulling together a full description of the planning manager's function. This is shown in Exhibit 2. This manager's department consists of six full-time planners, and many of the company's other 880 analyst-programmers and EDP employees are actively involved in its work.

The reader will recognize many of the items in the manager's job description as parameters defined by the pressures to plan which I have

Exhibit 2.   Job Description of a Planning Manager

POSITION TITLE: Manager of Divisional EDP Planning
REPORTS TO: Manager of Divisional EDP Department
WHO REPORTS TO: Controller

SUMMARY:

Develops and maintains a division-wide, short-range operating plan and long-range strategic plan by which to optimize the return on the investment of resources in information processing systems. Provides planning guidance and direction to EDP division management to maintain consistency of EDP planning and implementation with the overall objectives of the division.

PRIMARY TASKS:

1.   To develop and maintain, in consort with operations personnel, short- and long-range objectives and plans for systems to obtain maximum cost-effectiveness both in the EDP function and in the division facilities it services.

2.   To help corporate planning management integrate EDP objectives and plans developed at the division into general corporate objectives; and to help corporate planning management optimize cost-effectiveness.

3.   To see that resources allocated to the EDP function are adequate for maintaining a rate of technical progress that will enhance the division's competitive position.

4.   To see that resources allocated to the EDP function are directed to objectives that will result in maximum return to the division.

5.   To review all proposals and requisitions for consistency with established short- and long-range plans.

6.   To develop planning techniques and documentation methods that minimize planning effort and maximize planning utility.

7.   To review performance evaluations and identify the causes of differences between plans and achievement.

8.   To revise plans as dictated by division information requirements.

9.   To keep abreast of developments in information technology so objectives and plans of the division reflect the latest advances in the field.

been discussing. Before I go on to the details of the written plans themselves, I should mention one additional pressure of great importance.

Trend to Systems Integration

Systems design is currently evolving in the direction of integrated arrays of program packages. Failure to recognize and plan for interdependency and coordination of different packages can lead to major reprogramming in the future or, worse still, to complete revision of a system that cannot accommodate new requirements.

To install a new personnel information system in one major utility, for example, an employee had to add six pieces of information to the master record used in the payroll system (among other places). The original system design was not structured to accommodate this type of change; consequently, 50 programs had to be patched, requiring six months of straight time and 2½ worker years of effort.

Because of the inordinate expense incurred in accommodating these changes, the company inaugurated a systematic effort to plan its CBIS two months later.

Exhibit 3 indicates the various factors that must be creatively consolidated in the planning process:

☐ The evolving technology—the state of the art, forecasts of hardware and software improvements, and external computer utility resources.

☐ The company's EDP resources—its CBIS support base and the resources associated with it.

☐ The company as a working whole—its organizational structure, resources and capabilities outside the EDP area, its market opportunities, and its strategic planning.

The dynamic model in this exhibit is in some ways similar to that presented by Professor Zani in his article, "Blueprint for MIS."[1] However, Zani's point of view and my own differ in the following dimensions:

☐ I stress the need for a formal, periodic planning process as the driving mechanism which ensures that a company's CBIS will evolve as a viable entity. In a sense, Zani seems more concerned about covering all possible variables; I am more concerned with establishing an analytic process.

☐ I stress the importance of scanning the technological environment to ensure that new concepts are identified, and, when appropriate, assimilated.

☐ I distinguish sharply between CBIS planning and administration. When a company's CBIS plan and strategy have been formulated, as at the bottom of Exhibit 3, the administrative function takes over to make them operational. This administrative implementation naturally augments the company's systems support base (shown at the top of the exhibit); but this administrative function is essentially distinct from the planning function because the two have essentially different missions.

The Written Plan

The most significant factors differentiating the companies that are effective CBIS users from those that are not are the quality and content of their

Exhibit 3. Information Systems Planning Process

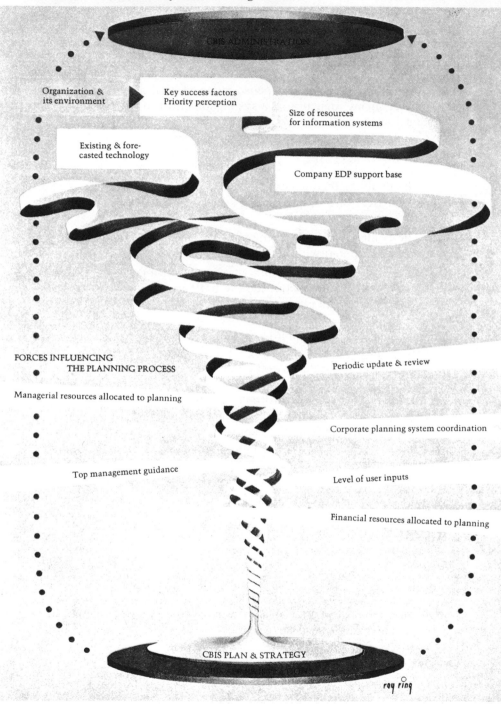

CBIS ADMINISTRATION

Organization &
its environment

Key success factors
Priority perception

Size of resources
for information systems

Existing & fore-
casted technology

Company EDP support base

FORCES INFLUENCING
THE PLANNING PROCESS

Periodic update & review

Managerial resources allocated to planning

Corporate planning system coordination

Top management guidance

Level of user inputs

Financial resources allocated to planning

CBIS PLAN & STRATEGY

roy ring

Exhibit 4. The Contents of a CBIS Plan

A. Introduction
   1. Summary of major goals, a statement of their consistency with corporate goals, and current state of planning vis-à-vis these goals.
   2. Summary of aggregate cost and savings projections.
   3. Summary of personnel requirements.
   4. Major challenges and problems.
   5. Criteria for assigning project priorities.
B. Project identification
   1. Maintenance projects, all projects proposed, and development projects.
   2. Estimated completion times.
   3. Personnel requirements, by time period and job category.
   4. Computer capacity needed for system testing and implementation.
   5. Economic justification by project—development costs, implementation costs, running costs, out-of-pocket savings, intangible savings.
   6. Project control tools.
   7. Tie-ins with other systems and master plans.
C. Hardware projections (derived from projects)
   1. Current applications—work loads and compilation and testing requirements.
   2. New applications—work loads and reruns.
   3. Survey of new hardware, with emphasis on design flexibility which will allow the company to take full advantage of new developments in hardware and in software.
   4. Acquisition strategy, with timing contingencies.
   5. Facilities requirements and growth, in hardware, tape storage, offices, and supplies.
D. Personnel projections (derived from projects)
   1. Personnel needed by month for each category.
      a. General—management, administrative, training, and planning personnel.
      b. Developmental—application analysts, systems designers, methods and procedures personnel, operating system programmers, and other programmers.
      c. Operational—Machine operators, key punchers/verifiers, and input/output control clerks.
   2. Salary levels, training needs, and estimated turnover.
E. Financial projections by time period
   1. Hardware rental, depreciation, maintenance, floor space, air conditioning, and electricity.
   2. Personnel—training and fringe benefits.
   3. Miscellaneous—building rental, outside service, telecommunications, and the like.

written plans. An outline of overall plan contents taken from the actual documents appears in Exhibit 4, but it is important to distinguish the following as the key features of the sound plan:

   ☐ The sound plan defines a two- to four-year time horizon, with detail declining in the later years. Most of the effective plans specify considerable detail concerning project features, personnel needs, and hardware timing requirements for the first year and then grow more general in format for each succeeding year.

☐ It embodies a series of detailed descriptions of specific projects. These descriptions include goals and economic analyses for the projects, the projects' aggregate personnel requirements by skills categories, its hardware time requirements for both program testing and ongoing operation), and gross project flow charts, accompanied by whatever volume of supporting material is necessary. This last is usually considerable.

☐ It states a strategy for CBIS development and a broad conceptual scheme for the "final form" of the CBIS. These statements are invariably general in nature; they are loosely related to substantive action proposals and loosely coordinated with the other components of the plan.

There is considerable concern within the companies about the utility of this section of the plan. On many dimensions, executives feel that the overall plan is best conceived as a sophisticated project management system that ensures effective use of resources, and hence it may be best not to try to state final objectives in too detailed a form.

☐ It develops a detailed exposition of future hardware and physical facility requirements. Specific pieces of equipment are identified, along with the optimum timing for their arrival, estimated usage rates, and so forth. These requirements have been systematically developed from existing work levels, new project plans, and specific assumptions concerning overall increases in activity. Software packages such as SCERT, which translates specific program descriptions into estimated running times and hardware requirements, are frequently used to assist in these analyses.[2]

☐ It includes technology forecasts that name assumptions about the pace of change in EDP hardware and software and assess their impact on the company's information systems activity. The sophistication of these forecasts varies widely.

☐ It also includes aggregate forecasts of future personnel and training levels, estimates of personnel requirements by job classification, employee turnover rates, and other like factors. These are derived from each specific project.

These key factors, once again, reflect the primary pressures to plan.

Naturally, the precise content, form, and quality of a company's CBIS plan are strongly molded by some additional factors, one of the most important of which is the quality of the company's corporate long-range planning. Top management participation and the planning structures used are also important.

Relation to Corporate Planning

We found a strong correlation between a company's ability to develop an effective CBIS planning process and the maturity and scope of its corporate planning process.

Four of the companies studied went so far as to postulate a formal relationship between the two planning activities, corporate and CBIS. The two activities are connected in the company budgets, of course, but the real relationship between them is far more meaningful than a mere formal budgetary connection would suggest. In fact, one company took its CBIS manager directly from its long-range planning department.

When this relationship is a strong one, it appears to contribute three concrete advantages:

1　The CBIS group is made explicitly aware of overall company objectives. This helps it develop priorities realistically.
2　In the reverse direction, a strong relationship helps executives in other areas to know and understand the goals and targets of the CBIS group. (Incidentally, this wider publicity and exposure enhance the commitment of EDP personnel at all levels to their work.)
3　Perhaps most important, the corporate planning group's expertise can be transferred to the CBIS planning and administrative groups.

These advantages can help to combat a very real communication problem. In one organization, for example—a large, successful bank—no one in the corporate planning department had ever spoken to, or even knew the name of, anybody in the CBIS group. The problems of planning are generic, to some extent, and it is a pity to isolate CBIS planning groups from experienced corporate planners if these are available.

Where no planning expertise is available, on the other hand, the company that is contemplating a CBIS should beware. The controller of one company I visited was particularly proud of his new budget system, the company's first in the 110 years of its existence. The company employed 50 analysts and programmers in its ordinary applications; but, not too surprisingly, its written plan consisted only of three pages of project titles. The EDP manager discoursed at great length on his company's CBIS plan for the future, but, while his verbal virtuosity impressed me, I could not help wondering if any vestige of the planning document would survive the next couple of months.

It seemed to me that this management was expecting too much from too little too soon. Developing a formal CBIS plan is a slow process; a company benefits from a secure base of planning skills and attitudes in the organization.

Relation to Top Management

Like corporate planning itself, CBIS planning stands a better chance of getting off the ground if the chief executive backs it personally. Also, the closer information systems activity is to the CEO, the more emphasis is placed on planning it formally.

Those organizations in which two or more layers of management lay between the CBIS department and the CEO ranked lower in effectiveness and planning ability. In this respect our findings are consistent with Neal J. Dean's.[3]

Structures Used for CBIS Planning

Of the 15 companies studied, 9 use a well-defined, formal planning structure to write and update their plans annually. This structure for creating and revising plans is laid out either as a series of operating procedures or as a corpus of job descriptions, or both.

There is, of course, wide variation among these nine companies, with respect to the specific methods used to develop plans and decide what personnel shall be involved at each stage of plan development. One large organization has gone so far as to print a 250-page manual that details the working procedures, reporting formats, and groups participating at each stage—committees, dates, printout formats, and the like are all well defined.

In another organization, judged equally effective as a user of CBIS, the EDP manager prepares the annual plan, consulting with a steering committee and with users throughout the company as he thinks necessary. This organization is small in size, and the manager has a genuine user orientation and excellent communication skills; so this informal procedure is entirely workable.

But in all nine cases, in addition to existing formal structures for planning, the companies have installed special informal procedures—safety valves, really—to accommodate unusual needs or circumstances arising during the year. Overall, the structures are characterized by flexibility and responsiveness, their primary function being to provide a framework for managing change, rather than to create ironclad documents to be administered regardless of consequences.

I shall have more to say about structures and their flexibility and responsiveness as these are reflected in two examples of CBIS planning. Before presenting these examples, however, I wish to discuss the critical issue of centralized versus decentralized planning of companywide CBIS. An understanding of this issue will help the reader to appreciate the examples.

Centralized Planning

In the companies in the sample, planning tends to be done on a decentralized basis around local computer centers or islands of automation. Companywide coordination between different centers is generally very weak, except when there is only one major computer center in the organization; this is particularly true when there is any significant geographic separation between computer centers within a company.

For example, in one electric equipment manufacturing company with $500 million in sales and 16 divisions, there is a very strong tradition of centralized financial control. All divisions use the same chart of accounts and standard procedures manual, and these materials can be altered only on direct instruction from corporate headquarters.

But, at the same time, IBM 360/25s and 30s and 40s are scattered through the divisions, and the EDP managers of the various divisions have little (if any) contact with one another. During my group's research, for example, it was discovered that no less than six of these installations were currently working to develop the same production scheduling applications. Parallel design teams in competition often produce a better result than an individual team, but with six groups competing, the company had obviously reached the point of diminishing returns. Some centralized coordination was obviously required.

Another large company has three EDP installations, each budgeted in excess of $10 million. The only formal communication and coordination between these installations is a really quite informal two-day meeting of eight to ten of the installation managers every three months. The key topics discussed in these meetings are:

- [ ] Salary and wage guidelines.
- [ ] Projects to develop classification standards for operators, programmers, and analysts.
- [ ] Joint purchase contracts and standards for items such as tapes and discs, for which economies of scale are obviously available.
- [ ] Systems to measure computer-room performance more accurately.
- [ ] Procedures for sharing reports on the failure rates of machine components.
- [ ] Limited joint development of program packages (Development of operating systems was felt to be a particularly appropriate topic for discussion.)
- [ ] Company hardware capabilities and personnel capabilities for specific studies.
- [ ] Evolving hardware technology and its implications.

Other companies in the survey also focused primarily on these topics, which, as a group, surely represent the bare minimum for planning CBIS administration and growth. They cover some basic operations, but do not touch the "big picture" at all.

In general, I sense, the companies realize this. More than half strongly expressed the sentiment that much more centralization of CBIS planning is desirable.

Attractiveness of Multiprocessing

In part, this desire for centralization is a consequence of companies' growing awareness of the new multiprogramming and multiprocessing environment, in which it is eminently feasible to connect a large central computer via telephone lines to remote batch-processing facilities. Many companies now have several medium-sized computers at discrete locations. The idea of turning them in for a central-control computer facility is becoming more and more attractive, for the following reasons:

☐ Large-machine economies mean more computation per dollar expended.

☐ Software development can be coordinated to serve several installations.

☐ Hardware-software planning and development can be more sophisticated.

☐ Integrating the data files from many discrete locations into a single file structure makes more data available for companywide use.

☐ There is a critical mass of programming and development activity that a company must reach before it can attract truly competent analysts. Large-machine installations are much more likely to achieve this critical mass than small or medium-sized installations.

Such arguments apply more readily to companies having several small, geographically proximate installations than to companies having two or three massive installations in which economies of scale have already been achieved.

Some companies, however, even among those for which multiprocessing should be attractive, are resisting the trend toward centralization, apparently because they either fear the task of managing a very large installation or are concerned that a centralized system will not be responsive to local needs. Companies that fear decreased responsiveness argue that poor communications with local management might warp application priorities and structures.

Thus, when to centralize and how rapidly to centralize are points that are far from clear. (They are now the subject of ongoing research.) For example, economies of scale are extremely complex to calculate when a company contemplates consolidating two installations, each with a budget in excess of $15 million.

One company studied, in exactly this position, decided *not* to consolidate, describing the situation as one in which a reverse critical mass would be created—that is, one that would create more disadvantages than advantages. On the other hand, other companies in closely similar situations have decided to proceed with consolidation, and have been glad they did so.

More work and research in the area may produce guidelines on when and how fast to centralize, but we found overwhelming evidence that companies are tending toward consolidation. This trend increases the need for, and the payoffs from, central CBIS planning.

Two Companies' Methods

To draw the foregoing analysis together and give the reader some feeling for the diversity of approaches a company can take to integrate the process of CBIS planning with its other operations, I present two case examples: one, a division of a major aerospace company, and the other, an international manufacturer of electrical and mechanical equipment. Both have sales in excess of $2 billion annually.

In Aerospace

This company division has been active in CBIS planning for four years. With respect to this relatively long planning history, it is significant that the division's information systems manager spent a large part of his early career working in the company's corporate planning department.

The division's CBIS operation is budgeted in excess of $20 million a year and has nearly 1,000 employees. For all practical purposes, it is completely independent of any other EDP activities of the company, all of which are a considerable distance away. Exhibit 5 indicates the principal groups involved in the division's CBIS activity.

The following points about the exhibit are particularly relevant to the planning process:

1. *A top management steering committee guides the overall process of budgeting and setting priorities.* Composed of eight vice presidents, this steering committee meets once a month to review progress and priorities. It continually faces the job of making broad policy for a very technical area, the underlying complexities of which are largely foreign to its members. Installed by the company, abandoned as unworkable, and then reinstated because of a sharp disruption in communication, this group serves primarily as a safety valve for pressures of extreme dissatisfaction from divisional users.

The same basic feature is present in 12 of the 15 companies studied; it ensures the participation of and guidance from the top.

2. *"Decentralized systems teams" link the vice presidential steering committee with the functional subgroups.* This is the key organizational mechanism in this division, so far as CBIS planning and administration are concerned. The EDP department is not laid out to correspond with its array of activities and systems. Rather, over one third of the division's analysts are on the staffs of the eight vice presidents and report directly to them, instead of reporting to the information systems manager. These staff members work both on special projects of particular interest to the vice presidents and on regular projects, where they join with departmental information systems analysts to form the so-called decentralized systems teams.

As members of these teams, their role is to communicate the peculiar needs and requirements of regular projects to the vice presidential level, and to assure the vice presidents that the system designs created for these regular projects are adequate.

Exhibit 5.   Framework of CBIS Activity in a Major Aerospace Company

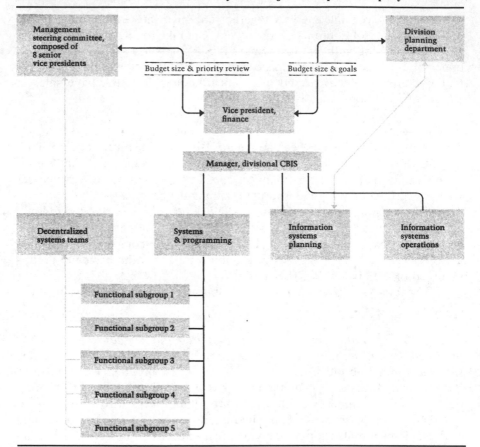

A small fraction of the decentralized team members have come originally from the information systems department. The great majority, however, have been either hired directly into the functional department to fill
this special role or transferred from some non-EDP position within the division and then trained. Division personnel judge this to be an extremely
effective arrangement.

3. *The existence of an information systems planning department.* This department of five people is directly responsible for coordinating and implementing the process of formal planning. The job description
of the manager of this department is the one given in Exhibit 3; that exhibit
provides insight into the scope of this manager's responsibilities and the
vital task of the group—to ensure that the planning process is carried out
in a timely and apt fashion.

4. *The influence of a strong bottom-up planning process.* CBIS planning begins in the five subgroups of the systems and programming area.

Working alone, or in conjunction with the analysts from the various vice presidential staffs and with user-managers, as they see fit, the members of these five subgroups have the basic responsibility for putting together a two-year plan.

They then forward these plans to the information systems planning department, which coordinates them and begins to integrate them, matching costs against available budget dollars. The manager of divisional CBIS and the vice president for finance participate in this process.

Within the divisional CBIS framework, there are three main issues to be resolved. The first is the degree of involvement vice presidents should undertake and how they can provide meaningful guidance to the CBIS activities as they evolve. By the time the consolidated plan is passed up to them through the levels, all the basic decisions have been made, in a very real sense, and it is most difficult for them to reverse this momentum and make substantive changes. As the company uses this framework, then, the real challenge is to find means to bring the vice presidents into the planning process in a meaningful way, given the enormous time pressures under which these people labor.

Second, the planning horizon currently being used is under fire. At present the period is two years, and in the start-up stages of planning (which are still in the recent past) this relatively close horizon made sense because it cut the planning job down to manageable proportions. But today the company can handle a more extended horizon, and there is considerable pressure to extend it by one year. It takes about 4½ years for this company to develop a new aircraft, and both the steering committee and the EDP department realize the desirability of extending the planning horizon toward this ideal limit.

Third, the divisional CBIS activity is isolated from similar activity elsewhere in the company. There is only limited coordination with the other company EDP centers, and it is possible that opportunities are being lost through not sharing hardware-software expertise and not working out joint applications.

On balance, however, this department provides an example of a highly organized, comprehensively planned organism built around a major computer installation.

In International Manufacturing

A quite different picture is presented by a major international manufacturing company.

Operating in over 60 countries, with the equipment of six different computer manufacturers, the company has an annual hardware rental bill which runs to nearly $100 million. More than 95% of this is spent in its 40 largest installations.

Until two years before our research project, these installations developed largely independently of one another. Concerned with rising aggregate costs of the company's CBIS activities, top management founded a control group, staffed from corporate headquarters, that was split 50–50 between personnel with user orientations and personnel with technical strengths. This group's role is currently threefold.

First, the group must approve acquisition of any hardware renting for more than $2,000 per month. When such an acquisition is contemplated, a feasibility study must be prepared and submitted to this group, which then draws on its knowledge of the hardware at other company installations and evaluates the economic justification presented in the study to make its decision. The company feels that this mechanism has significantly improved its technical decisions by bringing a quality of expertise to bear on them that was simply not possible before.

Second, and more to the point of this article, the group has installed, and now monitors, a formal planning system. Each division is required to submit a two-year CBIS plan to headquarters under the signature of the vice president in charge of the division. This procedure forces senior division management to review plans in detail, a fact that has produced startling results in several instances.

In one case, when division CBIS management presented its proposed plan to senior division management, the vice president made the startling discovery, about 15 minutes into the presentation, that the document, which represented one man-year's worth of work, had been prepared under a completely different set of assumptions about division goals from those contained in the division's strategic plan. Needless to say, it was resoundingly rejected, and there ensued a period of considerably closer relations between the headquarters control group and the division CBIS management.

As of now the group has developed standard procedures specifying plan format and contents to guide the individual division in preparing its plan. This guidance will hopefully improve the overall quality of the different divisions' efforts, which has varied widely in the past.

Third, the group visits at least once a year with the manager of each division's CBIS operation, either at corporate headquarters or at the division's offices. This helps extend the already strong informal contacts of the headquarters group with the individual installations, and enables it to monitor continually for opportunities for joint efforts between different installations.

This particular corporation does not have a geographical "home base" hardware facility to build on because its applications are diffused worldwide. Hence, in the foreseeable future it is unlikely to find physical consolidation an appropriate goal.

Rather, the company has found it effective to develop a planning and control structure that rations scarce technical expertise in hardware in a particularly efficient fashion, facilitates communication about EDP operations and goals between its far-flung divisions, and coordinates these divisions' EDP activities.

These two examples show that the nature of the CBIS plan and the structure that creates it must be tailored to company needs. The items covered by a CBIS plan are relatively constant, since the pressures to plan are relatively omnipresent, but they can and must be dealt with in a fashion that meets specific company operating requirements. The range of possible planning structures is clearly very great.

Key Issues for the Future

Information systems planning is still in an early stage of development in most organizations, and numerous critical issues must still be clarified—especially the following.

1. *What are the comparative benefits of the top–down and bottom–up approaches to planning?* The effective organizations studied to date have been primarily oriented to the bottom-up approach. With this approach, different interest groups, both inside and outside the EDP department, lobby for specific projects. As these groups and their projects achieve formal recognition from above, they are assigned priorities and receive more or less formal supervision to ensure optimum resource utilization.

The main difficulty of the bottom-up approach is that top management does not actively participate in structuring the projects themselves or the general plan that grows out of them. Thus the real challenge in this area appears to be how to channel top management guidance into the planning process right from the start.

2. *What level of detail can be meaningfully incorporated in plan formation?* The more complex plans now include flow charts and time estimates for computer runs (made via SCERT or similar packages). But for no significant projects are there comfortable guides either for assessing the appropriate level of detail for current-year plans or deciding how rapidly this level should decline for ensuing years.

3. *What should the time horizon of a sound plan be?* The effective companies believe it is appropriate to prepare detailed plans for one to two years, with additional statements for two to six years that encompass general goals, objectives, manning levels, and hardware strategy. Still, in all cases there is uncertainty concerning the appropriateness of these horizons and a desire to rethink them. Executives stated that a short horizon had been used to reduce the setup work required to develop an adequate initial plan, and that they intend to place more emphasis on the long-range aspects in the future.

4. *How should a company scan for outside EDP services?* Service organizations offer specialized data bases, statistical services, time-sharing services, and special program packages. Traditionally, coordination between

company CBISs and outside service has been minimal; flexible integration of the two may become a watchword in the future.

Additionally, the two companies studied that included outside services in their information systems planning feel that they thereby stimulated a broad, thorough review of such activities and the potential benefits which they might contribute, and that this review was in itself a great benefit.

Notes

1. *HBR*, November–December 1970, p. 95.

2. SCERT is a product of COMRESS, Inc. of Washington, D.C.

3. "The Computer Comes of Age," *HBR*, January–February 1968, p. 83.

Appendix A. McKinsey Study on Effective Users

In 1968 McKinsey & Company conducted a study of the computer systems employed in 36 major companies. The sample was designed to cover a wide range of sizes and types of industry, as shown in Table A.1. McKinsey then ranked the companies on three criteria—measurable return on the computer investment, range of meaningful computer applications, and the CEO's assessment of the computer effort—and divided them into "more successful" and "less successful." The results are shown in Table A.2.

Appendix B. What is "Effectiveness"?

The 15 companies in the study sample are a diverse group of heavy EDP equipment users. The size of their annual EDP manpower and hardware expenditures ranges from $2 million to $22 million; the size of their system and programming groups varies from 50 to more than 300 men. Exhibit 1 describes other characteristics of these important users. In our interviews in each of these companies, we focused on the scope of its EDP applications, its current approach to planning, and the overall *effectiveness* of its EDP activity.

Measuring effectiveness of information systems in such a wide variety of contexts is a complex task, and necessarily is heavily subjective. Still, we tried to give objective recognition to the following factors:

The comparative quality of a company's applications in its own critical problem areas—In my view, an application is successful if it is demonstrably profitable, in money or intangible benefits.

The level of service and support furnished by the central computer staff—The best criterion for judging this is user satisfaction.

Table A.1. Breakdown of Companies in the McKinsey Study

	Number of Companies
Sales volume	
Under $200 million	6
$200 million to $499 million	5
$500 million to $999 million	10
$1 billion to $1.9 billion	9
$2 billion and over	6
Computer outlay as a percent of sales	
Under 0.25%	7
0.25%–0.49%	7
0.50%–0.99%	14
1.0%–1.99%	7
2% and over	1
Industry	
Airlines	2
Apparel	1
Chemical	8
Feed	3
Forest products	1
Insurance	3
Machinery	6
Paper	1
Petroleum	3
Primary market	2
Railroads	1
Textiles	1
Transportation equipment	4

Table A.2. Ranking of the Study Companies

	More Successful Users	Less Successful Users
Companies that plan EDP activities and audit results against plan	9	3
Companies that plan EDP but do not audit results	7	3
Companies that neither plan EDP nor audit results	2	12

The innovativeness of the applications—The managerial excellence of a company's basic data flows and management reporting systems is a much more reliable yardstick here than sheer technological sophistication (which might be reflected in extensive real-time system simulation, linear program modeling, etc.).

The competence of the company's professionals—A specialist is best evaluated by his experience, the depth of his background, and his potential for assuming key leadership positions in other, highly progressive organizations.

The tautness, efficiency, and reliability of the EDP operations.
For maximum effectiveness, then, a superior professional group would devise clever, straightforward, up-to-date applications for the areas in which a company needs them most, and keep the data flowing on schedule to the satisfaction of every user in the company.

On these dimensions, we found 10 of the 15 companies highly effective—of these, 9 engaged in serious CBIS planning. Of the 5 marginal ("somewhat effective") companies, 2 engaged in serious CBIS planning. These figures themselves demonstrate the correlation between planning and effectiveness.

4

Management Audit of the EDP Department

F. WARREN MCFARLAN

The top managements of many companies are in the classic position, vis-à-vis EDP activities, of not being able to see the forest for the trees. The latest expensive machine, the latest controversial project, the latest budget dispute, the latest technical wrinkle, and similar quantities have distracted management from its real responsibilities where EDP is concerned; namely, auditing the *management control, resource allocation, operations and technology management,* and *project control* of the EDP department, and using the resulting information to shape and direct the growth of the activity. This article first sketches the impediments that make a real management audit of the EDP department difficult and then proceeds to outline the questions management ought to ask in the course of its investigation of each of the four areas of primary concern.

The recent flood of books and articles on EDP management practice has explicitly recognized the need both for an EDP planning system and for senior-management involvement in key decisions relating to the area. However, the manner in which these needs are fulfilled is also critically important, and this fact has been too often overlooked.

The essence of the problem was captured by a member of the computer steering committee of a large electric equipment manufacturer when he noted:

"I feel totally frustrated at these meetings. Every time I attend I see a two-hour presentation of some new project with flowcharts, file structure, and detailed cost/benefit analyses. I am always so overwhelmed by detail that I wind up voting for the project to avoid exposing my ignorance."

The existence of a steering committee, in itself, indicates that the company was at least trying to plan and manage its EDP function at a reasonably high level, but this effort was clearly not meeting with success.

In this particular company, as in so many others, an inadequate interpretation by the top-management group of how to execute its EDP-related responsibilities led to an initial, excessive preoccupation with operating detail, an area with which a steering committee has neither the time nor the necessary background to cope effectively. Consequently, in the process of its deliberations, this steering committee never even approached the more subtle policy issues, such as the validity of the EDP planning, the adequacy of the EDP management control system, and the practical structure of the resource-allocation process-issues on which its guidance was critically needed and with which it was well qualified to deal. Ultimately, the members' sense of growing frustration led to abandonment of the committee.

What business needs, in my opinion, is a broader definition of senior management's responsibilities in guiding the EDP resources and evaluating its relative effectiveness. To begin with, there are four key topics that top management must examine and raise questions about:

☐ Management control.
☐ Resource allocation.
☐ Operations and technology management.
☐ Project management.

In the discussion that follows, I have paid special attention to the aspects of these topics about which concepts are particularly poorly formed and where further thought and research are likely to offer significant benefit.

There are also some special considerations relating to the EDP area which top management should keep in mind:

☐ The dramatic growth both in dollar value of installed equipment (from $7.0 billion in 1965 to $25.5 billion in 1970) and in the number of people employed (there were in 1973 over 500,000 systems analysts and programmers) suggests an opportunity for economy through more efficient internal operations. As they audit the EDP activity, managers might keep in the backs of their minds that such rapid growth is often accompanied by the accumulation of fat.

☐ In most companies, EDP management practice has developed in isolation from the organization's other management systems and functions. This is true because the whole area has been progressing rapidly, because its technical content and skill requirements have been changing at a great rate, and because the forest of operating problems has prevented companies from integrating the EDP department properly with the other components of the organization.

Hence, beyond simply controlling, motivating, and evaluating the EDP department on a periodic basis, top management should devote part of its effort to encouraging coordination between the EDP department's management practices and those used in other departments of the company. Management practices are not as well formulated nor as well implemented in this portion of the business as in others; and senior management must take some care to ensure that the characteristically "messy" EDP department is as effectively controlled and planned as the older (and presumably neater) regular departments of the company.

☐ The early automation of clerical and physical-control systems has permitted a sequential evolution to more complex, more subtly interrelated EDP applications, and this has caused the number and variety of standard EDP technical skills to explode. The simple world of systems analysts and programmers has been supplanted by one populated with such diverse technical craftsmen as telecommunications specialists, operating systems specialists, and data-base administrators. In consequence, the levels of technical integration required *inside* the EDP department have grown sharply.

☐ At the same time, the exploding technical performance of new machines has opened new horizons. There are now physical-control applications that previously were not economically feasible, and the dynamics of these applications are more complex than those of the early applications. The stand-alone, batch-processing computer has been replaced by complex multiprogramming computers, computer networks, minicomputers, and many other devices. The increase in technological options this new generation of equipment represents is obscuring the boundaries of the territory to be covered.

Indeed, it has become difficult to define exactly where a computer begins and other entities leave off. One large organization, for example, wanted to find out why its research laboratories were using its large computer facility less and less frequently. Investigation revealed that the laboratories had recently acquired several large pieces of industrial testing equipment that contained their own built-in minicomputers. Although this fact had an impact on the company's EDP resource-utilization, it was never considered in the decision to acquire the testing equipment, simply because this equipment was to be used "for research purposes."

As it happened, there were other, cheaper ways of getting the same testing capability, by using simpler machines in combination with the company's central EDP facility. These alternatives were concealed from view by the laboratories, because they wanted complete control over all aspects of the testing environment. Such questionable and unnecessary duplication of facilities is far from infrequent.

With these special considerations in mind, let us look at the way management ought to approach its audit of EDP control, resource allocation, operations and technology, and special-project management.

Management Control

Top management needs two key structures to control EDP. The first is a financial reporting system that allows it to do the following things:

- ☐ Review the department's performance on a periodic basis.
- ☐ Compare the department's development against the formal plans for it.
- ☐ Check the functioning of the department's project control systems.

The second is a structure that links the responsibility for various departmental decisions to the operations of the users—ordinarily other company departments. Generally, this structure is a procedure to account for EDP expenses, either on a charge-out or an overhead basis.

Periodic Financial Reports

A financial reporting system should provide timely résumés of expenditures against budget for the different organizational components within the department. In particular, the reporting system should mesh neatly with the project control system so that the aggregate of project expenditures can be clearly related to the department's total expenditures.

One might think that EDP installations, which enable the development and operation of large corporate control systems, would have organized good control systems of their own; but this is frequently not the case. For example, the best financial reporting effort of the EDP department in one major insurance company is a six-week-old comparison of expenditures and budget which is so constructed that one cannot correlate the reported expenses by project with the aggregate expenditures. This same company has an efficient, imaginatively designed corporate control system, organized around its decentralized profit centers, that rapidly tracks and evaluates the performance of its agents.

Also, the system must identify financial performance variances. In volatile environments, to be sure, where there are wide fluctuations in transaction volumes, it may be necessary to put parts of the operations budget on a flexible basis. The important point is that a clear comparison between *expected* expense and actual expense is needed for control.

Finally, for large installations the system should include a software package that diagnoses the ways a given application uses the different components of the EDP configuration. This package permits the financial system to allocate hardware costs to an application in proportion to the demands that application makes on the whole computer resource. The advent of multiprogramming systems has made the design of this package a complex task—simple devices such as time clocks can no longer give meaningful data on how much of the computer resource is being consumed by a given application.

After management has seen to the installation of such a financial reporting system, it should periodically evaluate its effectiveness by raising these questions:

☐   Are the performance data delivered by this system of comparable quality and timeliness as those received from other departments?

☐   Has the structure of the financial reporting system been reviewed in the past three or four years with an eye to changing technology standards?

☐   Does the system provide its data in a form that permits management to compare the efficiency of the EDP department with that of outside service bureaus and other installations?

Overhead vs. Charge-out
Management makes a highly critical decision in choosing between the following alternatives:

☐   The EDP department will be a cost center whose charges are passed on to the operating departments as corporate overhead.

☐   The major part of its expense will be charged out to the various departments in proportion to their use of the facility.

Here are the arguments *for* overhead accounting and *against* chargeout accounting:

☐   Overhead accounting is cheaper than charge-out accounting. Both the design and implementation of cost-allocation systems are expensive, particularly for the computer operations, where special software packages must usually be installed.

☐   The overhead system leaves the responsibility for EDP department costs where it belongs—in the EDP department. The users of EDP should not be made responsible for EDP department costs. They generally do not have the background to make alternative resource-allocation decisions of EDP expenditures versus other items; these decisions must be made at the corporate level, and hence the quality and efficiency of the EDP department is a top-management responsibility.

   (This argument undercuts the rationale for charge-out—namely, holding the users responsible for their own demands—and overhead accounting is then the only fair choice. One may well question the validity of this argument. A similar case, after all, could be made against *all* systems of transfer pricing, of which charge-out is just a special variant.)

☐   The overhead system tends to keep the EDP department honest and within bounds, because the EDP department must account for its funds in a straightforward manner. A company that uses the charge-out system runs the risk that EDP department cost will be hidden under other department budgets, and this may encourage ungoverned growth of the EDP function.

☐   The overhead system brings EDP expenses directly under the eyes of the corporate controller; and he may feel that he can exercise better control over *all* company department expenditures under overhead accounting. There is some risk that the charge-out system encourages user departments to conceal expenses of their own in the expenditures of the EDP department.

The research division of a large pharmaceutical manufacturer, for example, is a heavy user of the company's central EDP resource. This division has chronic and severe difficulties living within its budget and is in constant conflict with the controller, who monitors the division's expenditures closely. The controller also monitors the EDP department's expenditures closely, which he can do easily because the company uses overhead accounting for EDP expenses. He feels that a change to charge-out would cause him to lose some of his control over the expenses of the research division and the EDP department as well— if these two segments of the company were left to do business with each other, he feels, the levels of their expenditures would grow in a significant and irresponsible way.

(Of course, misdemeanors under charge-out indicate poor management control, not necessarily a weakness inherent in the chargeout concept.)

☐   The overhead system tends to insulate the EDP operation from the fluctuations of corporate activity, and this has its advantages. The charge-out system, on the other hand, can lead to dramatic EDP department instability as corporate profits rise and fall. EDP billings are highly visible items on user income statements, and under a charge-out system user requests for reports and services are likely to drop sharply in a time of economic stress. This could have a devastating impact on the EDP department, whose long lead times for systems development and hardware shifts require some budgetary continuity if it is to make effective progress.

These arguments are primarily relevant where general management is weak, and where it is important to give a fledgling EDP department room to prove itself. Usually, they are outweighed by the reasons for using a charge-out system, particularly in organizations with strongly decentralized management control systems. The charge-out system offers the following advantages:

☐   It requires more meaningful analyses and commitments on the part of users, who must allocate financial resources among projects that demand EDP and projects that do not.

☐ It provides a rough map of the ways in which the EDP department is interacting with other segments of the company. Top management can use this map to check its impressions of the extent to which the EDP department is integrated into the company.

☐ It gives top and divisional management a framework for realistically assessing the relative competitive efficiency and capability of the company department vis-à-vis outside sources.

☐ Charge-out provides economic data that permit top management to evaluate its option to centralize or to decentralize EDP operations and systems design.

☐ Charge-out also provides data that are useful in deciding whether to add or delete applications. In practice this use of the data can be dangerous, since significant components of EDP-operations cost are fixed within relatively broad swings in production volumes. Thus, abandoning an application may appear to offer great savings to the user, under a charge-out system, while from the corporate view it will make little or no difference.

If one compares the arguments for overhead accounting and those for charge-out accounting, it is clear that charge-out frequently offers the more significant advantages where management is vigorous or the EDP department is becoming mature. Hence, corporate management should ask these questions:

☐ Do we have a charge-out system? If not, has the subject been recently and professionally reviewed?

☐ Does out charge-out system integrate effectively with the broader management control system of the organization? Is it being treated on a serious basis for decision making or is it just another bookkeeping exercise, one we might usefully consider a candidate for elimination?

☐ Have the charge-out data been structured to highlight costs of configuration changes and application shifts, or are they so highly aggregated and filled with arbitrary cost allocations that they are valueless for these purposes?

Resource Allocation

No topic in EDP administration is more critical or sensitive than the process by which the company allocates financial and manpower resources to the EDP department for its developmental activities and ongoing operations.

Ostensibly, these allocations are approved through a number of different mechanisms:

☐ The manager or lower level executives in EDP review detailed summaries of a project or a particular operation.

☐   Senior managements in user departments review project reports for activities that affect them directly. (This happens most often in situations where there is a charge-out system for allocating user costs.)

☐   A corporate steering committee hears presentations and reviews the project summaries.

In actual practice, however, the vast majority of resource-allocation decisions are no more made in this manner than capital budgeting decisions are made by the committee for capital budgeting in a large corporation.[1] But this fact is often not even recognized; indeed, people act as though it were not true.

In most large organizations, top management, top user management, steering committees, and such groups are so far removed, in sheer organizational distance, from the specifics of any proposed project or operation that they are effectively prohibited from applying analytic criteria to the EDP decisions they must make. Instead, their judgments are heavily influenced by highly subjective criteria relating to the company's financial position ("What can we afford?"), other commitments already made, and the quality of support a project or operation has received as it has moved upward on its way to the decision-making group or individual involved. The evaluation of this last criterion—quality of support—is heavily influenced by the track record of the activity's sponsors and their perceived understanding of corporate goals.

The sheer technical merits of the project have little relevance at this point, since neither time nor expertise is ordinarily available at these levels for such considerations. This clearly suggests that the guts of the resource-allocation process cannot be managed just by assigning responsibility for it to decision-making groups at the top of a company.

But it does suggest that these groups must pay attention to the process by which new project ideas are generated at the technical levels of the organization. They should carefully consider this question respecting lower organizational levels:

Does the planning process adequately involve the people who have sufficient understanding and credibility to both develop a new EDP application idea and evaluate its worth?[2]

Good Planning Style

The mere existence of a formal planning process is not enough; it is the quality of this process which is the key. This point was dramatically illustrated in a recent study of a research department, in which the investigators made an effort to evaluate the quality of ideas actually submitted to department management against ideas which were formulated but not submitted.[3] The results, which were compiled by a panel of knowledgeable judges, are shown in Exhibit 1—approximately 25% of the best ideas went unsubmitted.

Exhibit 1.   Quality of Projects

	Excellent–Good	Fair–Poor	Total
Unsubmitted	28 (24%)	19 (10%)	47 (16%)
Submitted	88 (76%)	168 (90%)	256 (84%)
Total	116	187	303

Next, management reviewed *both* the submitted and unsubmitted projects (without knowing the results of the prior analysis) and moved some into the active category and some into inactive categories. A subsequent study showed that of the 29 ideas that were now accorded active project status, 11 were project ideas that previously had gone unsubmitted (see Exhibit 2). These findings reinforce the importance of designing the planning process to encourage intelligent initiatives at the lower levels, and they strongly suggest that failure on this dimension can lead to significant inefficiencies in terms of new project identification.

As these data would indicate, a company that offers a low reward and high risk for an individual who openly sponsors a new systems development project may well be defeating itself. On the other hand, if sponsorship of a valuable new project for the company promises low risk with high personal career advantages, the company will probably find that it is receiving a richer stream of ideas. The incentive system, in other words, must be congruent with corporate goals.

Further, the company must ensure that the planning and project-approval processes provide feedback and criticism to those who submit ideas; this encourages an evolutionary approach to conception and development, rather than a go/no go approach.

Yet good planning and proper incentives are only the necessary conditions for effective resource allocation. They are not sufficient in themselves. At the beginning of this article I said that it is the style and manner in which a planning system and a top decision-making unit are used which are really critical. Thus a company needs *informal* as well as formal pro-

Exhibit 2.   Project Status After Full Management Review

	Active	Decision Postponed[a]	Rejected	Total
Unsubmitted	11	6	30	47
Submitted	18	43	195	256
Total	29	49	225	303

[a]Idea that was judged to be more relevant to another company division was communicated, but there has been no response.

cedures to meet its need for substantial collaboration and exposure of new
ideas during the formulative stages. Frequent presentations of evolving plans
to an EDP steering committee, lunches with key members of user management, and joint discussions between user staff and EDP staff are all important
elements. At the annual presentations of the formal plans, there should be
few surprises for anyone.

Finally, attention must be paid to the EDP project portfolio in terms
of its riskiness. It is extremely easy to veer either toward a set of low-risk/
low-payoff projects in the name of conservatism or, alternatively, toward a
series of high-risk projects which, if the worst happens, may so significantly
cloud perception of EDP performance that the department will subsequently
prevent other potentially attractive projects from being undertaken. A balanced portfolio of proposals must be maintained, including both modest sure
winners and high-risk items.

In auditing its resource-allocation procedures, then, top management
should keep the following questions in mind:

- [ ] Are the lower levels adequately involved?
- [ ] Is the incentive system for project development congruent with
corporate goals?
- [ ] Does the planning process allow for feedback from operations to
development?
- [ ] Is the company developing a viable, balanced portfolio of EDP
activities?

Technology and Operations

In-company technology and the management of the computer processing
environment have changed more rapidly in the 1960s and early 1970s than
any other aspect of EDP administration. In the hardware-software environment, the simple selection decision for a batch-processing computer made
once every two to three years has necessarily been replaced by a complex,
highly professional, and continuous decision-making activity. Computer configurations change almost monthly as parts are added and dropped, new
software packages are acquired, and new data-input devices installed. Too,
companies today deal with more than a single vendor—half a dozen vendors'
components may be attached to a company's family of configurations.

The expansion of EDP technology requires that top management review
the methods used to track the department's technological growth.

One place to begin is with a complete inventory of hardware and software resources. Many companies are continually surprised at what turns up
in the corridors, cabinets, and corners of their facilities. Recently, one company was shocked to find that it had acquired over 100 minicomputers, over
a period of two years, without any central coordination or knowledge of

other installations. These acquisitions had in fact led to significant excess capacity and to duplication of software expenses.

Next, there is the task of evaluating the configurations of hardware and software that the company is actually using. Given a certain hardware-software inventory and given a company's specific needs, management should inquire whether the resources are being used to full potential. This requires more than ordinary administrative expertise, in conjunction with up-to-date *technical* expertise.

The technical expertise of the 1960s, unless totally revamped and re-structed, is of little value in 1973; hence management should review its sources of technical knowledge. For example, does it have access to really to-notch, disinterested advice on hardware and software, or is it primarily dependent on homegrown, conventional wisdom? Has it evaluated its source of advice against other outside sources? Does it rely primarily on vendors for technical advice or is it self-sustaining? Is there a steady infusion of either new technical expertise or technical training in its EDP department? Is the department familiar with the technical accomplishments and failures of nearby companies facing similar technology challenges?

The following anecdote shows the importance of these points. A large manufacturing company recently undertook a detailed study of alternative methods of selectively reducing the size of its computer configuration while maintaining an acceptable level of service to its customers. One afternoon, as the opening step in this "study" process, the EDP management unhooked part of the capacity of the configuration; since the hardware monitors in-dicated that this capacity was largely unused, management anticipated it would have little impact on the machine's throughput.

Unfortunately, the computer system reacted violently; it slowed down by 50%, causing several disruptions in the operating schedule. Subsequent analysis indicated both that there were far less risky ways of seeing what would happen if that piece of capacity were disconnected, and that a knowl-edgeable technical specialist could have predicted the results in detail.

A hard-nosed reevaluation of the company's technical personnel in-dicated that all the specialists in the department had spent the bulk of their careers in the company, attended few seminars, and had very little major design experience with a vendor.

Hence, in auditing the company's technical expertise, management should raise the following questions:

- ☐ Is there a complete, periodic inventory of hardware and software?
- ☐ How efficiently is the inventory being used?
- ☐ Do the department personnel understand the problems and the potential of the latest technology?

Operations Management

The operating sections of the EDP department that perform the data-input and computing functions may be considered a factory; they form the locus where the basic product of the department is produced. Just as with any kind of factory, the existence of a well procedurized reporting system is absolutely mandatory for monitoring overall performance and identifying the sources of problems. How to set up this reporting system is a subject of some controversy, however, because there are two schools of thought as to what really constitutes the operations factory.

One school of thought seeks to strip operations proper of all programming and other technical skills and to pool these skills with the systems and programming group, or perhaps to split them off as a ward wing of the department. Proponents of this method of organization argue that purely technical functions ally themselves more naturally with the systems and programming area, and that putting them together, away from operations, leads to better coordination and better career paths for the individuals involved.

The opposing school of thought has moved toward an "integrated factory" concept, according to which operations includes not only the computer center and data input and output activities, but also program maintenance, operating systems maintenance, and other allied technical-support services. This school believes that since decisions must be made as to what volume and quality of computing resources should be devoted to operations proper, it only makes sense to keep personnel who are competent to analyze and evaluate these resources under the direct supervision of operations.

It seems reasonable to sympathize with the integrated-factory school— at least, to some extent. The group that manages EDP operations must be sufficiently aware of key issues and trade-off possibilities to articulate the full thrust of operations considerations when trade-offs between design alternatives must be made. The reason is simple; no one else is sufficiently conversant with the facts of operations to articulate them clearly, in firsthand fashion. This requires, however, significant hardware-software expertise in the operations group.

The Influence of Generations

Equally, advanced operations cannot work unless the operations management has a grasp of each succeeding technological innovation. For example, the installation of a newer and more complex operations system, while it may offer an improved capability in theory, in practice depends on such mundane things as rearrangements of peripheral machines in the computer room, more sophisticated and better-trained operators, and reworked schedules in the data input and output areas. Management of the dull and unattractive tasks entailed by new technology is critical, here, to the success of the technology itself.

The problem of organization design vis-à-vis operations is further complicated by the proliferation of subspecializations—such as telecommunications design, data-base management, and operating-system design—which also have to be integrated into the organizational design. One might think that such sophisticated applications would not bear too heavily on the more routine operations, but this is far from true. Each radical application of this kind generates additional processing requirements and higher work-load levels for a department.

The failure of many departments to alter their operating procedures to take account of these new factors has resulted, in many cases, in companies' owning fourth-generation hardware and hiring fourth-generation talent but still managing operations by methods suited to the first and second generations of computing.

One company still maintains a Gantt chart-scheduling mechanism left over from second-generation computing to schedule jobs through its two interconnected, multiprogrammed computers. A three-man group working only on the first shift (the company's computer operations runs three shifts a day) busily posts numbers to a board. But the numbers are obsolete before preparation and are mercifully ignored by both EDP users and other operations personnel.

A company may have a difficult time, then, in defining the proper scope for its operations control system and in seeing that this system meshes with the internal complexities of its EDP department. The best complement to any system of this kind, of course, and the best guarantee of its proper functioning, is an operations manager who has a management background, a technical background, and a salary level that are commensurate with those of the manager of systems and programming.

The disparity between these positions which could be justified a decade ago is no longer appropriate. Although it is now considered a position of great responsibility, the post of manager of computer operations is all too frequently staffed by an individual with less than impressive credentials. The necessity of dealing with technical options, large numbers of workers, and situations that have a strong impact on the company's ability to function on a day-to-day basis makes this a key managerial position.

In sum, top management should consider these questions respecting control of operations:

☐ Is there a concise, objective performance reporting system that embraces turnaround time, rerun time, hardware-software component utilization, and user complaints in such a way as to permit both senior EDP management and top management, itself, to quantitatively monitor performance?

☐ Are users satisfied with speed and quality of service? If not, why not? If they are, have operational procedures and capacities been studied to ensure that this is not being achieved through highly inefficient procedures which are hidden by the existence of too many computer personnel and excessive machine resources?

☐ Is the group that manages EDP operations fully involved in the hardware-software evaluation process—and are the members *competent* to be involved?

☐ Have the scheduling and control procedures been modified to become consistent with the technical options made possible by the most
recent generation of machines acquired by the department?

☐ Does the manager of computer operations have commensurate
salary, management, and technical background with the manager of
systems and programming?

☐ Is there a managerial career path with an opportunity for advancement in operations which is commensurate with that in systems and
programming?

"Hard" answers, I might note, will not be possible for all these questions.
More experience with and research on the best uses of subspecialization
options—for example, data-base management and telecommunications design—are urgently needed. A second area where research is needed is the
design and use of hardware and software packages for measuring and monitoring aggregate operations performance in terms of its use of technical and
personnel resources. As we acquire more insight on how to link management-
control concepts to operations activity, new improvements in operations
efficiency will be possible.

Still a third area for spadework is improvement of methods by which
a department can more effectively monitor the changing technological environment and translate its shifts into appropriate courses of action for the
company.

Project Management

An enormous number of controversies and broken promises have been created in project management. In response, a thriving literature of cookbook
approaches has developed. Without being unduly harsh and critical of work
to date, I have concluded that one can examine this area intelligently only
if one begins with the recognition that it is an elusive and complex topic.

First of all, only flexible, contingency-management concepts are likely
to be found useful in so fluid a context; standard procedures in one setting
often are useless in another. But there are basic elements which can be
brought to bear in varying combinations on the control and management of
a project. As the reader will note, I have classified them into four categories.
These categories may be subject to some discussion, but, on balance, they
have proved distinctive and useful groupings for me. Categories one and
two are primarily organizational in nature while categories three and four
are composed of specific tools and procedures.

If there is some agreement, however, that these categories present a
concise view of the elements of project management, there is considerable
disagreement about how they should be applied and the impact they can
make in different settings. The viewpoints of EDP managers range from the

opinion that "project management is an act of faith where there are no tools except the intuitive judgment" to the opinion that "the availability of the new tools and techniques and, above all, experienced managers has reduced most of the risk out of the process."

I do not wish to get involved here in the controversy about the absolute impact of these tools and techniques. Instead, I wish to identify certain critical dimensions that *limit* their effectiveness in any particular setting.

Dimensions of Risk

The criterion I have used to identify these dimensions is risk. As the reader will understand shortly, the farther a project moves out on any of these dimensions, the greater will be the inherent risk of the project's failure, and the less effective will be the contribution of any formal planning and controls. In other words, as a project moves toward high risk on any of these dimensions, two *management* questions—which can be stated, not quantified—must be asked:

☐ How much risk can we tolerate before the project becomes unacceptable, *regardless* of the tools and management techniques available?

☐ When a given project becomes unacceptable, should it be restructured on a more modest scale or should it be dropped completely?

For each project in the department's portfolio, management must answer the preceding questions as risk grows along these dimensions:

☐ The degree of absolute technological innovation vis-à-vis the state of the art for the project's application. As the project pushes the absolute state of the art—for example, using new data-base software, new telecommunications concepts, and new programming languages—cost estimates, time estimates, and likelihood of simple technical success all become steadily more uncertain and the number of potential, unforeseen difficulties soars.

☐ The degree of "company relative" technology. As a project pushes into technology with which the company is unfamiliar, it becomes more risky, even though such technology is being used routinely in other organizations. Project-control mechanisms, supported by outside consultants, can have a bigger impact on this dimension than on the first, but many of the more spectacular failures have occurred here.

☐ The degree of organizational differentiation between the EDP department and the departments being served. A department whose primary goals, time-span orientation, interpersonal-relationship patterns, and orientation to change in day-to-day operations are similar to those of the EDP department will be able to implement EDP projects with fewer controls and less difficulty than a department where these factors are at wide with those of the EDP department.[4] Thus EDP/R&D projects may require less control that EDP/marketing projects. Also, R&D will find its projects' output more useful, things being equal, than marketing.

☐ The degree of structure inherent in a project. Projects that involve simple automation of existing data-processing or clerical systems or well understood physical processes are far more tractable to planning and control than projects whose outputs are either information or automation of processes whose characteristics are only poorly understood. A strict project-design discipline, combined with strong integration procedures, is likely to offer great payoffs here.

One such project-design discipline calls for a two-stage design effort. During the first stage project personnel perform a complete systems analysis and design job; the documents are presented to senior management in the user department, and formally signed after the necessary modifications have been made. Only then does the second stage—the implementation stage—begin. It includes a formal procedure for handling any additional design changes that can be justified by the user.

Although it is hard to operate under such a severe system when it is first installed, continued use of this technique has paid strong dividends in diverse settings by forcing stronger analysis and commitment before the main expenditures are authorized.

☐ The sheer physical size of the project. As the size of the project grows, the importance of formal project planning and control, external integration, and internal integration grows. For small projects, informal controls are generally adequate; for very large projects, even elaborate controls may be inadequate, and here the extensive use of submodules is often the answer.

These dimensions are unmistakably qualitative; and control procedures for most EDP projects cannot be specified and handled by a simplistic uniform set of procedures. Project control, to be effective, must embrace the thinking and concepts of general management control and organizational behavior. Many of the elements of control in my four categories originated in these fields, and it is that type of broad thinking, as opposed to technical EDP expertise, which needs to be brought to bear on the problem.

In evaluating an EDP administration's efforts on project control, then, management should consider these questions:

☐ Has the problem of project control been systematically addressed? Do we have a meaningful, formal, project-control approach and strategy, or do we do it on an ad hoc basis?

☐ Is there a formal procedure for coping with the problem of restructuring a project? Does it take into account changes in technology, reassessments of resource potential, and shifting corporate needs?

☐ Is there a formal process for performing postaudits of projects to examine the effectiveness of the project management efforts and methods for communication?

☐ Are postaudit results used to improve the management of other projects?

☐ Have the key project managers been exposed to modern project-management concepts through seminars, training, and other methods?

☐ Does the company's management-control system reward effective project management?

Concluding Note

The technical complexity of the EDP field, its relative newness, the limited, nontechnical training of its managers, and its crisis atmosphere have often prevented the questions I have raised from being asked. Too often, other, tangential questions have been raised instead—for example:

☐ What does telecommunication technology mean to me?

☐ What do the newly developments in external memory imply for the department?

☐ What is "data-base software technology" and what are its implications for me and for my environment?

The danger to EDP administration lies in the fact that the expertise needed to answer these tangential kinds of questions, while also critical to the success of the EDP department, is quite different from the types of *management acumen* that can ensure the questions raised in this article are being handled appropriately.

On the other side of the coin, it is only through answering and acting on the questions I have raised that top management can approach the two main issues with which it must be concerned, vis-à-vis EDP:

☐ Are we spending too much or too little or just enough on EDP?

☐ Is the money we have allocated to the department being properly spent?

Notes

1. See Joseph L. Bower, *Managing the Resource Allocation Process* (Boston: Division of Research, Harvard Business School, 1970).

2. See my article, "Problems in Planning the Information System," *HBR*, March–April 1971, p. 75.

3. Norman R. Baker and James R. Freeland, "Structuring Information Flow to Enhance Innovation," *Management Science*, September 1972, p. 105

4. See Paul R. Lawrence and Jay W. Lorsch, *Organization and Environment: Managing Differentiation and Integration* (Boston: Division of Research, Harvard Business School, 1967).

Appendix: Elements of Project Control & Management

1. *Formal integration procedures, where the users of the project's output are located outside the EDP department:*

☐ Regular meetings between the users and an EDP project advisory committee.

☐ The appointment of a full-time manager in the user's department to coordinate and manage the interface with EDP.

☐ Assignment of one or more staff members from the user's department to the project design team.

☐ Distribution of the minutes of liaison meetings to all management in the user's department.

☐ Formal procedures for users to follow in approving the initial design and all subsequent changes.

☐ Assignment of a project leader and project personnel who have had significant, positive, personal contact with key members of the user's department.

☐ Charge-out of project costs to the user's department.

2. *Formal integration procedures within the EDP design team and between the various units of the EDP department:*

☐ Institution of a technical steering committee for the project, composed of key project staff.

☐ Selection of a project leader who has significant technical competence (for projects with relatively advanced technology).

☐ Use of formal flowcharts and other documents to highlight the interfaces between key systems components, when these are significantly differentiated.

3. *Formal planning tools:*

☐ Use of PERT or CPM to lay out the project.

☐ Detailed documentation of systems design and specifications prior to project implementation.

☐ Use of systems simulation or other hardware-resource planning tools.

☐ Use of modular approach to design, with strong limitations on the size of each module. (One large bank recently wrote off as a sunk cost over $5 million of investment in the development of a trust accounting package. The prime cause of failure appeared to be its decision to install, simultaneously, four massive modules of interwoven coding that constituted a single software package. Although this maneuver might have been appropriate in a sophisticated environment of highly skilled and experienced programmers, the approach failed at the bank because personnel in the EDP department lacked the necessary skills. A more modest, evolutionary approach would have offered far greater likelihood of success.)

4. *Formal control tools:*

☐ Use of PERT or CPM during project implementation.

☐ Formal procedures for collecting and measuring actual expenditures of time and dollars by project submodule.

☐ Regular use of formal postaudit procedures. (Post-auditing is often recommended but seldom implemented. No other commitment is easier to state but harder to deliver on.)

5

Managing the Crises in Data Processing

RICHARD L. NOLAN

Now that the experiences of many companies with advanced data processing systems can be analyzed, fresh and important observations can be made for the guidance of policy-making executives. For one thing, we can see the outlines of both the past and future, with six stages of DP growth standing out. Although no companies have yet entered stage 6, a few are approaching it, and a great many have entered the intermediate stages. Stage 3 produces a notable jump in already rapidly increasing computer costs; stage 4 features the rise to control of users of DP programs; and stages 5 and 6 feature the development and maturity of the new concept of data administration. For DP managers and program users, this evolution has significant implications. Planning, control, operations, technology, and costs—all are affected profoundly. Using the benchmarks described in this article, managers can see where their organizations stand in the evolutionary process. Turning to the guidelines described at the end, they can better understand how to manage the growth that lies ahead of them.

The member of the corporation's steering committee did not mince words:

> I'm telling you I want the flow-of-goods, computer-based system, and I am willing to pay for it. And you are telling me I can't have it after we have approved your fourth running annual budget increase of over 30%. If you can't provide the service, I'll get it outside. There are now reliable software companies around, and my people tell me that we should take seriously a proposal that we received from a large minicomputer vendor.

The reply of the vice president of information services was not well received:

> I'm at the edge of control. It isn't any longer a question of financial resources. My budget has grown from $30 million in 1975 to over $70 million in 1978. The technology is getting ultracomplex. I can't get the

right people fast enough, let alone provide suitable space and connections
to our sprawling computer network.

On returning to his office, the vice president knew that the steering committee
member would be going ahead with the minicomputer. There was no way
that the corporate technical staff could provide the flow-of-goods functions
for the money or within the time frame that the minicomputer vendor had
promised. Although he could not put his finger on it, he knew something
was not right.

The vice president mused at the irony of it all. Five years ago he was
brought in to set up a corporate computer utility after a similar period of
poorly understood growth (that growth had been the undoing of his predecessor). Now key questions were being asked about a similar growth pattern
of the data processing budget, and he did not have the answers. He wished
he did!

The plight of the vice president of information services is not singular.
The rapid growth in DP services that many companies experienced in the
mid- to late 1960s is occurring again in numerous companies. The resurgence
is confusing.

The senior managements of some of these companies thought that the
DP control structures put in place during the 1970s, such as charge-out,
project management, and consolidation of computing activities under tight
budgetary control, would contain any future budget growth. Nevertheless,
the annual DP budget growth rates are exceeding 30%. Further, just the
annual budget *increments* are equal to the total size of the budgets four or
five years ago. The confused top executives of these companies are searching
for answers to what underlies this growth. Is it good? Will it stop? What are
the limits?

The answers are not obvious, but a probing of the status of the DP
activities in different companies and of the current technological environment sheds light on the situation and provides insights into the management
actions that are needed to prepare for and manage the growth.

Six Stages of Growth

Studies I have made during the 1970s of a series of companies—three large
corporations early in this decade, 35 companies several years ago, and then
a large number of IBM customer concerns and other corporations since
then—indicate the existence of six stages of growth in a company's DP
function. These stages are portrayed in Exhibit 1.

The scheme shown in this exhibit supersedes the four-stage concept I
described in *HBR* in 1974.[1] The four stages described then continue to be
valid, but the experience of recent years reveals a larger and more challenging
picture.

This exhibit shows six stages of DP growth, from the inception of the

Exhibit 1. Six Stages of Data Processing Growth

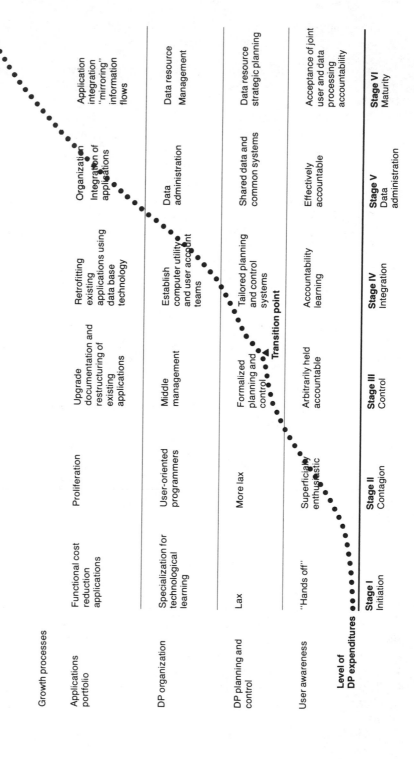

computer into the organization to mature management of data resources. Through mid-stage 3, DP management is concerned with management of the computer. At some point in stage 3, there is a transition to management of data resources. This transition involves not only restructuring the DP organization but also installing new management techniques.

To understand the new picture, one must look at the growth in knowledge and technology, at organizational control, and at the shift from computer management to data-resource management. I will consider each of these topics in turn.

Burgeoning of Knowledge

Organizational learning and movement through the stages are influenced by the external (or professional) body of knowledge of the management of data processing as well as by a company's internal body of knowledge.

The external body of knowledge is a direct response to developments in information technology. It is concerned with developments in the theory of DP management as well as with the collective documented experiences of companies. The internal body of knowledge, however, benefits from the external body of knowledge but is primarily *experiential*—what managers, specialists, and operators learn first-hand as the system develops.

It is important to realize how greatly DP technology spurs the development and codification of an external, or professional, body of knowledge. For this reason a company that began to automate business functions in 1960 moved through the stages differently from a company that started to automate in 1970 or 1978. The information technology is different, and the extent of professional knowledge on how to manage the DP technology is much greater in the latter years. Not only is the external body of knowledge more sophisticated, but the information technology itself is more developed.

Control & Slack

Organizational learning is influenced by the environment in which it takes place. One possible environment is what might be called "control"; a second might be called organizational "slack," a term coined by Richard M. Cyert and James G. March.[2]

In the *control* environment, all financial and performance management systems—including planning, budgeting, project management, personnel performance reviews, and charge-out or cost accounting systems—are used to ensure that DP activities are effective and efficient. In the *slack* environment, though, sophisticated controls are notably absent. Instead, incentives to use DP in an experimental manner are present (for example, systems analysts might be assigned to users without any charge to the users' budgets).

When management permits organizational slack in the DP activities, it commits more resources to data processing than are strictly necessary to get the job done. The extra payment achieves another objective—nurturing of innovation. The new technology penetrates the business's multifunctional areas (i.e., production, marketing, accounting, personnel, and engineering). However, the budget will be looser, and costs will be higher. Management needs to feel committed to much more than just strict cost efficiency.

The balance between control and slack is important in developing appropriate management approaches for each stage of organizational learning. For example, an imbalance of high control and low slack in the earlier stages can impede the use of information technology in the organization; conversely, an imbalance of low control and high slack in the latter stages can lead to explosive DP budget increases and inefficient systems.

Exhibit 2 shows the appropriate balance of control and slack through the six stages. In stage 3 the orientation of management shifts from management of the computer to management of data resources. This shift, associated with introduction of the data base technology, explains the absence of entries in the computer columns after stage 3.

Shift in Management Emphasis

In stage 2 more and more senior and middle managers become frustrated in their attempts to obtain information from the company's computer-based systems to support decision-making needs. Exhibit 3 helps to explain the root of the problem. The exhibit is based on a fictional corporation that represents a kind of composite of the organizations studied. The spectrum of opportunities for DP equipment is called the "applications portfolio."

The triangle illustrates the opportunities for cost-effective use of data processing to support the various information needs in the organization. Senior management predominantly uses planning systems, middle management predominantly uses control systems, and operational management predominantly uses operational systems. At every level there are information

Exhibit 2.   Optimum Balance of Organizational Slack and Control

Stages	Organizational slack Computer	Data	Control Computer	Data	Objective of Control Systems
Stage 1	Low		Low		
Stage 2	High		Low		Facilitate growth
Stage 3	Low	Low	High	Low	Contain supply
Stage 4		High		Low	Match supply and demand
Stage 5		Low		High	Contain demand
Stage 6		High		High	Balance supply and demand

Exhibit 3.   Applications portfolio Late in Stage 2[a]

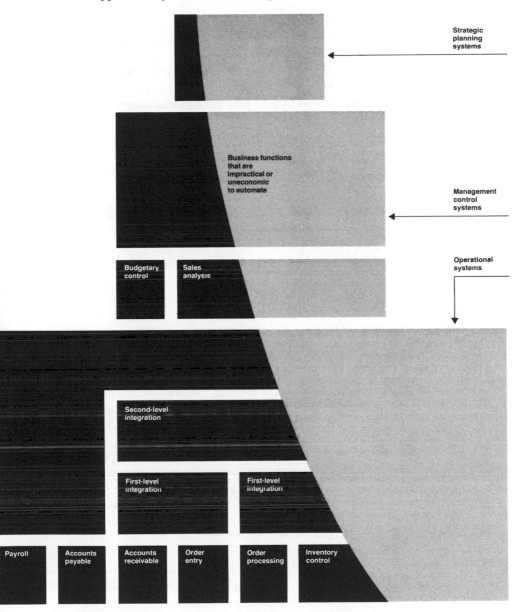

[a]An example of first-level integration is a purchase order application that uses order processing and inventory status information. An example of second-level integration is a vendor payment application that uses accounts payable and purchasing information.

systems that are uneconomic or unfeasible to automate, despite managers' desires for faster and better data.

In stage 1 in this organization, several low-level operational systems in a functional area, typically accounting, are automated. During stage 2 the organization encourages innovation and extensive application of the DP technology by maintaining low control and high slack. While widespread penetration of the technology is achieved by expanding into operational systems, problems are created by inexperienced programmers working without the benefit of effective DP management control systems. These problems become alarming when base-level systems cannot support higher-level systems—in particular, order processing, production control, and budgetary control systems. Maintenance of the existing, relatively poorly designed systems begins to occupy from 70% to 80% of the productive time of programmers and systems analysts.

Sometime in stage 3, therefore, one can observe a basic shift in orientation from management of the computer to management of the company's data resources. This shift in orientation is a direct result of analyses about how to put more emphasis, in expanding DP activities, on the needs of management control and planning as opposed to the needs of consolidation and coordination in the DP activities themselves. This shift also serves to keep data processing flexible to respond to management's new questions on control or ideas for planning.

As the shift is made, executives are likely to do a great deal of soul searching about how best to assimilate and manage data-base technologies. The term "data administration" becomes common in conferences, and there is much talk about what data administration controls are needed.

But there is little effective action. I believe there is little action because the penetration of the technology is obviously low at its inception, and a combination of low control and high slack is the natural balanced environment to facilitate organizational learning. However, at the same time the seeds are being sown for a subsequent explosion in DP expenditures.

Stage 3 is characterized by rebuilding and professionalizing the DP activity to give it more standing in the organization. This stage is also characterized by initial attempts to develop user accountability for the DP expenditures incurred. Usually these attempts take the form of charge-outs for DP services. Unfortunately, both the conceptual and technical problems of implementing user accountability lead to confusion and alienation; real gains in accountability are not made. Nevertheless, the trends of DP chargers in user budgets are rarely reversed.

Consequently, during stage 3 the users see little progress in the development of new control systems while the DP department is rebuilding, although they are arbitrarily held accountable for the cost of DP support and have little ability to influence the costs. Even the most stalwart users become highly frustrated and, in a familiar phrase, "give up on data processing."

Explosive Growth

As stage 3 draws to a close, the DP department accomplishes its rebuilding and moves the data base and data communication technologies into several key application areas, such as order entry, general ledger, and materials requirements planning. In addition, the computer utility and network reach a point where high-quality services are being reliably provided to the users. When these accomplishments are realized, a subtle transition into stage 4 takes place.

Just when users have given up hope that data processing will provide anything new, they get interactive terminals and the various supports and assistance needed for using and profiting from data-base technology. Already they have benignly accepted the cost of DP services. Now, with real value perceived, they virtually demand increased support and are willing to pay pretty much whatever it costs. This creates DP expenditure growth rates that may be reminiscent of those in stage 2, rates one may have thought would not be seen again.

It is important to underscore the fact that users perceive real value from data-base applications and interactive terminals for data communication. In a recent study of one company with more than 1,500 applications, I found that users ranked their data-base and interactive applications as far and away more effective than users of conventional or batch technology ranked their applications. This company has been sustaining DP expenditure growth rates of about 30% for the past four years. More important, the users of the new applications are demanding growth to the limits of the DP department's ability to expand.

The pent up user demand of stage 3 is part of the reason. But a more important part of the reason is that the planning and control put in place in stage 3 are designed for *internal* management of the computer rather than for control of the growth in use of it and containment of the cost explosion. Exhibit 4 shows the typical pattern of starting and developing internal and external (that is, user-managed) control systems. Late in stage 4, when exclusive reliance on the computer controls proves to be ineffective, the inefficiencies of rapid growth begin to create another wave of problems. The redundancy of data complicates the use of control and planning systems. Demands grow for better control and more efficiency.

In stage 5, data administration is introduced. During stage 6, the applications portfolio is completed, and its structure "mirrors" the organization and the information flows in the company.

Identifying the Stage

How can executives determine what stage of development their corporate data processing is in? I have been able to develop some workable benchmarks

Exhibit 4. Growth and Maturation of Data Processing Planning and Control

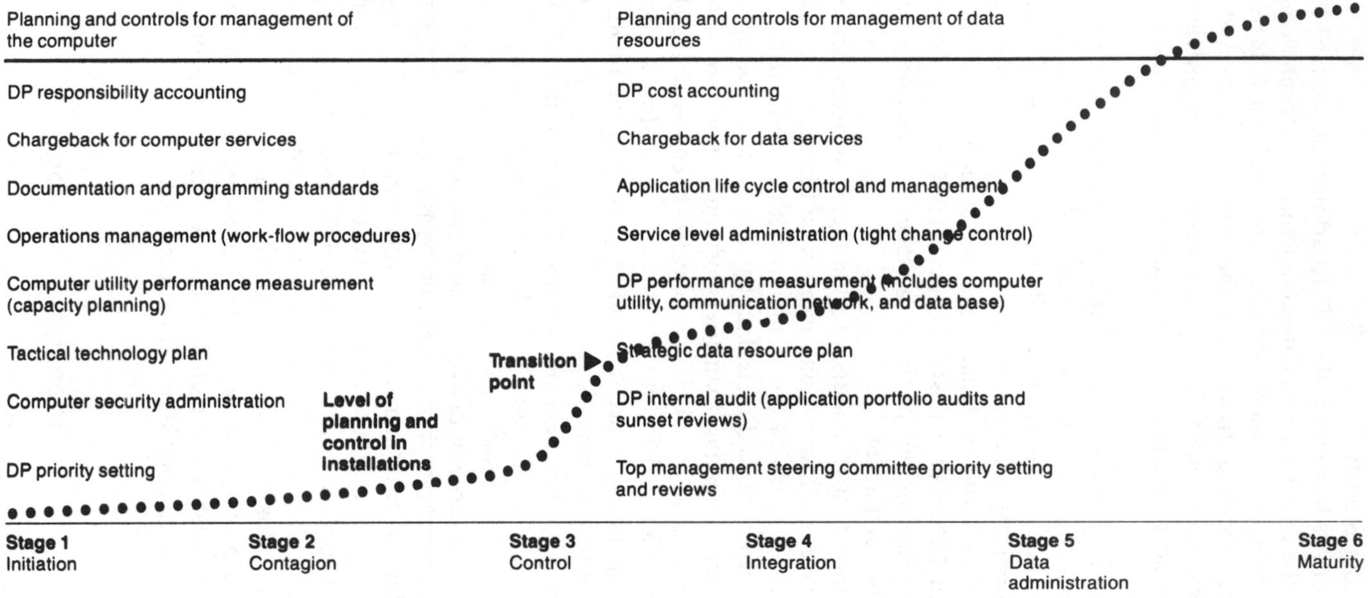

Planning and controls for management of the computer

Planning and controls for management of data resources

DP responsibility accounting

DP cost accounting

Chargeback for computer services

Chargeback for data services

Documentation and programming standards

Application life cycle control and management

Operations management (work-flow procedures)

Service level administration (tight change control)

Computer utility performance measurement (capacity planning)

DP performance measurement (includes computer utility, communication network, and data base)

Tactical technology plan

Strategic data resource plan

Computer security administration

DP internal audit (application portfolio audits and sunset reviews)

DP priority setting

Top management steering committee priority setting and reviews

Level of planning and control in installations

Transition point

| Stage 1 Initiation | Stage 2 Contagion | Stage 3 Control | Stage 4 Integration | Stage 5 Data administration | Stage 6 Maturity |

Exhibit 5. Benchmarks of the Six Stages

	Stage 1 Initiation	Stage 2 Contagion	Stage 3 Control	Stage 4 Integration	Stage 5 Data administration	Stage 6 Maturity
First-level analysis						
DP expenditure benchmarks.	Tracks rate of sales growth.	Exceeds rate of sales growth.	Is less than rate of sales growth.	Exceeds rate of sales growth.	Is less than rate of sales growth.	Tracks rate of sales growth.
Technology benchmarks.	100% batch processing.	80% batch processing. 20% remote job entry processing.	70% batch processing. 15% data base processing. 10% inquiry processing. 5% time-sharing processing.	50% batch and remote job entry processing. 40% data base and data communications processing. 5% personal computing. 5% minicomputer and microcomputer processing.	20% batch and remote job entry processing. 60% data base and data communications processing. 5% personal computing. 15% minicomputer and microcomputer processing.	10% batch and remote job entry processing. 60% data base and data communications processing. 5% personal computing. 25% minicomputer and microcomputer processing.
Second-level analysis						
Applications portfolio.	There is a concentration on labor-intensive automation, scientific support, and clerical replacement.		Applications move out to user locations for data generation and data use.		Balance is established between centralized shared data/common system applications and decentralized user-controlled applications.	
DP organization.	Data processing is centralized and operates as a "closed shop."		Data processing becomes data custodian. Computer utility established and achieves reliability.		There is organizational implementation of the data resource management concept. There are layers of responsibility for data processing at appropriate organizational levels.	
			◀ Transition point			
DP planning and control.	Internal planning and control is installed to manage the computer. Included are standards for programming, responsibility accounting, and project management.			External planning and control is installed to manage data resources. Included are value-added user chargeback, steering committee, and data administration.		
Level of DP expenditures ▷	User awareness.	Reactive: End user is superficially involved. The computer provides more, better, and faster information than manual techniques.	Driving force: End user is directly involved with data entry and data use. End user is accountable for data quality and for value-added end use.		Participatory: End user and data processing are jointly accountable for data quality and for effective design of value-added applications.	

for making such an assessment. Any one of the benchmarks taken alone could be misleading, but taken together these criteria provide a reliable image. I will describe some of the most useful benchmarks so management can gain a perspective on where it stands and on what developments lie down the road. For a visual portrayal of the benchmarks, see Exhibit 5.

It is important to understand that a large multinational company may have divisions simultaneously representing stages 1, 2, 3, 4, and perhaps 5 or even 6. However, every division that I have studied has its DP concentrated in a particular stage. Knowledge of this stage provides the foundation for developing an appropriate strategy.

First-Level Benchmarks

The first step is to analyze the company's DP expenditure curve by observing its shape and comparing its annual growth rate with the company's sales. A sustained growth rate greater than sales indicates either a stage 2 or 4 environment. Then, analyze the state of technology in data processing. If data-base technology has been introduced and from 15% to 40% of the company's computer-based applications are operating using such technology, the company is most likely experiencing stage 4.

In the light of International Data Corporation's research on the number of companies introducing data-base management systems technology in 1977 (shown in Exhibit 6), I believe that roughly half of the larger companies are experiencing stage 3 or 4. This is further corroborated by evidence that 1978 saw the largest annual percentage growth in the total DP budgets of U.S. companies—from $36 billion to an estimated $42 billion, or a 15½% increase.

As shown in Exhibit 6, about 55% of IBM installations in 1979 will have data base technology, compared with only about 20% in 1976. I feel that this means the explosive stage 4 in DP expenditures can be expected in the next two to five years in most companies; the increases may be somewhat moderated by continuance of the impressive technological advances that have improved prices and equipment performance.

Second-Level Benchmarks

The second step is to focus on the four growth processes shown in Exhibit 5. Each major organizational unit of the company, such as a subsidiary, division, or department, should be listed. Then the growth processes associated with each organizational unit should be identified. For example, a decentralized subsidiary generally has all four grwoth processes, from expansion in the applications portfolio to an increase in employees' awareness of DP potentials and functions (see the left-hand side of Exhibit 5). However, a division using the services of a corporate computer utility is likely to have only two of the growth processes—expansion in the applications portfolio and in user awareness.

Next, identify the stage (see the bottom of Exhibit 5) of each of the growth processes associated with the organizational unit. Use growth as an example in the applications portfolio. The approach used for this process is similar to that for any of the processes. The procedure is as follows:

1.   Define the set of business functions for the organizational unit that represents cost-effective opportunities to apply DP technology. I call this the "normative applications portfolio." It represents the business functions that would be receiving DP support if the company had achieved stage 6 maturity. Exhibit 7 portrays such a scheme.

2.   Taking each function in turn, indicate for each set of systems the support that data processing gives to the function in the organization. Ask, "What is it doing for our business?" I suggest doing this by shading the

Exhibit 6. Data-Base Management Software Installed and Projected to Be Installed on IBM Medium—To Large-Scale Computers in the United States*

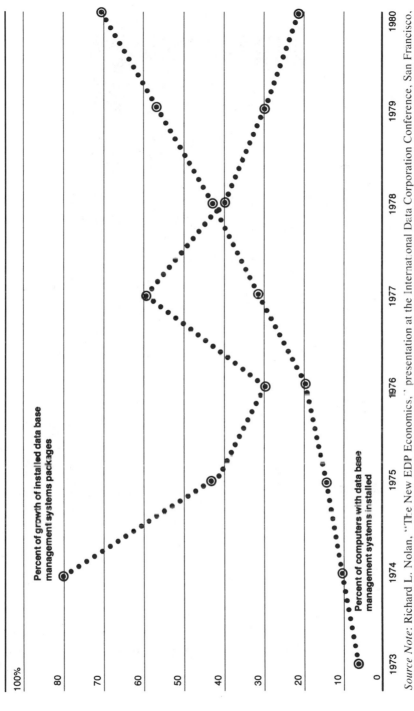

Source Note: Richard L. Nolan, "The New EDP Economics," presentation at the International Data Corporation Conference, San Francisco, April 3, 1978.

Exhibit 7.   Investment Benchmarks for DP Applications

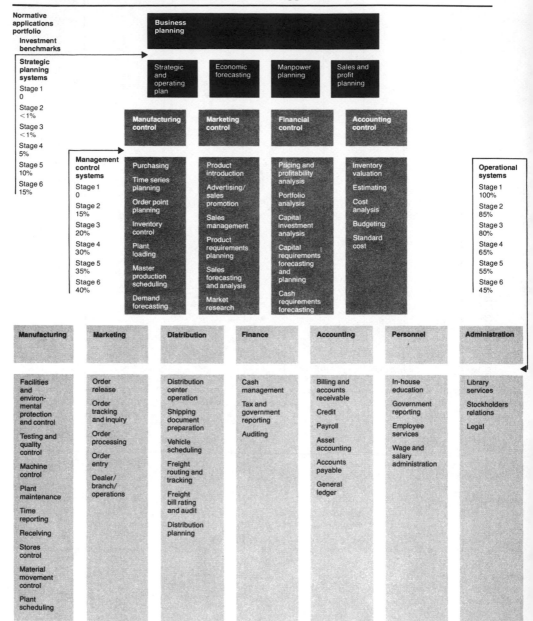

Normative applications portfolio	Business planning			
Investment benchmarks				
Strategic planning systems	Strategic and operating plan	Economic forecasting	Manpower planning	Sales and profit planning
Stage 1 0				
Stage 2 <1%	Manufacturing control	Marketing control	Financial control	Accounting control
Stage 3 <1%				
Stage 4 5%				

Management control systems	Purchasing	Product introduction	Pricing and profitability analysis	Inventory valuation	Operational systems
Stage 1 0	Time series planning	Advertising/ sales promotion	Portfolio analysis	Estimating	Stage 1 100%
Stage 2 15%	Order point planning	Sales management	Capital investment analysis	Cost analysis	Stage 2 85%
Stage 3 20%	Inventory control	Product requirements planning	Capital requirements forecasting and planning	Budgeting	Stage 3 80%
Stage 4 30%	Plant loading	Sales forecasting and analysis		Standard cost	Stage 4 65%
Stage 5 35%	Master production scheduling	Market research	Cash requirements forecasting		Stage 5 55%
Stage 6 40%	Demand forecasting				Stage 6 45%

Strategic planning systems: Stage 5 10%, Stage 6 15%

Manufacturing	Marketing	Distribution	Finance	Accounting	Personnel	Administration
Facilities and environmental protection and control	Order release	Distribution center operation	Cash management	Billing and accounts receivable	In-house education	Library services
Testing and quality control	Order tracking and inquiry	Shipping document preparation	Tax and government reporting	Credit	Government reporting	Stockholders relations
Machine control	Order processing	Vehicle scheduling	Auditing	Payroll	Employee services	Legal
Plant maintenance	Order entry	Freight routing and tracking		Asset accounting	Wage and salary administration	
Time reporting	Dealer/ branch/ operations	Freight bill rating and audit		Accounts payable		
Receiving		Distribution planning		General ledger		
Stores control						
Material movement control						
Plant scheduling						

space for the function on the normative applications portfolio; use a 10-point scale to shade the function at 10%, 40%, 80% or whatever amount seems appropriate. Looking at all the shaded functions as a whole, judge the level of support given the system as a whole.

3. Then, match the support given the system as a whole with the benchmarks shown to the right of Exhibit 7. For instance, 80% support of operational systems, 20% support of management control systems, and just a faint trace of support for strategic planning systems would show the organization to be at stage 3.

4. Next, look for matches and mismatches between DP investment and the key functions that contribute to the company's return on investment or profitability. For example, if the company's business is manufacturing, and if half of the DP system investment goes to support accounting, a red flag is raised. The possibility of a mismatch between expenditures and need should be investigated.

After the functional assessment, one should conduct a technical assessment of the applications. The technical assessment gets at the concern of whether the DP activity is using current technology effectively. Benchmarks used include individual system ages, file structures, and maintenance resources required.

Again using a scheme like that described for Exhibit 7, compare the support given by data processing to the different corporate functions with the technical assessment. Are the DP systems old, or are the file structures out of date, or are there other shortcomings indicating that up to date technology is being neglected? Such neglect may be the result of managerial oversight, of a shortsighted desire to make a better annual profit showing, or of other reasons. In any case, it means that a portion of the company's assets are being sold off.

During the definition and assessment of the applications portfolios for a company, a DP "chart of accounts" is created. The business functions identified in the applications portfolio are the "objects of expenditures." Creating the chart of accounts is an important step in achieving the level of management sophistication required to effectively guide this activity through stages 4 and 5 and into the stage 6 environment.

So much for the applications portfolio analysis. Using the same sort of approach, management can turn next to the other growth processes shown in Exhibit 5 for second-level analysis. When the analysis is completed, management will have an overall assessment of the stage of the organization and of potential weaknesses in its ability for future growth.

If complete analyses of this type are made for all important organizations—divisional and functional—of the company, management will have a corporation-wide profile. Exhibit 8 is an example. Such a profile provides the foundation for developing an effective DP strategy.

Exhibit 8.   One Company's Stage Analysis

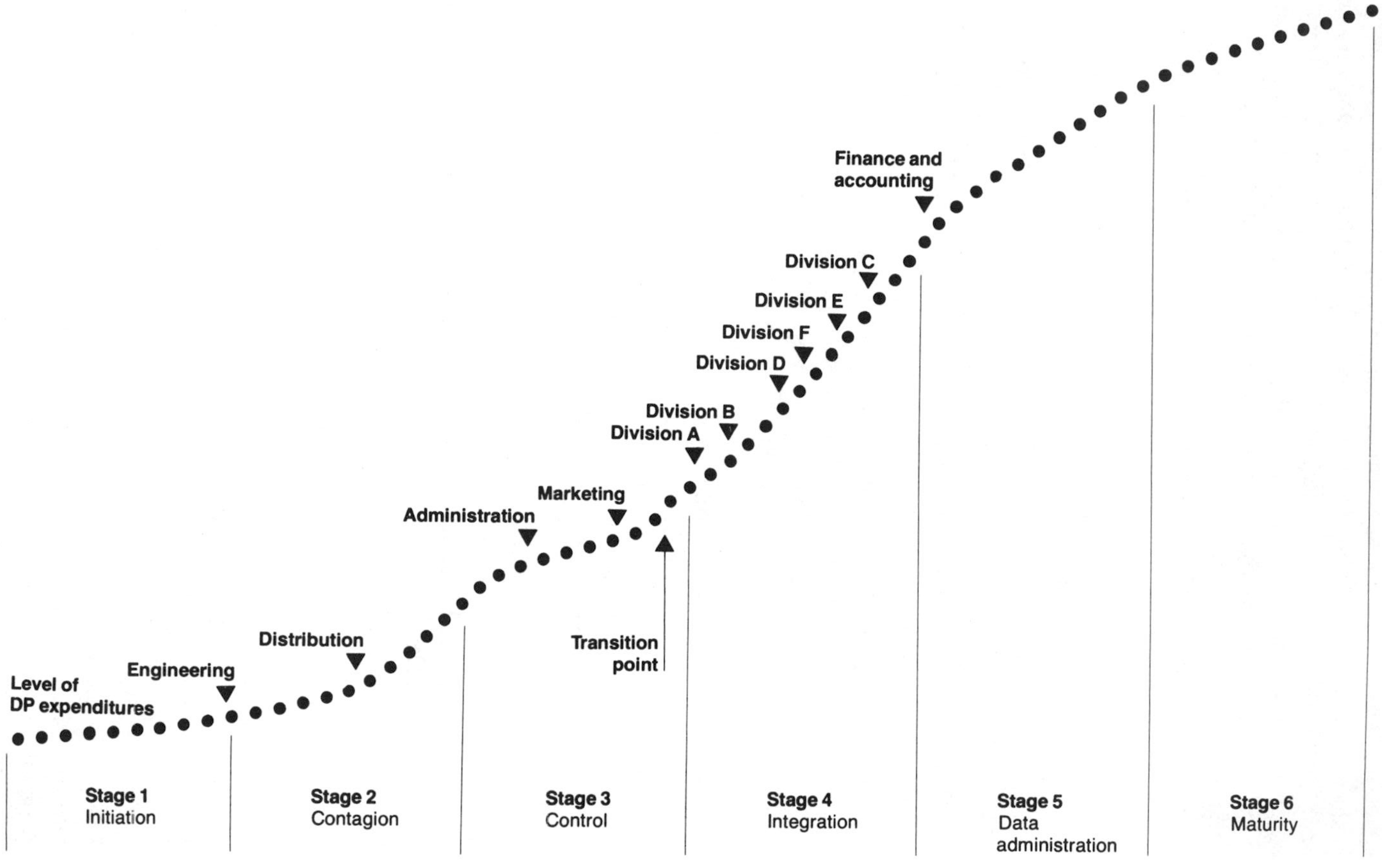

Guidelines for Action

In most sizable U.S. corporations, data processing is headed for an extremely rapid growth in the next few years. This growth is not necessarily bad; in fact, I believe that if the growth can be managed, it will be the most cost-effective growth experienced to date. Here are five guidelines for managing the growth successfully.

1. *Recognize the fundamental organizational transition from computer management to data-resource management.* With the introduction of data-base technology in stage 3, an important shift in emphasis occurs—from managing the computer to managing the company's data resources. Obviously, this transition does not occur all at once. It appears first in the analysis of the late stage 2 applications portfolio and is a result of the requirement to restructure it so that applications can be tied together efficiently.

The transition also becomes apparent during the implementation of controls. Difficulties with charge-out systems that are computer-oriented cause management searches for alternative ways to achieve user accountability. This often leads to the conclusion that the user can be accountable for the functional support, but data processing must be accountable for management of shared data.

The key idea is to recognize the importance of the shift in management emphasis from the computer to data and then to develop applications and planning and control systems to facilitate the transition. Applications should be structured to share data; new planning and control systems should be data oriented.

2. *Recognize the importance of the enabling technologies.* The emerging information technologies are enabling companies to manage data economically. It is important to emphasize the word *economically*. What companies did only a few years ago in establishing large central DP utilities is no longer justifiable by economic arguments. Data-resource management changes the economic picture.

Data-base and data-communication technologies are important from an organizational standpoint. Sprawling DP networks are enabling new approaches to management control and planning. We can now have multidimensional control structures such as function (e.g., manufacturing, marketing, and finance), product, project, and location. Managers and staff can be assigned to one or more of the dimensions. Through shared data systems, senior management can obtain financial and operating performance reports on any of the dimensions in a matter of hours after the close of the business day, month, quarter, or year.

Last but not least, developments in on-line terminals, minicomputers, and microcomputers are opening up new opportunities for doing business at the operational level. Airline reservation systems, for example, no longer stand alone in this area; we now can include point of sale (POS) for the retail industry, automated teller terminals (ATMs) for the banking industry, and plant automation for the manufacturing industry.

3. *Identify the stages of the company's operating units to help keep DP activities on track.* A basic management tenet is: "If you can't measure it, you can't manage it." The applications portfolios of a company provide data processing with a chart of accounts. In the past, management lacked a generic and meaningful way to describe and track a DP activity—that is, to locate it in relation to the past and future. However, there is now a generic and empirically supported descriptive theory of the evolution of a DP activity—the stage theory. One can use this theory to understand where the company has come from, which problems were a result of weak management, and which problems arose from natural growth. More important, one can gain some insight into what the future may hold and then can try to develop appropriate management strategies that will accomplish corporate purposes.

4. *Develop a multilevel strategy and plan.* Most DP departments have matured out of the "cottage industry" era. They have reached the point where they are woven into the operating fabric of their companies. There are many documented cases of the important impact that a computer failure of mere hours can have on a company's profitability.

Nevertheless, many DP departments continue to hold on to the cottage industry strategy of standing ready to serve any demands that come their way. This can have a disastrous effect when stage 4 begins to run its course. The extent and complexity of corporate activity make it impossible for data processing to be "all things to all users." Consequently, decisions will have to be made on what data processing will be—its priorities and purposes; when, where, and whom it will serve; and so on.

If the DP management makes these decisions without the benefit of an agreed-on strategy and plan, the decisions are apt to be wrong; if they are right, the rationale for them will not be adequately understood by users. If users do not understand the strategic direction of data processing, they are unlikely to provide support.

Development of an effective strategy and plan is a three-step process. *First,* management should determine where the company stands in the evolution of a DP function and should analyze the strengths and weaknesses that bear on DP strategies. *Second,* it should choose a DP strategy that fits in with the company's business strategy. And *third,* it should outline a DP growth plan for the next three to five years, detailing this plan for each of the growth processes portrayed in Exhibit 5.

It is important to recognize that the plan resulting from this three-step process is, for most companies, an entry-level plan. Thus the plan cannot and should not be too detailed. It should provide the appropriate blueprint and goal set for each growth process to make the data processing more supportive of the overall business plan. It should also be a spark for all those in DP activities who want to make their work more significant and relevant to corporate purposes.

5. *Make the steering committee work.*   The senior management steering committee is an essential ingredient for effective use of data processing in the advanced stages. It provides direction to the strategy formulation process. It can reset and revise priorities from time to time to keep DP programs moving in the right direction.

From my observation, I think that the steering committee should meet on a quarterly basis to review progress. This would give enough time between meetings for progress to be made in DP activities and would allow the committee to monitor progress closely. Plan progress and variances can make up the agenda of the review sessions.

Notes

1. See my article, written with Cyrus F. Gibson, "Managing the Four Stages of EDP Growth," Chapter 2, this book.

2. Richard M. Cyert and James G. March, "Organizational Factors in the Theory of Oligopoly," *Quarterly Journal of Economics*, February 1956, p. 44.

6

An Unmanaged Computer Can Stop You Dead

BRANDT ALLEN

Many businesses today are discovering that technology alone will not ensure the success of their information systems. In fact, the growing availability of computer-driven technology has made it harder for many companies to keep pace, and some have already fallen behind. Complicating this grim picture is a growing shortage of trained personnel. Such serious problems jeopardize not only the computer systems but the very existence of some companies, says Brandt Allen. Senior executives must become closely involved with their information systems to reassess and perhaps reorganize their computer resources. He details some measures for first aid and long-term care of the information system that should help to avert life-threatening situations.

Author's Note. The conclusions presented in this article are based largely on my experiences during the past three years as a consultant, researcher, or case writer with over 50 large and generally advanced computer users in the United States, Canada, Europe, and the Pacific Basin. Most of these businesses were one of the three largest in their respective industries; almost all had computer budgets in the $10 to $100 million range. Also during this time I've been able to discuss the observations and ideas in this paper with executives from over 200 other companies during seminars and short courses on information systems management.

Throughout this paper the terms "DP," "computer," "information resources," and "information systems" have been used interchangeably. Information resources is the more descriptive term as it encompasses functions ranging from traditional data processing and information reporting, to the technologies of office automation, networking, and process control in manufacturing as well as nontraditional applications such as decision support systems and the information center concept. The author wishes to acknowledge the contributions of Professor F. Warren McFarlan of the Harvard Business School, Mr. Phil Grannon of the IBM Company, and Professor Louis T. Rader, my colleague at the University of Virginia and former President of Univac, to the development of certain concepts in this article.

There may be slight stylistic differences in the article published in this book and the way it eventually appeared in the Harvard Business Review.

This should be the best of times for computer departments: installed capacity is increasing at better than 30% per year in the United States and even more in the largest and most advanced companies. Demand for new applications is rising even faster. Pressures for increased productivity in manufacturing, distribution, services, and, especially, the office, together with renewed emphasis on improved quality for American products, can only place even greater demands on computing organizations in the future. Indeed, the over-all picture reads like a technologist's dream: huge backlogs, increasing de-mand, constantly improving efficiencies of computers, new technology in-cluding that for the office, the plant, and probably the home promising even greater potential, with inflation enabling the justification of more and more applications. It sounds almost too good to be true—and it is! In spite of these glowing prospects, many businesses today face problems so serious in their use of our wonderful technology that they threaten to jeopardize not only the bright futures of many of those computer professionals, but also those of the firms which employ them. Matters are at a crisis point in com-puting for many corporations. Technology, by itself, is not enough. Busi-nesses face a tough set of computer problems today and in the future, prob-lems where the solutions are largely managerial in nature and typically beyond the scope of the executive charged with managing the computing function. Key to these solutions is the formulation of a comprehensive strategy for the deployment of information resources within the firm, something that can only be done by senior management. Unfortunately, many of these execu-tives don't yet understand the problem.

The Biggest Problems

Computer users today face a common set of problems and challenges. *The economics of computing have turned around—total costs for an application are now rising*. The costs of computing have dropped steadily since business use began some 30 years ago, driven primarily by the dramatic improvements in the performance/price of processors and memory. And continuing im-provements in this technology on the order of 25% per year can be expected for the rest of this decade, but these changes are nowhere near great enough to offset the rising cost of people necessary to support it all. The *total* cost of many applications today, including hardware, communications, software maintenance, and operations support has stopped declining and is about to rise even without considering the cost of applications development. An his-toric turning point in computing has been reached: the biggest cost element for an application today, or all applications together for that matter, is the cost of people.

For example, Exhibit 1 is a summary of the total costs of a standardized unit of computing—in this case a large, on-line, order entry application in three different years—1970, 1975, and 1980.[1] The figures are a composite of both pencil and paper studies of what the costs should have been at each

Exhibit 1. The Costs of a Standard Computer Application In This Example: A Large Order-Entry System

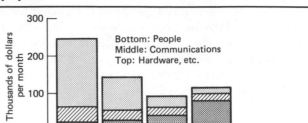

time period as well as studies of applications of similar size actually in use in a number of corporations in the U.S. *Hardware* costs include the costs of computers, environmental software and maintenance, *communications* costs include terminals, lines, and modems, *people* costs are for operations personnel, system programming, and applications program maintenance. (No applications development figures are included in this analysis.)

The total costs drop from 1970 to 1975 and again from 1975 to 1980, primarily due to the sharp price-performance improvements of computers during this time. But the support costs for people rose substantially. In the fourth column I've extrapolated these trends out to 1985. By then the computer itself will be only an insignificant part of the total cost of the application.

Most large, ongoing computer applications have total costs similar to those in Exhibit 1. Indeed by 1985 people can be expected to represent at least 80–90% of total information system costs—and probably more if proper accounting were to be given to the cost of user involvement. In Japan MITI came to a similar conclusion; its forecast is that Japanese computer department budgets by 1985 will be 85% of personnel costs.[2] The cost of the hardware will continue to drop steadily as a percentage of total costs; but the increasing cost of personnel will raise total costs of an application almost as rapidly as the underlying rate of inflation!

The shortage of applications and systems programmers is the major constraint for computer users today—it will become more severe in the years to come. The enormous demand for computing, even at increasing cost levels, requires growing numbers of new, entry-level employees; for example, the U.S. Department of Labor has forecast that the employment opportunities for new programmers and systems analysts will increase 20% in the U.S. throughout the eighties.[3] Other forecasts from the Bureau of Labor Statistics place the estimated jobs available for new entry-level computer programmers in 1990 to be 43% higher than that in 1980. In spite of these rosy forecasts of demand, the supply of such people may actually *decline* over this same time period due to changing demographics in the U.S. Between 1981 and 1988 the number of young people (aged 20) entering the workforce will fall 20%.[4] Along with this decline one can also expect a serious and depressing drop in aptitude for computer programming and systems work, at least insofar as can be measured by standardized tests. For example, math SAT scores of college-bound high school seniors dropped from 493 to 467 from 1968/69 to 1978/79.[5] Verbal scores dropped even more, from 463 to 427 for the same years. Compounding the problems of the present shortage of people as well as the shortfall to come is the alarming dropout or loss rate of employees from computing. For whatever reason, and there are many theories, the exodus of skilled employees from the ranks of programmers and systems analysts is very high. The shortage of people, particularly experienced professionals, not money or equipment or demand, will be the biggest constraint for computer users in the decade.

The pace of technological change exceeds the ability of many organizations to keep up—many today are falling behind; some are technologically obsolete. That we live in an age of rapid change is without doubt; that computers, communications systems, and office automation technology are some of the fastest changing parts of the business is also unquestioned. However, many managers seem unaware of the costs and dangers of such rapid change. First, this fast pace is a threat to employees. Many computer system personnel and their managers live in fear of the technology passing them by; too many have already fallen behind. To keep up requires a degree of training and education that many organizations are unable or unwilling to provide. Second, not only individuals, but entire companies are falling behind. Businesses and government agencies in certain industries with obsolete computers, old and outdated applications, and antiquated management practices based on late 1960s and early 1970s environments risk their own continued existences. As time goes by the best people leave, and they fall further and further behind to the point where they cannot benefit from technology without taking great risks. Increasingly, one's business is unable to incorporate the most modern and efficient manufacturing technology without up-to-date computer systems in place. Those who let their DP organizations fall behind endanger their companies. The pressure to keep information systems competitive and current will be especially important to organizations undergoing rapid change, particularly within industries facing fundamental restructuring. The predicted revolution in the U.S. banking industry and the deregulation of the airline and trucking industries are good examples of fundamental changes that take their toll of U.S. businesses unable to keep their information systems competitive. A good example already is that of one of this country's largest trucking companies is about to fold. Inflation, deregulation, and the recession have all been contributing factors in their demise, but a careful study of the company revealed that their information systems function was probably their biggest problem. Their systems for rating and routing were so out-of-date, so poorly designed, and so inflexible that they simply could no longer be used to support the business. If this company does indeed go under, the headlines will blame the recession or deregulation, but management knows that its inattention to its computer systems is just as significant a factor as these others.

Senior managers don't have confidence in their ability to manage information resources—and they don't have confidence in DP management either. The crisis in computer systems starts at the top. Of all the important functions of a business, information systems is the one area where senior management lacks real experience and understanding. There are several explanations: for many executives, the computer is a new technology that has been always treated as a specialized function in which their participation was minimal. Even today, an assignment in information systems is not on the career paths of general managers in most firms. Technology has changed so fast that what little managers do learn is quickly obsolete. Finally, few senior managers have come from the computing field. As a consequence, we find senior executives managing information resources either defensively (minimize budgets and risks, go slow, don't innovate, use strict controls) or by remote control (lost of consultants, heavy turnover of senior DP management, frequent changes of direction) always looking for some piece of magic that will suddenly make all the problems go away. The situation is made worse by the lack of comprehensive measures of performance and results that typifies most DP shops.

Backlogs of applications awaiting development are large and growing—trends in development productivity are disappointing. While there's little agreement as to what a three-year backlog actually is or what it means, most companies think they have such a situation or worse, and for most it's a big problem. Today some corporations claim their backlogs are measured in man-centuries! Businesses are creating and approving new computer projects at a rate faster than their ability to actually develop and install those applications. In many companies the delay in getting projects even begun is indeed measured in years, especially if the applications have to be programmed by conventional methods. If the problems caused by big backlogs and increasing demand were not enough, they have been compounded by the dismal record of productivity improvements many companies have realized in programming. Indeed, too often there has been no improvement at all. Today medium-sized computers cost about as much per hour as does a programmer; tomorrow the programmers alone will cause the bottlenecks, because we shall surely get increased productivity from the technology. If means cannot be found to improve development productivity dramatically, backlogs will grow and grow. This tends to drive users to outside vendors, service bureaus, and to software packages, or it makes them respond by pushing for their own systems or for higher priority on their own pet projects—thus putting great pressure on the dp organization, computer steering committees, or both. These alternatives to the traditional company-developed-and-operated computer applications are not necessarily ill-advised, but often users turn to them for the wrong reasons. Sometimes users simply give up and blame their failure to meet their business plans on lack of computer support.

Applications and data collections prove inflexible and difficult to change—a large part of the "computer problem" in most organizations stems from the poor products developed in the past. "Every change request gets to be a giant project that takes forever to complete and costs a fortune" is a universal complaint. Some blame it on programming languages; others claim it's because of their data-base system or even the data-base concept itself, while others say it's due to the shortsightedness of the original users and designers. Whatever the reasons, there is general dissatisfaction with the adaptability of information systems to changing requirements. Yet it is just this flexibility that is the crucial element of information systems, especially when one considers their high cost, long development time, and economic life—typically 10 years or more. "Overall, they're just not doing the job" is a judgment one hears everywhere.

Many backbone computer applications now need replacement—at a time when all resources are needed to whittle away at the backlogs. On top of large and growing backlogs, a great many companies now find many of their most fundamental applications sadly out of date and in need of replacement. The replacement projects, reflecting expanded requirements, more advanced technology, and more stringent controls, often are considerably larger than the applications they replace. These replacement projects now loom as big, costly, high-risk endeavors that will further delay work on the backlogs of totally new projects and yet will only marginally improve the results of delivered products as perceived by the users. The U.S. Social Security Administration is a good case in point. Its benefits payment system is quite old, primarily batch, with large tape files and programs mostly written in assembly language. A rewrite will be five years in the planning, seven in development and conversion, and, when completed, will then be expected to last late into the 1990s. The effort will require thousands of man years. While few businesses face conversions and rewrites of this magnitude, countless companies will be surprised at the burdens and risks of such big replacement projects.

Instead of establishing administrative procedures and tactical systems to manage information resources, steering committees have been formed to fill the gap—and they are not working well in many companies. Steering committees of one kind or another are widely used to review computer projects, set priorities, allocate scarce resources, propose budgets, and coordinate planning activities. Too often these committees are failures. Membership on such committees is often the most frustrating and time-consuming assignment the manager has. One of the questions I am asked most frequently is, "What is the role of a computer steering committee?" This question often comes not from companies just setting up a committee but from organizations that have been trying for years to make them work effectively. They recognize that their committees have failed, but they do not know why. Usually these failures result from a committee being used as a substitute for much needed administration practices, managerial systems, an overall structure, and a comprehensive information resources strategy, matters I will discuss later.

The related technologies of telecommunications, office automation, and computer-controlled manufacturing technology pose major integration challenges to many companies. While a few businesses have made great strides toward integrating not only their plans for this technology but major pieces of it as well, most still have not sorted out what they should do or how to go about it. It is quite common, even in large businesses, for computing and information systems to be under one head, word processing and other office automation projects under another, voice and message communications under a third, with no thought given to how, if at all, the various computer-controlled equipments and processes of manufacturing or distribution are to be related.

DP managers themselves are in trouble. Many DP managers today hold classic "no-win" jobs. They are caught in a squeeze between users who want more and more computer services and senior management concerned with costs and control. Many are trying to fight off outside service bureaus, minicomputer and microcomputer vendors who are courting their users, and even inside managers wishing to establish their own information systems groups. Unhappy users are the norm; irate users are common. In spite of increased budgets for development and new development tools, backlogs keep growing. There seems to be an invisible backlog at least as large as the visible one. Purchased packages prove difficult to implement to the user's satisfaction. Even with continued improvements in price/performance of processing and memory, and bigger budgets for equipment, capacity problems never go away. The squeeze is most apparent in the budget process: user budgets grow and flex with departmental and divisional requirements, but the dp or computer department budget is normally fixed or capped. Information resources becomes the battleground between growth-oriented users and defensive, reactive senior managers. Overriding all of these concerns is the realization on the part of many of the senior DP managers, if not the majority, that they are in dead-end jobs; there's no next, higher job for them in their company. As an example, the person to whom they report, executive vice president, vice president—administration, or chief financial officer, almost always holds a position he or she is not equipped to assume.

The Need for Strategy

Each of these problems is serious in its own right. Taken together they present a challenge so great as to jeopardize not only the computer systems of many companies but increasingly the very existence of the business itself. The 1980s will witness businesses in many industries that go on to succeed over their competitors due largely to their ability to manage the new technology and develop information systems of strategic importance to the company. Competitors will suffer and decline because they lack this ability.

Obvious examples of organizations where information resources will become the key strategic factor are American Express, MasterCard, and Merrill Lynch, but there are a great many others where the products and services that the company can design and produce, the quality and cost structures of those products and services, and speed and responsiveness to changing market conditions will depend in large part on the quality, creativity, and flexibility of their information systems.

If there ever was a time for senior executives to be closely involved with information systems this is it, yet too often we find such managers active with matters of secondary importance: approving new projects, allocating scarce budget dollars to competing departments, reviewing the status of development projects, selecting vendors, approving software packages, and the like. No doubt these activities are important and need to be decided with care, but they are largely operational or tactical and are not the most important issues for top management attention. These topics are frequently forced onto the agendas of steering committees because senior management has failed to perform its primary task: to establish an overall strategy for information resources. In my opinion senior executives should first spend their time addressing four key strategic questions:

☐ How should information resources be organized and deployed within the company?

☐ Where and how should information resources be controlled?

☐ What overall architecture should one have for applications and data?

☐ What overall architecture should one employ for technology?

Organization Design

The first strategic planning question for information resources today is: How should it be organized? Subsets of this question include:

☐ How many large or host data centers should there be and to whom should they report?

☐ How should the development groups be organized, how many should there be and where should they be located within the business?

☐ What role should the corporate information department play vis-à-vis divisional or regional departments?

☐ Should computing be brought together with office systems and communications and in what type of structure?

☐ Should DP planning be an activity separate from development and operations?

☐ How should the traditional data processing and basic business systems be organized relative to information reporting systems and decision support activities?

None of these questions can be answered until the company sorts out what responsibility for information resources each organizational participant (user department, systems developer, data center, business planner) is to assume. Each must have a clear and comprehensive statement of mission and responsibility. Few companies have such a strategy.

The key organizational question today for many large companies is that of segmentation: what information resources should be structured centrally, what located elsewhere but managed and designed centrally, what managed locally and how and where should the activities by linked? Difficult trade-offs are required to properly balance the advantages of integration with the costs of that integration. The costs are typically those of flexibility, adaptability, and the money and time required to respond to change.

Almost all organizations must decentralize more responsibility for information systems than was necessary in the past. Computers and their related technologies have become so pervasive that the simple organizational solutions of the past are no longer practical. Few central computer groups can hope to effectively manage all this technology in a large, or even medium-sized business. Even companies that have decentralized computing to a divisional or group level now find that they must go even further. End-user facilities, decision support systems, information centers, and many of the new nonprocedural programming systems all require that users assume more decision-making responsibility, yet to be successful many of these newer technologies depend for their effectiveness upon data bases and other centrally managed technologies such as networking.

A reassessment of organizational strategy is essential in view of the projected shortages in the critical MIS skill categories, the growing applications backlogs, and upcoming system rewirtes. Many companies will be reorganizing their central applications development and systems programming resources to concentrate on only matters of strategic importance. Typically these will be:

☐ Corporation-wide telecommunications networks.
☐ Data bases.
☐ A limited number of truly corporate applications.
☐ End-user facilities to be provided to divisional and corporate level departments.

At the same time, the responsibility for most of the companies' application design and programming or acquisitions will be further decentralized. For example:

☐ *Electronics Company.* This large multinational is organized in a traditional, decentralized-profit-center fashion with several dozen divisions. Data collections at a corporate data center include only those that support a few, limited, corporation-wide functions: contracting, external financial reporting, and legal. Applications related to that information are the responsibility of the corporate information systems group. All other data collections and supporting applications are delegated to the divisions except for an integrated order entry function that spans the divisions and performs the billing and collections function. Thus their segmentation is on three levels: corporate, distributed (linking the divisions for order entry), and divisional.

Control

The second element of computer strategy is that of control. Who is to control which aspects of information resources? How is control to be effected? And how is performance to be assessed and by whom? Key issues include:

☐ Who plans and approves applications and sets priority, and according to what criteria?

☐ Who selects and approves new technology, and on what basis?

☐ How are budgets set, and who determines spending levels and constraints?

☐ How are outside sourcing decisions (and all "make or buy" decisions) made, and by whom?

☐ Where and how are costs collected and charges rendered?

☐ What financial control structure is used for the data centers and development groups?

☐ How is performance measured?

☐ What corporation-wide standards are to be set, by whom, and how enforced?

☐ What is the role of audit?

The primary options are illustrated in Exhibit 2.[6] As depicted in the first column, responsibility for applications, budgets, and priorities is typically either: vested in the information services department or function; shared between that department and the end users but coordinated by a steering committee or several committees; or delegated to the users, either departmental or divisional (but definitely not an information services responsibility). The key control question is simply: Who is responsible for assuring that this company's information systems are effective?[7]

A few examples may help to illustrate these options. A DP manager of a large company came up to me at a conference recently and said, "I don't know why everyone here is so anxious to have steering committees. I'm the Director of Information Systems in my company and the title means just what it says. I'm responsible for seeing that we have the information systems that we need, just as the Director of Accounting has that responsibility for accounting systems. He doesn't have a steering committee for accounting and I'll be damned if we're gonna have one in my department."

Exhibit 2.   Elements of Control Strategy

	Decision responsibility for applications budgets, and priorities	Type of budget	Financial structure for Information resources	Objective of charge—out	Use of outside services
Centralized	Information services	Fixed	Cost center	Cost awareness	Decision of information services
Bureaucratic	Steering committee		Service center	Cost allocation	Approval of information services
Decentralized	Divisional or departmental user	Flexible	Profit center	Pricing	Local option

This is obviously an example of centralized control. At the other end of the spectrum are those companies where that same manager is called Director of Information Services and operates what amounts to an internal service bureau. Responsibility for identifying potential applications, evaluating and justifying them, and then funding or budgeting these applications is strictly a user responsibility. With decentralized control, company-wide systems become the responsibility of some corporate department, the so-called system "owner." In this situation, the corporate information services organization, if there is one, is not responsible for these key decisions on applications, priorities, and budgeting; they are not application owners. And there are a wide variety of organizations falling somewhere in between (bureaucratic) where a centralized DP function shares responsibility with various users for these key decisions. Such an approach to control is typically effected through the use of steering committees.

As depicted in the second column, the approach to budgeting reflects another important control choice for information services. In many companies the information services budget, once approved, remains fixed for the year, while in others it is variable or flexible depending upon user demand. In the latter situation, information services management has the authority to increase expenditures if demand increases over what was originally budgeted and also to cut back if the reverse is true, although this rarely happens today. For most businesses the key question is how fast will capacity grow. The type of budget employed is really a question of whether budgetary control for DP rests with a corporate information services function or the users.

An example of a company with a flexible DP budget is illustrated next:

☐ *Manufacturing Company* A large industrial products company provides information products and services to both divisions and corporate departments from a central telecomputer center in New York. Each division is a profit center; corporate staff departments are cost centers. Telecomputer charges these users for services provided and has no upper limit on their gross or total DP expenditures. However, they do have a limit or cap on the net or unrecovered portion of their budget for those activities that cannot be charged out. In effect they have a flexible budget. Budgetary control over computing in this company is decentralized; it is a function of the budgeting and decision activities of the users—various divisions and corporate staffs.

Closely related to the type of budget is the type of management control or financial control structure used for information services (Column 3). Centralized control is typically achieved by operating information services as a cost center with a fixed budget; in decentralized control structures it is more likely to be an internal profit center with a flexible budget. Charge-out practices are another key control device. As reflected in Column 4, the objective of charge-out under centralized control is to provide cost information to various parties short of actually charging out costs. There is either no charge-out at all for development or operations or it is of the "memo-record" variety. Bureaucratic control structures typically use cost allocation charge-out mechanisms either by monthly charge-backs of costs incurred or by budgeting machine rates and collecting job accounting statistics for billing. Charge-out in decentralized control structure is more often a type of transfer pricing accomplished either by adding a margin to costs or in some way reflecting standard costs or market prices. Pricing here is usually monitored or reviewed by some function other than computer services, such as the controller.

Last, another key control issue is that of sourcing: in centralized structures the decision to purchase outside or to provide services from within is made by information services or DP, in bureaucratic structures it is frequently a steering committee decision with advice or approval from DP, while in decentralized control forms it is a user's option, frequently within previously established guidelines or standards.

It is essential that these various options be selected consistently. Decentralized control over applications, budgets and priority-setting is best accomplished when information services has budget flexibility, is run more like a profit center than a cost center, and has an advanced pricing-oriented, charge-out system. It makes little sense and could lead to very serious problems if an organization were, for example, to delegate applications, budgeting, and priority decisions to users, but attempt to use a fixed budget for information services while trying to structure it as a cost center with a break-even, charge-out system.

Control issues will become increasingly important as firms experience the full effects of the changing computer economics and proliferating technology. Divisional data centers will frequently become inefficient when compared to large corporately controlled host machines and networking which can achieve more significant economies of scale—not so much on equipment as on people. At the other extreme many will find microcomputers spreading rapidly throughout the organization. Not all of these applications will be justified and control challenges here will be even more severe than when minicomputers began entering the business. Key professional and managerial employees will be "lost" for a week, two weeks, or a month as they disappear to master their new personal computers. The $3,000 purchase cost will quickly jump to double that as additional equipment is added (another diskette reader, a better printer, more memory, power smoothing) and software, lots and lots of software, is bought. Next will come requests for access to corporate data collections, and soon they will begin to find transaction processing systems being constructed with no ties to divisional or corporate information systems.

The Architecture of Applications and Data

Closely related to the issues of organization and control is the question of overall architecture for applications and data. Although the concept of a total information system or total data base has been long ago dismissed and with good reason, because most of those efforts bogged down in detail of corporate politics, the need for a master plan for information has never been greater. This grand design must answer these questions:

☐   What will be the major data collections?
☐   How, if at all, should they be related?
☐   What types of application systems will feed them and draw on them; how are these to be related?

Most large American businesses are organized on a decentralized or divisional basis, yet corporate and often group, or strategic business unit staffs are significant and growing in both size and involvement in both planning and coordination activities.[8] The same pressures are seen in computing. Data flows and information requirements typically mirror the organizational structure of the firm. The grand design for applications and data must not be merely an extension of the basic corporate structure and way of operating the business day to day, it must be a key element of the way in which the business structure is defined and operations prescribed.

The data architecture, for example, must address such issues as whether plant data such as inventory, orders, scheduling, shipping, billing, and purchasing should be located at the plant, or grouped together with other plants at the division or group level, or be at the corporate level. In other words, data architecture must settle the questions: How much data should be where?, How should the major elements be linked?, and Why should it be done that way? This architecture must specify the core data processing applications, how they should tie together, and how they are to be integrated with the data collections. Other key issues in planning the applications architecture include which functions to automate (or the scope of applications), the use of shared systems, and the mix of traditional data processing, information reporting, and decision-support applications.

Another strategic issue exerting a strong influence on applications and data architecture is the determination of what to attempt in-house through the use of traditional, custom-tailored programming, what to contract out, what to purchase in package form, and what to implement via end-user, through information-center or nontraditional programming means.

Two brief cases illustrate what I mean by strategic architectural planning:

☐ *The bank holding company.* This bank is expanding by acquiring other banks and expects to increase the pace of their acquisitions during the 1980s. Each bank has been run as an autonomous profit center. In the past each bank's DP operations were distinct, although they frequently shared application packages when convenient. Such a decentralized approach had been quite satisfactory during the 1970s and was largely the outgrowth of the holding company's acquisition program and method of operation. That strategy has not changed because of the anticipated changes in banking. In the future, operations of the banks will be consolidated so as to offer common services on a state-wide and probably a regional basis. A customer of one of the member banks will in the future be a customer of the integrated bank company. As a consequence, the new architecture envisions central collections of integrated customer information, probably segmented by type of customer, and integrated applications, bankwide, linking formerly quite separate applications such as the deposit accounting, consumer loans, and cash management services.

☐ *An energy company.* The situation at one of the large energy companies is considerably different. In the past all major applications were planned to support companywide needs, and all data collections were centrally managed and tightly integrated to avoid redundancies and to insure commonality and accuracy. But the business structure is changing and the firm, now organized into operating companies, finds its various business activities and information requirements increasingly diverse. As a consequence it has changed its architecture to one based upon operating company and divisional data collections for operational information leaving corporate systems and data bases only to support staff and corporate office needs. In time, even such core systems as general accounting and payroll will be broken up along divisional lines.

As these examples illustrate, the applications and data architecture of a company is the primary determiner of its future information services and products. In the words of Tregoe and Zimmerman, it is "the driving force" for information systems planning in the same sense as the master plan is for a city or a university.[9] Unfortunately, past architectual decisions or grand designs are also a major impediment to change. Such rigidity is often painful because the requirements for new applications and data arise quickly. Business segments change rapidly as markets and products evolve, as organizational units change and as managers come and go. Indeed, many vital aspects of the company change much faster than do information systems. It takes months to construct a data base, or to redo a major core application, or to convert DP operations from one type of technology to another. It takes years to restructure the applications and data architecture of a business. Witness many of the airlines today which cannot implement complex fare structures on their computer systems and may not be able to do so for three or four more years.

Many companies, because of their upcoming needs to rewrite their core applications, now have an opportunity to substantially revise their applications and data architecture that will not present itself again for many years. Indeed, if better architectures do not emerge, many of the companies I've been studying face only bleak prospects for substantially more responsive applications and little hope of reducing their mounting backlogs.

The Architecture for Technology

In the past most companies provided data processing services from a central site, primarily for reasons of economy of scale and to maintain control. If the organization was quite large, or operations geographically dispersed, or the company operationally decentralized, one often found multiple data centers again with large host machines centrally managed within a designated segment of the business. Technology planning was basically a process of determining the number of central sites, their size, and how, if at all, they were to be linked together, usually through some collection of dial-up and leased telephone lines. Today the technological options are so much richer and the scope of architectural planning so much broader, that companies need an overall architecture within which technology planning, the integration of computing, communications, office automation technology, and process control can occur, as they do for applications. Key issues today include:

☐ The general mixture of large host computers, minicomputers and microcomputers. Everyone requires some mixture of this technology— the question is what mix is best?

☐ The geographical siting of the technology.

☐ The technological plan for office systems. Again there is a question of mix: which office systems should be implemented on computers, which on traditional office machines, and which on the new technology just emerging from the laboratories?

☐ The technological plan for manufacturing, distribution, and services with respect to computer-controlled processes.

☐ How and where processing devices should be linked, how many networks there will be, and the mix of company and public carrier networking facilities to be used.

☐ Which software concepts to employ for operating systems, communications, data bases, and programming?

This type of architecture requires a level of planning without resort to the details and specifications of specific equipments, operating systems, or communication protocols. For example:

☐ A *university* has decided to continue to operate three primary data centers (research and academic computing, administration, and hospital/medical center) each with its own separate network, with a fourth and also separate network for voice and electronic mail, based on Rolm technology, and, finally, a mixture of stand-alone word processors, micros and minis for certain designated types of applications. This strategy was conceived and approved without specifying vendors, machines, operating systems, or data-base packages; indeed, they really do not know what the specifics will be, but there is considerable confidence in the architecture itself.

☐ A *U.S. government agency* is about to choose one of three options for a technological strategy: (1) a single large multiprocessor host configuration with nationwide communications network; (2) several regional host machines with regional networks and a central switching center, and (3) third option based on dozens of localized minis and a host-less interlinking network, probably employing satellite-based data transmission.

Summary

Computers and their related technology do indeed promise almost unlimited potential to businesses today, but only to those who learn to manage them well. Information systems are in trouble in many companies today because of inadequate management practices, attention, and direction. More will be in trouble tomorrow.

In view of the common problems most large computer users face, senior managers should take immediate action:

☐ To strengthen their own understanding of computers and the new information technologies. Most probably need a "crash course" to get started, and an ongoing educational program to stay current. Many companies need to bring to executive rank individuals with substantial information-system experience.

☐ To assess the status of their core information systems and to prepare life-cycle plans reflecting needed maintenance as well as cost and scheduling of replacement.

☐ To overhaul their personnel practices in information services with special emphasis on hiring, training, and education programs so as to insure at least a minimal staff of experienced professionals during the next few years of expected shortages in the people area.

☐ To restructure their costing and charge-out practices for information resources to properly reflect the changing computer economics.

☐ To sponsor research and development programs to keep the corporation up-to-date with the emerging technology, particularly the end-user based approaches to program development which now seem to provide the greatest potential for progress in both reducing the growing backlogs and improving the flexibility and responsiveness of those applications.

☐ To formulate a comprehensive organizational, control, and architectural strategy along the lines outlined here.

If managements do not act quickly they will discover that today's technology problems have a way of becoming tomorrow's business problems.

Notes

1. Unpublished study conducted by E. Bryan of IBM's Advanced Business Institute.

2. "Interim Report on Study and Research on Fifth-Generation Computers" *Japan Information Processing Development Center*, 1980.

3. "Occupational Outlook Handbook, 1980–81 Edition," U.S. Department of Labor, Bureau of Statistics, Bulletin 2075.

4. "Population Estimates and Projections," U.S. Department of Commerce, Bureau of the Census, Series P-25, No. 870.

5. *National Report, College Bound Seniors*, College Entrance Examinations Board, 1979.

6. Adapted from "Computer Strategy: A Philosophy for Managing Information Processing Resources," Brandt Allen, in *The Economics of Information Processing*, R. Goldberg and H. Lorin eds., New York, Wiley, 1982.

7. For additional perspective on the issue of responsibility assignment for information resources, see Jack R. Buchanan, and Richard G. Linowes, "Understanding Distributed Data Processing," *HBR*, July–August, 1980.

8. Richard Vancil, in *Decentralization: Managerial Ambiguity by Design,* Dow Jones-Irwin, Homewood, Ill., 1978, documents the apparent ambiguity of increasing decentralization of operational responsibility and increasing centralization of staff activities in large U.S. firms.

9. Benjamin B. Tregoe and John W. Zimmerman, *Top Management Strategy: What It Is and How to Make It Work,* New York, Simon and Schuster, 1980.

7
Catching Up with the Computer Revolution

LYNN M. SALERNO

Today's computer on a chip, smaller than a postage stamp, is the descendant of machines that filled a room and required miles of wiring. As this tiny wafer has fallen in price and grown in computing power, its applications have multiplied so that now the miracle chip touches most aspects of our lives in some form. Until very recently, the literature has not kept pace with the expanding technology, but writers are beginning to examine the possible effects of chip-based computers on jobs, on industrial production, on offices, and on education, among other areas. In this article, a specialist in computers and business reviews the current literature to show the experts' views of where we now stand in what some have called the computer revolution.

In almost every article on computers today, a picture of a tiny wafer of silicon poised on an index finger appears. This small chip has become the emblem of the "Computer Revolution." To call this rectangle, no larger than ¼ inch on a side, a miracle chip is no media hype. In fact, it is surprising that the popular press contains no more arm-waving articles than it does on the wonders we may expect from the chip and the new electronic era it has introduced.

The literature on computers is growing almost as fast as computer technology itself. Most books have the word *revolution* in their titles and treat the subject in a general or a popular way. Considering the richness of the subject matter, why is it that most of the public has had to gain its feel for the potential of computer technology from *Star Wars* and *The Empire*

Author's Note. I wish to thank Professor Michael Hammer of MIT as well as Frederic Withington and Martin Ernst of Arthur D. Little, Inc. for giving me their views on future uses of computers.

Strikes Back? The most obvious reason is the short half-life of the data, which makes both publisher and author fear that a book's "far-out" predictions will come true before it appears on the shelves.

As for the business literature, until recently writers in the field—like most executives—have seemed not to realize the potential applications of the new chip-based technology. When the microprocessor chip was developed at Intel Corporation in 1971, Robert Noyce, then chairman, saw its potential and encouraged the work that gave the company the lead in its field. Others, who could have started even in the race, hesitated to work with a component so small that it could get lost in a crack. Noyce, however, had already realized that chips could be so cheap that losing one would be irrelevant.

Recognizing the perishability of their data as well as the lag between technology and practice, many of the serious writers for business air their views in periodicals. More and more of these writers understand both the technology of computers and the workings of the businesses where it is applied.[1] Two such authors are Richard L. Nolan and Cyrus R. Gibson, who described the now classic four stages of computer growth, which provided managers with a scheme for finding out how well their organizations use computers as well as a guide for their productive growth.[2]

Other, more recent articles point to such important dimensions of computer management as control of computer growth,[3] spread of computers through decentralization,[4] and the move toward the office of the future.[5]

From these articles and others, we see that computers are spreading—some are stretching out by cable from the host computer, and others (the stand-alone minicomputer) have cut the cord and communicate with each other by telephone wire or cable. Some get in touch by satellite.

If we have no Paul Revere to warn that "The computers are coming! The computers are coming!" should we look for one? Should we plan for a computer revolution in whatever time we have left?

How Soon the Revolution?

Considering the fast pace of developments in electronics—whose description, with the chip on a finger, is the other hallmark of today's computer articles—what about the future impact of the computer on business? Almost everyone knows by now that the microprocessor chip grows ever smaller, ever cheaper, more powerful, and more portable; and most writers agree that the human imagination rather than technology will limit its future uses.[6]

Many of the spectacular applications that experts predict for computers are either completely possible today or clearly attainable with quite foreseeable stretches of available technology. Thus, understanding today's use of computers provides a glimpse of tomorrow's possibilities, and seeing the current difficulties may help us avoid future stumbling blocks.

Computers in the Factory

Because some of the thorniest problems show themselves there, let's start with the field of robotics. Such robot creatures as the endearing R-2 D-2 of *Star Wars* or the frightening HAL of *2001* may reflect efforts to deal with the disturbingly uncertain effects of computer technology, but the robot of reality bears no resemblance to fictional figures.

Robots first entered the factory not so much to do routine work as to perform dangerous tasks. They worked, for example, where it was too hot or where fumes were too noxious for human laborers. Among their main tasks today are spraying paint, feeding furnaces, and guiding machine tools basic to production processes, such as those for drilling and milling.

A description of an automated plant of today may give us a preview of the future factory:

> Your first impression when you view the McDonnell Douglas parts fab-
> rication plant in St. Louis is the sheer size and loneliness of it all. Some
> two dozen acres of milling machines noisily grind grooves, slots, and
> intricate patterns in airframe parts to a tolerance of 0.0025 inch. The
> machines, for the most part, work alone—watched by only a few men
> who glance occasionally at a control panel or sweep the cuttings.[7]

In the field of robotics, writers have examined the technology and its impact to a greater extent than in many other areas of the new electronics.[8] Attention to this subject arises both from the basic allure of robots and from the fact that they have been in use for more than 10 years, which is almost a lifetime compared with the general pace of developments in applied microelectronics and which permits some conclusions based on experience.

Despite the growing use of robots, the United States is still far from being a nation of automated factories. Many writers in the field agree that stumbling blocks to the adoption of this highly promising technology resemble those hindering the other new industrial technologies. One such barrier arises when the new fits poorly with the old. In industries with heavy capital investment in machinery, the costs loom large. The telephone equipment industry, for example, with its commitment to a network of coaxial cable, has had to phase in the use of more efficient optical fiber. The steel industry, with its difficulties of adopting continuous casting technology, is another obvious example.

Another barrier is that applying robotics and other advanced control systems requires the hiring of technical specialists who not only come from outside the factory but usually speak the language of electronics—to many, a foreign tongue. Added to this barrier is the lack of theoretical knowledge of how to integrate advanced control systems with the production process. Though there is a bountiful literature on production process, few theorists have the electronics background that would provide the understanding needed to prepare the ground for the magic seed. Too hasty an implementation of automation can obviously lead to failures that not only are costly but also inhibit a company's future adoption of computer-controlled devices.

Another constraint on the introduction of robotics and allied technology is the opposition of workers, particularly organized labor. Since demand for routine factory jobs is declining, automatons can move in to some extent. On the other hand, the industries where electronic advances can make the greatest contribution are also those that have the strongest unions, so any innovation in those plants will encounter resistance or at least the need for extra planning.

The White-Collar Robot

The literature on the electronic revolution in the office grows daily, and each technological breakthrough unleashes avalanches of glossy booklets from the vendors, pushing the advance guard of machines into the new electronic office.[9] The "miracle chip" has moved into the office largely in the form of the microcomputer. These desk-top machines have brought computers out from under the strict control of data processing departments and made them readily accessible to the end user. They draw their advantages from the microprocessor that is their brain—they are portable and cheap, and they consume small amounts of power. These qualities of the microprocessor have led to the concept of distributed data processing (DDP).

The impetus for DDP originally came from a need to prevent a complete shutdown of operations whenever the central computer failed. In the networks of large computers and minicomputers, various configurations have evolved to suit the requirements of the user. They involve at least one main computer and one or more minicomputers, so that failure in any part of the network has no effect on the remaining parts. Another advantage of DDP is increased computational power delivered at low cost to the place where it is needed. Such an arrangement allows divisions to acquire information, which headquarters can also retrieve.

Microcomputers have been well received in offices because they are "friendly"—they don't require the user to have the technical knowledge of a professional programmer. They excel at accumulating information, and, with various programs and peripheral devices, they can plot data and put out printed reports. As word processors, they allow the operator to delete, insert, and move text around on the page before, and after, printing. The minicomputer can store standard documents and retrieve them for suitable modification.

Minicomputer software can also create a multicolumn, multirow matrix that business managers can use for forecasting and inventory planning—functions that now consume huge amounts of paper and time.

Computers Get Together

Although as early as 1973 the Bell System reported that more machines were talking to one another than people were talking to people on its long distance lines, only recently have the larger computer makers begun to produce networks connecting various office machines. The literature has closely tracked these growing bonds in both books and articles.[10] Interoffice linkages among equipment and machines, the so-called local networks, use various kinds of cable (and even glass fibers) as connectors between computers, terminals, word processors, and "intelligent" copiers. The advantages of such systems are obvious: sharing of data bases, computing power, and time, to name only three. Beyond the area of the individual office or another building in close proximity stretch the external networks that allow distant offices and machines to communicate with each other.

These networks, which use either phone lines or satellites, will increasingly affect business communications through electronic mail and teleconferencing. Electronic mail, which is becoming increasingly cost effective as the postal service becomes less so, involves a document or letter sent from one word processor to a target microprocessor, where it can be displayed on a TV screen or terminal.

The Fabulous Future

Where the outlook for computers is concerned, we find not only articles but a goodly number of books in which experts have been willing to make forecasts. Though past predictions about computers have been so inaccurate that we laugh at them—for example, the unfortunate scientist who said 30 years ago that 10 computers would fill all our needs in the future—the exciting worlds, or woeful possibilities, lure many to stretch their imagination and ours.

Effects on Employment

The interest in the future of technology and its impact does not extend to forecasting the future of employment, except in fairly general terms. This reluctance arises partly from the inherent difficulty of predicting the adoption of any particular technology and partly from the rapidly changing technology itself.

Writing in 1954, Norbert Wiener, a pioneer in information theory and coiner of the term *cybernetics,* made a grim prediction about the effect of automation on employment:

> It is perfectly clear that this will produce an unemployment situation, in comparison with which the present recession and even the depression of the thirties will seem a pleasant joke. This depression will ruin many industries—possibly even the factories that have taken advantage of the new potentialities.[11]

Though most writers are less pessimistic, they largely agree that the new technology is likely to reduce employment. Estimates of the loss in blue-collar jobs range as high as 30% over the next 25 years, and writers see a shift of workers to the top and very bottom of the employment ladder. This polarization of factory jobs could arise in part from the fact that top managers could probably adjust to necessary changes brought about by technology, while the lowest-level workers would not need to. Middle-level workers would have the greatest difficulty in adapting their skills. Also, some of the jobs of the midlevel factory workers could disappear because electronic components mean that fewer workers would be needed for skilled machine operations.

In a study of companies making new, microprocessor-based products or using microprocessor-based tools in manufacture, Robert Lund and his coworkers at MIT made some revealing discoveries.[12] In the short term, companies making the new products had higher employment, which Lund attributes to increases in market share and general market expansion. Companies using the new tools had either no change or a reduction in employment. The productivity of some of these technology users increased by ⅓ or more. In these factories, some workers were shifted to monitoring tasks.

In supervisory jobs and the management of manufacturing, the Lund study found that the required skill levels had risen, particularly the analytic skills needed for diagnosing intangible problems. In addition, buyers, salesmen, and service people needed retraining to deal with the sophisticated products and product components they were using.

For the business office, a common view is that computerization may not reduce staff but will help a company to become more productive at less expense or at least to pay less for the same amount of work.

The appearance of the typical office will change as word processors more and more take the place of typewriters. The majority of office workers will be placed in central work stations and, according to some predictions, all but top managers will lose their private secretaries. Although such changes could lead to less office hierarchy, secretaries who have moved out of the pool may now feel they have returned to it.

The secretary's job will also change, for not only does the word processor reduce the degree of typing skill necessary to perform a creditable job, but also most of the machines will have, as many already do, a production monitor. Thus, time and motion studies will be a tempting possibility, and at the very least the machine could serve as a time clock for the job.

If lower-level jobs will demand less skill, what effects will higher managers feel from the introduction of computer-based machines into the office? Commentators on the impact stress the increased demands on middle managers that will result from automation. According to Victor Vyssotsky of Bell Laboratories, top managers have special informational needs, so far not met because of a shortage of subordinates with the skill to supply them.[13] He says that better managerial information systems will be coming as more computer-literate professionals enter the business world. And such systems will heighten the disparities of performance among managers.

The creative manager who asks the right questions of the computer will find a wider scope for his talents from a properly constructed management information system than he ever has. The CEO can gain little from such tools, says Vyssotsky, since the quality of available information on which his strategic decisions must be based is so poor that pen and pencil can be as helpful to him as a computer.

Commentators see managers at the middle level as psychologists often see the middle child—squeezed from both sides and showing adverse effects. In factories, they will lose their jobs through automation, and in the business office another form of computer will try to take their place. Even if neither of these things happens, middle managers may find themselves threatened by the increased visibility of their decisions, as recorded and/or printed out by the computer. Some writers, however, see the automation of routine decisions freeing the middle manager to do more creative work and to make more significant decisions.

Commenting on these various perspectives, Michael Hammer, computer specialist at the Massachusetts Institute of Technology, says of the middle manager: "On the one hand, according to some people, he's going to have more tools, so he'll be more creative; on the other, they say, he's going to be displaced by automation. I think both views are wrong, or rather they're both right and they're both wrong. First, the manager is not going to be displaced through automation. The manager's responsibilities of judgmental, intuitive decision making can only rarely be handled by a machine.

> Once upon a time economic reorder points in inventory control were surrounded by mysticism; now they are automatable. But most decision making is not of that character. On the other hand, the view that the manager will have more tools to be creative—that's the optimistic view of the vendor. In fact, many people suffer from information overload.[14]

MIS—Still a Mirage?

Though many managers may lose their secretaries, they will have gained "decision support systems." Most authors agree that the top-level manager already suffers from a glut of information, and they foresee no decline in the office of the future. They disagree, however, on whether computer-based systems will help managers make better decisions. Some see an enhancement of the executive's overall grasp of the organization coming from instantly available data, while others think such information will be at best useless and at worst a source of anxiety for the executive not attuned to computers and quantitative methods.

As far back as 1972, John Dearden pointed out the shortcomings of computer-based management information systems.[15] The possibility of using computers to back up decisions and to organize the corporation's information has always been alluring, but early attempts to introduce MIS led to high hopes followed by hot debate when much touted systems promised and then failed to deliver a new era of management productivity.

Arising from the ashes today is a phoenix that some call DSS (decision support systems), on which are placed similar but less grandiose expectations.

Such systems, whatever they are called, act as accumulators of information in a world where information may already be too abundant. Some writers point out that as more and more computers crank out more and more data, human beings must spend more and more energy dealing with these data and can absorb, retain, and use less and less information. Thus, information becomes, in Jeremy Rifkind's words, a kind of "social pollution."

In addition, Rifkind remarks, as computers proliferate into every social function, society becomes dependent on them for its survival—the human being becomes hostage to the technology.[16] A realistic view of MIS seems to depend, as John Rockart points out, both on development of more relevant systems and on managers' ability to use them.[17]

Moving Information, Not People

As it becomes possible to move information around much more quickly and increasingly more cheaply than people can travel, the way we do business is sure to change. Already a battle has been joined among giants for dominance in the field of teleconferencing—meetings that take place among participants linked by long-distance video and audio networks. AT&T and Satellite Business Systems (SBS)—a joint venture of IBM, COMSAT General Corporation, and Aetna Life & Casualty Company—plan teleconferencing as part of their satellite networks.

With the cost of travel climbing, corporations appear likely to take advantage of such facilities, and airlines, hotels, and other businesses that depend on the business traveler will feel the impact. But business people may not just stop traveling to conferences in different cities, they may even stop going to work. Most futurists include in their scenarios some form of electronic cottage that enables people to work at home.

James Martin, writing in 1978, pictured this environment:

> Imagine a city 10 or 20 years in the future, with parks and flowers and lakes, where the air is crystal clear and most cars are kept in large parking lots on the outskirts.. . . There is less need for physical travel than in an earlier era. Banking can be done from the home, and so can as much shopping as is desired.. . . Working at home is encouraged and is made easy for some by the videophones that transmit pictures and documents as well as speech.[18]

Calculating the Cost

The cornucopia of electronic marvels that business and industry can choose from dazzles the imagination. But what are the possible social and psychological costs of acquiring so many electronic helpers? By greedily grabbing more and more of them, are we striking some kind of Faustian bargain?

The Crowded Electronic Cottage

In the world of the futurist, everything is possible, but as some writers point out, the computerized cottage may become a little too cozy.[19] If the dull green efflorescence of the terminal screen replaces the rosy glow of the hearth, the continuous contact among family members able to work and learn at home together could lead to conflict.

Part-time work and shorter workweeks for most people are inevitable by the end of the decade, according to many writers. Some wonder how the greater leisure time and loss of work opportunity will affect the attitudes we refer to as the Protestant work ethic. Those who take a generally optimistic view of computer developments see increased free time as a chance to be rid at last of such constraining moral codes, while pessimists envision the loss of work as removing a mainstay of personal worth and dignity.

Everybody's Secrets

Giant data banks linked by ever-widening networks pose obvious threats to privacy. Thus, the writings in this field have many Cassandras.[20] With centralized data collection and numerous exchanges among agencies, not only do many more people have access to private records, but because computers can greatly magnify human error by constantly compounding it, there is greater possibility of harm to the individual from inaccurate or incomplete records.

Businesses have good reason to fear an increase in fraud and other crime by computer. In 1975, as many are aware, a $2 billion fraud drove the Equity Funding Corporation into bankruptcy. In that complex case, in which 22 persons were finally indicted, the role of the computer was to lend credibility to nonexistent insurance policies.[21]

The computer criminal does not even have to be a sophisticated data processing professional. School children in New York who were learning about computers and communications managed to provoke an international investigation involving the Royal Canadian Mounted Police as well as the FBI. They gained access to two international networks, seized control of the computer system used by Canada Cement Lafarge, and destroyed some of its data.[22]

Let Many Flowers Bloom

Despite warnings of the dire consequences computers can bring, some writers are seeing the other side of the coin—a golden age of information for all. They emphasize not the stealing but the sharing of information that the new technology makes possible.

Microprocessor technology today can compress literary information ten-thousandfold. Such developments make likely a new kind of publishing world wherein electronic books will be sold directly to the consumer, who will have the space for a huge private library. For the scholar, the benefits might be easy access to centers of learning anywhere in the world.

The computer optimists see the multiplication of information entering the home leading to a corresponding growth in the variety of ideas. Such increased diversity could lead to wider differentiation in products and services to appeal more accurately to more fragmented markets.

Undaunted by the image of the machine run amok, the optimists point out that many persons prefer to deal with a computer rather than another human being. In banks with automated tellers, customers often show a preference for the machine, and researchers have found that some patients are more open about their problems, both physical and psychological, when talking to a computer than to a doctor or some other professional.[23]

Business Implications

Authorities divide widely on their outlook for society if computers and their supporters have their sway. These authorities are equally divided in their prognostication for the impact of the new technology on business. Some believe that as computers proliferate throughout the corporation, hierarchies will tend to dissolve; as information perfuses through lower levels, subordinates will increasingly challenge their superiors with their computer models. Not exactly so, says Martin Ernst of Arthur D. Little: the top executive knows knowledge is power and will keep controls in place to maintain desired levels of authority.

Nevertheless, many commentators emphasize the importance of computer literacy, saying that many older managers, from CEO on down, will feel threatened by the increasing influx of younger persons who have grown up with computers and who use them with comfort.

Another area of disagreement concerns whether computers will tend to centralize or decentralize business. The technology pulls both ways: the computers themselves are clearly spreading like weeds, while companies are trying through centralized controls to bring coherence back into their data processing systems—to regather the information broadcast on many networks.

Centralization of some types of information is coming about through the growth of large, specialized commercial data banks. Such concentration could lead to antitrust suits, according to Ernst, who foresees the possibility of lawyers or doctors suing the relevant data bases for cornering the information they need to practice their professions.

Barriers to Implementation

Despite glorious promises of a technology whose costs will continue to decline by a factor of three each year, most experts don't envision wholesale adoption of all the facets of computer technology.

Labor Opposition

Many companies have already learned that labor unions expect their needs to be met as part of the cost of using the new technology. Among the current methods for smoothing the path of automation are the transfer, relocation, and retraining of workers. Some employees receive large incentives for early retirement; in other cases, companies use attrition to thin the ranks in accordance with diminished needs.

In the United Kingdom, where unemployment is high and labor unions are strong, the introduction of computer-based technology has met strong resistance. But Britain is already behind others, notably the United States, so it may need technology advances to keep up with the competition.

Some U.S. unions have demanded that the smaller work load be spread among all workers by reducing the workweek but not decreasing the pay. Such demands may foreshadow a general reduction in hours worked, which many observers see as the inevitable consequence of automation.

To overcome the possible forms of opposition, many writers think planning in conjunction with the employees who will be affected is crucial. An interesting exception to this philosophy is in greenfield plants, where, to avoid any dissention with established workers, new technology has been installed with an entirely new or a different work force from that in a company's other plants.

Robert Lund, in the MIT study mentioned earlier, attributed the successful introduction of a technology-based product—the Singer electronic sewing machine—to a strategy of secrecy, at least in the developmental stages:

> It is unusual for an established firm with a 100-year tradition of evolutionary change to develop a product so radically different; the climate within such a firm normally works against such attempts. A key factor in success was the firm's decision to protect innovation from in-house reactionary influences by isolating the Athena 2000 team from the rest of the firm. By making the team self-sufficient from inception to implementation, and by giving it direct access to top management, the company effectively bypassed the internal resistance that the project normally would have encountered.[24]

Further Constraints

Other often-cited deterrents to the adoption of computers are the software lag and the shortage of computer professionals. Although the advances in software and programming have not matched the spectacular progress of hardware technology, more effort will probably be devoted to this area. Promising results may come from an ever-increasing group of amateur and free-lance programmers. Research has not yet produced self-programming computers, but scientists agree the problem will eventually by solved. And the computer may supply the solution. Today, microprocessors help in the design of chips for specialized uses, and already many correct their own errors.

Finding Solutions

No matter which scenario the business person decides to believe, computers in some form will affect the way he or she does business. To ensure orderly development and to prevent the disruption that accompanies all revolutions, we need thinkers who will go beyond the futurists, who alternately intrigue and horrify:

> It may appear an exaggeration to say that evolution also depends on the social ingenuity of the technical specialists. But there is a lot of truth in it. Technical specialists must take the trouble to imagine the world of tomorrow. If they are unable to do this properly themselves, they must present their ideas and plans in good time to others who can help them to assess these.
>
> Much unnecessary resistance arises because engineers naively launch an idea, obviously without having thought very much about nontechnical aspects, after which people with vivid imaginations get a fixed idea in their heads and create panic, sometimes even justifiably. The building up of good communication with nonspecialists is the most important condition for a joint building up of a society in which everyone, even the simple worker with no interest in science, can feel at home.[25]

Many writers feel strongly that we need to close the gap between social scientists, technologists, and business people to realize the promise of the new technology, that we need, in an ever diminishing time span, to try to understand and plan for the electronic age.

To have information is indeed to have power, but, as one observer put it, information can have many combinations and permutations that affect that power:

> Change the form of information, or its quantity, speed, or direction, or accessibility, and some monopoly will be broken, some ideology threatened, some pattern of authority will find itself without a foundation. We might say that the most potent revolutionaries are those people who invent new media of communication, although typically they are not aware of what they are doing.
>
> When Gutenberg announced that he could manufacture books, as he put it, 'without the help of reed, stylus, or pen but by wondrous agreement, proportion, and harmony of punches and types,' he could scarcely imagine that he had just become the most important political and social troublemaker of the Second Millennium. Unless that dubious title be given to Professor Samuel Morse who, in sparking the electronic revolution under whose conditions we must now live, at least had the good grace to wonder, What hath God wrought?
>
> Well, God hath wrought plenty, and, although there is no Plato anywhere in sight to help us find the answer to Morse's question, we are obliged

for our own sakes, if not for God's, to pursue the matter with the utmost vigor and attention.[26]

Notes

1. See Russell L. Ackoff, "Management Misinformation Systems," *Management Science,* December, 1967, p. B147; and Peter G.W. Keen and Michael S. Scott Morton, *Decision Support Systems: An Organizational Perspective* (Reading, Mass.: Addison-Wesley, 1978).

2. Richard L. Nolan and Cyrus R. Gibson, "Managing the Four Stages of EDP Growth," Chapter 2, this book.

3. Frederic G. Withington, "Coping with Computer Proliferation," *HBR,* May–June 1980, p. 152.

4. Jack R. Buchanan and Richard G. Linowes, "Understanding Distributed Data Processing," Chapter 21, this book; and "Making Distributed Data Processing Work," Chapter 22, this book.

5. Richard J. Matteis, "The New Back Office Focuses on Customer Service," *HBR,* March–April, 1979, p. 146; and Louis Mertes, "Doing Your Office Over—Electronically," Chapter 29, this book.

6. See, for example, Christopher Evans, *The Micro Millenium* (New York: Viking Press, 1979).

7. Neil P. Ruzic, "The Automated Factory," in *Microelectronics Revolution* (Cambridge: MIT Press, 1981), p. 165.

8. See, for example, John F. Young, *Robotics* (New York: John Wiley, 1973); and Michael L. Dertouzos, "Individualized Automation" in *The Computer Age: A Twenty-Year View,* edited by Michael L. Dertouzos and Joel Moses (Cambridge: MIT Press, 1980).

9. See, for example, James R. Bell, "Future Directions in Computing," *Computer Design,* March, 1981, p. 95.

10. See, for example, Starr R. Hiltz and Murray Turoff, *The Network Nation* (Reading, Mass.: Addison-Wesley, 1978); David Copithorne, "The Wired Office," *Output,* May 1981, p. 38; and Howard Cravis, "Local Networks for the 1970s," *Datamation,* March 1981, p. 98.

11. Norbert Wiener, *The Human Use of Human Beings* (Garden City, New York: Doubleday, 1954), p. 162.

12. Robert T. Lund, "Microprocessors and Productivity: Cashing in Our Chips," *Technology Review,* January 1981, p. 33.

13. Victor A. Vyssotsky, "Use of Computers in Business," in *The Computer Age: A Twenty-Year View,* edited by Michael L. Dertouzos and Joel Moses (Cambridge: MIT Press, 1980).

14. From a conversation with the author.

15. John Dearden, "MIS Is a Mirage," *HBR,* January–February 1972, p. 90.

16.   Jeremy Rifkind, *Entropy* (New York: Viking Press, 1980).

17.   "Chief Executives Define Their Own Data Needs," *HBR*, March–April 1979, p. 81.

18.   James Martin, *The Wired Society* (Englewood Cliffs, N.J.: Prentice-Hall, 1978), p. 8.

19.   For a generally pessimistic view of the home of the future, see Joseph Weizenbaum, "Once More: the Computer Revolution," in *The Computer Age* (Cambridge: MIT Press, 1981).

20.   See, for example, Hiltz and Turoff, *Network Nation;* also Joseph L. Sardinas; Jr., *Computing Today* (Englewood Cliffs, N.J.: Prentice-Hall, 1981).

21.   For a thorough analysis of the case, see Donn B. Parker, *Crime by Computer* (New York: Charles Scribner's Sons, 1976), p. 118.

22.   "The Great Dalton School Computer Tie-In Mystery," *New York Times*, May 7, 1980.

23.   For a good example of such interaction, see Pamela McCorduck, *Machines Who Think* (San Francisco: W.H. Freeman, 1979), p. 254.

24.   See Lund, "Microprocessors and Productivity," p. 38.

25.   J.J.A. Vollebergh, "Microelectronics and the Evolution of Society," *Microprocessing and Microprogramming*, January 1981, p. 11.

26.   Neil Postman, "The Information Environment," *ETC: A Review of General Semantics*, Fall 1979, p. 234.

PART TWO
DESIGNING AND MANAGING THE SYSTEM

AN OVERVIEW

In this section, managers will learn the most effective ways of setting up their data processing or, more properly, their information systems. These systems in many companies now include telecommunications and office automation besides data processing, areas that have added several layers of complexity to the problems of design and management. The issues raised by the addition of these new technologies are addressed by McKenney and McFarlan in the piece that begins this section. They point out that many managers are stuck in the mold of the 1970s, dealing separately with the three components of telecommunications, office automation, and data processing.

Now they must free themselves from this straitjacket to move flexibly into the new information environment. McKenney and McFarlan, like most other authors here, believe that integration of the various islands of technology should now be first on the planning agenda. They know the task will not be easy, since managers' familiarity with each kind of technology will vary considerably, so they propose a step-wise approach for moving toward full integration that takes into account a company's experience in each area.

After coming to grips with the problems of merging the technologies in a company's information system, managers still must cope with an issue of equally daunting proportions—what data and what hardware will be located centrally and what of the two should be distributed over the organization. This issue arises again and again in various forms and with various ramifications in this book, though it has overriding importance in this section because planning can help avoid so many of the possible difficulties that sometimes result from spontaneous, *ad hoc* procedures and projects.

McFarlan and McKenney endorse the top-level policy committee as the best way for an organization to handle these knotty problems, and this notion lies at the heart of one of Richard Nolan's pieces in this section. Nolan again nudges top managers to get involved in setting the strategy for their information systems. Pointing out that the opportunities for using computers cost effectively have increased fourfold over the last decade, he urges managers to make good use of this "strong economic and entrepreneurial tool" to improve virtually all aspects of business operations.

Since budgets and personnel are limited, companies often must make tough choices among the various possible uses for their computer-based technology. Such strategy considerations demand high-level perspective, which can be expressed in the executive steering committee. This committee, in Nolan's view, is a kind of board of directors for the computer function. But despite the seemingly obvious advantages of the top-level committee to guide this ever more pervasive aspect of a company's business operations, many of these groups have had such a poor record of success that some companies have abandoned them, and at least one author of this book, Brandt Allen, raises serious questions about them.

In Nolan's study of steering committees, he found that they often took on too many important functions in too short a time. He thinks a more measured approach, adapted to the company culture and organizational design, will make the committees work. To ensure that a newly formed committee, or one that has been revived, will stay on the right track, Nolan gives managers a blueprint that details membership, functions, and evolution of the group. The success of the steering committee is vital, he says, because a leadership vacuum has developed in the wake of decentralization. Because of wider knowledge and dispersal of computers, in addition to their greater strategic importance, the company can no longer depend on the data processing manager to run the operations that now make up information processing in its multiple forms. On a broader scale, Martin Buss sees the same need for executive intervention. In surveying the international scene, he discovered that the head office often prefers to ignore the corporation's overseas information systems, that is, until the reports top managers depend on are chronically late or some other symptom arises to warn that the system is in serious trouble.

For various reasons, the information systems of many muiltinational corporations have become a patchwork of computers and applications, not to mention management styles. But changes in the business environment may force the top players' hands, unless they decide to declare a new deal. Among these sometimes hostile trends are pressure for regulation of transborder data flow and for unionization of data processing departments. Also, as most of the authors here point out, new technology, especially advances in data communications, can change the appropriate structure for an area or a country by making it economically feasible to use smaller computers rather than a central hub—again the issue of decentralization.

Buss tells managers what measures they can take to make their international systems more responsive to the needs of the business, including even the organizational charts for the reorganized responsibility. However, he, like McFarlan and others, urges the corporation to maintain a certain amount of flexibility in its approach. For example, where possible, he favors leaving systems development to affiliates, since they best understand their own needs. The overall goal of top-level attention to international IS is coordination of effort and of systems. To this end, Buss suggests that larger international divisions should have their own data processing function unless such a change would prove too disruptive, in which case one or more systems coordinators would have to help achieve the common focus that their organization should be seeking.

The central message of Buss's piece is that international IS operations must be integrated, a task that becomes both easier and more difficult, as we have seen, because of the development of data communications, which, by linking computers, make both operations and data interdependent. It is this last aspect of computer networks that concerns Richard Nolan in his discussion of data bases. Though when he was writing the data-base concept was not as familiar as it is today to most top executives, the concerns Nolan expresses are completely relevant now. As in the international information systems Buss was discussing, domestic information management has developed in an unintegrated and wasteful way. And, like the international manager, the top-level executive at home often finds the data he needs too fragmented either by level or by application to be useful. Nolan describes how the situation in most corporations came to such a pretty pass, and shows the reluctant manager the inevitability of the data-base concept as the next natural milestone in the evolution of electronic data processing.

For companies that may have heeded Nolan's message and for those who have not yet embraced the data-base concept, McFadden and Suver's advice will be welcome. With the knowledge of some monumental failures, they tell managers how to build on other's mistakes so that they can move successfully into the data-base era.

8

The Information Archipelago – Maps and Bridges

JAMES L. McKENNEY and F. WARREN McFARLAN

As a result of their very different technological development, the islands that make up an archipelago of information—office automation, telecommunications, and data processing—have usually been under separate rule. In this article, Messrs. McKenney and McFarlan say that managers must now attempt to draw the maps and build the bridges that will bring the islands under integrated control. The authors point out how taking account of such factors as organization structure and leadership style can smooth the process, and they give examples of typical blocks to progress.

☐ The vice president of services of a large durables manufacturing company recently faced a dilemma. Her request for a stand-alone word processor to solve operating problems in her fastest-growing sales office had been denied. It had seemed a trivial request; yet having to do without the word processor would cause delays, and she thought that the decision set a dangerous precedent. The reason the accounting department gave for denying the machine was its incompatibility with the division's information services network. When she questioned this, an incomprehensible series of technical arguments ensued that appeared to have no relationship to her very real productivity problem. Should she fall in line, fight the decision, or resubmit the request as an operating expense instead of a capital expenditure?

☐ A major manufacturing company has reduced the processing capacity and staffing of its corporate data processing center by 60% over the past four years. The divisional data centers have grown to such an extent, however, that overall corporate data processing expenditures have risen more than 50% during the period.

☐   After careful analysis, the senior staff of a decentralized insurance company recommended an orderly dissolution of the company's $25 million data center and the creation of eight, smaller, diversified data centers over a 30-month period.

These actual incidents are not unusual. Repeatedly over the past 10 years, technological change has made organization structures for information services obsolete in many companies and has forced, or will force, major reorganization. There are several reasons for this.

First, for reasons of both efficiency and effectiveness, in the 1980s information services must include office automation, telecommunications (data and voice communications), and data processing, and these must be managed in a coordinated and, in many companies, integrated manner. This coordination is not easy in many organizations, as each of these activities in the 1960s and 1970s not only had different technical bases but also were marketed to the company separately. In addition, the organization structures and practices that developed for handling the technologies are quite different from what are now needed. The different managerial histories and decision-making habits associated with each of these technologies makes integration today exceptionally difficult.

Second, it has become increasingly clear that information services technologies that are new to the organization require different managerial approaches than do technologies with which the organization has had more experience. For example, the problems of implementing new office automation technology projects are quite different from those associated with more mature technologies.

Third, companies must rethink where data and computer hardware resources belong organizationally in the corporation. The dramatic improvements in hardware cost and performance for all three technologies in the past decade permit this issue to be addressed in the 1980s in a manner quite different from that of the early 1970s.

These improvements have occurred as computers have moved from vacuum tubes to very large-scale integrated circuits. These technology changes continue to improve productivity as still smaller, more reliable, and more useful circuits are being developed. Exhibit 1 shows the cost trends per individual unit and circuit over the past 20 years, trends that will continue for the next decade. The cost reduction and capacity increases caused by these changes have reduced computer hardware cost as a fraction of total DP department cost to below 30% in most large data processing installations.

Today, computer cost often does not exceed corporate telecommunications (including telephone) expense and for many companies is much less than software development and maintenance charges. Equally significant, technology has permitted development of stand-alone minicomputer systems or office automation systems that companies can tailor to provide specific service for any desired location.

Exhibit 1.   Costs and Performance of Electronics

Year	1958	1965	1972	1980
				Large-scale
			Integrated	integrated
Technology	Vacuum tube	Transistor	circuit	circuit
Cost per unit	$8	$0.25	$0.02	$0.001
Cost per logic	$160	$12	$200	$.05
Operation time (in seconds)	16×10^{-3}	4×10^{-6}	40×10^{-9}	200×10^{-12}

Source Note: W.D. Fraser, "Potential Technology Implications for Computers and Telecommunications in the 1980s," *IBM System Journal,* vol. 18, no. 2, 1979, p. 333.

This improved technology has caused a dramatic shift in both the types of information services being delivered to users and the best organizational structure for delivering them. The most desirable structure has involved and will continue to involve not only the coordination of data processing, teleprocessing, and office automation but redeployment both physically and organizationally of the company's technical and staff resources that provide information services. By technical resources we mean computers, word processors, private telephone exchanges, "intelligent" terminals, and so on. In staff resources, we include all the persons responsible either for operating these machines or for developing and maintaining new applications

Merging Islands of IS Technology

The problems in speedily integrating the three technologies of data processing, telecommunications, and office automation are largely a result of their historically very different management (as shown in Exhibit 2). Let us analyze these differences.

In 1920, in most organizations the manager and his secretary were supported by three forms of information services, each based on a different technology. For word processing, the typewriter was used to generate easily legible words. A file cabinet served as the main storage device for paper output, and the various organizational units were linked by secretaries who moved paper from one unit to another.

Data processing, if automated at all, depended on card-sorting machines to develop sums and balances using punched cards as input. The cards served as memory for this system. The telecommunications system comprised wires and messages that were manipulated by operator control of electromechanical switches. This telecommunication system had no storage capacity.

In 1920, the organizational designers of each of the three islands had

Exhibit 2.   Islands of Technology

Functions of Technology	Islands of Technology		
	Word Processing	Data Processing	Communication
1920			
Human-to-machine translation	Shorthand, dictophone	Form, keypunch	Phone
Manipulation of data	Typewriter	Card sorting	Switch
Memory	File cabinet	Cards	None
Links	Secretary	Operator	Operator
1965			
Human-to-machine translation	Shorthand, dictaphone	Form, keypunch	Phone
Manipulation of data	Typewriter	Computer	Computer
Memory	File cabinet	Computer	None
Links	Secretary	Computer	Computer
1980			
Human-to-machine translation	Shorthand, dictaphone	Typewriter	Phone, typewriter
Manipulation of data	Computer	Computer	Computer
Memory	Computer	Computer	Computer
Links	Computer	Computer	Computer

significantly different roles, as shown in Exhibit 3. For word processing, the office manager directed the design, heavily influenced by the desires of his or her manager. Although formal office systems were beginning to emerge, word processing remained primarily a means of facilitating secretarial work. The chief means of obtaining new equipment was through purchasing agents and involved the selection of typewriters, dictaphones, and file cabinets from a wide variety of medium-sized companies. Standardization was not critical.

Data processing was the domain of the controller-accountant, and the systems design activity was carried out by either the chief accountant or a card systems manager, who set the protocols for the flow of information processing. The machines for both data processing (the card sorters) and teleprocessing (the telephone) were so complex and expensive that managers had to develop a plan for their use.

Exhibit 3.   Evolution of Islands of Technology

Function	Islands of Technology		
	Word Processing	Data Processing	Communication
1920			
Design	Office manager	Card design	AT&T
Operation	Secretary	Machine operator	AT&T
Maintenance	Many companies	Single supplier	AT&T
User	Manager	Accountant	Manager
Design	Office systems analyst	Systems analyst	AT&T
Operation	Secretary	Operator and analyst	AT&T
Maintenance	Many	Single supplier	AT&T
User	Manager	Manager and accountant	Everybody
1980			
Design	Systems analyst	Systems analyst	Systems analyst
Operation	Manager, secretary, and editor	Manager and secretary	Manager and secretary
Maintenance	Many or single	IBM and other	AT&T and other
User	Everybody	Everybody	Everybody

Starting in the 1920s data processing services—that is, card sorting machines—were normally purchased and maintained as a system from one supplier, so that from the beginning a systems relationship existed between buyer and seller. Teleprocessing (telephones), however, were a purchased service requiring no capital investment. All three islands, therefore, were served differently in 1920: one by many companies, one by a systems supplier, and one by a public utility.

In 1965 the servicing and management of the three islands still functioned in the 1920 pattern. Word processing was still largely influenced by the manager and centered around the secretary. Services such as typewriters and reproducing systems (mimeographs, for example) were purchased as independent units from a range of competitors offering similar technology. There was little long-term planning, and such systems as existed evolved in response to newly available machines.

Data processing, however, had emerged as an ever more complex process. In that area, systems and planning were dominated by the need for serious evaluation of major capital investments in computers and software, as well as for multiyear projects. In addition, so that companies could take advantage of the productivity of the new system, all employees and users had to undergo extensive training. At times, as in the insurance company example at the beginning of this article, even the corporate organization was changed to accommodate the new potential and problems caused by computer technology. In regard to communications, however, in 1965 AT&T still completely dominated the supply of services; the equipment a company bought determined how the service was managed. In some organizations, managing communications implied placing three-minute hourglasses by phones so that employees would reduce the length of their calls.

By 1980, however, management's concerns for word processing and teleprocessing had become integrated with those of data processing for two important reasons. First, both areas now required large capital investments, large projects, large and complex implementation, and extensive user training. But the managers of these activities lacked the expertise to handle these types of problems.

For office automation, a special problem now is the move from multiple vendors and relatively small individual cost to, in many cases, one vendor that will provide integrated support to many units through a large capital purchase. The size of the purchase is several orders of magnitude larger and the applications much more complex than those of a decade ago.

For telecommunications, now managers need to break the reliance on a service purchased from a public utility and to look at multiple sources for large capital investment for equipment. These developments in word processing and teleprocessing represent a sharp departure from past practices and create the need for new management skills, which were added to the data processing function years ago.

The second reason for linkage of word processing and teleprocessing to data processing is that key sectors of all three components—data processing, teleprocessing, and office automation—are increasingly physically linked in a network; consequently, managers cannot address the problems of one component independently of those of the other two. For example, in one manufacturing company over a 24-hour period the same WATS line is used for voice transmission, on-line data communications, and an electronic mail message-switching system.

The situation is complicated by the fact that in 1982 a dominant supplier in each of the three islands of technology is attempting to market its products as the technological base from which a company can develop its coordinated automation of the other islands. IBM, for example, is extending its data processing base into various products supporting office automation and communications. AT&T is extending its communications base into products supporting data processing and office automation, and Xerox is expanding its office automation effort into communications and data processing.

Failure to address this issue of coalescing technologies poses great risk to an organization. Over the next few years, we believe most organizations will consolidate at least policy control and perhaps management also of the three islands into a single information services unit. The following are key reasons for such a move:

1   Decisions in each area now involve large amounts of money and complex technical and cost evaluations.
2   The types of analytic skills and project management skills and staff need to plan and implement applications are similar for each of these technologies.
3   Many systems call for the combination of these technologies into networks that handle computing, telecommunications, and office automation in an integrated way.

A company can follow multiple paths in effecting the merger of the three islands of technologies as it moves toward a single information services function. We will discuss the three most common and most practical approaches.

DP & Telecommunications

In many larger organizations data processing and teleprocessing of data merged under DP leadership some years ago. In these cases, the DP staff had to become familiar with the technical aspects of data communication. In the early 1970s the technical issues were formidable, and there was a clear separation technically between voice and data transmission. But in the mid-1970s technical changes in telecommunications systems permitted voice and data to be dealt with similarly so that the same line could be used for voice and data without the need for special equipment. On several non-technical dimensions, however, initially voice and data communications continued to pose separate management problems: the telephone (voice) was still part of a carefully regulated utility and required little planning for purchase and use, while data communications, sold by many vendors, demanded increasingly sophisticated means for evaluating capital investments.

As the market for data communications has expanded, the economic advantages of merging voice and data communications, for example, in the WATS line, have become significant. In 1982, the trend is toward merging voice and data communications policy and operations in a single unit, usually located in the DP department. For example, a large bank recently installed an integrated network to replace the previously separate voice and data networks. The system reduced the bank's communication bill 35% and improved service to both the data processing installation and the telephone system.

Telecommunications and Office Automation

New technology has made possible the joining of word processing and office automation to telecommunications. Designers of word processing equipment now include in their machines the ability to communicate both to other machines and to storage devices through telecommunications systems. With these features, word processors are no longer merely automated typewriters but links to word storage files, other employees, and data files. The communications process has been vastly accelerated by development of telecommunications storage capacity, which permits the sender to leave messages. In many offices, this capability has equaled or exceeded word processing use in importance, but the real potential of these linkages is only partially exploited today. Development of this potential is slowed when telecommunications and office automation report to widely separated parts of the corporation.

DP and Office Automation

In many companies today, technologically innovative DP managers are linking their data processing and their word processing by extending their DP terminals to remote sites. As these companies began to move words (as opposed to just numeric data) through computers from one site to another, demand arose for systems to store and forward large volumes of words to other sites.

Often, employees used the remote terminals more for word than for data communications. Soon DP assimilated all communications, voice and data, as well as word processing. The success of this arrangement depends on whether the mature DP organization can nurture the new technologies instead of smothering them with excessive controls.

In summary, at present a number of organizational patterns are possible as companies move toward adopting and combining all information services. This heterogeneity is transitional, and most organizations will eventually merge these islands into a central hub, certainly for policymaking, planning, and control purposes, and, in many settings, for line control and execution. The timing of these moves in any organization depends on such factors as corporate structure and leadership style, the speed at which a company usually adopts new technologies, flexibility in staff assignments (for example, to remove deadwood), and current development priorities.

Phases of Assimilation

The merger of the three technologies is complicated by managers' need for different approaches to a particular technology as their organization gains experience with it. For example, the approach to planning and using relatively mature DP technology, such as new batch systems, may be inappropriate for new office automation or new DP technologies. Failure to recognize this difference has led to mismanagement of major projects and missed opportunities for projects that should have been started but were not because no one knew enough about the technology to perceive the possibilities.

Organizations change much more slowly than technology. As Richard L. Nolan and Cyrus F. Gibson showed for data processing, an organization goes through stages in assimilating technology.[1] Recent work in office automation and data processing has revealed this model to be a special case of the situation of the learning cycle of adapting a technology to an organization's needs.[2] That companies have been surprisingly poor in transferring skills learned in managing the DP stages to office automation is shown in a recent study of 37 companies, of which 30 had not built on their DP technology experience when moving into word processing and office automation.[3] Of equal importance, more than two-thirds had not progressed beyond Nolan's stage 2 of office automation of tasks and experimentation with respect to word processing and were in a state of arrested development.

Another study tracing an organization's use of information services technologies in all three components found four phases of evolution that relate both to Nolan's original stages and to concepts of organizational change developed by Edgar Schein.[4] These phases can be characterized as, (1) investment or project initiation, (2) technology learning and adaptation, (3) management control, and (4) widespread technology transfer (see Exhibit 4).

The first phase begins with a decision to invest in an information processing technology that is new to the organization and involves one or more complementary projects, as well as training users. The second phase usually follows, unless there is a disaster in Phase 1, such as failure of the vendor or poor user involvement. Such a setback results in a delayed phase, which is shown as Assimilation Block A in Exhibit 4.

A company would normally decide to "disinvest" if the system increased the work and provided few benefits. Such problems, in turn, result from lack of management attention, incompetent project management, major unanticipated technical problems, or bad choice of hardware. Managers are usually slow to recognize problems leading to this type of assimilation block.

The complexity and time requirements of implementing new information technology normally prevent discovery of the developing failure for 18 to 36 months. The project is usually not a clear technological disaster but rather an ambiguous situation that managers see as adding more work to the organization, with little measurable benefit. Hence, they reject the system.

All projects studied that were stalled in Assimilation Block A had significant cost overruns. Each failure created anxieties and prevented any coordinated momentum. Organizations frozen in this state usually end up purchasing more services based on a familiar technology and become adept

Exhibit 4. Use of Technology in a Corporation

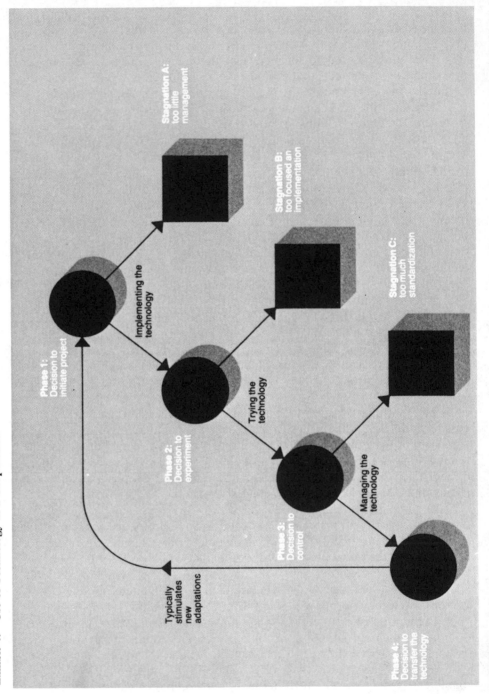

at adapting it to their use; for example, they might try to work with batch sales reports as opposed to learning how to use on-line sales updates. A two-year lag usually follows this assimilation block before new investments in this technology are tried again, often along with a complete change of personnel.

The second phase of adapting technology to an organization involves learning how to use it for tasks beyond those mentioned in the initial proposal. In none of 37 office automation sites studied was the technology implemented as originally planned.[5] In each case, managers learned a lot during implementation. If the second phase is managed so as to permit managers to develop and refine their new understanding of this technology, the organization moves to Phase 3. Failure to learn from the first applications and to effectively disseminate this learning leads to Assimilation Block B (see Exhibit 4).

A large manufacturing company experienced such an assimilation block during automation of clerical word processing activities that were under the control of a very cost-conscious accounting function. Highly conservative in its approach to technology in data processing, the company had automated accounting systems that were centrally controlled in a computer operating system that was becoming outmoded, but it had not yet adopted data-base systems.

Having developed this narrow word processing application to reduce costs, the accounting department showed no interest in expanding its scope beyond simply automating the editing function of a typewriter. The experience the department had gained was not disseminated; thus, over several years the lessons from introducing this technology were lost.

Phase 3 typically involves a change in the organization (when one company reached this point, for example, it transferred projects using a technology from an entrepreneurial system group to a control-oriented group) continued evolution of the uses of technology, and, most important, development of precise controls to guide the design and implementation of systems using these technologies to ensure that later applications are made more cost efficiently than the first. If, in this phase, control for efficiency is not all important and room is left for broader objectives, then the organization moves into a Phase 4, which involves broad-based communication and spread of technology to other groups in the organization.

Assimilation Block C comes when a company develops controls that are so onerous that they inhibit the legitimate, profitable spread of the use of technology. An example of this block with respect to data processing is a manufacturing company that entered into large-scale centralization with distributed input systems. To justify the expense, it focused on gaining all the benefits of a standardized, highly efficient production shop. In this process, the organization lost its enthusiasm for innovation and change with respect to this technology and actively discouraged users. Further, the rigorous protocols of these standard programs irritated users and helped set

the stage for local offices to experiment surreptitiously with automation—
Phase 1 in a different technology. The first incident described at this article's
beginning was from that company.

As time passes, new technologies emerge that offer the opportunity
either to move into new applications areas or to restructure old ones (see
Exhibit 4). Each of the three components of information services thus involves waves of new technologies, and companies must continually adopt
different approaches to managing and assimilating them, as each component
of technology is in a different phase.

For example, in 1981 a manufacturing company was in Phase 4 in terms
of its ability to plan for and deal with enhancements to its batch systems
over a period of years. At the same time, it was in Phase 3 in terms of
organizing protocols to solidify control over the efficiencies of its on-line
inquiry and data systems, whose growth had exploded in the past several
years. Finally, it had made an investment in several word-processing systems
and was clearly in Phase 1 with respect to this technology.

Thus, as the islands of technology merge, managers must not try to
use the same approach to technologies that are in different phases. A mismatch may be a reason to change the speed of reorganization.

The significant implications of these phases for organizations of IS
technologies include the following:

1 Where possible operationally, Phase 1 and 2 technologies should
   be kept organizationally separate from Phase 3 and 4 technologies
   so the efficiency goals of one do not blunt the effectiveness of the
   other. This suggests that policy may be ahead of operations when
   companies seek to merge, for example, office automation with DP.
2 The full operational integration of IS technologies will be a long
   time maturing, but companies may have to tolerate a certain dis-
   orderliness during integration in order to gain technical experience.
3 Dispersion of technology into the hands of the users in Phase 2 may
   be appropriate (although inefficient). However, managers may appropriately install tighter control after the original dispersion and
   make organizational shifts at a later phase.

Patterns of Distribution

As the three islands of technology coalesce and as structure and procedures
emerge to manage the phases of technology assimilation, the question that
remains is where the data and hardware elements should be located in the
organization. At one extreme is the company that has a large, centralized
hub connected by telecommunications links to remote input–output devices.
At the other is a small hub, or none at all, with most or all data and hardware
distributed to users. Between these extremes lies a rich variety of intermediate alternatives.

In the past, hardware costs heavily influenced resolution of this organization problem. Because the cost per arithmetic operation was higher for small hardware (as opposed to large hardware) in the early 1960s, the first large investments in computing were consolidated into large data centers. In contrast, rapidly falling hardware costs and the introduction of the minicomputer and microcomputer in the early 1980s permit, but do not demand, cost-effective organizational alternatives.

To retain their market shares as the difference in efficiency between large and small computers erodes, vendors of large computers are suggesting that many members of an organization need access to the same, large, data files; hence, according to them, the ideal structure for an information service is a large central processing unit with massive data files connected by a telecommunications network to a wide array of intelligent devices (often at great distances). While this holds true in many situations, for some companies the problem is unfortunately more complex, as we will discuss later. The factors influencing the final decision on structure include management control, technology, data professional services, and organizational fit (see Exhibit 5, below).

Exhibit 5. Pressures on Placement of the IS Function

Pressure	For Centralization	For Distribution
Management control	More professional operation	Better user control and response
	Flexible backup	Simpler control
	Efficient use of personnel	Improved local reliability
Technology	Large-scale capacity	Efficient size
	Efficient use of capacity	Reduced telecommunications costs
Data related	Multiple access to common data	Easier access
	Assurance of data standards	Better fit with field needs
	Better security	Data relevance
Professional service	Specialized staff	Stability of work force
	Reduced vulnerability to turnover	Better user career paths
	Richer DP career paths	
Organizational fit	Corporate style is central or functional	Decentralized corporate style
	History of IS	Meets business needs, e.g., for multinationals

Pressures Toward a Central Hub

Multiple pressures, both real and illusory, can cause companies to use a large hub with a distributed network.

Need for Management Control.   The ability to attract, develop, manage, and maintain staffs and controls to ensure high-quality, cost-effective operation of systems is a compelling reason for a strong central unit. A single large unit permits a more professional, cheaper, and higher-quality operation than would a series of much smaller units. These advantages caused the major decentralized company mentioned at the beginning of this article to retain its corporate data center rather than move to regional centers. The company was unconvinced that eight small data centers could be run as efficiently in aggregate and, even if they could, that it was worth the cost and trauma of making the transition.

Better backup is available through multiple central processing units in a single site. When hardware failure occurs in one CPU, pushing a button will switch the network from one machine to another. Obviously, this does not address the possibility that an environmental disaster could affect the entire center.

Available Technology.   The availability of large-scale processing capacity for users who need it only sometimes is another strong reason for a company to have a large hub. In a day when cheaper and more powerful computing has become available, it is easier for users to visualize doing some of their computing on their own personal computer, such as an Apple, or a stand-alone minicomputer. At the same time, however, some users have other problems, such as the need for large, linear programming models and petroleum-reservoir-mapping programs, that require the largest available computing capacity. In such cases, the larger the computer capacity available, the more detail the company can profitably build into its computer programs.

Also, many companies see an opportunity to manage aggregate computing more efficiently, thereby reducing hardware expenditures. With many machines in the organization, and with each loaded to 70%, managers may feel that consolidation would make better use of the available processing power. Although it was clearly an important cost issue in the 1960s, it is largely irrelevant in the 1980s.

Control of Data.   Another argument for the large central hub is the ability it gives users to control access to common corporate data files on a need-to-know basis. This access, absolutely essential from the early days for organizations such as airlines and railroads, is now economically feasible in many other companies because of the sharp reductions in storage and processing costs.

Personnel Services.   The large staff that is necessary in a major IS data center provides an opportunity to attract a specialized technical staff and keep it challenged. The opportunity to work on a variety of problems and to share expertise with other professionals provide the requisite air of excitement. Having these skills in the organization also permits individual units to undertake complex tasks as needed without incurring risks of uncontrolled use. Further, since such skills are generally in short supply, consolidating them in a single unit permits better deployment from a corporate perspective. Finally, the large group's resources at a hub permit more comfortable adaptation to inevitable turnover problems; resignation of one person in a three-person group of a decentralized system is normally more disruptive than five persons leaving a group of a hundred professionals.

Organizational Fit.   In a centralized organization, the factors just mentioned take on particular weight since they lead to a good fit between IS structure and overall corporate structure, and they help eliminate friction for organizations where IS hardware was introduced in a centralized fashion and whose management practices developed accordingly. Reversal of such a structure can be tumultuous.

Pressures Toward Distribution

In 1982 significant pressures argue for placing processing capacity and data in the hands of the users, and placing only limited or no processing power at a hub.

Management Control.   Most important among these factors is satisfaction of users' desire for control. Locally managed data files enable users to hear first about deviations from planned performance of their unit, and giving them an opportunity to analyze and communicate their understanding of their operations on a regular basis.

Also, by being removed from the hourly fluctuations in demand on the corporate network, the user has a better chance of stability in response time. Most users find predictable response time very important in at least some of their applications.

The distribution of hardware to users helps them remove or insulate themselves from the more volatile elements of the corporate charge-out system. They can better predict their costs, thus avoiding the necessity of describing embarrassing variances. Often costs will actually be lower.

With distribution of processing power, the corporation is much less vulnerable to a massive failure in the corporate data center. Companies with very large IS budgets, by which computers support essential parts of the operations, have found it increasingly desirable to set up two or more large data centers and split the work between them so that if something happened to one data center, the core aspects of the company's operations could run at the other. These companies have in general been such large users of data processing services that arrangement of backup at some other neighboring site is impractical.

Medium-sized companies have had the practical option of making backup arrangements with other organizations (which often sound better in theory than they turn out to be) or of buying into something like the remote-site solution (where for about $6,000 per month they have emergency access to a fully equipped, unloaded data center). In case of less dramatic events causing a service interruption at the main location, a network of local mini-computers can keep crucial aspects of an operation going.

From the user's perspective, the distributed network simplifies operations both in the construction of the operating system and in feeding work into it. The red tape involved in routing work to a data entry department is eliminated and the procedures can be built right into the operations of the user department, although, surprisingly, some users regain this control with trepidation. Similarly, with the right type of software, the machines in the distributed network are user friendly.

Technology Related.   Although in the early days large central processing units were more efficient than smaller machines, in the 1980s several important changes make this no longer true:

☐   The size of CPUs and memories no longer governs their power,[6] and their cost is a much smaller percentage of the total hardware expenditure in 1981 than in 1970.

☐   Grosch's Law (that computer processing power increases as the square of computer costs) was never intended to apply to peripheral units and other elements of a network.

☐   The percentage of hardware costs as a part of the total IS budget has dropped sharply over the past decade, as personnel, telecommunications, and other operating and development costs have risen. Thus, efficiency of hardware use is not the burning issue it was 10 years age. Taking these factors in conjunction with the much slower improvement in telecommunications costs (falling 11% per year) and the explosion of user needs for on-line access to data files that can be generated and stored locally, in many instances the economic case for a large hub has totally reversed itself.

Data Related.   Because of telecommunications costs and the very occasional needs of access to some data files by users other than those originating the data, many companies will find it uneconomical or undesirable to manage all data by central access. Further, ability to access and relate data may not be necessary to corporate strategy.

A case in point is the large company we mentioned at the outset, which recently considered abandoning its corporate computing center. The center is a service bureau for its eight major divisions, where all development staff members reside. No common application or data file exists between even two of the divisions (not even for payroll). If its survival depended on it, the company could not identify in less than 24 hours its relationship with any customer.

In senior management's judgment, this organization of the development staff and the lack of data relationships among divisions reinforces the company's highly decentralized structure. Thus, no pressure for change exists anywhere in the organization. The corporate computing center, an organizational anomaly, is considered simply a cost-efficient way of permitting each division to develop its own network of systems. Changing this approach would have had no practical use and could even threaten a soundly conceived organizational structure.

Professional Service.   Moving functions away from the urban environment toward more rural settings can reduce employee turnover, which is the bane of metropolitan-area information service departments. While recruiting may be complicated and training facilities may not be available in such locations, once the employees are there, the lack of "head hunters" and attractive employers nearby can reduce turnover.

When the IS staff is closely linked to the user organization, it becomes easier to plan employee promotions that may move technical personnel out of the IS organization to other user departments. This is an important advantage for a department with low turnover, as technical staff members may develop burn-out symptoms. Such transfers also aid relations between users and IS.

Organization Fit.   In many companies, the controls implicit in the distributed approach better fit the organizational structure and general leadership style. This is particularly true for companies with highly decentralized structures (or organizations that wish to evolve in this fashion) and/or for those that are geographically very diverse.

Finally, highly distributed facilities fit the needs of many multinational structures. While airlines reservation data, shipping container operations, and certain banking transactions must flow through a central location, in many cases the overwhelming amount of work is more effectively managed in the local country. Communication to corporate headquarters can be handled by telex, mailing tapes, or a telecommunications link, depending on the organization's management style, the size of the unit, and so on.

Assessing the appropriateness of a particular kind or size of hardware and the data configuration for an organization is very challenging. All but the most decentralized of organizations have a strong need for central control over standards and operating procedures. The changes in technology, however, both permit and make desirable in some companies distribution of the *execution* of significant portions of hardware operations and data handling.

Reexamination of the deployment of hardware and software resources for the information services function has high priority in the 1980s. Changing technology economics, merging of formerly disparate technologies with different managerial traditions, and problems of administering each phase of IS technology assimilation in different ways have made obsolete the decisions appropriate to 1970. To ensure appropriate handling of these issues five steps must be taken.

1.   Companies must make the development of a program to implement these decisions part of the mission of a permanent, corporate policy group. This policy group must assess the current move toward merging the islands, ensure a balance of the desires for a central hub against the advantages of a distributed approach, and ensure appropriate guidance of different technologies.
2.   The policy group must make sure that uniformity in management practice is not pushed too far and that diversity exists where appropriate. Even within a company, it is fitting that different parts of the organization have different patterns of distributed support for hardware and data. Different phases of development, with respect to specific technologies, and geographical distance from central service support are among the valid reasons for approaches to differ.
3.   The policy group must show particular sensitivity to the needs of the international activities. It may be inappropriate to enforce common approaches to these problems internationally, either for companies operating primarily in a single country or for the multinational that operates in many countries. Each country has a different cost and quality structure for telecommunications, a different level of IS achievement, different reservoirs of technical skills, and a different culture, at least. These differences are likely to endure. What works in the United States often will not work in, say, Thailand.
4.   The policy group must address its issues in a strategic fashion. The arguments and reasoning leading to a set of solutions are more complex than simply the current economics of hardware or who should have access to what data files. Corporate organizational structure, corporate strategy and direction, availability of human resources, and operating administrative processes are additional critical inputs. Both in practice and in writing, the technicians and information theorists oversimplify a very complex set of problems and options.
    A critical function of the group is to ensure adequate research and development investment (Phases 1 and 2). A special effort must be taken to make appropriate investments in experimental studies, pilot studies, and development of prototypes. Similarly, the group must ensure that proved expertise is being distributed appropriately within the company, especially to departments that may be unaware of IS potential.
5.   The policy group must establish a proper balance between long- and short-term needs. A distributed structure optimally designed for the technology and economics of 1982 may fit the world of 1989 rather poorly. Often it makes sense to postpone feature development or to design a clumsy approach in today's technology in order to be able to adapt more easily and inexpensively to the technologies of the late 1980s. As a practical matter,

the group will work on these issues in a continuous, iterative fashion rather than implement a revolutionary change.

Notes

1. "Managing the Four Stages of EDP Growth," *HBR*, January–February 1974, p. 76.

2. James McKenney, "A Field Study on the Use of Computer-Based Technology to Improve Management Control" (*HBS* Working Paper 7–46).

3. Kathleen Curley, "Word Processing: First Step to the Office of the Future? An Examination of the Evolving Technology and Its Use in Organizations," unpublished thesis, June 1981.

4. Edgar Schein, "Management Development as a Process of Influence," *Industrial Management Review*, 1961, Vol. 2, p. 59.

5. Kathleen Curley, *op. cit.*

6. Edward G. Cole, Lee L. Gremillion, and James L. McKenney, "Price/Performance Patterns of U.S. Computer Systems," *Proceedings of the ACM*, April 1979.

9

Information Archipelago – Plotting a Course

F. WARREN McFARLAN, JAMES L. McKENNEY, and PHILIP PYBURN

Information systems applications now resemble those of a decade ago—they cost a lot, are technically complex, and take a long time to develop. Moreoever, as the technology continues to change rapidly, managers find themselves continually squeezed by a shortage of the technical staff and financial resources they need to keep up. A company can use knowledge of its particular strengths and weaknesses in regard to IS to steer its way onto a safe course, say these authors, in the second part of a series dealing with the "islands" of information: computers, telecommunications, and office automation (see "The Information Archipelago—Maps and Bridges," Chapter 8 of this book). This requires a new planning approach, for which the guideposts are the company's familiarity with any one technology, how important the technology is to corporate strategy, and certain business characteristics such as size, complexity of product lines, and the general approach to corporate planning.

☐ A major manufacturing company eliminates its five-person IS planning staff, reassigning three to other jobs in the IS organization and letting two go. In commenting on this, the vice president—finance stated, "We just didn't seem to be getting a payoff from this. After three years of trying, we thought we could find a better place to spend our money."

☐ The executive vice president—operations of a large financial institution, in speaking of a recently completed business systems planning effort, stated that this effort has been the key to conceptualizing a new

There may be slight stylistic differences in the article published in this book and the way it eventually appeared in the Harvard Business Review.

and important direction concerning both the amount of IS expenditures and where they should be directed during the next five years. "We would be lost without it," he noted.

☐   The head of IS planning of a major financial services organization, in discussing his recent disillusionment with planning noted, "When I started IS planning two years ago, I was very enthusiastic about its potential for invigorating the company. It worked for a while, but now the effort seems to have gone flat."

These comments seem typical of a number of organizations where an IS planning effort is launched with great hopes and apparent early results but, in some cases, subsequently runs into difficulty. This article shows how IS planning can be approached to yield better results.

IS refers to the technologies of computers, telecommunications, and office automation. In the early 1970s, these could be planned and managed as largely separate entities. By 1982, however, increasingly they are being managed together. This is, first because more and more new applications require the interconnection of all three technologies; second, because the project management problems of applications using any one of these technologies have become quite similar. These applications are characterized by the words of the professionals "large purchase cost," "technical complexity," and "long systems development lead times." While these words were applicable primarily to computer projects in the early 1970s, they now divide both telecommunications and office automation projects as well.

As information systems applications have grown in both size and complexity over the past two decades, the job of planning the types and amounts of IS applications and services to be offered has grown steadily more important to ensuring that the right amounts of staff, hardware, and financial resources be available. A rapidly changing technology, a scarcity of corporate staff, limited financial and managerial resources, a trend toward database design, and need to validate the corporate plans are the key driving forces for this increased importance.

This article will show that the best approach to planning the use of a specific IS technology is contingent on the organization's familiarity and experience with the technology. Technologies new to the company require quite different planning approaches than those with which it has had great familiarity. Further, it is becoming clear that the strategic impact of IS technologies on a company varies widely from one setting to another. These differences significantly influence how IS planning can best be done. Finally, a number of factors specific to a firm such as its size, complexity of product lines, and approach to corporate planning influence how IS planning can best be done.

Pressures to Plan—General Considerations

There are a variety of critical pressures which force one to plan ahead in the information systems field. The more important include:

Rapid Changes in Technology.   Hardware/software technical and cost characteristics have and will continue to evolve rapidly, thereby offering substantially different and profitable approaches to applications development. On the one hand, this requires continued meetings of the IS staff and management groups to ensure that they have properly identified shifts significant to the company and developed plans to manage them. On the other hand, it is equally important that potential users, such as office managers or analytical staffs (often quite different from the traditional users of data processing systems), be made aware of the implications of these changes (as well as potential problems), so that they can be stimulated to identify appropriate, profitable new applications in their areas of responsibility that would not necessarily occur to the IS staff.

As the technology changes, planning becomes increasingly important to ensure that the organization does not unwittingly fall into a proliferation of incompatible systems. It is also important because the lead time for acquiring and updating equipment is often long. Also, integration of new equipment such as laser printers into a company's existing technical configuration and network of administrative procedures frequently forces implementation schedules to be extended by up to four years.

A recently studied regional bank has a three-year installation program to manage its transition from 140 on-line terminals to over 1,100 terminals on completion of its on-line teller network. Preparation of a detailed plan was absolutely critical in developing senior management's confidence in the integrity of the installation program and insuring sound operations would continue during the implementation.

Personnel Scarcity.   The scarcity of trained, perceptive analysts and programmers, coupled with the long training cycles needed to make them fully effective is a major factor restraining IS development.

These do not appear to be cyclical problems, but rather long-term difficulties which will endure throughout the 1980s. Not only will increasing amounts of software have to be obtained from outside the firm, but tough, internal resource allocation decisions must be made. In 1981, not only is the computer services industry booming but an increasing number of U.S. firms are looking overseas for English-speaking technical personnel to meet existing shortages, at attractive U.S. salaries.

Scarcity of Other Corporate Resources.   Another critical factor inducing planning is the limited availability of financial and managerial resources. IS is only one of many strategic investment opportunities for a company, and cash invested in it is often obtained at the expense of other areas. This is intensified by the overwhelming financial accounting practice in U.S. companies of charging IS expenditures directly against current year's earnings. Hence, a review of both the effectiveness and efficiency of these expenditures is a matter of great interest and is a critical limiting factor for new projects, particularly in companies under profit or cost pressures.

The scarcity of IS middle-managers, particularly on the development side, is also a significant constraint. Companies' inability to train sufficient project leaders and supervisors has significantly restrained IS development. This has forced either significant reductions in many application development portfolios, or the undertaking of unduly high-risk projects with inadequate human resources.

Trend to Data-Base Design and Integrated Systems. An increasing and significant percentage of the development portfolio involves the design of data bases to support a variety of different applications. A long-term view of the evolution of applications is critical in order to select, appropriately, both the contents of the data bases and the protocols for updating them to adequately support the family of application systems using them.

Validation of Corporate Plan. In many organizations, new marketing programs, new product design, and introduction and implementation of organizational strategies depend on the development of IS support programs. It is critical that these points of dependency be understood. If the corporate strategy is infeasible due to IS limitations, this message should be highlighted and the problem's resolution be forced when alternatives are still available. In organizations where the IS products are integral to elements of the corporate strategy this linkage is more important than in organizations where IS plays an important but distinctly support function. For example, a large paper company recently had to abandon major new billing discount promotions, a key part of its marketing strategy, because it was unable to translate the very complex ideas into the existing computer programs with its present level of staff skills. Coordination with IS in planning sessions would have identified both the problem and more satisfactory solutions to it.

Pressures to Plan—Situational Considerations

It is important to note that at different points in the evolution of an IS technology, the balance between these pressures shifts, and planning begins to serve substantially different purposes. Reflecting upon the advent and growth of business, data-processing data bases, distributed systems, telecommunications, and other new technologies, one can identify four different phases of technology assimilation. Each poses quite a different planning challenge.

Normally a firm simultaneously deals with a number of technologies, each of which is at a *different* phase of assimilation within the firm.

Phase 1—Technology Identification and Investment Phase. The basic focus of planning in the initial phase of a new technology for a company is both technically oriented and human-resource-acquisition oriented. Key planning problems include identification of an appropriate technology for study, site preparation, development of staff skills, and managing development of the first pilot applications using this technology.

In this phase, short-term technical problem resolution issues are so critical and experience so limited, that long-term strategic thinking about the implications of the technology is limited. This is not bad, since those involved usually do not yet have a strong enough background in the technology and its implications for the company to think long term. As the organization gains experience, selection of appropriate applications for this technology become more equal to technical issues and one evolves to the second phase.

Phase 2—Technological Learning and Adaptation Phase. Planning in this phase is focused on developing consciousness in users of the new technology's existence and communicating a sense of the type of problems it can help solve, sequencing projects, and providing coordination. The initiation of a series of user-supported pilot projects is a key to success. As a secondary output, planning focuses on numbers and skills of staff to be hired, equipment to be acquired, and the generation of appropriate financial data supporting those projects. The plan is not an accurate indicator for predicting the pace of future events because individuals engaged in a learning process do not yet have the insights to be both concise and accurate concerning what their real desires are in relation to this technology and how practical these desires are. It is important to note that, since technology will evolve, for the foreseeable future, there will usually be a Phase 2 flavor to part of a company's IS development portfolio. Our observations of successful practice at this phase suggest clearly that:

1   Planning for introducing new technology best starts with a rough and dirty test to educate both IS and users rather than with years of advance introspection concerning design and potential benefits.
2   The critical success factors in Phase 2 involve attracting the interest of some potential users of the technology on their terms. Success here leads later to more crisply articulated requests for service.

Phase 2 has a heavy strategic focus to planning for technologies. However, as is true in companies which are in a rapid growth phase in new industry sectors, precision of such planning suffers from both the user's and developer's lack of familiarity with the technology and the environment being supported. Hence it does not have the same predictive value as planning for technology at a later phase. What the technical developer thinks are the implications of the new technology often turns out to be quite different after the users have experimented.

Phase 3—Rationalization. Effective planning for technologies at this phase has a strong focus on efficiency. Where technological learning and adaptation planning has a long-range, if not terribly accurate flavor to it, planning in Phase 3 is dominated by short-term one- to two-year efficiency and organization considerations. These include getting troubled development applications straightened away and completed, upgrading staff to acceptable knowledge levels, reorganizing to develop and implement further projects, and efficiently utilizing this new technology. During this phase, planning's objective is to draw appropriate limits concerning the types of applications which make sense with this technology and to ensure they are implemented cost efficiently. During this phase, effective planning has much more of a management control and operational control flavor to it and less of a strategic planning thrust to it.

Phase 4—Widespread Technology Transfer. The final phase is one of managed evolution by transferring the technology to a wider spectrum of systems applications within the organization. At this phase, with organizational learning essentially complete, a technology base installed with appropriate controls in place, it is appropriate to look more seriously into the future and plot longer-term trends. Unfortunately, if one is not careful, this can become too rigid an extrapolation of trends based on business and technology as we now understand it. Unexpected quirks in the business and evolution of technology often invalidate what has been done during Phase 4 planning.

Given the current dynamic state of IS technology, a mix of technologies across all four phases can be found in a typical organization. The planning for business batch data processing for most companies, for example, is Phase 4, while word processing and office automation is Phase 2. This suggests that uniform orderliness and consistency in planning is not appropriate because of organizational variances in familiarity with particular technologies. The planning approach must evolve for a particular technology over time. Also a consistent, uniform process for the aggregate portfolio of applications for an organizational unit is unlikely to be appropriate since it is dealing with a cluster of different technologies, each of which is at a different phase of assimilation with the organization. For example, one manufacturing company studied was Phase 4 in terms of its ability to conceptualize and deal with enhancements to its batch systems over several years. At the same time, it was Phase 3 in terms of developing control over its on-line inquiry and data input systems whose growth had exploded in the past several years. Finally, it had made an investment in several word-processing systems, was beginning to examine several different methods of office automation, and was clearly in Phase 1 with respect to this technology.

In summary, planned clutter (as opposed to consistency) in the approach to IS planning for an organizational unit is desirable rather than undesirable. Similarly, the approach to IS planning for different organization units within a company should vary, since each often has quite a different familiarity with specific technologies.

Challenges in Implementation Planning

As new products appear, as the competitive environment shifts, as the laws change, as corporate strategies change, and as mergers and spinoffs take place, the priorities a company assigns to its various applications also evolve. Some previously considered low-priority or new (not even conceived of) applications may become critically important, while others previously vital may diminish in significance. This volatility places a real premium on building a flexible framework that permits change to be managed in an orderly and consistent fashion, to match evolving business requirements.

Technical Forecasting Inaccuracies

In a similar vein, every information systems planning process must make some very specific assumptions about the nature and role of technological evolution. If this evolution occurs at a different rate from the one forecasted (as is often the case) then major segments of the plan may have to be reworked in terms of both scope and thrust of work.

For example, if the present speed of access to a 100-million character file were suddenly increased in the coming year by an order of magnitude beyond current expectations, with no change in cost, most organizations' plans would require careful re-examination, not just concerning the priority of applications, but more importantly, their very structure.

Some individuals have used this as a reason not to plan, but rather to be creatively opportunistic on a year-to-year basis. We have found the balance of evidence supporting this viewpoint unconvincing.

Planning as a Resource Drain.   Every person's time, or part of that time, assigned to planning, diverts resources away from systems and program development. The extent to which financial resources should be devoted to planning is still very much in question. Not only will the style of planning evolve over time, as parts of the organization pass through different phases with different technologies, but the amount of commitment to planning will also appropriately shift. This suggests that there is incompatibility between the notions of stability in an IS planning process and its role of stimulating a creative view of the future. If not carefully managed, IS planning tends to evolve into a mind-numbing process of routinely changing the numbers instead of a stimulating, sensitive focus on the company's real problems.

Strategic Impact of IS Activities.   For some organizations, IS activities represent an area of great strategic importance while for other organizations they play, and appropriately will continue to play, a cost-effective and useful role but one which is distinctly supportive in nature. It is inappropriate for organizations of this latter type to expect that the same amount of senior management's strategic thinking be devoted to the IS organization as to organizations of the former type. This issue is complicated by the fact that, while in some organizations the IS function may not have strategic importance in meeting today's goals, its application portfolio may have great significance for the future and, thus, senior-management involvement in planning is very important. The opposite, of course, could also be true where IS plays a strategic operational role in the company's operations, but the future IS applications do not seem to offer the same rewards. Here a less intensive focus on strategic planning is in order with clearly different people involved than in the previous case.

Exhibit 1 summarizes these points by identifying four quite different IS environments and identifying where some companies fall in this categorization.

Strategic. There are companies that are both critically dependent on the smooth functioning of the IS activity to operate on a daily basis and whose applications under development are critical for their future competitive success. Banks and insurance companies are examples of firms which frequently fall into this category. Appropriately managed, not only do these firms require considerable planning, but the organizational distance between IS and senior management is very short. In fact, in some firms, the head of the IS function, broadly defined, sits on the Board of Directors.

Recent comments by the CEO of a large financial institution to his senior staff captured this perspective as he noted:

Exhibit 1. Information Systems Planning—A Contingent Focus

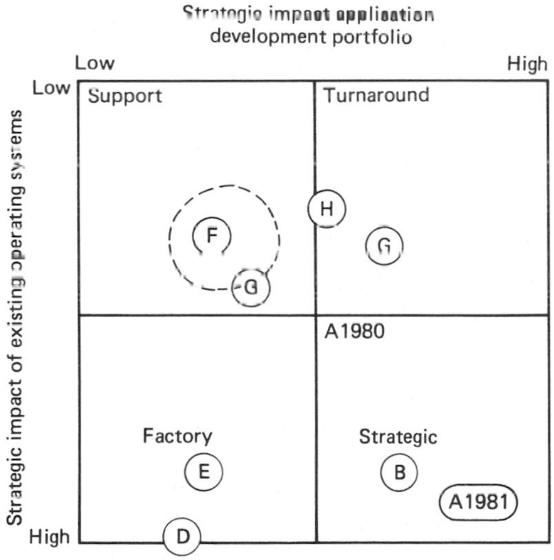

A—Major bank 1980—1981
B—Major insurance company
C—Medium—size grocery chain
D—$100 million distributor
E—Major airline
F—Major chemical company
G—Major process industry manufacturer
H—Insurance broker

Most of our customer services and much of our office support for those services involve some kind of systematic information processing. Without the computer hardware and software supporting these processing efforts, we would undoubtedly drown in a sea of paper—unless we were first eliminated from the market because our costs were so high and our services so inefficient that we had no customers to generate the paper. Either way, it is abundantly clear that information systems are critical to our survival and our success.

In our businesses, the critical resources which ultimately determine our marketing and our operating performance are *people* and *systems*.

Turnaround.   These are firms that may receive considerable amounts of IS operational support, but where the company is not absolutely dependent on the uninterrupted cost-effective functioning of this support to achieve either short-term or long-term objectives. The impact of the applications under development, however, are absolutely vital for the firm to reach its strategic objectives. A good example of this was a rapidly growing manufacturing firm. IS technology imbedded in its factories and accounting processes, while important, was not absolutely vital to their effectiveness. The rapid growth of the firm's domestic and international installation in number of products, number of sites, number of staff, etc., however, had severely strained its management control systems and had made its improvement of critical strategic interest to the company. Enhanced IS leadership, new organizational placement of IS, and an increased commitment to planning were all steps taken to resolve the situation. Companies in this block not only have an increased need for IS planning, but frequently fulfill the need along with a number of other changes to enhance senior management's overview of IS.

Factory.   These firms are heavily dependent on IS operational support for smooth operations. Their application development portfolios, however, are dominated by maintenance work and applications which, while profitable and important in their own right, are not fundamental to the firm's ability to compete. Planning for these firms has a shorter-term, more operational flavor, balancing service, cost, and efficiency issues. Some manufacturing, airline and retailing firms fall into this category very nicely. In these organizations, even a one-hour disruption in service from existing systems has severe consequences on the performance of the business.

Support.   These firms, some of which may have very large IS budgets, are firms that are neither fundamentally operationally dependent on the smooth functioning of the IS activity nor are their application portfolios aimed at the critical startegic needs of the company. A recently studied large manufacturing company fit this category perfectly. Spending nearly $30 million/year on IS activities, with more than 500 employees involved, it was clear that this sum was being well spent and the firm was getting a good return on its investment. It was also clear that the firm could operate, albeit unevenly, in the event of major operational difficulties and that the strategic impact of the application portfolio under development was limited. IS was at a significantly lower organizational level than in other settings and the commitment to planning, particularly at the senior management level was quite low. The director of Corporate Planning recently noted:

> There is no payoff in my spending time here. Any conceivable improvements in this department's performance will have negligible impact on the company as a whole. Our research has uncovered a surprisingly large number of companies in this category.

Not only should the planning approach differ for each of these environments, but it should take into account the more complicated situation when a mismatch exists between where an organization is in the grid and where senior management believes it should be.

The following example describes such a situation recently faced by a large financial institution. The institution's senior management was very comfortable with the company's IS performance although it came up only infrequently on their agenda. Its IS management team, however, was deeply concerned that it lacked the necessary conception of what the firm's goals were and what its products would be four to five years hence, to ensure that they could provide the necessary support for the achievement of these goals.

The institution is a large, international one with a very sophisticated, but closely held, corporate-planning activity. Appropriately in a world of potentially major shifts in what financial institutions can and should do, there was great concern at the top about the confidentiality of this information, and only four or five individuals knew the full scope of this direction. Neither the IS manager, nor his boss, were among this handful. Consequently, they were substantially in the dark about the future direction of the organization and could only crudely assess it in terms of trying to guess why some projects were unfunded while others were funded.

The company had a full-time IS planning manager who had three assistants and who reported to the IS manager. For the last two years, the IS planners had worked closely with both middle-management users and the DP technologists to come up with strategies and applications portfolios which were commonly seen by both sides to be relevant to their needs. Because there was little direct linkage, formal or informal, between the IS planning activity and the corporate planning department (repeatedly corporate planning had communicated "don't call us, we'll call you"), the IS staff had two overriding concerns:

1 The plans and strategies developed for IS might be technically sound and meet the needs of user middle-senior management, but could be unproductive or indeed counterproductive in terms of their ability to support the institution's corporate image.

2 The corporate plans, as developed by the four or five at the top in

the know but also isolated from IS, could unwittingly place onerous or unworkable pressures on IS in terms of future support requests.

At this stage, senior management perceived IS as a factory, believed it was staffed appropriately, was being managed appropriately, and had no concerns about its planning process. IS saw itself as strategic, but couldn't sell the concept to anyone. This frustration was recently resolved when an outside review of the institution's overall strategy convinced senior management that they had misunderstood the role of IS and that IS should be treated as strategic. Unfortunately, in the process of evolution, IS management who were perceived as being satisfactory to run a factory, were quickly perceived as being inadequate for this newly defined challenge and were personally unable to survive the transition.

IS planning on the surface had looked good when one read the written plan. However, in fact, it had failed to come to grips with the realities of the corporate environment and left an organization where extremely important IS activities are in a state of potential unpreparedness and risk. This was fatal to IS management where on multiple dimensions, IS activities were belatedly perceived as being critical to the organization's achievement of its product and productivity goals.

The IS criticality segmentation (see Exhibit 1) is useful not just for categorizing a company as a whole, but also for characterizing the position of the different business units inside the company, which quite appropriately can be at very different positions on the grid. Both the actual positions of the units and the perceptions, from the perspective of IS management and senior management, of where they should be represent critical inputs to the design of IS planning.

Exhibit 2 contains a questionnaire used by one firm to analyze the strategy of the development portfolio for each of its organizational units. These questions are designed to uncover whether on balance the development work being done is *critical* to the firm's future competitive posture or whether it is useful but not at the core of what has to be done to be competitively successful. Similarly, Exhibit 3 contains a questionnaire used by the firm to analyze how critical the existing systems are to an organizational unit in achieving its basic operating objectives. Both exhibits are used by the firm as rough, diagnostic tools.

Exhibit 4 suggests that not only does a firm's placement in this matrix influence how IS planning should be done but has numerous other implications in terms of the role of the executive steering committee, organizational placement of IS, type of IS management control system appropriate, and so on. Further, since different organizational units within a company may be at quite different points on the grid, the planning organization and control approach suitable for one unit may be quite inappropriate for another. Finally, since an organizational unit often migrates over time on the grid, the planning organization and control approach suitable at one time may be quite unsuitable at another time.

Exhibit 2. Information Systems Planning—A Contingent Focus

Portfolio Analysis	Percent of Development Budget
1. Projects involved in researching impact of new technologies or anticipated new areas of applications where generation of expertise, insight, and knowledge are the main benefits.	0–5% 5–15% Over 15%
2. Projects involved in cost displacement of cost avoidance productivity improvement.	Over 70% 70–40% Under 40%
3. Do estimated aggregate improvements of these projects exceed 10% of firm's after-tax profits or 1% of sales?	Yes No
4. Projects focused on routine maintenance to meet evolving business needs (processing new union contract payroll data) or meeting new regulatory or legal requirements.	Over 70% 70–40% Under 40%
5. Projects focused on existing system enhancements which do not have identifiable hard benefits.	Under 10% 10–40% Over 40%
6. Projects whose primary benefit is providing new decision support information to top three levels of management. No tangible identifiable benefits.	0–5% 5–15% Over 15%
7. Projects whose primary benefit is to offer new decision support information to middle management or clerical staff.	0–5% 5–15% Over 15%
8. Projects which allow the firm to develop and offer new products or services for sale or enable additional significant new features.	Over 20% 10–20% 5–10%

Exhibit 3. Information Systems Planning—A Contingent Focus

Operational dependence questions
1. Impact of a one-hour shutdown—main center
    Major operational disruption in customer service, plant shutdown, groups of staff totally idle.
    Inconvenient but core business activities continue unimpaired.
    Essentially negligible.

Exhibit 3. (*Continued*)

2. Impact total shutdown—main center—two to three weeks
   Almost fatal—no ready source of backup.
   Major external visibility, major revenue shortfall or additional costs.
   Expensive—core processes can be preserved at some cost and at reduced quality levels.
   Minimal—fully acceptable, tested backup procedures exist, incremental costs manageable, transition costs acceptable.

3. Costs of IS as percent total corporate costs
   Over 10%
   2–10%
   Under 2%

4. Operating systems
   Operating system software totally customized and maintained internally.
   Major reliance vendor-supplied software but significant internal enhancements.
   Almost total reliance on standard vendor packages.

5. Labor
   Data center work force organized—history of strikes.
   Nonunionized work force, inexperienced and/or low morale.
   High morale—unorganized work force.

6. Quality control—criticalness
   Processing errors—major external exposure.
   Processing errors—modest external exposure.
   Processing errors—irritating, modest consequence.

7. No. of operationally critical on-line systems or hard-line batch systems
   10 or more
   3–5
   0–2

8. Dispersion of critical systems
   Critical systems—run by multiple departments. Geographic dispersion of processing.
   Critical systems—2–3 installations.
   Critical systems—1 location.

9. Ease of recovery after failure—six hours
   3–4 days—heavy workload. Critical system.
   12–24 hours critical systems.
   Negligible—almost instantaneous.

10. Recovery after quality control failure
    Time consuming, expensive, many interrelated systems.
    Some disruption and expense.
    Relatively quick—damage well contained.

11. Feasibility coping manually 80–20% basis
    Impossible.
    Somewhat possible.
    Relatively easy.

Exhibit 4. Examples of Different Managerial Strategies for Companies in Support and Strategic Boxes (assuming they are appropriately located)

Support	Activity	Strategic
Middle-level management membership. Existence of ←——— committee less critical	Steering Committee	———→ Active senior management involvement, committee key
Less urgent, mistakes in resource allocation not ←——— fatal	Planning	———→ Critical. Must link to corporate strategy. Careful attention to resource allocation vital.
Avoid high-risk projects ←——— because of constrained benefits. A poor place for corporate strategic gambles.	Risk profile— project portfolio	———→ Some high-risk/high-potential benefit projects appropriate if possibility exists to gain strategic advantage
Can be managed in a ←——— looser way. Operational headaches less severe	IS capacity management	———→ Critical to manage. Must leave slack.
Can be lower ←———	IS management reporting level	———→ Should be very high.
A conservative posture ←——— one to two years behind state-of-art appropriate	Technical innovation	———→ Critical to stay current and fund R&D. Competitor can gain advantage.

IS Management Climate

In an environment of great management turmoil, turnover, and reassessment, it is unlikely that the same intensity and commitment of effort to planning IS can be productively unleashed as is possible in more stable environments where individuals have a stronger emotional attachment to the organization.

In aggregate, while these factors make execution of planning complex, they do not eliminate its need. Rather, they identify the importance of tailoring the planning approach to a particular situation. A general-purpose planning approach is unlikely to be successful.

Corporate Environmental Factors Influencing Planning

Recently completed research has identified four factors that influence how IS planning must be structured to improve the likelihood of success within a specific company.

1. *Importance and status of the IS manager.* Proper alignment of status of the IS manager to the role IS plays or should play in the overall operation and strategy formulating process of the company is very important. In environments where IS is in a "strategic" or "turnaround" role, a low status IS manager (reporting-level and/or compensationwise) makes it hard to get the necessary inputs from general management into planning. If the corporate communication at the top is heavily informal, this is apt to be fatal, as IS is outside the key communication loop. If the corporate communication is more formal, development and management of appropriate committees and other formal processes can alleviate the situation. For companies where IS is and should be in the "support" role, lower status of the IS director is appropriate and less effort needs to be made to assure alignment of IS and corporate strategy. Further, a lower level of investment (dollars and type of staff) in IS planning is appropriate for these situations. This is illustrated by the recent comments of a director of strategic planning for a large process-oriented manufacturing company.

> We relate to IS by giving them insight on what the corporate goals are and what the elements and forms are of a good planning system. Because of their role in the company, we do not solicit feedback from them as to what the art of the possible is. The nature of their operation is such that they can provide no useful input to the selection of corporate strategy.

2. *Physical proximity of systems group and the general management team.* For organizations where many important decisions are made informally in *ad hoc* sessions, and where IS is playing a "strategic" or "turnaround" role, then it is important to keep key IS management staff physically close to senior line managers. Regardless of the systems manager's status, it is difficult for him or her to be an active member of the team in this type of organization if he or she is geographically distant. In the words of one manager in such a company "when a problem surfaces, those people who are around and easily accessible are those who solve it, and we don't wait to round up the missing bodies." When the management communications are more formal, physical proximity becomes less important. In these situations, the formal written communications and the scheduled formal meetings largely substitute for the informal give-and-take. In informal organizations, where IS is strategic or turnaround even if the systems groups must be located many miles from headquarters for other reasons, it is critical that the IS managers, and preferably a small staff, be at corporate headquarters. For "support" and "factory" organizations in informal organizations, location at corporate headquarters is much less critical.

3. *Corporate culture and management "style."* In organizations where the basic management culture is characterized by the words "low key" and "informal" and where an informal, personal relationship exists between systems manager and senior management, then formal IS planning procedures do not appear to be a critical determinant of systems effective-

ness. Development of this relationship is assisted (as mentioned here) by the geographic proximity and IS manager status. As an organization becomes more formal in its business practices, the role of formal IS planning disciplines becomes more significant as a countervailing force, even for systems environments which are not highly complex.

4. *Organizational size and complexity.* As organizations increase in both size and complexity, and as applications of information systems technology grows larger and more complex, more formal planning processes are needed to ensure the kind of broad-based dialogue essential to the development of an integrated "vision of IS." Of course, this is not unrelated to the previous discussion concerning management culture and style, as greater size and complexity often leads to more formal practices in general. In environments where the business unit size is small and relatively simple, formal planning approaches become less critical, irrespective of the other factors. Similarly, for business units where the systems environment is not terribly complex, IS planning can safely take place in a more informal fashion. However, as the portfolio of work increases in size and integration across user areas, more discipline and formality in planning become necessary.

In aggregate, these corporate culture items highlight on another dimension why selection of a planning approach is so complex and why recommendations on how to do IS planning "in general" almost always turn out to be too inflexible and prescriptive for a specific situation. (Even within a company, these issues may force considerable heterogeneity of practice between organization units.)

Corporate Environmental Factors—An Example

The following example shows how these issues have shaped IS planning in a billion dollar manufacturing organization. This company has both a medium-sized corporate IS facility and stand-alone IS facilities of some significant size in each of its six major U.S. divisions. These divisional IS facilities report straight line to the divisions and dotted line to the corporate IS function. The corporate IS group is part of a cluster of corporate staff activities in an organization where traditionally some considerable power has been located at corporate level.

The vice president of corporate IS also has the corporate planning activity reporting to him. In addition, he has had a long personal and professional relationship with both the chairman and chief executive officer, extending over a period of many years, in a company that could be described as having an informal management culture. He was initially given responsibility for IS because the number of operational and development problems had reached crisis proportions. While under normal circumstances, the criticality of IS might be termed "support," these difficulties pushed the firm into the "turnaround" category.

The closeness of relationships between the division general managers and their IS managers varies widely. The size of the application portfolios in relation to the overall size of the division also varies considerably, with IS activities playing a more significant role in some settings than in others.

IS planning begins at the divisional level within the framework of some rather loose corporate guidelines concerning technological direction. At the divisional level, planning culminates in the preparation of a divisional IS plan. The planning involvement and dialogues vary widely from division to division in terms of line managers. Some line managers are intimately involved in developing the plan, with the division general manager investing considerable time in the final review and modification to the plan. In other divisions, however, the relationship is not so close and IS plans are developed almost entirely by the IS organization with very limited review by the general management. The relationship of IS activities to the strategic functioning of the various units varies widely.

Critical to IS planning is an annual three-day meeting of the corporate IS director and key IS staff, where the divisional IS managers present their plans. The corporate IS director plays a major role in these sessions in critiquing and modifying plans to better fit corporate objectives. The director's understanding of the corporate plan and the thinking of the divisional general managers (in his or her capacity as head of corporate planning), as well as his or her first-hand knowledge of what is on the chairman's and president's minds enables this IS director to immediately spot shortfalls in IS plans, particularly for those divisions where there are weak IS line management relationships. As a result, plans evolve which fit the real business needs of the organization, and the IS activity is well regarded. A planning approach which in other settings might have led to disaster, has worked out well because of the special qualities of the IS director, and development of a communication approach between the director and general management which is appropriate for this firm's culture.

Summary

There continues to be evidence that there is a clear link between planning and effectively perceived IS activity for many organizational settings. Quite apart from the generation of new ideas, etc., a major role of IS planning is stimulation of discussion and exchange of insights between the specialists and users. Effectively managed, it is an important element in avoiding potential conflict.

For example, a major financial institution that we studied attempted at least four different approaches to IS planning over a six-year period. Each was started with great fanfare with different staffs and organizations, and each limped to a halt. It was, however, only when the firm abandoned efforts to plan, that deep and ultimately irreconcilable differences arose between IS and the user organization. Communication of viewpoints, and exchange

of problems and potential opportunities (key to developing shared understanding) are as important as the selection of specific projects.

In this context our conclusions are:

1. Organizations where the IS activity is critical to corporate strategy
implementation have a special need to build links between IS planning and
corporate strategy formulation. As indicated earlier, accomplishing this is
complex. Key aspects of this linkage are:

Testing elements of corporate strategy to ensure that they are possible
within IS resource constraints. On some occasions, the resources needed
are obtainable, but in other settings, resources are unavailable and painful
readjustments must be made.

Transfer of planning and strategy formulating skills to the IS function.

Ensuring long-term availability of appropriate IS resources.

In other support and factory settings, this linkage is less critical. Appropriately, over time the need for this linkage may change as the strategic mission
of IS evolves.

2. As organizations grow in size, complexity of systems, and formality, IS planning must be directly assigned to someone to avoid resulting
lack of focus and the risk of significant pieces dropping between cracks. This
job, however, is a subtle and complex one. The task is to ensure that planning
occurs in an appropriate form. A strong set of enabling and communication
skills is critical if the individual is to relate to the multiple individuals and
units touched by this technology and cope with their differing degrees of
familiarity with it. Ensuring involvement of IS staff and users for both input
and conclusions concurrence is key. The great danger is that frequently the
planner evolves the task with more of a *doing* orientation than an enabling
one and begins to interpose, inappropriately, his or her sets of priorities and
understanding. To overcome this problem, many organizations have defined
this job more as a transitional one than a career one.

3. Planned clutter in the IS planning approach is appropriate to deal
with the fact that the company is in different phases with respect to different
technologies and the technologies have different strategic payout to different
organization units at different times. While it is superficially attractive and
orderly to conceive planning all technologies for all business units to the
same level of detail and time horizon, in reality this is an inappropriate goal.

4. IS planning must be tailored to the realities of the corporate style
of doing business. Importance and status of the IS managers, geographic
placement of IS in relation to general management, corporate culture and
management style, and organizational size and complexity all influence how
IS planning can be best done.

5. IS planning must be considerably broader in the range of technologies it covers than just data processing. It must deal with the technologies
of electronic communications, data processing, office automation, stand-
alone minicomputers and others both separately and in an integrated fashion.

10
Portfolio Approach to Information Systems

F. WARREN MCFARLAN

Despite business's more than 20 years of experience with information systems, disasters in that area still occur with surprising regularity. According to this author, managers, both general and IS, can avert many of these fiascoes by assessing the risks—singly and as a portfolio—in advance of implementation. Also he notes that difficult projects require different management approaches. The chief determinants of risk are the size and structure of the project and the company's experience with the technology involved. Companies can use a series of questions to assess risk and to build a risk profile that will help them choose the best management tools for projects with differing risks.

☐ A major industrial products company discovers 1½ months before the installation date for a computer system that a $15 million effort to convert from one manufacturer to another is in trouble, and installation must be delayed a year. Eighteen months later, the changeover has still not taken place.

☐ A large consumer products company budgets $250,000 for a new computer-based personnel information system to be ready in nine months. Two years later, $2.5 million has been spent, and an estimated $3.6 million more is needed to complete the job. The company has to stop the project.

☐ A sizable financial institution slips $1.5 million over budget and 12 months behind on the development of programs for a new financial systems package, vital for the day-to-day functioning of one of its major operating groups. Once the system is finally installed, average transaction response times are much longer than expected.

Stories from the Stage 1 and Stage 2 days of the late 1960s and early 1970s?[1] No! All these events took place in 1980 in *Fortune* "500" companies

(I could have selected equally dramatic examples from overseas). In a fashion almost embarrassing to relate, the day of the big disaster on a major information systems project has not passed. Given business's more than 20 years of IS experience, the question is "Why?"

My analysis of these cases and first-hand acquaintance with a number of IS projects in the past 10 years suggest three serious deficiencies in practice that involve both general management and IS management. The first two are the failure to assess individual project risk and the failure to consider the aggregate risk of the portfolio of projects. The third is the lack of recognition that different projects require different managerial approaches. This article focuses on these deficiencies and suggests ways of redressing them.

Elements of Project Risk

The typical project feasibility study covers exhaustively such topics as financial benefits, qualitative benefits, implementation costs, target milestones and completion dates, and necessary staffing levels. In precise, crisp terms, the developers of these estimates provide voluminous supporting documentation. Only rarely, however, do they deal frankly with the risk of slippage in time, cost overrun, technical shortfall, or outright failure. Rather, they deny the existence of such possibilities by ignoring them. They assume the appropriate human skills, controls, and so on, that will ensure success.

By *risk* I am suggesting exposure to such consequences as:

- [ ] Failure to obtain all, or even any, of the anticipated benefits.
- [ ] Costs of implementation that vastly exceed planned levels.
- [ ] Time for implementation that is much greater than expected.
- [ ] Technical performance of resulting systems that turns out to be significantly below estimate.
- [ ] Incompatability of the system with the selected hardware and software.

These kinds of risk in practical situations, of course, are not independent of each other; rather, they are closely related. In discussing risk, I am assuming that the manager has brought appropriate methods and approaches to bear on the project (mismanagement is obviously another element of risk). Risk, in my definition here, is what remains after application of those tools.

In my discussion, I am also not implying a correlation between *risk* and *bad*. These words represent entirely different concepts, and the link between the two normally is that higher-risk projects must yield higher benefits to compensate for the increased downside exposure.

At least three important dimensions influence the risk inherent in a project:

1. *Project size.* The larger it is in dollar expense, staffing levels, elapsed time, and number of departments affected by the project, the greater

the risk. Multimillion-dollar projects obviously carry more risk than $50,000 projects and also, in general, affect the company more if the risk is realized. A related concern is the size of the project relative to the normal size of a systems development group's projects. The implicit risk is usually lower on a $1 million project of a department whose average undertaking costs $2–$3 million than on a $250,000 project of a department that has never ventured a project costing more than $50,000.

2. *Experience with the technology.* Because of the greater likelihood of unexpected technical problems, project risk increases as familiarity of the project team and the IS organization decreases with the hardware, operating systems, data-base handler, and project application language. A project that has a slight risk for a leading-edge, large systems development group may have a very high risk for a smaller, less technically advanced group. Yet the latter group can reduce risk through purchase of outside skills for an undertaking involving technology that is in general commercial use.

3. *Project structure.* In some projects, the very nature of the task defines completely, from the moment of conceptualization, the outputs. I classify such schemes as highly structured. They carry much less risk than those whose outputs are more subject to the manager's judgment and hence are vulnerable to change. The outputs of these projects are fixed and not subject to change during the life of the project.

An insurance company automating preparation of its agents' rate book is an example of such a highly structured project. At the project's beginning, planners reached total agreement on the product lines to be included, the layout of each page, and the process of generating each number. Throughout the life of the project, there was no need to alter these decisions; consequently, the team organized to reach a stable, fixed output rather than to cope with a potentially mobile target.

Quite the opposite was true in the personnel information project I mentioned at the beginning, which was a low-structure project. In that situation, the users could not reach a consensus on what the outputs should be, and these decisions shifted almost weekly, crippling progress.

Assessing Risk

Exhibit 1, by combining the various dimensions of risk, identifies eight distinct project categories, each carrying a different degree of risk. Even at this gross intuitive level, such a classification is useful to separate projects for quite different types of management review. IS organizations have used it successfully to distinguish the relative risk for their own understanding and as a basis for communicating these notions of risk to users and senior corporate executives.

A legitimate concern is how to ensure that different people viewing the same project will come to the same rough assessment of its risks. While the

Exhibit 1.   Effect of Degree of Structure on Project Risk

	High	Low
Low company relative technology	Large—low risk	Large—low risk (very susceptible to mismanagement)
	Small— very low risk	Small—very low risk (very susceptible to mismanagement)
High company relative technology	Large— medium risk	Large—very high risk
	Small— medium-low risk	Small—high risk

best way to assess this is still uncertain, several companies have made significant progress in addressing the problem.

Exhibit 2 presents, in part, a method one large company developed for measuring risk: a list of 54 questions about a project that the project manager answers both prior to senior management's approval of the proposal and several times during its implementation.

This company developed the questions after carefully analyzing its experience with successful and unsuccessful projects. I include some of them as an example of how to bridge concepts and practice. No analytic framework lies behind these questions, and they may not be appropriate for all companies; however, they represent a good starting point and several other large companies have used them.

Both the project leader and the key user answer these questions. Differences in the answers are then reconciled. (Obviously, the questionnaire provides data that are no better than the quality of thinking that goes into the answers.)

Exhibit 2.   Risk Assessment Questionnaire (sample from a total of 54 questions)[a]

Size risk assessment		Weight
1. Total development man-hours for system[b]		5
100 to 3,000	Low-1	
3,000 to 15,000	Medium-2	
15,000 to 30,000	Medium-3	
More than 30,000	High-4	

Exhibit 2. *(Continued)*

Size risk assessment		Weight
2. What is estimated project implementation time?		4
12 months or less	Low-1	
13 months to 24 months	Medium-2	
More than 24 months	High-3	
3. Number of departments (other than IS) involved with system		4
One	Low-1	
Two	Medium-2	
Three or more	High-3	

Structure risk assessment		Weight
1. If replacement system is proposed, what percentage of existing functions are replaced on a one-to-one basis?		5
0% to 25%	High-3	
25% to 50%	Medium-2	
50% to 100%	Low-1	
2. What is severity of procedural changes in user department caused by proposed system?		5
Low-1		
Medium-2		
High-3		
3. Does user organization have to change structurally to meet requirements of new system?		5
No	-0	
Minimal	Low-1	
Somewhat	Medium-2	
Major	High-3	
4. What is general attitude of user?		5
Poor—anti data-processing solution	High-3	
Fair—some reluctance	Medium-2	
Good—understands value of DP solution	-0	
5. How committed is upper-level user management to system?		5
Somewhat reluctant or unknown	High-3	
Adequate	Medium-2	
Extremely enthusiastic	Low-1	
6. Has a joint data processing/user team been established?		5
No	High-3	
Part-time user representative appointed	Low-1	
Full-time user representative appointed	-0	

Exhibit 2. *(Continued)*

Technology risk assessment		Weight
1. Which of the hardware is new to the company?		5
None	-0	
CPU	High-3	
Peripheral and/or additional storage	High-3	
Terminals	High-3	
Mini or micro	High-3	
2. Is the system software (nonoperating system) new to IS project team?[c]		5
No	-0	
Programming language	High-3	
Data base	High-3	
Data communications	High-3	
Other—specify	High-3	
3. How knowledgeable is user in area of IS?		5
First exposure	High-3	
Previous exposure but limited knowledge	Medium-2	
High degree of capability	Low-1	
4. How knowledgeable is user representative in proposed application area?		5
Limited	High-3	
Understands concept but no experience	Medium-2	
Has been involved in prior implementation efforts	Low 1	
5. How knowledgeable is IS team in proposed application area?		5
Limited	High-3	
Understands concept but no experience	Medium-2	
Has been involved in prior implementation efforts	Low-1	

Source: This questionnaire is adapted from the Dallas Tire case, no. 9–180-006 (Boston, Mass.: HBS Case Services, 1980).

[a]Since the questions vary in importance, the company assigned weights to them subjectively. The numerical answer to the questions is multiplied by the question weight to calculate the question's contribution to the project's risk. The numbers are then added together to produce a risk score number for the project. Projects with risk scores within 10 points of each other are indistinguishable, but those separated by 100 points or more are very different to even the casual observer.

[b]Time to develop includes systems design, programming, testing, and installation.

[c]This question is scored by multiplying the sum of the numbers attached to the positive responses by the weights.

These questions not only highlight the risks but also suggest alternative ways of conceiving of and managing the project, If the initial aggregate risk score seems high, analysis of the answers may suggest ways of lessening the risk through reduced scope, lower-level technology, multiple phases, and so on. Thus managers should not consider risk as a static descriptor; rather, its presence should encourage better approaches to project management. Numbers 5 and 6 under the section on structure are particularly good examples of questions that could trigger changes.

The higher the score, the higher must be the level of approval. Only the executive committee in this company approves very risky projects. Such an approach ensures that top managers are aware of significant hazards and are making appropriate risk strategic-benefit trade-offs. Managers should ask questions such as the following:

- [ ] Are the benefits great enough to offset the risks?
- [ ] Can the affected parts of the organization survive if the project fails?
- [ ] Have the planners considered appropriate alternatives?

On a periodic basis, these questions are answered again during the undertaking to reveal any major changes. If all is going well, the risk continuously declines during implementation as the size of the remaining task dwindles and familiarity with the technology grows.

Answers to the questions provide a common understanding among senior, IS, and user managers as to a project's relative risk. Often the fiascoes occur when senior managers believe a project has low risk and IS managers know it has high risk. In such cases, IS managers may not admit their assessment because they fear that the senior executives will not tolerate this kind of uncertainty in data processing and will cancel a project of potential benefit to the organization.

Portfolio Risk Profile

In addition to determining relative risk for single projects, a company should develop an aggregate risk profile of the portfolio of systems and programming projects. While there is no such thing as a correct risk profile in the abstract, there are appropriate risk profiles for different types of companies and strategies. For example, in an industry that is data processing intensive, or where computers are an important part of product structure (such as banking and insurance), managers should be concerned when there are no high-risk projects. In such a case, the company may be leaving a product or service gap for competition to step into. On the other hand, a portfolio loaded with high-risk projects suggests that the company may be vulnerable to operational disruptions when projects are not completed as planned.

Conversely, in less computer-dependent companies, IS plays a profitable, useful, but distinctly supporting role, and management often considers this role appropriate. In such cases, heavy investment in high-risk projects appropriately may be smaller than in the first type of company.

Even here, however, a company should have some technologically exciting ventures to ensure familiarity with leading-edge technology and to maintain staff morale and interest. Thus the aggregate risk profiles of the portfolios of two companies could legitimately differ. Exhibit 3 shows in more detail the issues that influence IS toward or away from high-risk efforts (the risk profile should include projects that will come from outside software houses as well as those of the internal systems development group).

In summary, it is both possible and useful to talk about project risk during the feasibility study stage. The discussion of risk can be helpful both for those working on the individual project and for the department as a whole. Not only can this systematic analysis reduce the number of failures, but, equally important, its power as a communication link helps IS managers and senior executives reach agreement on the risks to be taken in line with corporate goals.

Exhibit 3.   Factors that Influence Risk Profile of Project Portfolio

	Portfolio Low-Risk Focus	Portfolio High-Risk Focus
Stability of IS development group	Low	High
Perceived quality of IS development group by insiders	Low	High
IS critical to delivery of current corporate services	No	Yes
IS important decision-support aid	No	Yes
Experienced IS systems development group	No	Yes
Major IS fiascoes in last two years	Yes	No
New IS management team	Yes	No
IS perceived critical to delivery of future corporate services	No	Yes
IS perceived critical to future decision-support aids	No	Yes
Company perceived as backward in use of IS	No	Yes

Contingency Approach

Now the organization faces the difficult problem of project operation. Much of the literature and conventional wisdom about project management suggest that there is a single right way of doing it. A similar theme holds that managers should apply uniformly to all such ventures an appropriate cluster of tools, project management methods, and organizational linkages.

While there may indeed be a general-purpose set of tools, the contribution each device can make to planning and controlling the project varies widely according to the project's characteristics. Further, the means of involving the user—through steering committees, representation on the team, or as leader (not DP or IS professional)—should also vary by project type. In short, there is no universally correct way to run all projects. The general methods for managing projects fall into four principal types:

☐ *External integration tools* include organizational and other communication devices that link the project team's work to the users at both the managerial and the lower levels.

☐ *Internal integration* devices ensure that the team operates as an integrated unit.

☐ *Formal planning tools* help to structure the sequence of tasks in advance and estimate the time, money, and technical resources the team will need to execute them.

☐ *Formal control* mechanisms help managers evaluate progress and spot potential discrepancies so that corrective action can be taken.

Exhibit 4 gives examples of the tools in each category commonly used by companies. The next paragraphs suggest how the degree of structure and the company-relative technology influence the selection of items from the four categories.

High-Structure—Low Technology

Projects that are highly structured and that present familiar technical problems are not only the lowest-risk projects but are also the easiest to manage (see Exhibit 1). They are also the least common. High structure implies that the outputs are very well defined by the nature of the task, and the possibility of the users changing their minds as to what these outputs should be is essentially nonexistent. Consequently, the leaders do not have to develop extensive administrative processes in order to get a diverse group of users both to agree to a design structure and to keep to that structure. External integration devices such as inclusion of analysts in user departments, heavy representation of users on the design team, and formal approval by users of design specifications are cumbersome and unnecessary for this type of undertaking. Other integrating devices, such as training users in how to operate the system, remain important.

Exhibit 4. Tools of Project Management

External Integration Tools	Internal Integration Tools
Selection of user as project manager	Selection of experienced DP professional leadership team
Creation of user steering committee	Selection of manager to lead team
Frequency and depth of meetings of this committee	Frequent team meetings
User-managed change control process	Regular preparation and distribution of minutes within team on key design evolution decision
Frequency and detail of distribution of project team minutes to key users	
Selection of users as team members	Regular technical status reviews
Formal user specification approval process	Managed low turnover of team members
Progress reports prepared for corporate steering committee	Selection of high percentage of team members with significant previous work relationships
Users responsible for education and installation of system	Participation of team members in goal setting and deadline establishment
Users manage decision on key action dates	Outside technical assistance

Formal Planning Tasks	Formal Control Tasks
PERT, critical path, etc., networking	Periodic formal status reports versus plan
Milestone phases selection	Change control disciplines
Systems specification standards	Regular milestone presentation meetings
Feasibility study specifications	Deviations from plan
Project approval processes	
Project postaudit procedures	

The system's concept and design, however, are stable. At the same time, since the technology involved is familiar to the company, the project can proceed with a high percentage of persons having only average technical backgrounds and experience. The leader does not need strong IS skills. This type of project readily gives opportunity to the department's junior managers, who can gain experience that may lead to more ambitious tasks in the future.

Project life cycle planning concepts, with their focus on defining tasks and budgeting resources against them, force the team to develop a thorough and detailed plan (exposing areas of soft thinking in the process). Such projects are likely to meet the resulting milestone dates and keep within the target budget. Moreover, the usual control techniques for measuring progress against dates and budgets provide very reliable data for spotting discrepancies and building a desirable tension into the design team to work harder to avoid slippage.

A portfolio comprised of 90% of this type of project will produce little excitement for senior and user managers. It also requires a much more limited set of skills for the IS organization than might be needed for companies whose portfolios have quite a different mixture of projects. An example of this type of project is the agent's rate book project mentioned earlier.

High Structure—High Technology

These projects, vastly more complex than the first kind, involve some significant modifications from the practice outlined in project management handbooks. A good example of this type is the conversion of systems from one computer manufacturer to another with no enhancements (which is, of course, easier said than done). Another example of this kind of project is the conversion of a set of manual procedures onto a minicomputer with the objective only of doing the same functions more quickly.

The normal mechanisms for liaison with users are not crucial here (though they are in the next type of project), because the outputs are so well defined by the nature of the undertaking that both the development of specifications and the need to deal with systems changes from users are sharply lower. Liaison with users is nevertheless important for two reasons: (1) to ensure coordination on any changes in input-output or other manual procedure changes necessary for project success and (2) to deal with any systems restructuring that must follow from shortcomings in the project's technology.

It is not uncommon in this kind of project to discover during implementation that the technology is inadequate, forcing a long postponement while new technology is chosen or vital features pruned in order to make the task fit the available technology. In one such situation, a major industrial products company had to convert some computerized order-entry procedures to a manual basis so that the rest of an integrated materials management system could be shifted to already-purchased, new hardware.

Such technological shortcomings were also the main difficulty in the financial institution I described at the start of this article. In such a case, where system performance is much poorer than expected, user involvement is important both to prevent demoralization and to help implement either an alternative approach (less ambitious in design) or a mutual agreement to end the project.

The skills that lead to success in this type of project, however, are the same as for effective administration involving any kind of technical complexity. The leader needs this experience (preferably, but not necessarily, in an IS environment) as well as administrative experience, unless the project is not very large. The leader must also be effective in relating to technicians. From talking to the project team at various times, the ideal manager will anticipate difficulties before the technicians understand that they have a problem. In dealing with larger projects in this category, the manager's ability to establish and maintain teamwork through meetings, a record of all key design decisions, and subproject conferences is vital.

Project life cycle planning methods, such as PERT (program evaluation and review technique) and critical path, identify tasks and suitable completion dates. Their predictive value is much more limited here, however, than in the preceding category. The team will not understand key elements of the technology in advance, and seemingly minor bugs in such projects have a curious way of becoming major financial drains.

In one company, roughly once an hour an on-line banking system generated garbage across the CRT screen. While simply hitting a release key erased this screen of zeroes and x's, four months and more than $200,000 went into eliminating the so-called ghost screen. The solution lay in uncovering a complex interaction of hardware features, operating system functions, and application traffic patterns. Correction of the problem ultimately required the vendor to redesign several chips. And formal control mechanisms have limits in monitoring the progress of such projects.

In summary, technical leadership and internal integration are the keys in this type of project, and external integration plays a distinctly secondary role. Formal planning and control tools give more subjective than concrete projections, and the great danger is that neither IS managers nor high-level executives will recognize this. They may believe they have precise planning and close control when, in fact, they have neither.

Low Structure—Low Technology

When these projects are intelligently managed, they have low risk. Over and over, however, such projects fail because of inadequate direction. In this respect they differ from the first type of project, where more ordinary managerial skills could ensure success. The key to operating this kind of project lies in an effective effort to involve the users.

Developing substantial user support for only one of the thousands of design options and keeping the users committed to that design are critical. Essential aspects of this process include the following:

- ☐ A user either as project leader or number 2 person on the team.
- ☐ A user steering committee to evaluate the design.
- ☐ An effort to break the project into a sequence of very small and discrete subprojects.
- ☐ Formal user review and approval on all key project specifications.
- ☐ Distribution of minutes of all key design meetings to users.
- ☐ Strong efforts to keep at least chief subproject time schedules below normal managerial and staff turnover times in the user areas (since a consensus on approach with the predecessor of a user-manager is of dubious value).

The personnel information debacle I mentioned at the start of this article is an example of what can happen when this process does not take place. Soon after work started, the director of human resources decided that his senior staff's participation in the design was a waste of their time, and he made sure none of them was involved.

Instead of immediately killing the undertaking, the IS manager attempted to continue work under the leadership of one of his technically oriented staff who had little experience dealing with the human resources department. Bombarded by pressures from the human resources staff that he did not understand, the project manager allowed the systems design to expand to include more and more detail of doubtful merit until the system collapsed. The changing design made much of the programming obsolete. Tough, pragmatic leadership from users in the design stage would have made all the difference in the outcome.

The importance of user leadership increases once the design is final. Almost inevitably, at that stage users will produce some version of ''I have been thinking.. . .'' Unless the desired changes are of critical strategic significance to the user (a judgment best made by a responsible user-oriented project manager), the requests must be diverted and postponed until they can be considered in some formal change control process.

Unless the process is rigorously controlled (a problem intensified by the near impossibility of distinguishing between the economies of a proposed alternative and those implicit in the original design), users will make change after change, and the project will evolve rapidly to a state of permanent deferral, with completion always six months in the future.

If the project is well integrated with other departments, the formal planning tools will be very useful in structuring tasks and helping to remove any remaining uncertainty. The target completion dates will be firm as long as the systems target remains fixed. Similarly, the formal control devices afford clear insight into progress to date, flagging both advances and slippages. If integration with outside departments is weak, use of these tools will produce an entirely unwarranted feeling of confidence.

By definition, the problems of technology management are usually less difficult in this type of project than in the high technology ventures, and a staff with a normal mixture of technical backgrounds should be adequate.

In fact, in almost every respect management of this type of project differs from the previous two. The key to success is close, aggressive management of external integration, supplemented by formal planning and control tools. Leadership must flow from the user rather than from the technical side.

Low Structure—High Technology

Because these projects are complex and carry high risk, their leaders need technical experience and knowledge of, and ability to communicate with, users. The same intensive effort toward external integration described in the previous class of projects is necessary here. Total commitment on the part of users to a particular set of design specifications is critical, and again they must agree to one out of the many thousands of options.

Unfortunately, however, an option desirable from the user's perspective may turn out to be infeasible in the selected hardware-software system. In the last several years, such situations have occurred particularly with stand-alone minicomputer systems designs, and they commonly lead either to significant restructuring of the project or elimination of it altogether. Consequently, users should be well represented at both the policy and the operations levels.

At the same time, technical considerations make strong technical leadership and internal project integration vital. This kind of effort requires the most experienced project leaders, and they will need wholehearted support from the users. In approving such a project, managers must face the question whether it can or should be divided into a series of much smaller problems or use less innovative technology.

While formal planning and control tools can be useful here, at the early stages they contribute little to reducing uncertainty and to highlighting problems. The planning tools do allow the manager to structure the sequence of tasks. Unfortunately, in this type of project new tasks crop up with monotonous regularity, and tasks that appear simple and small suddenly become complex and protracted. Time, cost, and resulting technical performance turn out to be almost impossible to predict simultaneously. In the Apollo moon project, for example, technical performance achievement was key, and cost and time simply fell out. In the private sector, all too often this is an unacceptable outcome.

Contingency Approach

Exhibit 5 shows the relative contribution that each of the four groups of project management tools makes to ensure maximum control, given a project's inherent risk. It reveals that managers need quite different styles and approaches to manage the different types of projects effectively. Although the framework could be made more complex by including more dimensions, that would only confirm this primary conclusion.

The usual corporate handbook on project management, with its unidimensional approach, fails to deal with the realities of the task facing today's managers, particularly those dealing with information services. The right approach flows from the project rather than the other way around.

The need to deal with the corporate culture within which both IS and project management operate further complicates the problems. Use of formal project planning and control tools is much more likely to produce successful results in a highly formal environment than in one where the prevailing

Exhibit 5.   Relative Contribution of Tools to Ensuring Project Success

Project type	Project Description	External Integration	Internal Integration	Formal Planning	Formal Control
I	High structure, low technology, large	Low	Medium	High	High
II	High structure, low technology, small	Low	Low	Medium	High
III	High structure high technology, large	Low	High	Medium	Medium
IV	High structure, high technology, small	Low	High	Low	Low
V	Low structure, low technology, large	High	Medium	High	High
VI	Low structure, low technology, small	High	Low	Medium	High
VII	Low structure, high technology, large	High	High	Low +	Low +
VIII	Low structure, high technology, small	High	High	Low	Low

culture is more personal and informal. Similarly, the selection and effective use of integrating mechanisms is very much a function of the corporate culture.

Thus the type of company culture further complicates may suggestions as to how different types of projects should be managed. (Too many former IS managers have made the fatal assumption that they were in an ideal position to reform corporate culture from their position!)

The past decade has brought new challenges to IS project management, and experience has indicated better ways to think about the management process. My conclusions, then, are threefold:

1   We will continue to experience major disappointments as we push into new fields. Today, however, the dimensions of risk can be identified in advance and a decision made whether to proceed. If we proceed, we will sometimes fail.

2   The work of the systems development department in aggregate may be thought of as a portfolio. Other authors have discussed what the appropriate components of that portfolio should be at a particular moment. The aggregate risk profile of that portfolio, however, is a critical (though often overlooked) strategic decision.

3   Project management in the IS field is complex and multidimensional.

Different types of projects require different clusters of management tools if they are to succeed.

Notes

1. Richard L. Nolan and Cyrus F. Gibson, "Managing the Four Stages of EDP Growth," Chapter 2, this book.

11
Managing Information Systems by Committee

RICHARD L. NOLAN

In the majority of companies today, the large, centralized data processing department is no longer an isolated bastion of arcane knowledge. DP managers have
seen their power erode as cheaper and smaller computers have spread throughout
the organization and as opportunities have expanded for computer-based technology. The whole structure and importance of data processing have changed over
the past ten years, according to Richard Nolan, whose survey reveals that many
managers are still stuck in the mold of the 1970s. Though management by committee generally has a bad name, in the case of computers the executive steering
committee is the most efficient way to ensure the fit of information systems with
corporate strategy.

"I'm concerned that we are missing the boat; shouldn't we be more
distributed?"

In the past year or so, CEOs of large corporations have been asking
this question about their data processing. Behind it is a feeling that their
organization of computers is wrong and that it should probably be more
decentralized. Their intuition is correct on both accounts. Continued growth
of centralized DP activities has resulted in services of such size and diversity
that companies are losing opportunities for cost-effective use. Managers
naturally respond to this type of complexity by breaking the organization
into smaller pieces and decentralizing. The heart of the issue is when and
how to decentralize, not whether to do so.

The most effective mechanism for restructuring DP when this proves
necessary is the executive steering committee. Of 127 companies I surveyed,
85% had functioning corporatewide executive steering committees. This is
a dramatic change from the mid-1970s, when less than half of companies

There may be slight stylistic differences in the article published in this book and the way it
eventually appeared in the Harvard Business Review.

had such committees. At that time, respondents to another survey said that in many cases their companies had tried the committee approach but senior management had let the committees die.

Two forces are leading companies to establish committees: decentralization and strategic choice.

The Move to Decentralization

Expansion of uses for computers in business and the essential role of users in defining new applications have increased the pressure to decentralize responsibility and control. Following large-scale introduction of computers into the office in the last decade, minicomputer and microcomputer technology and communications technology were developed to permit the construction of large computer networks and thus to bring geographically dispersed operations into instant contact with one another.

Expenditures for business computing have expanded dramatically to make use of the available technology. Although the business-computing expenditures in one manufacturing company increased from $25 million in 1970 to $90 million in 1980, the DP manager, who in 1970 had direct control over all of the $25 million business-computing expenditure, directly controlled only 60% of the 1980 expenditure. Such a situation makes it difficult to build an integrated, efficiently functioning corporate computer network.

In the late 1970s, the widespread use of computers to attack the productivity problem added complexity to computer management. As a measure of this growth, the manufacturing company's expenditure for scientific computing rose from $3 million in 1970 to $24 million in 1980, and process control expenditures rose from $2 million to $15 million, reflecting the adoption of CAD/CAM (computer-aided design and computer-aided manufacturing) and robotics. (See Exhibit 1 for more details.)

Many senior executives are still responding to the 1970 environment. In the same manufacturing company, the DP manager directly controlled and was accountable for 80% of the overall computer expenditure in 1970, and scientific computing and process control were narrowly focused in engineering and manufacturing. All capital expenditures for computers over $50,000 required approval of the DP manager; and, of course, functioning computers costing less than $50,000 were rare at that time. All in all, the DP manager was effectively responsible for the company's use of computers.

Sweeping changes have taken place in the last ten years. Functioning computers for less than $50,000 are commonplace. In the manufacturing company, the vice president of data processing is now directly accountable for only 36% of the annual computer expenditure, and that 36% includes only 60% of the business computing. Further, the new computers can support functional specializations that the vice president and his staff understand only superficially.

Herein lies a real danger of computer expenditures bounding out of control. Exhibit 2 illustrates the problem. On a spectrum between central-

Exhibit 1. Changing Computer Technology and Responsibility

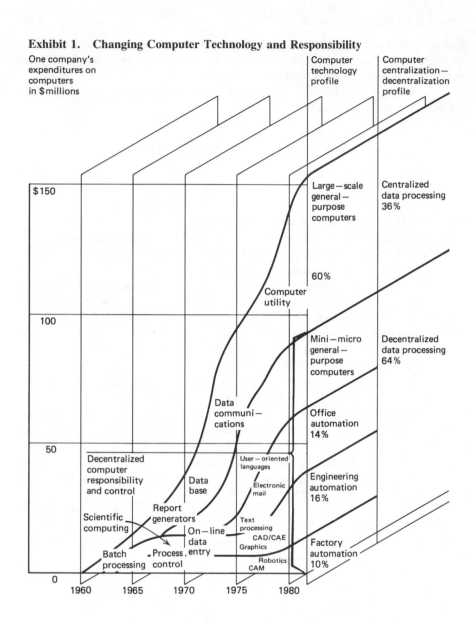

Exhibit 2. Degree of Centralization

Centralized	X	Y	Z	Decentralized
	Top management's perception of computer organization structure	Facts of actual computer organization structure	Business structure	

ization and decentralization, an X marks the judgment of a typical top management as to the degree of its company's centralization. In most companies, top managers perceive the organization structure for computers as much more highly centralized (Y in Exhibit 2) than the facts warrant (i.e., the correct mark would be point Z). The business structure of a company acts as a magnet pulling the DP structure toward it. Until now, economies of scale in computer hardware often justified centralized DP. Currently, however, smaller and cheaper computers make a new structure possible.

An executive steering committee is well suited to the task of determining the new policy. It should be made up of managers who are knowledgeable about diverse uses of the computer, who can make computer policy, and who can choose the appropriate organization structure and degree of decentralization of the company's computers.

Strategic Choice

The opportunities for using computers cost-effectively to support a business have increased easily fourfold over the opportunities of the last decade because of orders-of-magnitude leaps in the cost-performance ratio of computer technology. Today's powerful computer technology, from robotics in the factory to electronic mail in the office, offers a strong economic and entrepreneurial tool for improving virtually every aspect of business operations. Emphasis has shifted from narrow support of administrative business functions when justified by cost savings to wide-ranging attacks on the productivity problems businesses universally face.

Today, as we have already seen, computer technology has been integrated with such technologies as communications, graphics, optics, and voice recognition so that highly specialized applications penetrate almost every functional aspect of a business. Exhibit 3 shows the expanded technology of the 1980s compared with that of the 1970s. It also shows that planning for computers has changed its objectives from linking DP strategy with business strategy to linking computer-technology strategy with business strategy.

No productivity gains result, however, without skilled people and management, and the exponential growth in computer use has created a severe shortage of computer professionals. In addition, employee turnover rates range from 15% to 35%. Thus, companies must make choices among the many possible uses of computers. In many cases, these choices are of strategic importance to the company.

For example, a heavy-equipment manufacturer may have to redirect priorities and make use of robotics to meet a competitive threat surrounding product quality; a high-technology company might decide to invest in computer-aided engineering (CAE) to reduce the product design cycle; a financial institution might choose to invest in automated-teller terminals to gain market

Exhibit 3.   Changing Objectives in Planning for Computers

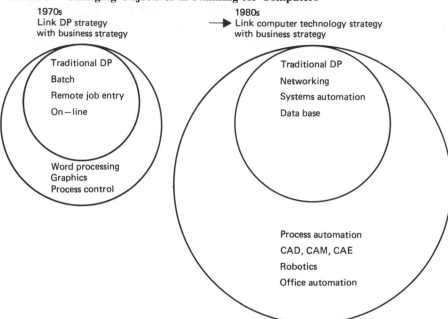

1970s
Link DP strategy
with business strategy

1980s
→ Link computer technology strategy
with business strategy

Traditional DP
Batch
Remote job entry
On–line

Word processing
Graphics
Process control

Traditional DP
Networking
Systems automation
Data base

Process automation
CAD, CAM, CAE
Robotics
Office automation

share; and a grocery business might choose to defer point-of-sale technology so that it can direct its computer capability to warehouse automation and thus achieve lower warehouse inventories with higher turnover rates than its competitors have.

The information required to make such strategic choices effectively must come from senior managers, who can maintain a high-level perspective. Indeed, the need for top management to make strategic choices is the second main force behind the formation of an executive steering committee.

It is easier to see why executive steering committees should be formed than it is to determine what makes some successful and others not. Two considerations are important here. First is the charter of the steering committee and second is how this fits within the organization in regard to both timing and design.

Functions of the Committee

The most useful analogy for the executive steering committee is the company's board of directors: the committee functions as the computer activity's board. It links business strategy with computer strategy by setting a strategic direction and determining the multiyear financial commitment. It provides a forum where senior managers and users can discuss this direction, match corporate concerns with technological potential, and build commitment to policies.

The company's "board of directors" for its computer activity has five essential functions: direction setting, rationing, structuring, staffing, and advising and auditing. Exhibit 4 shows how senior managers and DP managers in 127 companies rated their steering committees on these functions.

Direction Setting

The direction-setting function links corporate strategy and computer strategy. It consists of setting objectives for the use of computers, formulating strategy to focus on these goals, devising policies to ensure that the organization's actions are consistent with these objectives, and reviewing and approving the long-range plan for computers to guarantee that the approach for achieving these goals is workable and is in line with the company's priorities and capabilities. An important part of the long-range plan is the technology plan, which identifies the computer-based technologies important to the company's competitive position and draws up guidelines for implementing these technologies.

Exhibit 4. Ratings of Executive Steering Committee Functions[a]

Function	Importance			Percentage Carrying Out Function	Relative Effectiveness
	Senior Management (SM)	DP Management	Overall Rating		
Direction setting			1		
Establish companywide objectives and policies for computer technology	1	1		82	Effective
Review and approve long-range plan	2	2		90	Effective
Rationing			2		
Review and approve annual budgets	6	5		69	Effective
Review and approve major computer-	5	4		73	Effective

Exhibit 4. (*Continued*)

Function	Importance Senior Management (SM)	DP Management	Overall Rating	Percentage Carrying Out Function	Relative Effectiveness
related capital appropriations (e.g., facilities, hardware)					
Major project screening and approval	3	3		85	Most effective
Structuring			SM, 4; DP, 3		
Develop, maintain, and revise steering committee charter	7	7		67	Effective
Review and approve organization structures and changes	8	8		46	Less effective
Staffing			5		
Selection of key managers for the computer activity	10	10		28	Least effective
Advising & auditing			SM, 3; DP, 4		
Monitor and review major projects	4	6		84	Effective
Advise and audit key managers' performance	9	9		33	Less effective

"Questionnaires were sent to 202 companies, and 127 were returned; thus, there was a 63% response rate. Thirty-three percent of these companies had DP expenditures of less than $10 million; 44% had DP expenditures ranging from $10 million to $50 million; and 23% had DP expenditures of over $50 million.

In my survey, both senior management and DP management said that their executive steering committees carried out the direction-setting function effectively. My own experience is that DP departments complain more than any other area about the failure of senior management to give them essential information on where the company is going. Perhaps the plain fact is that the information, though provided, is too general to be of much direct help to DP managers.

Rationing

The rationing function reconciles the commitment of company resources to computers with commitments to other business activities. Our respondents ranked it second in importance. The company's budgeting process and capital appropriations process should govern the computer activity, as they do other business functions. However, both of these financial processes must have the benefit of a long-range plan since the effective management of computers is a multiyear proposition.

Screening of computer projects is related to capital appropriations, but it has another important dimension: risk assessment. The implementation of computer projects involves high technology and extensive organizational change. Since both of these aspects involve risk, it is essential to develop a process as an integral part of capital appropriations whereby the potential benefits of proposed computer projects are assessed against their potential risks.[1]

Structuring

The structuring function focuses on an appropriate organization design to ensure effective use of computers in the organization. It deals directly with the centralization-versus-decentralization issue and establishes charters for various organizational units.

The research results for this function are revealing. First, DP management ranked it of higher importance than senior management did. Second, less than half of the committees carried out structuring, and respondents with this function indicated that it was carried out less effectively than others.

In a follow-up to the study, a number of DP managers said that the decentralization issue was confused by the related concept of distributed data processing (DDP). In their opinion, since DDP has been accepted as inherently "good," decentralization was considered good also.

Staffing

The structuring and staffing functions are closely related, because the ideal organization structure should make the best use of the computer activities most important to the company's business objectives and should build around key personnel. Of all the committee functions, structuring and staffing should be the most comfortable for senior managers, since they are what top executives spend most of their time doing. Yet in the survey they ranked "selecting key managers for the computer activity" lowest in importance. Moreover, only 28% of the committees even carried out the function. Respondents whose committees did concern themselves with staffing ranked it the least effective of their functions.

There is, of course, a "newness" problem that executives readily admitted in the follow-up discussions. Senior managers, in particular, found it hard to define desirable attributes for top computer managers. In one interview, the executive vice president who chaired the steering committee indicated that he thought staffing was the committee's most important function. He went on to discuss the advantages the company had gained by selecting the right managers for essential computer-related positions and the opportunities it had lost when it made mistakes. Executive steering committees seem to grow into the staffing function after they have been in existence for two or more years.

Advising and Auditing

The advise-and-audit function keeps the computer activity on track. Through advising, the committee assists top computer managers with problem solving. In execution of a long-range plan, the unexpected inevitably happens. It can take the form of failure of a vendor to deliver a piece of hardware on schedule or even completion of an important project *ahead* of the due date. Since only the issues that significantly affect the long-range plan or policy should come to the executive steering committee for its advice, a structure for presenting issues is necessary. The advice function is analogous to the role a company's outside directors perform for the president.

The audit function evaluates the company's performance in using computers. Having a good statement of objectives and a long-range plan is essential to this function. The audit is best done annually and should be conducted by an outsider to ensure objectivity. All aspects of the computer activity should be audited against the long-range plan. In addition to evaluating performance, the audit review plays a central role in helping the committee learn about opportunities and issues in applying computer technology.

Senior managers ranked the advise-and-audit function higher than DP management did. They also ranked project monitoring and review higher than advising and auditing key computer managers' performance. Apparently both senior management and DP management were uncomfortable with the latter task. Historically, senior managers have been gun-shy when evaluating any technical manager's performance. This was quite apparent in questions concerning responsibility for such emerging technologies as computer-aided engineering or office automation.

Empirical Guidelines

By far the most frequent comment in the survey responses was that the first year is the most critical for the executive steering committee. Indeed, failure in the first year was commonplace. Apparently, the members simply become frustrated because they lack at the outset the knowledge to set effective computer strategy. To help companies avoid the pitfalls of the critical first year, I have drawn several guidelines from the survey results.

Frequency of Meetings

A typical suggestion from those who had formed executive steering committees was to "get on with it." Executive steering committees initially meet with enthusiasm weekly or biweekly. This almost guarantees their demise. The members simply cannot get enough assistance from staff to deal with strategic issues in this much detail, nor can they assimilate the pertinent knowledge and framework well enough to deal with the issues. Frustration inevitably rises to intolerable levels.

Of the 127 companies surveyed, 50% found quarterly meetings best. This frequency is enough to meet the constraints of senior managers' time while giving them sufficient opportunity to deal with important matters. This interval has the added advantage of not straining their tolerance for tackling the complex issues of computer strategy.

In 25% of the companies, the steering committees met monthly, 2% met more often than monthly, and 23% held semiannual or annual meetings.

Length of Meetings

As important as the frequency of meetings is their length. Half of the companies found one to two hours sufficient, and my experience is consistent with this. When sitting through half-day and all-day steering committee meetings, I have often thought to myself that even Bob Hope doesn't attempt to engage an audience for longer than an hour. Nevertheless, 25% of the companies held meetings that lasted from three to four hours, and 17% had sessions that went on for more than four hours. Only 8% held meetings for less than one hour.

Number of Members

The size of the committee also affects results. In the companies surveyed, 64% had committees ranging from 5 to 10 members, with 16% having more than 10 members and 20% having fewer than 5. The 5-to-10 range is also consistent with experience with other committees. Having more than 10 members results in one-way rather than two-way communication, which prevents the committee from accomplishing its objectives. Simple office meetings usually work well when there are fewer than 5 members.

Staff Support

If the executive steering committee is to deal with issues effectively, staff must be available to do pertinent background work, including quantitative data analysis. In addition, the issues the committee handles must be corporate-level matters.

Companies in our survey that had corporatewide executive steering committees usually had a hierarchy of lower-level steering committees also. In fact, 90% had divisional steering committees, and 80% also had functional steering committees (e.g., for personnel, finance, and manufacturing).

The DP planning department generally provided staff support for the executive steering committee. The committees that reportedly operated most successfully cited the long-range plan, prepared by such a staff, as the principal management tool for working with the executive steering committee. This plan documented objectives, specified costs and milestones, and provided a basis for measuring performance.

Chairing

There has been a surprising shift in the chairing of executive steering committees over the past five years. I would guess that in the mid-1970s the corporate DP manager served as chairperson in at least half of such committees. The DP manager's expertise was generally the rationale for making him or her chairperson. In the survey, however, the corporate DP manager chaired only 19%. Other corporate managers chaired 74% (the president or CEO chaired 38%). The remaining 7% were chaired by managers outside the corporate office, such as a major user. As the use of the computer intertwines more with the strategy of the company, the trend toward top-management chairing will probably continue.

Evolution of Functions

It sounds obvious to say that the functions of the steering committee evolve over time, but failure to understand this is a frequent reason for the demise of committees in the first year. The pitfall seems to be in chartering. Most of the charters I have reviewed are comprehensive and include, in one way or another, the five functions already discussed. The problem begins when the executive steering committee schedules all these functions on its initial agenda, assuming that it will be able to handle all of them. Frustration then results, primarily because the members lack adequate conceptual frameworks or models with which to execute all the functions.

Exhibit 5 shows a more successful stepwise approach, in which the functions evolve over time, starting with direction setting. The vertical axis

Exhibit 5.   Evolution of Functions & Activities of Executive Steering Committee

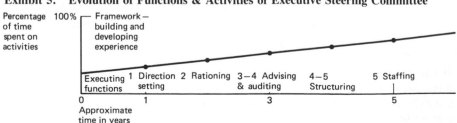

represents the time during committee meetings that should be devoted to framework building and execution.

For example, the first function to be tackled by the steering committee is direction setting. Indeed, the committee might usefully dedicate as much as 90% of meeting time to examining frameworks for direction setting—namely, the long-range plan, ROI analysis, or evaluation of competition. The committee can then spend the remaining 10% of its time discussing and documenting an appropriate direction. The charter can evolve in this way as the committee masters each function and decides how best to execute it.

Another point, rather obvious when one thinks about it but too often forgotten in designing the steering committee, is that the strategic importance of computer activities to the company influences the amount and level of senior-management involvement needed. Further, strategic issues involving computers do not remain constant over time; they tend to change. Thus, the composition and calendar that were appropriate for the committee in 1981 may be inappropriate in 1983 or 1984. In addition, while the guidelines for making the committee work are sound in the aggregate, organization design is highly company-dependent. What works well in one business may be disastrous in another. Thus, it is particularly important to consider the corporate culture when structuring and employing committees.

Changing Dimensions

The walls surrounding the large, centralized DP function are breaking down. Rapidly developing and diverse opportunities to employ computers to increase productivity and gain competitive advantage have brought strategic importance to the application and management of computer technology. Accordingly, the management problems for computers have changed. No longer can the company look to its corporate DP manager to provide *the* leadership. Instead, the executive steering committee is emerging to fill the leadership vacuum.

Though the committee structure has always been cumbersome, and the executive steering committee is no exception, it is proving to be the most effective way to deal with the forces of computer decentralization without dissipating the company's investments in building a computer capability. It has also proved to be the most effective vehicle for making strategic choices among computer-based technologies and for deciding how fast the company should move toward their adoption.

Notes

1. See F. Warren McFarlan, Portfolio Approach to Information Systems," Chapter 10 of this book.

12
Managing International Information Systems

MARTIN D.J. BUSS

Faced with a confusion of approaches, hardware, and applications in their international operations, some U.S. multinationals have chosen to "let sleeping dogs lie" where information processing is concerned. But increasing costs, greater interdependence of affiliates, and a more hostile regulatory environment are among the factors that may cause managers to question this benign neglect. Mr. Buss discusses the mistakes senior managers often make in trying to remedy their problems in managing international data processing and shows how they can refocus and coordinate their efforts.

For the international division of a $1.7 billion U.S.-based consumer products company, management reporting was often a hectic process. The monthly comparisons of operating results and product margins were always late, despite a steady stream of telexes between the international head office in New Jersey and the six regional offices scattered around the globe. Occasionally, the delays in putting the numbers together had serious implications, particularly for the management of the division's foreign currency positions.

After repeatedly observing missed deadlines, the head of the international division finally intervened. After some digging, he discovered that his staff's inability to deliver was the fault of the company's international, information-processing capabilities, which woefully lagged behind its needs. Although the division's financial requirements were uniform throughout the world, nearly every regional office approached information processing differently. There were no corporate standards for international data processing. Computers, programming languages, operating systems software, and telecommunications equipment varied greatly among the affiliates.

As a result, the application systems used to produce the financial information for each country functioned quite differently. Some were batch

There may be slight stylistic differences in the article published in this book and the way it eventually appeared in the Harvard Business Review.

systems; others were more modern, making extensive use of terminals. Yet a third group had purchased accounting packages from different outside vendors and had modified them to suit corporate needs. With such diversity it was hardly surprising that the division's management information system had finally failed.

This situation is by no means unique; similar examples abound in other industries. Often for good reasons, affiliates use different computers and different application systems. The regional offices may be at different stages of maturity in their information systems operations when they are acquired. Diverse products and markets in each country may create a need for different types of systems. The computers available in some countries may not be available in others, or sophisticated and expensive DP systems used in one region may not be economically justifiable in others.

This diversity in hardware and applications is also apparent in the organization of data processing on an international scale. Depending on the people involved, accidents of history, and the importance of data processing to the corporation, the role of U.S. IS management in international information processing can range from "not involved at all" to "totally responsible," with all shades in between.

For example, the U.S. technical staff in the parent headquarters of a $5 billion manufacturing company exercises total control over data processing in Europe. However, in a similar-sized chemical company, where the European DP activities are run by a forceful vice president, data processing staff people from the United States are not allowed anywhere near the European affiliates. As the senior executive for information systems said, "The only way people can help me is by staying where they belong—back in the U.S.A." In yet a third company, a pharmaceutical manufacturer, the U.S.-based staff intervenes in some European countries but not in others.

This diversity of approaches is confusing, and there are few models to follow. Further clouding the issue is the fact that many regional and country managers have backgrounds such as marketing and have had little exposure to information-processing management issues. The executive vice president of a $1 billion international subsidiary recently commented, "It is hard for us marketing people to get a handle on such an esoteric subject."

In the face of these problems, some U.S. multinationals have adopted a "let sleeping dogs lie" policy toward their information processing. Others, out of operational necessity and like the consumer products company mentioned initially, are rethinking their approaches. During the next five years, increasing costs and a changing business environment, both discussed later, will force more and more corporations to do likewise. The aim of this article is to help U.S.-based multinational managers face the upcoming changes more confidently.

Issues Accelerating Change

Higher costs and a changing business environment will speed up changes in the organization and management of international information processing.

Of these two factors, rising costs may be more readily apparent today, particularly to top management.

Payroll costs and fringe benefits are already higher outside the United States for a comparable level of experience, and the gap may be widening. A programmer with three years of experience in West Germany makes about twice as much as his or her U.S. counterpart. Four weeks vacation is common in Europe, compared with two weeks in the United States, and this may now increase to five or even six weeks in some countries. (Incidentally, these wide differences in payroll costs and benefits are also true for some Latin American countries, for example, Venezuela.)

Hardware costs can be 60% more than those in the United States for a comparable computer. This variance arises from currency differences, the costs of importation, the higher cost of the manufacturer's selling effort overseas, and, in some cases, the higher costs of local manufacture.

Data communications costs are many times greater than in the United States, particularly if the lines cross countries. One international manager in Spain noted that his two lines to Germany—1,000 miles long—cost six times more than a comparable network in the United States.

In some cases, however, costs may be a secondary motive for change. New developments in the international business environment itself are starting to affect the management of information resources in many multinational companies. Four trends are particularly important: (1) the growing interdependence of overseas affiliates, (2) the increasingly hostile legal and regulatory environment for business, (3) the unionization of data processing departments, and (4) recent developments in computer and communications technologies.

Increasing Interdependence

In Western Europe in particular, with the Common Market growing (albeit slowly), affiliates that have historically operated autonomously are becoming interlocked. However, while management may now view international business operations as an integrated whole, it has not necessarily ensured that the underlying information systems follow suit. A regional vice president for Europe, Africa, and the Middle East of a $1.2 billion division of a consumer products company noted:

"Until three years ago my six European affiliates were very much self-contained operations. Today, however, I see these companies as an integrated set of manufacturing resources that supply different markets with products made wherever my cost advantage is greatest. Specialization and automation are key to lowering my manufacturing costs in each country. Some countries now have to concentrate on a limited number of components and/or products. Rarely can one country, or even one plant, manufacture a complete product. The plants in one country now must supply others located elsewhere."

This executive acknowledged, however, that the division's management information system was designed for an earlier era in which each regional office acted autonomously. The system was not integrated across country lines. There was no central coordination of data for the manufacturing operations, and the transfer of production information between plants was a slow, mostly manual, process. It was, therefore, difficult for country managers to find out what was going on elsewhere. In fact, the executive was facing an issue on an international scale similar to the problem that has often confronted managers running domestic operations spread throughout the United States—an obsolete information system.

Hostile Environments

New legislative and legal developments regarding corporate record keeping and the flow of information across national boundaries are also shaping the direction of information processing.

The Foreign Corrupt Practices Act includes requirements for effective record keeping and internal controls. Furthermore, according to the Securities and Exchange Commission these restraints apply both to the parent company and to foreign subsidiaries. Since most record keeping in large multinational corporations is computerized, companies are scrutinizing their affiliate information systems more closely than before.

One large multinational, at the request of the audit committee of its board, carried out a broad review of its international data processing operations. The report presented to the audit committee revealed a diversity of approaches for processing accounting data in each regional office. Overall, the controls were considered inadequate: the audit committee asked for remedial action, and a plan to tackle the issue is now being implemented. New standard application systems for accounting are a part of this program.

Transborder data flows. In less than a decade, more than a dozen countries, including the United States, either have passed legislation or have begun considering bills to regulate the collection, storage, transmission, and disclosure of data. There is, however, a fundamental problem. Although the legislation has a common purpose—to define the rights of people regarding the information collected about them—the European approach to data protection differs considerably from that in the United States. This is a typical "conflict of laws" issue.[1]

In Europe, laws cover both public and private sectors. In the United States, the laws apply only to federal agencies. Then again, in Europe the laws make no distinction as to the citizenship of those entitled to protection, whereas in the United States protection is extended primarily to U.S. citizens and to aliens with permanent residence status.

European countries with data protection legislation do not allow name-linked data to be transmitted outside national boundaries unless they are satisfied that the laws of the receiving country are in harmony with their own. This applies to data going not only from Europe to the United States but also between different European countries, where legislation also often differs.

The vice president of information systems for the Eaton Corporation said before a congressional subcommittee that national data protection legislation was impeding his whole data processing strategy:

> We have been moving gradually from an organizational structure, which required stand-alone computing facilities in each of our plants, to a networking structure that ties together England, Germany, Italy, France, and Monaco into a European system. If the 25 countries in which we operate insist on their own separate measures by legislating the flow of data, it is conceivable that we would be forced to revert to processing our data within each country of operation at a 30% greater cost per year.[2]

Similar concerns also were expressed at the hearings by executives from other large multinationals, including American Express, Control Data, and IBM.

Are such concerns really justified? Is transborder data regulation an issue with which top international managers ought to be concerned, or is the whole subject an intellectual "ho hum"? My view is that data regulation will indeed affect data processing in the following types of MNCs:

1   Those whose data processing for European affiliates is centralized in the United States.
2   Those who transmit name-linked data such as personnel records, credit card information, and customer details from Europe to the United States.
3   Those whose European data processing is centralized in one European country or whose European affiliates interchange electronically name-linked data among themselves.

Many MNCs will fall into one or more of these threatened groups. However, given the efforts being made in Europe to harmonize the data protection laws, the impact on this third group is likely to be less severe than on the first two.

A possible avenue of escape for MNCs in the first two groups—accord between the U.S. legislative approaches and those in Europe—seems highly improbable in the foreseeable future. It is, therefore, dangerous for them to adopt "business as usual" attitudes. Data protection laws could one day be invoked against them, seriously disrupting one or more of their computer applications. It may, for example, prove impossible to run a payroll in Chicago for a German affiliate or to update the central personnel records and career planning system in New York with information about a company's French employees. Management must work out alternative systems approaches if only on a contingency basis.

Unionization of DP Departments

Traditional assumptions about DP strategies may not hold up in the face of unionization. In the United States, data processing installations have so far been free from the influence of powerful labor unions. In the United Kingdom, Germany, and France, however, many DP employees, particularly lower-level data entry and computer operators, belong to militant trade unions that occasionally strike. When they do, the impact is dramatic. The vice president for data processing in Europe of a $2 billion corporation with computer installations in the United Kingdom, France, and Germany said:

> Data processing unions have a great hold over our operation. I'm planning to build new computer centers in Switzerland where the strike risks are, today at least, negligible and to transfer the work there. I know my ongoing costs will be higher. But my board believes the risk of a strike paralyzing our entire European operation warrants the expense.

Technological Developments

Information technology can creep up on a multinational company and render a carefully prepared data processing strategy obsolete. Hardware costs have changed dramatically, making it less costly to put a small computer in a regional office that had previously used a large, centralized resource. At the same time, advances in data communications make it more feasible to link isolated affiliates. For the future, we can expect more of the same cost reduction. As a result, long-range information strategies will have to be more flexible to account for changing economics.

A $2.5 billion chemical manufacturer's current situation well illustrates this problem. In 1975 the new executive in charge of information systems reviewed the data processing strategies for his affiliates in Western Europe. He decided, first, to reduce the number of computer centers from eight to two and, second, to use terminals to link each location to one of them. That decision was justified at the time by the fact that the two large computers were much cheaper than eight smaller ones.

Now, five years later, he finds that implementation is difficult because he lacks the full support of the regional managers. They believe that each affiliate should have its own computer. Furthermore, they argue that the lower costs of computers drastically alter the original, mainly economic, justification for the two-center approach.

This corporation is not alone; many multinationals face similar problems as their technical and planning staffs wrestle with the issues posed by information processing's rapidly changing technology. The office of the future, satellite processing, and new, data transmission networks further complicate information planning for the next five years.[3]

Where Companies Go Wrong

There is a common thread in the efforts of multinationals to change their data processing operations. Many are stepping up efforts to implement the same applications software—generally called common systems—in all their affiliates, a move that has met with only limited success so far. The executive vice president for international operations in a $1.5 billion electronics company noted that during the past three years his European affiliates have made good progress in laying the groundwork for common systems.

In this first phase, the company appointed regional data processing coordinators to develop corporate standards for procedural issues such as budgeting and monitoring information systems activities of the affiliates in each country. But he also reported little success in getting systems up and running in several locations. Some affiliates, particularly the larger ones, still preferred to develop their own computer programs.

Why will one regional office not readily accept an application programmed in another? The answer seems to be that management is making the following three mistakes:

Defining Objectives Poorly.   The business objectives and the data processing plans at the global, regional, and country levels are rarely integrated. In some corporations, managers make no clear statement of the business objectives, and data processing professionals have to guess what they are. Not surprisingly, they are sometimes mistaken in their assumptions.

A country manager of a $2 billion pharmaceutical company in Spain could not understand why the corporate DP staff was spending so much time installing a general ledger system for him. His business problem, which he shared with many other regional offices, was to retain market share in a very competitive and highly fragmented market. To help his sales force do this, he urgently needed a modern information system to track sales calls made on doctors. The new general ledger did not relate in any way to this objective. Further discussions with top management of international later showed that it did not fulfill the business needs of the international division as a whole either.

With objectives poorly defined, it is hardly surprising that country managers give low priority to implementing information systems that do not seem to relate to their immediate needs. They may be unaware, for example, that a common order-entry system is required by the company's marketing program and competitive corporate goals, and therefore transcends national interests.

Failing to Define Responsibilities.   Implementation of common systems implies new, coordinated roles for several powerful groups of people, many of whom are accustomed to acting autonomously. For example, country or regional managers generally have done things their own way; data processing professionals have taken their instructions from local rather than corporate management; and planners have characteristically ignored the information systems function in the long-range plan.

All these groups and others now will have interrelated roles to play. There is little chance of success unless the roles are defined, understood by all, and generally accepted. The common approach, appointing information systems coordinators, does not go far enough.

Misunderstanding DP Capabilities.   Many companies assume that installing the same application programs in several affiliates across national boundaries is a task for the technical staff. This is, however, only partly true. Some important operational problems require the commitment and intervention of top managers who need to "persuade" affiliates to follow a new corporate policy, especially when the policy requires changes in the ground rules concerning their administrative autonomy. Sometimes new corporate policy will mean closing down all the DP operations in a particular locale. Such a broad issue is beyond the experience, authority, and leadership of managers to implement by themselves. Support from senior management is essential.

In addition, senior international managers need to take a more active interest in information processing. The complexity of international data processing, often compounded by differences in language and culture, demands more attention from them than that characteristically given to DP by managers in the domestic business.

Guidelines for International Managers

As a first step, senior international managers should assess their organization's status in information processing. They need to find out in very general terms whether things are on track or whether their intervention is necessary.

To get a quick perspective on the situation, I suggest they answer with a *yes* or *no* the 15 questions in Exhibit 1.

A score of 12 of more yeses indicates that information processing operations are sound and well coordinated. A score of 6 to 11 yeses suggests that management intervention in some areas is needed. Fewer than 6 yeses indicates serious problems; senior international managers should almost certainly take action in the following three ways:

1   Orchestrate the process by which the organization plans its approach to international data processing.
2   Create the right organizational framework for the international information system activity.
3   Define the roles of the key players.

Orchestrate the Planning Process

Managers should first determine what should be done to make international data processing more responsive to the needs of the business. This is a one-

Exhibit 1.   Rating the International DP Operation

		Yes	No
Nature of the information provided			
1	Can I compare operating results across affiliates in a way that helps me form conclusions on relative product costs, margins, and sales volumes?	☐	☐
2	Do I know whether my subordinates are satisfied with their information resources?	☐	☐
3	Do I know whether my competitors have better information systems than I do?	☐	☐
Business and data processing planning			
4	Have I approved a long-range information systems plan?	☐	☐
5	Do I know whether the data processing plan supports my business plans for the key regions?	☐	☐
6	Has data processing been on the agenda of high-level operations reviews in the past 6 months?	☐	☐
7	In the past 12 months have I been involved in any major decisions on an information processing issue?	☐	☐
8	Have I been briefed in the past 12 months on the implications of new information processing technology for my business?	☐	☐
Organization of data processing			
9	Do I know how international data processing responsibilities are organized?	☐	☐
10	Do I have the authority and responsibility to get the information processing I want?	☐	☐
11	Do I have a source that keeps me informed as to how well data processing is working?	☐	☐
Cost of information processing			
12	Do I know how much I am spending on data processing in my key regions?	☐	☐

214

Exhibit 1.   (*Continued*)

		Yes	No
13	Do I know whether these regions are spending enough, too much, or too little?	☐	☐
14	Do I know on which functions data processing emphasis is being placed for the current levels of expenditure?	☐	☐
15	Do I think this emphasis is in the right place?	☐	☐
Total			

time effort to prepare a blueprint for the future. A systematic approach is essential, and three steps will help managers:

Create a Task Force to Make Recommendations on the Approach to Be Followed.   A mixed team is essential for thinking creatively about new approaches to information processing. The task force should have representatives from the key region, one or more countries, corporate planning, corporate and/or international data processing, and, in larger corporations, representatives from the legal department. Such a team would not only bring the depth of experience that the subject requires but also have high credibility throughout international operations.

Focus Efforts.   A good part of the task force's work will be technical and will require little guidance from senior management. Nevertheless, a manager must ensure that the task force also considers broader issues, including the following:

☐ The nature of the business in each country (whether products are similar, for example), its maturity, and the role of information processing in realizing business objectives.

☐ Corporate structure and style and the degree of power vested in corporate domestic and international staffs.

☐ Personalities and cultural characteristics of key international executives and of their data processing professionals.

☐ History of affiliates (particularly the larger ones) and the roles they have played in data processing.

☐ The information policy of host governments on such issues as privacy.

☐ Sophistication of technology and its availability in the various countries.

Examine the Proposal.   First, although recommendations for centralizing data processing in one region or country may be theoretically valid, they may also be difficult to implement. They may lack support from country managers because users will not want to give up their autonomy. Also, legal restrictions on transborder data flows may make a centralized approach unworkable. Second, a global solution that covers all countries may also be hard to implement. The international manager will almost certainly have to handle the large affiliates with long experience in data processing differently from those that are medium-sized and relatively inexperienced in data processing. Also, it will generally be easier to start by working with one geographical region or a few countries. Third, managers should focus effort on the two or three applications that are key to the business (e.g., inventory control), as opposed to purely administrative support systems such as general accounting.

Create the Framework

After establishing a blueprint for the future, the international manager should take a look at the organization. In most corporations, the organizational framework does little to encourage an integrated approach to international, information-processing activities. Many corporations run the international division separately from the U.S.-based or domestic businesses. The international division has staff departments such as planning, finance, and marketing assigned to coordinate worldwide activities in their respective areas (see Exhibit 2).

By contrast, it is rare to find an international division (particularly one headquartered in the United States) with its own data processing department. Instead, U.S. companies usually assign the function to the U.S.-based corporate data processing department within finance (see Exhibit 3).

But the corporate department probably has its hands full with the more immediate needs of domestic data processing. Meanwhile, international managers assume that the corporate department is managing all information activities. The result is that no group really focuses on the needs of international data processing, and, in turn, the affiliates take up the slack. Thus the country-by-country approach emerges.

A common focus—a corporate pattern of control—is becoming increasingly important if corporations are to respond effectively to higher costs and other pressures for change that I have discussed. To achieve this, three changes in framework will help.

First, where responsibility for international data processing rests with the corporate organization and modifying the structure is just too difficult an undertaking, the head of international should appoint a systems coordinator. In a large, international corporation, more than one may be needed (for example, one for each region). These coordinators would have responsibility for ensuring the effective use of data processing among affiliates and for resolving international information-processing issues. Ideally, the co-

Exhibit 2.   Separate International Division Without Responsibility for Data Processing

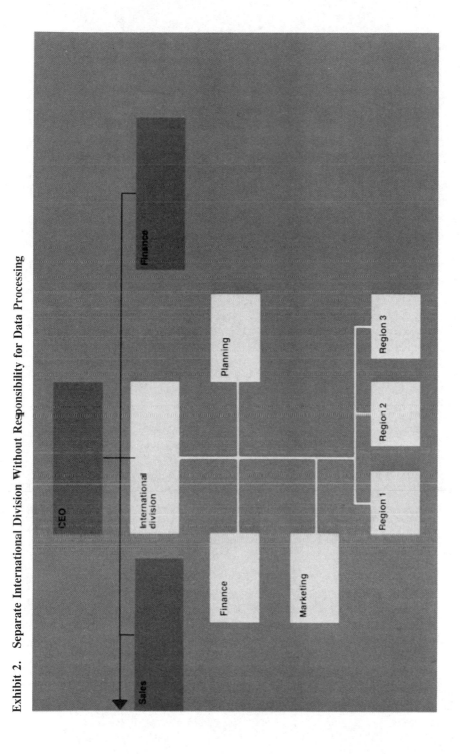

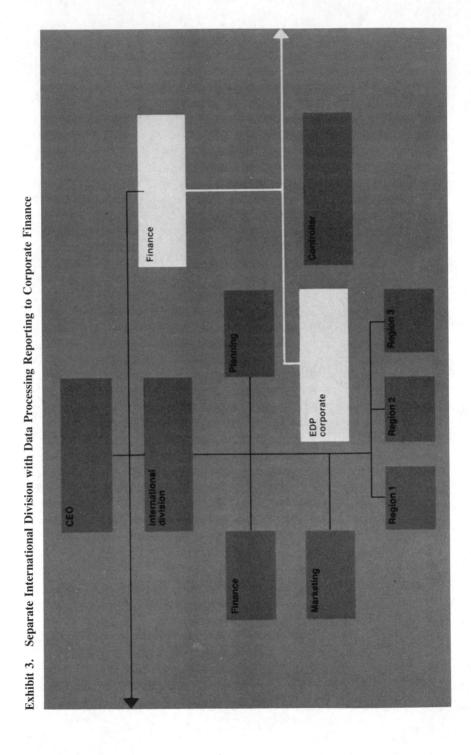

Exhibit 3. Separate International Division with Data Processing Reporting to Corporate Finance

ordinator should report to the head of the international division or to the planning staff, giving international greater control over IS activities (see Exhibit 4).

Appointing the proper person is critically important, since the coordinator must be perceived as competent in the countries in which he or she will work. Coordinators should have excellent business skills, a broad enough understanding of data processing to be able to identify where it can be used effectively, and high interpersonal skills to help cement relationships across national boundaries. A sensitivity to corporate politics and a facility for foreign languages are also pluses. Sometimes international coordinators are "rejects" from the corporate department, and, lacking credibility, they are ineffective.

Second, an international division with sales of more than $500 million should have its own data processing function. This function should have a dotted-line relationship to corporate data processing (see Exhibit 5) and might well pull the nucleus of its staff from there. This new international department would play a role in international data processing similar to that typically played by the corporate data processing function in the domestic business. The department's role would include the following particularly important aspects:

It would have overall responsibility for establishing international DP policies and standards relating to hardware (for example, which vendors and what computers), to software, and to systems development. Of growing importance in the case of standards, for example, is the need to move toward a central coordination of data to permit greater flexibility in the interchange of information between countries. For example, where one country defines product cost as one thing and another uses the term differently, management information will be wrong—not an uncommon situation today.

It would determine from country managers and/or the head of international whether affiliates should use systems already in use elsewhere, and, if so, what systems and which affiliates. This role is important in the case of small affiliates that have a need to install many systems quickly. The international DP department, literally wired into the international division, can be an effective mechanism for corporations to avoid costly reinventions of the wheel.

It would provide technical support for the small affiliates that lack in-house resources. Although this is not as serious a problem in Western Europe as it is in Latin America, for example, some of the smaller European countries (for example, Spain) do have problems because of a lack of technically qualified personnel. For these countries, an international data processing function can help with the development of local systems and can also act as the clearing house for information about systems that already exist elsewhere or for the purchase of packaged software.

An international DP department should not necessarily have its own data center. Nor should it have a large staff of analysts and programmers

Exhibit 4. Separate International Division with an EDP Coordinator Responsible to Planning and a Dotted-Line Relationship to Corporate Data Processing

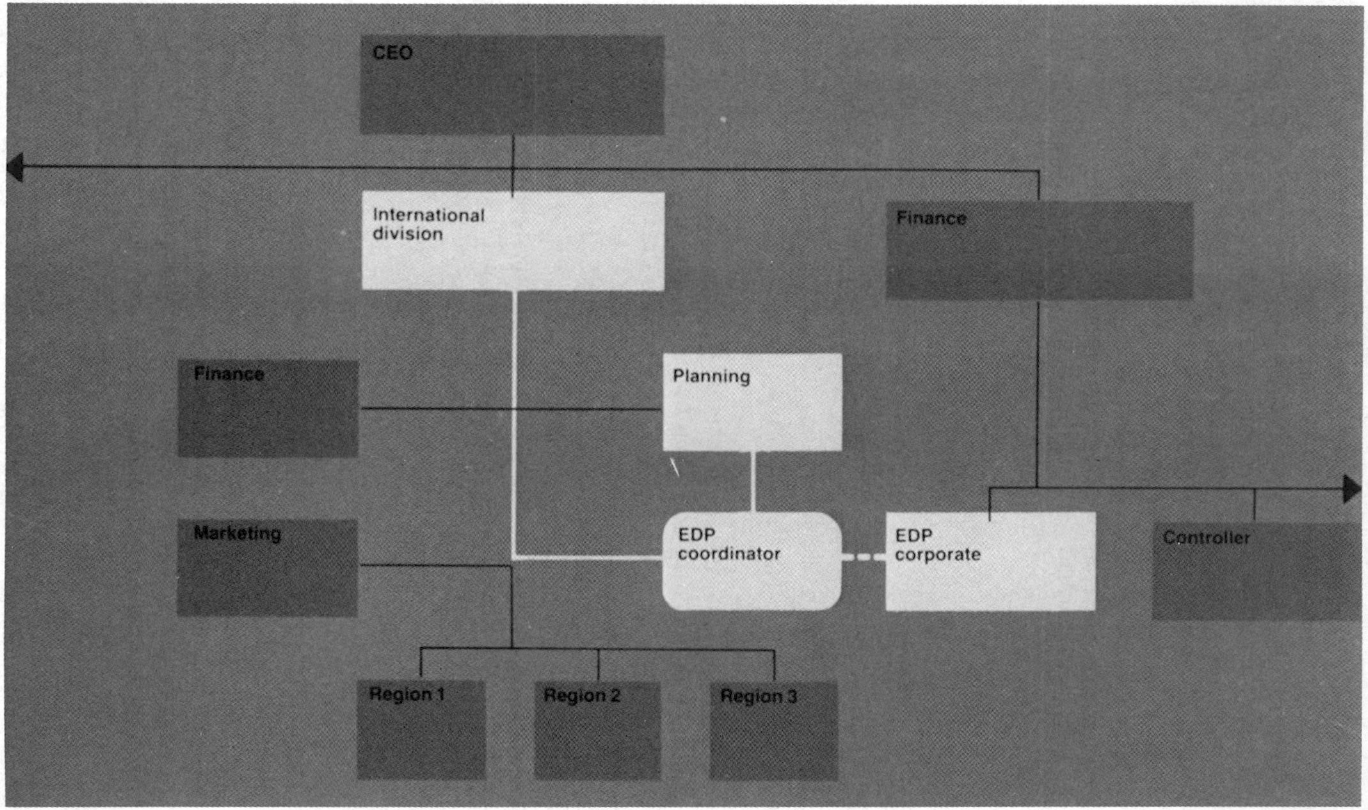

Exhibit 5. Separate International Division with Its Own Data Processing and Dotted-Line Relationship to Domestic Data Processing in Finance

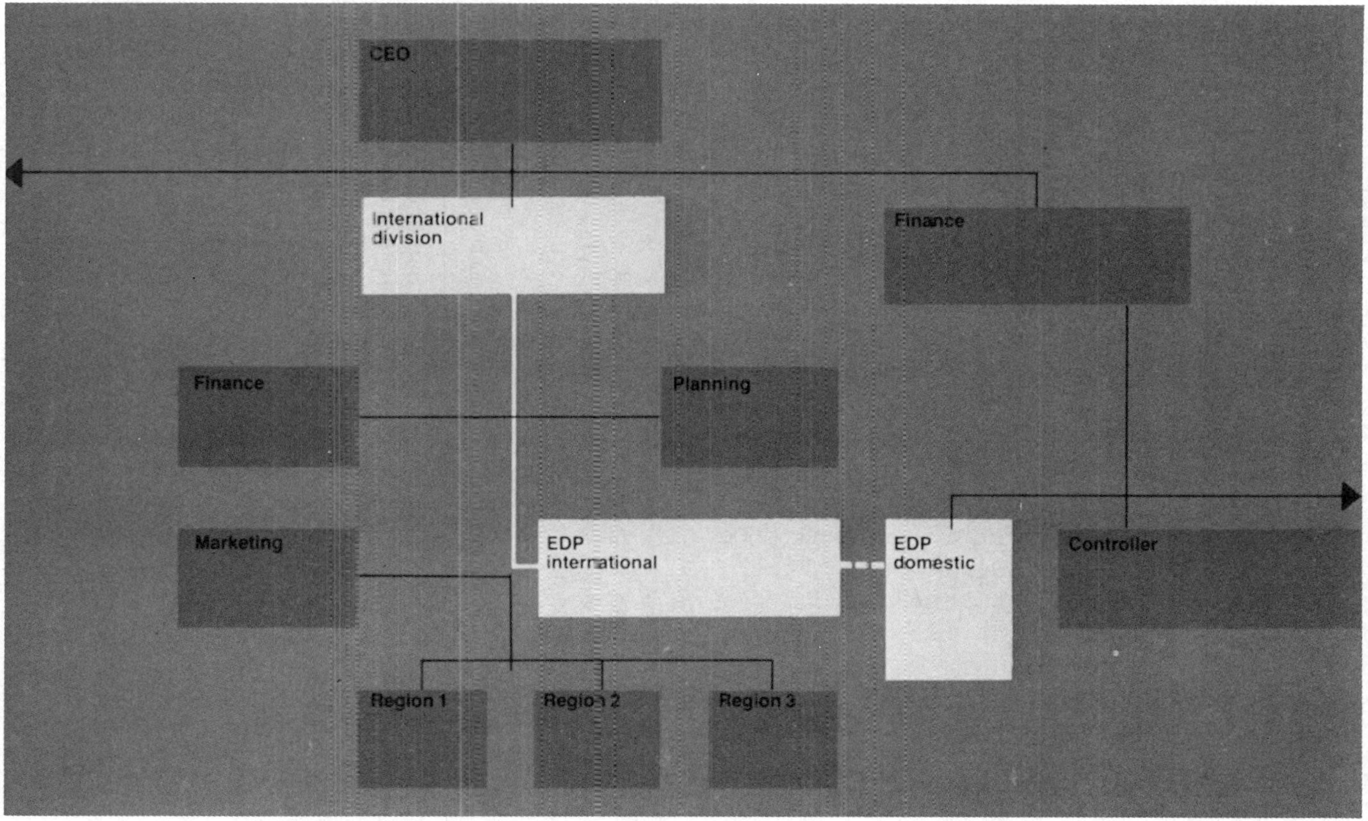

located in the corporate international offices in the United States and charged
with developing systems for the affiliates. Where possible, it is preferable
to leave systems development to the affiliates, which have greater understanding of their own needs. The role of the international data processing
department is to collaborate with the affiliates to try to ensure future port-
ability to other countries.

Third, management should create an international computer council to
oversee the conduct of information processing internationally. Many companies accept the idea of a domestic computer steering committee, and I
believe that it can be usefully extended to the international scene. It should
have representatives from the key regions, from international data processing, from corporate data processing, and from corporate planning.

The council would consider issues related to information processing
that have potentially broad impact internationally. These might include how
international data processing plans fit with corporate objectives to ensure
their compatibility, the corporate stand on transborder data-flow issues,
funding for major new applications, implementation of important common
systems where stumbling blocks have occurred in particular regions or countries, and allocation of technical resources where opinions differ among
country managers. Also, a council could usefully monitor progress on major
international data processing projects.

The IS professionals (whether corporate or international) would be
responsible for the staff work for the council meetings, and the international
coordinators just mentioned would provide most of the information about
the situation in each country. To keep costs down, meetings should coincide
with periodic regional and country managers' meetings.

Define the Roles

The effectiveness of information processing internationally revolves around
four tasks; every organization has to decide who carries them out. In fact,
international managers should view a definition of these roles as a chief
product of the original task force's study and one that will ultimately influence the approach a company finally selects. A discussion of the most important tasks follows.

Stating Objectives.   The chief international executive must issue the statement of objectives in a direct manner like this: "During the next three years
as recommended by the international computer council, we will standardize
our spare parts inventory system in the European region and improve our
average availability by 5%." Moreover, top management of the international
division must show support for these objectives by including information-
processing topics on the agendas of operating committee meetings. Such
forums can also be useful for briefing managers on new technology and its
impact, and for monitoring performance on the corporate objectives.

Implementing Policy.   Country managers generally control the local IS resources and have the ultimate responsibility for implementing corporate policy for international data processing. Their considerable power and autonomy also allows strong managers to resist certain policies. For this reason, the international chief executive should spell out the objectives clearly in advance, and the international computer council should make its wishes known.

Identifying Problems and Opportunities.   International IS coordinators should be the catalysts for change and the eyes and ears of the international computer council. They have to communicate formally and informally with a spectrum of international executives and data processing professionals and look for possible synergies in the use of information processing across national boundaries.

They need to find ways to overcome the "not invented here" syndrome and convince country managers that it makes business sense to use application programs developed elsewhere. And once these opportunities are found, coordinators need to keep abreast of implementation. Rarely can they be responsible for implementation, since the control of the technical resources normally rests with DP management.

Executing Technical Work.   Data processing managers are responsible for designing, developing, and installing application systems. But in many organizations, data processing professionals are scattered among corporate offices in several countries. When a coordinated effort is required, it therefore becomes most important to stipulate exactly who is responsible for each part of the applications development process. The international computer council is the appropriate forum for discussing such issues when the DP managers in each location have worked out the details.

A number of business and economic issues, and the increasing interdependence among international businesses, complicate the challenge of managing worldwide data processing operations, and data processing itself certainly poses its own inherent complexities.

It is becoming apparent, furthermore, that IS professionals alone cannot cope with the way international data processing function is evolving. Success depends on the more active involvement of senior international management. To ensure that the full potential of information processing is realized in foreign operations, most companies with global interests should examine their structures and procedures for managing data processing and determine whether a new approach is needed. Management must be willing to question established organizational relationships, focus energies on a few key areas, and intervene when necessary if the competitive advantages associated with well-managed, information-processing operations are to be realized.

Notes

1. For a comparative analysis of the U.S. and European legislative approaches, see Adrian Norman, ''The Regulation of Transnational Data Flow,'' Arthur D. Little Decision Resources, March, 1981, ref. no. R810301; and see also Royal Parker, ''Handling Transborder Data Flow—a Global Concern,'' *Financial Executive,* December 1979, p. 41.

2. Subcommittee on Government Information and Individual Rights, U.S. House of Representatives, March 13, 1980, p. 141.

3. See Louis H. Mertes, ''Doing Your Office Over—Electronically,'' Chapter 29, this book.

13
Computer Data Bases: The Future Is Now

RICHARD L. NOLAN

There has been considerable debate among specialists about what a data base is, if such a thing exists at all; about the elements of information that ought to go into it; about the administrative complexities created by the concept; and about the real value of the concept as the central organizing principle for a company's EDP operations. To the extent that top management has overheard this debate, it has probably become confused and highly skeptical about the whole idea. This article shows that the concept is real, viable, and beneficial. It also shows that EDP evolution is leading companies with significant EDP operations in the direction of a data-base form of information organization. The author's purpose here is to clarify for top management the essential facts about the nature of a data base, its construction and administration, in such a way that top managers can grapple with the notion and guide lower levels of managers, especially in the EDP department, to a standard of operations that is adequate to the company's need for management information. As documentation, the author uses the results of a survey designed to find out what the data-base concept means in strategic and operational terms today.

On July 1, two sets of forecasts from the planning department arrived on the desk of the marketing vice president. The first set forecasted sales for the company's existing line of industrial products for the year beginning the following January. The second set forecasted sales over the same period for a new line of industrial products, similar to the company's established line, to be introduced in January.

The company expected that the two lines would complement each other, permitting an in depth coverage of its markets which would place the company in an extremely strong competitive position. This was particularly important at this juncture; competition had been making inroads into the company's traditional turf, and the higher level of sales that could be expected would give the company some much-needed profits.

With pleasure, the vice president of marketing noted that the forecasts were more promising than he had dared to hope. The forecasting staff had an excellent track record—there was no reason not to take the high projections seriously. So some thought would have to be given to increasing production for both lines over the next months.

Production was really not much of a problem. In preliminary talks with manufacturing, the fact had been well established that existing plant and personnel could stretch to produce higher quantities on short notice with relatively little sweat. The forecasts gave adequate indications, too, of just how high a level of production would be needed each month for the succeeding nine months.

Inventory, on the other hand, did present something of a problem. Company sales had distinct regional characteristics; they were made from regional warehouses which the company held on leaseback arrangements. In preparation for the new product line, some provision had already been made to increase the company's regional warehouse facilities, but these high sales forecasts made the marketing vice president wonder whether the expansion had been large enough. It seemed to him that a good many of the regional warehouses might well be severely squeezed—both in sheer physical space and in manpower. With these high projected volumes, he thought, the company could be marketing itself right into a warehousing bottleneck.

Also, the regional variations in sales patterns had not been taken fully into account in making the forecasts, for "technical" reasons—here was the one "soft" area he had agreed to tolerate in the forecasts. Hence he was not clear on which warehouses would be the worst hit and where there might be some excess capacity in closely adjoining regions.

He thought next of the aggressive marketing and promotion strategies he had just approved, for both product lines, to be carried out in various regions over the next few quarters. If they were as effective as he expected them to be, there *would* be a problem in the warehouses. Perhaps he could cut back on his preferred marketing and sales strategies, but this alternative conflicted with the company's need for increasing sales as quickly as possible.

Definition of a Problem

He did some simple arithmetic and then headed for the CEO's office. After outlining the situation in light of the final forecasts from planning, he boiled it down to this: "If things work out the way we expect them to, the Chicago warehouses, at least, will have to operate at four times their capacity for at least three months. That's only one group of warehouses. And we really don't have the cash in hand to contract for additional outside space."

They argued about a number of possibilities, making a few calculations and thinking out various consequences aloud. After an hour's discussion, they concluded that they simply had to have a better picture of the impact of the new marketing strategy on sales of both lines, and they also had to have a better picture of the impact of projected sales on inventory turnover and warehouse crowding. They needed, in short, to pull all three of the threads together.

At this point, the CEO pointed out that parts of the puzzle were already on the computer:

☐ The company had inventory simulation programs which had been developed recently to help adjust inventory policies. Several years' actual data on inventory turnover were also available.

☐ The sales department had a number of forecasting programs designed to provide sales reports and forecast information by region and product.

☐ On behalf of marketing, the forecasting staff had developed a model for market penetration of the new product line, based on the sales of the existing product line, which it was intended to supplement.

So the two men went to see the vice president of computing services and laid the problem out for him. Then they asked, "Can you get us a printout that will tell us what impact marketing and sales are going to have on the warehouses?"

His answer was *no*. He pointed out that the company had no program for running such a simulation. He also pointed out that while the company had most of the data that such a simulation would require, none of the data were in readily available form. The inventory data had been specially prepared for the inventory simulations and would have to be completely recoded before they could be used for such a radically different purpose. The programs for forecasting sales did provide regional projections, but they had not been adjusted to mesh with the new inventory systems as yet—that development was still some months away. Further, the several years' sales data used by the programs, once again, were specially coded for the sales programs and could not be used in different programs without a massive reorganization of the data.

Finally, he pointed out that their computer system could not handle the sheer volume of data required by a simulation that attempted to combine all the necessary inventory data, sales data, and market-strategy data. At a minimum, more main memory for the computer would be required.

The CEO looked glum: "I'm not worried about the size of the computer. If we need a bigger memory, we'll get our hands on a bigger memory. How long will it take you to clean up the data and write a simulation program that will give us some answers?"

"Nine months, maybe a year," said the EDP manager.

"Because all our data are frozen into these other programs?" the CEO asked.

"That's the main reason," the EDP manager replied.

"That's a hell of a reason," the CEO said and stalked toward the door.

"Of course, we could have done it the other way," the EDP man called after him. "But now what we'd have to do is. . . ."

But the two men were gone.

What's the Answer?

The problem in this vignette is not one that has an easy solution. Management asked for a computer simulation that cut across three different departments, and was frustrated primarily because each department's data were locked up into its own applications. Even if time had permitted, the cost of recoding all the data for a cross-departmental simulation would probably have been too high for the company to bear. In other words, the company's own data were a frozen asset—a highly constrained resource, analogous to money which could be used to purchase only one type of asset.

Management requests for such ad hoc processing are increasing. As a consequence, companies are beginning to realize that data are a valuable resource, to be managed like any other basic resource.

What the EDP manager wanted to explain to the CEO, and what the CEO did not wait to hear, is that the company could have been managing its data in such a way that the CEO's request could have been fulfilled.

If the company had maintained all its computer-readable data in a single pool or bank—in a so-called "data base"—and if the company had structured this base of data so that a program for virtually any feasible use could have been run from this data base, then it would have been a matter of sheer expertise and flair for a good, experienced programmer to concoct a program that pulled the desired information together. Further, if the company had been maintaining a data base, its programmers would already have developed the expertise and capability to write such a program, with the aid of a "data-base language," on reasonable notice.

The ability to deal with such *ad hoc* requests is the special benefit of the data-base approach. It has a more mundane benefit too: in an EDP facility of any size and complexity, it is feasible, and much more efficient over the long haul, to create *any* program—whether big, small, complex, routine, or *ad hoc*—and to run it from a data base rather than from a lot of separate files of data locked to specific applications.

The truth of this rather strong statement derives from the fact that the data-base approach frees the programmer from the constraint of working over, under, around, and through the structures of separate data files, an expensive fact of life implicit in the traditional approach to EDP operations and planning. With a data base, he need only work with a single structure, that of the base itself.

This one-main-structure feature also makes it easy to decide how data can be obtained and integrated into the base most efficiently and economically—that is, it eases the data-maintenance problem, once the data base has been set up. Considering the extraordinary percentages of EDP budgets that companies allocate to maintenance today, usually over 50%; this benefit is a highly significant one.

Thus the concept of a companywide data base has emerged. It has two key aspects:

1   The data that computer programs use are considered an independent resource in themselves, separate from the computer programs.
2   There is an art and an approach to managing and structuring a company's computer-readable data as a whole, so that they constitute a resource available to the organization for broad-range applications—especially on an *ad hoc* basis.

Because of its potential benefits, the data-base concept has received much attention recently in the professional press. What I hope to do in this article is explain it in management terms and present some survey results that indicate how the concept is being received and implemented in a small sample of companies.

A Historical Pattern

As the matter now stands, most managements would be hard put to manage— and *use*—their data to full potential, for reasons that are largely historical. Because of the rapid growth of computer technology, management of data has developed haphazardly and in laggard fashion over the years. A general approach to data management has emerged only very recently, and, consequently, applications have developed discretely from one another in an unintegrated and wasteful fashion. Further, each increase in the complexity and capabilities of computers has brought new generations of applications, but these applications still, for the most part, have been specialized in nature, designed for a specific operational use or for a specialized staff function.

Hence management of data has continued to develop in fragmented fashion and at rather low organizational levels—at a subdepartmental or substaff level.

Today, upper levels of management are seeking information that can be generated only from properly structured, companywide pools that include data from the narrower applications located farther down in the organizational hierarchy. That is, management information today requires that a company have a data base which can be used, in conjunction with broad-range programs, to generate information on a broader and more comprehensive scale than the single, isolated applications of the past could usually do.

Notwithstanding the new demands, tradition is still strong; indeed, it has barely been challenged. Exhibit 1 represents the traditional way of doing things—collecting and coding data for specific programs and thereby gluing

Exhibit 1.   The Traditional Approach to Programs and Data

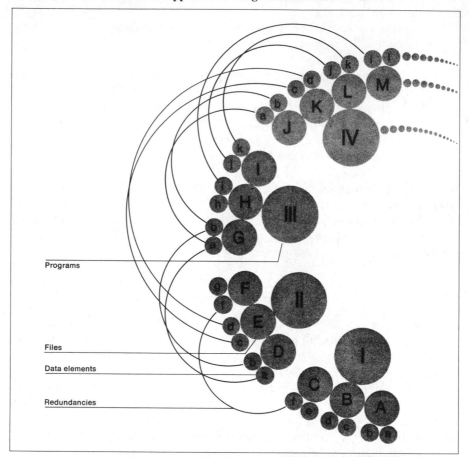

Programs

Files

Data elements

Redundancies

them more or less permanently and exclusively to those programs. In retrospect, this approach has had three significant disadvantages.

1. *Files and records have tended to become redundant.*   Suppose Company X originally *had* only a single, computer-based system—say, for accounts receivable—which is represented in Exhibit 1 as Program I. (At this point, please pay attention to Exhibit 1 only. I shall explain its companion, Exhibit 2, subsequently.)

Program I has three data files: A, B, and C. File A contains customer records, each consisting of data elements *a* and *b; a* might be the customer name and *b* his outstanding balance. Files B and C contain other data elements needed for the accounts receivable program.

Assume that now the company wishes to implement a second program—Program II, as illustrated in Exhibit 1—with Files D, E, and F comprehending elements *a, b, c, d, f,* and *g.* Note that the company already has all these elements, except *g,* on file for Program I. In all probability, however, its programmers coded Files A and B (including all the elements *a, b, c,* and *d*) expressly for Program I, and hence cannot now use A and B intact for Program II. Thus the programmers have to make a choice:

☐ They can recode A and B so that these files can be used by either Program I or Program II. *But* this would mean rewriting Program I to take account of the recoding.

☐ Alternatively, they can build two "new" files, consisting of data from A and B but coded for the special convenience of Program II.

In the past, when faced with this kind of choice, an EDP department has usually just gone ahead and constructed the two "new" files. Going back over Program I ordinarily seems like too much trouble, so making up the new files seems the easiest way out. It is—*in the short run.*

But in the long run, as the exhibit shows, Company X might easily find itself creating more and more quasi-duplicate files as it adds new programs. For example:

☐ It will need two new versions of File B for Programs II and IV— that is, Files E and K.

☐ It will need three new versions of File A for Programs II, III, and IV—that is, Files D, G, and J.

☐ It will need a new version of File I for Program IV—that is, File L.

And so on. The redundancy of data is obvious. In just this little, highly simplified example, seven out of twelve (58%) of the data elements in the files are redundant.

Initially, redundancy does not cause a great deal of trouble. As soon as pieces of data must be *updated,* however, it *does* cause a great deal of trouble. In an EDP department of any size, it is virtually impossible to update all the redundant files and reports in systematic and synchronized fashion. Consider what must happen if Company X adds a customer: it must update A, B, D, G, and J, and that would only be the beginning.

Once files, records, and reports have begun to overlap and updating becomes a serious chore, updating procedures begin to sag of their own weight and different parts of the organization begin to receive inconsistent reports generated from files that are in various states of disrepair. In one large company, the inconsistencies between sales reports at the division level and sales reports at the branch level were so extreme that the salesmen began to keep very elaborate *manual* sales records. These two sets of reports were, in fact, generated in large part from redundant files that were updated at different times.

These particular inconsistencies resulted from a mere difference of organizational *level*—that is, the divisional versus the branch level. Severe redundancy problems can arise even more easily when reports from one function must be meshed with reports from another function. For example, there is absolutely no reason to expect that a company's inventory-control report will jibe with its accounting report unless the updating disciplines for the files of both functions are synchronized with each other.

Even slight variations in the data used for the two functional reports can cause glaring inconsistencies:

In a large retail chain whose applications had developed in the traditional fashion, the needs of the business forced management to request the integration of a number of different functional programs and systems. With great effort, the job was done. However, it was done in such a way that many quasi-duplicate files were created and many separate, but essentially similar, programs were patched together. The company suddenly found itself spending 90% of its programming labor-hours just keeping the programs running in concert and the files up to date.

At the very least, redundancy spells confusion and expense for any sizable operation. Perhaps its worst feature is that the longer a company follows the traditional pattern and keeps adding new programs and redundant files of data, coded specifically and exclusively for those programs, the greater the task it must face when it finally assembles all its data in a single pool, so structured and coded that new programs can be run without extensive recollection or recoding of data.

2. *The traditional approach undercuts or aborts the advances of computer technology.* Computer memory was once a great deal more expensive than it is today. A major computer manufacturer is now predicting that semiconductor technology will reduce the present cost of main memory by many orders of magnitude in the not-too-remote future. Even now the costs of random-access storage have been greatly reduced by the development of extremely large disc devices. Furthermore, new software has introduced new dimensions to computing, dimensions that make possible the more advanced kinds of information systems. For example, virtual-memory techniques allow one to explore, cheaply, relationships between elements in a relatively huge pool of data, not all of which need necessarily be present in literal fact.

Originally, the relatively high cost of on-line storage ("memory," in a rough sense) was a main factor that induced companies to delimit the scope of programming and therewith the amount of data needed during any given run. In effect, this reinforced the practice of creating and maintaining separate files for each application in the company's portfolio—companies tended to store no more data than were needed for the run at hand.

Today, however, many companies that have followed the traditional route, but have acquired up-to-date, on-line storage systems, find they have the capacity to keep relatively huge amounts of data alive in the system.

But their data are still organized and coded along first-generation computer lines—that is, by specific programs. From a rational viewpoint, this is as awkward, expensive, and absurd as keeping modern accounting records wholly in Roman numerals.

3. *The traditional approach obstructs upper management's growing demands for applications that require a data base.* The reason for this unfortunate condition is locked into the history of the computer. A brief review of the evolution of computer-based applications runs as follows:

☐ The computer was first used to replace existing manual functions, primarily within the accounting function.

☐ Next came the integration of computer-based systems within and between functional areas—this was the cross-functional stage.

☐ Now cross-functional/interlevel systems are being developed to serve middle and upper-middle management; or, to put it another way, management is now demanding the benefits of computer innovations.

At this third stage, the redundancies and inefficiencies that result from the traditional approach to the management of data become so signal and so extensive that applications can be adequate only if they are developed in such a manner that specific programs are separate from the data. That is, the whole body of a company's data must be structured into a flexible data base.

A Modern Concept

As Exhibit 2 shows, the data-base concept structures EDP activity in such a way that all of a company's computer-readable data are merged in a single pool, which is used to run both routine programs and programs written in response to ad hoc requests. Note that no files appear in this exhibit— the base of data elements constitutes the general file for the company, and specific files are by and large unnecessary. Note also that two additional software systems are in evidence here which were not in evidence in Exhibit 1:

☐ *The data-base interface system.* This enables a specialist data-base programmer to organize and structure the data elements in a manner that minimizes or eliminates redundancy and optimizes the economic costs of data storage and accessibility.

☐ *The interface system for special programming.* This includes a high-level programming language especially designed for manipulating data elements contained in the data base, solving problems, and producing reports. To write an ad hoc program, the programmer works successively through the interface for special applications and the general interface system to the data base itself.

Exhibit 2.   The Data-Base Approach to Programs and Data

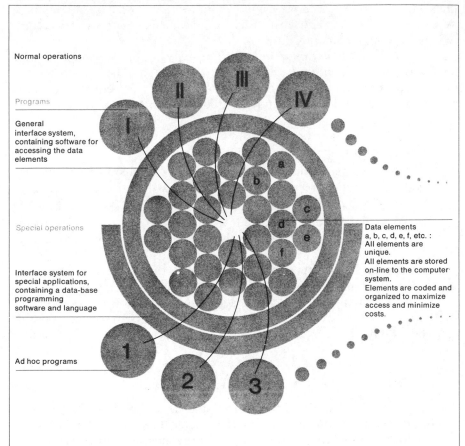

Comparing Exhibits 1 and 2, one can see an immense contrast between the traditional concept and the data-base concept, both theoretical and practical. If the company described in the vignette with which I opened this article had had a working data base, the CEO might merely have asked his EDP manager to set a programmer to work on an *ad hoc* program. No question of data availability would have arisen; the only variable in the case would have been the time required to actually write the program, and this time might only have been a matter of hours.

One can more fully appreciate the contrast if he looks forward to the fourth stage of development in computer applications—applications that senior executives will use in corporate management. This development will most likely emerge from the union of the data-base concept and the corporation-model concept; and while this union is still but a gleam in the specialist's eye, the company that adjusts its EDP policies to the data-base concept now will enjoy a very significant advantage over the company that pursues the traditional patterns until the day of reckoning has actually arrived. (Just *how* a company should pursue this adjustment is a problem I shall consider later.)

Since much of the computer technology necessary to implement the data-base concept exists and the rest of the technology is being developed rapidly, a strong case for adopting the data-base approach can now be made. Yet, in operational terms, the concept is still novel. To what degree is it being used? What are the issues and problems involved in implementing it? By what strategies can a company work toward a data base? And what benefits can we realistically expect from it?

An Interview Study

To answer these questions I administered a pattern interview to the data-processing managers of ten companies in six diverse industries. The questions permitted unrestricted responses, and hence the information these managers provided (summarized in Exhibit 3) is not as clear-cut as one might wish. However, it is informative. It provides some operational perspective from EDP managers on the following topics:

☐ Current impressions of what a data base should be and do.

☐ Approaches to structuring and organizing a data base.

☐ Strategies for building a data-base system.

☐ The assignment of responsibility for the base's scope and contents—that is, data-base administration.

☐ The role of the data-base administrator.

☐ Access and security.

☐ Organizational and technical problems associated with the data-base concept.

The opinions expressed on these topics varied considerably among the EDP managers I interviewed. By and large, a given manager's opinions reflected the particular stage his company had reached in the evolutionary progression toward full use of the data-base concept.

For the reader's convenience I have organized the material in Exhibit 3 in evolutionary sequence. One manufacturing company, Company 1, at the far left, has barely begun to understand and use the concept; in Company 10, at the far right, one finds a fairly sophisticated example of a data base in operation.

Let me now discuss the topics listed, one by one, with some attention to the way the data base shapes up at various stages of its maturity.

Exhibit 3. Evolutionary Stages of the Data Base

	Company 1—Manufacturing	Company 2—Public Utilities	Company 3—Banking	Company 4—Manufacturing	Company 5—Manufacturing
Evolutionary stage	Low	Low	Low-medium	Medium	Medium
Data-base concept	All computer-readable data	All computer-readable data	Tape and disc files	Disc files	All computer-readable data
Data-base structure	Individual applications	Individual applications	Operational, by products	Operational, by functions	Individual applications
Degree of integration across level	Minimal	Minimal	Low	High	High
Degree of integration between levels	Minimal	Minimal	Minimal	Minimal	Minimal
Data-base strategy	Brute force	Brute force	Brute force	Piggyback	Key task
Decision maker for data-base contents and designs	Systems analyst	Systems analyst	Steering committee, with an administrative position planned	Systems analyst, with an administrative position planned	Systems analyst
Personnel with direct data-base access	Programmers	Programmers	Programmers	Programmers	Programmers

Company 6—Insurance	Company 7—Manufacturing	Company 8—Manufacturing	Company 9—Wholesale/Retail Food	Company 10—Manufacturing
Medium	Medium-advanced	Medium-advanced	Advanced	Advanced
Shared random-access files	Shared random-access files	Shared random-access files	All computer-readable data	Shared random-access files
Operational, by products	Operational, by functions	Operational, by functions	By key tasks in accounting and distribution	By key tasks in planning and manufacturing
Medium	High	Medium	High	High
Minimal	Minimal	Low	Medium	Medium
Piggyback	Piggyback	Piggyback	Key task	Key task
Data-processing manager	Data-processing manager, with an administrative position planned	Steering committee, with an existing administrative position	Steering committee, with an existing administrative position	Data-base administrator
Programmers	Programmers	Programmers, analysts	Programmers, analysts	Programmers, analysts

Nature of the Data Base

First of all, I found a certain amount of confusion about what "data base" means. My open-ended question, "What is the data base in your company?" usually brought first a puzzled expression to the manager's face, and then a request for clarification. I answered that I wanted a statement on how he views his company's data base, if, indeed, he views it at all.

Responses ranged all over the lot. Some managers included all the computer-readable data in their company. Others defined the base more narrowly—for example, as including only the random-access disc files used for routine reporting and analysis.

The common thread in the responses was "computer-readable." Since all the interviewees were data-processing managers, this common thread is not surprising. But, obviously, the great majority of an organization's data are noncomputer-readable; they are maintained in file cabinets as well as in the minds of management.

Although more and more data are being put into computer-readable form, as the technology improves and makes more sophisticated computer-based applications both feasible and economic, much of the literature on data bases falsely assumes that companies have already translated all the data needed for these applications into machine-readable terms. This simply has not yet happened—indeed, most companies have not even begun to collect the data needed for these applications, in machine-readable form or otherwise.

In general, the more advanced a company's use of the data-base approach, the less naïve and more realistic the manager's definition of what the base ought to contain—for example, "shared random-access files used for [periodic] production programs and *ad hoc* management requests." Such a definition reflects the two key characteristics of the data base: (a) sharing data between programs, and (b) structuring data so that *ad hoc* management requests can be served. As Exhibit 3 shows, the more advanced companies conceive their data bases in this light.

One data-processing manager articulated the criterion of responsiveness to *ad hoc* management requests especially well. He said that his company will realize the data-base approach fully when he has incorporated the technology that will permit him to respond to any reasonable request by management for reporting or analysis within one day, and without undue degradation of his continuing data processing. He further described a reasonable request as one that draws on existing computer-readable data.

Structure & Integration

Companies 1, 2 and 5 in Exhibit 3 viewed their data base as structured under the single criterion of individual applications, in the fully traditional manner. Companies 1 and 2 had a minimal degree of cross-functional integration— that is, sharing data between such functional applications as manufacturing and accounting.

Company 5, in the middle of the spectrum, had a high degree of cross-functional integration, as Exhibit 3 shows. In my interview with its EDP manager I had been led to believe that cross-functional integration was minimal. However, further discussion with their lead systems analyst pointed to high integration. With more probing, I found out that this man had taken it on himself to design files to accommodate sharing between programs. He was quite active in the EDP professional societies and expressed strong feelings that this was the "right" approach.

Still, all three of these companies had minimal sharing of data between levels of management. In fact, there were very few programs developed for management in any of the three companies.

In addition to Company 5, four other companies (4, 7, 9, and 10) indicated a high degree of cross-functional integration of their data bases, and they had very well-developed computer applications in the operations aspects of their businesses as well. But I should note a significant difference between Companies 4 and 7, and Companies 9 and 10:

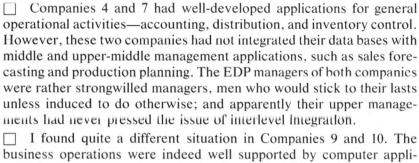

☐ Companies 4 and 7 had well-developed applications for general operational activities—accounting, distribution, and inventory control. However, these two companies had not integrated their data bases with middle and upper-middle management applications, such as sales forecasting and production planning. The EDP managers of both companies were rather strongwilled managers, men who would stick to their lasts unless induced to do otherwise; and apparently their upper managements had never pressed the issue of interlevel integration.

☐ I found quite a different situation in Companies 9 and 10. The business operations were indeed well supported by computer applications; the operational aspects related to the product flows were supported by highly developed computer applications (for example, the ordering of raw materials, sales distribution, accounting for accounts payable and receivable, and inventory control).

More significantly, however, under strong direction of upper management, the EDP managers in Companies 9 and 10 both used *key-task criteria* to integrate their data bases. Company 9 viewed distribution and efficient accounting for billing, product movement, and pricing as key tasks, while Company 10 viewed manufacturing and planning as the keys to the overall profitability of the company. In addition, both companies had integrated their data bases for managerial reporting and analysis with their operational data bases.

In both companies one can see the beginnings of interlevel integration—both have been ranked as "medium" on this parameter in Exhibit 3. Interlevel integration must soon appear, after all, where planning is considered a key focus for company and data-base development, as in Company 10, and where pricing decisions are considered a key focus, as in Company 9.

Without this impetus from upper management to focus integration around key tasks, Companies 9 and 10 could never have reached the advanced stage of computer usage and data-resource management which they have attained. Management's choice of and insistence on this particular strategy was all the more fortunate, considering the popularity of other, far less viable alternatives.

Three Strategies

Thus a main characteristic of the key-task strategy is the capability to respond to management's *ad hoc* requests for reports and analyses. A company can pursue a couple of other strategies to satisfy such requests without recourse to the data-base concept; but the alternatives are not likely to be very successful.

These are the strategies I can identify: the brute-force strategy, the piggyback strategy, and the data-base/key-task strategy. The strategy of each company interviewed is specified in Exhibit 3; and in Exhibit 4 I have attempted to define the three diagrammatically.

Exhibit 4.   Three Strategies for Responding to *Ad Hoc* Requests

Brute force   Piggyback

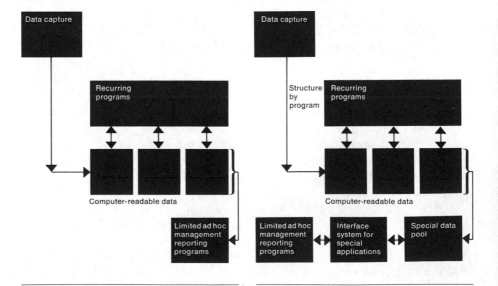

Exhibit 4. (*Continued*)

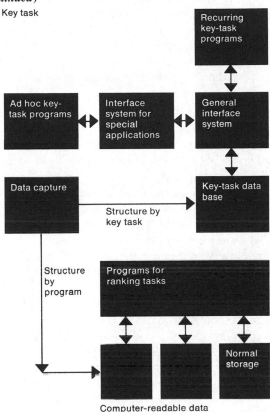

Suppose an EDP manager is suddenly given an assignment of the kind I described at the beginning of this article—that is; an *ad hoc* request for management information that draws across the functions and levels of the company. These are the possible ways he can do the job.

☐ *Through brute force.* He can start from scratch, collecting all the needed data, coding them, writing special programs, and acquiring hardware capability, if it is required. The effort demanded by this approach is likely to be huge, the expense prohibitive, and the time demand wholly impossible. This approach is, as a consequence, very rarely followed.

Now, Exhibit 3 would indicate that companies 1, 2, and 3 service ad hoc management requests through just this approach. The manager of one of these companies even stated emphatically that this approach is cheaper than any other—and notably cheaper than the data-base approach, which I shall come to presently.

However, he admitted that he has virtually never received such a request for ad hoc reporting. This is no small wonder; such a request would disrupt his department completely, and I suspect that this fact is known to upper management in the company.

The other two companies in this group, equally, have had virtually no experience and no success at all in servicing such requests. Claims for the virtues of brute force should be taken with grains of salt.

☐ *Through piggyback.* Using this strategy, the manager attempts to "ride the special project through" on more-or-less existing capabilities. What he does is strip data from existing files, structure them into a special data pool, augment this pool with new data as necessary, expand old programs and write new ones, and increase his hardware capability, if this is required. This approach has two signal disadvantages: it requires the construction of a totally redundant data pool, and, while it consumes less money and time than the brute-force technique, the money and time are still substantial indeed.

The piggyback technique is somewhat more common than the brute-force technique. Companies 4, 6, 7, and 8 have all used it, as Exhibit 3 shows. But since in every case this approach represented a special effort to obtain a special kind of information, its uses were marked by a certain narrowness and shallowness. Possible projects were limited by the quantity and nature of existing data; and the programming skills developed in these companies were not really adequate to create programs tailored to the companies' specific needs. In fact, commercially available data management systems were generally used to structure the new data pools and to generate the programs that produced the reports for management.

☐ *Through a data-base/key-task strategy.* I have already described how an EDP manager would attack the problem of a management request for information; the reader may wish to look back at the organization shown in Exhibit 3. The diagram for data-base/key-task response in Exhibit 4 is a close parallel to the general data-base organization, but it contains some new terms and options. To explain what these mean, let me return to a discussion of companies 9 and 10, which have evolved furthest toward a full data-base mode of operation and have used it most successfully.

Both these companies, 9 and 10, had highly integrated data bases, as I remarked before. These bases were structured according to the companies' key tasks, and were sufficiently developed so that the companies could use commercial data-base software packages. They used one software package for data organization, defining records and files to support multiple applications (the General Interface System of Exhibit 2, and a different software package to produce *ad hoc* management reports and analyses (the Interface System for Special Applications in Exhibit 2).

Both data-processing managers were reasonably satisfied with the commercial software they were using. Nevertheless, they both commented that even the most sophisticated data-base software commercially available did not incorporate the more advanced, data-structure methods. Such methods coordinate theoretical data structures (for example, things resembling immense decision trees) with the access constraints of physical storage devices, such as rotating magnetic discs. Suffice it to say that data organization is extremely complex and technical.

It is so complex, in fact, that one is virtually forced into using commercial software. One of the data-processing managers stated that structure technology is so complex today that he could not possibly support an in-house effort to develop the software. The other manager had initially hoped to develop his own data-base soft-ware, but, after a preliminary investigation of the costs and problems, he decided to acquire a commercially available package.

However, this complexity ultimately derives from the nature of the key tasks for which top management wants the data base to be used. If upper management focuses on key tasks that embrace all the company's data and require very extensive vertical and horizontal integration of reports and analyses, the job of organizing the data base is tougher than when the key tasks embrace only a part of the data and require less than the complete integration of all functions.

In addition, my interviews led me to a conclusion that may be directly useful to top and senior managers, as they set their sights on the issue of data-base organization: the more closely related the functional uses of the data, the easier it is to design a nonredundant, integrated data base. For example, Company 10, which structured its data base on the key tasks of planning and manufacturing, seemed to be incurring fewer problems in data-base design than Company 9, which structured its data base on the key tasks of accounting/distribution.

The planning manufacturing structure used by Company 10 focused on vertical integration of the data base. Its manufacturing data were organized at the operations or transaction level; many of the planning data were obtained by summarizing the manufacturing data. The data base was designed to explicitly accommodate the information needs of different levels of management. Also, there was a strong linkage between organizational objectives and use of the data resource through a computer-based planning model. The model provided continuing guidelines for determining important data to be collected at the manufacturing level.

On the other hand, the accounting/distribution structure used by Company 9 required integration of data from two functional areas at the operational level. Although the structure reflected information flow, it did not explicitly recognize middle-management information needs. Thus there was not a continuing source of guidelines and benchmarks for determining which data and which analyses were important, as there were for Company 10.

Generally, then, the data-base/key-task strategy is more effective than brute force and piggyback because it forces cross-functional and interlevel integration in a manner that will suit upper management's needs. For its part, once it has decided that this strategy is the right one, upper management must take a careful look at what it considers its key tasks and make sure that it has settled on the ones that (a) make sense for the company and (b) are clearly understood by the EDP personnel responsible for structuring and maintaining the data base.

Let me return for a moment to the key-task diagram in Exhibit 4. This diagram makes provision for the fact that some application, *ad hoc* or otherwise, may be remote from the key tasks of the business. If such applications are really required, and if they are *really* remote from the organizing principles used to structure the data base, a company can always have recourse to special files and special programs, in the traditional fashion. However, it seems clear enough that a company that wants to follow the data-base/key-task concept and at the same time succumbs to the temptation to create a "special"or tangential application every time it needs a new program may find that it is doing neither effectively.

Data-Base Administration

In addition to good decisions on data structure and organization, good decisions on what information will be included in a company's data base are central to the successful use of the concept. The total sum of data must be usefully large, but not ungovernably large, or the system will collapse under its own weight.

In all 10 companies I studied, the systems analysts responsible for the various user areas initiated all requests to develop new sets of data or to change old ones. However, the processing of the requests varied considerably:

☐ Companies 1 and 2, still in the early stages of data-base development, permitted the individual systems analysts to decide what files would be developed and how they should be structured for different applications. These companies had not yet begun to consider data independently from the programs for which they were collected and coded.

☐ Companies 4 and 5 were just becoming aware of the need to separate data from applications and to recognize a "data resource function," but the systems analyst was still the primary decision maker.

☐ Companies 3, 6, and 7 assigned decisions on what data should be maintained to a higher and more centralized authority than the systems analysts—namely, to the data-processing manager or to the EDP steering committee.

☐ Companies 8, 9, and 10 had advanced to the stage at which they had formal data-base administrators who played a central role in monitoring the content and standards of the data base. In these companies, a request for data for a particular application was studied from a number of viewpoints: necessity, redundancy, cost/benefit, procurement methods, EDP planning, and so forth. These analyses had become sufficiently specialized to give rise to another formal administrative position—data-base analyst.

The Role of the Administrator

Exhibit 3 shows that data-base administrators actually exist in three companies—8, 9, and 10—and that Companies 3, 4, and 7 plan to fill such a position in the foreseeable future (in two to five years).

However, in none of these cases has the company fully delineated the administrator's exact responsibilities or authority. Companies seem to agree that the administrator should concentrate his energies in the areas of planning and designing the data base; and they seem to view the administrator as a useful focal point from which the whole issue of computer data can be viewed as an integrated whole. Too often companies have waked to find a plethora of fractured repositories of data scattered all over the organization.

I might note also that EDP managers with purely technical backgrounds often want to include all possible data—the president's personal files, traffic rates, and so on—in the data base, whereas managers with some executive experience in broader areas tend to take a more realistic view of the elements that ought to be included in a company's working library of data. I have argued elsewhere for the wisdom of injecting the broader managerial viewpoint into EDP department decision making.[1]

The interview discussions on the data-base administrator's responsibilities raised an interesting dichotomy. In the comments on what the responsibilities *should* be, data were talked about as a corporate resource. In the comments on what the responsibilities actually *are*, data were viewed merely as computer-readable items.

However, this dichotomy really should not be surprising. The data resource function is being carved out of the general management function. Specialization in data associated with computers is warranted at this time; the conditions for specialization exist.

But the activities for managing data as a corporate resource have not yet developed to the point where specialization is warranted. Senior management within the EDP department can still carry out these activities better than can a specialist.[2] I have already pointed out upper management's responsibility to give guidance on key tasks. Moreover, since the data-base administrator represents a relatively rare, advanced stage of development in the data resource function, it behooves top management to supervise this area closely.

A note on access: Exhibit 3 shows that the groups that either directly or indirectly had access to the data base are programmers and analysts. None of the companies provided either managers or their analysts *direct* access to the data base. Companies 8, 9, and 10 provided an *indirect* access for analysts through a data management system. Here the analyst communicated a request to a programmer who, in turn, used the data management system to obtain a rapid response.

In all the other companies I studied, the analyst and manager were forced to work through the process of satisfying their needs through a programmer. This process will be changed and greatly simplified as the quality of interface software improves.

Organizational & Technical Issues

The EDP managers expressed concern over these major organizational issues associated with the data base:

☐ Acquiring personnel that can handle its technical aspects.
☐ Funding and developing suitable charge-out systems to support it.
☐ Setting and enforcing companywide standards.
☐ Using the data resource to best advantage.

The major associated technical issues for which they expressed concern were these:

☐ Converting data to data-base form.
☐ Providing appropriate software for the interfaces.
☐ Designing a data base which will permit *ad hoc* responsiveness without degrading normal computer processing.
☐ Building in reliability and the ability to reconstruct lost data.

Both the organizational issues and the technical issues were generally felt to be of such magnitude that aggressive action on implementing the data-base concept fully was not warranted at the time. The consensus was that the concept is sound, but that much more needs to be done administratively before it can be effectively realized in practice.

What Should Management Do?

Use of the data-base concept is the next natural milestone in the evolution of EDP applications. It embraces the specialization of EDP functions; it allows management real flexibility in satisfying its need for information; and it permits companies to view and use their data as a real resource. Yet caution and patience are advised in pursuing the concept. What should managers do to deal with this push-and-pull condition?

1. *Take the idea seriously.* Upper management should provide direction to the EDP manager by identifying key tasks of the business and setting priorities for an improved information capability. Perhaps the single most important factor that permitted companies 9 and 10 to break out of a parochial treatment of data was upper management's guidance and its insistence on exploiting data for the interests of the business.

2. *Set up a data administration function.* The issue is when to set up a data administration function, rather than whether to have such a function. Ultimately, an administrator will be needed to implement the data-base concept, anyway. For those companies currently without such a position, an administrative structure is needed for formulating a data-base implementation plan, regulating the pace of implementation, and establishing data-base standards, controls, and access procedures. At a minimum, a data-base specialist should be acquired now to provide decision-making guidance for the EDP manager and steering committee. This person can also provide guidance in evaluating and selecting appropriate software.

3. *Incorporate data-base technology into the computer system.* The hardware technology, as well as the software technology, for data bases has matured to the point that the data-base concept can be both feasible and cost-effective for many organizations. While the company will not be noticeably hurt in the short run by ignoring data-base technology, it will in the longer run

Also, the data-base concept cannot be implemented overnight. If a company begins to plan and act now, it can assimilate even drastic, technological improvements into its existing systems in a slow, comfortable, and orderly fashion.

To incorporate the technology that will permit data-base operations, an organization must identify its key computer-based systems and restructure them (a) to remove redundancy and (b) to facilitate their use by higher levels of management. For the present, companies must probably acquire commercial software for structuring data and responding to management requests for ad hoc analyses and reports.

4. *Think of data as a resource.* For the longer term, management should begin to think of data as a basic resource. It should accept this idea as a natural consequence of functional specialization of the general management function. Since the data-resource concept is closely associated with a fast-moving computer technology, management should expect to see the movement toward specialized data-management activities proceed at a faster rate than, say, specializations in the human resource function. My survey of the 10 companies indicates that the emergence of the data-base administrator is a key event in the specialization.

5. *Estimate your own company's position in the evolutionary sequence.* If you find that your company is still at a rudimentary stage of development, plan for development. If your company is fairly advanced, press forward a little harder. The only thing to lose is redundancy.

Notes

1. See my article, "Plight of the EDP Manager," *HBR*, May–June 1973, p. 143.

2. John Dearden, "MIS Is a Mirage," *HBR*, January–February 1972, p. 90.

14
Costs and Benefits of a Data-base System

FRED R. McFADDEN AND JAMES D. SUVER

Since a data-base management system is, in effect, simply a more logical way for an organization to store information, it seems only a matter of time until most companies adopt one. Until now these systems have been most useful in larger corporations because of both the power of the computer installations and the complexity of organizations' informational needs. In the next five years, however, a majority of medium-sized and smaller companies are expected to find them advantageous also. What can be learned from those who have gone before? Plenty, the authors of this article show, not the least of the lessons being that a carefully designed preliminary analysis of the systems' costs and benefits is wise. Using a hypothetical company with $50 million in sales to represent several companies familiar to them, the authors illustrate how such an analysis can involve both operating and data processing managers. This dual involvement is necessary because of the assumptions that must be made and the effect the change will have on the decision-making process.

Business is at the threshold of a new era that will feature an explosive growth in the use of data-base management systems, or DBMS. After the initial trials, errors, and false starts, the concept of a data base as a corporate resource is becoming a reality. In the United States approximately 3,000 companies—or somewhat less than 10% of all data processing (DP) organizations—have implemented DBMS at this time, and the number of installations worldwide is probably close to 5,000. However, some experts predict that within five years 75% of all DP organizations in this country are likely to be using this approach.

As might be expected, most of these systems have been installed in large corporations, but this pattern is also expected to change in the near future. Since data-base management systems are or soon will be available for most of the popular minicomputers and small business computers, many smaller companies will also begin to realize their advantages.

Why the rush to data base? There are a number of important potential benefits. A data base is a collection of data logically organized to meet the information and time requirements of an entire organization (or division). The data-base approach makes the sharing of data easier, thereby helping to eliminate its duplication, improves productivity in the DP organization, and provides better and more timely information to management.

Companies that use data-base systems have in essence recognized that data represent a major corporate resource. Thus they have taken three steps in order to standardize the processing of data throughout the corporation:

1 Establish a data-base administrative function. The data-base manager develops standards and procedures for the creation, processing, and safeguarding of all corporate data.
2 Develop structured data bases to replace the individual files.
3 Install the set of computer programs required to create and manipulate the data bases.

Much of the enthusiasm for data-base systems is justified. However, experience clearly indicates that a cautious approach—accompanied by careful analysis and planning—is essential.

In a recent survey, for example, data processing managers already using data-base management systems indicated that if they were to repeat the process, they would devote more time and attention to evaluating the systems, their impact on operations, and hardware needs. The managers were not unhappy with their systems; in fact, they all reported benefits such as improved quality of design and faster programming and implementation. However, they all also agreed that satisfaction went hand in hand with careful planning, preparation of a detailed proposal, and use of bench mark tests.[1]

Not so well publicized is the fact that there have been some monumental failures among would-be data-base builders. According to one author, "Some of the overenthusiastic and inadequately perceived projects have cost their corporations appalling sums of money and have seriously set back the needed evolution of corporate data bases."[2]

One of the most important elements in planning for a data-base system is an analysis at the outset of potential costs and benefits. It is also one of the most difficult. Although direct costs are readily estimated, DBMS benefits reflect quantities such as ease of access to and value of information that are difficult to measure. Also there are intangible costs such as organizational and procedural changes that must be considered.

Despite these measurement difficulties, such an analysis is worthwhile for a number of reasons:

☐ It becomes a focal point for management involvement at all levels, which is indispensable to any data-base development efforts and, at the same time, helps managers set realistic expectations.

☐ It permits decision makers to apply tested measures, such as prospective rates of return, in addition to using their intuition.

☐ As a by-product, it can help management to identify the operations that would most benefit from data base and to develop priorities accordingly.

☐ Finally, it provides a set of quantitative objectives that can be used to check progress and serve as targets in a management-by-objectives environment.

What follows is an outline, together with some guidelines, that management can use to conduct a cost/benefit analysis for data base. We will illustrate the concepts involved by means of a hypothetical company called Apex Products, which is a composite of several companies we are familiar with, to show how the approach can be tailored to suit the needs of a particular company.

Preliminary Analysis

Apex Products manufactures and distributes consumer products nationwide. Its sales, which totaled $50 million in 1976, had been growing at a real rate of about 10% per year during 1970–1973, but had declined during the 1974 recession. During the last two quarters of 1976, sales had recovered but still lagged behind the previous 10% growth rate.

Apex has a centralized, data processing organization. Its annual budget, about $750,000 in 1976, includes rental on a medium-scale computer with 256,000 bytes of memory and 200 million bytes of disk storage. The data processing staff includes the manager, nine systems analysts and programmers, three administrators, and twelve persons in operations.

Major data processing applications at Apex are order processing, inventory, accounting, and production reporting. At present, the company is developing plans for installing a material requirements planning (MRP) system. All applications developed to date have conventional file-processing systems.

Apex management has been considering data base for about three years for a number of reasons. One reason is that while the present batch-oriented system has satisfactorily supported the daily operations of the company, the rapid rate of growth in the data processing budget is alarming. The analysts and programmers devote most of their time to modifying and maintaining existing systems rather than to developing new ones.

Another reason is that, aside from the standard financial reports, management seldom uses the information to support its planning and decision making. It is just too difficult to obtain information in a useful format. Typical lead time for obtaining specified reports is three to six weeks, and these reports upset priorities in data processing. Overall, management believes that the return on investment on the data processing dollar is quite low and is deteriorating over time.

The present upsurge of interest in data base at Apex is the result of the proposed MRP system. The manufacturing vice president has called attention to the fact that installing this system will entail building an extensive data base for bills of material, inventory, open orders, and so forth.[3] Apex has the choice of building this data base using conventional software or using a generalized data base management system. The manufacturing vice president supports the latter approach, pointing out that Apex has reached a crucial decision point in managing its data.

Apex managers are somewhat divided. Although a majority favors data base, some are skeptical and insist on more information. They have been burned in the past by new systems that never quite delivered on promised improvements.

As a result of this difference of opinion, Apex has formed a survey team composed of the data processing manager, materials manager, a marketing analyst, a financial analyst, and a data base specialist to prepare a preliminary analysis of the costs and benefits of the data base approach. This team interviewed key managers to determine the probable impact of data base in each area.

Benefits of Data Base

The potential benefits of data base were divided into two major categories: performance improvement, and cost avoidance and reduction. Performance improvement would take place in the following areas: marketing and sales, production, purchasing, finance and accounting, and general management.

In Marketing and Sales. The team's discussions with marketing people indicated that there was a need to improve customer service, a need for improved market-analysis capability, and a need for more accurate cost information concerning products, advertising, sales, and distribution.

The Apex sales manager routinely receives information on sales and gross margin by product line. This report is furnished on a monthly basis. However, the information is not sufficiently detailed or timely to support marketing decisions in today's environment. A marketing data base would link together information concerning customers, dealers, products, salesmen, and advertising and promotional expenditures. Once the data base is established, information such as the following could be obtained at frequent intervals or on demand:

- ☐ Sales breakdowns by product, salesman, and territory.
- ☐ Sales and advertising costs.

☐ Distribution costs.

☐ Credit sales and past due accounts by product, by territory, and by customer group.

☐ Customer service levels and number of delayed shipments.

With this information readily available, the marketing managers would be able to detect market shifts and sources of shipping delays, more effectively allocate advertising and promotion, and identify and train inefficient salespeople.

As a consequence, these managers feel that Apex's sales growth rate could be increased from its current 5% to 10% over a three-year period. That is, the growth rate would be 5% during the first year, 7.5% during the second year, and 10% during the third year.

But they are skeptical that a 10% compound growth rate, or at least a rate attributable to improved data handling, can be maintained indefinitely. Therefore, they make the assumption that during the fourth and fifth years sales would grow by the same dollar amount as during the third year. Exhibit 1 shows the result of the analysis based on these assumptions.

The survey team stresses that these benefits are by no means certain to be an automatic consequence of installing a DBMS. Apex still must contend with a competitive market, and the product still has to be made and sold.

However, if management fully understands and capitalizes on the improved information system, there will be an impetus to increased sales and production—even when routine bottlenecks to sales and delivery do turn up.

In Production, Apex's production manager now receives daily reports on production completed during the past 24-hour period. He also receives weekly

Exhibit 1.   Expected Increases in Sales and Profits

	Year				
	1	2	3	4	5
Forecasted sales (present system)	$52,500,000	$55,100,000	$57,900,000	$60,800,000	$63,800,000
Forecasted sales (marketing data base)	52,500,000	56,400,000	62,000,000	67,600,000	73,200,000
Increased sales	0	1,300,000	4,100,000	6,800,000	9,400,000
Profit improvement (8% of sales before tax)	0	104,000	328,000	544,000	752,000

reports on labor and material costs and a comparison of actual versus planned production. Marketing reports on finished goods inventory levels are furnished routinely by data processing.

He feels that there are two major information system needs at present: first, a net-change, MRP system to determine gross and net material requirements, maintain production priorities, and control manufacturing inventories. Second, an on-line, shop floor control system to monitor work flow, pinpoint yield problems, and settle day-to-day questions such as who worked on which lot, which operators were ahead or behind schedule and below standards.

Although a generalized data-base management system is not absolutely essential to either of these systems, it would make their implementation easier and provide more timely information concerning inventories, schedules, and costs. This would allow production management to discern trends and take corrective action much sooner than is currently possible.

The production manager and other production specialists estimate the following major benefits of a manufacturing data base:

☐ *Reduction of manufacturing lead times and late orders.* Increased production complexity and the volume of orders in recent years have led to increased lead times and a high incidence of late orders. To compensate for these factors, marketing and distribution have had to increase finished goods inventories to meet desired customer service levels. The production and marketing manager agree that aggregate finished goods inventories could be reduced from 5% to 10% as production schedules are brought under control. Applying the 5% figure to an average finished goods inventory of $5 million would result in an overall reduction of $250,000. Applying the standard corporate inventory carrying cost of 20% would result in an annual savings of $50,000.

☐ *Increased utilization of personnel.* Improved scheduling and shop floor control would eliminate much nonproductive time for direct employees and reduce the need for expediting and stock chasing. This would result in a net reduction of several direct and indirect laborers (to be met through attrition) over a period of five years.

☐ *Reduced manufacturing inventories.* A disciplined MRP system should lead to reduction in manufacturing inventories (raw materials and work-in-process) of from 20% to 35%. During the past year, manufacturing inventories at Apex Products have averaged about $3 million. Applying the 20% reduction and an inventory carrying cost of 20% would result in a prospective annual saving of $120,000.

Exhibit 2 is a summary of the forecasted benefits of improved information systems in the manufacturing area. A portion of these benefits would result from installing material requirements planning, and shop floor control

Exhibit 2. Savings in Production

	Year				
	1	2	3	4	5
Savings, finished goods inventory	0	$ 50,000	$ 50,000	$ 50,000	$ 50,000
Savings, wages	0	120,000	120,000	120,000	120,000
Savings, manufacturing inventory	0	75,000	75,000	110,000	125,000
Total savings	0	$245,000	$245,000	$280,000	$295,000
DBMS savings, 25%	0	61,250	61,250	70,000	73,000

systems, while the remaining portion would result from using the DBMS. To be conservative, the Apex team decided to assign ¼ of the total benefits to the data-base system.

In Purchasing. A purchasing data base would provide up-to-date information on vendor performance in terms of quality, cost, and lead time. The purchasing manager estimates that there would be three tangible benefits:

1   Reduction of inspection costs and of returning below-standard lots to suppliers, for an estimated annual savings of $10,000.
2   Reduction in time and effort spent expediting and following up purchase orders, with an estimated annual savings of $5,000.
3   Better vendor selection and ability to take advantage of quantity discounts, for a conservative estimated annual savings of $10,000.

The purchasing manager is also a strong supporter of the proposed material requirements planning system since it should provide much more accurate information on the timing and needed quantity of purchased items.

In Finance & Accounting. Financial accounting systems at Apex include accounts receivable, payable, and general ledger. These systems are operating satisfactorily and provide management with standard financial reports, including monthly income statements and balance sheets.

At the planning level, however, financial managers see several potential advantages to the data-base approach. A financial data base would simplify budget preparation and provide on-demand reporting of performance versus budget. On several occasions, the president has asked for projections of the financial condition of the company under various economic conditions. These projections have generally required a time-consuming, manual effort and have gradually forced the financial manager to add to his staff. He wants an on-line, source-and-application-of-funds budget which can be used to evaluate the financial impact of various decisions.

The financial manager estimates that he could reduce his annual operating budget by 10% (a savings of about $15,000) if these aids were available. In the long run, he thinks that a financial data base coupled with simulation programs could have a great impact on corporate financial decisions. However, these benefits would be difficult to evaluate, and he does not foresee a substantial impact during the next few years.

In General Management.   Possibly the greatest payoff could come in this area. The current standardized reporting system does not allow for *ad hoc* "what if" questions. Apex's president is very hesitant to ask for many specialized reports because they generally lead to an increased budget request by the data processing manager the next year. In addition, much of the desired information cannot be obtained in a timely fashion.

Recently, for example, the president wanted to evaluate an increase in the advertising budget in light of the company's pricing strategy and distribution channels. The data were available in the files but could not be retrieved in a useful fashion without considerable reprogramming. In a similar fashion, the finance manager wanted to evaluate current cash requirements by simulating several alternative strategies. Unfortunately, the model could not be developed in time to be useful because of the necessity for rearranging the data files. Although top managers at Apex can see the potential long-term benefits of data base in making decisions, they are reluctant to attempt to quantify these benefits.

Cost avoidance and reduction would take place in the following areas: analysts and programmers and seeking information.

Analysts & Programmers.   During the past few years, Apex has steadily increased its staff of system analysts and programmers. Without a common base, application programs depend entirely on input and output data requirements. Even relatively minor changes in data files or reports can lead to major reprogramming efforts. Apex has found that an increasing portion of analyst and programmer time is required to modify and maintain existing programs, leaving little time to develop new applications.

This trend is common for companies that use traditional system development. With a data base, however, a high degree of independence is possible between application programs and the data base. Control and maintenance of the data-base structure can be centralized in a data-base management function. As a result, there is far less need for system analysts and programmers to define files and to modify existing programs. The productivity of analysts and programmers often doubles, or even triples, once they become thoroughly familiar with the DBMS.

Apex's data processing manager projects the current growth in technical staff and estimates that with present EDP development procedures at least two more system analysts and two programmers will be needed during the next five years. With a data-base system, he feels that by hiring a data-base manager and assigning one of the present analysts to assist that person, he can get by with the present staff during this period.

Seeking Information.   Like most managers, those at Apex spend a significant portion of their work time seeking information. At the top management level, much of this information comes from outside sources such as business contacts and competitors. At the middle and lower management levels, managers seek information concerning customers, orders, inventory levels, and the like.

The DBMS survey team believes that as data bases are established, managers will have an increasing body of information on hand. This would tend to free their time for other things. However, since the study group is not sure just what the value of this freedom would be, it decides to use a conservative figure of $10,000 to represent the annual benefit to all managers of improved information availability.

A summary of the team's forecast of benefits to be derived from installing a data-base management system at Apex Products is shown in Exhibit 3.

Costs of Data Base

Having estimated the benefits of data base, the Apex survey team turned its attention to the costs. This proved to be somewhat easier, although it found a number of subjective factors had to be considered. The principal costs are software and conversion, hardware, and personnel.

Software Program.   The major software cost is the data-base management system itself. A number of commercial systems are available that could potentially satisfy the needs of Apex Products. If Apex decides to convert

Exhibit 3.   Benefit Forecast

	Year				
Type of Benefit	1	2	3	4	5
Performance improvement					
Marketing/sales	—	$104,000	$328,000	$544,000	$752,000
Production	—	61,250	61,250	70,000	73,750
Purchasing	—	25,000	25,000	25,000	25,000
Finance/accounting	—	15,000	15,000	15,000	15,000
General management	—	—	—	—	—
Other	—	—	—	—	—
Cost avoidance and reduction					
System analysts		25,000		30,000	—
Programmers	$20,000		20,000		
Seeking information	—	10,000	10,000	10,000	10,000
Other	—	—	—	—	—
Total benefits	$20,000	$240,250	$459,250	$694,000	$875,750

to a data base, a detailed evaluation will be made of each of these candidate systems.

For purposes of the study, the survey team has selected a system that is an implementation of the CODASYL recommendations and that is comparable in price and performance to others. (CODASYL is an acronym for Conference on Data Systems Languages. This organization standardized the COBOL language—which Apex uses—and is now developing a set of proposed standards for data-base languages and structures.) This system costs $100,000, a price that includes several facilities recommended by the database specialist, including a data dictionary and a user-oriented query language.

As Apex moves into on-line processing, a communications monitor will be required to interface with user terminals. The cost of this software module is about $15,000.

Apex plans to send several managers as well as data processing personnel to training programs conducted by the vendor. Some of these courses will be conducted in-plant, while others will be held at vendor locations. The costs for these programs are shown in Exhibit 4.

Conversion Effort. Moving from a conventional file-processing system to a data-base processing system normally entails a large-scale conversion ef-

Exhibit 4. Cost Forecast

Cost Element	Year				
	1	2	3	4	5
Software and conversion					
Data base management system	$100,000	—	—	—	—
Communications software	15,000	—	—	—	—
Training programs	10,000	$ 5,000	$ 5,000	—	—
Other software	—	—	—	—	—
Conversion costs	20,000	20,000	25,000	$ 25,000	$ 25,000
Hardware					
Central memory	75,000	—	—	50,000	—
Central processing unit	150,000	—	—	—	—
Storage devices	60,000	40,000	—	—	—
Terminals	15,000	15,000			
Other hardware	—	—	—	—	—
Personnel					
Data base administration	75,000	80,000	80,000	85,000	100,000
Information analysis	—	—	—	—	—
Consultants	5,000	—	—	—	—
Other personnel	—	—	—	—	—
Total costs	$525,000	$160,000	$110,000	$160,000	$125,000

fort. Data must be filed in a new format and application programs must be modified.

Management at Apex Products does not visualize a large-scale conversion effort. For one thing, many of the application programs under data base will be new. These include programs for on-line sales order processing and for the manufacturing applications. For another, it is believed that the present customer file can be easily restructured. Also, Apex intends to seek a vendor who will provide software conversion aids to simplify the process. The survey team has assigned the equivalent of one full-time analyst to cover the cost of the conversion effort.

Hardware Demand. The present hardware configuration will have to be upgraded to support the new demands. Although the exact needs will not be known until an actual system is selected, the survey team projects three needs:

☐ *Upgrading the central processing unit and adding additional central memory.* Considering the present workloads as well as the resources required by the new system, the team recommends that an additional 256,000 bytes of main memory be added, which will result in a doubling of present capacity to 512,000 bytes. To accommodate this change, the team recommends that the central processing unit be upgraded. The cost of the additional memory will be $75,000, while the upgrading will cost about $150,000. The team allows an additional $50,000 for add-on-memory for the fourth year. These hardware additions, the data processing manager points out, will probably be necessary during the next two or three years, whether or not a new system is acquired. However, the survey team uses the conservative approach of assigning their costs to the data-base installations.

☐ *Additional mass storage capacity.* Present disk storage capacity is fully utilized. An additional disk storage unit and storage control unit will be needed as soon as the new system is installed. The cost of these units will be about $60,000. In addition, another disk storage unit ($40,000) will be needed in the second year, primarily for the manufacturing data base.

☐ *Additional visual display terminals.* Apex uses only a limited number of terminals in its present batch-oriented environment. However, the company has definite plans to install an on-line system for order entry in the near future. The company has estimated that from six to eight terminals will be required for this purpose. However, the on-line system will be installed whether or not the company uses a DBMS, so the cost of these terminals is not charged to data base.

In the course of interviewing managers concerning the new system, the Apex survey team has preached the advantages of on-demand availability of information, especially through the use of a user-oriented query language.

However, the DBMS specialist did inject a note of caution: the type of information available will depend on the design, and guidelines concerning the use of terminals will have to be established to safeguard information and to prevent unreasonable demands on computer resources.

Nevertheless, several of the managers have expressed an interest in having terminals available in their offices. Thus the team has factored in six display terminals over the first two years of the project. The cost of each terminal (including direct-line connection costs) is estimated at $5,000.

Personnel Staffing.   The principal addition to personnel costs under the DBMS would be for the data-base manager. The team believes that the company should hire a manager with proven experience rather than train an individual from within the company. One of the present system analysts would become a full-time assistant to the manager, and a small clerical staff would also be needed. Total estimated costs for staffing the function range from $75,000 in the first year to $100,000 by the fifth year.

The team also recommends that Apex create a new "information analyst" position for each functional area. Each of these people should be well qualified in one or more functional areas such as marketing and finance and should also have a thorough understanding of the data base system and its use. Each would serve as liaison between data processing and functional managers, helping to define information requirements, formulate information requests, and the like. Rather than hire new people for this position, Apex plans to select an existing employee for training from each functional area.

As a final element of personnel cost, the survey team allocated $5,000 for outside assistance and advice during the first year of the data base project. The forecast of costs for the new system is shown in Exhibit 4.

Summary of Benefits & Costs

Exhibit 5 summarizes the benefits and costs for the proposed data base implementation at Apex Products.

Although estimates will of course differ from one company to another, the following general conclusions apply:

Exhibit 5.   Summary of Benefits and Costs

	Year				
	1	2	3	4	5
Total benefits	$ 20,000	$240,250	$459,250	$ 694,000	$ 375,750
Cumulative benefits	20,000	260,250	719,500	1,413,500	2,289,250
Total costs	$525,000	$160,000	$110,000	$ 60,000	$ 25,000
Cumulative costs	525,000	685,000	795,000	955,000	1,080,000

☐ *Installing a data-base system is a major undertaking, requiring a substantial investment of resources.* At Apex, the projected cost over a five-year period is about $1 million.

☐ *The investment does not pay for itself immediately.* The reason for this is that major expenditures occur at the outset while significant benefits do not occur until later. At Apex cumulative benefits are predicted to equal cumulative costs after three years. In many companies the payback period might be longer.

☐ *The potential return on investment is large.* In the Apex case, the prospective internal rate of return over the five-year period exceeds 50%.

In Conclusion

The analysis of benefits and costs can provide a firm foundation for companies to move into the data-base era. Obviously this analysis is just the beginning of a long process which requires the major commitment of all managers. The next steps are to select a well-qualified data-base manager and then to develop a set of detailed requirements for the new system. Beyond that lie the design and implementation of data bases that will support the hoped-for benefits.

One major advantage of such a study is the involvement of key managers. The benefits can be estimated by the managers themselves rather than the study team.

Another major advantage of this kind of analysis is the development of a preliminary set of priorities for data-base development. For instance, Apex's management might give priority to the design and implementation of a marketing data base because of its enormous potential. At the same time, a company can also evaluate critical subsystems such as, in Apex's case, the material requirements planning system, and begin to lay the foundations for their applications.

Notes

1. "Users Wish They Had Taken More Time Picking DBMS" *Computerworld,* October 25, 1976, p. 17.

2. James Martin, *Principles of Data Base Management* (Englewood Cliffs, N.J.: Prentice-Hall, Inc., 1976).

3. See Jeffrey G. Miller and Linda G. Sprague, "Behind the Growth in Material Requirements Planning," *HBR,* September–October 1975, p. 83.

PART THREE

KEEPING CONTROL

AN OVERVIEW

As computer budgets have grown to become a significant financial consideration in all but the smallest companies, managers have begun to cast about for ways to bring expenses under control and to ensure that the company is receiving value for its money. The authors in this section look at this problem from differing perspectives. Warren McFarlan leads off by suggesting that in most companies data processing is a characteristically "messy" department that hasn't received the attention from top management that other departments have benefitted from. With wider distribution of computers, this problem is likely to worsen, unless top management takes firm measures. Among the criteria McFarlan suggests for use in choosing among prospective projects are the degree of risk the company bears in the event of the project's failure and the amount of experience the company has with the technology involved in a given project.

In Paul Strassmann's view of cost control, failure to consider all the expenses associated with handling of data is the chief shortcoming of most company's efforts to contain information-processing costs. With this focus on the entire bureaucracy of information suppliers and handlers in the organization, the manager can properly identify costs and establish standards for them. In Strassmann's experience, based on the practice at the Xerox Corporation, the proper way to manage information-processing functions is as accountability centers, in effect as little businesses, buying and selling goods and services as they are needed. Further, principles of competitive pricing can be applied in the adoption of new technology in the various centers.

Surprisingly, Strassmann recommends that companies deemphasize technology by concentrating their efforts and investments in methods, procedures, and training. The aim is to make versatile generalists out of narrow specialists by rearranging the accountability for work functions. In this way job satisfaction is increased and more efficient use is made of technical people since they are freed to move up to administrative systems positions. In this "rebalancing of talent," money formerly spent on computer problems can go for such uses as standardizing technologies, automating programming, and improving quality control, among others.

Richard Nolan takes up where Paul Strassman leaves off in the discussion of how to control costs by showing why efforts to make users accountable for the information services they use have not been a resounding success. Since a large part of the difficulty arises from failure in communication between data processing and users, a primary objective must be to make managers aware of and responsible for the economic costs of the services they use. Nolan agrees with Strassman that the DP department should neither design nor implement the management control and charge-out strategy. They feel that the greatest degree of control results when such responsibilities are moved organizationally as close as possible to the ultimate user, though Nolan emphasizes the role of the high-level steering committee in ratifying the users' strategy.

In his "Penny-Wise Approach to Data Processing," Martin Buss looks at cost control from again another perspective. He points out that top executives' ignorance or disregard of their companies' information systems often leads them to install rigid budget controls. But this can have disastrous consequences in a company that depends heavily on its computer systems. When software becomes outdated because of inadequate funds to replace it, some businesses could face disaster. Buss tells executives who may have kept a too-heavy hand on the purse strings how they can mend their ways as well as their tattered software.

In another piece, Buss deals with an area that, although it involves costs more indirectly, contributes directly to the overall effectiveness of information systems: the setting of project priorities. Buss says, in fact, that so-called tangible, or financial, benefits often wrongly determine the priority of project funding. Other factors, such as certain intangible benefits, business objectives, and technical implications, must also be considered. He shows senior managers how to proceed step by step through the evaluation process.

Another kind of guide is provided by Brandt Allen in his irreverent approach to computer crime, "Embezzler's Guide to the Computer." In this detailed study of opportunities for unearned reward, he shows where a company's weak spots are generally found. He starts with disbursements fraud, in which a voucher is the next best thing to money, and gives five steps to success in this most promising type of theft from computer-based operations. Going next to inventories, he points out that controls here are ordinarily lax, thus making them an easy mark for the potential thief. Manipulation of shipments, sales and billing procedures offer further scope for the fertile, if dishonest, mind. Add to the list payroll fraud, theft from pension benefits and annuities, and manipulation of accounts receivable, and you have some of the best ways of making money by computer. Of course, turned around, Allen's schemes become the company's manual of protection against computer crime, but his approach is informative—and amusing—either way.

15

Personal Privacy Versus the Corporate Computer

ROBERT C. GOLDSTEIN and RICHARD L. NOLAN

Americans have long abhorred the specter of a faceless, bureaucratic Big Brother. As computerized personal data systems have grown more and more sophisticated, many people have become concerned about the threat these systems pose to the privacy of individual data subjects. Recently some regulations were passed to counter that threat, and, the authors say, the passage of laws to eliminate it throughout the country is imminent. But the cost of complying with them will be high. After looking at the probable shape of these laws, the authors discuss what the laws' impact will be on five actual personal data systems—consumer credit, health, personnel, insurance, and law enforcement. Finally, they suggest that organizations using or contemplating the use of such systems take four steps in adjusting to the new environment.

A senior executive of one of the country's largest retail chains recently told us that his company is seriously considering closing down its credit authorization department. Because of what it would cost to comply with proposed laws, not to mention existing regulations, ensuring that computerized information about people will not be handled or used in such a way as to invade their privacy, an organization even as large as his will no longer be able to afford to make its own credit checks, he said. And so he is planning to contract with a national consumer credit company to perform this function for his chain.

When we talked with the general manager of a major consumer credit company, however, he told us that these regulations could drive *his* company entirely out of business.

While both of these executives are worried about how computer privacy regulations will affect the field of consumer credit, their impact extends far beyond that field to all organizations that use data systems containing personal information. These regulations will affect government organizations at every level, as well as those in the health or insurance fields. In fact, since virtually every organization collects and uses personal information about its own employees, the impact of proposed privacy regulations will be sweeping indeed.

Concern over the privacy invasion potential of computerized data banks is picking up momentum reminiscent of the environmental protection activities of a few years ago. A sampling of recent headlines indicates current governmental thinking about this problem:

- ☐ "Senator Ervin charges 858 data banks show regulation a must"
- ☐ "Ford council pushes federal regulation, takes 14 privacy initiatives"
- ☐ "Right-to-privacy bill backed at Senate hearing"

Several states and foreign countries have already enacted privacy laws, and about 100 privacy bills are currently pending before the U.S. Congress and the various state legislatures. We can now safely predict that within the next year or two privacy will affect every organization that has computerized data about people, for either the federal government will act to impose uniform laws throughout the country or the states will take action on their own. If the federal government does not win this race, another level of complexity will be added to the already difficult process of developing and maintaining useful computer-based systems. With the possibility of having to comply with different requirements in every state, it is no wonder that many forward-looking executives like the two mentioned are worried.

In this article, we shall first look at what the responsibilities of organizations and the rights of data subjects are or no doubt will be under privacy regulations. Then, using a computer model, we shall examine what it will cost various kinds of organizations operating some actual systems to comply with the regulations. Lastly, we offer four steps to take in planning for the new environment.

Privacy and Power

Privacy proposals recently passed and others currently under consideration go far beyond any strict definition of privacy. For example, giving someone the right to restrict the use of information about himself or herself falls within a limited notion of privacy. But the right to examine information about oneself and add to it if it is felt to be incomplete or inaccurate has little to do with privacy per se. It is a direct effort to increase the power of individuals in their dealings with large organizations, which often seem remote, domineering, and unconcerned about individuals.

Appendix A gives several excerpts from two regulations already on the books in Minnesota and California. Generally, privacy proposals cover three main categories: controls on operating procedures, access rights of data subjects, and usage control by data subjects.

☐ *Controls on operating procedures.* An organization using a personal data system must (1) take appropriate precautions against natural hazards and other threats to the system and its data, (2) publish descriptions of it periodically in a medium likely to be seen by most of its subjects, (3) establish procedures for responding to inquiries from individuals about their records and for settling complaints about their accuracy, and (4) keep a log of all uses of each person's record.

☐ *Access rights of data subjects.* A person may (1) examine his own record, (2) request the correction of any information in it that he believes to be erroneous, and (3) append a statement to the record if the error is not corrected to his satisfaction.

☐ *Usage control by data subjects.* At the time information is collected from someone, he must be told what it will be used for and given the opportunity to refuse to provide it. The subject's permission must again be sought for any new use of the data not covered by his original consent.

One consequence of granting veto power to data subjects is that companies that have sold their mailing lists in the past will no longer be able to do so without the consent of the subjects. Hence these lists may no longer be available to those who have used them as prime sources of sales prospects. Another consequence is that such veto power partially offsets the efficiency gained through data-base technology, which essentially unlocks data from a specific application for wider use.

Although these rights substantially increase the cost of using personal data, everyone will probably benefit from the increased accuracy that should result from giving data subjects access to their records.

Model of Systems

To determine what it will cost an organization operating a personal data system to comply with privacy regulations, one of us constructed a computer model to analyze their impact on some systems already in use.[1]

The model calculates costs in six categories—programming, computer processing, information storage, data communications, administration, and capital equipment—and analyzes both those costs incurred at the time of conversion to the regulated environment and those associated with the ongoing operation of the system in that environment.

The ruled insert on page 68 gives descriptions of five of the systems analyzed. Exhibit 1 shows some of their characteristics, along with what their conversion and annual operating costs to comply with privacy regulations will be. Although some interesting comparisons can be drawn from

Exhibit 1. The Cost of Privacy

	System 1 Medical	System 2 Insurance	System 3 Personnel	System 4 Credit	System 5 Law enforcement
System characteristics					
Number of subjects (in thousands)	1,000	3,300	10	35,000	31
Number of characters in data base (in thousands)	3,500,000	3,600,000	20,00	3,500,000	19,000
Number of users	50	60,000	45	500,000	5,000
Transaction volume per year (in thousands)	2,500	12,000	50	10,000	55
Mode	Batch	On-line	On-line	On-line	On-line
Data-management package	No	Yes	Yes	No	Yes
Development cost (in thousands)	$726	$5,000	$200	$800	$3,000
Annual operating cost before converting to comply with privacy regulations (in thousands)	$4,000	$13,000	$340	$14,000	$2,000
Privacy conversion and annual costs					
Privacy conversion cost (in thousands)	$543	$573	$142	$1,416	$348
Annual privacy cost (in thousands)	$1,797	$1,882	$40	$20,453	$216
Annual privacy cost per subject	$1.80	$0.57	$4.00	$0.58	$6.97
Annual privacy cost per transaction	$0.72	$0.15	$0.80	$2.05	$3.93
Annual privacy cost as percent of annual operating cost	45%	15%	12%	146%	11%
Comparison of record-existence notifications with record-existence inquiries					
Cost per record-existence notification	$0.24	$0.09	$0.10	$0.20	$0.48
Cost per record-existence inquiry	$2.76	$1.27	[b]	$1.40	[b]
Inquiry/notification break-even point[a]	9%	7%	[b]	14%	[b]

[a]If more than this percentage of data subjects would be expected to inquire about their records in a given year, it would be cheaper just to notify all subjects.

[b]The precision of the model and data do not permit the determination of inquiry costs for System 3 because of its small size. Inquiry costs cannot be computed for System 5 because of the nature of this system. Without an inquiry cost, it is impossible to compute break-even points for these two systems.

this data, it is important to bear in mind the different uses of each system as well as the differences in number of subjects, record size, and transaction volume.

Notification vs. Inquiry Response

The exhibit shows, for each system, the cost of notifications and inquiries for making data subjects aware of their records. Some early legislative proposals required that organizations notify each data subject at least once a year. Because notification seemed prohibitively expensive even without detailed analysis, most later proposals specify that system operators need not notify subjects of their records but must stand ready to respond to subjects' inquiries about them.

Even though it costs more to process a single inquiry than to issue one notification as part of a large batch, the former alternative is generally believed to be cheaper because it is assumed that relatively few individuals will initiate such inquiries. The exhibit shows the fraction of subjects who would have to inquire about their records before it would be cheaper to simply notify all of them.

This break-even point may seem relatively low for all of the systems; however, evidence currently available to the consumer credit company, for example, suggests that the actual number of inquiries it can expect to receive will be even lower—in the range of 1% to 3%. Thus, if these estimates are reliable, the model's break-even analysis supports the belief that inquiry processing will be cheaper than mass notification.

Weighing the Costs

Exhibit 1 clearly shows that the effect of privacy laws on a personal data system will depend on what it is used for. In discussing these effects, we shall divide the systems into three general classes of use—internal, financial, and governmental. In our study, the respective examples for each of these systems were a personnel file, a retail credit information clearinghouse, and the automobile registration and license records maintained by a state police department.

Impact on Internal Systems

Systems used only within a company offer excellent opportunities for unilateral action on the privacy front. A company can gain significant experience while working under regulatory conditions without having to contend with external cooperation or actual regulations. At the same time, it can get the necessary mechanisms and procedures in place for the time when they will be required.

Such action can also serve as a positive demonstration of the organization's social responsibility in protecting the privacy of its employees. Because all of the data subjects of a personnel system are in one place, or in a relatively small number of places, many of the difficulties of implementing the privacy regulations in a more complex environment do not exist, and consequently costs are lower.

For example, the conversion cost of the one personnel system we studied (*System 3*) is $142,000, and its annual incremental operating cost is $40,000. These figures are far lower than those for any other systems in the study. In addition, securing the computer installation, a step which should probably be taken regardless of privacy regulations, accounts for slightly more than 80% of the conversion costs. The existence of a free intracompany mail system (free insofar as its marginal cost is concerned) is a major factor in keeping the privacy costs low for an internal system since one of the highest compliance costs is associated with mailing

Rights in Conflict.   Two difficulties arise from the provision specifying that data subjects may examine their own records, because each record usually includes evaluations of the employee by present and past supervisors. First, to allow an employee to see information that was assumed would be kept from him violates the privacy of those who provided it. Second, once a new policy has been established, anyone asked to provide an evaluation will know that it will be available to the subject. Thus privacy rights of the evaluator will not be affected, but he is not likely to be as candid as he would be otherwise.

So, on the one hand, this policy could result in bland evaluations that would be virtually useless for personnel planning purposes. On the other hand, of course, it could help eliminate unfavorable reports based strictly on personal dislike. Since such reports could have a significant effect on the subject's career, this protection is rather important. While this is a tough trade-off, the benefit of airing constructive criticism should, in addition to protecting all concerned, more than outweigh the lost benefits of "confidential" information.

Impact on Financial Systems

Privacy regulations will hit financial information systems even harder than personnel systems. Financial information contains some of the most sensitive and most widely circulated data about people. Almost every family has bank accounts of various types, credit cards, charge accounts, mortgages, or other loans. In fact, the statement that you have to give Americans "credit" for their standard of living is more truth than jest. The negotiation of credit requires a person to supply information about his personal financial condition, and in many cases this is supplemented by reports from other creditors or investigative agencies. A complex but nevertheless workable credit information network underlies this essential economic activity.

The data in Exhibit 1 show how severe a strain compliance will place on one consumer credit company. The actual amounts of both the conversion and the annual privacy costs ($1.4 million and $20 million, respectively) are far higher for its system (*System 4*) than for any of the others. This is primarily because of its greater number of data subjects. Thus, while physical security is the dominant cost for personnel systems, dealing with people (obtaining consent, making notifications, and processing inquiries) is the dominant cost for credit systems.

More specifically, the regulatory variables used in this study indicate that each credit transaction will cost $2.05 more than a current transaction, which costs less than $1.50.

Who Will Pay?   In fact, because credit is so central to the American economy, these numbers raise an important question: Who should bear the cost of protecting the privacy of credit records? The credit company executive we interviewed feels that he cannot add $2.00 to his price for a credit check without losing a major share of his business. It is his belief, at least, that retail stores, banks, and loan companies—his major customers—will not pay that additional price for a credit report.

But Exhibit 1 also shows that the increased cost per data subject is $0.48 per year. This does not seem to be an unreasonable amount for people to pay to protect their records, but, of course, collecting it from them would probably be a very complicated and expensive business in its own right.

Unilateral Action Foolish.   The provisions included under the general heading of privacy regulations increase the power of individuals in dealing with large organizations. As such, these provisions probably deserve the support of most people as individuals. However, the appropriate response for the affected organizations is not a simple matter for corporate executives. It would be foolish for a bank or a credit company to adopt the proposals unilaterally.

In the first place, the costs involved would be substantially greater because of the organization's relatively indirect relationship with data subjects. More important, however, is the fact that unilateral action in this area is simply uncalled for because the major market for credit information is an intercompany one. Unless all involved follow the same set of rules, the protection of privacy will be minimal, and so there is no reason for a single company to handicap itself by incurring the associated costs before its competitors do.

Impact on Government Systems.   It is likely that personal information systems within the government will be subject to privacy regulation before those in the private sector. There are two reasons for this. First, members of both the legislative and the executive branches have expressed the view that governmental systems are a more appropriate target for such regulation. Enforcement is probably easier within the government, as well. Second, the government affects virtually everyone, so moving first in the public sector makes sense.

A great deal of highly personal data is collected by government. The story headlining the existence of 858 data banks was about a survey that covered only the federal government. The systems included contain nearly one billion records on individuals, and these numbers understate the actual situation since several government agencies declined to cooperate fully in the survey.

As a result of the Census and Internal Revenue acts, the personal data banks of the federal government include information on nearly every citizen. In addition, anyone who has ever served in the armed forces is the subject of extensive records relating to his or her service and status as a veteran. All beneficiaries of government-supported health programs have medical information on file, and if a national health insurance for all citizens is established, this particularly sensitive information will be collected about everyone. Information about an individual's brushes with the criminal justice system, another very sensitive type of data, is maintained by government, much of it by the federal government through the National Crime Information Center and the National Criminal History System.

Transaction Costs High.   The government system in this study (*System 5*), an automobile registration and license file used by a state police department, shows some particularly interesting results. The annual privacy cost for this system, while relatively low overall ($216,000), is the highest of all the systems studied when prorated to the individual data subject ($6.97) or to each transaction ($3.93). These results occur because this system requires a relatively large complex of equipment to handle a rather small data base and to process a very small number of transactions. In fact, privacy considerations aside, it costs more than $36 each time a state police officer picks up his microphone and asks for a license check.

While in a commercial enterprise a transaction cost of this magnitude and the concomitant large privacy cost would probably be considered unacceptable, it is characteristic of many governmental systems to consider the benefits so important that cost becomes a relatively minor factor. In fact, of all the data-processing executives interviewed in the five organizations we studied, the executives associated with the two governmental systems were the least concerned about the potential cost of privacy regulations. "If Congress imposes the regulations, then Congress will have to put up the money to implement them"—that seemed to be their general attitude.

Corporate Policy Guidelines

In the United States, we are at a crucial point in developing and institutionalizing the concept of personal privacy. The necessary momentum appears to have been achieved, and it seems likely that some sort of federal legislation will be adopted within a year. It is definitely time for those with personal data systems to begin planning for the new environment. What exactly should be done? At least four steps that organizations should take are to:

1. *Prepare a "privacy impact statement."* A statement analyzing the potential privacy implications should be made a part of all proposals for new or expanded systems. The three categories of privacy proposals we mentioned earlier provide a structure for this analysis: (a) controls on operating practices, (b) access rights of data subjects, and (c) usage control by data subjects. Such a statement should cover not only the system's impact on individuals' privacy but also the effect of privacy regulations on the system.

2. *Construct a comprehensive privacy plan.* The input for planning is the privacy impact statement, which specifies what has to be accomplished. For new systems, the purpose of the plan is to make sure that the necessary privacy controls are integrated into the design of the system at the very beginning. This procedure will not only be cheaper than grafting controls on later, but it will also ensure that the company will take no steps that are incompatible with privacy objectives. For existing systems, the plan should cover needed changes in programs, equipment, and procedures. Where existing practices will become illegal or excessively expensive, alternatives should be devised.

3. *Train employees who handle personal information.* The next step in preparing for the privacy regulations is to begin a program of making employees who handle personal data aware of the importance of protecting privacy and the specific policies and procedures to be followed.

4. *Make privacy part of social responsibility programs.* Finally, data subjects should be kept informed about whatever an organization plans to do on the privacy front without regulatory pressures or in addition to them. Informing subjects will demonstrate a company's awareness and concern for the privacy of its data subjects and may also be of significant help later in obtaining data and the authorization to use it.

Problems to Anticipate. Taking these steps may reveal that some privacy restrictions will render some systems or portions of them entirely infeasible or unjustifiably expensive, especially those restrictions requiring that all proposed uses of personal data be authorized by the subjects in advance. The need to go back to data subjects to obtain permission for a new use of data already collected may make it almost impossible to expand the usefulness of a system. Organizations should consider this constraint both in deciding whether to go ahead with a new project and in creating initial master plans so that the need for further permission will be minimized.

Capabilities Expanded. The acquisition of new programs and data-processing equipment usually involves fairly long lead times. This may be particularly true in meeting privacy objectives since some capabilities that will be needed to do so are not widely available yet. For example, much of the effectiveness of many of the regulations depends on being able to accurately and reliably identify the source of an inquiry. On-line computer systems, especially, will require additional hardware and perhaps operating software. Suppliers should begin now to develop products to meet these new needs.

Another inadequacy of most systems currently in use is in controlling access to data-bank records. Because the law will require permission from the subject for each use, it will no longer be valid to assume that every record in a system can be used for all purposes. In particular, it will be necessary to keep permission information on each person's record and to have computer systems that can interpret and enforce the restrictions implied by that information.

This problem, like the user identification one, is not technically too difficult to deal with. Current systems handle both problems in ways that will surely be satisfactory. However, for the most part, these are specialized military or research systems. The relevant capabilities have not been included in normal commercial systems up to now because there has been little demand for them.

Data-Management Packages Useful.   Our research supports the use of data-base technology in responding to privacy regulations. Of the five systems we have described, the three commercial data-management systems have significantly lower programming costs than the two that do not use them. Much of the specialized-access control programming can be done in a data-management system, and using a standardized version will make it easier to verify implementation of required controls.

Moreover, the law will surely require organizations to provide data to an enforcement agency. Those using data-base technology should find it easier and cheaper to respond, just as did the oil companies who reported with the aid of a data-management package during the oil crisis in 1973.

For virtually all organizations, the new regulations imply the need to carefully reconsider the technical and economic feasibility of existing and proposed applications. It is not too early to begin planning to reduce the cost and the adverse impact that may result from this legislation.

Notes

1.   Robert C. Goldstein, *The Cost of Privacy*, Harvard Business School doctoral dissertation, 1974 (Boston: Honeywell Information Systems, Inc., 1974.)

Appendix A

Examples of Privacy Regulations
Minnesota Privacy Act, Chapter 479, Section 4

Paragraph E
Upon request to a responsible authority, an individual shall be informed whether he is the subject of stored data and if so, and upon his additional request, shall be informed of the content and meaning of the data recorded about him or shown the data without any charge to him.

Paragraph F
An individual shall have the right to contest the accuracy or completeness of data about him.. . . The responsible authority shall within 30 days correct the data if the data is found to be inaccurate or incomplete and attempt to notify past recipients of the inaccurate or incomplete data, or notify the individual of disagreement.. . . Data in dispute shall not be disclosed except under conditions of demonstrated need and then only if the individual's statement of disagreement is included with the disclosed data.

The California Fair Information Practice Act of 1974

Chapter Three:
Rights of Data Subjects

Every governmental body maintaining an automated personal data system in California shall do each of the following:

Item B
Inform in writing an individual, upon his request and proper identification, whether he is the subject of data in the system, and if so, make such data fully available to the individual in a form comprehensible to him.

Item E
Maintain procedures that allow an individual who is the subject of data in the system to contest their accuracy, completeness, pertinence, and timeliness.

Item F
If the accuracy, completeness, pertinence, or timeliness of personal data is disputed, and such dispute is directly conveyed to the governmental body maintaining the personal data, the governmental body shall reinvestigate and record the current status of that personal data.. . . If the governmental body maintaining the system and the data subject fail to resolve their dispute after

reinvestigation of the data, the dispute may be resolved one of three ways to be elected by the governmental body maintaining the system:

1   The data subject may file [a complaint with] the governmental body maintaining the system, [that is,] a brief statement setting forth his views on the dispute.. . . Whenever a statement of dispute is filled, the governmental body maintaining the system shall, in any subsequent disclosure or dissemination of the disputed data, clearly note that it is disputed by the data subject and provide with the data either a copy of his statement or a clear and accurate summary thereof.
2   The parties to the dispute may agree to binding arbitration of the dispute.
3   The data subject may seek injunctive relief ordering the governmental body maintaining the data to amend, correct, or purge the disputed data.

Appendix B

Description of Personal Data Systems Studied

System 1 processes records of the treatments given one million people at a large network of hospitals. In regular weekly runs, it adds new records to the master file and prepares a large variety of reports. The hospitals use this system almost exclusively for management control and planning purposes. Virtually all its output is in the form of aggregated statistical reports. Only on very rare occasions is information about a single individual retrieved.

System 2 is an on-line system operated by a large casualty insurance company. Its data base covers 3.3 million policyholders and can be queried interactively from any of the company's branch offices around the country. The records may contain financial, legal, medical, or other descriptive information on an individual.

System 3 is an on-line, data-base personnel system for an organization with about 10,000 employees. The company can handle inquiries about any employee's record interactively. Although, like many other companies, it plans to eventually add a skills inventory and other evaluative records to its file, the company is currently using the system only for routine payroll and employee-benefit activities.

Although System 3 is the smallest one in the study, it is one of the most interesting because nearly every organization has one like it. Most of these systems got their start with the payroll function. Over the years, they have been added to, patched up, and modified to meet governmental reporting requirements, provide information for the collective bargaining process, and otherwise facilitate management of the organization's human resources. Expanding personnel systems to serve these additional functions has resulted in the addition of liberal amounts of personal information covering such topics as performance reviews, medical histories, and grievances filed.

System 4 processes information for one of the largest consumer credit companies in the country. This company acts as a clearinghouse for retail credit information, collected from subscribers and stored in an on-line system where any subscriber can obtain a virtually instantaneous credit report on any individual in the data bank. Subscribers can either phone terminal operators, who interrogate the data base and report back verbally, or interrogate the data base directly themselves from small terminals in their own stores.

System 5 is an on-line, real-time system operated by a state police organization with a file of about 30,000 records—some being outstanding warrants on individuals and others stolen car reports. This system is set up in such a way that a state police officer can report a license number to his dispatcher and have it checked in a few seconds against registration and license files as well as against a "wanted and warrants" file. Some police vehicles in the state have even been equipped with mobile keyboard printers so that officers can directly query the files themselves.

16
Embezzler's Guide to the Computer

BRANDT ALLEN

Do not let it bother you that the only reports of embezzlement schemes you have heard about have ended in the thieves being caught. Do not be discouraged by the fact that the takes reported in the press are so small. The really big, successful embezzlement schemes are still out there working, and working well. Most of the people who have been caught owe their capture not to the lack of their computer skills but to bad luck and mismanagement. You can be smarter. The author of this quick guide provides you with a rich sampling of embezzlement schemes that will work, and does a good job of allaying some old fears about the difficulties of taking your company for a ride. His message is to take heart, learn from others' mistakes, and be clever.

With the assistance of an on-line computer system, a young graduate student stole about a million dollars' worth of inventory from a large utility in California. The student acquired knowledge of the system by posing as a magazine interviewer, retrieving computer manuals from wastebaskets, and phoning employees. Eventually he was able to accumulate enough data, including system instructions and practices, ordering and operating instructions, catalogs, passwords, and the like to gain access to the equipment order system.

With his knowledge of company procedures and his access to the on-line system used for part of the inventory control system, the student was able to place orders for equipment to the utility's central supply division. The equipment would then be shipped to various designated warehouses,

Author's Note. I wish to acknowledge the painstaking and creative contributions made by my research assistant, L. Price Blackford, to the research and drafting of this article.

278

where, at early hours in the morning, in a disguised truck, he would pick it up, along with the bill of lading. He spread his thefts over a number of field locations so that no single loss would arouse suspicion, and sold the equipment through a company he had formed.

> *By entering fraudulent data into the bank's computer from a remote terminal in his branch office, a chief teller of a major New York savings bank stole a million and a half dollars from hundreds of accounts. When quarterly interest was due, he would simply either redeposit some of the money or indicate that it had been redeposited. The manual auditing and the computer controls failed to show any fraudulent manipulation. The teller was not detected until a police raid on a gambling operation revealed that he was betting up to $30,000 a day on professional sports. Even then the teller had to explain his manipulations to the bank executives for them to fully understand what he had done.*

As you can see from these examples, embezzlement may be the best game in town; it certainly beats the market for yield and return, and it is probably less risky. In fact, it is estimated that embezzlers take two to three billion dollars a year in the United States. (Since many if not most embezzlers never go public, only a sixth of the winnings and related incidents ever get reported in the press.) If embezzlers are detected, their penalties are almost always small. They rarely go to jail. The young graduate student in California, for instance, spent less than a year in detention.

As businesses and other organizations have automated more and more of their accounting and record keeping, embezzlers have found themselves faced with the problems of mastering and profiting from the new technology. Fortunately, the prognosis is good. Virtually all of the traditional peculation opportunities of the past may be safely run through the computer, and a host of exciting new schemes is possible as well.

To sweeten the pot, computer technology tends to confound auditors and managers to the extent that they are rarely in a position to detect or prevent computer-based embezzlement. For example, of the more than 50 case examples I have studied, fewer than half were first detected by auditors or internal controls.[1] A great many of these cases involved very simple schemes that could have continued to be successful for much longer, or for indefinite periods of time, had the perpetrator been a little more clever.

This guide is written both for the accomplished embezzler who wishes to polish his skills with computer technology and for the novice who correctly sees this field as a ripe new opportunity. The schemes most likely to be successful will be discussed, along with explanations of just how the computer must be manipulated. Examples of once successful but recently detected cases will be presented. Finally, a list of common misconceptions and important truths about computer fraud will be outlined. This is important since you, a would-be embezzler, may often profit from others' misconceptions.

The Best-Laid Plans

To steal from an organization, it does not really matter what industry you are in or whether you work for a profit-oriented, governmental, or not-for-profit group. It does help, however, if you are in a position of responsibility and are a "trusted" employee—the greater your responsibility, the better. Knowledge of basic accounting, record keeping, and financial statements is also necessary, though the same is not so of the computer. You are in the ideal position of not needing to know a lot about computer technology in order to beat it. The auditors and management must, however, know a great deal in order to catch you at it. The best embezzlement schemes have to be well executed to work, but the ideas are simple.

Disbursements Fraud: 'A Voucher Is the Next Best Thing to Money'

Without a doubt, the best place to start is with the fraudulent disbursements game. This fraud has historically accounted for more embezzlement losses than all others. The approach is actually quite simple: your company, bank, or organization is fooled into paying for goods and services that it did not receive or did not receive in full measure. Payment is made to your bogus company. Arranging to cash checks issued to your company is certainly no problem; fooling your employer into issuing those checks is a bit tougher. Here are five things to remember when you start:

1.   Carefully examine the accounting and record-keeping systems of your company. This can be done by personal inspection, unobtrusive questioning, and often simply by reading policies and procedures manuals or computer system documentation.

2.   Study the purchasing function. Most organizations use a "purchase order" or similar document to order merchandise. Determine: who has access to blank forms; who is authorized to approve them; where copies are stored once the order is prepared and sent (in companies with advanced computer systems, the "image" of the purchase order is kept in the computer and may be read by authorized personnel in various departments; in this case there may be no written copies of the order); how form numbers are controlled (if at all); and what procedures are used for partial receipt of goods, cancelled orders, changes to unfilled-outstanding orders, and for all unusual transactions. This last item is particularly important; because the controls for nonstandard procedures are often the weakest, you should concentrate your efforts there.

3.   Study the procedures for receiving merchandise. Often someone at the warehouse or receiving terminal verifies that the shipment corresponds to what was ordered by comparing the shipment to a file of open purchase orders. You must determine what verification is made and with respect to which documents, and what notification of receipt of merchandise is prepared, to whom it is sent, and where all the copies are maintained.

4.   Watch out for vouchers. At this point in a purchase transaction, organizations often initiate a voucher record or document that uses vendor, purchase order number, account code, amount, receipt of merchandise document number, and related information. Learn as much as you can about this process and about the vouchers and the voucher file, because a voucher is the next best thing to money.

5.   Find out how invoices are processed. The invoice is matched against the voucher to ensure that the invoice is correct and that the merchandise has been received; normally, a check is then prepared. Generating an invoice is the least of your problems, of course, since it comes from your bogus company through the mails.

The key point of the purchase transaction is this: whenever an approved purchase order is matched with a receipt of merchandise and with an invoice from the vendor, a check will be issued. You must be in a position to alter or fabricate both a purchase order and a merchandise receipt. After that, it is a simple matter for you to see that the invoice is rendered.

Exactly how you arrange to falsify the two key documents or records is, of course, the difficult part. If you work in purchasing, you can generally find some way of generating fraudulent purchase orders by forging names of legitimate buyers, altering otherwise proper orders, or cancelling an outstanding order and using that purchase order number and authorization to issue a fraudulent order to your bogus company. Your problem will be to generate the merchandise receipt or record. The easiest method is, of course, to collude with someone in the receiving terminal, but many other devices, short of collusion, may be used. Sometimes this is as simple as printing either packing slips for your bogus company or merchandise receipts (employer's), forging them, and sending them through the company mail to data processing or accounting.

It is often much easier to establish both the purchase order record and the merchandise receipt if you work in accounting or data processing. Sometimes it is as simple as punching a few cards and entering them as if they were legitimate into a batch of transactions. The danger of doing this in second-generation computer systems is that the computer files of open purchase orders and merchandise receipts would not correspond to the various duplicate files maintained elsewhere—a constant threat. More modern computer systems often lack duplicate files because "purchase orders" and "merchandise receipts" are entered into a centralized set of computer files through computer terminals or data-collection devices. Here's an example to get you thinking:

> Over a six-year period, the chief accountant of a large fruit and vegetable shipping company embezzled more than a million dollars. While running the accounting work at a computer service bureau, he developed a model of the company on which he experimented with both real

and fraudulent disbursement transactions. He determined which company accounts he could take large amounts of money from without being detected. He then charged these accounts with phony purchase orders and receipts from punched cards he had prepared. By increasing these expense and inventory accounts, the accountant made the difference between what was actually owed and the recorded amount payable to a dummy company he had established.

The embezzler must be aware that his scheme is not complete just because he has been able to close the purchase order/merchandise receipt/vendor/invoice circle, and his dummy company has received the check. He has left behind "footprints" that are a potential threat to him in the company records. One footprint is that some account was charged for merchandise or services not received. It may have been an inventory account, in which case the book inventory figure is higher than the actual physical inventory by the exact amount of the theft. When the count of the physical inventory is made, your speculation should be exposed. There are, of course, many steps you can take to minimize such occurrences; these four stand out:

1. Select inventory accounts with high activity and high value, accounts that are physically difficult to count, where security is a continuing problem, where responsibility is shared among many, and where a certain amount of loss is "expected."
2. Do not "hit" any account too hard. Try to find out how much shortage will be tolerated in each account before someone triggers a thorough investigation. Remember that there are likely to be other white collar thieves at work (as well as thieves without collars).
3. Select accounts supplied by many new and constantly changing vendors.
4. Be aware of managerial style. Some managers are detail oriented. They pore over the financial statements, analyze the operating variances, and scrutinize the purchases, prices, terms, and inventory levels. Other managers are just the opposite. When charging a fictitious purchase to an inventory account, pick on the latter.

Many of the same arguments also hold for charges to expense accounts. Pick accounts that are difficult to monitor—ones such as freight, taxes, employee benefits, indirect labor, supplies, services, and so on. Avoid charging to small departments, departments run by detail men, and basic accounts, such as fuel, that tend to be watched closely.

Remember that all your efforts must be conducted through an accounting system with a number of tests and controls, checks and balances, cash totals, and batch counts. Fortunately, most of these controls are documented in the computer system descriptions or are the major topic of conversation of the data control group. You can also test for them by occasionally rearranging proper transactions; when the "real" test occurs, "they" will just think it is an error.

Inventory: 'It Is Easier to Convert Goods to Cash'

Do not ignore inventories as a possible source of revenue. In many cases, it is easier to convert goods to cash than it is fraudulent checks, especially since the former are harder to trace. Although smaller, homogeneous articles might be easier to steal, size should not be a primary consideration, as the following example at an East Coast railroad suggests:

> One or more employees in a railroad's computer center allegedly altered input data to aid in the theft of over 200 boxcars. It is thought that the rolling stock inventory file was altered to reflect that the cars were either scrapped or wrecked when they were actually shipped to another company's yard and repainted. The U.S. attorney handling the case stated that the actual thefts could not have gone undetected without the collusion of someone who had access to and was able to manipulate the railroad's computer records. If they can take 200 boxcars—just think what you can do!

Computerized inventory systems lend themselves to penetration for two basic reasons: they account for a large amount of material, and the controls on access systems are normally lax. Depending on the company and the location of its warehouses, inventory transfers or shipments are either recorded on supporting documents first and later keypunched and entered into the computer, or they are entered directly into a central system via computer terminals. Both systems are vulnerable to theft. (By this time you have probably noticed that I use the terms *fraud*, *theft*, and *embezzlement* interchangeably. See the appendix on page 292 for more complete descriptions of the terms, and some idea of the penalties connected with the crimes.)

The computer can assist you because it lessens the visibility of your acts and may make it easier for you to gain access to the inventory files. Also, as in the example described at the beginning of this article, interwarehouse transfers are often subject to less control because no one outside the company is usually involved in the transaction.

One day soon you will read about the following now-hypothetical inventory fraud:

> A large manufacturing/wholesale company operating through a number of geographically separated warehouses linked by computer-communications to a centralized order-processing system found that several of its warehouses had been virtually "cleaned out." Apparently a computer other than that of the corporation was connected to the system and used to send shipping instructions to the warehouses. Be-

cause the company had relied on its central computer to keep records of all shipping instructions, there were no extra copies other than the bill of lading and the mailing labels, which were printed at the warehouse. As a result, there was no record of where the goods had been shipped.

Sales Manipulation: 'Shipping Documents Are Vulnerable'

Another fruitful area for the embezzler is the manipulation of shipments, sales, and billing procedures. Your objective here is to confuse your company into:

☐ Shipping a product to a customer without sending the bill.

☐ Shipping one thing and billing the customer for something else.

☐ Billing a shipment at the wrong price.

☐ Granting improper credits or adjustments on returned or damaged products.

☐ Manipulating the sales commissions, allowances, and discounts on merchandise shipped.

For homework, prepare a flow chart of sales-order processing. Determine how all sales orders are received, written up, logged, and checked; how logs or registers are prepared, verified, and checked; and how sales commissions are processed. Study the flow of sales orders to the warehouse or plant and observe how orders are picked, packed, and shipped, and how all logs and registers are maintained there as well.

From your research you should have little difficulty in determining how to place an order (through a dummy company or one controlled by an accomplice). Your key task will be to intercept the shipping document or processed sales-order statement after shipment but before it is processed by the accounting department. For example, in many warehouses one can simply destroy a processed sales order after the order has been shipped. A helpful hint: most of the checking, logging, and registering controls you will have to beat were set up to ensure that the customer receives his order, *not* to ensure that your company bills correctly. Shipping documents are vulnerable to manipulation all the way from the warehouse to the accounting records in the computer.

In many computerized, order-entry systems, the sales-order record is maintained on a computer file and is not normally updated or maintained until the order is shipped. When word is received that the order has been shipped, the sales-order record becomes the primary source of data on the shipment to accounts receivable and billing. The weak point in these systems is that the sales-order record can be changed after the shipment has been made but *before* the billing processes are triggered. The time delay here may be hours or just seconds, but in all systems there is still a point of vulnerability. For example:

A middle-level manager in one large manufacturing company had ac- cess to the company's on-line order-entry, billing, and shipping sys- tems. He was able to place bogus orders, which initiated the shipping of merchandise to a cover address. Then he would initiate billing can- cellations due to alleged loss, damage, or destruction of the shipment in transit.

As I have noted, some companies have such weak controls that you can simply destroy the sales-order record after shipment and it will not be detected. In most cases, however, a register of sales orders filled is main- tained, and a missing record would be noted. In this case, you may have to destroy the document after it has been checked against the log, or you might alter the record so that the eventual bill is much lower than what it ought to be. For example:

In a large Canadian department store, a systems analyst, using his knowledge of the sales-order processing system, was able to place orders for expensive appliances and have them coded as "special pric- ing orders." He was then able to intercept these orders in data pro- cessing and change the price to only a few dollars. When the appliances were delivered, he paid his account and closed the loop.

In most cases it is best to stick to only a few items per order and to order only items you know are in stock. In some cases, however, where a company's control over back orders and partial shipments is weak or non- existent, just the reverse is true.

Payroll Fraud: 'It Is Easiest in Companies with a Large, Varying Work Force'

If you apply yourself, the payroll processing function in most large organ- izations with computerized control systems is a ready source of funds. There are a number of ways to manipulate your organization's payroll, but probably the most popular are:

☐ Padding the payroll with nonexistent employees.
☐ Leaving former employees on the payroll after termination.

Once you understand the payroll process thoroughly, you are ready to start. Employees in data processing, payroll, and programming are in ideal posi- tions for these schemes. Perhaps the simplest method is to pad the payroll with extra hours, for oneself or for others as well, by altering input data; this does not require forging time records, or any other details. For example:

Over a five-month period a computer center employee who had both input and monitoring duties initiated checks payable to herself. Al-

though she regularly deleted the check from the disk record, a surprise audit revealed that overpayments had been made, and she was discovered.

Such payroll schemes are, however, limited as to the amount it is possible to take, and involve more and more risks as the number of people involved increases. These schemes are also the ones payroll managers fear the most, and thus the ones they know how to control the best. As a result, unless controls are extremely lax, these schemes should be avoided. There are better ways.

Data processing employees are often in the best position to create fictitious personnel, which is usually easiest to do in companies with lax controls and a large, varying work force. Supervisors of large departments often have neither the time nor the desire to verify the existence of each individual listed on the periodic check register (which they may or may not receive). In addition, the personnel department's employee data files are usually maintained in the EDP department and are subject to similar manipulation so that both files can be made to reflect the same fictitious employees. For example:

An employee in the data center at the welfare department of a large city entered fraudulent data into the payroll system and stole $2.75 million over a nine-month period. He and several of his friends created a fictitious work force identified by fake social security numbers that were processed weekly through the payroll routine. The computer would automatically print a check for each fake employee, then the conspirators would intercept the checks, endorse them, and cash them. The conspirators were uncovered when a policeman discovered a batch of over a hundred of the fraudulent checks in an overdue rental car he found illegally parked.

In those companies that have numerous branches employing a varying number of employees, like opportunities exist. A branch manager can easily submit to the central processing group fraudulent information on temporary employees he has "put on the payroll." When the periodic checks are delivered, all he has to do is pocket those for the fictitious members of his work force.

Programmers who have complete understanding of payroll system controls and auditing methods have many, and often much more subtle methods that they can employ. A payroll program may be written to take a few pennies from each person's check and add them to that of the programmer. A better approach is to use the same scheme with income tax withholdings. The programs should, however, be designed so that the fraud segments can be activited or deactivated at will.

Pension Benefits and Annuities: 'Keep a Deceased Pensioner on the File'

You can often embezzle from funds destined for the payment of pensions, employment benefits, and annuities. While insurance companies and pension funds are the most fertile grounds for such frauds, a surprising number of other organizations also handle pensions, even if only on a small scale. Many businesses have small groups of special employees who, for one reason or another, have pension and benefit programs that are administered directly by the company rather than being taken care of through a pension fund.

The actual steps to be taken will vary depending on the size of the company and the extent and type of the pension and benefit programs. Regardless, you will first need to become familiar with the details of the operation to be embezzled: the numbers and list of beneficiaries, how beneficiaries are validated and revalidated, how benefits are determined, the addresses changed, and so on.

One of the most elegant frauds in the pension area—one that can run undetected for a considerable period of time—involves changing the address of a legitimate beneficiary to that of the embezzler or an accomplice at the time of the beneficiary's death. It is best to select beneficiaries with no life insurance. Also, since particular attention should be paid to how death notifications are received and processed, employees of the computer center are often in the best position to operate this embezzlement. For example:

> *In a West German company, an employee operating a pension fraud left the deceased recipients' records in the computer system files but changed their bank account numbers, to which the checks were paid, to his own. When the pensioners were required to verify their existence, auditors uncovered the scheme.*

If you are to be successful here, you must keep a deceased pensioner on the file only for a limited time, and then "kill" him.

If an estate does not claim death benefits after a beneficiary dies, you can claim them yourself through an accomplice. Again, personnel in the data center are often in the best position to know the status of each account, the requirements for processing claims, and if there has been communication between the company and the estate.

Rather than claim death benefits, it may be possible for you to claim the annuity or retirement benefits of a former employee who, for whatever reason, has not applied for his legitimate benefits after a period of time. To protect yourself, you can make private inquiries as to why the person has not applied and, if the risk is low, proceed to claim them yourself.

Accounts Receivable: 'The Computer Can Be Your Scapegoat'

Theft from accounts receivable "robs Peter to pay Paul" by making good on one account with payments diverted from another. Popular long before the advent of computer systems, this "lapping" method does not necessarily require access to cash, though it does require constant vigilance; the amounts involved can mount up. The computer improves on the old scheme in several ways: in most cases, access to computer records is easier than to old manual records; your actions have less exposure when committed through a computer system; and the computer accepts all input as truth. Should a customer become suspicious because of repeated billings of a previously paid bill, a computer foul-up can be your scapegoat.

To succeed in this fraud, your main concern will be to shuffle the accounts continually. In addition to the accounts receivable section, ideal positions from which to operate this scheme are in the keypunch, data control, or computer operations departments. For example:

> *Two men diverted over $61,000 in bill payments sent by insurance companies to a university medical center and deposited them in dummy accounts they had established. To cover their scheme, which lasted for 10 months, the men deleted accounts from the medical center's computer records by making them uncollectible, or by purging them from the files. This fraud, like so many others, was uncovered by accident. One account was mistakenly left in the system, causing a second bill to be sent to an insurance company. A complaint followed which led to the discovery of the culprits.*

If you install what is commonly called a program "patch" into a computer program, you can alter the program so that thefts can be more permanent. To accomplish this, you will need a good working knowledge of computer programming, to know how to alter a program, and access to the program library.

It may also be necessary to "pass inspection" by the internal audit group, but this is not as difficult as it might appear since, as a practical matter, computer programs can only be tested by checking the results of test data. This method of inspection can ensure only that the program "does what it's supposed to do" not that it "doesn't do anything else" under unusual conditions, such as perform a different task when a particular switch is set "improperly" at the machine console, or when "unusual" transactions appear. In the trade, these are called "triggers."

An "unusual" transaction might be a debit and a credit of the same amount on the same day where the amounts are equal to the numeric data, e.g., a debit and a credit of $112.75 on January 12, 1975 (01-12-75) might trigger a secret patch. The best trigger is one that, like the "unusual transaction," can be controlled from outside the organization. In theory, a complete test procedure should detect such tricks, but there is no guarantee; the internal auditor is always playing catch-up ball against you. Here is a good example of a patch.

A bank programmer patched a program in such a fashion that it added 10 cents to every service charge less than 10 dollars and 1 dollar to those greater than 10. The excess charges were credited to the last account, which he had opened himself, under the name of Zzwicke. He was able to withdraw several hundred dollars each month until the bank, under a new marketing campaign, tried to honor the first and last names on their customer list, and discovered that Mr. Zzwicke did not exist.

Since they have the potential to enable the thief to prove that two plus two equals five, program patches, in spite of their difficulty and complexity, may be the embezzlement technique of the future. Companies have developed extensive controls over the processing of input data, in both receivable and payable accounts, primarily to detect and correct errors, but secondarily to prevent fraud. The "books" are assumed to be in balance at the beginning of the day, and if the day's transactions are clean and balanced, the ending totals are assumed to be correct and in balance. Thus the focal point of the controls is on the processing of inputs.

Using a program patch to cover fraudulent increases or decreases in balance can be especially profitable in large banks. The computer can be made to perform the old "adding machine trick" of the manual bookkeeping days in which bookkeepers totaling a series of ledger accounts could cover up a theft by advancing the tape, adding the stolen amount, and then repositioning the tape before finally punching the total key to get a desired but erroneous "balance." The computer program can also be made to "add" to the "correct amount," although not correctly.

A Little Learning Is a Dangerous Thing

There has been a paucity of published material about computer-related fraud, and because of this there are perhaps too many misconceptions about just how difficult it is to carry off. For some time, embezzlement has been the social disease of corporations, and they go to great pains to avoid any publicity when incidents occur. As a result, there is only skimpy knowledge on how to do it successfully. Perhaps some of the following truths and fictions will help you.

Fiction: It's Best to Stick to Banks

A number of computer frauds and embezzlements have indeed been detected in banks, insurance companies, brokerage houses, and other financial institutions. In fact, perhaps the first detected case of computer fraud was in a Minneapolis bank in 1966.

Embezzlement in financial institutions has received more publicity, probably because these organizations are, in many cases, regulated and investigated by federal agencies. But computer fraud has not been limited to financial institutions. There have been a number of examples of detected, computer-related frauds in manufacturing companies, wholesalers, utilities, chemical processors, railroads, mail-order houses, department stores, hospitals, and government agencies. Given the reluctance of corporations and other organizations to publicize their own problems with embezzlement, these case histories, at the least, are examples of detected fraud in organizations that were unable to prevent publicity. However, it is evident, even from this small sample, that computer embezzlement works in places other than financial institutions.

Truth: Any Organization Can Be a Target

Fortunately for you, many executives believe just the opposite; they think embezzlement is something that happens to the other guy. This is, of course, the classic rationalization, and is the reason that general security in many organizations is poor. The potential for embezzlement varies with the type of firm, size, extent of controls, degree of audit, capability of the management and auditing personnel, as well as a host of other factors that are often unique to the organization. But there is probably no business organization, government agency, foundation, or not-for-profit organization that cannot be a successful embezzlement target. (Furthermore, the executive who says it cannot happen to him always makes the best patsy.)

Fiction: You Need Access to Cash

Probably the most strongly held and most dangerous misconception executives hold is that the successful embezzler has access to cash or cash equivalent items, such as securities, in his day-to-day-activities. Do not believe it. Many of the most exciting and lucrative embezzlements have been conducted by individuals who had absolutely no access to cash. Of all of the embezzlement schemes in this guide, only one involved people who had access to the "real thing." In fact, as most organizations have better control over cash and the people who handle it than any other part of their accounting system, there is a greater chance of embezzling funds if you do not have access to cash in your job assignment.

Truth: Collusion Is Beautiful

Corporations act as if there were some unwritten law of business that holds them responsible for embezzlement losses incurred by single individuals, but leaves them blameless if such losses are due to collusion. This is, of course, a ridiculous but nevertheless advantageous belief for the embezzler. Furthermore, if you are willing to take the added risk, collusion can mean a many-fold increase in the take.

A good place where collusion works well is in banks. Employees in positions to make noncash, uncleared deposits appear as if they had been cash can and do bilk banks of thousands of dollars a year. With help, those thousands can become millions. There is nothing that a wise controller fears more than collusion between key individuals, and with good reason. For example:

> *Five men, including a vice president of one big New York bank and a branch manager of another, stole $900,000 by running a float fraud between the two banks for four years. Deposit records were altered in the banks' data-processing centers so as to appear as cash deposits; the men would then withdraw cash. The fraud was detected only after a bank messenger failed to deliver some checks for a fraudulent "cash" deposit, and they overdrew one of their accounts by $440,000. Otherwise the scheme could have continued indefinitely.*

Fiction: Small and Poorly Managed Companies Are the Best

It is true that small companies are not able to maintain the same degree of internal control and separation of job responsibility and job assignments that a larger one can handle. It is also true that the internal controls and financial-system designs of poorly managed companies are more easily exploited than are those of well-managed ones. However, it is certainly a misconception that computer frauds have taken place only in small, poorly managed organizations. Some of the largest losses have occurred in the large companies. Furthermore, big companies are less apt to become suspicious of large losses than smaller companies are.

Truth: Look for Special Circumstances

One good rule of thumb is to always be on the watch for special circumstances that create opportunities for fraud, such as when a company converts from manual processing to a computer system or switches from one system to another. At these times unusual activities are less noticeable, and improper transactions and manipulations can be covered up. Exactly what you do is dependent upon what changes are being made and what position you occupy at the time.

Fiction: The Old Schemes Will Not Work any More

Many age-old embezzlement schemes work just as well today as they did before computers were commonplace; many are even more successful because the computer makes transaction processing more predictable and reliable. Theft from dormant bank accounts is a good example. Long before computer systems were installed, bank embezzlers transferred money from accounts that showed very little activity to their own or to that of an accomplice. Today, the task is easier because more persons have access to the subsidiary ledger files, via the computer, and money can be transferred through a number of accounts at a faster rate. This makes the embezzler's actions harder to trace. For example:

A computer systems vice president and a senior computer operator of a New Jersey bank, along with three nonemployees, stole $128,000 from little used savings accounts by transferring the funds to newly opened accounts. The actions were uncovered when the bank switched to a new computer, disallowing the culprits a chance to erase their withdrawls as had been planned.

Truth: Some Schemes Are Never Detected

By definition, the only schemes known of are the detected ones. Considering the fact that a great many schemes are uncovered by chance, there must be a large pool of undetected embezzlement operations. For example:

A large bank in New York recently suffered a severe setback in trading in foreign currencies. That loss, together with certain other conditions within the bank, led to the suspension of dividends, a large run on the deposits of the bank, and eventual collapse. In the course of a full and complete examination of the bank, investigators discovered a large embezzlement scheme, unrelated to the losses on securities trading, that had escaped detection by the bank auditors and examiners. In the absence of the securities trading losses, this embezzlement scheme could have run undetected for a long period of time.

This and other accidental discoveries of embezzlement schemes lead one to believe that there is a great deal of embezzlement that goes undetected. In fact, *all* successful embezzlement is undetected.

A final word of encouragement: In just the few examples mentioned in this article, embezzlers stole over $15 million with the computer's help. They were caught—but you can be smarter!

Notes

1. See Lee Seidler, "What Will They Think of Next?" (Ideas for Action), *HBR*, May–June 1974, p. 6.

Appendix A

Know What You Are Doing, or Let the Punishment Fit the Crime!

If you are going to steal in style, it would be wise for you to understand the nature of your thefts, their legal classifications, and the statutes involved. Although the laws and statutes vary from state to state, the following are generally accepted descriptions of the illegal activities you will undertake.

1.   **Larceny** is the theft of assets, with the intent to convert them into cash without the consent of their lawful owner.

2.   **Embezzlement** involves the theft of property by someone to whom the property has been entrusted (i.e., "larceny after trust").

3.   **Collusion** occurs when more than one person is involved in cooperation for a fraudulent purpose.

4.   **Fraud** involves the intentional misrepresentation of the truth to deceive the owner. In computer crimes the fraud occurs (a) when a thief attempts to conceal his actions through incorrect entries or changes in the company's records or files, and (b) when he is not entrusted with the assets that he actually steals. Most computer crimes fall into the fraud category.

If you simply steal inventory, it is theft, and if detected you may be charged with larceny. If you are an employee who steals and you disguise the theft, as was allegedly done at the railroad, that is fraud. If, however, you are the individual charged with responsibility for the inventory, your fraud is an embezzlement. If there is more than one of you, your embezzlement is collusion. For some delightful reason having to do with blue collars and white collars, thieves go to jail when caught, but embezzlers generally do not.

In a large percentage of cases, embezzlers are not even prosecuted. Because embezzlement is a crime against an entity and not an individual, a concept dating back to English common law, the criminal is often absolved if he or she simply returns the money. Also, because embezzlers are in positions of trust, they are often high up in the organization and friends of the top management, if they are not top managers themselves. Organizations naturally preferring to hang their dirty laundry inside settle such matters between friends.

17 Managing the Costs of Information

PAUL A. STRASSMANN

As organizations begin to harness the full power of information technology, the framework for analyzing information systems requires broadening. To make any sense of further computerization, all labor costs surrounding the computer—at both the input and the output end—must be accounted for. By means of nine steps toward total management of information resources for greater productivity, the author offers help to information managers seeking trade-offs among office automation, office labor, and office performance.

Industries and governments all over the world are currently struggling to contain rising administrative and clerical overheads by automating information handling in the office. In the past 20 years, white-collar labor has been the fastest growing component of the work force in every industrialized country. Yet this labor segment consistently shows lower increases in productivity than such blue-collar employment sectors as farming, manufacturing, and mining, where the management of capital versus labor investments is much better understood.

If bureaucracy (in the most benign sense of the word) is indeed the premier growth industry of the foreseeable future, then the dollars spent on white-collar automation must assume prime importance, particularly for the top information-systems executive in an organization. My purpose here is to show that managing information systems now goes far beyond just managing computers and to suggest a series of steps for managing this enlarged function effectively.

Information processing in today's large, complex organization really encompasses three sectors. The first is the by now well-understood and well-defined data-processing sector. Aside from the costs of computers, terminals, and peripherals, this sector includes expenses for such things as computer services, time sharing, data processing supplies, data communication, programming support, operating labor, and consulting. It has been estimated that, in 1973, organizations in the United States spent about $26 billion in this area of information processing.

Now the problem is that all too many of today's information-processing executives define their jobs largely within the context of data processing—they focus their energies on integrating the explosive data processing technologies into their organizations. This task has not been easy, but overemphasis on it has led managers into the trap of ignoring a second major sector of information processing, which for lack of a better term I call "administrative processing"—a sector on which an estimated $42 billion was spent in the United States in 1973.

This sector is rarely aggregated under a single expense heading, yet it accounts for the largest and most frequently used set of tools and facilities for handling information transactions. It includes everything from typewriters, word processors, and dictating equipment to telephone and Telex networks, recording devices, copiers and duplicators, facsimile-transmission devices, microfilm equipment, and even such relatively mundane necessities as office supplies, mail, and simple filing systems.

These administrative tools are quite diverse and often isolated from one another, so that the expense involved in their use tends to become highly diffused. Historically, little trade-off has been possible among such individual office "technologies."

Indeed, only rarely is an organization dedicated to the vital task of integrating these noncomputer aspects of information handling. But it is precisely here that the fastest expense growth is occurring in today's office environment; competition across several new administrative processing technologies is already here. This means that if we are to control rising expenditures for white-collar automation, careful expense accounting for these technologies must come under the rubric of information systems management.

The third sector of expense that should fall within the purview of the modern information systems manager involves people. After all, neither data processing nor administrative processing is an end in itself. The payoff from all sorts of office devices and facilities, from computers to mail rooms, lies in increasing the productivity of office labor—secretaries and typists, switchboard operators and clerks, administrative personnel and people who process applications, claims, orders, and inquiries of all sorts—that host of office employees classified as nonmanagerial and nonprofessional.

What makes the office labor sector so important for information systems people is the fact that it is the largest single occupational category—approximately 22%—in the U.S. labor force. What's more, in 1973 the total annual expense associated with such personnel, including benefits, pensions, office space, and other allocated overhead, has been estimated at about $350 billion.

The work that these people do, while vital to our organizations, represents almost entirely an overhead burden—and a fast growing one, too. From 1950 to 1970, the proportion of employees in these "overhead" categories as a percentage of the total U.S. labor force grew by more than 6%, while those in categories representing "direct" labor in areas of high productivity (for example, farming and manufacturing) decreased their share by more than 9%. Thus office labor represents a rich source of cost saving indeed for the information systems manager. If the myriad information transactions that this huge segment of our work force performs can be systematized and made efficient through modern information-handling techniques, the financial benefits will be great.

To accomplish this, we must abandon the traditional practice of managing excessive overhead labor growth by periodic pruning. Data processing, administrative processing, and the work that office labor does have become too intertwined and interdependent for the one-shot surgical approach to work anymore. Rather, we will have to design self-adaptive cost-control methods into each organization's systems and procedures. We must learn how to install advanced office automation techniques that will safeguard productivity improvements as conditions change.

In the face of uncertainties about the future volume of information transactions, the relative importance of various cost elements, rapid changes in technology, and shifting attitudes toward office automation by labor and government, we must harness the power of information technology through a more responsive control mechanism. Let us explore briefly the objectives of such a mechanism and then move on to the action I recommend to achieve it.

Once we accept the notion that the top information executive's job encompasses much more than managing data-processing expense, we still have to articulate, in terms of precise objectives, just what the job calls for in today's business environment. In my view, the new job definition would include the following objectives:

☐ Ensuring the integration of data processing, administrative-processing, and office labor productivity programs.

☐ Instituting accounting, cost-control, and budgeting innovations that will subject *all* information systems overhead activities to the disciplines traditionally applied to direct labor.

☐ Subjecting office labor automation programs to analyses comparable to those applied to all other forms of capital investment.

☐ Conceiving organizational designs that will permit information to be handled as a readily accessible and easily priced commodity rather than as a bureaucractic possession.

☐ Creating within the organization an internal market for alternative information systems products, so that trade-off decisions, even technologically complex ones, can be decentralized into the hands of local user management.

☐ Fostering a technique of pricing that will allow decisions on introducing new technology, or abandoning obsolete technology, to be made on a decentralized basis.

☐ Installing and monitoring measurement methods that will protect improvements in productivity achieved by automation programs.

These objectives are far from easy to achieve. However, from experience with information systems in several large organizations, I have developed a set of nine guidelines, or steps, that have proved helpful in my work. They have been sufficiently tested to make me feel quite confident in offering them here as a practical route for any organization to follow in an effort to control its own information systems programs.

I should emphasize, however, that all of them may not be valid, or even acceptable, in every organization, for they do involve some major restructuring. Nor can they all be instituted quickly. Changing a whole organization's perspective on information systems management to the broader view I have set out here must be a gradual process. Thus the steps outlined in the balance of this article constitute a rough road map to guide an organization toward the total management of its information resources.

Managing Costs

The sequence should start with the budgeting process. It must identify all of the components of information processing cost and segment them by (1) *function,* for example, the total cost of performing the billing function, from order entry until receivables are reconciled, (2) *technology,* for example, what portion of the billing cost is done clerically and what portion by computer, and (3) *organization,* for example, what the various billing systems of one organization are.

Step 1: Identify Costs
Identifying computer and telecommunication costs is relatively easy. The tough part begins in identifying budget elements of corresponding administrative processing and office labor cost. Classifying expenses and people can be difficult, since organizational boundaries do not translate readily into functional or technological definitions. This step will probably require major modifications in the organization's job classification scheme, so that job categories for white-collar personnel become more detailed and comparable job functions become consistent across organizational lines.

In addition to this internally oriented, personnel cost analysis, careful attention must be paid to external purchases of services and technology. Because the budgeting process focuses on expense levels of a particular organizational element, costs incurred outside do not readily surface when an attempt is made at a functional profile of costs.

For instance, in arriving at the total cost of the billing function, you need to make sure that the costs of mail and banking services are included. The overall billing expense should include investment costs as well as new systems-programming or minicomputer-development expenses that are to be amortized over a period of years. Since for accounting purposes most information systems costs are now expensed rather than capitalized, it is important that your cost identification process discriminate between these different classes of costs.

Finally, a word of caution: step 1 is not an easy, one-shot effort. Depending on the size and complexity of the organization, it may take up to five years of continual changes in the budgeting process before consistent data are obtained. The new cost identification scheme must become the accepted way of looking at the cost structure of *all* information activities. And this takes time.

Step 2: Keep Score on Unit Costs

Knowing what each information transaction costs is critically important for all that is to follow. It is the only way to monitor productivity trends independent of changes in volume, work element mix, and inflation.

After wrestling for years with the problem of getting comparable data on the consequences of computer automation, I have concluded that, to really control administrative costs, one must begin by tracking "real," deflated unit costs for discrete, output end products. By these, I mean items like cost per service call, cost per payment, cost per purchase order, cost per printed page, and cost per inquiry. Only by keeping score over a number of years on such consistently defined unit output measures is it possible to observe real improvements in cost performance.

In unit costing, it is important to define the measurements in sufficient detail that assigning responsibility for them at the working level is easy. Defining a measurement too broadly forces excessively high aggregations such as one finds in divisional overhead-burden ratios, where little can be done to trace the consequences of specific productivity improvement programs.

Also, be sure to include total unit costs for each unit output measure you choose. For instance, the cost of management overhead, employee benefits, and capital must flow into unit transaction costs before you can make valid comparisons between various means of improving productivity through office automation.

In describing these first two steps, I am considering information-processing services as an *industrial process* rather than as an undifferentiated overhead. This is quite deliberate, for in my experience it leads to a much better understanding of how costs can be controlled in this rather amorphous and "messy" domain.

Step 3: Establish Standard Costing

Setting a standard cost for each element of measured information output is essential for several reasons.

First, when cost reductions are planned, they must be locked into the planning and budgeting system by means of standards against which operating management can be measured. All too often, existing charge-out or full-cost-absorption costing systems disguise cause-and-effect relationships in expensive information processing activities and make it practically impossible to look at period variances from planned expense levels in a way that keeps management accountable for results.

Second, standard costing for information services is essential for making long-term commitments to users. If they have a predictable cost picture, users can feel more confident in making new investments and in decentralizing systems investment decisions.

A third reason for standard costing is its ability to reflect variability, so that the organization supplying information services can no longer cite "fixed costs" or "undisplaceable overhead commitments" as excuses for not achieving productivity improvements.

The basic tool for achieving standard costing is a job process sheet containing the cost profile for every resource used to create an output transaction. Each job step is costed out just as if it were part of a manufacturing assembly operation. The job process sheet should focus on all pertinent costs, such as those for handling, editing, output preparation, mailing, and reproduction or storage. In this way, analysts searching for cost reductions can do a thorough evaluation of the thousands of discrete activities that make up the total information processing budget.

In a well-run operation, such improvements do not come easily; saving a penny here or a nickel there is typical of most paper-work activities. This situation means that the basic tool—the job process sheet—must be designed with sufficient detail to permit an ongoing review of operating costs for every information transaction involved.

Aside from making it easier to track operating costs and thus to highlight opportunities for savings, the most important consequence of standard costing is that it changes the attitudes of managers supplying central information services. Standard costing also tends to shift the staff and planning people to the working levels of the organization, where they are closer to being a part of direct product cost. Also, such managers become more wary of commitments to fixed technology costs.

The reasons for both of these attitudinal changes lie in the imperatives of standard costing—that indirect overhead be kept small and that technology costs be responsive to changes in volume or to obsolescence in methods.

The experience with standard costing of Xerox has so far been good. We now operate over 40 internal information services groups that derive a large part or all of their revenues from standard revenue per unit of output.

As a minimum, each of these groups must liquidate its entire cost structure, including all overheads and management charges, from a changing revenue mix. The overall result has been a sharpening of the ability of managers to respond to a changing information-systems environment, while maintaining good accountability for cost performance.

Organizing Functions

The action steps discussed so far—identifying costs, tracking unit costs, and establishing standard costs—are all procedural aspects of information systems control. To be effective, they need an organizational focus. Cost-accountability centers, in which people engaged in functional office activities are assigned to product-oriented units, will provide this.

Step 4: Set Up Accountability Centers

The rationale for this approach stems from the recent tendency in business, industry, and government to centralize information-processing functions. Centralization, so goes the argument, puts the information-processing specialist under one umbrella, consolidates the technology, and concentrates expert management—all this in the guise of "economies of scale."

But the real problem occurs after centralization takes place. Simply put, it is this: How do you manage large agglomerations of clerical and administrative people without sacrificing the attributes that make them effective in their local environments? For instance, how do you justify taking personal secretaries away from individual managers and grouping them into better equipped word-processing centers without losing in motivation what you gain from computerized text-editing typewriters?

The answer seems to lie in finding an organizational compromise between centralized efficiency and decentralized effectiveness of people. At Xerox, we have achieved this middle ground by creating small teams—sometimes as few as 10 people but never more than 50 to 80—to handle well-defined information-output tasks.

For example, our manager of the payroll-processing center has complete control over his products, which are payroll checks and payroll-related reports. He is, in effect, an entrepreneur in the payroll-processing business. He is responsible for his cost reductions per payroll check—weighed against error rates, document turnaround time, cash management, and so on. He seems himself, in turn, as being in a highly competitive payroll business, in which he must not only optimize his total resources but also aggressively seek opportunities for providing new and better services.

More important, we encourage this manager to make trade-off decisions among a variety of resource deployment choices that are available for improving his overall financial results. Thus he may trade off such options as training investments versus salary levels, information investments versus personnel expenses, teleprocessing cost versus data-processing expense, and in-house service versus external procurement.

In my view, the true test of "decentralization" is not an organizational one; rather, it is whether a manager responsible for an end product has the freedom to make trade-offs like those just cited in getting the job done. In such an environment, it is then possible to charter data processing or administrative-processing activities without getting bogged down in organizational definitions. Output becomes the proper focus. When information-processing functions become the accountability centers, they are in effect little businesses, buying and selling goods and services as needed.

For instance, our payroll-processing center (to use the same example) "buys" batch processing and time-sharing from our "centralized" computer service units, and "sells" the reports and analyses that are by-products of its payroll work to decentralized personnel departments within the company. Although people in computers and personnel may regard the payroll-processing center as a centralized function, it operates in the independent, decentralized way I have described.

In short, one person's centralization becomes another's decentralization. The labels become meaningless after a while. In the end, it is accountability for the cost of information processed that matters.

Step 5: Apply Competitive Pricing

In information-processing operations, it is not easy to establish standard costs and create accountability centers. There are two reasons for this: technologies can change radically, and the costs of computerization are hard to set realistically. Let me explain briefly what I mean.

When a new technology such as data-base management software or time-sharing appears, the cost of converting to it, learning how to use it, and getting "customers" to employ it will make it appear noncompetitive with established methods. Thus the manager of an information-processing operation may be reluctant to try the new technology. In contrast, obsolescent technologies always appear more attractive in the short run, since they are well established and it does not really cost much to add to the bag of tools already being used.

Comparing the cost of computerization with the cost of the human wages that will be displaced is also a very tricky business. Employees are always valued at the going "market" rate for salaries plus benefits, whereas the cost of computerization varies according to the company's cost-accounting practices in allocating the initial introduction cost.

The up-front cost of buying a computer is usually written off separately, with the result that the price of computer time—at "marginal cost"—is almost always substantially lower than the market price offered by commercial service bureaus. We then have the incongruous situation that, when labor and machines compete, labor savings are valued at market price, whereas computer time is costed at a heavily subsidized level. It thus becomes impossible to compare the two costs realistically.

The solution to both of these difficulties—accommodating new technology and making valid cost comparisons—is to open internal information processing operations to competitive market forces by basing their revenues on prevailing competitive prices for equivalent services.

Establishing a market price for each information service rather than pricing it at "cost" accomplishes several ends: (1) it simplifies cost accounting by avoiding complex overhead allocations, since all automation facilities become fixed expenses if viewed from a sufficiently short-term standpoint; (2) it stimulates the introduction of new technologies because it permits cost averaging of such innovations over program life; and (3) it allows simulated "profit" objectives to be assigned to the lowest levels of an operation, so that even first- and second-level management has a clear understanding of what it can and cannot do.

An example of this last advantage is our experience with word-processing centers. When we first created them, we found it difficult to establish their scope and performance measures. Using competitive prices from local firms, we then allowed the text-preparation technicians (that is, the former secretaries who now operate word processors) to charge their "clients" for secretarial services. The results were gratifying, because we found that, to remain competitive, we had to back off from many fancy technical solutions.

There are, however, two serious disadvantages to using market pricing formulas for internal transfer of information services. Automation opportunities may be turned down that would be justifiable under a marginal costing approach. Second, an efficient internal information-processing operation may accumulate a large surplus of revenues over costs, and most bureaucracies simply do not have accounting conventions for dealing with internal profits.

The issue of too little automation can be easily resolved by regarding new automation investment opportunities as a part of the conventional capital funds budgeting process and applying the same criteria for choice used there. The recent progress in the technology of information processing suggests that there will be no dearth of automation investment opportunities over the next decade or so.

Establishing comparability between office automation and other capital investment opportunities should simplify the decisions on how to allocate scarce resources. The cutoff level between approved and disapproved automation projects will then be roughly consistent, regardless of the way investments are priced.

As for the issue of accumulated profits, each organization must resolve it within the context of its own rules. One way of looking at such profits is to use them as an indirect measure of how efficiently a particular service unit is investing in information technology over the long term. If it invests its funds wisely—in technology that makes its people really productive—

the unit should not only be able to keep up with rapidly dropping market prices for information transactions (and thereby garner new customers) but also to use the accounting surpluses for making new investments (and thereby prepare for the future).

Step 6: Plan for the Long Term

Here I want to focus briefly on a basic dilemma facing the manager of an information systems department in a large organization. The people using the services he provides usually want some new task done right away—in three months or at most a year. The trouble is, meeting such a new demand often requires information technology or processing methods that take a long time to install.

This, plus the fact that total information-processing costs can exceed 15% of a large organization's expense budget these days, is why the planning of long-term information strategies warrants the same processes as are applied to functions like marketing, manufacturing, distribution, procurement, and personnel.

In this step, therefore, I strongly recommend that information systems investment decisions be shifted from an annual funding basis to two- to five-year planning commitments initiated by the functional user departments in the organization. This suggestion means that the information systems department, even if it is completely decentralized, should not contend for corporate budget funds as an independent cost center.

Rather, its budget levels should be set through renewable long-range contracts with the *users* of its services, that is, with the people accountable for end product costs containing various elements of information transaction expense.

Step 7: Let the Users Control

This step is a logical outgrowth of the shift of planning initiatives regarding information systems from the suppliers of information services to the users. Users should control not only the initial procurement but the execution as well. After all, they are the ones who understand the trade-off opportunities between information and other variables in functions as diverse as manufacturing, engineering, marketing, personnel, and procurement. Computer people and administrative specialists like to claim that they know what is best for their clients, but information systems are just too important to the success of an organization to be left entirely in the hands of the suppliers of information services.

To achieve the necessary degree of control, I recommend that key aspects of information systems management—business analysis, methods planning, and applications training—be moved organizationally as close to the ultimate user as possible. This arrangement not only enables the user to make intelligent procurement of data processing and administrative-processing services but also creates a powerful mechanism for balancing the business needs of the user against the claims of the information technicians.

I am frequently asked how to structure the user's organization to accommodate the systems-planning and systems-implementation personnel. There are many possible organizational combinations. However, my experience leads me to favor assigning business systems analysts to the planning mission for each functional area, since these are the people who are concerned about the future or about methods for changing the operating environment.

In preparing for new ways of doing business, we must increasingly rely on information systems as a means of achieving goals. Therefore, I am convinced that the user's planning area is the logical place to put information systems development and control staffs.

Redirecting Emphasis

Over the past few years, I have become convinced that the greatest opportunities for lasting productivity in information processing lie in job redesign and job enrichment rather than in improving the efficiency of existing data-processing operations. To be sure, new computer technology and new systems approaches are frequently essential in improving the work done in offices. But there should be no mistake about what should come first—human work needs, not technology.

Step 8: Deemphasize the Technology

I am recommending here a significant deemphasis of technology in information-processing operations. This reorientation means that top information executives face a new challenge. Whereas their primary skills have been focused on technical management, the enlarged scope of information processing calls for a humanistic, nontechnical, and general management perspective rarely found among more specialized executives.

How can the transition from an excessively computer-oriented attitude be engineered? Perhaps our experience at Xerox can point the way. Recently, we have begun increasing our investments in methods, procedures, and training. For years, these activities atrophied as talent moved into the more glamorous and better paying, computer-related activities.

The payoff from this redirection has been gratifying. For instance, in the information network we are currently installing, analysis of methods and work flow has shown that computer terminal access to central data bases allows us to rearrange accountability for work functions. Under the old system, work had to be broken up into specialties: accounts receivable specialists handled accounts receivable; equipment order entry clerks handled customer orders; credit was still another specialty. The new approach allows us to make versatile generalists out of narrow specialists. Since our people can now see the total results, job satisfaction has increased substantially.

Such a change is not free. I estimate that the costs involved in changing procedures, redesigning jobs, and training people to do them (all of which I call the "soft software") have exceeded the technical costs for setting up the computer terminals network itself (which I call the "hard software").

The important fact, however, is that the soft software aspects of the project have been given the same care and attention as the heretofore more glamorous hard software aspects. We have been our own campaign of deemphasizing technology by increasing the importance and influence of the people who develop the soft software.

I should point out that deemphasizing technology in information-processing operations does not necessarily mean getting rid of your technical people. It does mean, however, that you can shift many of them into administrative systems positions, where there is plenty of systems work to be done.

A goodly portion of the money formerly spent on computer problems can thus finance efforts to standardize technologies, to automate programming and testing tasks, to devise output measurements, and to improve quality control—all of which will increase the productivity of your technical resources. What this step comes down to, then, is a rebalancing of talent, not a purge.

Step 9: Use Job Enlargement

This recommendation elaborates a bit on the previous step. I single it out for emphasis because it calls for transforming our current rigidly designed information systems, with their emphasis on single-task work stations, into a different mode—one in which systems tasks are enlarged to include many of the attributes of computer-aided learning.

One of the problems I see in most existing information systems that rely mainly on computer terminals is their relatively narrow task orientation. People do not fit readily into such an environment. The training levels of individuals vary, and their attitudes toward work fluctuate. Therefore, designing terminal procedures to the lowest acceptable performance level, and leaving output volume as the only performance variable over which the operator has control, is clearly unsatisfactory, since it lessens productivity and discourages the operator.

For this reason, I recommended that terminal operating procedures be designed as a combination of tutorial and job execution devices—a combination that permits changes in both task content and job scope. As I see it, terminal systems should encourage people to deal with situations of increasing complexity as organizations and individuals continue to grow in their experiences.

As organizations perceive that increasing portions of their expense budgets are being devoted to information processing, judgments will have to be made about where to place the responsibility for overall information systems management. Making such decisions requires that both information systems executives and top management take time to reappraise their roles. To be specific:

☐ Top management will have to decide whether to strengthen its control over increasing complexity and interdependence by gathering the functional costs related to information processing.

☐ Explicit choices will have to be made among investments in computers, software development, training, methods development, telecommunications, job design, technologies available, and compensation levels.

☐ Most important, top management will have to decide whether some of the steps presented in this article can be applied in their own organizations. Even if it is found, for example, that information-processing, cost-accountability centers and productivity improvement through job enlargement are desirable, will there be adequate management talent available in the existing information-processing operation to support such a major change?

☐ The information systems manager will also have to reappraise his role. Can he learn to delegate the management of technology to others? Can he break free of the disciplines that shaped his entire career and enter into competition with management generalists? Can he acquire the new skills needed to motivate white-collar workers toward greater involvement in their work? Can he broaden his background to include the complex economics of information handling?

There is no doubt that arriving at answers to such questions will be difficult. Initially, only a small number of organizations will find switching to information-cost management sufficiently urgent to make these issues matters of central concern. In all likelihood, they will become central in information-intensive organizations like insurance companies, banks, credit card organizations, government social service agencies, income tax departments—places where information processing is a principal occupational concern. But as the pace of technology quickens and as shrinking margins make it necessary to employ resources more economically, most large organizations will have to consider the issues of information cost management as inseparable parts of overall business planning.

18

Controlling the Costs of Data Services

RICHARD L. NOLAN

Most companies by now have centralized their data processing activities to some degree. In doing so, they have found that they need more formal arrangements for providing services to operating units. Because of the press of day-to-day operations, formalizing arrangements for providing services usually take priority. Satisfying this requirement seems straightforward: develop a transfer-pricing or "charge-out" system for data processing services similar to those used by other units, such as product divisions, for internal transfers. While this logic is generally followed, its application has been fraught with problems, often bringing communications between managers and those in data processing to a grinding halt. In this article, the author discusses seven steps that companies can take to design an effective charge-out system whereby they can place more control in the hands of those who use data services and hold them accountable for the services they use.

Without exception, the companies that I have studied for the past four years have found it difficult to make their transfer-pricing, or charge-out, systems for data processing services understandable to the managers who use them.

The root of this problem is not the inherent technical complexity of computer technology—it is a historical error made in the management of data processing. To date, we have designed our DP management systems around the *computer* instead of the *data*. Consequently, charge-out systems have been designed to hold the manager who uses the data accountable for computer-related resources such as processing time, main memory time and space, and input/output accesses.

However, the user works with output units, such as invoices processed, inventory reports, and production schedules. Thus the user is forced to somehow translate input and processing charges into the information for which he or she receives value. Only then can he take appropriate control and be held accountable. In a sense, what is being asked of the user is

307

analogous to asking a car buyer to make a decision on several automobiles by being given a bill of materials on the different types of cars. The car buyer makes the decision on information such as performance of a V-8 versus the economy of a six-cylinder engine; the convenience of an automatic versus manual transmission; economy, safety, and wear of radial versus belted tires, not on kilos of steel, cast iron, and rubber.

Take, for example, this all too common vignette. On July 1, the vice president of marketing had just received his third monthly bill for his department's use of the order entry system. The bill he received is shown in Exhibit 1.

Although he did not understand the detail of the bill (for example, he had no idea what CPU, kilobytes, and EXCP stand for), he felt that it was way too much. In fact, the charge represented a good 25% of his budget. He also knew from the president's recent memorandum that he was now accountable for these expenses. So he picked up the telephone and made an appointment to talk with his newly appointed "data-processing coordinator."

Management's experience with data processing had followed the pattern of many other companies. After starting out in the early 1960s by automating payroll, the company had experienced extremely rapid growth in its DP budget as applications were developed for almost all parts of the business. The order entry system was one of the early applications.

It was close to a disaster when the devised estimate of development costs skyrocketed from $100,000 to $275,000 with less than half of the originally promised capability. Nevertheless, the marketing department stuck with it, and the costs were treated as corporate overhead. The bugs were shaken out by 1967, and the system was gradually expanded to the point where the vice president of marketing said that the company couldn't carry on business without it.

A year ago, management had become concerned with ever-rising DP expenses and seemingly declining performance, as maintenance problems with existing applications seemed to have got out of hand. Therefore, the

Exhibit 1.   Data Processing Services Bill

Resource	Use	Charge per Unit	Total
Elapsed time on computer (minutes)	243,000	$0.04	$ 9,720
CPU (seconds)	2,430,000	0.0167	40,500
Kilobytes (1K memory/minute)	14,515,000	0.0016	23,220
EXCP (I/O accesses)	105,000,000	0.0002	21,000
Total due			$94,440

company centralized data processing under a new vice president of information services, and there was a general consensus that users should be held accountable for the services they were using. With the support of the president, the vice president of information services had his staff design a system for charging out all costs on the basis of resources used to support the various applications. He also established data-processing coordinators for each major user group.

It was in this context that the vice president of marketing opened the meeting with his data processing coordinator:

> Although I really don't understand this bill, it has to be too high. Order entry cost us less than $30,000 per month before the computer system was installed. Not only is the $94,400 too high, even taking inflation into account, but the cost has varied from $78,000 to $104,000 in the three short months that the charge-out system has been in effect. How is a manager supposed to plan in such a volatile environment?

> You are absolutely right about the variance,'' the coordinator responded. It is due partly to the volume of orders processed and due partly to the upgrade in the computer operating system software last month. We have also incurred technical difficulty in measuring kilobyte minutes in an MVS operating system environment. You see we have a "meg" of main memory, but with virtual memory software we have a lot more. Our problem in charging equitably is one of.. . .

The vice president didn't understand this explanation and felt that he was getting the same waffle treatment that he had come to expect from data processing. Somewhat irritated, he said he didn't give a damn about the technical problems but wanted the bill to be reduced by 25%.

The coordinator reminded him that the information services division was only a service department and that it was the vice president's responsibility to provide the guidance for making such cuts. He then asked him what component of the bill he would like to attack: CPU seconds, elapsed time, kilobytes, or EXCPs?

At this point, the vice president of marketing became very angry. Shoving the coordinator out the door with instructions not to come back, he got the president on the telephone: "I'm strapped. Data processing is charging me for services that are essential, and I can't do anything about the cost. When I try to get down to how to control the costs, all I get is technical gibberish.. . ."

Design for Charge-Outs

Data services have become much too important to companies to be left to technicians. Management must devote the time necessary to understand data processing's current and future impact on the business so that it can provide the guidance that both data processing and users need.

In a sense, the charge-out systems that I have studied (see the ruled insert on this page) have been attempts to provide this guidance. Unfortunately, many of them were built on shaky DP accounting systems and implemented without a clear understanding of what was expected from the user.

As a result, both DP management and users became frustrated. The extent and intensity of the frustration are reflected in the vignette. The vice president of marketing was confused about what actions he should take to be accountable, and what the control rationale was. Another dysfunctional result is that the user gets too involved in the operational details of data processing.

One manager told me, "I now demand internal reports from data processing to check up on just how well they are running their operation."

How can a company develop an effective charge-out system? Obviously, no one system can work for all companies since the needs of companies vary tremendously. However, I think that one good approach to designing an effective system is to follow these seven steps:

1 Assess the overall status of data-processing services within the company.
2 Sort out how data processing is organized.
3 Evaluate capacity of accounting systems to support a DP management control system.
4 Assess current charge-out approach.
5 Develop charge-out system objectives and strategy.
6 Develop implementation goals and milestones.
7 Implement and review.

Let's look at each of these seven charge-out system steps in turn.

Assess Status of Data Services

The search for alternatives begins with a careful analysis of the characteristics of a company's industry and management philosophy. For example, managements of companies in high technology industries, such as electronics and aerospace, are more tolerant and understanding of technical complexities than managements of companies in service industries, such as insurance and banking. Also, managements of companies with sophisticated budgeting and financial controls are more receptive to similar systems for data processing. The general rule is that management control systems for data processing cannot be significantly more advanced than the management control systems used for the company as a whole.

Management's next task is to determine the status of its services. What I call the "stage process audit" is a useful way to structure this analysis.[1] Based upon the status of the applications portfolio, data processing organization, control mechanisms, and user awareness, an organization's data services can be thought of as being in one of four stages: initiation, contagion, control, or integration. Exhibit 2 shows the attributes for each of these stages. This detailed audit provides the foundation for tailoring the design of a control system.

A frequent mistake in designing an effective system is to impose sophisticated controls upon organizational units that are not "ready." The organizational unit is not ready if controls hinder its operation or if personnel cannot clearly see the relevance of the controls to their problems.

For example, one user in my study was charged for programming services that he did not fully understand because a new on-line system was being developed. Nevertheless, he was asked to make judgments on the resource commitments being made on the project, as well as to accept an accountability for those judgments even though the development process was largely out of his hands.

Sort Out the Organization Structure

Although many companies for the most part have centralized their data processing, there are usually pockets of activities still embedded within the organization that have not been dislodged.

The question of what constitutes an effective organization is complicated by wide disagreement on which activities should be centralized, even when they are only broadly categorized into systems development and operations. The majority of DP personnel I interviewed agreed that operations should be centralized, at least enough to support the specialists necessary to run and maintain the computer facility. However, proponents of minicomputers believe decentralization is preferable. The main disagreement concerns the location of systems development personnel, even though for the 18 research sites studied, 90% of the central DP departments had programmers and 60% had systems analysts—and over half of the user organizations had programmers and systems analysts.

Organizing data processing becomes even more complex and difficult when activities are sorted into maintenance, data entry, batch processing, on-line services and processing, and telecommunication facilities.

A study of an organization's structure will expose irrational locations for various data-processing activities. The majority of these locations can probably be changed; others may have to be viewed as constraints in the short run.

Even when an irrational structure cannot be altered, the structure must be understood because almost every control action taken for the central DP group will also affect the splinter groups.

For example, in one company I studied, the corporate data-processing department decided to charge users the full cost of providing services. The divisional data processing department charged less than full costs because occupancy and employee benefits were excluded from the calculation of costs. The effect of the corporate decision was to shift users to the divisional

Exhibit 2. Stage Process Audit Criteria

Criteria	Stage I: Initiation	Stage II: Contagion	Stage III: Control	Stage IV: Integration
DP organization				
Objective	Get first application on the computer	Broaden use of computer technology	Gain control of data-processing activities	Integrate data processing into business
Staffing emphasis	Technical computer experts	User-oriented system analysts and programmers	Middle management	Balance of technical and management specializations
Structure	Embedded in low-functional area	Growth and multiple DP units created	Consolidation of DP activities into central organizational unit	Layering and "fitting" DP organization structure
Reporting level	To functional manager	To high level functional manager	To senior management officer	VP level reporting to corporate top management
User awareness				
Senior management	Clerical staff reduction syndrome	Broader applications in operational areas	Crisis of expenditure growth Panic about penetration in busines operations	Acceptance as a major business function Involvement in providing direction
User attitude	"Hands-off" Anxiety over implications	Superficially enthusiastic Insufficient involvement in applications design	Frustration from suddenly being held accountable for DP expenditures	Acceptance of accountability Involvement in application, budgeting, design, and maintenance

Communication with DP	Informal Lack of understanding	Oversell and unrealistic objectives and schedules Schism develops	Formal lines of communication Formal commitments Cumbersome	Acceptance and informed communication Application development partnership
Training	General orientation on "what is a computer"	Little user interest	Increase in user interest due to accountability	User seeks out training on application development and control
Planning and control				
Objective	Hold spending at initial commitment	Facilitate wider functional uses of computer	Formalize control and contain DP expenditures	Tailor planning and control to DP activities
Planning	Oriented toward computer implementation	Oriented toward application development	Oriented toward gaining central control	Established formal planning activity
Management control	Focus on computer operations budget	Lax to facilitate applications development activity growth	Proliferation of formal controls	Balanced formal and informal controls
Project management	DP manager responsibility	Programmer's responsibility	Formalized system DP department responsibility	Formalized system tailored to project DP and user/management joint responsibility

Exhibit 2. *(Continued)*

Criteria	Stage I: Initiation	Stage II: Contagion	Stage III: Control	Stage IV: Integration
Project approval and priority setting	DP manager responsibility	Multi-functional managers First in, first out	Steering committee	Steering committee Formal plan influence
DP standards	Low awareness of importance	Inattention	Importance recognized Activity aggressively implemented	Established standards activity Published policy manuals
Application portfolio				
Objective	Prove value of computer technology in organization	Apply computer technology to multi-functional areas	Moratorium on new applications Consolidate and gain control of existing applications	Exploit opportunities for integrative systems Cost-effective application of advanced technology
Application justification	Cost savings	Informal user/ manager approval	Hard cost savings Short-term payout	Benefit/cost analysis Senior management approval

data processing facility, even though the best interests of the company were not served. If these responses are anticipated, systems may be designed to avoid dysfunctional relationships between the central and splinter groups, as well as between corporate and divisional management.

Evaluate Capacity of Accounting System

Since accounting systems provide the foundation for management control, management control can only reflect the quality of the accounting system. As shown in Exhibit 3, a logical progression exists in the development of the accounting systems, from after-the-fact, object-of-expenditure control to budgetary control responsibility center, by program (or job), and by quantitative measure of output units.

Although all 18 companies studied had developed meaningful classifications for expenditures—that is, charts of accounts, 4 companies still had not integrated the DP chart of accounts into the company's general ledger system. In addition, the DP accounting systems were of varying quality, which influenced their reliability.

The development of data processing accounting systems is initially an accounting problem rather than a data-processing problem because basic accounting concepts are most important. Unfortunately, this need for accounting skills does not seem to be fully recognized in the beginning. Over half of the companies studied reported that their technical personnel played the dominant role in designing the initial accounting systems. Systems analysts and programmers were usually assigned this task on the assumption that their technical skills were needed to measure computer system resource usage. Rather quickly, however, it became apparent that the real problems were accounting problems concerning responsibility centers, costing, and allocating costs to responsibility centers. Accounting personnel then would be brought into the project.

Cost centers, too, seemed to have evolved from the existing structure of the data-processing department rather than from an analysis of basic DP functions. Consequently, organizational changes often have a detrimental effect on control. In addition, costs are not consistently categorized by type—direct, indirect, and overhead.

These fundamental problems seriously hindered the effective design, implementation, and administration of the charge-out systems. Simply stated, you cannot build a sophisticated control system on a sandy foundation of weak accounting systems.

Assess Current Charge-Out Approach

A useful charge-out system communicates to managers the consequences of their decisions concerning use of services. Cost responsibility will tend to motivate users to employ the resources more effectively and efficiently. Four criteria can be used for determining the usefulness of a charge-out system—understandability, controllability, account-ability, and cost/benefit inci-

Exhibit 3. Evolution of Accounting and Control Systems

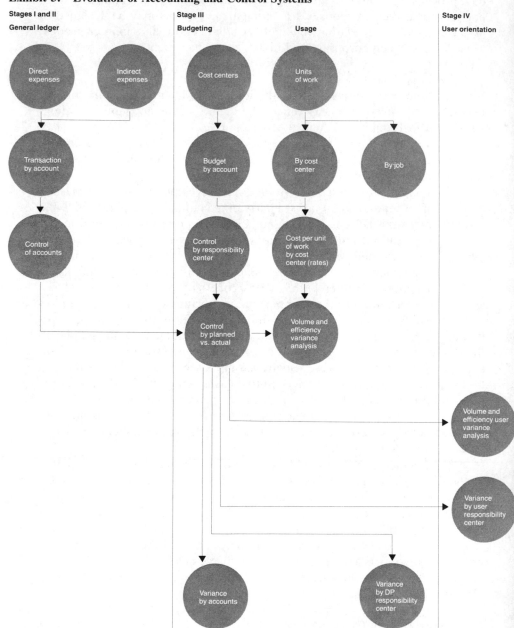

316

dence. Exhibit 4 shows the criteria and questions for determining the maturity of the charge-out system.

As shown in Exhibit 4, charge-out systems initially are directed at high-level managers. Summary data processing bills are sent to divisional controllers without much information on the charges being conveyed to end users. With maturity, the charge-out systems become more sophisticated and permit detailed bills to be sent directly to low-level users. It is important that the charge-out system evolve through successive phases so that users and DP managers can learn how to interpret and use the information. It is

Exhibit 4.   Criteria for Charge-out Systems

Understandability:
To what extent can the manager associate charge-out costs to the activities necessary to carry out his or her tasks?
Attributes:
High—Manager can associate costs with functions and determine variables accounting for costs.
Medium—Manager can roughly associate costs with functions, but cannot directly determine major variables accounting for costs.
Low—Manager cannot associate costs with functions.

Controllability:
To what extent are charges under the control of the user?
Attributes:
None—No control. The manager has no influence on acceptance or rejection or the charges. These decisions are made at a higher level.
Indirect—Through communication with others, such as divisional or departmental controllers that receive charges, the manager can influence the charges.
Direct/arbitrary—Charges are allocated directly to the manager, but his decision is to either accept or reject the application charges. Little information is provided on controllable versus noncontrollable data-processing costs.
Direct/economic—Charges are directly charged in a manner that allows the manager to make decisions that actually reduce controllable data-processing costs.

Accountability:
Are costs and utilization of computer-based systems included in performance evaluation of the user?
Attributes:
None—Not included in performance evaluation.
Indirect—Included indirectly in performance evaluation; costs can be related to user, but not done routinely.
Direct—Included directly in periodic user-performance evaluation.

Cost/benefit incidence:
Does the user responsible for task accomplishment also receive the charge-out bill?
Attributes:
Yes.
No.

especially important that the means for accountability be coordinated with the expectations for accountability.

After assessing the status of the existing charge-out system, management's next objective is to develop a strategy that will increase the maturity (and effectiveness) of the charge-out system at an appropriate pace for the major user groups. It is likely that several charge-out strategies may be required for the different user groups.

Develop Objectives and Strategy

In the companies I studied, objectives for the charge-out systems were rarely articulated. Or, if they were articulated, the objectives were often narrowly defined short-term goals. For example, eight of the companies stated that their charge-out system objective was to allocate data-processing costs. No mention was made of providing the cost information to users that they needed to make effective decisions about services. In other words, using data accounting systems to allocate costs for financial reporting and budgeting purposes should not be confused with charge-out. Charge-out brings the user into the realm of control and accountability.

In my opinion, the absence of a clear statement of objectives or an excessively narrow statement was the single most troublesome factor inhibiting chargeout system effectiveness. Consequently, systems were not well thought out, but were designed to provide minimal information for accounting, or to support other management tools such as project management systems.

Charge-out objectives should be stated in terms of desirable results for user accountability. Examples of such objectives include:

☐ Make managers aware of the economic (full absorption) costs of data-processing services provided to them.

☐ Make managers responsible for the economic costs of services they use.

☐ Motivate managers to make decisions about the use of data processing on the basis of the direct costs of providing the services.

☐ Charge costs in understandable volume units to facilitate data-processing capacity planning.

☐ Charge costs in a manner to facilitate manager product (service) pricing.

Each of these examples specifies a particular result, and taken together they imply the design of a system much broader than one that simply charges for computer services. Alterations in organization structure, budgeting, and performance review and measurement are often necessary. Once management has articulated an appropriate set of objectives, it should formulate a strategy to achieve them that takes into account the necessary changes in organization and administrative practices.

Develop Implementation Goals

The stage audit I discussed earlier provides an idea of how advanced a company is in respect to data processing. It also specifies a long-term objective.

Keeping in mind that a great deal of difficult organizational changes are required to first synchronize the status of the applications portfolio, organization, control system, and user awareness, and second, to progress through the advanced stages, management can lay out short-run goals and a schedule for longer term goals. A common mistake is to go too fast or to attempt to leap-frog a stage. It is important to remember that learning at all levels within the organization is involved in progressing through the stages.

The more detailed analysis of the organization's charge-out status and specification of management control objectives provide the groundwork for establishing short-run and long-run goals. These goals should also be realistic in terms of schedule and sequence. In addition, they should be initially tailored to the individual user groups with the long-term goal of progressing toward a common charge-out system for the entire organization or, at least, a common charge-out system for each of the major divisions.

Implement and Review

The data processing department should never take it upon itself to implement a management control and charge-out strategy. Implementation of the strategy will have far-reaching effects on the overall management control system of the company, as well as immediate effects on users. It is clear that managers must be able to evaluate information system alternatives since it is the development and operation of *their* applications that will determine what the costs will be. The charge-out system effectively brings the user into control by matching costs and benefits by responsibility center. Of course, there are complicating factors where applications serve several users in more than one responsibility center.

High-level steering committees play a crucial role in providing a forum for shaking down and ratifying a management control and charge-out strategy. Just as important as ratification is management's agreement on implementation goals and schedules. Organizational changes associated with a realistic strategy will inevitably result in some conflict and disagreement. To constructively negotiate through obstacles that arise, management needs to have a plan or road map on direction and destination.

The steering committee, or some type of quarterly review board, should ensure that the organization maintains progress. In addition to its role of approval and guidance, such a group provides a source of commitment that is necessary for successful management control programs.

The Future

The 18 companies that I studied are at the forefront of data processing. Their DP organization charts, trends, and plans provide a glimpse of future organization structures and control systems. The extensive incorporation of data-base technology is the most important trend, leading toward a structure that facilitates data-oriented management.[2]

For example, one of the more advanced companies had explained especially well the role of data-base technology in this orientation. The company used a facsimile of Exhibit 5 to compare the traditional computer-oriented accountability scheme with the data-oriented accountability scheme for two applications: an order entry system and an inventory control system. Traditionally, both the definition of data (inventory part numbers, reorder points, customers) and function (the way an order is processed) is contained in the application, using programming languages such as COBOL or PL/1. Charge-out is based on the computer-related resources used, and the user is held accountable for both data and function.

But data-base technology enables management to separate function from data. As a result, users can be held directly accountable for function, and data processing can be held directly accountable for management of the company's data resources.

Exhibit 5.   Comparison of Traditional Computer-Oriented Accountability with Data-Oriented Accountability

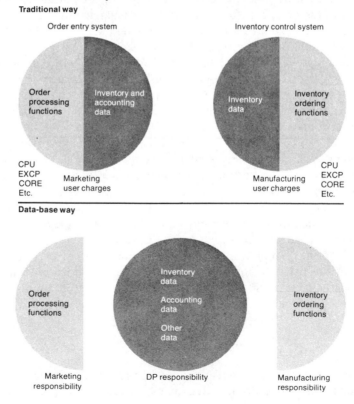

This company envisions a charge-out system including both simplified user bills and data-processing bills from users. In other words, data would be purchased from functional groups that originate them, as well as from outside sources. In responding to requests from users, data processing would provide value-added services by combining, processing, and distributing data. The users would be charged for the cost of the data plus the value-added services of processing them. The value-added concept solves a basic problem of current charge-out systems; it provides a quid pro quo for those who bear the costs of collecting the data but who are not the end-users.

The rapid development of data-base technology will most likely lead to specialized components for data management. Exhibit 6 shows the three main components: data, processing, and control.

To start with, current processing systems will be relieved of data management functions and will be designed to carry out value-added functions of combining, mutating, and distributing data. Both the data and processing systems will incorporate large-scale and mini/microcomputer technologies.

This division of functions will then lead to a separate control system to facilitate specialized management necessary to account, bill, schedule, monitor, and control the efficiency of the company's data-processing installation. Although this control component is at present at a rudimentary state, one manufacturer has already entered the market and has delivered such systems to the Social Security Administration and the General Electric Company.

The impact of the evolving data-processing installation is distinctly visible on several of the organization charts of the companies I studied. One of the first signs is the incorporation of data administration positions. Data administration separates the management of data from the development of user applications. Another sign is the emergence of the controller position.

Exhibit 6. Components of Future Data Services Installation

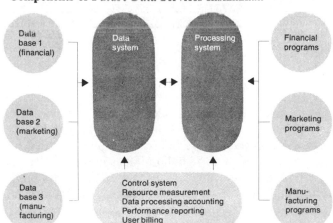

This position is created to recognize the need for more formal management of data processing, as well as to cope with the need for bringing about effective user accountability. Exhibit 7 shows my projected organization chart for the future data processing installation.

In Summary

The role and position of data processing has now taken sufficient form to mount effective management programs to fit it into the modern organization. It is clear that organizations progress through stages of maturity for data-processing management and the next apparent stage is to establish three separate functions for this management.

In order for it to better control these functions, it is important that top management first understand the natural shift from computer management to data management. This shift cannot and will not take place overnight. It is, and for each organization will be, a gradual shift beginning with the incorporation of data-base technology and an elaboration of control systems.

Next, top management needs to realize that an effective chargeout system is essential if those who use data processing are to be in control and held accountable for the services they receive. It is the users that ultimately justify and obtain the potentially lucrative returns from the company's investment in data processing.

It is this simple fact that should determine top management's orientation and decisions concerning data processing.

Notes

1.   See my article, "Managing the Computer Resources: A Stage Hypothesis," *Communications of the ACM,* July, 1973, p. 300.

2.   See my article "Computer Data Bases: The Future is Now," Chapter 16, this book.

Appendix A

Description of Research

This article is based on a study I conducted in 18 organizations. All were considered large in their respective industries. Four were major banks with assets ranging from $1 billion to $8 billion. Sales in the remaining companies ranged from $50 million for a division to over $6 billion for a large retailer. Data-processing budgets varied from $750,000 for a division to over $120 million for an aerospace company that commercially sold computer services. In the course of the research, I interviewed 21 executives, 56 managers who

Exhibit 7. Future Data Services Organization

Exhibit 7. Future Data Services Organization

- Vice president data resources
  - Data resources planning
  - Data resources controller
  - Data architecture planning
    - Data processing planning
  - Data administration
  - Data base technical services
    - Data analysis and programming
  - Data processing
    - Operations
    - Data processing technical services
    - Functional systems analysis and programming (Project teams)

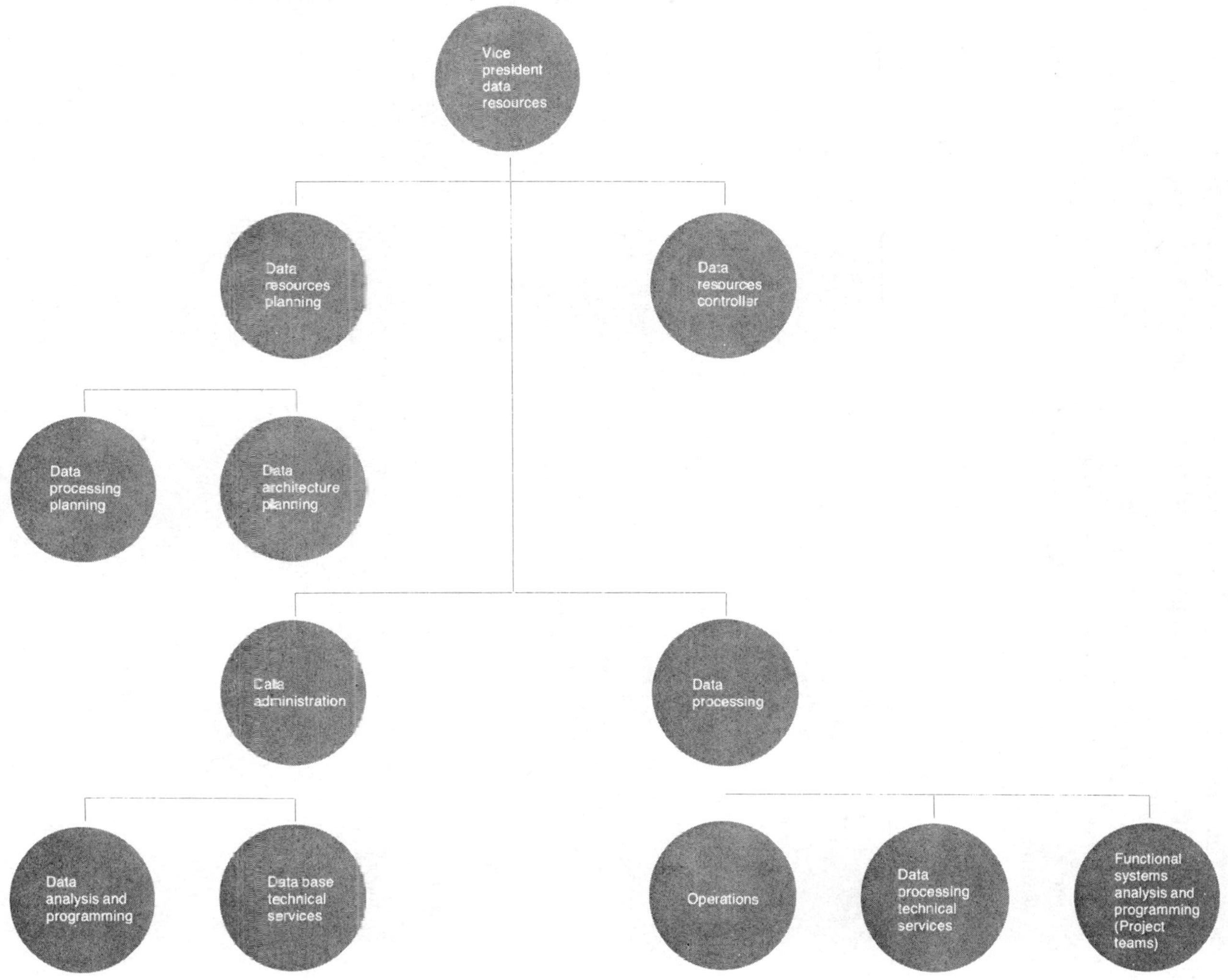

used DP services, and 38 DP managers. Following the visits, I sent a questionnaire to a sample of managers to determine their attitudes toward charge-out systems. Thirteen of the companies participated in a follow-up questionnaire that I sent to 222 users; 170 usable responses were returned. The full report on this research is contained in my book, *Management Accounting and Control of Data Processing* (New York: National Association of Accountants, 1977).

19
Penny-wise Approach to Data Processing

MARTIN D.J. BUSS

Top executives are usually the last to know when things are going wrong in a company's data-processing operation. Because they often control the department in the only way they know how—by watching the total budget—they remain unaware that serious problems are developing. The rude awakening comes when such key elements of the computer operation as sales order processing and inventory control break down completely. Such fiascoes arise from outdated applications software, says this author, who shows top managers how to read the danger signs.

"You ask me how we control data processing? Well, we have tried everything, and the only thing that works is to take a really hard line on costs. We control these rigorously." In this comment by the senior vice president of finance and administration in a billion-dollar corporation, the seeds of trouble lie.

Controlling data processing by controlling costs can have unexpected consequences, as a number of companies have found out. These companies have discovered that they have devoted insufficient resources to data processing, and, as a result, they are now faced with a large investment in new programming. This happened because the interrelated sets of programs that make it possible for the corporation to conduct day-to-day business—those that process orders, maintain inventories, or produce payrolls (key applications, as they are often called)—and that have been running for years have simply worn out.

Like an often-patched suit that finally falls apart, computer programs can be patched until they wear out and need to be replaced. With more and more patches they become more and more unwieldy. Users have increasing difficulty obtaining information, and programmers find it hard to modify programs to cater, for example, to management's new pricing policies or the government's latest rules for investment credits.

Changes take longer and longer to make because the programs have been so modified since they were first written, perhaps 10 years previously, that their logic becomes extremely hard for any programmer to follow. Also, each additional change becomes more difficult to test before it is put into effect.

Replacing key applications programs can take months or years, and the investment can be considerable. This is because such sets of programs are usually very large, involve several departments and many people, and consume a lot of computer resources, people as well as hardware.

One may well ask why the situation gets so out of hand. Surely data-processing management is responsible for keeping key applications programs running even though funds may be limited. In fact, data-processing managers often do a magnificent job of keeping these programs running. The problem is that strict budgetary control limits the funds for investment in new programs needed to replace those that are wearing out. Faced with a budget squeeze, the DP manager has little choice but to take measures that, in the long term, can harm the competitive position of a corporation. Especially vulnerable are airlines, insurance companies, and some banks, where data processing is a vital part of their operations.

Typically, the DP manager tries to reduce the investment and time spent on old but still usable programs by inserting a patch here and there as necessary to accommodate some change in company policy or a new legal requirement. Since a small staff can often keep them working, the manager can dedicate his scarce systems development staff to new areas either that promise a quick payoff or that enhance the image of data processing in the corporation by making automated systems available to more users—those who are not involved in the older key applications.

Why CEOs Wait Till It's Too Late

Top managers fail to see and correct the situation I have described for a couple of reasons. The first is that the chief executive and his aides receive financial signals to indicate all is going well with data processing. Rarely do those at the top of the corporation track how the money is spent, so if these executives see an increase in the total budget, they may assume that some of it is going toward replacement of old software. The purchase of new, cheaper, and more powerful hardware will strengthen their belief that DP is keeping up with the latest developments—including replacement of old software.

The second reason obsolete systems do not get replaced soon enough is that the deterioration process is slow—it extends over years. A sudden breakdown is rare. Evidence of an obsolescent application comes to light when program changes have to be made quickly to meet a deadline. In a mutual fund management company, for example, a hurried change in a much-patched and very old program accomplished its objective: modifying the basis for sending out premium-renewal notices for one group of clients. In the process, however, it generated 250,000 renewal letters for a different group that should not have been involved at all.

A manufacturing company ran into a similar problem when a change in an inventory system suddenly produced shop orders for every item in stock because the quantities in stock had inadvertently been set to zero by a change in another, linked system.

Such problems with old, patched programs get worse over the years. Data-processing staff and users have to work longer and longer hours under increasing pressure until finally the situation becomes unacceptable to everybody. At last top managers recognize the fact that the data-processing department can no longer maintain the applications on which the daily life of the corporation depends. At this late stage, the chief executive finally hears about it.

In addition to devising a plan of action, the CEO will want to avoid a recurrence of the problem. In the next section, I will discuss the importance of keeping applications up-to-date and then suggest four questions to help top managers determine the status of data-processing activities and avoid unpleasant surprises. Finally, I offer guidelines for getting back on track when this proves necessary.

So What If Key Applications Are Out-of-Date?

There are three dangers in outmoded computer software. First, it places the corporation at considerable risk technically. Second, it can make things easier for the competition. Third, it is not cost effective.

1. *Old software is risky.* Primarily from the technical point of view, in terms of personnel, hardware, and the software itself.

☐ The corporation comes to depend on one or two data-processing technicians for its survival. Earlier, I mentioned that changes to old software take longer and longer to make. This is partly because of difficulties in tracing through the logic. And partly it is due to a decline in the number of programmers capable of doing the tinkering, either because no one is familiar with the program or because no one has the expertise necessary to deal with such a convoluted application.

In the end, possibly only one programmer knows how to introduce changes in the system. If he or she fails to make the changes correctly, the corporation may be exposed to financial or legal repercussions. If, for example, a new SEC requirement is not properly programmed into the securities application, the company is liable. Furthermore, when it happens that several important changes are needed simultaneously, the job can become impossible.

☐   The longer replacement of outmoded software is delayed, the greater the possibility of a major breakdown at the most inopportune moment. No software lasts forever.

When software is first developed, users estimate the maximum volumes (of clients, daily orders, inquiries, and so forth) that the programs will have to handle. From this information, the technical staff designs the computer files and the processes. When the volumes start to exceed these limits, problems appear with the way the computer handles the data. After a time, the difficulties become serious. Finally they become insuperable.

Often the final collapse results from large increases in volume. For example, the system may fail while processing the orders that result from a successful sales drive or, as in the case of one Wall Street brokerage house, while processing data from a series of high-volume days on the stock exchange. In computerized back-office systems of this type, the only solution to such a problem is an entirely new applications program designed for larger volumes.

☐   It becomes increasingly difficult, also, to maintain outdated hardware. A multibillion-dollar insurance company over the years found itself with 15-year-old hardware whose manufacturer was threatening to discontinue maintenance of the equipment. Moreover, it was almost impossible to find technical staff prepared to work with the system. There was a serious risk of collapse.

☐   The conversion problem grows worse over time. It is far easier to write new software from programs that are in reasonable shape than from monsters that only a few programmers still understand.

2. *Outdated software helps the competition.*   If a competitor's system is in better condition than yours, you may suffer several setbacks.

☐   Losing customers. A large insurance company lost business after a major sales effort when it took weeks to respond to the simplest client request for policy information.

☐   Failure to attract customers. This trouble occurs particularly when data processing has high visibility among customers (in banking, insurance, car rental, and credit cards, among other businesses). Hertz had to redesign its approach when the "Wizard of Avis"—a car rental system—revolutionized the rental procedure.

☐   Catching up under pressure. It is never pleasant to play catch up ball, and it is even less so when the competition is breathing down your neck. A few years ago, a leading Spanish bank with at least 600 branches installed a nationwide, on-line, real-time computer system for its demand deposit accounts. The new system offered its clients a far higher level of service and represented a major change in approach to processing customer accounts. Until then, real-time computer systems had been used only for savings accounts.

The change caught the competition completely unaware, and two banks launched a crash program to prevent a switch of their deposits to a "real-time bank." Although they caught up, the effort drained resources from other of the banks' important activities.

3.   *Outmoded software is not cost-effective.*   The costs of using older software show up both directly and indirectly.

☐   User costs are higher. To circumvent the unsatisfactory service, users turn more and more to costly clerical procedures, preferring to trust their own staff to handle certain types of transactions rather than have them incorporated into the computer system.

There are three reasons for this attitude. Managers involved with old software often say it takes too long to get the programs changed (in companies with really old software, it may take months). Another reason is that user managers have had unfortunate experiences with results in the past and are unwilling to try again. Last, it may be impossible to make the change in the computer system, owing to the complexity of the problem.

☐   Programming costs are higher. Such costs usually stem from poor documentation of the many programs that make up an application or from poor overall design. The older the software, the truer this tends to be. In the past 10 years there have been significant advances in programming techniques, facilitating efficient design of programs and easing the continuing problem of documentation. Therefore, it is now much simpler to maintain modern collections of programs. The task can be done by fewer programmers and often by junior people with lower salaries.

☐   Hardware used inefficiently will sooner or later translate into higher costs. In the late 1960s, programmers designed software with the currently available hardware in mind. But computing technology has changed tremendously in the past 10 years, and often using old software with the new, more sophisticated hardware is like using a Ferrari to drive only to the grocery store. It can be done, but it costs a lot.

Sometimes, as is the case with a major U.S. steel company, such inefficient use translates directly into increased cost. The company has many 15-year-old programs that by today's standards are inefficient because they take too much computer time. Although the hardware would be adequate if the software were rewritten using today's technology, this task has been left too long.

The rewriting problem has become so complex that the company has decided that the only solution is to buy another computer—the same remedy it adopted three years ago, and then three years before that. In the long run, it would have been much cheaper to replace the old software when it first became outdated.

☐ Personnel costs are higher. Data processing professionals have the reputation of following the technology. Old software and hardware make it hard to recruit and hold staff; high turnover is inevitable.

If a company underinvests in replacement of its key applications software, the heavy price it may eventually pay probably will be compressed into a short time frame. One large brokerage house that had underinvested faced an outlay of more than $30 million in three years for new applications software. A life insurance company found it would have to invest $25 million in hardware and software in 2½ years. And some federal government agencies face even more costly conversions.

Are You Heading for Trouble, Too?

Top managers can find out whether their key applications software is getting out-of-date by answering four questions relating to the status of their data processing. The questions concern corporate data processing costs, the effort being expended on maintenance, the turnover rates of the technical staff, and the general use of terminal-based systems.

1. *What has the five-year trend of your data-processing costs been?* The criterion here is how fast your data-processing costs have increased in comparison both with the rate of inflation and with the rate at which your business is growing. Increases in inflation and growth rates should be reflected in growing DP budgets. It will also be useful to compare the growth in your DP budget to that of other companies. If your expenditures significantly lag behind inflation, revenues, or what's normal in your industry, you are probably underinvesting.

Specifically, the percentage annual increase in your data-processing costs should be compared with the rate of inflation and with DP budgets in your industry. If you are 25% below the rate of inflation, take a closer look. The overall trend is most important. As in Exhibit 1, graphs that show annual percentage changes and the equivalent dollar expenses on a cumulative basis will help clarify your position.

Figures on the rate at which data-processing expenses have been increasing in similar industries are often difficult to obtain. However, Exhibit 2, which shows the approximate rate of increase across all industries, can be used as a rough guide. Trade journals usually review budget trends by industry. As a rule, if your rate of increase is 35% below that of your industry, a warning bell should sound.

Moreover, if your data-processing costs are consistently increasing more slowly than the revenues the DP department supports, you may be underinvesting. In general, if your revenues are growing 1.5 times faster than your data-processing expenses, you may have a problem.

For manufacturing companies, capital expenditures can also be revealing, since they are a warning of things to come.

Investment in new plant will nearly always have implications for data processing. For example, changes may be needed in some key applications software to accommodate the new products to be manufactured in the new plants. Changes of a different sort may be needed if the new facilities are going to mean large increases in volume that old systems cannot handle and may in fact be the trigger for a rewrite of some applications software because the changes are simply too hard to make. By tracking the capital investment rate, senior managers will get a forewarning and can take the right steps in time.

Chief executives should ask for a chart showing these three comparisons. Exhibit 2 shows the experience of one corporation—a clear case of underinvestment.

2. *Is the technical staff spending an increasing percentage of its time maintaining software?* Here again, management must look for a trend, perhaps over the last five years. Increasing dedication to maintenance may be a sign that systems are getting old and inefficient. On the other hand, continuing dedication to new development may be a positive sign, provided

Exhibit 1.   Comparisons of Annual Growth Rates and DP Expenses: XYZ Company

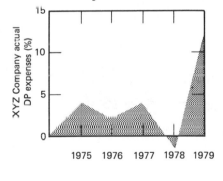
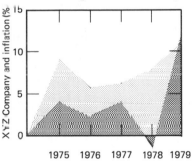
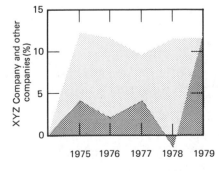
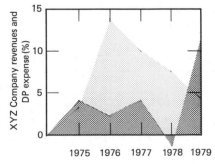

Exhibit 1. (*Continued*)

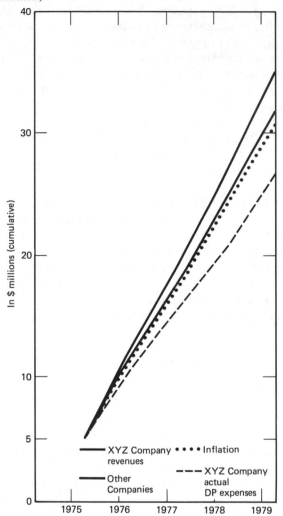

Source Note: *Datamation,* CPI, and Arthur D. Little, Inc., estimates.

the real problems are being addressed. Exactly how the time has been spent needs checking, too.

3. *What is your turnover among analysts and program-mers?* Turnover figures provide a useful guide to the technical adequacy of the data-processing activity, since most DP professionals prefer to work in "state of the art" environments or at least in companies that show clear signs of moving in that direction.

Turnover may be related to maintenance problems, since this type of work is boring compared with the development of new systems. As a guide, in my experience, turnover rates above the 17% level indicate a DP center

Exhibit 2. Percentage Changes for Costs Comparisons 1974 = 100

Year	Inflation CPI		All Industry DP Costs	
	% Change	Indexed	% Change	Indexed
1975	9.1	109	13	113
1976	5.8	115	12	127
1977	6.5	123	10	139
1978	7.6	132	12	156
1979	11.5	147	12	175
1974–1979	47%		75%	
5-year combined growth rate	8%		11.8%	

Sources: Datamation annual budget surveys and Arthur D. Little, Inc. estimates

that is becoming dated or requiring high levels of maintenance, although the percentage will vary according to the location.

4. *Are you adding remote terminals fast enough?* Although not a guide by itself, the number of terminals often indicates the age of the system. The older systems, introduced before telecommunications capabilities improved, tend to have fewer terminals. Most people, however, prefer systems using terminals because such systems are fast and enable the user to take greater operational responsibility for the result.

Growth of the terminal base is usually an encouraging sign; a 25% growth rate is favorable. However, the cost of terminals must not get out of hand, as it did in a $1 billion steel company whose terminals increased from 20 to 200 in less than 18 months without reasonable economic justification.

It should be easy to find answers to these four questions. When analyzing results, however, managers must look at the pattern rather than at individual answers. The combination of below-average expenditures, increasing maintenance load, high turnover, and a small number of terminal-based systems almost certainly points to underinvestment in new software to replace key applications. Although this represents an extreme case, it is by no means an uncommon situation today.

If you still have doubts, one further question about key applications software, rather than DP generally, is instructive.

5. *When were your key programs designed?* Sometimes it is good strategy to keep old programs—to support an obsolete product line at low cost, for example. However, a portfolio of such programs is a bad sign. Age is a relative term, of course, but experience shows that if key programs are more than eight years old, they may well not meet user needs cost effectively. Technology will have passed these programs by. So a rewrite could well be due, particularly if competitors are using more modern approaches.

How Can the Company Get Back on Track?

Most companies completing this exercise will discover that, to some degree, underinvestment is a problem and key programs are out-of-date. What should management do? There are some simple rules.

On the Negative Side

Don't fire the person responsible for data-processing. Too often this has been the remedy for DP problems. Although a fresh perspective may help, changing the staff can do more harm than good. First, lack of guidance and tight budgets may have hampered the effectiveness of the DP manager. Second, the manager is perhaps the only person capable of rebuilding the system in a short time. He or she knows the technical and business environments, priorities, and tasks that have been neglected, as well as the skills available. Then, too, managers dealing with obsolete systems should be given the opportunity to do what they have almost certainly been saying for a long time needs doing.

Don't give up on in-house data processing. All is not lost. The chances are you can easily replace the older software. The DP staff knows much about your software from both the technical and the user requirements sides. Techniques for developing new programs are significantly better today; and there is a vast market of ready-made packages to provide quick, cost-effective solutions for various user needs.

On the Positive Side

Do prepare a plan for replacing your key programs. The problem has to be approached in an orderly way. Review alternatives, investment requirements, and priorities, and then allocate resources. The data-processing manager must understand that you intend to go through with a long-term investment and that you expect the plan to be implemented.

Do ensure that the same thing does not happen again. Once you have put the house in order, three things need doing to make sure you stay on track:

☐ Instruct your computer steering committee or senior executive with general responsibility for data processing to monitor the investment in the replacement of old applications software. Often computer steering committees focus almost exclusively on the issue of priorities. In setting priorities, the committee should prepare an annual report on the corporation's key applications, perhaps including graphs like those in Exhibit 1, together with a brief analysis of the state of each of your major programs and recommendations for replacements.

☐ Direct your chief financial officer to establish a task force to review the cost-accounting principles applied to data-processing expenditures. Large outlays for new software development are, in effect, capital rather than revenue expenditures. Give more thought to monitoring them as such. Probing questions can be asked about programs that are still operational, though fully depreciated.

A useful basis for the task force's approach is the federal government's accounting pamphlet, "Guidelines for Accounting for Automatic Data Processing." This pamphlet suggests (page 13) that software systems in use more than two years and costing more than $100,000 should have their costs capitalized and depreciated. While one can argue about the amount, the principle is sound.

☐   Ensure that your strategic planners, as part of their annual review of the competition, include a brief statement of the significance of any major changes expected in the competitors' approach to information processing. An interesting example of such a possible competitive advantage is the proposed modification of the American Airlines computer system to allow for peak-hour surcharges on some routes. This change, complex when applied to such a large computer operation, may well give American a strategic advantage if it is not matched by the competition.

Business today is devoting major resources to the creation, storage, manipulation, and interpretation of information. Modern software systems are vital to the efficiency of this process. Yet key programs, which are the source of much of this information, are rapidly becoming outdated.

New investments, made in a selective manner to help improve productivity and competitiveness, are necessary. Chief executives can find out where they stand and, armed with the facts, can initiate programs to put their corporations back on track. In so doing, they can improve their competitive position and increase operating efficiency.

20
How to Rank Computer Projects

MARTIN D. J. BUSS

How does your organization decide which information-processing project gets top priority? If it comes down to a decision between a new data communications network, a new word-processing application, or a new inventory control system, which one is likely to win out? One thing is sure, information systems managers, executive management, and users will all have quite different perspectives on which is the most important. Attempts to resolve their conflicting views can raise everyone's blood pressure.

Differences of opinion can become particularly acute in periods of organizational change when, for example, a new vice president for finance and administration takes over responsibility for information systems, or when a newly formed computer steering committee holds its initial meetings. Likewise, a new DP manager assuming responsibility for an existing activity may well feel the pressure from the new boss "to come up with something" on the vexing question of priorities. Even mature, relatively quiet, DP installations are not immune, say, when the new mover and shaker in manufacturing, fresh on the scene, asks the CEO, "How are our priorities determined? Is there a formal approach, or are we flying by the seat of the pants, as in my last company?"

This article will discuss the issues involved in setting priorities for information-processing projects and describe an approach which has proven successful.

The article is organized into three sections. The first reviews the policy issues that affect the decisions on priorities and some common misconceptions about how priorities should be determined. The second describes an approach that takes into account the policy issues, and the last identifies the key factors for successfully implementing such an approach.

There may be slight stylistic differences in the article published in this book and the way it eventually appeared in the Harvard Business Review.

Policy Issues Affecting Priorities for Computer Projects

Corporations run the risk of adopting an overly simplistic view when setting priorities for computer projects. Undue weight is often given to financial benefits, "tangible benefits," in determining the order in which projects are funded. Thus, a project that pays for itself (either on a pay back or a DCF basis) in one year may well be placed higher in the queue than one taking two years.

Such an approach is likely to be favored when the basic corporate philosophy is focused as it is in many companies today on immediate, short term, financial performance. However, it is becoming increasingly recognized that such a view can have an adverse effect on long-term results.

The same is true for information-processing projects. Tangible benefits by themselves are not enough to determine priorities. Three other important factors intervene.

☐ *Business objectives.* Information-processing projects must first and foremost further the overall goals of the organization. Yet, translating this ideal into practical reality often presents a real headache for IS managers. In some corporations business planning itself is not well developed and there may be no formal statement of objectives. In others the quality of the information systems planning falls behind that of business planning. And in others, where there are formal IS and business plans, there are inadequate mechanisms to link the two. Furthermore, not all corporations need to plan their IS activities to the same degree.[1] The characteristics of the IS plan depend on the nature of the organization. For some, such as banks, where IS is a strategic weapon, fully integrated IS plans are vital, yet in others, where IS projects have less impact on corporate performance, the need for careful planning is not so great.

However, if the end result of any priority setting process is to have real meaning, the need to relate IS projects to business objectives never completely goes away. All organizations need to make some attempt to factor in this critical relationship.

☐ *Intangible benefits.* Some important benefits cannot be readily quantified (for example, improved decision support, fulfilling some operational urgency, accuracy, better presentation of information, or whatever). Rather than attempting to quantify the unquantifiable and forcing calculations to prove benefits, it seems to be more sensible and practical to accept the premise that information processing can sometimes benefit the corporation in important but unmeasurable ways. In fact, sometimes the unquantifiables can be more important than the quantifiables. This is particularly true, for example in the case of information-processing software projects such as the conversion of operating systems, the design of data networks, and the creation of data bases to serve multiple applications.

☐ *Technical dependencies.* This is a question of practical realities. It is sometimes either essential or highly desirable to undertake one project before another, if for no other reason than the practical limitations imposed by the abilities of the technical staff. Also, considerations about the overall architecture of the system may intervene. Thus, the design of a new network may logically precede a system using data communications, or a new client master file may precede the introduction of a revised demand deposit system for a bank. Where organizations have a pronounced tangible benefit/bottom line focus—the "support" type described by Warren McFarlan—executive management may not appreciate just how important the technical questions can be in setting priorities. As a result, astute information systems managers are forced to obscure the issue by creatively combining projects into a single, saleable package, or by assigning resources to the technically important projects without executive management's knowledge.

All these four categories—tangible benefits, intangible benefits, business objectives, and technical dependencies—have impact on the priority-setting process. Yet, they may well present contradictory information. For instance:

☐ A project may have zero tangible benefits although it clearly supports the business objectives (e.g., a mailing campaign to support a corporate image building program).

☐ A project with high tangible benefits, such as a new inventory system for project line (X), may not support the business objectives of increasing market share in product line (Y).

☐ A technically important project such as developing specialized software to increase computer security may have few tangible benefits and a questionable direct fit with certain business objectives. Yet it may well deserve higher priority because, for example, the audit committee of the board expressed serious concerns about the issues.

Further clouding the issue is the question of *who* should define computer priorities. Consider these three common misconceptions:

☐ *Users should decide the priorities.* They shouldn't; at least not alone and not at too low an operating level. Although they clearly are important to the priority-setting process, lower-level operating managers will generally have insufficient knowledge of the overall business objectives and of the technical issues to make the right decisions alone. Senior managers are, of course, better placed to decide the priorities, though even they may not always be informed about all the factors. The technical dependencies may escape them, for example.

☐ *Operating managers and IS managers should jointly define priorities.* No! This view overlooks the fact that executive management should be an integral part of the process. This is particularly true when IS has strategic importance and in "turnaround" situations.[1] In such cases closely relating the IS projects to the business objectives will be critical. Moreover, in any organization, only executive management can make the final decision about the allocation of scarce resources between two equally attractive projects. After all, it can decide to do both and add resources accordingly. Leaving executive management out preempts that decision.

☐ *A computer steering committee can decide the priorities.* Sometimes! One problem here though is that the committee is likely to become involved in political negotiations and end up focusing on tangible benefits only. Moreover, the committee will not be a useful forum for discussion unless it includes the right representatives from users, DP, and executive management and has good staff support.

The best way, without doubt, to set priorities is to make them a by-product of some formal planning processing at the corporate or business unit level. Unfortunately, few organizations have planning processes so explicit and orderly as to be extremely reliable for determining information systems priorities. Furthermore, even when business unit and IS planning are formalized, priority issues can still present serious problems.

A multi-billion-dollar food company recently went through a detailed planning exercise for its consumer food division. The planners and division controllers made serious efforts to translate the systems implications of the 10 business unit plans into IS projects with dollars and cents, and suggested priorities. Yet the consolidation of the plans at the divisional level has resulted in friction and misunderstandings between the group head of the $2 billion division and the IS staff over the whopping 30% budget increase in IS expense, and the need for the new systems being proposed.

Realistically speaking, in most organizations, it is the information systems manager who has to take the most active role in establishing priorities. He has to try to reconcile conflicts regarding key criteria. Clearly, the process not only requires consideration of more than tangible benefits, but the involvement of people who understand a broad perspective. How then can the IS manager measure the relative importance of tangible and intangible benefits, assess the fit with objectives, and express the technical importance of a range of information-processing projects in a readily understandable way?

An Approach to Setting Computer Priorities

Exhibit 1 describes the process in a conceptual way. Key is the solid, analytical framework and the simple, visual representation to senior management of the basic issues involved. Interaction along the way is highly desirable both to get guidance—on objectives, for example,—and to sensitize

Exhibit 1. The Process

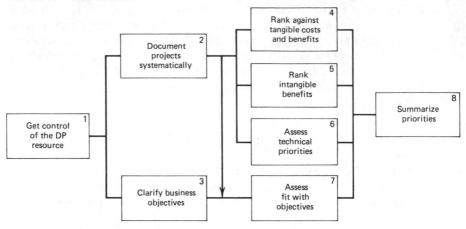

senior managers to the policy issues which influence the final decisions on project priorities.

The eight steps in Exhibit 1 are quite detailed and will probably only apply to those companies with a chaotic situation in information systems. Companies that have well-documented, information-processing activities and clear statements of business objectives should be able to focus immediately on steps 4–7. These four describe the ranking process itself. They are not sequential. Overlapping them will speed up the process. Furthermore, an early start on Step 7—assessing the fit between the projects and the business objectives—may shorten the project list, since it should be practical to eliminate marginal projects. Also, if the objectives have a striking "bottom line" focus, the analysis of intangible benefits may too be curtailed.

One last point before discussing the whole process in more detail. Although the methodology as described has eight discrete steps, in practice it has, to some extent, to be iterative. This is particularly so, for example, when looking at the tangible costs and benefits of developing each project (Step 4).

Step 1: Get Control of the Data Processing Resource

Where a formal priority-setting process has not been adopted, there are likely to be a number of problems. One may well find individuals fixing priorities, the "them against us" syndrome, misinformed users, and data processing management acting unilaterally out of necessity.

Clearly, in such a situation, no methodology can be effective. The newly appointed information-processing manager must first gain control by taking one or more of the following actions:

☐ Establishing improved mechanisms for interacting with users
☐ Reorganizing data processing and hiring new people

☐ Creating some sort of computer steering committee

☐ Improving the information base about the outstanding projects

This last point leads directly to Step 2.

Step 2: Document Systematically

Part of the problem in sorting out priorities stems from inadequate documentation of project requests. There may be several deficiencies: an outdated approach, total randomness in the way projects are documented, deficient authorization procedures, or poor communication about projects either within the information systems department and/or between users and management. As a result, the information systems manager may not have the facts needed to evaluate and rank the projects. By contrast, proper documentation requires:

☐ Establishing, in broad terms, the data required for the various classes of projects, for example, data processing, office automation. Complete uniformity across all IS projects is likely to be impossible because organizations will be at different stages in their use of the various technologies. They may be obliged to estimate data for some projects (prototypes, for example), while having a more solid base for calculating costs, for example, accurately for others. Some flexibility will, therefore, always be essential.

☐ Publishing procedures by which projects are identified and submitted for approval. Here too variations to take into account the different classes of projects will be necessary.

☐ Converting informal outstanding project requests to the new procedures and standardized formats and including the intangible benefits, the fit with objectives, and the technical importance of each project.

☐ Insisting on adherence to the new procedures for all projects. Much has been written about project documentation, so this article will not elaborate further on this important issue. Suffice it to say that, without a systematic process for identifying and documenting projects, it will be impossible to make informed decisions about priorities.

Step 3: Clarify Business Objectives

As mentioned earlier, clarifying the business objectives may prove to be difficult since the importance assigned to planning will differ from organization to organization. Some have formal statements of objectives, others do not. Yet, to ignore the objectives can result in devoting scarce resources to projects which only have a marginal impact. And this can be a double loss since the potential benefits that would result from deploying them on projects that really serve the business objectives will also be foregone.

In an environment where formal planning is not well developed, the proactive IS manager will have to take the initiative and attempt to state them him/herself for later review by senior management. A pragmatic, big picture approach is essential since there is no way the IS department can suddenly transform itself into a full-fledged corporate planning department, nor is there any intention that it should. This is a one-time exercise carried out to place the IS projects in their business context.

The best way to proceed is to combine judicious interviewing of business managers, division heads, territory managers, and soon with a careful reading of internal documents, and a quick review of information processing in key competitors. The most critical element, though, is the interviewing of the decision makers.

The IS manager is looking for guidance on essentially two issues; namely what the organization is trying to achieve, and what the nature is of the key constraints. In looking at the first, the IS manager will want management's perspectives on such issues as increasing market penetration, reducing operating costs, expanding internationally, accelerating product development, and the like. In looking into the constraints, such questions as time horizons, resources, possible competitive responses, and so forth, will be important.

Although views will differ among the decision makers, there will almost certainly be some measure of consensus on the top three or four objectives. The IS manager can build on these through discussion and through review meetings with an appropriate high-level management group such as an operating committee, a policy committee, or a computer steering committee, where one exists. The end result of perhaps a series of meetings will be an agreed list of objectives which, although not perfect, can later serve as a guide for evaluating and ranking the information processing projects in Step 7 (assessing fit with objectives).

Step 4: Rank Against Tangible Costs and Benefits

The prerequisite for this step is the classic analysis of costs and benefits on a project-by-project basis. Since the results will be different, it will be necessary to calculate the numbers under a series of assumptions such as in-house developmemt, subcontract programming, purchased package, and so on. The aim must be to arrive at the optimum balance between all the various means of getting applications up and running, not just the cost of doing the projects internally.

The level of detail required will, of course, depend on corporate policy, time, availability of information, and so forth. Where there are no standards or procedures, the only practical course is to estimate gross numbers. Once these are known, their relative priority status can be easily shown by using the nine-square grid on Exhibit 2, which illustrates the ranking of a series of computer applications for the European bank mentioned above. The same methodology applies, however, to any set of information processing projects (that is, word processing, data communications, software engineering) and not just to those using the computer.

In Exhibit 2, the vertical scale indicates the total costs associated with each project (investment); the horizontal scale reflects the level of anticipated

Exhibit 2. Rank by Tangible Costs and Benefits

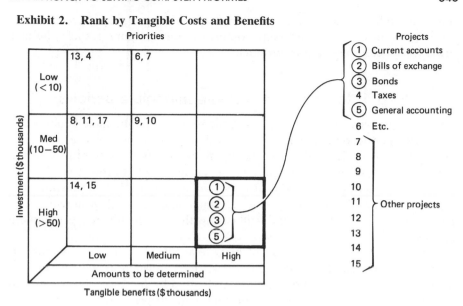

tangible benefits. Fifteen projects, identified by number, are listed. Project 1, "current accounts" is positioned at the bottom right of the grid because it has high tangible benefits and requires a high level of investment. On the other hand, Project 4, taxes, appears at the top left because it offers low tangible benefits and requires a low investment.

With such an array of projects, senior managers can, at a glance, determine the relative costs and tangible benefits of the entire portfolio of projects. They will, of course, be attracted by the projects that fall into the square at the top right—those with high tangible benefits and low investment needs. Unfortunately, these are likely to be few and far between. Many companies, for example, that have started to tackle the problem of obsolete key applications caused by under investment[2] in data processing in the past have found that such projects are more likely to be positioned bottom right; that is, they require significant investment and yield little in the way of tangible benefits. A mining company, for example, faced with quantifying the benefits of redoing its 1956 payroll system is finding that the exercise requires a good blend of witchcraft and financial analysis! Most such analyses are highly questionable.

This same company, however, has reaped an unexpected benefit from its long hard look at information systems and at the costs, benefits, and priority issues. Its senior management became convinced that it had a serious problem in the staffing of the function—it simply didn't have enough people to do anything other than the bare minimum. Given the hostile economic environment, management made an informed decision to delay projects rather than add staff. It knew the consequences and the IS manager could do his job without unwarranted pressure to perform the constant miracles he had previously been expected to produce.

Step 5: Identify and Evaluate Intangible Benefits

This is a four-part process. Part 1 is to identify which intangible benefits are acknowledged to be achievable by both data processing and user management. Part 2 is to determine the scoring methodology to be followed for the evaluation. Part 3 is to assign numerical values to each project so that the benefits can be ranked in order of importance. Finally, Part 4 positions the projects on the nine-square grid in a similar manner to that shown in the preceding step. Exhibits 3 and 4 illustrate the end result of the complete process.

The work is best carried out by a team made up of user personnel, such as departmental operating managers and information systems professionals, knowledgeable about the areas affected by the projects. It can also be helpful to include the head of internal audit to bring added impartiality to the exercise.

A mixture of group sessions and team members working independently will be the most effective way of conducting the evaluation. Thus, Part 1— the identification of the intangible benefits—is best done in a group, each team member bringing to the table his perception of what these are (quicker information, improved image, better decision process, and so forth). Some will probably be rapidly agreed upon, whereas others may need thrashing out.

Exhibit 3.   Determine and Score Intangible Benefits

Intangible benefits	Projects					
	1	2	3	4	5	6
Improve client service	6	3	8	9	0	0
Improve financial control	1	7	6	0	10	10
Provide management information	8	6	5	0	10	5
Standardize manual processes	3	8	7	3	10	7
Speed up decision—making	4	3	0	0	10	5
Improve quality of information	3	7	6	0	7	7
Speed up information	9	6	7	5	10	7
Total	34	40	39	17	57	41
Ranking	11	9	10	15	1	8

Exhibit 4. Rank by Intangible Benefits

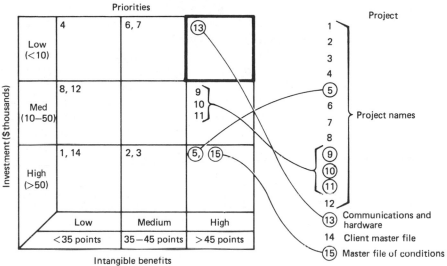

The group approach will also be the best for Part 2— the definition of the scoring methodology to be followed. Several systems are possible. However, beware of overcomplicating the process by adapting one that is very complex or spuriously scientific. In the illustration in Exhibit 3, for example, the team adopted a very straightforward system. It assigned to each intangible benefit a maximum of 10 points, deciding after a short discussion not to weight or score some benefits higher than others. Weighting benefits can result in interminable arguments that serve little purpose. This is not an exact science; the objective is to arrive at a broad measure of the relative importance of each project.

For Part 3—the actual scoring of the projects against the benefits—it is preferable to have each team member work independently and then have everyone iron out differences in a group meeting. However, at these meetings each person should be prepared to support his or her evaluation with qualitative opinions. Thus, if one project scores five out of ten, and another scores the maximum, the team member ought to be able to explain what makes one twice as good as the other.

The end result of the group meeting be the summary sheet illustrated in Exhibit 3. This shows for each project its scores for each individual tangible benefit, its total score, and its overall ranking, the project with the highest score being No. 1.

With the projects ranked in this way, Part 4—positioning each on the nine-square grid—is an easy last step. All that remains to be done is for the team to determine the ranges of values along the horizontal axis for high, medium, and low intangible benefits. These will, of course, vary depending

on the scoring system chosen. Using the development costs calculated previously, each project will then automatically fall into one of the squares,
thus enabling senior management to see the entire portfolio of projects arranged in a consistent and intelligible manner.

Not suprisingly, the value of a project as defined by its intangible
benefits can be quite different from its tangible benefits. For instance, in
Exhibit 2, Project 1, "current accounts," is rated quite high by tangible
benefits. Yet, in Exhibit 4 it is perceived as a project yielding low benefits
when its intangibles are measured. Just the opposite movement occurs with
Project 13, "communications and hardware." It is unlikely to generate cash
savings, but promises strong intangible benefits.

Step 6: Assess Technical Dependencies

Some projects must logically be completed before others. It is relatively
straightforward for data processing management to reflect the technical importance of each of the projects in the nine-square grid format as shown in
Exhibit 5. In this figure, the vertical axis again represents investment, whereas
the horizontal axis shows low, medium, and high levels of technical importance. This is a subjective judgment of data processing management, but
represented in this consistent way it is easier for executive management to
understand.

Exhibit 5. Rank by Technical Priorities

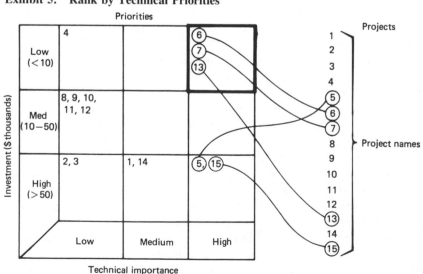

Step 7: Assess Fit With Objectives

Once the business objectives are clarified (see Step 3), user and data processing management together can review the quality of fit between the projects and the objectives. The work sheet in Exhibit 6 offers a convenient and simple way of doing this. A check mark indicates a fit between a project and an objective. It is also possible to develop a quantitative approach in which a project's contribution to an objective is indicated numerically in each column. Thus, for example, 10 might be the maximum score for a project which coincided completely with the objective.

With the quality of fit between the project and objectives established, the IS manager can then use the same nine-square grid format to depict these relationships. The vertical axis continues to show the investment required, and the horizontal axis now shows the degree of fit between the projects and the objectives. Once again, this ranking of priorities yields quite different results. Project 4, taxes, has a high degree of fit with objectives, whereas Project 1, current accounts, ranks only medium.

Step 8: Summarize the Priorities

The use of the preceding figures will give senior management a good picture of the various ways to measure a project's value, and, accordingly, of the complex issues involved in establishing overall priorities. But the process also raises a question: how can the sometimes conflicting information be

Exhibit 6.   Fit Projects to Objectives

Division	Objectives	Projects			
		1	2	3	4
Planning and finance	Improve financial control over • Interbank accounts • Bond processing • General accounting	✓		✓	✓
Industrial	Implement an MIS system Establish budgetary control Improve treasury management	✓ ✓	✓		✓ ✓ ✓
Consumer banking	Expand the client base Develop an international capability Implement an MIS system	✓	✓	✓	✓ ✓

Exhibit 7. Rank by Objectives

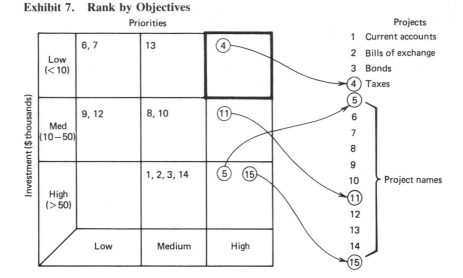

reconciled? The solution is to summarize the priorities on a single, nine-square grid (Exhibit 8).

In this summary, the vertical axis, as in each of the preceding examples indicates investment; the horizontal axis shows low, medium, and high priority projects. The final assessment is determined by the number of times any one project appears in a particular square in the nine-square matrix. For example, Project 5, accounting, appears in the bottom right-hand corner in every case, and Project 15, master file of conditions, appears three out of four times. Evidently these two projects should have high priority.

If priorities were assigned measured only by tangible benefits, the results would have been very different. In fact, three other projects would have been placed above Project 15: Project 1, current accounts, Project 2, bills of exchange, and Project 3, bonds. Yet all three "top priority" projects had only a medium fit with the business objectives, and two of the three had low technical importance and medium intangible benefits.

This approach highlights such inconsistencies and gives executive management the data necessary to decide upon priorities. Thus, in the example, executive management could still decide to ignore everything except tangible benefits but would do so with a full understanding of the implications, namely that most of the projects did not serve effectively the business objectives.

One further point about the summary. Knowing how the four factors affect the priority decision, executive management can change the degree of emphasis given to each one depending on the circumstances of the corporation. In hard times, for example, they might decide that only tangible benefits should be considered.

Exhibit 8. Summary of Priorities

Tangible benefits

	L	M	H
L	13, 4	6, 7	
M	8, 11, 17	9, 10	
H	14, 15		1, 2, 3, 5

Intangible benefits

	L	M	H
L	4	6, 7	13
M	8, 12		9, 10, 11
H	1, 14	2, 3	5, 15

Technical

	L	M	H
L	4		6, 7, 13
M	8, 9, 10, 11, 12		
H	2, 3	1, 14	5, 15

Objectives

	L	M	H
L	6, 7	13	4
M	9, 12	8, 10	11
H		1, 2, 3, 14	5, 15

Overall priorities

Investment ($ thousands)	Low	Medium	High
Low <10	4 Taxes	6 Correspondents / 7 Branches / 13 Communications	
Med 10–50	8 Int'l / 12 Personnel		
High >50		1 Current accounts / 2 Bills of exchange / 3 Bonds / 14 Client master file	5 Accounting / 15 Master file of conditions

349

Key Factors for Success

In this process of setting computer priorities, success depends on the inter-action of three groups of people, namely executive management, users, and data processing management. Each of these has important roles to play.

Executive Management Must:

☐ Demonstrate a willingness to commit resources to approved high priority projects.

☐ Participate in the priority-setting process, and, in particular, in the determination of which aspect of priority setting should be of the most importance in any one time period.

☐ Help clarify the business objectives so that the whole process can be related to the underlying needs of business.

☐ Be willing to exercise judgment and make decisions in areas that have not traditionally involved top management.

Users must:

☐ Commit to the benefits stated in the analysis of the costs and benefits of each project.

☐ Involve themselves actively in the process so that the final deci-sions reflect a consensus.

Particularly important here, for example, is the statement of the intangible benefits and a commitment to achieving them.

DP Management Must:

☐ Lead the project
☐ Provide analytical capabilities
☐ Esnsure progress
☐ Develop the alternative priority-setting schemes for executive decision

Finally, one comment on this overall approach. It is important to build on an existing framework for setting priorities—rarely should it be necessary or even desirable to start from scratch.

Conclusions

Analysis and programming resources are continuously getting scarcer and most costly. We have to use them effectively by assigning them to important, high-priority projects. A structured approach will help the harassed IS manager and the executive management think through these issues.

Notes

1. See F. Warren McFarlan, James L. McKenney, and Philip J. Pyburn, "The Information Archipelago—Plotting a Course," *HBR*, January-February 1983, p.377.

2. See "Penny-Wise Approach to Data Processing" Chapter 19, this book.

INVOLVING THE USER

AN OVERVIEW

As users become more familiar with computers and their companies can afford to have more of them, conflicting pressures arise inside the organization—often from users eager for more access to and control of these smaller and cheaper machines but sometimes from managers anxious to get their more reluctant employees to accept them. The articles in this section address the problems that result from such tensions.

Buchanan and Linowes analyze the developments that have made the distribution of computer systems feasible for many companies, pointing out that so-called distributed data processing (DDP) implies more than the spreading out of hardware and data. By their definition, DDP should mean that authority over various areas of responsibility has been vertically or horizontally decentralized; that is, authority has been delegated downward or assigned laterally. They point out, further, that proper design of these newer decentralized systems has become vital for some organizations, since their administrative systems are now often embodied in computerized information systems. Finally, Buchanan and Linowes sound a theme that is heard often in this book: managers must stop viewing their information systems simply as labor-saving devices that support the activities of one or more departments; they should see them as control and coordination devices that should fit an organization's formal structure and enable it to achieve its business goals. Thus DDP goes beyond the conventional approaches of simply applying computers to business.

Like Buchanan and Linowes, Frederic Withington sees users as one of the forces behind the spread of computers into all levels of the organization. He understands their impatience with the poor response time and uncertain results from central data processing, but he worries about their inexperience and the possible duplication of effort, the lack of standards, and laxity of control in such areas as accountability and auditability that could result from unplanned computer proliferation. To ease the tension most effectively between the organization's central data processing management on the one hand and the possible anarchy of uncontrolled decentralization on the other, Withington proposes the concept of distributed responsibility. According to this notion, responsibility for each information-processing activity should lie with the unit most closely associated with it. However, and equally important, the units should have technical assistance as needed and they should have management oversight. To keep control over the whole process, Withington thinks a combination of three conventional management methods will suffice: the management steering committee, project management techniques, and assignment of "global staff responsibility" to the corporate DP manager. Under Withington's system, the corporate DP function acts as a kind of clearinghouse and coordinator of the activities of all parts of the information-processing system. The DP manager prepares the actual budget, but the steering committee sets the limits and approves the projects. Withington agrees with Buchanan and Linowes that the best arrangement for DDP in most companies will not involve total distribution—at least not in the sense that they will abandon completely hierarchical management practices.

According to Withington, few organizations will want to rush into any type of distributed responsibility. He suggests that experiments with local responsibility first be conducted in the more novel areas of office automation and computer-aided design. It is the possibilities of this latter technology that Hirotaka Takeuchi and Allan Schmidt explore in their piece on computer graphics. If any of the newer technologies has captured the imagination of users, this is it. Whereas a decade ago only engineers used computer graphics, today many managers are discovering the applications of this technology to their business problems. Although the hardware and data bases that computer graphics requires have been available for some time, the software to produce the actual graphic output has been lacking until fairly recently. Takeuchi and Schmidt see the promise of computer graphics expanding even further in the next decade through the use of intelligent terminals, which will permit local storage of data bases, with access to larger remote computers for their data bases and greater computing capacity.

If, as these authors say, the applications of computer graphics are, or soon will be, limited only by the imagination, why do these and other electronic marvels sometimes gather dust on the suppliers' shelves? Harvey Poppel provides some of the answers to that question. In a survey of large U.S. organizations, he discovered that although knowledge workers accounted for the largest and fastest growing segment of the work force, the amount of the corporate budget devoted to any kind of information technology support for them was minuscule. In fact, you could say about the new office technology that most companies wouldn't give a nickel for it, since they spend less than five cents on it of every dollar that goes to knowledge worker salaries and internal support costs.

Poppel's study also showed that neither the workers themselves nor their managers were satisfied with their productivity. Given the high costs and less than satisfactory performance of this group, office automation would seem to be a ready-made answer. The chief reason for the slow acceptance of such a solution seems to be negative experience with earlier innovations, such as MIS, plus lack of confidence in the possible benefits of the newer technology. However, since most of the managers and professionals Poppel interviewed were eager to improve the quality and quantity of their work, he thinks that with the proper mix of electronic enhancements—ranging from word processors to video conferencing facilities—most companies could increase productivity and demonstrate the financial soundness of their investment.

The resistance among workers that Poppel refers to becomes the subject of a piece that explores what happens when managers fail to notice the negative feelings that working with computers may give rise to. In fact, this piece, by Shoshanna Zuboff, is the perfect complement to Poppel's. If top managers do decide to get off the bench and get into the big leagues of the completely automated office, they would do well to take into account the wide-ranging effects on almost every area involving workers. Since the introduction of computers and their related technologies will affect the skills that an organization needs, the training, career paths, control, authority, and even the overall organizational design, most businesses will want to consider very carefully what kind of organization and what kind of work place they want to foster as they move into the automated office.

21

Understanding Distributed Data Processing

JACK R. BUCHANAN and RICHARD G. LINOWES

Declining hardware costs, increasing self-confidence of users, and developing technologies have provided compelling reasons in the minds of many managers to bring distributed data processing (DDP) into their organizations. Rather than let it spread almost randomly, managers who recognize the strengths as well as the pitfalls of DDP are seeking to establish coherent policies and procedures. The authors define DDP in terms of responsibilities for managing all phases of information processing. They also provide a framework companies can use to evaluate alternatives and to develop a DDP strategy that both matches their organizational structure and enables their business to plan.

The data processing profession has generated a new set of buzzwords that purportedly describe the next generation of information systems. A new development, referred to as "distributed data processing," or "DDP," will figure in major expansion plans both now and throughout the 1980s. Managers in many organizations are eager to bring some of this state-of-the-art technical capability into their own operations, for distributed data processing, as they see it, is an opportunity to distribute computing facilities and allow access to a machine in a way that was never possible before.

Is distributed data processing just a new technological fad or does it represent a new concept that will enable organizations to make more effective use of their data processing resources? If DDP entails the spread of computing around an organization, what are the hazards of such proliferation? Is there some systematic way for managers to plan and monitor the introduction of DDP into their organizations? In this, the first of two articles, we shall attempt to answer these questions by developing a framework that enables managers to understand DDP and to identify opportunities for its use.

DDP is a concept that has only recently come of age. Technological, economic, and educational developments now allow us to design information systems that may achieve the objectives of matching the organizational structure, supporting the business strategy, and, in general, providing a more natural use of information processing. In essence, DDP involves the exciting prospect of assigning responsibility for DP-related activities so that both business and technical knowledge can be applied more readily to the achievement of an organization's goals.

Underlying Developments

The move to distributed data processing is possible today in large part because of the drop in the cost of computer hardware. Minicomputers and now microcomputers are becoming so inexpensive that it is quite reasonable for a company to buy three or four small computers to do the work previously performed by one central computer or to automate activities previously performed manually. Whereas, in the past, economics of scale may have driven a company to use one large data processing center to perform a wide variety of services, a company now might employ several different computers in different locations to provide more specialized services. Management can now arrange data processing facilities with much less concern for hardware costs.

Technical developments are also responsible for the recent practicality of distributed data processing. Major innovations, primarily from the areas of telecommunications and data-base systems, have ushered in many new capabilities. Improvements in both equipment and software have made possible the building of very sophisticated computer networks, and direct links from computer to computer are becoming more common. Tasks that have been handled in large centers may now be partitioned into subtasks, and these in turn may be farmed out to remote sites.

When information systems are designed in this fashion, a whole network of computers often becomes involved in carrying out an operation. Such systems represent prototypes for the distributed data processing of the future; they show how technical developments, perhaps for the first time, permit the decentralization of many data processing activities.

The DP manager has traditionally been responsible for cost center management, capacity planning, systems administration, and adaptation of new technology. Since DDP will increase direct access to the system by the end user, the administrative process of the user must be reflected in system design, and information systems must focus on business tasks.

The DP manager will participate with end users in more joint enterprises and consequently will have to be more concerned with how the user defines productivity. Where computer operations are decentralized, the manager must establish charge-out methods that are understandable to the user and that measure service to the organization. For example, the DP manager should translate from kilocore seconds, computer resource units (CRUs), or other technical terms into measures such as number of transactions processed and reports produced so that both user and top management can make practical use of them. If a user group manager is to have any control over the computer resource, he or she must have this type of information as well as the means to effect change.

Finally, the exposure that most managers have to computerized information systems grows all the time, and their increasing familiarity with data processing leads them to make better use of the systems they have and to demand more from their systems. Thus many of these managers can be expected to set up some kind of data processing activities in their own departments and to become involved in delivering some of their own data processing services.

Declining hardware costs, improving communications and data base capabilities, and the growing data processing experience of users are prime factors behind our projection that distributed data processing, including the extensive use of data bases,[1] will be the hallmarks of the computer era.

Common Pitfalls

To take advantage of the power of DDP, managers need a clear conception of the complexities of using and managing the computer resource. Yet managers at all levels too often find themselves in difficulty because of their overly simplistic understanding of data processing, which they see chiefly as a collection of machines and technical issues; and oddly enough, DP managers sometimes are the worst culprits. This narrow view has led to a number of common fallacies.

One manufacturing manager recently pulled us aside to show us a new microcomputer hidden away in his office. He said proudly that it permitted him to do a few small applications unencumbered by the red tape and priority system of the corporate data center, where such applications officially should be done. He was delighted with the department's new toy, and he was eager to expand his operation and bring all his data processing activity in-house. "After all," he argued, "we already have one machine operating successfully. And there is a young engineer upstairs who took some computer courses in school, so we're all set."

In another company, a division general manager was perturbed at the high data processing charges appearing in his monthly income statement, charges that supposedly reflected his actual use of the corprate data center. He felt particularly disgruntled when he stumbled onto an advertisement for a new minicomputer that seemed capable of performing all the processing his division required yet whose monthly fee was signficantly less than the figure he was paying. At the next quarterly meeting he complained, "For what we are paying for the data center, we could have our own minicomputer system and control our own priorities."

In a highly diversified conglomerate that has grown by the acquisition of other companies, the corporate controller was concerned about the alarming increase in data processing expenditures by the divisions. He appointed a corporate systems planner to investigate the problem. The planner returned with a suggestion: take data processing away from the divisions and place it in regional centers under corporate direction. The plan was rejected out of hand by the controller, who knew that the design would be unacceptable to division managers in the company because they would not give up data processing to a corporate group. The corporate controller exclaimed, "I don't want to *manage* data processing, I just want to *control* it."

Finally, in the federal courts, administrators were planning how computers should be distributed around the country to provide computer support for various administrative functions of the courts. The design of the new system could take any form because there was no existing data processing activity with which to conform. The leadership and development of the project were centered in Washington, and systems analysis and implementation were carried out jointly with district and appellate court administrators. The study team was considering two possible arrangements of data processing facilities: local court minicomputers or regional centers.

Proponents of regional data centers argued that the configuration they favored would permit more responsive systems and more effective control by the courts. Those favoring local minicomputers, on the other hand, felt it was *their* configuration that offered these benefits, primarily because they saw that physical custody of the machines established effective control of the information-processing resource: "How could a court have more control over its information processing at regional centers than it would within its own four walls?"

In all four of these examples, the managers' positions regarding use of computer systems appeared quite reasonable at the time. Only later did the problems or unrealistic features of their stands emerge. As we shall see, their arguments rested on the conventional image of data processing and its role in an organization, a view too limited for data processing planning in the 1980s.

Acquiring a Broad View

How can a manager avoid the pitfalls of the narrow view and systematically plan the placement of DP responsibilities? Primarily, he or she should recognize and work with two fundamental assumptions: (1) information systems should match a company's structure and strategy; and (2) activities that support information systems are wide ranging and separable. These basic notions are not only a good general way to understand the data processing resource, but they also allow us to construct a framework for describing and planning distributed data processing systems.

To most technicians, DDP simply means the spread of computer hardware and data to multiple sites around an organization. This definition is deficient, however, because it overlooks a wide range of activities that help make information systems work, and furthermore it neglects the linkage of information systems to strategy and structure. In effect, its technical orientation leaves general managers out of discussions about the design of DDP systems.

A broader definition acknowledges that data processing is an organizational resource consisting of many areas of activity, each of which may be executed or controlled by various individuals. These activities, or areas of responsibility, can be spread across an organization in a variety of ways, and a manager should carefully consider the appropriate degree of decentralization for each of them. Assignment of responsibilities by default seldom works.

To facilitate a systematic approach to organizing data processing, one should identify the areas of responsibility that may be operationally assigned in an organization. Exhibit 1 shows suggested areas of activity, grouped rather loosely into the major categories of control and execution, with execution further divided into development and operations. The content of each area may be intuitively clear. Given this division of responsibilities, the major challenges of DDP planning lie, then, in determining the extent to which each should be decentralized, in understanding the interdependencies among them, and in assuring that the appropriate degree of authority and necessary level of competence coexist at the designated locations in the organization.

The areas of execution are the easily identifiable kinds of activities that are commonly associated with data processing. In most companies, technically trained persons, such as programmers, systems analysts, and com-

Exhibit 1.   Areas of Managed Activity

Execution (Development)	Control
Data base administration	Providing security
Applications programming	
Systems analysis	Setting priorities
System documentation	Standardizing tasks
User training	
	Accessing data
Execution (Operations)	Scheduling tasks
Hardware operation	
Telecommunications	Personnel planning
Systems programming	
Application system	Budgeting
maintenance	Evaluating products

puter operators, have responsibility for delivering the data processing product or service. The areas of control activity regulate the delivery of data processing in terms of dollars, people, time, quality assurance, and access to data, but they do not require a detailed level of technical knowledge of computers.

To describe the data processing in an organization as "distributed" is to say that authority over one or more of the areas of responsibility shown in Exhibit 1 has been vertically or horizontally decentralized; that is, authority may be delegated downward or assigned laterally. This definition is more inclusive than the definition commonly used. It can imply the spreading out not only of hardware and data but of the whole array of activities associated with managing information processing.

Before describing decentralization of activities within these areas in greater detail, we first consider the forces that shape the design of distributed information systems.

Roots of Decentralization

What causes an organization to decentralize? We have identified three general motivations that might lead a company to decentralize or distribute its data processing. These are the pressures for differentiation and the resulting needs for selective integration, the desire for direct control, and the wish to reallocate or lend support to authority. Heterogeneity or variability in task, function, or local situation leads to a state of differentiation, which, according to Paul R. Lawrence and Jay W. Lorsch,[2] means the organizational units will differ in goals, time perspectives, interpersonal relationships, and structure. Such differentiation creates the need for various integrative devices. Information systems are common integrative tools which are often used to coordinate operations that span functions, products, divisions, and geographic locations.

Also, uncertainty about such aspects of centralized control as setting of priorities might motivate user group managers to seek control over all system services they see as critical to their operations. When volume permits suitable economies of scale, managers who feel sufficiently competent will have strong motivation to control and even to run their own data processing groups.

Finally, because power to make decisions tends to rest at the level where the necessary information is accumulated[3] and because information support is one of the necessary conditions for effective power,[4] managers can use distributed information systems strategically to bolster the authority of system users in the organization.

Strategy, Structure & Information Systems
Since Alfred D. Chandler's landmark book, *Strategy and Structure*, describing the history of America's first great corporations,[5] writers have noted

how organizations alter their formal structure to facilitate achievement of goals. But the relationship between structure and business plan has many dimensions. The key to a good design for an organization is not only the match between strategy and structure but the more complex match involving strategy, structure, and other administrative systems. Today many of these administrative systems are embodied in computerized information systems, which assist management in controlling and coordinating most of the activities of modern, large-scale organizations—tying together the efforts of diverse departments that pursue different but complementary ends.

Yet computer applications in general have been so specialized that many organizations—the data processing profession along with them—have overlooked potential, and more general, roles for information systems. Information systems are not simply labor-saving devices that support the activities of people in one or more departments. Rather, they are control and coordination devices that should fit an organization's formal structure and help it achieve its business goals.

Most information systems are designed to play such roles, and it is worthwhile to reexamine them in that light. Consider the following typical situations:

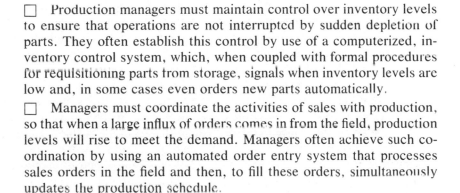

☐ Production managers must maintain control over inventory levels to ensure that operations are not interrupted by sudden depletion of parts. They often establish this control by use of a computerized, inventory control system, which, when coupled with formal procedures for requisitioning parts from storage, signals when inventory levels are low and, in some cases even orders new parts automatically.

☐ Managers must coordinate the activities of sales with production, so that when a large influx of orders comes in from the field, production levels will rise to meet the demand. Managers often achieve such coordination by using an automated order entry system that processes sales orders in the field and then, to fill these orders, simultaneously updates the production schedule.

In the first case a computerized information system is used to *control* an important facet of operations, whereas in the second a system is used to *coordinate* different activities. In both cases the information systems fit the structural and stragegic features of the organization.

In general, information systems can *support* the organizational structure by providing the information necessary to carry out the assigned responsibility. They can also *make* the structure more elaborate by providing project-based information in a functional organization or function-based information across divisions. Ideally, systems offer managers access to information that can help them fulfill their roles in the formal organizational structure.

What happens if the systems do not fit exactly? What occurs when the design of an information system no longer matches stragegy and structure? Of even greater concern, how elastic is the fit of current systems to ever-changing organizations?

The elasticity of an information system may be explored by studying its ability to meet the reporting requirements placed on it. The typical evolution of a system might be: (1) at the outset, the new information system meets the needs of users; (2) changes occur in information requirements, and informal information channels develop as a result; (3) difficulties arise when analysts attempt to modify the system to match current needs—and the system thus becomes distorted, subverted, and inappropriately used, a situation marked by "information overkill"; and (4) eventually the system is replaced, with varying degrees of disruption.

Let us see how this evolution occurs in an example from an actual company that manufactures a variety of products in several plants. The central data processing department developed an information system for plant managers, and most users were happy with the reports that they received. Later, top managers formulated a more comprehensive marketing strategy, creating new product lines that grouped products from different plants. Then they appointed new corporate-level product-line managers to monitor both the manufacture and the marketing of each product line.

The information needs of this new group of managers overlapped those of the plant managers to some extent, so they made minor changes in the plant managers' reports, using informal communication channels to meet their remaining needs. As time went on, unrelated additional products were added, so that the old information system became unsatisfactory even for the plant managers. Yet, ironically, nearly all managers clung to the system because they knew it so well and felt they had to have the same data they had always received. These people never stopped to realize that the system had become an encumbrance to rather than an enabler of the business strategy.

Information systems that do not fit the organization they were designed to serve are not uncommon. But with DDP, companies can organize their data processing support groups to better use the competence that exists and to better serve the formal structure. Systems so designed and operated will be less likely to suffer problems such as those just recounted.

Given the ideal that information systems should match an organization's strategy and structure, we can expect that companies with diversified interests and with greater autonomy among their operating units will find DDP particularly useful. DDP will offer them new opportunities for formal control and coordination.

The general influence of corporate structures[6] and product diversification[7] on decentralization of information systems is shown in Exhibit 2. The exhibit suggests that the motivation to distribute computer resources will be felt most keenly in highly diversified conglomerates but will be less important to single-produce companies that are organized according to function. Though other factors, of course, will be important in deciding how and when DDP

Exhibit 2.   Tendency toward Distributing Data Processing in Relation to Product Diversification and Corporate Structure

Increasing tendency for data processing distribution

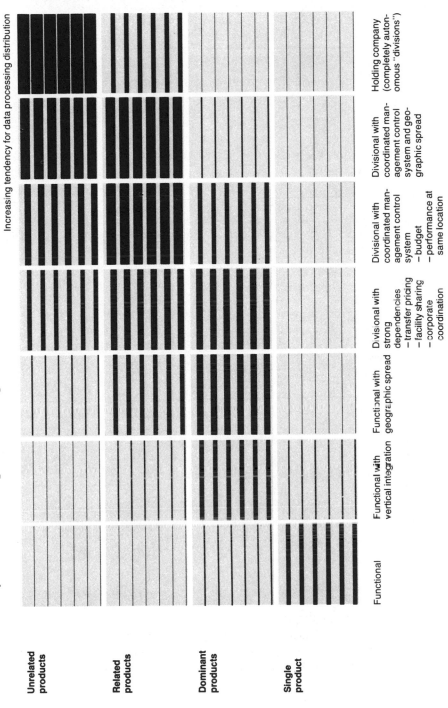

| | Functional | Functional with vertical integration | Functional with geographic spread | Divisional with strong dependencies
– transfer pricing
– facility sharing
– corporate coordination | Divisional with coordinated management control system
– budget
– performance at same location | Divisional with coordinated management control system and geographic spread | Holding company (completely autonomous "divisions") |

Unrelated products

Related products

Dominant products

Single product

is appropriate, Exhibit 2 reminds us that efficient information systems are inexorably linked to the strategy and structure of a company.

Framework for Analysis

To match information systems with the organization they serve, careful attention must go into planning the arrangement of the data processing resources that develop and operate information systems. All of the different activities appearing in Exhibit 1 are assigned to different groups in the organization, and it is useful to analyze systematically who has what responsibilities. We shall develop here a multidimensional framework that we can use to evaluate the way a company locates its data processing resources.

The purpose of such a framework, in general, is to divide the overall problem into interrelated subproblems so that each can be solved separately while it contributes to an overall solution. A framework may also be used to provide a system of measures by which to compare organizations or assess the impact of organizational change. The spectra in Exhibit 3 achieve both these ends.

For each of the areas listed in Exhibit 1, we develop a spectrum of feasible positions, shown in Exhibit 3, representing the variety of alternative arrangements of activity ranging from complete centralization in a data processing unit to complete decentralization to user groups. Each spectrum shows an increasing and cumulative level of responsibility for the user group manager as the line is traversed from left to right. The ordering of the specific functions is normative, in that if a user participates in some way in a given function as described by a single point along a continuum, he or she will probably participate in all functions shown to the left along that continuum (though some mechanism may be employed to coordinate a shared responsibility). The functions to the right of a given user's position may be carried out by the company's data processing groups or be shared as well.

For example, if the user has technical people who perform data-base administration activities up to and including the physical design of the data base, then, according to the fifth spectrum in Exhibit 3, he or she is most likely responsible for logical data-base design, the determination of data requirements and conventions, and the control of source documents. Similarly, the DP manager at some data center performs the remaining tasks, setting and enforcing conventions for data access based in part on the design and, in general, managing all data bases.

The spectra for controlling activities shown in Exhibit 3 are designed to be applicable to either operational or developmental activities under different interpretations. The dual interpretation of the control spectra is a useful feature of the framework. Using the same set of lines, we can analyze control of system development work and control of operations. In most situations, however, control of these two groups of activities is handled in such different manners that it makes sense to discuss them separately.

Hardware operation

Prepare source documents	Manage data entry	Operate satellite processor without data base	Operate satellite processor with data base	Manage independent facility

Telecommunications

Specify communications needs	Design network configuration	Specify interface protocols	Implement network	Maintain network

Systems programming

Use operating system, compilers, and utilities	Interface application programs to systems software	Maintain updates to systems software	Develop & modify systems software

Application systems maintenance

Document system errors	Diagnose system errors	Correct system errors

Data base administration

Control source documents	Determine data requirements & conventions	Carry out logical data base design	Carry out physical data base design	Set & enforce conventions for data access
				Manage all data bases

Application programming

Turnkey system	Communicate needs to programmers	Participate on programming team	Supervise development	Select & develop system-building tools

Systems analysis

Conduct preautomation analysis & procedure revisions	Define user data & functional specifications	Evaluate system relative to functional specifications	Participate in high-level system design	Carry out program-level system design

System documentation

Write functional specifications	Write user's manual	Write program design specifications	Write detailed description of all data structures & routine

Exhibit 3. (Continued)

User training

| Conduct preautomation interviews | Prepare user training materials | Conduct user training | Maintain adequate user competence |

Providing security

| Comply with security procedures | Devise security measures | Authorize security procedures | Manage security facilities |

Setting priorities

| Accept imposed priorities | Identify needs for system services | Rank alternatives | Authorize commitment of resources |

Standardizing tasks

| Carry out standards | Propose standards | Devise standards | Authorize standards | Enforce standards |

Accessing data

| Identify available data | Specify data needs | Authorize data collection & distribution privileges | Enforce data collection & distribution privileges |

Scheduling tasks

| Specify tasks | Determine feasibility of tasks | Sequence tasks | Allocate time to tasks | Approve schedule |

Personnel planning

| Determine system's impact on user staffing | Designate liaison staff for development & operation | Administer personnel assignments | Evaluate personnel performance |

Budgeting

| Specify needs in nonfinancial terms | Set upper bounds on system expenditures | Prepare detailed budget | Monitor complete budget |

Evaluating products

| Collect performance data | Define performance requirements | Monitor performance | Determine appropriate response |

For example, "accessing data" as a developmental activity represents managements' desires and restrictions on the kinds of data that will be collected within a system. As an operational activity, it is a statement of policy defining authorized access to information within the organization.

The area of "providing security" addresses the engineering (during development) and enforcing (during operation) of mechanisms that prevent unauthorized access. Finally, "tasks standardizing" is a control area whose purpose is to coordinate, without direct supervision, a control role that is relevant to all stages of the system's life cycle. It is usually a staff activity designed to magnify the efforts of the line managers and may apply to tasks ranging from defining the phases of system development, including authorization protocols, to developing programming conventions.

One should recognize that management can control and coordinate activities not only by direct supervision but also by the establishment of comprehensive guidelines or standard operating procedures. The technical concerns of data-base administrators, for example, are commonly controlled in this fashion. Their responsibilities can be either centralized in an individual or a group, decentralized but constrained by centrally designed standards,[8] or decentralized with virtual independence. In the future, the second approach, that is, decentralizing the data-base administration activity while using centrally established standards, will probably become increasingly important. In this way, the DP manager can define comprehensive standards that can be enforced by top managers or a highly placed steering committee and that can be used in a decentralized organization to protect the data processing department from excessive control by the user.

Given this introduction to the spectra of data processing responsibilities, consider how the spectra can be applied to a typical application. Exhibit 4 describes the inventory control system of a medium-sized manufacturing company that currently plays a critical role in production operations. The system is run at the corporate computer center located at headquarters, and the records are kept up-to-date via terminals located in the plants.

A team of programmers and analysts who came from both the user departments and the centralized systems development group originally developed the system. Exhibit 4 shows how responsibilities for this system have been and are now distributed across the organization. Note that the control spectra appear twice, once for operations and once for development, because the nature and arrangement of control activities changed significantly when the inventory control system became operational.

In general, user group managers will select the level of responsibility they want for their information processing activities as they traverse the spectra from left to right. This decision is analogous to a company's decision about how far back from the market it wants to be vertically integrated. DP managers, in turn, will determine how much of each user's operation they want to be responsible for. The general manager must then arbitrate between the DP manager and the end user. The general manager must understand

Exhibit 4. Assigned Responsibilities for a Typical Application: a Manufacturing Company's Inventory Control System

Execution (Operations)

Hardware operation
The user prepares source documents and manages data entry through terminals to DP center.

Telecommunications
The user specifies his volume and scheduling requirements for communications through his configuration of terminals.

Systems programming
The user only uses the DP center's operating system, compilers, and utilities.

Application system maintenance
The user both documents and assists in diagnosing system errors.

Control (Operations)

Providing security
The user simply complies with security procedures.

Setting priorities
The user identifies his needs for system services.

Standardizing tasks
The user proposes operating procedures and performance standards.

Accessing data
The user authorizes data collection and report distribution.

Scheduling tasks
The user participates in sequencing the tasks.

Personnel planning
The user manages only his own data entry personnel.

Budgeting
The user controls his expenditures by limiting DP use.

Evaluating products
The user defines his performance requirements.

Execution (Development)

Data base administration
The user determines his data requirements and develops a logical data base design.

Applications programming
The user assigns some internal personnel to participate in the programming team.

Systems analysis
The user is quite involved in most analysis work, including some program-level system design.

System documentation
The user develops his own manuals and shares in writing program design specifications.

User training
The user alone is responsible for all internal training activities.

Control (Development)

Providing security
The user devises and authorizes security procedures.

Setting priorities
The user ranks alternative designs for his system.

Standardizing tasks
The user proposes standards and participates in an authorizing steering committee.

Accessing data
The user authorizes data collection and access privileges.

Scheduling tasks
The user participates in approving the schedule.

Personnel planning
The user jointly administers and evaluates all personnel.

Budgeting
The user jointly prepares and monitors the total budget.

Evaluating products
The user decides whether to use the system.

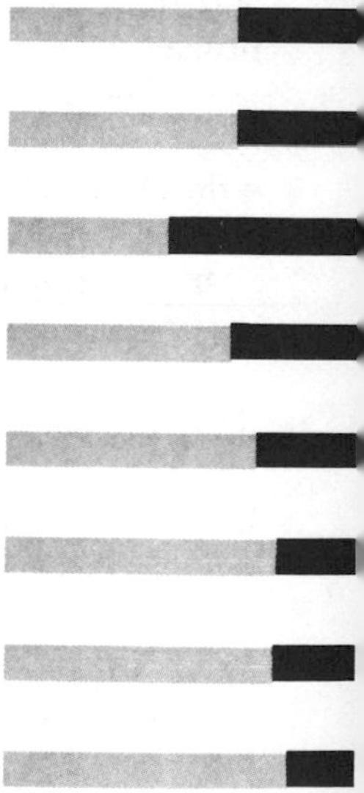

Distributed

Centralized

370

the issues well enough to allocate responsibility so as to best achieve the organization's objectives.

How Much Decentralization?

The framework just described equips us to look inside our own organizations to see to what extent each area of data processing activity is decentralized. By examining the complete set of activities, we see that decentralization of some tasks—be they technical or managerial—is a common occurrence and that even classic types of information systems, such as inventory control applications run on centralized computers, are supported in part by a variety of decentralized, or user, activities. Thus we can say that even these classic information system applications represent a distribution of information-processing responsibility.

As we have seen, DDP has implications that go beyond conventional approaches of applying computers to business. Although on the surface it appears to concern itself solely with the arrangement of computer hardware and data around an organization, at a deeper level it involves the management of a wide array of activities that go into the development and operation of computerized information systems.

Managers can organize these activities in many ways, and the choice they make should reflect the strategic and structural decisions they have made before. Thus, even if their information system design leaves hardware at some central site while assigning a few data processing tasks to users, their system is in some sense distributed.

According to this more general definition, nearly all computer applications are distributed. And, indeed, to ensure that information systems fit an organization, data processing *should* be distributed. Managers should concern themselves now with the question of how they can best distribute data processing for the information systems they require.

The next article in this series will provide tools for managers to help them in this undertaking. For now, however, let us summarize the implications this article has for the role of DDP in organizations:

☐ Data processing involves distinct types of technical activities and managerial or control activities. Managers can assign responsibility for these activities to different groups in the organization; usually they divide the responsibilities between a data processing manager and a user manager.

☐ Managers' assignment of data processing responsibilities should create a DP-support organization that can efficiently develop and operate information systems well suited to the organization. Assignment of data processing responsibilities thus may involve considerations more critical than those relating to cost alone.

☐ Organizations will face competing forces that push for and against decentralization. User groups may argue for more independence to design and operate their own systems, to escape what they see as the uncertainties posed by completely centralized operations, or to bolster their own power in the organization. Central data processing groups may counter with arguments for an arrangement that offers economies of scale, ensures a higher level of technical competence, and permits corporate managers closer scrutiny of data processing activities. Both arguments sound compelling.

☐   Although it is sometimes advantageous to assign control responsibility along with execution responsibility, separation of control activities from execution activities can in fact resolve the dilemma between competing forces. Controls may be distributed throughout an organization to provide checks and balances on activities performed by other groups, to share responsibility between cooperating units, or to assure that the behavior of various units is consistent with organizational objectives and guidelines.

The troubles described earlier came about because decision makers were unaware of these crucial considerations. They had only a limited understanding of data processing and so were unprepared to grapple with the problems inherent in the expanded role of computers in their organizations. Managers should seek to understand distributed data processing because, now that it has come of age, they have much to gain by using it to improve the inner workings of their organizations.

Notes

1.   Richard L. Nolan, "Computer Data Bases: The Future Is Now," Chapter 13, this book.

2.   Paul R. Lawrence and Jay W. Lorsch, *Organization and Environment*, Chapter 2 (Homewood, IL: Richard D. Irwin, 1967).

3.   Ibid., Chapter 3.

4.   Rosabeth Moss Kanter, "Power Failure in Management Circuits," *HBR*, July–August 1979, p. 65.

5.   Alfred D. Chandler, Jr., *Strategy and Structure* (Cambridge, Mass: MIT Press, 1962).

6.   Richard P. Rumelt, *Strategy, Structure, and Economic Performance* (Boston: Division of Research, Harvard Business School, 1974), p. 33.

7.   Leonard Wrigley, "Divisional Autonomy and Diversification," (Ph.D. diss., Harvard Business School, 1970).

8.   Jack R. Buchanan, Rob Gerritsen, and David Root, "Automated Data Base Programming," *Communications of the Association for Computing Machinery*.

22
Making Distributed Data Processing Work

JACK R. BUCHANAN and RICHARD G. LINOWES

In this article, the second of a two-part series, the authors build on the basic understanding of distributed data processing that they developed in the first part. With the methods presented here, a manager can examine DP resources, compare his DP organization with that of other companies, and decide what modifications are desirable. Armed with such information, executives can better decide what degree of decentralization fits with company strategy and where to place responsibility for control and execution of the various data processing activities.

Recently, a marketing manager defended a key point in his three-year plan thus: "It's crucial that we put minicomputers in each of the regional sales offices. We're planning to install a sophisticated customer-support information system for tracking orders and storing service records, and we'll need half a dozen minicomputers to make this system work. If we have to depend on the big old machine at the corporate data center, we won't be able to provide our customers the kind of service we claim to offer."

The executive committee listened attentively. Several people looked skeptical, but the controller seemed particularly troubled. He pointed to an unusually large number on the planning document in front of him and retorted: "Look at this figure! I'm not convinced we need to spend that much. I think you can get the responsiveness and sense of independence you need at the branch offices without giving each region its own machine."

Then he continued, "We can't go around giving minicomputers to any group in the company who wants them. We've authorized too many such plans already, and frankly, I think the whole situation is getting out of control. Right now we're only talking about *buying* machines, but we don't know what these guys will do with them once they *get* them. There could be some serious consequences. We need some general policies for handling this kind of proposal."

Variations of this discussion are occurring frequently these days. In many companies, there is a growing call for the large-scale acquisition of minicomputers to serve the needs of a broad cross section of functional areas. This newly surfaced "computer urgency" puts corporate planners in an awkward position. Many groups are demanding scarce resources for very different hardware and software projects that all look attractive on paper but whose benefits are hard to measure. How can managers plan for the acquisition and use of minicomputers in their companies? What policies should guide them as they enter the era of distributed computing?

This article, our second in a two-part series (see Chapter 21), will explore the need to plan for DDP and present a set of planning tools for managers. All levels of management should be involved in planning for distributed computing needs because the decisions have too broad an impact to be left in the hands of functional users or technicians alone.

How can managers get more involved in the planning for the next generation of information systems? The answer is simple: they must understand what DDP is and they must be able to evaluate the implications of various ways of organizing it. Our previous article tackled the first task; it defined the term *distributed data processing*.

In this second article, we introduce some powerful new techniques for evaluating all possible arrangements for data processing resources. These methods will enable nontechnical general managers to contribute to the important data processing planning meeting of the future.

The Need For Planning

DDP is the systematic decentralization of data processing activities—including a wide range of technical tasks and management responsibilities. It offers an organization the opportunity to develop and operate computerized information systems that both match the organizational structure and promote organization goals. This definition draws on the fact that data processing, in general, is more than just computer hardware and the work of a handful of programmers; it is a composite of a whole host of activities.

Information systems can support an organizational structure by strengthening communication lines and clarifying measures of performance. To achieve this, managers may choose to decentralize systematically the component activities of data processing within their organizations while paying close attention to overall business plans.

But once managers agree on the advantages of DDP, where do they go from there? How do they plan for distributed computing to ensure that strategy, structure, and information systems all match? Too often either management's planning sessions consist of intense technical advising, not to mention lobbying, or there is no planning at all. In some cases, management involvement and approval are carefully skirted. When managers *are* involved, often their thoughts are overly influenced by cost considerations.

They tend to approve some plans solely on the basis of the potential for reducing operating expenses, and they tend to accept other because they are easy to use and do not require a staff of computer professionals.

Whereas promises of cost reduction or work simplification may be paramount in a go-ahead decision for a new information system, other factors are also critical, such as the availability of technical talent, the degree of coordination between users and programmers on project teams, and the careful construction and enforcement of standards. Unless managers have analytic techniques for assessing these other factors of a DP strategy, they will be severely hampered in their planning; success will depend on luck or on prodigious effects to rescue a badly planned venture.

In the following sections, we shall introduce some new analytic methods that can simplify the planning process. They use a set of charts and tables that enable managers to describe and plan, with minimal technical terminology, the company's approach to arranging and managing its DP resources. Briefly, these analytic methods embody the following:

1. *The DP activity spectra.* A set of lines, one for each area of activity of the data processing function, showing the various degrees of involvement that a data processing user may have in managing an information system.

2. *The DP participation table.* A tabular presentation of the responsibilities assigned to key persons who participate in managing an information system, highlighting the roles they play at each decision point in the system's life cycle.

3. *The DP decentralization pattern.* A one-dimensional pictorial representation focusing on technical resources and showing the relative degree of decentralization of all technical data processing activities that support an information system.

4. *The DP distribution chart.* A two-dimensional pictorial representation focusing on both technical and managerial resources. It displays on a summary level the strategic placement of responsibilities for technical and management activities that support an information system.

We shall illustrate these four tools with several examples and then discuss how they are useful in a DDP planning situation. First, we shall describe some dynamics that influence systems planning at a fundamental level.

Dynamics of Systems Management

In developing systems to support administrative activities, companies tend to go through a process that reflects, among other things, management's growing sophisticaion in the use and control of computer technology and the organization's ability to use new management methods, a process often referred to as "organizational learning."[1] The finding that the data processing budget of a number of companies follows an S-shaped curve over time prompted the hypothesis that there are four major stages of data processing growth, each with its own characteristics, problems, and opportunities.[2]

The introduction of administrative innovations often produces these growth curves, and, of course, where we find them depends on what we measure and control, and what kind of changes are possible. However, the use of DDP as one form of administrative innovation has the potential of producing complex innovative disturbances, or dynamics, within the organization. These dynamics are difficult to sort out.

To account for extra "ripples" in otherwise mature organizations and to explain the impact of data-base systems, Richard L. Nolan proposed a six-stage hypothesis.[3] The "stage hypotheses" will continue to be useful for characterizing a particular application area for a particular user, but in the extensively distributed organizations of the future, an organization as a whole is not likely to show a coherent stage behavior.

Managers will need to understand the causes as well the results of the forces they experience. Results such as growth in the application portfolio, expansion in size of the data processing organization, and increased use of planning and control methods are important issues for management's attention. However, for planning purposes, there are more basic dynamics that underlie these organizational responses. Some of the more important dynamics may be summarized as follows:

1.   Changes in business strategy or organizational structure will create disruptions for DP management. Some may be due to reorganizations of data processing resources as part of a general corporate reorganization. This occurred recently at Citibank, where operations were decentralized to place greater control in the hands of the banking groups.[4] Other changes may come with a reshuffling and redefinition of product lines. Recently at Dun & Bradstreet, computer technology—above and beyond its contribution to management as an administrative tool—became the essence of a brand-new product and the delivery vehicle for an existing product using online database systems.[5] Structure and strategy changes of this sort usually generate a flurry of demands for new information.

2.   An organization as a whole displays some stage-like behavior as it evolves over time.[6] The stages of data processing growth evolve within a larger organizational context. For example, consider a company moving from a functional structure to one organized by product line. Managers working within such transition plans may choose DP departments that are organized by data processing function—for example, programming, telecommunications—or operations dedicated to particular users' needs. Some blend these two approaches, using a matrix organizational structure.

3.   Changing external and internal technology creates challenges and opportunities to use the appropriate technology. It is often difficult to sort out the differences between the stages of data processing growth in a par-

ticular company and the stages of data processing growth in a particular company and the stages of data processing technology in general. First, technical competence must be available to handle the innovation in-house. Second, organizational learning must have progressed to the stage where assimilation of new applications is feasible.

4. Managing multiple projects at various life cycle phases becomes increasingly difficult as the number and sophistication of projects grow and as the need arises to integrate systems with business functions.

Managers can view the growth stages of data processing as a composite of these dynamics. If executives learn to monitor these forces over time and to recognize their implications for DDP planning, crises will be less devastating or may not even arise.

Tools for Analysis & Planning

Effective information systems depend on the careful assignment of responsibility for areas of data processing activity. The following tools will assist managers in their planning.

Tool No. 1: Activity Spectra

We introduced the first tool—depicting multiple scales of responsibility for data processing activities—in our previous article, and we shall use it here as a measuring stick to assess the way a company organizes its data processing resources. (For the reader's convenience, we reproduce that exhibit here as Exhibit 1.)

The data processing function involves many kinds of activities. Some are technical and some managerial, and the analytic separation of execution activities from control activities reflects this distinction (see Exhibit 2). For execution activities, we then distinguish the technical tasks associated with systems development from those supporting systems operation. The result is a four-way split of data processing activities into execution of development, control of development, execution of operations, and control of operations.

To visualize where these activities are performed in an organization, we must examine them in further detail. Exhibit 2 will help us here. At the extreme left, a user of an information system is an uninvolved recipient of the services of a completely centralized data center. At the other extreme, the user performs all the tasks himself, and the centralized group—if one exists—is completely uninvolved. At points in between these extremes, activity is divided between the user and the data processing center. In constructing the lines in the exhibit, we followed conventional practices closely, so (usually) if a user performs a task corresponding to one point on a line, he or she probably performs all tasks to the left of that point.

Exhibit 1. Responsibility Spectra

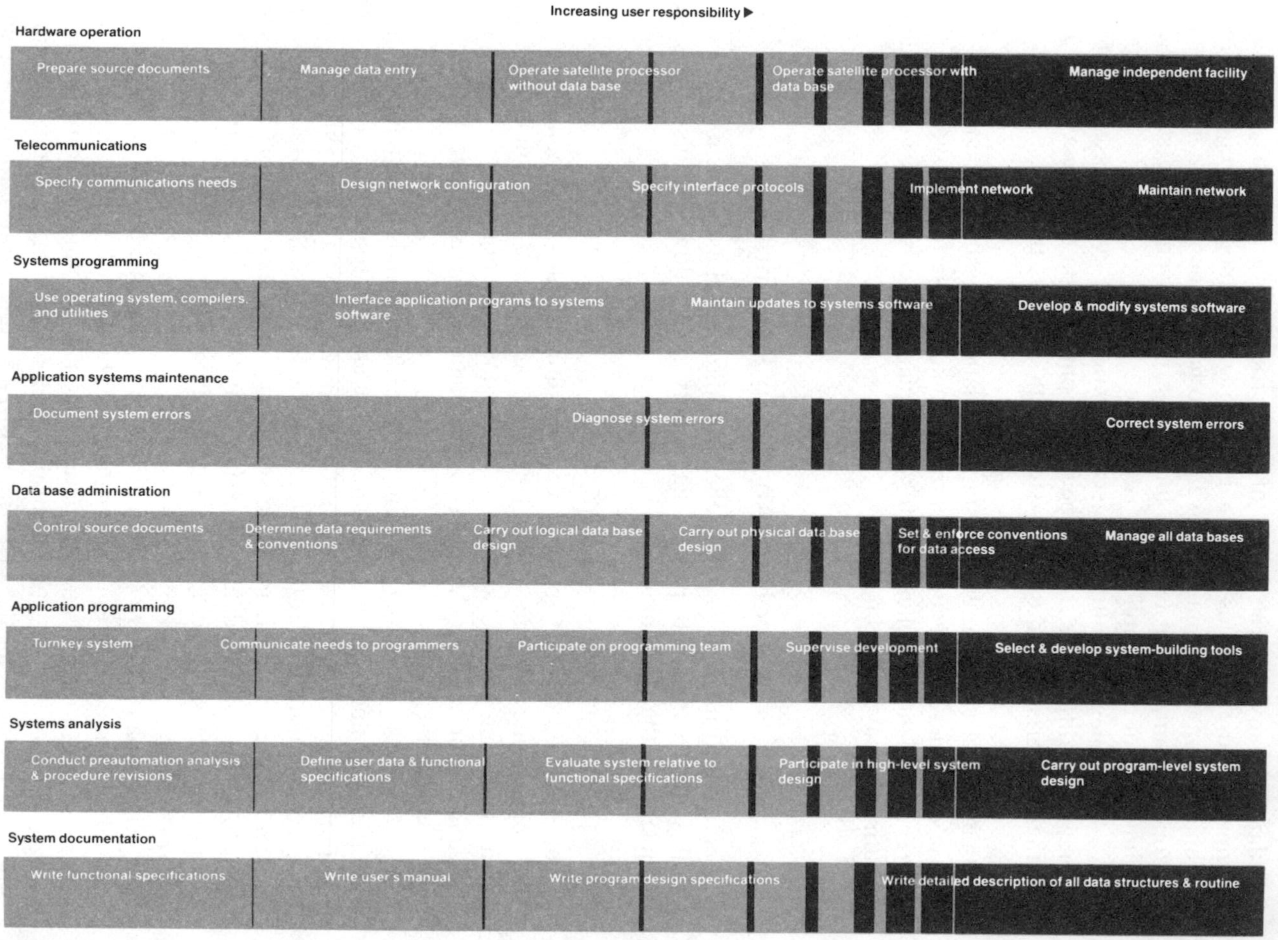

Increasing user responsibility ▶

Hardware operation
Prepare source documents | Manage data entry | Operate satellite processor without data base | Operate satellite processor with data base | Manage independent facility

Telecommunications
Specify communications needs | Design network configuration | Specify interface protocols | Implement network | Maintain network

Systems programming
Use operating system, compilers, and utilities | Interface application programs to systems software | Maintain updates to systems software | Develop & modify systems software

Application systems maintenance
Document system errors | Diagnose system errors | Correct system errors

Data base administration
Control source documents | Determine data requirements & conventions | Carry out logical data base design | Carry out physical data base design | Set & enforce conventions for data access | Manage all data bases

Application programming
Turnkey system | Communicate needs to programmers | Participate on programming team | Supervise development | Select & develop system-building tools

Systems analysis
Conduct preautomation analysis & procedure revisions | Define user data & functional specifications | Evaluate system relative to functional specifications | Participate in high-level system design | Carry out program-level system design

System documentation
Write functional specifications | Write user's manual | Write program design specifications | Write detailed description of all data structures & routine

User training

Conduct preautomation interviews | Prepare user training materials | Conduct user training | Maintain adequate user competence

Providing security

Comply with security procedures | Devise security measures | Authorize security procedures | Manage security facilities

Setting priorities

Accept imposed priorities | Identify needs for system services | Rank alternatives | Authorize commitment of resources

Standardizing tasks

Carry out standards | Propose standards | Devise standards | Authorize standards | Enforce standards

Accessing data

Identify available data | Specify data needs | Authorize data collection & distribution privileges | Enforce data collection & distribution privileges

Scheduling tasks

Specify tasks | Determine feasibility of tasks | Sequence tasks | Allocate time to tasks | Approve schedule

Personnel planning

Determine system's impact on user staffing | Designate liaison staff for development & operation | Administer personnel assignments | Evaluate personnel performance

Budgeting

Specify needs in nonfinancial terms | Set upper bounds on system expenditures | Prepare detailed budget | Monitor complete budget

Evaluating products

Collect performance data | Define performance requirements | Monitor performance | Determine appropriate response

Exhibit 2. Areas of Managed Activity

Execution (Development)	Control
Data-base administration	Providing security
Applications programming	
Systems analysis	Setting priorities
System documentation	Standardizing tasks
User training	
	Accessing data
Execution (Operations)	Scheduling tasks
Hardware operation	
Telecommunications	Personnel planning
Systems programming	Budgeting
Application system	
maintenance	Evaluating products

Using all of the lines in the exhibit, we can describe the placement of responsibility for a particular information system. We simply go through the list checking off on each spectrum the right-most point that accurately describes the user's role. For a complete analysis, we must use the eight control activities twice, once for development and once for operations, because control of development is separate and often quite different from control of operations.

Exhibit 3 shows the results of this analysis for a marketing information system of a medium-sized manufacturer. The system currently has centralized computers at the corporate data center, but it was developed jointly by marketing and corporate DP. During development, marketing had responsibility for many of the control tasks—primarily personnel planning, budgeting, and evaluation. But now, during operations, it controls only the distribution of computer reports.

How are these DP activity spectra useful to management? First, as a descriptive tool; they provide a simple way to describe the placement of DP responsibilities. With minor alterations, they can be used in more complex situations in which more than two groups provide the service necessary to support an information system. When the functions described are assigned to specific organizational units, they show quite well who does what DP-related activities.

Second, the spectra suggest ways to modify the organization of DP. For a given arrangement of activities, such as that presented in Exhibit 3, simple shifts in the selected points represent a slightly altered organization and represent transfers of technical tasks or control responsibilities in either a centralized or a decentralized direction.

Suppose now that a manager wants to alter the structure of the DP support organization. He or she should first rank order the spectra of the different activities according to their decreasing degree of rigidity or per-

Exhibit 3. Assigned Responsibilities for a Typical Application: A Manufacturing Company's Marketing Information System.

cution (Operations)

dware operation
user prepares source documents manages data entry through ter-ials to DP center.

communications
user specifies his volume and eduling requirements for com-nications through his configuration erminals.

tems programming
user only uses the DP center's rating system, compilers, and ties.

plication system maintenance
user both documents and assists iagnosing system errors.

ecution (Development)

ta base administration
e user determines his data require-nts and develops a logical data se design.

plications programming
e user assigns some internal per-nnel to participate in the program-ng team.

tems analysis
e user is quite involved in most alysis work, including some gram-level system design.

stem documentation
e user develops his own manuals d shares in writing program design ecifications.

er training
e user alone is responsible for all ernal training activities.

Centralized

Distributed

Control (Operations)

Providing security
The user simply complies with secu-rity procedures.

Setting priorities
The user identifies his needs for system services.

Standardizing tasks
The user proposes operating proce-dures and performance standards.

Accessing data
The user authorizes data collection and report distribution.

Scheduling tasks
The user participates in sequencing the tasks.

Personnel planning
The user manages only his own data entry personnel.

Budgeting
The user controls his expenditures by limiting DP use.

Evaluating products
The user defines his performance requirements.

Control (Development)

Providing security
The user devises and authorizes security procedures.

Setting priorities
The user ranks alternative designs for his system.

Standardizing tasks
The user proposes standards and participates in an authorizing steering committee.

Accessing data
The user authorizes data collection and access privileges.

Scheduling tasks
The user participates in approving the schedule.

Personnel planning
The user jointly administers and eval-uates all personnel.

Budgeting
The user jointly prepares and moni-tors the total budget.

Evaluating products
The user decides whether to use the system.

manence. Activities that are easily transferable should appear last, while those that are fixed or relatively immobile should appear first.

Next, the manager should step through the newly ordered set of spectra, carefully evaluating the possible shifts that might create the intended effect of redesigning the organization. Clearly, different sets of small shifts may produce similar general effects, so management should explore the consequences of many alternative designs. The spectra organize this exploration process; they structure a manager's search for and evaluation of new options.

Third, the spectra provide the foundation for the other tools we shall describe. By consolidating the spectra in a variety of ways, we shall generate other conceptual devices that involve less technical terminology and hence are more geared toward general management.

Tool No. 2: Participation Table

The second tool is useful in the assignment of specific responsibilities for the DP administrative process. By creating a table that plots both responsibility assignments and the system life cycle, we obtain an outline of how each group participates in the system development process. The resulting DP participation table specifies which tasks and checkpoint responsibilities each group in the organization must bear over each stage.

The table follows nicely from the description of responsibilities provided by the activity spectra. Once a manager has used the spectra to characterize the organizational support for a given informational system, he or she can evaluate the roles of key players in the organization over time. The time element appears in the use of the well-established concept of the system life cycle, which captures the important fact that there are distinct phases in the life of an information system: work begins with the planning and design phases, passes through the programming and implementation phases, and enters an operational mode during the production phase.

(Systems also pass *out* of operation, moving through a period that we might call the senescence phase, but those involved in DP are loath to describe this phenomenon as a universal fact of life.)

By examining responsibility assignments over the system life cycle, a manager obtains a table such as the shown in Exhibit 4. This table corresponds to the marketing information system described in the previous section and in Exhibit 3. We see that at the end of each life cycle phase some milestone document is prepared and passed around to all concerned parties.

The participation table tells us what role each party plays in the overall evaluation of each document. The term *approve* applies to those who assume responsibility for the commitment of resources based on the plans and estimates of those who *prepare*. *Review* is provided for information and comments only. *Concur* requires agreement with the proposed course of action, although the individual assumes no responsibility for the actual commitment of resources.

Exhibit 4.   DP Organization Participation Table

Phase	Milestone document	User		Data Processing		
		Manager	Systems analysis	Manager	Analysis-Programming	Operations
Planning	Business application plan	approve	prepare	review	review	review
	System definition	approve	prepare	concur	concur	concur
Design	System design specifications	approve	prepare	approve	concur	concur
	Technical specifications	review	approve	concur	prepare	concur
Programming	Program libraries	review	approve	concur	prepare	
	Test data & procedures	review	approve	concur	prepare	
Implementation	File conversion	approve	concur	approve	concur	prepare
	Procedure manuals System	review	approve	concur	concur	prepare
	User	approve	prepare	review	concur	
Production	Production report	review	concur	approve	concur	prepare

The organization participation table has value for managers primarily because it clarifies roles to be played over time. Since each company or even each application within a company may have its own distinctive version, the table serves as useful documentation of the administrative processes that have been established to launch and operate a new information system. It also functions as a simple reference sheet to remind all those involved in DP activities about the administrative procedures and protocols that affect their work.

Tool No. 3: Decentralization Pattern

This tool defines a pattern for the organizational arrangement of technical DP activities. It is based on the fact that not all execution activities are decentralized to the same extent. For any given information system, we can enumerate supporting technical activities in a sequence that reflects the degree of their decentralization. As we shall see, such a pattern can function as a shorthand notation in discussions about the organizational features of specific DP plans. For some companies, it may even form the basis of a general design for DP organization.

Exhibit 5 repeats the spectra for the execution activities associated with the marketing information system example of Exhibit 3. Clearly, the points on the different lines do not line up perfectly. Some points appear more toward the centralized end of the spectrum ("hardware operations" and "telecommunications"), and others appear more toward the decentralized end ("systems analysis" and "user training").

When these points are projected down to a summary line, the sequence of points reveals neatly the pattern of DP activities arranged according to degree of decentralization. This pattern, henceforth called the *DP decentralization pattern*, characterizes the detailed spread of activities for a single application system. Exhibit 6 shows a common decentralization pattern found in many companies. "Hardware operations" tend to be most centralized, "user training" and "staff activities" tend to be most decentralized, and "systems analysis" and "data-base administration" are usually shared in some manner corresponding to the level of user involvement.

The DP decentralization pattern can aid managers in formulating and clarifying their policies for organizing DP resources. By means of a pattern, or "strip," managers can state succinctly for their organizations the general arrangement of responsibilities that characterizes relationships between DP groups and user groups.

Exhibit 6 shows one such pattern for a single application system for a single user group. It is highly likely that the decentralization patterns of other information systems of this user look quite similar. In effect, then, this single decentralization pattern represents a standard decentralization policy for all application systems of this user.

There are a number of reasons to expect such a standard arrangement. First, resources collected in one place can serve as a pool for a variety of applications. Expertise required on one project can be extended readily to other projects.

Second, any regularities that appear in the relationship between a user and a central group often become a cultural norm, and any new projects are then expected to conform.

Third, the relationship may be so structured and formalized that it is explicitly reflected in the organizational structure. For example, a user who has established a programming group for one project will probably tend to assign this group to other projects. If separate groups perform each activity, these groups may be staffed so that the degree of user participation remains relatively fixed.

Now, assuming some typical pattern for the relationship between a user and a DP center, consider the situation of multiple users sharing a

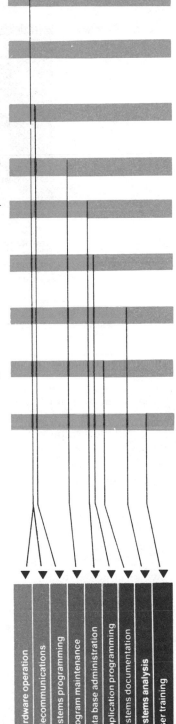

Execution

Hardware operation
The user prepares source documents and manages data entry through terminals to DP center.

Telecommunications
The user specifies the volume and scheduling requirements for communications through his or her configuration of terminals.

Systems programming
The user only uses the DP center's operating system, compilers, and utilities.

Application system maintenance
The user both documents and assists in diagnosing system errors.

Data base administration
The user determines his data requirements and develops a logical data base design.

Applications programming
The user assigns some internal personnel to participate in the programming team.

Systems analysis
The user is quite involved in most analysis work, including some program-level system design.

System documentation
The user develops his own manuals and shares in writing program design specifications.

User training
The user alone is responsible for all internal training activities.

Decentralized

Centralized

Hardware operation
Telecommunications
Systems programming
Program maintenance
Data base administration
Application programming
Systems documentation
Systems analysis
User training

Exhibit 5.   Development of the DP Decentralization Patern

Exhibit 6. A typical DP Decentralization Pattern

User manager

Staff activities	Systems analysis	Data base administration
User training		
System documentation		
Application programming		
Program maintenance		
Systems programming		
Telecommuni-cations		
Hardware operation		

Data processing management

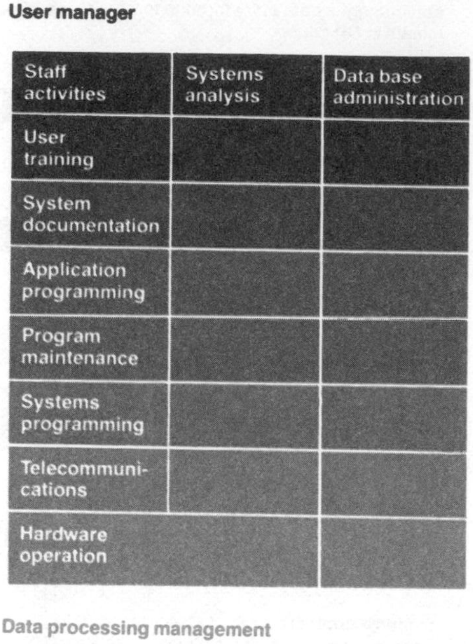

common DP center. In many cases, we can expect the pattern for one user to resemble the pattern for most other users. The differences among the patterns involve not the ordering of activities but the specific point at which responsibilities change hands.

What does this mean? Exhibit 7 illustrates this situation for a company with separate engineering, marketing, and manufacturing groups. The decentralization patterns are the same for all three, but they are positioned differently. Engineering handles the largest protion of its own technical DP tasks; manufacturing, the next largest portion; and marketing, the least. These organizational variances are most likely due to differences in the technical competence and data processing experience of the users and to the different requirements of the information systems.

Exhibit 7 shows that a company may use a decentralization pattern as a general policy while actual participation in technical work differs considerably from user to user. In general, it is possible to establish uniform policies for decentralization of data processing activities while maintaining the flexibility to vary users' responsibilities.

The example in Exhibit 7 shows how the decentralization pattern is useful for expressing policies for DP organization. A company may use it as an expression of its approach to decentralizing DP activities. In the event that a uniform pattern does not hold across all applications of a particular

Exhibit 7. DP Decentralization to Multiple Functional Areas—A Typical Distribution

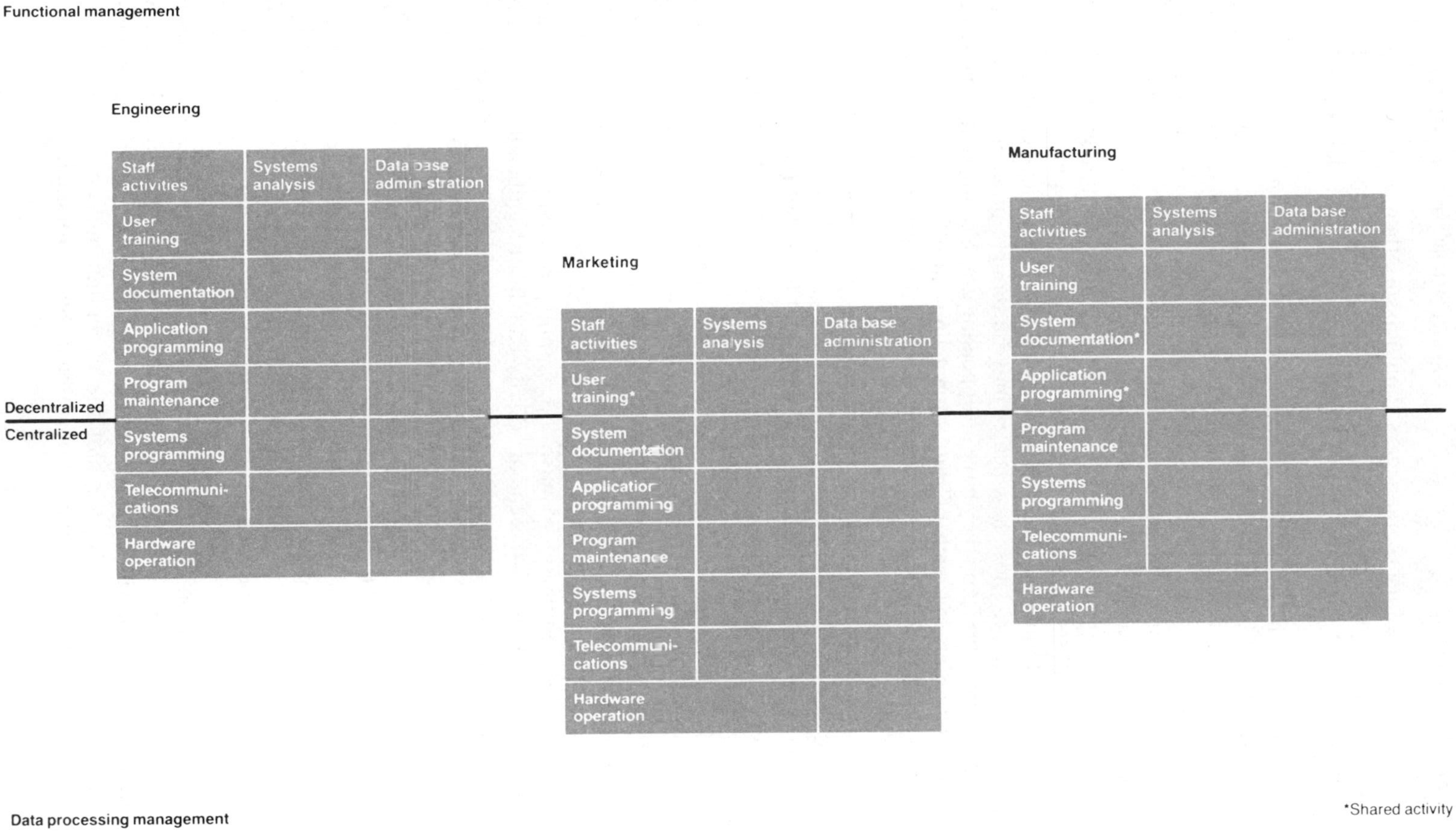

Functional management
Engineering
Staff activities
Systems analysis
Data base administration
User training
System documentation
Application programming
Program maintenance
Systems programming
Telecommunications
Hardware operation
Marketing
Staff activities
Systems analysis
Data base administration
User training*
System documentation
Application programming
Program maintenance
Systems programming
Telecommunications
Hardware operation
Manufacturing
Staff activities
Systems analysis
Data base administration
User training
System documentation*
Application programming*
Program maintenance
Systems programming
Telecommunications
Hardware operation
Decentralized
Centralized
Data processing management

*Shared activity

user or across all users, managers should assure themselves that such variations are justified. In this way, the tool can help managers adopt organizational policies that are formulated consciously rather than be default.

Tool No. 4: Distribution Chart

The spectra of activities shown in Exhibit 1 can be combined in a simple manner to give a concise summary of a company's data processing activities. The separate scales, when consolidated as suggested in Exhibit 8, generate a two-dimensional picture portraying how a company distributes its data processing resources among organizational subunits.

How are the multiple scales condensed into a simple graph? The multiple "execution" measures of operations and development activities are consolidated into two single summary measures, one for operations and one for development. These new scales may be thought of as projections of the original measures, and they have an appealing graphic simplicity: the selected point or points on each of the original lines in effect "map down" onto corresponding points on the summary lines, defining intervals on the summary lines.

The resulting spread of points in the intervals represents the spread of operations and development activities for a given system within an organization. The summary lines portray what will be called the "execution distribution." These projections and the resulting summary lines appear at the top and the bottom of the exhibit.

The two summary measures obtained so far, however, provide only half the picture. A more complete description of a company's handling of its DP resources must show not only where resources are located but how they are controlled. Consequently, the eight control spectra must appear in the picture. To include them, we must separate control of operations from control of development because the methods, procedures, and philosophy of control for these two areas of activity can differ significantly in any given company. The eight control measures are thus used twice when a company's handling of the DP resource is evaluated—once for operations and once for development.

For each area of activity, now, the multiple control measures are projected on summary lines on the sides of Exhibit 8 as we did at the top and bottom. Exhibit 8 also diagrams this process for a sample company. The resulting pattern of points describes the spread of control responsibility for the DP resource. These summary lines therefore portray what will be called the "control distribution." They appear on the left and right sides of the exhibit.

The execution distribution and the control distribution for both operations and development can be visualized simultaneously by using the two-dimensional graph shown at the center of Exhibit 8. Treating operations and development separately, we plot the execution and control distributions against each other, creating regions of distribution for each of the two major

Exhibit 8.   Development of the DP Distribution Chart

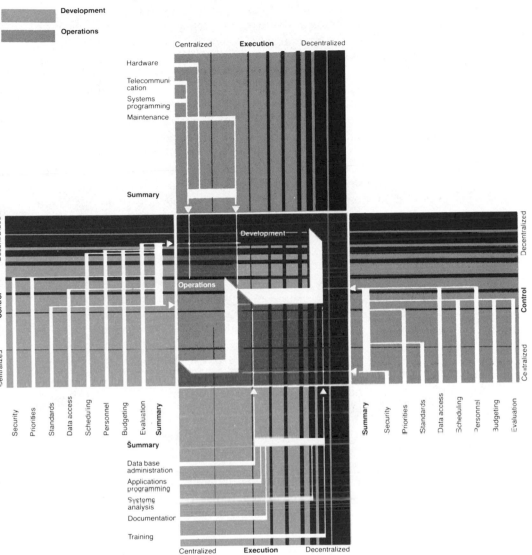

areas of activity. The resulting diagram succinctly displays essential features
of the decentralization of the information processing resource in an organization. We shall refer to this diagram as the *DP distribution chart* because
the location and shape of its regions reveal in summary form the special
features of a company's approach to distributing its DP resource.

Exhibit 8 illustrates how one can consolidate into a simple visual display
the multiple dimensions that underlie the data processing resource (according

to conventional practice). Managers can use this worksheet to ascertain (and describe) the company's approach to managing its data processing resources.

Here's how: (a) assess the company's practices for a given application system or network by determining the company's position on each of the spectra (while addressing control of operations separately from control of development); (b) determine the summary distributions by projecting the results of the multiple spectra analysis onto the summary lines; and (c) plot the execution and control distributions against each other in the DP distribution chart. The resulting arrangement of shapes presents a summary of conditions in the company that is readily communicable.

One can easily extend this approach to handle the case in which more than two organizational units have responsibility for the DP resource. For example, data center operations can be distinct from systems development work groups even though both are centralized relative to user groups. Such a situation can be handled in the distribution chart by assuming that the tasks on each spectrum completely describe the activities of each area. Intervals within each spectrum represent the activities that separate organizational units might perform.

To apply this notion to the distribution chart, one simply projects the intervals onto summary lines—as was done with points in the earlier situation. The result is a more general strategic view of distributed data processing.

How is this method of summarizing the handling of DP in a company useful? What does it tell managers that will help them plan and better manage the DP resource? In the next section, we shall use the chart to describe the variations in DP practices across a wide array of companies, an exercise that will give more meaning to the patterns appearing in the distribution chart and will help managers characterize their own situations.

Descriptive Use

As is the case with any new tool, one should apply it to many situations in order to become familiar with its descriptive powers. Here we shall present the distribution chart of several companies for just this purpose. The companies display widely varying approaches to distributing data processing, and some of these differences are captured in the charts.

Exhibit 9 presents the distribution charts for DP applications in six different companies, with key DP tasks labeled. These companies use some of the most common arrangements found in industry and government.

The three examples in the upper half of the exhibit illustrate arrangements that are encountered perhaps most frequently. In the first chart (which describes an airline), both development and operations activity are centralized, and they are controlled centrally also. This company depends on a widely dispersed network of terminals tied in to a very large computer center to maintain its on-line ticket reservation system. The users play some role in operations, but on the whole the show is run centrally.

Exhibit 9.   Illustrative Examples of DP Distribution Charts

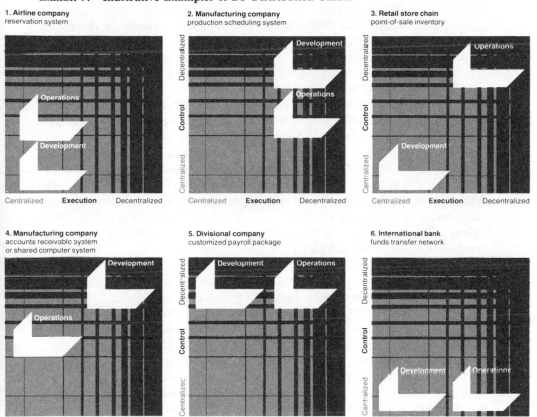

1. Airline company
reservation system

2. Manufacturing company
production scheduling system

3. Retail store chain
point-of-sale inventory

4. Manufacturing company
accounts receivable system
or shared computer system

5. Divisional company
customized payroll package

6. International bank
funds transfer network

The second chart, in contrast, depicts a highly decentralized situation in a manufacturing company. Both development and operations are again executed and controlled at the same place, only now the user group does it all. The production department of this manufacturing company develops and runs its own production scheduling system without drawing heavily on corporate resources. The diagram is also typical of divisionalized companies that permit their divisions largely to develop and execute their own applications.

In the third example (a retail store chain), development is executed and controlled centrally while operations are executed and controlled by the user group. The diagram portrays the features of a point-of-sale inventory system that was developed at corporate headquarters and installed in each branch store. The system operates independently in each store under the control of local management.

These first three charts show that operations and development are often placed primarily along the main diagonal of a chart, extending from the lower left corner to the upper right. This placement is quite natural because it is most often the case that execution responsibility is handled by the group that also handles control responsibility. For example, systems analysts and programmers usually report to technical managers who also budget, schedule, and evaluate their work. It is no surprise to learn that most companies would show distribution charts with placement along the main diagonal.

The fourth chart is the first example of a company that shows a slight deviation from pure alignment along the diagonal. Some of the other examples in the lower row show even greater deviations.

The fourth chart displays the most common arrangement of DP resources. It presents the features of a company that has a centralized computer center whose costs are charged out to the users on the basis of their actual use of the facilities. By this administrative device, the users maintain some budgetary control over the central site (if they are free to choose their extent of involvement with the central group). Thus operations are partly controlled by the user and partly controlled centrally.

The development of new applications is undertaken by the users themselves; they have their own computer analysts and programming staffs who can design and implement new information systems as required. The chart depicts a manufacturing company's accounts receivable system, which was developed by the accounting department's DP personnel but is now run by the corporate data center—a joint facility that is paid for by its users.

The fifth example shows a divisionalized company that has adapted a payroll package for use in a division. The division has its own small computer on which to carry out the payroll processing, but it depends on a corporate development group to make the necessary adaptations. In this case, operations are decentralized for execution and control, whereas development is executed centrally under the control of the division. The division controls development by setting priorities, scheduling activities, formulating the budget, and evaluating the work.

In some settings, it makes sense to have centralized development and decentralized operations in DP even though the nature of the application is too critical for its operation to remain under the control of local management. In such cases, the arrangement in the distribution chart of example six might be more appropriate. This chart depicts DP in a large international bank that has developed a sophisticated international computer network to handle the transfer of its funds from bank to bank. The development work is all done at the bank's headquarters, but operations must go on around the world. Control is essential, however, and therefore the company has established procedures that would place both development and operations squarely in the lower portion of the chart.

These six examples illustrate some basic approaches to organizing data processing. Using the distribution chart as a tool, a manager can get a quick overview of his or her organization today and pinpoint similarities with other companies.

User Involvement

How do managers decide how much to decentralize execution and control activities? Or when they do have an idea of the appropriate degree of user involvement in the design and operation of the information system, how do they achieve it? The DP distribution chart can help answer such questions.

Turning to Exhibit 10, note that the diagonal in the chart moves from centralized to decentralized execution and control. This diagonal shows the possible degrees of user involvement in DP. The range goes from essentially no involvement all the way to complete responsibility for a given system.

We will speak of *user involvement* henceforth to refer to the combination (or "sum") of decentralized execution and decentralized control. The concept is applicable to all regions of the chart, and by definition all points in the lower left offer less user involvement than points in the upper right.

The definition further suggests the idea of lines of "equal user involvement," also identified in the exhibit, which show that a wide variety of organizational arrangements of DP activities can give a user an equivalent of involvement in meeting his or her DP needs.

How are these lines of equal user involvement meaningful to management? They allow managers to consider systematically the alternative combinations of responsibilities that they may assign to user groups to obtain the desired amount of involvement in data processing. For instance, when

Exhibit 10. Planning with the Concept of User Involvement

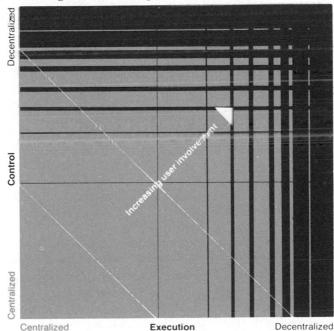

users experience critical or constantly changing needs for specialized information in their normal business operations, a high degree of user involvement is probably warranted. But what responsibilities should management assign to this user?

An answer to this question begins with the distribution chart. Thinking at a fairly abstract level, we begin by sketching some diagonal equal user-involvement line on the chart that seems to reflect—on the basis of management's judgment of the user's business and information requirements—the general degree of involvement that the user needs to develop or operate an information system. The more critical the system is to business operations, the greater the desire for involvement.

Once the desired level of involvement is known, managers must assign responsibilities that will produce a figure in the distribution chart that falls on the corresponding line of equal user involvement. They are free to choose both the kinds of tasks and the variety of subtasks to assign so long as the corresponding distribution chart reflects their decentralization strategy. Many possible mixes of execution and control activities satisfy this requirement, so managers have a host of options for achieving the same effect. Now, with the aid of the chart, they may evaluate their full range in a very systematic manner. The example that follows will illustrate this point more clearly.

An Example

Let us return to the planning meeting we described at the outset. There a marketing manager is expressing the need of his regional sales offices for greater involvement in data processing. He argues that the company's sales representatives must have more timely customer information in order to improve their performance in the marketplace. The solution, as he sees it, is to put minicomputers in the hands of the regional sales offices. With these machines, he says, local offices can obtain all types of data on their customers and thus create more responsive sales and service teams. Closing his case in a humble manner, the marketing manager credits a local minicomputer salesman for dreaming up this brilliant remedy to his current performance problems.

Although this manager has justifiable reasons for wanting greater sales force involvement in data processing, these concerns by themselves do not imply that regional sales offices should have their own minicomputers. The company can increase user involvement in data processing without giving users their own hardware. The concepts and tools developed in this article make this point clear.

Turning to Exhibit 11, we see the DP distribution chart for the customer information system now in operation at the corporate data center. The current system is the one we have seen before in Exhibits 3 and 8, so we are already familiar with its organization. As noted, operations are predominantly centralized for both execution and control, offering users relatively little involvement in DP. This lower degree of user involvement is reflected

Exhibit 11.   Increasing User Involvement: An Example

Increasing user involvement: an example

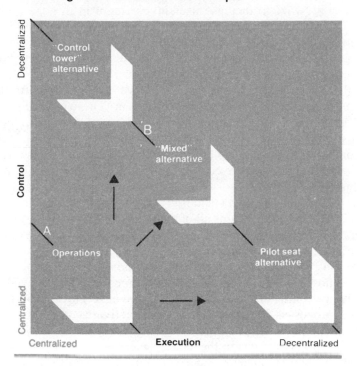

by the position of the operations square, falling as it does on line A in the lower left-hand corner of the chart.

If we now want to increase user involvement in the operations of a customer information system, we must rearrange the DP-related activities so that the operations square falls on a line of higher user involvement; that is, the organization should change so that the distribution chart shows operations along some line B, rather than line A.

As the diagram illustrates, there are several possible shifts that will bring about this state of greater user involvement. These include movement in the directions of pure execution, pure control, or a combination of each. It is a question of putting the user in the "pilot's seat," the "control tower," or in a combination of these roles. Under the shifts that commonly occur, involving a combination of execution and control, the user will probably acquire his own computer.

The pilot seat shift might entail giving the user a computer also, but here the corporate center retains all of the control it had previously, creating a state of affairs that might seem threatening or oppressive to new technical employees at the regional sales offices.

The control tower shift is perhaps the most interesting of the three, for it shows how a state of greater user involvement can be achieved without notable changes in the arrangement of hardware or technical activities. Only managerial processes are changed. Control activities such as budgeting, personnel planning, and task scheduling are put in the hands of the user, while the computer remains in the same place.

If the marketing manager is correct about the need for increased user involvement, the company should consider all possible paths it might take to meet that need. The original proposal—namely, buying minicomputers— probably would have led to a decentralization of both execution and control, some form of "mixed" shift. Though the company may ultimately endorse this particular approach, this shift is clearly not the only one to consider.

Suppose now that management has decided to decentralize some of its DP execution activities to the marketing organization and it rejects the pure control path. If Exhibit 7 accurately describes the way technical resources are distributed in the company, then decentralization of execution involves simply sliding the decentralization pattern for marketing out toward marketing, as shown in Exhibit 12. The pattern probably is pulled out to a position roughly alongside manufacturing's pattern.

This kind of shift still leaves "hardware operation" primarily under the direction of DP management, and so we see that it makes sense to discuss decentralization of execution—that is, technical activities, without requiring the proliferation of computers. As long as an organization's decentralization pattern retains the form presented in Exhibit 6, decentralization of execution can go a long way before computers are actually moved out into the field.

The fact that so many departments in this company are requesting minicomputers suggests that the company's implicit decentralization pattern may require conscious modification.

Exhibit 12. Decentralizing Execution: An Example

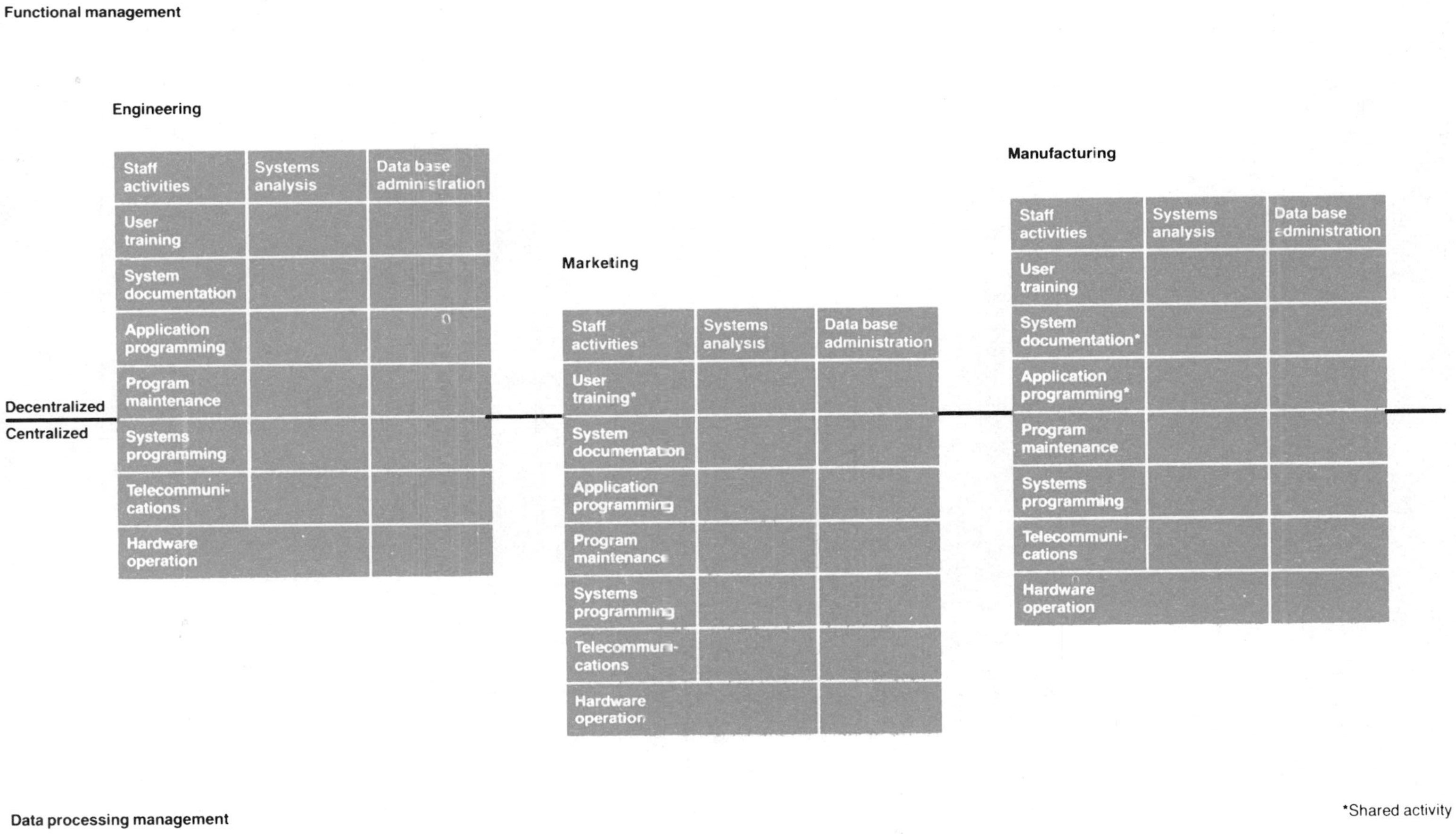

Functional management

Engineering

	Staff activities	User training	System documentation	Application programming	Program maintenance	Systems programming	Telecommunications	Hardware operation
Systems analysis								
Data base administration								

Decentralized

Centralized

Marketing

	Staff activities	User training*	System documentation	Application programming	Program maintenance	Systems programming	Telecommunications	Hardware operation
Systems analysis								
Data base administration								

Manufacturing

	Staff activities	User training	System documentation*	Application programming*	Program maintenance	Systems programming	Telecommunications	Hardware operation
Systems analysis								
Data base administration								

Data processing management

*Shared activity

Once the managers of this company have decided to increase marketing's involvement in data processing and have worked out some general path to this end and once they have agreed on a pattern for decentralizing technical resources, they then turn the project over to others for more detailed planning. Most likely, representatives from the DP and marketing departments will get together to hammer out the details and to ensure that the plan is consistent with top management's directives. Tools such as the DP activity spectra and the DP organization participation table can guide them in their deliberations.

In Conclusion

Companies are finding that distributed data processing offers great potential for improving the performance of individual departments and for promoting the success of an organization as a whole. Managers within these companies are turning to DDP to help solve long-standing, administrative problems and to help improve the control and coordination of fundamental business tasks. Enthusiasm is indeed strong for the decentralization of computing, and the call to acquire more computers is bound to increase.

Because of the demand, managers will be wise to plan carefully how their organizations will use information systems in the future. Along with these general plans, they should promulgate corporate policies establishing how they will arrange data processing resources to support their information systems. Only with such plans and policies can they assure that information systems will fulfill their potentially powerful roles in the overall success of their businesses.

Notes

1. James L. McKenney, "A Field Research Study on Organizational Learning," Harvard Business School Working Paper 78–23.

2. Cyrus F. Gibson and Richard L. Nolan, "Managing the Four Stages of EDP Growth," Chapter 2, this book.

3. Richard L. Nolan, "Managing the Crises in Data Processing," Chapter 5, this book.

4. Richard J. Matteis, "The New Back Office Focuses on Customer Service," HBR, March–April 1979, p. 146.

5. "Computer Revolution at Dun & Bradstreet," Business Week, August 27, 1979, p. 72.

6. Larry E. Greiner, "Evolution and Revolution as Organizations Grow," HBR, July–August 1972, p. 37.

23

Who Needs the Office of the Future?

HARVEY L. POPPEL

The office seems to be the last outpost of resistance to automation, if one can judge by the small amount of money companies are now spending on it. Yet more than a trillion dollars a year will go for salaries and support of white-collar workers in 1982. Booz, Allen & Hamilton studied so-called knowledge workers to determine how they spend their work day and whether the enhancements of the office of the future could make them more productive. Harvey Poppel discusses the results and points out that many of the frustrating, unproductive activities of these workers could be reduced by the appropriate mix of office systems.

"Dammit, Mary, I was within 20 minutes of Quick Industries this morning."

"Well, Mr. Coldcall, I tried to reach you at the field office. It's lucky that you just phoned in. Anyway, a Mr. Buysome at Quick said that if you still want to bid on their contract, you've got to see him tomorrow at the latest and your proposal has to be in by Friday."

"Which proposal? We've talked about three different jobs."

"He said it was the one with the new specs."

"Oh, no! Peter in sales engineering has those at the district office along with the pricing sheets. Please transfer me to Peter. I'll get back to you."

"Sorry, he's on his line; it's busy."

"I guess I'll have to hold, but I'm in a phone booth."

Some minutes later: "Pete? Fred. Listen. I need the Quick specs and pricing. Can you get them to the field office by noon tomorrow? I'll make a special trip in to pick them up."

"Those old things! I suppose I can find them somewhere, but we've changed some of the components and the pricing so I'll have to update them. I'll try to get them to you by the end of the day."

"Pete, you've got to do better than that."

There may be slight stylistic differences in the article published in this book and the way it eventually appeared in the Harvard Business Review.

"Sorry, Fred. I'm already working on three other rush proposals, and I'm expediting two other jobs through some bottlenecks in the factory."

"Pete, for Fred's sake, do your darndest! Now please transfer me back to Mary."

"Mary, two things: arrange the delivery with Pete. Then call Joan at the field office. Tell her we're going to have to work late tomorrow night after I come back from my meeting with Buysome. Tell her also to pull the Quick files and proposal boilerplates. She's the only one there who knows where everything is, how to work the word processor, and the high quality copier, and . . ."

"Oh, Fred, Joan just called me from O'Hare. Remember, she's off to Acapulco? Fred . . . Fred . . . are you there?"

Sound familiar? Fred Coldcall's plight is not peculiar to traveling salesman. Most "knowledge workers"—professionals like Fred, Pete, Mr. Buysome, and their bosses—find themselves frustrated daily by a seemingly diabolical scheme that scrambles information, information handling equipment, and business people so that they fail to work together at the right place and time.

Yet organizational success hinges largely on how well workers perform their assigned tasks and communicate with one another. The key workers—those who manage, analyze, market, and provide creative thrust—are its know ledge workers, the people who could benefit most from accurate and comprehensive business information and effective communications channels.

U.S. businesses will spend more than $1 trillion on white-collar personnel in 1982, and $600 billion of that will go to compensate knowledge workers (see Exhibit 1).

Exhibit 1. Annual Cost to U.S. Business of White-Collar Workers (in billions of dollars)

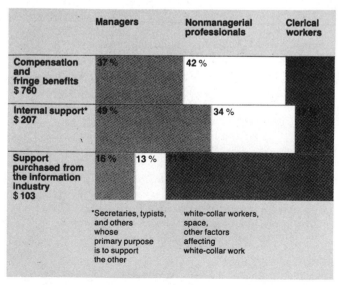

A few years ago, some executives became intrigued with office auto-mation as the magic formula that would revitalize white-collar functions. Despite the allure, however, businesses are spending less than a nickel for such technology of every dollar of knowledge-worker salaries and internal support costs.

The availability of technology is not the stumbling block. Vendors are already offering a powerful range of electronics devices, software, and com-munications networks. The fact is that most decision makers are skeptical about what managerial work stations, personal computers, videoconference rooms, and the other, newer icons of office automation can do for their businesses. These executives, disenchanted by their previous exposure to ill-conceived forays into management information systems and word pro-cessing, doubt that knowledge workers will embrace the new technology, and they lack confidence that their organizations can channel and measure the intended benefits. In addition, members of the computer-illiterate ma-jority are worried about whether, when, and how they themselves will deal with these new electronic tools.

The evidence from a few innovative organizations, including the U.S. Air Force and several large banks, that have made significant office auto-mation investments offers early, albeit fragmentary, signs that readily ac-cessible information technology can be an antidote for the professional per-formance malaise.[1] But if most businesses avoid investing in a broadly based office automation program, the electronic office concept could become an-other overpromised and undelivered remedy, while frustrations and expenses mount.

To determine whether performance improvements from office auto-mation are widely achievable and justify the costs and potential trauma of implementation, Booz, Allen & Hamilton recently completed a year-long study of 15 representative large U.S. organizations.

Study Methods & Systems

We focused on two vital aspects of knowledge worker performance: (1) how these workers now spend their time in achieving their business objectives and (2) how likely they are to raise their productivity through office auto-mation over the next five years. We did 15 case studies in a mix of functional areas such as marketing, purchasing, finance, design and analysis, and per-sonnel. Each study concerned a different type of manufacturing or service business. Six of the seven manufacturers were among the *Fortune* top 100 industrials. Aetna Life & Casualty and the First National Bank of Chicago typified the size and diversity of the eight service businesses we studied.

We treated each case as a detailed feasibility study, reinforced where possible by experiential data. In their automation sophistication the com-panies ranged from "high" to "nearly none." Each of these organizations, which included a government agency, partially funded the study. More than

25 information industry organizations, including AT&T, IBM, ITT, and Xerox, also partially funded our efforts but did not participate directly.

We considered five categories of automated office systems:

☐ *Conferencing.* Telecommunications systems that facilitate human interaction, ranging from basic telephone service to video conferencing.

☐ *Information transfer.* Electronic message systems in the form of keyboarded characters, facsimile images, or voice.

☐ *Information retrieval.* Computer-assisted recall of previously stored information, in the form of data, text, graphics, or audio or video input.

☐ *Personal processing.* Interactive, computer-assisted writing, editing, calculating, and drawing, including applications commonly known as word-text processing, personal computing, and interactive graphics.

☐ *Activity management.* Systems such as electronic tickler files and automated, task-project management, which track, screen, or expedite schedules, tasks, and information.

For all these systems, we assumed that knowledge workers could use the technology directly by means of newer, easy-to-use techniques such as touching display screens, manipulating multiaxis control levers known as joysticks and mouses, and by having the system recognize their spoken commands. However, when the system was too complex or expensive to use widely at the individual level, we configured an operator-driven system.

To determine how well the five categories of systems fit the 15 subjects, the study team used both quantitative and qualitative techniques. During the 10 to 12 weeks of each case study, the team worked with the executives of the particular departments to isolate the critical success factors (CSFs) in their operations and to become thoroughly familiar with the job characteristics, activities, and attitudes of the nine to twenty-five participants.[2]

The participants used a pocket-sized recorder to list and assess their work activities at 20-minute intervals over a three-to-four-week period, and after the study each participant filled out an anonymous questionnaire concerning his or her receptivity to potential office automation changes. Nearly 300 knowledge workers recorded about 90,000 time samples over 3,700 worker-days.

These participants closely resemble the U.S. knowledge-worker population: 59% were nonmanagerial professionals, 28% were lower- and middle-level managers, and the rest were senior managers, including 20 at the level of vice president or above. The average age was 41, although 29% were under 35. A plurality (40%) had from six to fifteen years of tenure with their companies, and the others were evenly divided between those with less than six years and those with more than fifteen years of service. Of the 78% who had graduated from college, nearly half held advanced degrees.

To establish a broad statistical base of information about current office automation status, plans, and perspectives, the team concurrently conducted two mail surveys of several hundred representative user organizations.[3]

Results of Study

We were not surprised that the study revealed no work pattern that nearly fit all levels and types of knowledge workers. Like Henry Mintzberg, who studied the manager's job to separate folklore from fact, we found knowledge workers acting much differently from the classical model of the highly systematic professional who plans, organizes, coordinates, and controls.[4]

Nevertheless, five findings concerning time use amplify Mintzberg's results and have broad managerial implications:

1. *Many of the subjects spend less than half their work time on activities directly related to their functions.* To understand this performance leakage, let's look at how the field sales professionals involved in four of our case studies spend their time. Whether called "account executives," "loan officers," "estate planners," or just generically "salesmen," sales professionals like Fred Coldcall are the spigot for the revenue stream of most businesses. Yet we found that they spend an average of only 36% of their work time on prospecting and selling—activities directly related to generating incremental revenue (see Exhibit 2). Moreover, they squander much of this 36% on traveling, calling on low-probability prospects, and working through the paper clogged proposal process.

Both sales professionals and their managers expressed frustration over

Exhibit 2. How Field Sales Professionals Spend Their Work Time

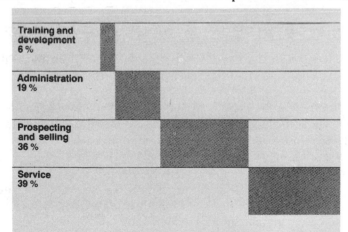

Training and development 6%

Administration 19%

Prospecting and selling 36%

Service 39%

this poor productivity. Furthermore, they were concerned that their non-revenue-generating chores were keeping them from cultivating a more lucrative customer base. They thought they had exhausted all the traditional time management techniques they knew but had failed to improve their use of time.

We found that the gremlin is not time management but the awkwardness and imprecision of today's information handling and communication processes. It is easy to see how information problems cost most sales professionals an hour or two a day.

In the first place, many sales professionals select and schedule their calls haphazardly because they lack access to information that might screen and geographically array high-probability prospects. In addition, they often make repeated trips between their offices and customers because they are unable to summon the requisite product, pricing, or delivery information when face-to-face with the customer. As if this were not enough, they are often obliged to handle, at the behest of customers, such clerical chores as determining the status of an outstanding order or resolving invoice discrepancies. Salespeople are usually pushed into such time wasting because of inadequate clerical support and faulty data processing systems. We found, on average, that such servicing of existing accounts consumed more time than prospecting and selling (39% versus 36%).

Purely administrative chores, such as time and expense reporting, chew up another 19% of work time. And much of this paperwork requires wearying trips to and from the office to receive, file, and mail reports and forms. Finally, training activities—keeping sales professionals up to date on new products, pricing changes, and sales techniques—eat up the remaining 6% of the work day. While continuous training is vital to performance, the communications techniques used today force sales professionals to take lengthy treks to the home office and to wade frequently through a stream of new product specifications, pricing, warranties, and other Brobdingnagian documents.

2. *The subjects spend 25% of their work time on "less productive" activities. (see Exhibit 3).* Three "generic" types of activities, which by our defintion are chronically less productive, consume from 18 to 30% of all professionals' time across all the functions in the 15 cases:

☐ *Totally unproductive.* Mainly the time spent traveling outside or within a building or waiting for meetings to start or a machine to become available. On average, each hour spent at an external site requires an additional 40 minutes of idle travel time.

☐ *Quasiprofessional.* Such activities as seeking information and expediting assigned tasks. These usually require some professional knowledge or interpersonal skills but are often inefficient because either automated or clerical support systems are unavailable.

Exhibit 3.   How Knowledge Workers Spend Their Work Time

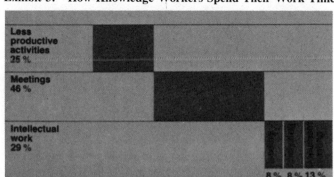

□ *Productive only at a clerical level.*   Professionals who lack adequate support and must therefore type, make copies, file, and make reservations and appointments themselves. In one case, highly paid R&D administrators were queueing up at an overloaded word processor to type their own progress reports.

Underscoring the importance of inadequate secretarial and clerical support, the results showed that organizations so handicapped consume more than twice as much time on less productive activities as offices that are better supported. In one case, professionals spent 42% of their time on such activities. Their communications-intensive mission was to coordinate operational services for an international commercial banking function. Such findings stress the penny wise and pound-foolish nature of needlessly harsh cutbacks or across-the-board head count controls of office support staffs.

3.   *Meetings, in person and by telephone, are the commonest form of professional activity.*   Meetings range from formal training seminars to bull sessions in the hall. Participants spent nearly half (46%) of their working time in meetings, senior managers exceeding 60% and nonmanagerial professionals slightly under 40%. Overall, they conducted 20% of their meetings by telephone. As one might expect, groups with heavy meeting time spent less than average time communicating through exchanges of documents.

4.   *Professionals spend an average of 21% of their work time in document-related activities and only 8% on analysis.*   Document preparation and review profiles varied widely, owing in part to differences in the availability and quality of word processing for less senior professionals. Nonmanagerial professionals spent nearly twice as much time composing documents as managers did. Also, younger people dictated fewer documents, and professionals who were newcomers spent about 65% more time editing than those who had been in the organization longer.

''Pure'' analytical time (time spent contemplating, problem solving, or conceptualizing) is perhaps the most precious and self-rewarding professional activity. But participants spent only 8% of their time in this way. Knowledge workers with some tenure, regardless of their organizational status, spent about 30% more time analyzing than those with little tenure.

5. *Most knowledge workers would like to reshape their time profiles.* Even though most participants and their department heads had distorted perceptions of how they spent their time, many of the managers and professionals we interviewed were eager to find ways of improving their productivity and work quality. For example, in interviews before the time sampling, well over 90% underestimated the time spent in meetings. While a similar percentage overestimated the time they subsequently recorded in analytical tasks, 35% felt they needed to spend considerably more time analyzing (even more time than they had mistakenly estimated). They also considered the time spent in planning and in professional development inadequate.

Despite these needs, participants felt blocked by the hours they squandered on the less productive activities. They especially criticized poorly trained and undermanned support staff, unproductive use of telephones and dictation systems, and inefficient means of document production, which often triggered unplanned and disruptive activities. The participants perceived the widely available computer-generated management reports as being unwieldly, unfocused, and containing out-of-date information.

Office Automation Recommendations

Clearly, many of these findings have implications beyond the feasibility of office automation. The time profiles suggest possible useful adjustments in organizational structure, ways of strengthening supervisory effectiveness, and the assignment of new priorities to activities closely linked to CSFs. Nevertheless, we concluded that within just five years knowledge workers could save an average of 15% of their time through more highly automated support. Roughly half the saving would come from reducing time spent in less productive activities. The balance would derive from selective reductions in certain meetings, analytical tasks, and document handling.

Since field sales is a highly eclectic function that usually embraces most generic activities of other business functions, let us examine a composite of our four field sales cases to illustrate how time savings can be gained.

A sales professional like Fred Coldcall would be equipped with an easy-to-use, portable intelligent display terminal enabling him to access information and contact people in a variety of time saving ways. First, Fred would scan publicly available data bases to select his prospect lists. Next, a ''traveling salesman'' algorithm could be used to display a minimum-time travel path among prospects and existing customers. Fred and his office based assistant, Mary, would use an electronic mail system operating through Fred's terminal to stay in close touch as she scheduled Fred's appointments to match the minimum-travel path. Naturally, the system would reconfigure the path should any appointments be unavailable or cancelled. Mary would use her desk-based, communicating word processor to send and receive such messages.

Next, Fred would use his terminal while visiting Quick Industries to access the Quick file, as well as the latest specifications and pricing information. Thus he could elicit Mr. Buysome's reaction to the main points of his proposal on the spot and adjust accordingly instead of wasting substantial time and effort preparing a formal proposal. In simpler situations, such as selling personal home insurance, the sales professional could display and print a complete proposal in front of the prospect.

In addition to a portable data terminal, Fred would have a portable telephone that he could use "hands-free" in his automobile and thus convert idle auto travel to productive time. Not only would this unit enable Fred to place and receive telephone calls while he was on the move but it would also connect him with a central voice message computer. Since this type of system can send and receive messages to and from any telephone, it would enable Fred to communicate with customers and the internal support people who did not have access to a data terminal.

Without having to leave his car, Fred could check the status of an order, coordinate invoice reconciliation efforts, arrange proposal preparations or sales engineering assistance, and even change his appointment schedule at any hour of the day.

Video technology would also help Fred. Full sound and motion product demonstrations on a videodisc would be accessed, along with standard pricing and availability, through an inexpensive videodisc player attachment to Fred's intelligent data terminal. Depending on the type of product, he could view this material with prospects or use it solely to prepare himself. Fred could also keep current with new product and marketing plans by attending video conferences available periodically at a nearby motel.

Certainly, not all these office systems would be useful for every sales force or in other situations. But we did find enough office automation applications (including some not described here) in each case to save at least 10%, and in one case more than 30%, of knowledge workers' time. The two commonest reasons for the savings variations among the 15 cases were the intrinsic differences in functional objectives, company cultures, and work practices and the effectiveness of office support staffs and equipment.

In addition to time savings, we found many opportunities in each case to raise the quality of output. Most of the qualitative benefits link directly to the four CSFs most commonly identified during interviews with executives and other participants:

1 Direct, timely access to accurate product, customer, and internal performance information, primarily by making it accessible through terminals or other types of automated work stations.

2 Effective intradepartmental communications, mainly through electronic mail systems.

3 More effective interaction with customers (both external and interdepartmental), through higher-quality documents and faster message systems.

4 Adequate, uninterrupted time for work activities most directly related to functional objectives, by taking the time saved from less productive activities and reinvesting it in high-priority tasks.

Because of the promise of both time savings and qualitative benefits, we recommended a mix of interdependent applications sufficient to justify a display terminal for 80% of the knowledge workers studied within five years. Few businesses, however, are likely to move that rapidly. As a base point, in 1980 there was only one such device for every 25 U.S. knowledge workers. Nevertheless, Texas Instruments, one of the leading-edge users, reported in 1980 that it already had one electronic information device (a computer terminal or a programmable calculator) for every three white- and blue-collar employees.

Acceptance of Automation

We found that acceptance varied according to two criteria: participants' familiarity with the application and the potential for reduction of less productive activities. For example, most participants, especially those who did heavy analytical work and created many documents, were enthusiastic about using such well-known aids as electronic information retrieval and word-text processing. Conversely, less familiar applications, such as video conferencing and electronic mail, appear to face greater resistance (see Exhibit 4). A recent market survey indicates, however, that persons who attend many task-oriented meetings are more receptive to video conferencing because of the time it will save them.[5]

Only a handful of participants would be likely to resist all applications. Those with more company tenure, less education, and lower-level positions tended to be less receptive. Surprisingly, once separated from tenure, age was only a minor factor.

On the basis of these findings, we think that organizations can gain maximum acceptance of office automation among knowledge workers by:

☐ Using it to reduce less productive time, which is the greatest source of dissatisfaction.

☐ Involving users and getting their opinions early when selecting and developing new automated systems.

Exhibit 4.   Receptivity of Subjects to Selected Office Automation Applications*

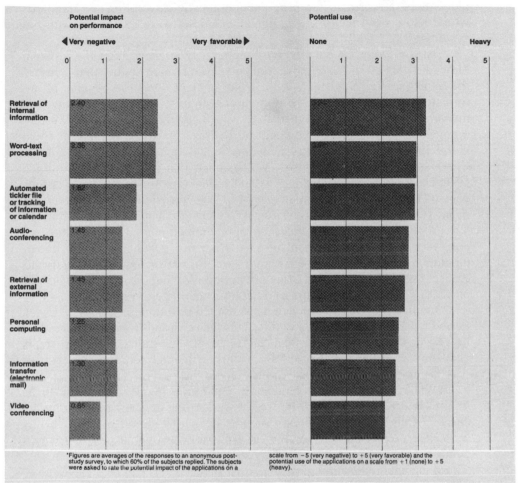

*Figures are averages of the responses to an anonymous post-study survey, to which 60% of the subjects replied. The subjects were asked to rate the potential impact of the applications on a scale from −5 (very negative) to +5 (very favorable) and the potential use of the applications on a scale from +1 (none) to +5 (heavy).

☐   Making no demands for universal acceptance, avoiding personnel shifts that might appear to reduce support service levels, beginning with easy-to-use applications, and starting with intensive user training.

Potential Obstacles

Many of the middle managers we surveyed complained that the technology seemed to be getting out-of-date too fast to ensure a payback. Obsolescence and the incompatibility with newer technology that often comes with it are real prospects. But we concluded that organizations can justify packaged systems, even if the systems' economic levels of use do not exceed four years. True, some key technological developments—which we did not assume to be fully mature in our study—bear watching during the 1980s. Among the most potent are large-vocabulary speech recognition; multiple-panel, high-resolution displays; and the joining of personal computers with video discs. Nevertheless, a program of compatible evolution and standards would allow new networks, equipment, and software to coexist with old systems.

As for senior executives, they seem fairly relaxed about the problem of obsolescence. They are more troubled about how to control and measure the benefits. We found that, with strong management, the benefits of automation can be brought to the bottom line. In as soon as one to two years, investments could yield an attractive return. In the case studies, we recommended that businesses commit an average of $8,200 per professional within the first 18 to 24 months, including $6,000 each for new office systems. For financial analysis purposes, we assumed that the cost of new office systems would be amortized as a $1,500 annual operating expense over four years. The remaining one-time costs of $2,200 consisted of project management, physical renovation, software development or acquisition, and training.

As the compensation value of the estimated annual time savings we derived a gross annual benefit of $3,400 per professional after the implementation period. To be conservative, we did not factor in any salary increase over this initial 18- to 24-month period. We found a net annual benefit of $1,900 after the subtraction of $1,500 for amortized systems.

On this basis, the average nondiscounted postimplementation payback period works out to 14 to 15 months. This figure varied from 3 to 48 months, however. A more demanding financial test, capitalizing all new office systems costs as part of the investment base, yields an average return on investment of 41%, or well over the hurdle rate of most businesses.

While in theory an organization could stop investing after 18 to 24 months and harvest its returns, we found a strong case for reinvesting the early savings in further systems support over a 60-month period. On this basis, the nondiscounted break-even point for the overall program would occur between the fourth and fifth years.

Financial realization of professional time savings can be elusive, however. Indeed, our researchers found that nearly all the companies we studied were already at least two to four years behind in installing available office systems, chiefly because they lacked guidelines for measuring the gains. What is the solution? An organization can reap tangible benefits from time saving by steering the improvements toward overall business goals. For example, a business concerned primarily with cutting operating expenses, as in our information systems' case, could use time saving to reduce personnel such as extraexpensive contract programmers.

Businesses will probably seek gains with more strategic leverage. "Most companies," notes David Ness of the University of Pennsylvania's Wharton School, "would prefer a 15% improvement in managerial effectiveness to a 10% cut in clerical overhead."[6] In our field sales cases, we recommended that the time the sales professionals saved by simplifying or off-loading servicing and administrative tasks and by reducing travel and time spent with low-probability prospects be reinvested in revenue-generating activities.

Simple arithmetic shows that we could increase prospecting and selling time from 36% to 51% of total time by rechanneling the 15% time savings derived from nonprospecting and selling activities we identified. In theory, this would amount to a 40% boost in revenue-generating potential, so we focused our recommendations for reinvestment on prospecting for new customers and on more thorough sales engineering, and "handholding" with existing customers.

The key to justifying office automation lies in selecting business indicators that best describe the results of either intended reductions in the work force or directed reinvestments of time savings. These indicators are usually integral elements of a management control system, such as revenues and expenses as well as such nonfinancial reinvestment indicators as the number of new products in R&D or the level of customer service and satisfaction in marketing situations.

Staffing Problems

Once an organization develops an appealing business case, it will probably find it lacks qualified designers and implementors. More than 80% of the businesses we surveyed cited this lack as either a major or a minor obstacle. For example, Lincoln National Life Insurance Company recently reported that it had only four full-time people assigned to user training and assistance, despite a well-publicized 1978 commitment to reduce the use of paper 90% by 1984. By early 1980, only 15% of the major U.S. businesses had reported having more than five, qualified, full-time office automation professionals on their staffs.

Further, most existing office automation units are attuned not to knowledge-worker performance but rather to secretarial use of word processing and other support systems. And reassigning already scarce computer systems analysts will not fill the entire gap because office automation differs too greatly from conventional data processing.

To overcome the downstream obstacle of inadequate staff capabilities, planners should anticipate the staff they will need to design and implement office systems as well as to guide fledgling end users. As a general guideline, a diversified manufacturer will want to have at least six to ten full-time specialists per billion dollars of revenue. Recognizing the diversity of technical, organizational, and behavioral skills required, companies should cross-train its employees or recruit new talent. They should also study the successful experiences of others to accelerate their experience curves.

Where to Begin

No single approach to performance improvement through office automation can meet the needs of every business or government agency, but successful programs share three features:

1. *Firm Commitment From Senior Management.* A good way of showing early support is to organize a steering committee of senior line and staff end-user executives to ensure that performance benefits are consonant with business strategy and that compatible systems are implemented across organizational lines. Management should then establish, one level below the steering committee, a full-time task force, including general managers thoroughly familiar with business operations, human resource specialists, office facilities experts, and information systems analysts, all of whom would be responsible for planning the knowledge-worker performance improvement program.

2. *Balance of Implementation and Planning.* Pilot studies often test the wrong tools on the wrong people and lack the proper controls and measurements. For instance, one manufacturer hurriedly installed an expensive electronic mail system across several dispersed departments only to find that determining and extrapolating the system's impact on professional performance was impossible. Moreover, since the system could not guarantee timely receipt of messages, end users were only lukewarm. Accordingly, the company had no firm basis for extending the program or salvaging its investment.

But realistic, comprehensive plans require some hands-on experience. The most successful experiences, such as those at Continental Illinois Bank and in the Air Force, were the result of long-range programs implemented only after careful assessment of pilot studies.

Before implementing even the simplest pilot study, any task force should develop at least a planning white paper, which would establish a general sense of strategy direction and pace and include gross estimates of potential benefits, one-time and continuing cost, and resource requirements. The task force should, above all, select initial showcase work groups and applications, along with a path of how, where, and when to expand applications and the user base.

3. *Time and Behavior Studies.* Detailed studies will sharpen the gross estimates of time savings, how to reinvest them, and how to anticipate potential impacts on work and work-life quality. Then, controlled introductions of off-the-shelf office equipment and software can contribute meaningful before and after data. Moreover, as we found in several case studies, the study process leads department managers to important and immediate, nonautomated improvements, such as reallocation of office support work loads and heightened emphasis on high-priority business missions.

These first steps are necessary to gain widespread, internal support and generate a grounds well of demand. Continental Illinois Bank controlled initial access to its new officer-level, information-retrieval system until management was convinced of the system's practicality. When success was demonstrable, other envious knowledge workers queued up to get on the system. Conversely, hasty attempts to force typing productivity may not only cause performance to fall but also create lingering hostility.

**Exhibit 5.   Likely Evolution of Office Automation in a Typical Large Company
During the 1980's**

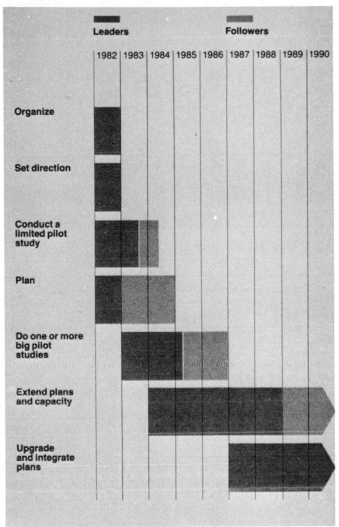

Urgency of Automation

Despite strong economic arguments, only a few businesses are likely to
hurdle all the obstacles described in the previous sections and achieve larger-
scale, intradepartmental installations over the next year or two. Most will
probably not install many interdepartmental, multiapplication systems until
the second half of the decade. Even then, only highly aggressive businesses
will have companywide installations by 1990 (see Exhibit 5).

Nevertheless, by starting serious planning now, organizations can
benefit early and lay the groundwork for long term payoffs. Conversely, a

laissez-faire approach is likely to result in a flood of localized, ad hoc, and dysfunctional activities.

Even now, some organizations without plans, such as one of the banks we studied, are beginning to suffer from the many personal computers, electronic mail systems, and word processors that have not been justified, that add little to professional performance, and that are often incompatible with each other as well as with valuable company data bases.

The most valuable lessons to be learned from our research project and the published experiences of others are twofold. First, businesses can improve the performance of knowledge workers significantly and measurably through a carefully conceived and executed office automation program. And second, the patterns of professional activity are complex, eclectic, and dynamic, so any attempt to change them should be approached sensitively, systematically, and at a controlled pace.

Hang in there, Fred Coldcall, help is on the way!

Notes

1. See Richard J. Matteis, "The New Back Office Focuses on Customer Service," *HBR*, March–April 1979, p. 146; Louis H. Mertes, "Doing Your Office Over—Electronically," Chapter 29, this book.

2. John F. Rockart, "Chief Executives Define Their Own Data Needs," *HBR*, March–April, 1979, p. 81.

3. Two surveys conducted by Booz, Allen & Hamilton Inc. during March–April 1980, one in conjunction with the National Office Automation Conference, the other with the Society for Management Information Systems.

4. Henry Mintzberg, "The Manager's Job: Folklore and Fact," *HBR*, July–August, 1975, p. 41.

5. Karen File, Alan Kuritsky, Robert Forrest, Sally Leiderman, "The Future of Videoconferencing: There's More than the Meeting to Consider," *Teleconferencing and Interactive Media* (Madison: University of Wisconsin Extension Center for Interactive Programs, 1980), p. 37.

6. Parker Hodges, "Fear of Automation," *Output*, August, 1980, p. 38.

24

New Promise of Computer Graphics

HIROTAKA TAKEUCHI and ALLAN H. SCHMIDT

As costs of hardware have declined and the necessary software has become more readily available, managers are discovering the special virtues of computer graphics. According to these authors, not only does computer graphics enable managers to see in one picture what they might otherwise have to glean from a stack of computer printouts, it also presents the material in a form that is easily grasped. In addition, computer graphics aids decision making because it presents trends and deviations accurately and clearly, permitting the user to discover the answers to "what if" questions at various stages in a project.

In studying what managers actually do in their jobs, Henry Mintzberg observed the following:

> I was struck during my study by the fact that the executives I was observing—all very competent by any standard—are fundamentally indistinguishable from their counterparts of a hundred years ago (or a thousand years ago, for that matter). The information they need differs, but they seek it in the same way—by word of mouth.[1]

The increased use of computer graphics technology within business has made this statement less true, for some managers now seek information through pictures.

Although computer graphics technology has been readily available in the past 10 years, only a few companies were willing to invest the substantial time and money required to make the technology useful for them.[2] Recently, however, with the decline in the costs of hardware and software and the availability of service organizations that commercially produce computer-generated graphic displays, more and more companies are discovering computer graphics. In addition, more managers are now using computer graphics to make better business decisions, as opposed to the engineers who used it for scientific applications a decade ago.

415

Computer graphics satisfies certain unfulfilled needs of managers. Overloaded with work and pressured to make quick decisions, most managers would prefer scanning a single picture to reading through reams of printouts that pile up on their desks. To these managers, a computer graphics picture is worth a thousand printouts. Less numbers-oriented managers would happily trade a statistical output printed in tabular form for one that is graphically presented. To these managers, keeping it simple is a virtue. More research-oriented managers, who need to analyze a multitude of critical factors for success (and acquire data bases associated with them), would most likely consider it worthwhile to supplement their elaborate mathematical equations with a visual overlay of different sets of original data bases. To these managers and to whomever they are reporting, seeing may be believing.

Computer graphics technology offers two basic benefits to all managers. First, it saves on one of the most coveted resources available to managers—time. Such savings occur in the time required to (a) interpret the data, (b) communicate a complex set of findings to others, and (c) supervise the production of a final report. Because the time used in processing data is essentially nonproductive, these savings free managers to engage in other, more productive functions.

Second, computer graphics helps managers better perform one of their most important functions—decision making. This happens because (a) visual information can be digested more readily, so that managers would, in a given amount of time, be able to acquire a larger pool of relevant information; (b) trends or deviations from the norm are easier to depict through graphics, so that managers would have access to a more accurate system of exception reporting or trend analysis; and (c) the rapid response of the interactive computer graphics systems enables managers to ask the "what if" questions without feeling guilty about having to consult others and helps them personally test out several contingency plans in a relatively short period of time. This broader, more accurate, and more contingent information reduces the uncertainties associated with making decisions.

The plan of this article is first to introduce a series of applications that are suitable for business organizations. We present two scientific and several marketing applications. Then, after demonstrating what computer graphics can accomplish, we turn to briefly describing how it actually works. We do so by outlining the three basic requirements of computer graphics—hardware, data bases, and software. We next describe three basic options for these requirements so that managers can carry out a simple cost-benefit analysis. The article concludes by anticipating what lies ahead for computer graphics.

Our objective throughout is to familiarize more managers with the technology that is currently available. The challenge to managers is to assess, for themselves, whether computer graphics can truly deliver the hoped-for benefits of making managers more productive and effective.

Scientific Applications

Within the sciences of design engineering and geology, acceptance was readily accorded to computer graphics. In the case of design engineering, the computer displays a prototype of a new product, most likely on a cathode ray tube (CRT) terminal, while in the case of geology, the computer displays a map of certain regions, most likely on a plotter.

General Motors and McDonnell Douglas have used computer graphics extensively for design engineering purposes for more than a decade. At General Motors clay models of a proposed design are scanned by the computer and stored in its memory. The designer uses a special pencil or the computer's keyboard to alter various features of the design. From the computer he obtains a quick response on how the change affects the car's weight, stability, and so forth. McDonnell Douglas has used graphics in building the Navy's new F-18 fighter plane. With the basic design on the computer's screen, engineers can find out the effects of various changes.

Both of these applications allow an engineer to use pictures to ask the what-if questions. Because answers and facts are displayed in a matter of moments, decision making is faster and more analytic.

Standard Oil Company of Indiana (AMOCO) has used computer graphics for more than 15 years to reduce uncertainties associated with geologic explorations. Robert Dupree of AMOCO estimates that 10,000 computer maps are produced in the oil industry every month. Although each map may run between $20 and $50 in computer cost, Dupree argues that it is well worth the investment:

> It can cost $10 million to drill a single oil well on land with no guarantee that it will produce. Our information system (which includes data on wells, seismic locations, land and water, etc.) is predicated on the belief that better information through computer technology can improve our odds in the search for energy. So, through an information system, if we improve our odds only a fraction of a percentage point through dry holes not drilled or new discoveries found, then it's well worth the cost not only to us, but to everyone.[3]

St. Regis Paper Company has recently begun to use computer graphics to manage its forest inventory. By displaying two sets of different forest maps (generated through computers) on top of each other, management can discover where and why disagreements are occurring. The two sets of overlaid maps are (a) data on hardwood availability provided by LANDSAT satellite (launched in 1972 by the National Aeronautics and Space Administration) and (b) internal data on hardwood availability obtained by field surveys. By resurveying areas of disagreement only, St. Regis will be able to realize substantial savings on the time and cost required for updating its forest inventory.

Marketing Applications

As companies become more market oriented, they need to monitor more closely consumer behavior, competitive conduct, and environmental trends. In the process of gathering such information, the marketing arm could easily become swamped with data. Bob Leavens, dealer survey manager of General Motors' Cadillac Division, discussed the buildup of computer printouts in his division. He recalled that a few years ago "a truck came with all this paper one day, and there it sat for a year. The problem arose because the computer's ability to spew out voluminous amounts of data far exceeded the human ability to examine, interpret, and put the data to use." As a means of correcting this imbalance, computer graphics was introduced to the marketing managers of the Cadillac Division two years later.

Like General Motors, more companies are turning to computer graphics to redress the imbalance between the overflow of market information and the overload on human resources it is creating. Since marketing applications are one of the fastest-growing areas of use, we describe them in the following sections.

Site Location

One of the most frequently mentioned uses of computer graphics is to determine the optimal location of a store, plant, or warehouse. At the Cadillac Division of General Motors, the computer plots out all Cadillacs registered in a certain region and the locations of all its dealers within that region.[4] Exhibit 1 shows by a small dot each car registered in the Chicago region that is competitive with Cadillac. Existing Cadillac dealers are shown by large lettered dots. The plot demonstrates a region with a high density of Cadillac competitors that is not served by any dealer (pointed out by an arrow).

"Looking at the map, we asked ourselves whether we should add a new dealer or relocate an existing dealer," said Bob Leavens. "Assuming we decided to relocate an existing dealer, we could ask the computer to plot out census tracts within that particular region that satisfy our criterion for dealer location on such variables as traffic flow, population density, land value, and others."

Arthur D. Little was asked by the Department of Housing and Urban Development to recommend possible experimental sites for locating a five-year demonstration program concerning residential solar heating and cooling. As part of this project, computer graphics was used to show the percentage of housing units using fuel oil for home heating in the United States (Exhibit 2).

Jerry Wasserman, who worked on this study for Arthur D. Little, sees three advantages of computer graphics in such a case: (a) the ability to analyze geographic information derived from both public and private data sources, (b) the power to easily convince clients of the study, including

Exhibit 1. Determining Optimal Locations for Cadillac Dealers in Chicago

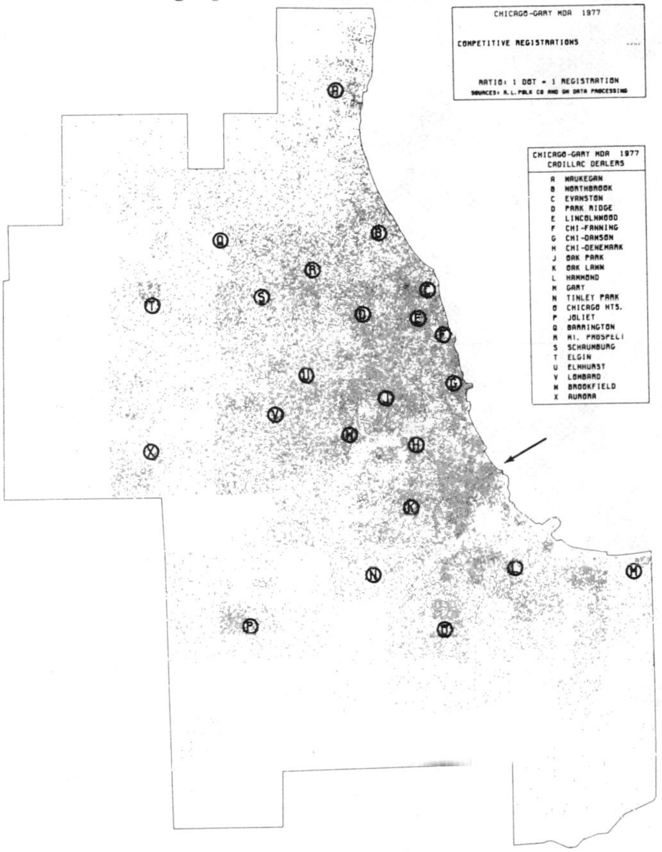

CHICAGO-GARY MOA 1977

COMPETITIVE REGISTRATIONS

RATIO: 1 DOT = 1 REGISTRATION
SOURCES: R. L. POLK CO AND SM DATA PROCESSING

CHICAGO-GARY MOA 1977
CADILLAC DEALERS

A	WAUKEGAN
B	NORTHBROOK
C	EVANSTON
D	PARK RIDGE
E	LINCOLNWOOD
F	CHI-FANNING
G	CHI-DAWSON
H	CHI-DENEMARK
J	OAK PARK
K	OAK LAWN
L	HAMMOND
M	GARY
N	TINLEY PARK
O	CHICAGO HTS.
P	JOLIET
Q	BARRINGTON
R	MT. PROSPECT
S	SCHAUMBURG
T	ELGIN
U	ELMHURST
V	LOMBARD
W	BROOKFIELD
X	AURORA

Source Note: Graphics prepared by Urban Science Associates.

419

Exhibit 2. Percentage of Housing Units Using Fuel Oil for Home Heating

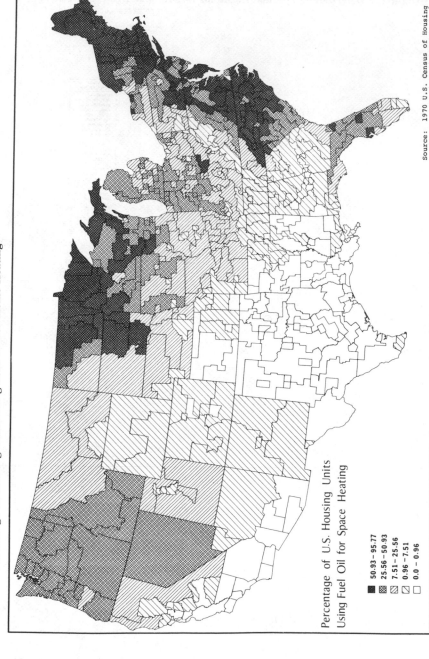

Percentage of U.S. Housing Units
Using Fuel Oil for Space Heating

■ 50.93 – 95.77
▨ 25.56 – 50.93
▧ 7.51 – 25.56
▨ 0.96 – 7.51
☐ 0.0 – 0.96

Source: 1970 U.S. Census of Housing

Source Note: Graphics prepared for Arthur D. Little, Cambridge, Massachusetts, by Harvard University's Laboratory for Computer
Graphics and Spatial Analysis.

municipal leaders and members of Congress, and (c) the increased chance of spotting anomalies, such as Seattle, and a pocket in Florida centered around Tampa, Orlando, and Jacksonville, which may not be obvious as high oil-using areas.[5]

Market Analysis

Analysis of current market performance and future market potential is another popular application of computer graphics. To assess current areas of strength and weakness, *Time* magazine plots the subscription rate of its regional circulation edition as shown in Exhibit 3 for the Boston area. The unique feature of this map is the use of zip codes as the basis for geographic segmentation. In addition to internal use, some of *Time*'s advertisers (especially those in the mail-order and telephone-order businesses) will find

Exhibit 3. Market Penetration Rates by *Time* Magazine in Boston

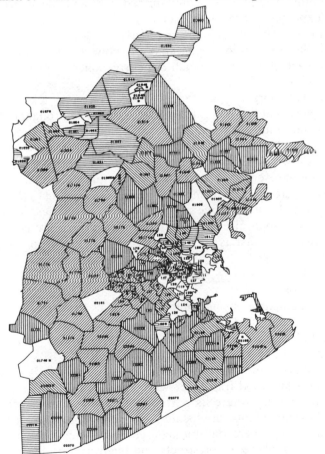

Source Note: Graphics prepared by Demographic Research Company.

these penetration rates displayed by zip codes an added attraction of the magazine.

Insurance Company of North America (INA) uses computer graphics to determine market areas that offer the best potential.[6] Using (1) internal survey results of the 10 most promising target industries by standard industrial classification codes and (2) Dun's Market Identifier list of names and addresses of companies within industries designated as prospective targets, INA's system shows the concentration of prospective customers in each census tract. Such a display helps INA to determine more exactly where the greatest marketing effort should be deployed.

Competitive Analysis

The Cadillac Division of General Motors uses computer graphics in a similar way to gauge the impact of competition on its business. Combining the syndicated data on competitive registrations for such cars as Mercedes, Lincoln Continental, and other high-priced cars and the internal data on Cadillac's expected share of market in each census tract, the computer calculates the distribution of sales, given expected total sales of 6,000 Cadillacs in the San Francisco area. Exhibit 4 shows the location of expected sales within each census tract (each dot corresponds to one registration).

Product Planning

A food company that has more than 60 sales districts throughout the United States and a multitude of product lines and brands found computer graphics a sensible means of managing the onslaught of numbers generated by sales reports. As shown in Exhibit 5, sales reports for each of the company's brands are now presented graphically. Notice that sales data are available on the basis of percent change and are indicated according to the company's sales districts and not by some predetermined boundaries. Top managers can quickly focus their attention on those districts that are not at par with or are not growing as fast as others and discuss what remedial actions need to be taken.

Media Planning

Two cases of companies using computer graphics to determine which geographic areas would yield the most return for their advertising investment were presented at the second annual Harvard Computer Graphics Week, held in Cambridge, Massachusetts, during July, 1979.

Joseph Weissmann of Demographic Research Company discussed the experience of a fast-food franchiser who developed a mapping system capable of displaying (a) where its best customers—defined in terms of age, income, and dwelling unit—are located, (b) where competing fast-food outlets are located, (c) where the trading-area boundaries are with respect to its stores, and (d) where major streets and highways are located. Looking at an overlay of such maps, the fast-food franchiser was then able to determine the areas of best advertising opportunities.

Exhibit 4.   Cadillac's Projected Sales in San Francisco Area

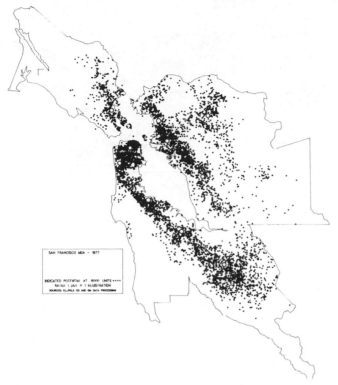

Source Note: Graphics prepared by Urban Science Applications.

Exhibit 5. A Product Planning Application (Brand A, pack #3, percent change, sales per 1000 persons, 1977–1978)

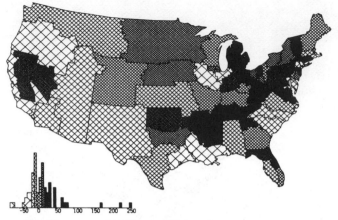

Source Note: Graphics prepared by Harvard University's Laboratory for Computer Graphics and Spatial Analysis.

Exhibit 6. Retail Productivity Analysis for a Hypothetical Shopping Center

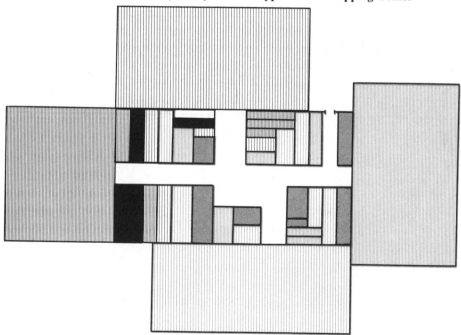

Note: Retail productivity is defined as sales per square foot of selling space. Gray codes are defined such that black signifies high productivity and color signifies low productivity.
Source Note: Graphics prepared by Urban Science Applications.

Allan Paller of Applied Urbanetics reported on a large publisher who, among other things, displayed the penetration rate of its periodicals on the basis of A.C. Nielsen's Designated Marketing Areas (DMA). Using this method, the publisher was able to visually determine which DMAs had the highest likelihood of success for television and newspaper advertising.

Retail Productivity Analysis

Developing regional shopping malls was one thing, but analyzing the performance of hundreds of tenants was another story for Bob Schout, vice president of marketing for the Taubman Company. Schout recalls that sales reports were growing too long to draw meaningful conclusions as the number of tenants in each shopping mall increased from 30 to 40 in the early 1960s to nearly 200 in the 1970s.

But with the newly added computer graphics capability (developed by Urban Science Applications Inc.), his task has been greatly simplified. Having produced a map of the mall floor plan, the computer now shows productivity of tenants space using color codes. One of the indexes for a hypothetical mall, retail sales per square foot of selling space, is displayed in Exhibit 6.

Such a system, Schout hopes, will lead to better management of Taubman's existing retail operations as well as better planning for future tenant space allocation. "After all," he says, "we are in the retail business as well as in the real estate business." (Computer-generated visuals are currently available in two shopping malls.)

Summing up the computer graphics applications presented so far, several advantages become clear:

☐ An appeal to a broad spectrum of companies in different businesses.

☐ Even within marketing, a number of varied uses in formulating better strategies.

☐ A custom-made unit of analysis—whether it be geographic (county, zip code, sales district, A.C. Nielsen's DMA) or nongeographic (such as a shopping mall).

☐ A multitude of graphic output formats, ranging from two-dimensional color to three-dimensional black and white (see Exhibit 7 for an example of the latter based on a study by one of the authors [H.T.] on grocery store productivity).

☐ A wide use of various statistical data (syndicated data and internal company data) in conjunction with a cartographic data base.

These observations all point to one of the major product attributes of computer graphics—versatility. To satisfy the ever-changing needs of consumers, computer graphics should have something for everyone at this stage of the product life cycle. Having described computer graphics from the user's perspective in this section, we now turn to discuss the requirements from a production or supply outlook.

Exhibit 7.   Example of a Three Dimensional Output Format Projected 1977 Grocery Store Productivity (in thousands)

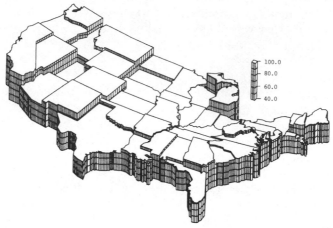

Source Note: Graphics prepared by Harvard University's Laboratory for Computer Graphics and Spatial Analysis.

Essentials for Computer Graphics

Three resources are needed before a computer-generated picture can appear for the user: hardware, data bases, and software. Although the first two resources have been available for some time, it is the development of packaged or proprietary software (as opposed to an in-house development of software) that has stimulated an expanded use of computer graphics in recent years.

Hardware Devices

In addition to a medium-sized computer (e.g., IBM 370 series), graphic-display devices such as pen ploters and CRT terminals are needed as part of the hardware. CRT terminals are becoming increasingly popular because the user can directly interact with the computer—that is, by creating a display, erasing it, and seeing a different display in a matter of seconds. The cost of CRT terminals ranges from $10,000 to $50,000, with a color CRT terminal costing about $25,000. An optional device for CRT terminals is a hard-copy unit in either black and white ($4,000 to $40,000) or color ($15,000 to $60,000).

Data Bases

Two types of data bases are required for successful generation of computer graphics: a cartographic (or x-y coordinate) data base and a statistical data base. A cartographic data base allows the shape of geographic zones to be defined in terms of states, standard metropolitan statistical areas, counties, census tracts, and other determinate geographic boundaries.

Publicly available cartographic data bases include the U.S. Bureau of Census DIME files for street patterns and Urban Atlas files for census tract outlines within metropolitan areas. The U.S. National Technical Information Service also distributes World Data Bank I and II files for international boundaries. Various commercial organizations can provide zip code boundaries as well.

Tailor-made, cartographic data bases, such as sales districts or shopping mall locations, can be created in-house through the use of a graphic data recording device or, alternatively, can be purchased from commercial organizations.

The second type of data base is statistical and consists of commercial data provided by private companies, census data and other public data available from the government, or internally generated data. Private companies such as A.C. Nielsen, Selling Areas-Marketing Inc., Dun & Bradstreet, Donnelly Marketing, Market Statistics, CACI, Urban Decision Systems, R.L. Polk, Data Resources, and many others offer a wide range of statistics on the market, consumers, competition, products, economy, and much more.[7] The government is an exceptionally rich, but often neglected, source for diverse statistics on population, labor force, specific industries, and other demographics. Internally generated data often consist of information on sales and financial performance as well as information obtained through surveys or other studies.

Software Packages

Computer graphics software is the "black box" that takes in the *where* information from the cartographic data base and the *what* information from the statistical data base to produce a graphic output on either paper, photographic film, or CRTs. The black box is actually a combination of computer programs typically written in Fortran. A computer graphics user can either write the program in-house or purchase a proprietary program from commercial software companies, government agencies, or universities.

One of the most advanced software packages has been developed by the Laboratory for Computer Graphics and Spatial Analysis at Harvard University and is being distributed by a commercial software company. This software can create and manipulate a cartographic data base, analyze and overlay a large number of statistical data bases, and enable users to specify exactly how they want their output to be displayed.

Acquiring the Capability

A company interested in acquiring a computer graphics capability has three basic options available. These are (a) use of service bureaus that specialize in producing computer graphics, (b) use of computer time-sharing companies, or (c) development of in-house capability. A company's choice will depend on the level of anticipated use, prior experience in the preparation and use of graphic displays, and current in-house availability of computer graphics equipment.

Service Bureaus

Service bureaus specializing in computer graphics provide custom-made visual outputs to the client company. One of the chief advantages of working with such an organization is the availability of graphic-display professionals who can consult with the client in specifying what data sources are required and what graphic format is best suited for a given task. Once these decisions are made, the service bureau will create high-quality graphic products in minimum time.

Because these organizations have made prior investments in hardware, data bases (with the possible exception of internal corporate data that the client company has to supply), software, and professional staff, initial investment requirements on the part of the client company are minimal. The price per graphic product, however, tends to be relatively high. A client company can expect to pay from $100 to $1,000 per product depending on the number and the complexity of the graphics being produced.

Time-sharing Companies

A computer time-sharing company provides the interim step between hiring a service bureau on the one hand and installing a computer graphics capability in-house on the other. When using a time-sharing company, the commitment on the part of the company in terms of time, people, and initial investment is less than installing the capability in-house but more than using service bureaus. As with service bureaus, time-sharing companies provide customer assistance through their service personnel. However, unlike service bureaus, these representatives do not actually provide the computer graphics product for the client company. That responsibility rests on the company itself.

Although time-sharing companies have all the resources available (hardware, data bases except for internal company data, and software), it is not uncommon for the client company to acquire its own display equipment. With display equipment such as a graphic CRT, the company can experiment with alternative sets of data or analyses in an interactive mode. The computer time-sharing charges for preparing a computer graphics product usually range from $50 to $500 per display. The charge varies with the volume and complexity of the displays and the availability of display equipment (including a hard-copy unit) on the part of the client company.

In-house Installation

Companies that already operate a large computer center may find it desirable to add to it a computer graphics capability. This add-on option requires the purchase of the hardware, data bases, and software necessary to produce computer graphics. Companies should also plan on assigning one or more persons specifically to the task of becoming proficient in the use of graphic-display software. Vendors of commercially available software provide companies only with the necessary initial instructions.

One of the advantages of in-house installation is that it eliminates the need to release sensitive corporate data bases to an external organization. It also has the advantage of providing maximum flexibility to the user at minimum operating costs. The operating cost under this option should range from $5 to $50 per graphic display.

But what about the initial investment? Assuming that the company has a computer and a fairly sophisticated data processing department employing integrated data-base technology,[8] initial incremental investment for hardware, software, and a cartographic data base is estimated to be $70,000. The investment is estimated as follows: $25,000 for a color CRT terminal, $20,000 for an optional color photographic hard-copy device, $20,000 for computer graphics software, and $5,000 for various cartographic data bases. Although $70,000 may not sound like a large investment, this incremental estimate does not include fixed developmental costs associated with staffing, interfacing with existing data bases, or building new statistical data bases.

An alternate approach to building a computer graphics capability is to acquire only a CRT terminal and use the services of a commercial computer time-sharing service. A service organization (such as Data Resources) provides access to the computer and all data bases over a telephone line. When needed, hard copies are sent by mail.

The Future for Computer Graphics

Since the publication of Shostack and Eddy's article on computer graphics in 1971, major changes have taken place in terms of availability and cost-effectiveness of hardware, data bases, and software. From the supply side of the picture, the outlook for the next few years is bright:

☐ *Hardware*. Further reduction in cost and increasingly widespread use of advanced display devices (such as high resolution, large-screen color displays; black and white and color hard-copy devices for paper and film output; and large-screen projectors).

☐ *Software*. Development of improved packaged programs that can handle larger data bases and be run with mini- and microcomputers.

☐ *Data bases*. Explosive growth in the construction and use of both cartographic and statistical data bases.

The single most important contribution, however, is expected to come from CRT terminals with built-in microprocessors (known as "intelligent terminals") that will help to integrate the three resources. These terminals will be able to store software and data bases locally at the user's site while communicating with larger remote computers (for purposes of accessing large data bases or performing heavy computational tasks) when necessary. Such a distributed-processing hardware coupled with data-base management system software will complement and facilitate the use of computer graphics by managers.

From the demand side of the picture, computer graphics is seeing application in areas besides marketing. It has been put to use in the following fields:

☐ *Public safety.* For allocating resources in high-crime areas.

☐ *Public transportation.* For evaluating the effects of alternate routes.

☐ *Environmental analysis.* For assessing the impact of proposed projects and resulting land-use decisions.

☐ *Public health.* For predicting the possible diffusion of an epidemic or depicting the incidence of cancer.

☐ *City and regional planning.* For predicting potential use of proposed public facilities or determining the effect of shadow cast by proposed skyscrapers on housing.

These and other applications of computer graphics suggest that the areas of potential use are limited only by the imagination.

The outlook is for user demand to snowball in the 1980s. Managers, who are the principal beneficiaries of the new technology, will continue to serve as the nerve center of information within the organization with the problem of information overload. They will also be expected to continue making effective decisions after having considered as many critical factors for success as possible and having evaluated as many contingency plans as possible. But, in the process of doing so, managers may become more engulfed with the problem of analysis paralysis. Computer graphics is one of the means of resolving these dilemmas for managers.

By helping managers become more productive and effective, computer graphics may possibly provide the answer to one of the critical problems perplexing the United States—namely, the lag in productivity growth. Seldom has anyone asked the question, "Is management partly to blame for the slowdown in productivity?" One American Management Associations study revealed that productivity in the executive suite is not much better than that on the production line, suggesting one of the first steps toward improving productivity should be for top management to heal itself.[9]

If Mintzberg's observation—that the procedures managers now use to make decisions are the same as the procedures of the nineteenth century manager—is true, then what we need is much more like open heart surgery than simple healing.

Fortunately, managers have new technology to assist them. With computer graphics, the computer's job description has changed from a resource that can read and write to one that can also see and draw. Now the ultimate question is whether managers can change *their* way of performing as well.

Notes

1. Henry Mintzberg, "The Manager's Job: Folklore and Fact," *HBR*, July–August, 1975, p. 49.

2. See Kenneth Shostack and Charles Eddy, "Management by Computer Graphics," *HBR*, November–December 1971, p. 52.

3. Robert L. Dupree, "AMOCO Graphics System," in Harvard University's Laboratory for Computer Graphics and Spatial Analysis, *Management's Use of Maps* (Cambridge, Mass.: Harvard Library of Computer Mapping, 1979).

4. Car registration data for each census tract were acquired from R.L. Polk Company.

5. Jerry Wasserman, "Commercial Applications of Computer Graphics," *Management's Use of Maps*.

6. Ken Hoffman and John Whitnell, "The Application of Computer Mapping in Marketing," a paper presented at the Harvard Computer Graphics Week '79, Cambridge, Mass., July 1979.

7. For a detailed list of commercial statistical data bases available for computer graphics application, see William Moult and David J. Reibstein, "Commercial Statistical Data Bases Available for Computer Cartographical Applications," a paper presented at Harvard Computer Graphics Week '79.

8. Richard L. Nolan, "Managing the Crises in Data Processing," Chapter 5, this book.

9. "Productivity Hampered by Executives' Failings," *Industry Week*, July 22, 1974, p. 17.

25
Coping with Computer Proliferation

FREDERIC G. WITHINGTON

As computers get cheaper, smaller, and more versatile, managers are demanding their own facilities. This demand can lead to duplication, lack of standards, and generally poor control. To avoid these pitfalls, this author suggests the concept of distributed responsibility, by which ambitious managers are given the responsibility for their own success, with technical experts assigned as needed to their project teams. At the same time, a top-level steering committee approves projects and monitors their progress.

Computers are cropping up everywhere. Once safely confined to computer centers, they are now appearing as distributed systems in every kind of business facility. As computers get smaller and cheaper (business versions of the so-called personal computers cost as little as $5,000), they will spread even further because people want them.

Supervisors and middle managers everywhere now have enough computer knowledge to give them confidence. Impatient with central data processing's poor responsiveness, inflexibility, and high cost (fancied or real), they believe they can be more productive with their own facilities. Maybe they can, but it is reasonable to worry about their inexperience.

Other legitimate concerns about computer proliferation include duplication of effort, lack of standards, and various aspects of control: accuracy of data, protection against fraud, and compliance with legal requirements for privacy of data, for retention of records, for accountability, and for auditability.

At the same time, office automation has begun in some form in most organizations, and computers are being used in devices that process text, graphics, images, and even voice. Computer-assisted engineering design and direct computer control of manufacturing facilities are spreading at an ac-

celerating rate. These novel applications of computers have exciting potentials for enhancing productivity, but they are even harder to plan. They
generally affect behavior and work habits more directly than data processing
applications do. It is difficult to know ahead of time whether they will be
accepted or rejected, or whether the hoped-for productivity enhancement
will materialize or be worth the cost. Data processing planning was never
easy; these new applications have made it much more difficult.

To complicate the picture, the shortage of trained people is more acute
than it has ever been. Programmers experienced in conventional data processing are hard to find, and people experienced in office automation, integrated digital communication systems, and design automation are essentially
nonexistent. Even if there were no such shortage, the products in these
newer areas are changing so fast that yesterday's experience becomes obsolete quickly.

It would be reasonable to hold the line and refuse to permit computer
proliferation until the dust settles—until the products are mature, reliable
planning processes have been developed, and enough experienced people
are available. But this could be decades from now, and, in the meantime,
what near-term opportunities will have been forgone for improved managerial and professional as well as clerical productivity, for better use of
money and materials, and for improved responsiveness to customers and
opportunities? Some feel that any business failing to rise to the challenge of
computer proliferation will become noncompetitive.[1]

The Best Responses

Many organizations have been facing this challenge and experimenting with
various management responses. The following four measures appear to be
the best overall that have emerged. They are stated briefly and not justified
in detail, mainly because their desirability (when broadly stated) is more or
less self-evident. The problem is how to implement these responses, which
is the main subject of this article.

Disperse Technical Expertise

Spread the programmers, systems analysts, and other information technicians around. Arrange for them to work with the increasing numbers of
"interested amateurs" among professional, supervisory, and middle management ranks. The amateurs will learn some technical aspects and be able
to do increasing fractions of the work, thereby making wider use of the
technicians' expertise. The technicians, in turn, will learn more about the
organization and its people.

One large pharmaceutical firm, for example, is reorienting its central
data processing group.

In the past, all the systems analysts and programmers worked on projects assigned by central data processing management and designed to provide complete, finished services to end users. Now, nearly half the systems analysts and programmers are "consultants" assigned to a project to help user groups implement their own systems. The consultants work under user project directors but return to the consulting pool as the project ends.

Experiment but Don't Waste

Expect some systems development projects to fail, but don't repeat mistakes. Support experiments with corporate money and people when desirable (to relieve subordinate management of some of the risk), but make sure the experimental project is finite and that results will be clear. Make sure, too, that the results (good or bad) are clearly identified and communicated broadly within the organization.

Experiments with interoffice mail systems at IBM illustrate this principle. In White Plains, New York, managers were given terminals with keyboards and visual displays. A central computer stored and forwarded messages entered by the managers or their secretaries, maintained files and indices, and performed other related functions. At the same time, in another experiment conducted in Poughkeepsie, New York, a central computer stored and forwarded digitized voice messages. This system offered a more limited range of services than the text-processing system in White Plains, but, because it processed voice instead of text, managers did not have to type their messages and any telephone could serve as a terminal.

Both experiments were terminated after their designated trial periods. The results (including user surveys) were carefully analyzed. The digitized voice system received the more positive response, but indications were that the best features of both should be combined in future systems. Work has proceeded on new systems for more widespread, operational use.

Standardize but Don't Ossify

Each successful experiment must be phased into the evolving, information-processing environment of the organization. It should be compatible with the existing communications environment, with existing data standards and data bases, and (as far as possible) with existing equipment, organizational knowledge, and behavior. This means that experimental systems should be developed in accordance with preexisting standards. However, the standards must not be so rigid that they preclude desirable innovation. The set of standards must itself evolve.

Hewlett-Packard, for example, has a distributed data processing network. From time to time, changes are made in the location of processing and file storage nodes in the network. Because standards for data, communications, and processors have been established throughout the network, such changes are relatively easy to make.[2]

Guide but Don't Direct

In most organizations, there is no shortage of ideas for new information systems; ideas often appear at low organizational levels and in unexpected places (for example, the tool crib supervisor in one manufacturing plant caused "personal computers" to be provided for all his counterparts in his company). Such ideas should be exploited. A balance should be sought between exclusive direction of an organization's information processing activities by central data processing management on the one hand, which may prove undesirably parochial, and anarchy, waste, and uncontrolled duplication on the other. Standards must be maintained, and the direction of the whole must be guided.

As previously noted, the desirability of these responses is more or less self-evident. The problem lies in implementing them because each involves a compromise between conflicting forces. Adopting the organizational concept of distributed responsibility may help.

Distributed Responsibility

This concept involves two principles: first, that every information-processing activity should be the responsibility of the unit most closely associated with it and, second, that the units should be provided with a uniform processing environment, with technical assistance as needed, and with management oversight.

This is not as simple as saying that all information-processing responsibility should be decentralized. The following are examples of the degree of centralization appropriate to typical information-processing activities:

☐ *Management information systems.* The managers who are going to use the information must be responsible for setting the specifications for these systems and for evaluating the results; only they can state their own needs and degrees of satisfaction. However, the implementation and operations of the systems are usually carried out by specialists in conjunction with operations support systems because operational activities produce most of the data that become management information.

☐ *Operations support systems.* These include the conventional data processing applications (payroll, inventory control, order entry). The functional management served has always been responsible for specifying operations support systems. A specialized data processing function has usually been responsible for the implementation and operation of these systems, but with use of distributed data processing networks functional management takes over most of the responsibility for implementation and operation as well as for specification.

Many organizations (e.g., Citicorp) have found that this change is feasible as long as appropriate skills and standards are applied to the functionally led activities.[3] This subject is discussed further later. Text processing, electronic mail, and computer-assisted design systems also become operations support systems once they have passed the experimental stage; their behavioral implications imply that the functional users must mainly implement and operate them (again with appropriate support).

☐ *Experimental systems.* In most organizations today, systems handling digitized text, images, and voice are still in the experimental stage. The success of these systems depends heavily on the attitudes, reactions, and preferences of the persons served (much more than data processing systems usually do). It has thus proved advisable to delegate the responsibility for such experimental systems to the units served (to the "guinea pigs" who have volunteered to try something out). They are in direct touch with the individuals affected and have the greatest motivation to succeed. Again, however, appropriately trained people must be available, and the entire organization must learn the results of each experiment, good or bad.

☐ *The processing environment.* The organization must be knit together by communications. The design, implementation, and operation of a wide-band, multimedium communications network become complex responsibilities. Also, economies can be obtained through central planning and procurement of a communications network to meet the pooled corporate need. For these reasons, in two large conglomerate organizations with strong divisional data processing managers, the divisional managers have recently volunteered to turn over their responsibility for communications planning to the corporate data processing manager—examples of the principle of distributed responsibility resulting in recentralization of a function at a higher level.

Most organizations also find it advisable to set some limits on the diversity of tools that can be employed for operations support (e.g., they may establish a "catalog" of acceptable computers, text processors, and software packages that users may procure). These limits constrain users' freedom somewhat, but they ensure the development of common skills and interconnection standards, provide for economies in procurement, and reduce the chance of selecting an unsatisfactory vendor.

Perhaps most important, the organization must speak a common language. Any information to be communicated between nodes in the network must be precisely defined in advance so that the software at all the nodes will be able to process the data received. This is the "data-base administration" function of the central information system facility, which many organizations already have.

A central authority must be responsible for these three aspects of the processing environment (providing communications, selecting acceptable tools, and administering the data base) because corporatewide interests are involved. If a division or a subsidiary has a completely isolated processing environment, it may perhaps make its own specifications, but these should be subject to the same principles within its own structure.

Distributed responsibility for information systems, then, may involve the assignment of functional responsibilities to numerous levels and parts of an organization. The appropriate assignment can be made roughly by classifying a function within one of these four categories. Actually, as the following examples show, it is usually not hard to tell where a specific function belongs.

How It Works

To see how distributed responsibility works for individual functions, we can examine four examples of specific system projects (one from each of the types of activity I have defined). The same hypothetical multinational company is carrying out all four projects at the same time. All four are slightly generalized from current projects of real companies. Although they are not all being carried out within the same one, they could be.

Exhibit 1 shows the hypothetical company, a manufacturer with subsidiaries in the United States, Canada, and Great Britain. The subsidiaries make nearly the same products and have similar, conventional structures, except that only two of them (U.S. and British) have engineering activities. Each subsidiary has a data processing activity. In the United States and Great Britain, data processing reports to finance; in Canada, the management chose to have data processing report to a central administrative officer.

The corporate management has several staff functions reporting to it (not all shown), including a central strategic planning group. The largest are the corporate research laboratory and the finance function, which manages a corporate data processing and communications activity.

Exhibits 2–5 show the four projects as overlays to this structure. Each project has a leader, a team, and a review committee. The circles in the overlays identify the lead unit and the units providing resources to the project team, and the squares identify the additional units having representatives on the review committee.

The first project (shown in Exhibit 2) has the responsibility for designing a new management information system for the company and for defining the data needed to support it. On the basis of the market and competitive position (embryonic, growing, mature), the company's planners (on corporate and division staffs) have recently worked out with management new strategic plans for products and subsidiaries. The planners now must work out appropriate performance measures—growth measures for embryonic activities, profit contribution measures for mature activities. These new measures are to be defined in terms of standard data that are to be reported by all three subsidiaries as outputs from their operations support systems.

Members of the four planning groups make up the management infor-

Exhibit 1.   Basic Management Structure in a Hypothetical Manufacturing Company

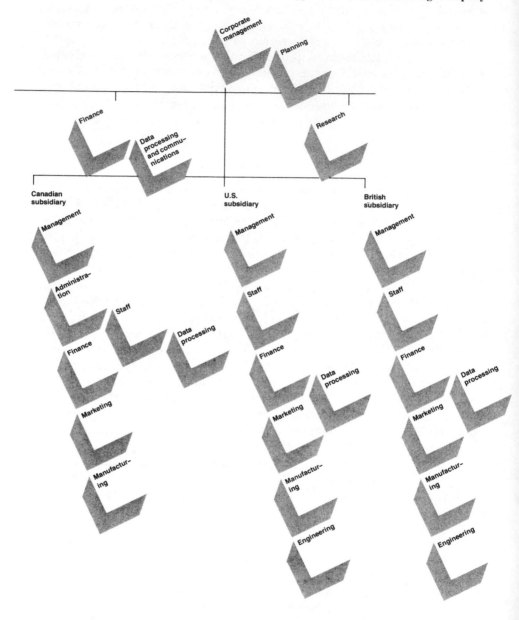

Exhibit 2.   Management Information System Project Responsibility in Hypothetical Company

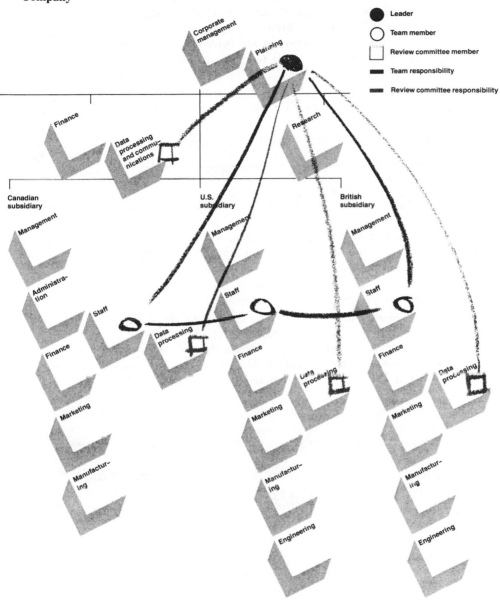

- ● Leader
- ○ Team member
- ▭ Review committee member
- ▬ Team responsibility
- ▬▬ Review committee responsibility

mation systems (MIS) project team because they are most directly involved in the process of translating the management measures into operational terms. A member of the corporate planning staff leads the project because the primary purpose of the new MIS is to serve corporate management. Representatives of the four data processing activities serve on the project review committee but are not part of the team. Their role is to ensure that the data required can be provided without major changes in the operations support systems or the existing processing environment. They may request that the project team rework its data requirements, but they do not participate in defining them.

When the project later moves to an implementation phase, it is anticipated that leadership will move to data processing and that the new data definitions will become part of the data-base structure administered by corporate data processing.

The measures and data definitions that the project members are working on are those needed by corporate management (e.g., aggregate product cost data). Because it is expected that the subsidiary managers will want other, more detailed measures and data (e.g., raw material cost information), the team members from the three subsidiaries have already formed a subgroup to start work on these lower-level definitions. The corporate staff representative will then be a reviewer of the subgroup's work but will not participate because he is not involved. The relationship of the data processing representatives to the subgroup will be the same as before.

The approach used in this project is very much like the "critical success factors" approach developed at the Massachusetts Institute of Technology's Sloan School, which incorporates distributed responsibility for determining MIS needs.[4]

The second project (shown in Exhibit 3 is a major reworking of an existing operations support system. Several years ago, the U.S. subsidiary developed a nationwide order entry system consisting of a network of data entry terminals connected to a central computer. The marketing department wrote the specifications for the system and operated it, and the U.S. subsidiary's data processing unit implemented it and maintains it in compliance with corporate processing environment standards. The Canadian and British subsidiaries opted not to implement the system.

Now the U.S. subsidiary wants to expand the system. It wants to put minicomputers in all the regional marketing offices to control the order entry terminals and to maintain local customer records and allocate local resources (inventories of products and parts, service personnel). The Canadian subsidiary intends to implement this expanded system as soon as it has been proved in the United States, and the British subsidiary will adopt it after that.

The U.S. marketing department leads this project, the U.S. data processing unit providing most of the technical resources. Several technical people will also join the team from corporate data processing and communi-

Exhibit 3. Order Entry System Project Responsibility in Hypothetical Company

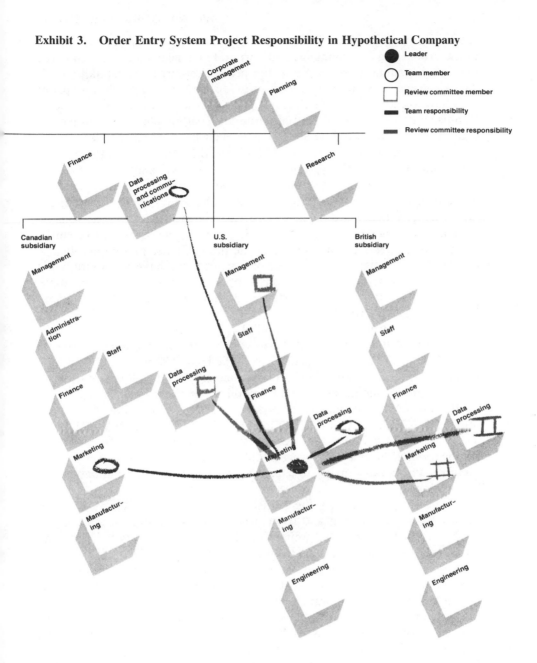

441

cations, for two reasons. First, the new system will bring substantial changes to the processing environment, and corporate management wants to participate in designing these. Second, the project requires special skills in the data base and telecommunications software, and the relatively few people who have these skills are in a central pool of experts at the corporate level. Representatives of Canadian marketing also participate in the project because the system should be able to meet their needs from the start.

British marketing is represented only on the review committee because it will not implement the system until later. Canadian and British data processing are also represented on the review committee. They will have to implement the system later, but they should have no great difficulty if corporate management has done its work of keeping the processing environment standard. The vice president of the U.S. subsidiary has decided to chair the review committee himself, in view of the project's size and importance.

By now, a significant number of organizations have successfully distributed responsibility for operations support systems. Excellent examples are Citicorp's letter of credit system and Hewlett-Packard's functional advisory councils approach.

The third project (shown in Exhibit 4) is experimental. The engineering department of the British subsidiary wants to try out a computer-assisted design system developed by a company in the United Kingdom. If the project is successful, the system will sharply reduce product development time and cost and permit increased product flexibility. Such an undertaking will be costly, however: not only is the system itself expensive but also its use implies the availability of new computer-controlled tools in manufacturing. The experiment will also take several years to complete because both the engineers and the manufacturing people will have to learn new skills and methods and because many new procedures and technical data bases must be developed.

This project is led by the British engineering department and staffed mainly by people from it and from British manufacturing. Because of the project's size and potential impact on the company, additional personnel have been assigned to the team from U.S. engineering and from the research laboratory. On the review committee, in addition to members of these units, are representatives of U.S. and Canadian manufacturing (who may be affected later) and of corporate data processing and communications. While the computer system involved is separate and specialized, management feels that some overall technical guidance from the corporate data processing experts may be helpful. General managers at both subsidiary and corporate levels are interested in the project but are waiting for initial results before becoming directly involved.

The fourth project (shown in Exhibit 5) involves a major change in the corporate telecommunications environment. Hoping to facilitate management and project communications and reduce mounting travel costs, corporate data processing and communications wants to try out high-speed

Exhibit 4. Computer-Assisted Design System Responsibility in Hypothetical Company

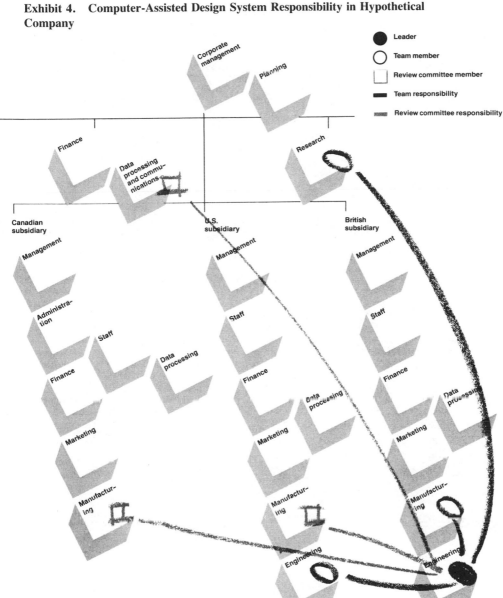

● Leader

○ Team member

□ Review committee member

▬ Team responsibility

▬ Review committee responsibility

Exhibit 5. Digital Telecommunications System Responsibility in Hypothetical Company

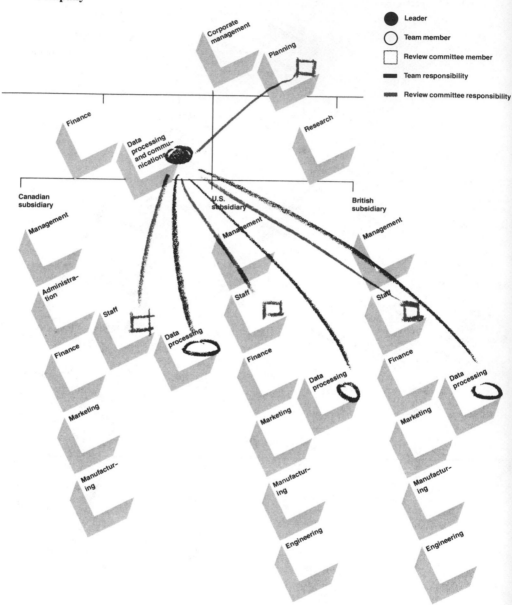

facsimile transmission of documents and teleconferencing. Because the necessary high-speed communications lines are expensive, they will be used also for lower-speed data and voice traffic now handled separately. The overall objective is to have a single, all-purpose digital communications network.

Leadership of this project resides in corporate data processing and communications. Each of the three subsidiaries' data processing units also participates. Each will have to acquire new equipment and software and to convert some present software. Also, each is the point of contact with the provider of communications lines in its country (each provider offers different services and rates, a complicating factor). The project's review committee also contains representatives from the four planning staffs. They have agreed to speak for their respective managements in estimating communications needs, determining cost-benefit trade-offs, and setting up short-term experiments within the overall project.

Tying It Together

The examples discussed show how it is possible to manage individual projects by means of distributed responsibility but not how the whole can be managed. To this end, methods are needed to accomplish the following tasks:

☐ Measure and budget the total costs of information-processing development and operation.

☐ Decide which projects to initiate, monitor their progress, and terminate those that are unsuccessful.

☐ Provide and enforce standards for project management and life cycle planning, and for financial control, auditability, and compliance with legal requirements.

☐ Allocate costs, funds, and personnel, and approve hiring and capital outlays.

A combination of three relatively conventional management means should be adequate to do the job. They are a management steering committee, project management techniques, and assignment of a global staff responsibility to the corporate data processing manager.

Management Steering Committee

This committee would consist ideally of the corporate chief executive officer and of the CEOs of each major division or subsidiary. If the CEO himself is not present at any meeting, a deputy with full voting authority should substitute. In some instances general managers of lesser rank may suffice, but experience consistently shows that the organizations with the most successful information processing services are those with CEOs directly involved.[5]

The steering committee makes all the major decisions. It reviews and approves the annual budget. It approves all major projects, reviews their progress, and decides when to terminate them. It also approves all major hiring and expenditure decisions. This may sound like too much for such a high-level committee to do, but experience has again shown that it is not if the project management and staff work are properly done.[6]

For each new project, a proposal (which may be prepared by any organizational unit) is presented to the steering committee. The proposal should contain a brief definition, set of objectives, and justification (a division or a subsidiary manager may add his endorsement to the justification— indeed, for smaller projects he or she probably has approval authority delegated by the steering committee). It contains a project plan with schedule, milestones, and resource requirements. It contains a management plan identifying the leaders and key members of the project and of its review committee, by name. This forces compliance with an important rule: that the resources for each project be tentatively committed (or negotiated, if provided from outside) in advance.

A self-ordering of priorities and work loads among the people recruited therefore occurs automatically, partially relieving the steering committee of the need to set detailed priorities. Also, this rule requiring tentative commitment of resources in advance of project approval exposes any shortages. If a proposed project is going to require hiring additional personnel or spending unbudgeted money, management will inevitably know it before approving the project.

If the project proposal is well prepared, it can be dealt with easily and (usually) relatively briefly.

After initiation, regular project management techniques are applied to each project; it is not necessary to detail them here. The steering committee need not concern itself much with the progress reports of small projects or of larger ones that are near schedule. If a major project appears to be in difficulty, however, the steering committee may wish to appoint a special fact finder (probably from the corporate planning or audit staffs). In no instance do the members of the steering committee have to get involved directly.

The steering committee also reviews plans for continuing operation of existing operations support systems on an annual budget cycle basis. Zero-based budgeting techniques are often used for projecting the costs of such ongoing operations.

The corporate data processing manager is responsible for coordinating the activities of all parts of the information-processing system. He receives reports of project progress, of ongoing information processing operations, and of technical personnel work loads and availability from every part of the organization (not necessarily in full detail; organization size is a factor). On the basis of these data, he prepares for the steering committee a periodic "steady state" summary and projection of future work loads, costs, and resource availabilities before the initiation of any new projects: the steering committee knows what it has to work with (a cross-check on the resource plans of the individual new project proposals).

On the basis of this and the steering committee's subsequent project approvals, the data processing manager can prepare the actual annual budget. He is responsible not for the approvals underlying the annual information-processing budget but only for reporting the total effect of the steering committee's approvals

The corporate manager can also perform a useful staff role in corporatewide data processing personnel management: he or she can coordinate recruiting, training, rotation, and establishment of career paths.

The steering committee also approves major hardware acquisitions (large computers, communications, switches, and batches of minicomputers or text processors). In the management environment just described, such decisions should be well anticipated and routine. The acquisition of equipment called for by a project is essentially authorized in advance as one of its milestones. The actual acquisition on schedule is a sign of success. Acquisition of equipment required by increasing total work load should also be anticipated—an expected consequence of the committee's project approvals added to the steady state projections made by the corporate data processing manager.

This description of the three management methods for tying together the distributed responsibilities has been brief, but the methods are familiar and are practiced in some form by many organizations. Each organization will have to adapt them to its style of planning, profit center management, and cost allocation. Each organization will also have to decide what to exclude (e.g., conventional office machines and telephone service) and how much to delegate. However, there is little question of the general workability of these methods.

Evaluating the Concept

Like any other organizational concept, distributed responsibility is a two-sided coin. Following are some possible advantages and disadvantages.

Possible Advantages
Distributed responsibility implements the organizational responses described earlier in the following ways:

☐ It disperses expertise by putting the technical people into teams with others throughout the organization who understand needs but are less technically expert. Memberships on review committees and assignments to team membership and leadership help to spread familiarity with information-processing technology and applications.

☐ It fosters experimentation with innovative information processing techniques but provides review mechanisms at both the project and the corporate levels to maintain control.

☐ It requires all projects to be implemented according to a set of corporate information-processing standards. At the same time, by having the standards setters participate in the projects, it provides continuous feedback of information about needs for new and changed standards.

☐ It enables management to guide the evolution of information processing in the organization through budget setting and project management but encourages subordinates to propose innovative projects (and to make them succeed; the responsibility for project success or failure is clear and highly visible). Allocation of effort can be locally determined, but within the context of overall corporate guidelines and strategies.

Distributed responsibility is likely to have two other significant benefits. First, it tends to break down organizational barriers (e.g., it no longer matters so much whether data processing reports to financial management, administrative management, or elsewhere, or whether an individual is a member of one subsidiary or another). Second, it fosters the self-imposing of new disciplines. Any new information system is likely to require that its users follow specific operating procedures. Under distributed responsibility, it is these users who themselves define the new systems. They are therefore more likely to abide by the systems' operating disciplines than if the information-processing systems were imposed from above.

Potential Disadvantages
Distributed responsibility has some significant potential disadvantages when compared with conventional hierarchical information-processing management methods, and these should be weighed by any organization considering it:

☐ The isolated nature of the individual projects is likely to lead to installation of many small, dedicated computer systems. Their intercommunication is assured by the standards, but economies of scale derived from using fewer, larger computers (which still exist) tend to be lost. As Hewlett-Packard, Citicorp, and others have concluded, however, networks of small computers can be preferable on an overall basis.

☐ People will waste time attending numerous team and review committee meetings, reading unnecessary papers, and trying to establish consensus on matters that an expert might decide quickly. Furthermore, many of these people can ill be spared from their basic jobs to work on information-processing projects.

☐ Data processing professionals will have to change their behavior in ways that may be unwelcome. They will have to work for what they see as amateur project leaders, spend time patiently educating the ignorant, and generally learn to be diplomats instead of just technicians.

☐ The process is difficult to control. Despite the overall budget and the two levels of project review provided, the distribution of responsibility and the amateur leadership many of the projects will have are bound to lead to some failures of both conception and execution, which might be avoided in a more hierarchical organization. (Hierarchical structures also have failures however, usually resulting from the evils of bureaucracy. Distributed responsibility is designed to provide stronger motivation for people at many levels and may in the end work out better.)

☐ There is no overall long-range plan for information processing. The large, ongoing operational support systems can continue to have multiyear development plans, but the experimental systems cannot. Only the standards are certain to last a long time, and they may prove to be the wrong ones.

These disadvantages are significant: few organizations will want to rush totally into distributed responsibility without considering them carefully. Fortunately, though, no sudden or total adoption is required. Experiments with distributed responsibility can be conducted, most easily in novel areas such as office automation and computer-assisted design. Success can then lead to more distribution of responsibility, in a slow process that may never require total abandonment of hierarchical management practices. In fact, many organizations such as Citibank have already distributed much of the responsibility for their information processing, though few, if any, have the combination of central standards and decentralized system management that is discussed here.

If conventional data processing were the only issue, distributed responsibility might not be necessary at all. Traditional data processing management methods have proved reasonably adaptable to such trends as distributed data processing. The new media—digital text, image, and voice processing—make the difference, interwoven as they will certainly be with data processing and organizational evolution. It is hard to imagine any organization phasing these into its structure without some form of distributed responsibility.

Notes

1. See Harvey L. Poppel, "The Information Revolution: Winners and Losers," *HBR*, January–February, 1978, p. 14.

2. See Cort Van Rensselaer, "Centralize? Decentralize? Distribute?" *Datamation*, April, 1979, p. 88.

3. See Richard J. Matteis, "The New Back Office Focuses on Customer Service," *HBR*, March–April, 1979, p. 146.

4. See John F. Rockart, "Chief Executives Define Their Own Data Needs," *HBR*, March–April 1979, p. 81.

5. See Richard L. Nolan, "Managing the Crises in Data Processing," Chapter 5, this book.

6. Ibid.

26
New Worlds of Computer-Mediated Work

SHOSHANA ZUBOFF

When managers make changes in the ways employees perform their work it's only natural for the employees to resist. Managers themselves are famous for the not-invented-here syndrome that is a disguised way of resisting change. It's not surprising that when they hear about resistance to working with the new information technology managers dismiss it as normal and to be expected. The author of this article maintains that managers should heed the resistance, however, because it is telling them something about the quality of the changes that are taking place. Computer-mediated work is more abstract and can demand new conceptual skills while deem-phasizing the importance of direct experience. Information technology can poten-tially depersonalize supervision, alter social communities, and often means that technology absorbs much of the judgment that routine jobs used to entail. The author suggests ways that managers can use the new technology as an opportunity to re-envision job responsibilities and develop new approaches to the problems of supervision.

One day, in the 1860s, the owner of a textile mill in Lowell, Massachusetts, posted a new set of work rules. In the morning, all weavers were to enter the plant at the same time, after which the factory gates would be locked until the close of the work day. By today's standards this demand that they arrive at the same time seems benign. Today's workers take for granted both the division of the day into hours of work and nonwork and the notion that everyone should abide by a similar schedule. But, in the 1860s, the weavers were outraged by the idea that an employer had the right to dictate the hours of labor. They said it was a "system of slavery" and went on strike.

Eventually, the owner left the factory gates open and withdrew his demands. Several years later, the mill owner again insisted on collective work hours. As the older form of work organization was disappearing from other plants as well, the weavers could no longer protest.

In general, industrialization presented people with a fundamental challenge to the way they had thought about behavior at work. The employer's desire to exploit the steam engine as a centralized source of power, coupled with the drive to closely supervise workers and increase the pace of production, resulted in a greater degree of collectivization and synchronization in the workplace. Employers imposed an exact discipline on workers that required them to use their bodies in specified ways in relation to increasingly complex forms of equipment. By the early 1900s, "scientific management" had given supervisors a systematic way to measure and control the worker's body.

Although most workers have accepted the work behavior that industrialization fashioned, the issues behind the New England weavers' resistance lie at the heart of modern labor-management relations. Using collective bargaining, later generations of workers have developed elaborate grievance procedures and work rules that carefully limit an employer's right to control a worker's body.

New forms of technology inevitably change the ways people are mobilized to work as well as the kinds of skills and behavior that are critical for productivity. These changes are rarely born without pain and conflict—nor do they emerge exactly as planners envision them. Instead, new conceptions of work organization and behavior emerge from an interaction between the demands of a new technology, its social organization, and the responses of the men and women who must work with the new technological systems.

In this regard, the weavers' example is doubly instructive. First, it illustrates that during a period of technological transition people are most likely to be aware of and articulate about the quality of the change they are facing. When people feel that the demands a new technology makes on them conflict with their expectations about the work place, they are likely, during the initial stage of adaptation, to resist. Many managers maintain that employees are simply denying change when they cling to familiar patterns and complain as these forms of sustenance are threatened. But resistance can also reveal an eloquent appraisal of the *quality* of change—a subtle commentary that goes beyond a stubborn attachment to custom.

Second, the weavers' example shows that as a major technological transition recedes into the past, and with it the sense of psychological crisis, older sensibilities tend to become subsumed or repressed. However, original sources of resistance, if they are not properly resolved, can continue to influence the management-labor agenda for many years, even though employees may accommodate the demands of a new technology.

Business is now witnessing a period of technological change that shares some important features with the first industrial revolution. Information technology is rapidly reorganizing the kind of work people do across industries and organizational strata. It is affecting clerical workers through the automation of high-volume, back-office operations as well as with word processing and electronic mail. Managers are more frequently making use of computer conferencing, decision-support systems, sophisticated modeling procedures, and new on-line management information systems. Blue-collar workers are increasingly required to interact with computer technology in order to monitor and control a variety of manufacturing and continuous-process operations. During the past year, business people bought one million data terminals, worth $2.6 billion, to supplement the four million terminals already in use. The market for intelligent terminals is expected to grow 25% annually during the coming decade.

This increased use of information technology is altering the technological infrastructure of the work place. More and more production in office and factory depends on the computer and large-scale information systems that can control increasingly complex sets of data. And just as with industrial technology, people who are required to use information systems often resist their introduction. When managers allow employee discontent with new computer-based technology a voice, they can learn a great deal about the more subtle effects of this technology and the issues that are likely to challenge their practices in the coming decade.

During the last few years I interviewed approximately 200 employees, supervisors, professionals, and managers from several different organizations in three countries to discover how people at distinct organizational levels respond to their work when it has been fundamentally reorganized by information technology. (See ruled insert for a description of the organizations and their information systems.) In this article, I outline the principal themes that emerged repeatedly from my interviews and observations, both as they pertain to employees' experiences of information systems and as observable, often unintended, consequences for the organization. Finally, I identify some of the implications of these findings for human resource management policies.

Management Policies Toward Automation

In many ways, management policies can determine the effectiveness of automation and the quality of the workplace culture that emerges. In this regard, my discussions with employees and managers reveal two primary concerns.

Substitution & Deskilling of Labor

The purpose of the intelligent technology at the core of a computer system is to substitute algorithms or decision rules for individual judgments. This substitution makes it possible to formalize the skills and know-how intrinsic to a job and integrate them into a computer program. As decision rules become more explicit, the more they are subject to planning, and the less they require a person to make a decision at each stage of execution. For some jobs the word "decision" no longer implies an act of human judgment, but an information-processing activity that occurs according to rules embedded in a computer program.

At present, most programmed decision making has been limited to the most routine jobs in an organization such as high-volume operations where tasks can be simplified and rationalized to maximize outputs and minimize skill requirements. For example, partly by limiting a collector's discretion regarding how or in what order he or she should work on an account, an automated collection system makes it possible to increase production goals and reduce the time spent on each account.

Thus for that activity the key to revenue generation becomes volume instead of collection skills. Collection managers I interviewed believe that the system enables them to recoup more funds while reducing their dependence on skilled collectors. One collection manager described the value of the system:

> It gives us a tighter lock on the collector, and we can hire less skilled people. But there's a real loss to the job of skills and know-how. You are being told what to do by the machine.

But job deskilling is not exclusive to the most routine jobs in the organization. A decision-support system installed for a bank's 20 credit analysts was supposed to free them from the most mechanical and boring aspects of the job. Six months after the system was in place, not a single analyst had used it. As one analyst explained it, "I think, then I write down my calculations directly. I know the company and the problem. With this system, I am supposed to type into the machine and let it think. Why should I let it do my thinking for me?"

Automation of Managerial Assumptions

Information systems can embody management's assumptions and values about its employees, especially about their commitment and motivation. The automated collection system provides an example of how this happens.

Bill Smith had managed collection activities for 30 years, and management considered his perspective invaluable. In creating the system, designers spent long hours debriefing Smith, and he helped them make many important design decisions. Senior managers explain key design decisions by saying: "We tried to build Bill Smith's brain into the computer. If we did not build it into the system, we might lose to the competition."

When I talked to Bill Smith, some of the reasons the system eliminated most discretion from the job became clear. As Smith put it:

> I like to see people work. I'm a good worker. I don't like to see people take time off. I don't do it.

The depth of memory and extent of communications that computer systems are capable of mean that managerial biases can surround the employee as never before. The cost of Smith's managerial assumptions in the collections operations system was high. A year after the system was in place, turnover had reached almost 100%, and the corporate personnel and employee counseling offices were swamped with complaints from replacements. The new and less-educated collectors presented a different set of problems for management and training. Even with the new staff, turnover remained about three times higher than in the rest of the back-office organization.

Computer Mediation of Work

As the Bill Smith example illustrates, managerial assumptions can easily get embedded in information systems. But what impact do the new systems have on the organization of work and what actually happens to the people who interact with them?

Work Becomes Abstract

When information technology reorganizes a job, it fundamentally alters the individual's relation to the task. I call the new relationship "computer mediated." Usually, this means that a person accomplishes a task through the medium of the information system, rather than through direct physical contact with the object of the task.

Computer mediation can be contrasted to other forms of task relationships in terms of the way in which one *knows* about the object of the task. The potter who turns a pot with his or her own hands has direct experience of the task's object through continual series of sights and tactile sensations. These sensations form the basis for moment-by-moment judgments regarding the success of the process and any alterations that the potter should make. Machines, such as a press or a welding torch, usually remove the worker as the direct source of energy for the labor process, but leave the task's object within sensuous range.

Those who work with paper and pencil usually feel "in touch" with the objects of their tasks through the activity of writing and because they are the sources of what they write.

With computer-mediated work, employees get feedback about the task object only as symbols through the medium of the information system. Very often, from the point of view of the worker, the object of the task seems to have disappeared "behind the screen" and into the information system.

The distinction in feedback is what separates the linotype machine operator from the clerical worker who inputs cold type, and the engineer who works with computer-aided design from one who directly handles materials, the continuous process operator who reads information from a visual display unit from one who actually checks vat levels, and even the bill collector who works with an on-line, real-time system from a predecessor who handled accounts cards. The distinctiveness of computer-mediated work becomes more clear when one contrasts it against the classic image of work from the nineteenth century in which labor was considered to be the transformation of nature by human muscle. Computer-mediated work is the electronic manipulation of symbols. Instead of a sensual activity, it is an abstract one.

Many employees I spoke to reported feeling frustrated because in losing a direct experience of their task it becomes more difficult to exercise judgment over it. In routine jobs, judgment often becomes lodged in the system itself. As one bill collector said:

> In our old system, come the end of the month, you knew what you were faced with. With the automated system, you don't know how to get in there to get certain accounts out. You have to work the way the system wants you to.

People in even more complex jobs can also lose direct experience of their tasks. The comptroller of a bank that was introducing information systems to a variety of functions commented:

> People become more technical and sophisticated, but they have an inferior understanding of the banking business. New people become like systems people and can program instructions that don't necessarily reflect the spirit of the operation.

The auditor at one bank is working with a new information system that frees him from traveling to regional branches. The branches feed financial data directly into the information system that he can access in real time. He described his job this way:

> The job of auditing is very different now. More imagination is required. I am receiving data online. I don't go to the branches if I don't want to. I don't see any books. What do I audit in this situation? I always have to be thinking about what is in the system. I may be auditing, but it doesn't feel like it.

The auditor now has access to a new level of complexity in his data. He has the possibility of comparing branches according to criteria of his choice and searching out new relationships in the data. But in order to do this, he must now develop a theory of the auditing process. He needs to have a conceptual framework that can guide him through the mass of available information. Theoretical insight and imagination will be the keys to his effectiveness on the job.

By creating a medium of work where imagination instead of experience-based judgment is important, information technology challenges old procedures. Judging a given task in the light of experience thus becomes less important than imagining how the task can be reorganized based on new technical capabilities. In the banking industry, for example, planners are not automating the old, but inventing the new.

While working through information systems seems to require a more challenging form of mental effort, it can also induce feelings of frustration and loss of control.

A collections supervisor described the difference between the manual and computer systems:

> If you work with a manual system and you want to see an account on a given day, you have a paper file and you simply go to that particular section and pull out the file. When you're on the computer system, in a sense all your accounts are kind of floating around in space. You can't get your hands on them.

Some people cope with this frustration by creating physical analogues for their tasks. In one bank branch, an on-line system had been installed to update information on current accounts. Instead of making out tickets that would be sent to a data center for overnight keypunching, operators enter data directly into terminals; the system continuously maintains account information. Despite senior management's efforts to persuade them to change, the branch manager and his staff continued to fill out the tickets. When asked why, they first mentioned the need for a backup system. The real reason came out when the branch manager made the following comment: "You need something you can put your hands on. How else can we be sure of what we are doing?"

People are accustomed to thinking of jobs that require employees to use their brains as the most challenging and rewarding. But instead, the computer mediation of simple jobs can create tasks that are routine and unchallenging, while demanding focused attention and abstract comprehension. Nevertheless, the human brain is organized for action. Abstract work on a mass scale seems likely to create conditions that are peculiar if not stressful to many people. While it does seem that those who shift from conventional procedures to computer-mediated work feel this stress most acutely, it's impossible to forecast what adaptation to the abstraction of work will do to people over the long term.

Social Interaction Is Affected

Doubtless, once information technology reorganizes a set of jobs, new patterns of communication and interaction become possible. In time, these patterns are likely to alter the social structure of an organization.

When resources are centered in the information system, the terminal itself can become employees' primary focus of interaction. This focus can lead people to feel isolated in an impersonal situation. For example, because functional operations in the back office of one bank have been reorganized, a clerical worker can complete an entire operation at his or her "professional" work station, rather than repeat a single procedure of it before passing the item on to someone else. Although employees I talked to were split in their attitudes toward the new back-office system, most of them agreed that it created an uncomfortable isolation. Because they had few remaining reasons to interact with co-workers, the local social network was fragmented.

Decades of research have established the importance of social communities in the work place and the lengths to which people will go to establish and maintain them. Since people will not easily give up the pleasures of the work place community, they tend to see themselves at odds with the new technology that transforms the quality of work life. The comments of one employee illustrate this point:

> I never thought I would feel this way, but I really do not like the computer. If a person makes a mistake, dealing with the computer to try and get that mistake corrected is so much red tape. And it's just taken a lot of feeling out of it. You should have people working with people because they are going to give you what you want, and you're going to get a better job all around.

In a very different kind of application, professionals and managers in the R&D organization of a large consumer goods company find the range of their interaction greatly extended with computer conferencing. While there is some evidence of reduced face-to-face interaction, the technology makes it relatively easy to initiate dialogues and form coalitions with people in other parts of the corporation. Clearly, information technology can offset social life in a variety of ways. It is important to realize, however, that this technology has powerful consequences for the structure and function of communication and social behavior in an organization.

New Possibilities for Supervision & Control

The dream of the industrial engineer to create a perfectly timed and rationalized set of activities has never been perfectly realized. Because face-to-face supervision can be carried on only on a partial basis, employees usually find ways to pace their own activities to meet standards at a reasonable rate. Thus, traditionally, supervision depended on the quality of the relationship between supervisor and worker. If the relationship is a positive one, employees are likely to produce quality work without constant monitoring. If the relationship is adversarial, the monitoring will be continual.

But because work accomplished through the medium of video terminals or other intelligent equipment can be recorded on a second-by-second basis, the industrial engineer's presence can be built into all real-time activities. With immediate access to how much employees are producing through printouts or other visual displays, supervisors and managers can increase surveillance without depending on face-to-face supervision. Thus the interpersonal relationship can become less important to supervision than access to information on the quality and quantity of employee output. One bank supervisor described this new capability:

"Instead of going to someone's desk and physically pulling out files, you have the ability to review peoples' work without their knowledge. So I think it keeps them on their toes."

Another variant of remote supervision involves controls that are automatically built into systems operations, as in the collections system described earlier. These rules are substitutes for a certain amount of supervisory effort. Because the system determines what accounts the collector should work on and in what order, a supervisor does not have to monitor collectors' judgments on these issues. Managers also see automatic control as the organization's defense against the potentially massive pollution of data that can occur through access by many people to an on-line real-time system.

Remote supervision, automatic control, and greater access to subordinates' information all become possible with computer-mediated work. In some cases, these capabilities are an explicit objective, but too often management employs them without sufficiently considering the potential human and organizational consequences.

With remote supervision, many employees limit their own risk-taking behavior, such as spotting an error in the data and correcting it, developing a more effective approach to the work than the procedures established by the information system, or trying to achieve quality at the expense of keeping up with new production standards.

One reason the initiative to design a custom-made approach to a particular task has become too risky is that many people have difficulty articulating why their approach might be superior to other alternatives. Usually, management has developed a clearly articulated model of the particular task in order to automate it, and if employees cannot identify their own models with equal clarity, they have little hope of having their views legitimated.

Another reason for decreased employee initiative is that the more an information system can control the details of the job, the less even relatively trivial risk-taking opportunities are available. Finally, the monitoring capabilities increase the likelihood that a supervisor will notice a deviation from standard practice. As one bank employee noted.

> Sometimes I have a gut feeling I would rather do something another way.
> But, because it is all going to be in the computer, it changes your mind.
> If somebody wouldn't listen to the reason why you did it that way, well,
> it could cause you quite a problem.

Another frequent response to the new relationships of supervision and control involves perceptions of authority in the work place. Employees can tend to see technology less as an instrument of authority than as a source of it. For instance, one group of bank employees with an especially easygoing manager described the work pace on their computer-mediated jobs as hard-driving, intense, and at times unfair, but thought the manager was friendly, relaxed, and fairminded.

One collector told about the difference in her attitudes toward her work under the manual system and under the automated system:

> When I worked with the account cards, I knew how to handle my responsibilities. I felt, 'Hey! I can handle this!' Now I come in every day with a defeatist attitude, because I'm dealing with the tube every day. I can't beat it. People like to feel not that they are necessarily ahead of the game, but that they have a chance. With the tube I don't have a chance.

While this employee knows that her manager is the actual authority in the office, and that he is in turn accountable to other managers, she has an undeniable feeling that the system, too, is a kind of authority. It is the system she must fight, and, if she wins, it is the system she vanquishes.

In the Volvo plant in Kalmar, Sweden, a computer system was installed to monitor assembly operations. A feedback device was programmed to flash a red light signalling a quality control problem. The workers protested against the device, insisting that the supervisory function be returned to a foreman. They preferred to answer to a human being with whom they could negotiate, argue, and explain rather than to a computer whose only means of "communication" was unilateral. In effect, they refused to allow the computer to become, at least in this limited situation, an authority. Yet clearly, the issue would never have arisen in the first place were the technology not capable of absorbing the characteristics of authority.

Finally, these capacities of information systems can do much to alter the relationships among managers themselves. A division or plant manager can often leverage a certain amount of independence by maintaining control of key information. Though a manager might have to present the data in monthly or quarterly reports, he or she has some control over the amount and format. With information technology, however, senior managers in corporate headquarters increasingly have access to real-time systems that display the day-to-day figures of distinct parts of the company's business. For instance, a division vice president can be linked to the information system that transmits raw production data from a processing plant in another state. Such data can provide the vice president with a view of the plant that only the plant manager or mid-level managers in the operation previously had.

This new access raises several questions for a corporation. First, some policy decisions must be confronted that address the kind of information appropriate to each level of management. Top managers can quickly find themselves inundated with raw data that they do not have the time to understand. It also creates a tendency for top managers of focus on the past and present when they should be planning the future.

It would seem that this new access capability would expand top management's opportunities to monitor and direct and, therefore, improve the performance of subordinate managers. But as the online availability of such information reaches across management hierarchies (in some companies all the way to board chairpersons), reduced risk taking and its effects begin to take hold. Managers are reluctant to make decisions on the basis of information that their superiors receive simultaneously. As one plant manager said to his boss in division headquarters: "I'm telling you, Bob, if you're going to be hooked up to the data from the pumps, I'm not going to manage them anymore. You'll have to do it."

Birth of the Information Environment

Another consequence of information technology is more difficult to label, but its effects are undeniable. I call it the "information environment." It refers to a quality of organizational life that emerges when the computer mediates jobs and begins to influence both horizontal and vertical relationships. In the information environment, people generally have greater access to data and, in particular, data relevant to their own decision making. The capacity for follow-up and reorganizing increases as information retrieval and communication can occur with greater ease and convenience than ever before.

One effect of this immediate access to information is a rise in the volume of transactions or operations. This increase, in turn, compresses time and alters the rhythm of work. While people were once satisfied if a computer system responded in 24 hours, those who work with computers now are impatient if information takes more than five seconds to appear. Timely and reliable functioning of the system determines workers' output, and these effects extend up the managerial ladder. Once managers become accustomed to receiving in two hours a report that once took two weeks to compile, they will consider any delay a burden. This speed of access, retrieval, and information processing is allegedly the key to improving the productivity of the organization, but few organizations have seriously considered the appropriate definition of productivity in their own operations. In the meantime, more transactions, reports, and information are generated in an ever-shorter amount of time.

Responses to the information environment usually are accompanied by feelings about power and orderliness. To some people, the increased access to information enhances their power over the contingencies of their work. An account officer for one bank states:

> I never had such a complete picture of a particular customer before. I can switch around the format of the base for my reporting purposes and get a full picture of where the bank is making money. This gives me a new power and effectiveness in my work.

While most people agree that the information environment makes the work place more orderly, responses to this orderliness tend to be bipolar. Some see the order as "neat and nice," while others perceive it as increasing the regimentation of the workplace. Responses of two collections managers illustrate these differences. The first described the system this way:

> The computer simply alleviates a lot of paperwork. Everything is lined up for you instead of you having to do it yourself. If you are sloppy, the system organizes you.

Another manager in the same organization regards the collections system in a different way:

> Things were a lot more relaxed before the tubes. Before, you scheduled your day yourself; now the machine lines it up for you. This means a more rigid environment because we can track things better.

Greater regimentation can also affect the environment of the professional. A vice president in one organization where professionals have come to rely heavily on electronic mail and computer conferencing puts it this way:

> I used to make notes to myself on things I had to follow up. Now those notes go into my electronic mail system. The system automatically tracks these things and they are there in front of me on the screen if I haven't followed up yet. Nothing slips through the cracks, but certainly for the way professionals usually operate, it's more regimented.

Many of the managers and professionals I talked to are wary of systems that seem to encroach on their judgment, their freedom, or the "artistry" of their professional assessments. Instead of feeling that increased information augments their power, these people resist information systems that they see limiting their freedom or increasing the measurability of their work.

At present, most professionals and managers function in fairly ambiguous environments. Information is imperfectly exchanged (often in corridors, washrooms, or over lunch), and considerable lag time usually occurs before the quality of decisions can be assessed. A continual flow of complete information, however, reduces ambiguity. For example, in the marketing area of one bank, an information system provides complete profiles of all accounts while it assesses their profitability according to corporate criteria. Top management and systems developers believed the system could serve as a constant source of feedback to account officers and senior managers, allowing them to better manage their account activities and maximize fee-based revenues. But some bankers saw the flow of "perfect" information as not only reducing ambiguity but also limiting their opportunities for creative decisions and resisted using it.

Limited information may create uncertainty in which people make errors of judgment, but it also provides a "free space" for inspiration. This free space is fundamental to the psychology of professional work. The account officers in the bank had traditionally been motivated by the opportunity to display their artistry as bankers, but as increased information organizes the context of their work, the art in their jobs is reduced.

Employees in back-office clerical jobs also tend to perceive the increased time and volume demands and the measurability of operations as limits on their opportunities to experience a sense of mastery over the work. To overcome these effects, many of the collectors keyed fictitious data into the system of account files. Their managers were confronted with high productivity figures that did not match the size of monthly revenues.

Many managers first respond to such a situation by searching out ways to exert more control over the work process. I am convinced that the more managers attempt to control the process, the more employees will find ways to subvert that control. This response is particularly likely when outsmarting the system becomes the new ground on which to develop and test one's mastery. Managers may dismiss these subversive activities as "resistance to change," but in many cases this resistance is the only way employees can respond to the changes they face. Such resistance can also be understood as a positive phenomenon—it is evidence of an employee's identification with the job.

Listening to the Resistance

Critics of technology tend to fall into one of three camps. Some bemoan new developments and see them as a particular form of human debasement and depersonalization. Others are ready to applaud any form of technology as progress toward some eventual conquest of dumb nature. Finally, others argue that technology is neutral and its meaning depends on the uses to which human beings press its application. I have found none of these views sufficient.

It is true that information technology provides a particularly flexible set of technical possibilities, and thus can powerfully embody the assumptions and goals of those whom it is designed to serve. Yet, while the value and meaning of a given application must be read, in part, from management's intentions, beliefs, and commitments, this does not imply the ultimate neutrality of the technology itself. To say that information technology is neutral is like saying an airplane is neutral because it can fly to either Washington or Moscow. We know that airplanes are not neutral because we all live in a world that has been radically altered by the facts of air travel—the globe has been shrunk, time and space have collapsed.

If one accepts that technology is *not* neutral, it follows that information technology must have attributes that are unique in the world view they impose and the experience of work to which they give shape. The flexibility, memory, and remote access capabilities of information systems create new management possibilities and, therefore, choices in the design of an application.

This argument suggests three general areas for management deliberation and action in the deployment of new information systems. The first concerns policies that shape the quality of the employment relationship. The second involves attitudes toward managerial control, and the third concerns basic beliefs about the nature of an organization and the role of management.

The Quality of the Employment Relationship

Because the computer mediation of work can have direct consequences for virtually every area of human resource management including skills training, career paths, the social environment, peer relationships, supervision, control, decision making, authority, and organization design, managers need to think through the kind of work place they want to foster. They need to make design choices that reflect explicit human resource management policies.

For example, consider the automated collections system I described earlier. Although the system minimizes individual decision making, most managers I interviewed in that organization believe that collector skill and judgment are critical variables in the organization's ability to generate payments and have compelling financial data to support that view.

A management policy commitment to maintaining skill levels, providing challenging jobs, and promoting collector loyalty and motivation could have resulted in an information system that preserves the entrepreneurial aspects of the collector's job while rationalizing its administration with on-line recordkeeping. But to assess the likely consequences of an approach to automation that strictly rationalizes procedures, managers need to understand the human logic of a job. In many cases, this human logic holds the clue to the motivational aspects of the job that should be preserved in the conversion to new technology.

What do managers do when faced with some of the more intrinsic features of information technology? First, they need to understand the kinds of skill demands that the computer mediation of work generates, and to construct educational programs that allow employees to develop the competencies that are most relevant to the new environment.

If a more theoretical comprehension of the task is required for effective utilization of the information system, then employees should be given the opportunity to develop this conceptual understanding. If an information system is likely to reduce the sense (if not the fact) of individual control over a task, is it possible to redesign the job to reinvest it with a greater self-managing capacity? As elements of supervision and coordination are loaded into jobs that have been partially drained of challenge, new learning and career development opportunities can open up. The astonishing quantity of information that is available can be used to increase employees' feedback, learning, and self-management rather than to deskill and routinize their jobs or remotely supervise them.

New systems are often presented with the intention of providing "information resources" for more creative problem solving. Unless employees are actually given the knowledge and authority to utilize such resources in the service of more complex tasks, these systems will be undermined, either through poor utilization or more direct forms of resistance.

The Focus of Managerial Control

Because of the many self-management opportunities the information resource makes possible, managers may have to rethink some classic notions of managerial control. When industrial work exerted stringent demands on the placement and timing of physical activity, managers focused on controlling bodies and stipulating the precise ways in which they should perform.

With the burgeoning of office work, physical discipline was less important than reading or writing and, above all, interpersonal behavior. Because people needed to learn how to behave with superiors, subordinates, and the public, managers began to control less what people did with their bodies and more what they did with one another—their communication, teamwork, meeting behavior, and so forth.

With computer-mediated work, neither physical activity nor interpersonal behavior appear to be the most appropriate targets of managerial control. Instead, patterns of attention, learning, and mental engagement become the keys to effectiveness and high-quality performance. Obviously, people have always had to "pay attention" to their work in order to accomplish it properly. But the quality of attention computer-mediated work requires is essentially different.

For instance, in almost all accounts of routine work, researchers report that employees are daydreaming and bantering with one another while they accomplish their tasks. Of course, they must pay attention with their eyes, but not so much with their brains. In contrast, people concentrating on a visual display unit must pay a very different sort of attention. If employees are to understand and properly respond to information, they must be mentally involved.

Managers can experiment to find how to make the most of people's attending and learning qualities as well as their overall engagement in the information environment. One observation that emerges from my current field research is that imposing traditional supervisory approaches on the computer-mediated environment can create considerable dysfunction. Supervisors and managers who concentrate on the physical and interpersonal behavior of employees working with information systems simply exacerbate tensions instead of creating an environment that nurtures the kind of learning and attention computer-mediated work makes necessary and compensating for some of its less obvious but potentially negative attributes.

The Nature of Organization & Management

With information technology, managers will do a variety of tasks that others once did for them. Because of this, we are likely to see a gradual shift in the overall shape of the organization from a pyramid to something closer to a diamond shape—with a diminishing clerical support staff, swelling numbers of professionals and middle managers, and a continually more remote, elite, policy-making group of senior managers.

While these considerations should be of central importance to management policy in the coming years, as a society we are sure to see a continuing challenge to the salience of work and the work place in our daily lives. The traditional importance of occupational distinctiveness may be further eroded as what it means to "accomplish a task" undergoes a fundamental change. When a person's primary work consists of monitoring or interacting with a video screen, it may become more difficult to answer the questions, "Who am I?" and "What do I do?" Identification with an occupational role may diminish, while the transferability of on-the-job skills increases. Will this have implications for individual commitment to an organization and for the relative importance of work and nonwork activities?

Information technology is also likely to introduce new forms of collective behavior. When the means of production becomes dependent on electronic technology and information flows, it is no longer inevitable that, as in the case of the weavers, work be either collective or synchronous. As long as a terminal and communications links are available, people will be able to perform work in neighborhood centers, at home, or on the road. At the same time, electronic technology is altering the traditional structure and function of communication within the organization. Who interacts with whom in the organization? Can the neat chain of command hierarchy be maintained? Should it be? What does it take to lead or influence others when communication itself becomes computer mediated? Finally, who is likely to gain or lose as we make the transition to this environment?

These developments make it necessary to rethink basic conceptions of the nature of organization and management. What is an organization if people do not have to come face to face in order to accomplish their work? Does the organization itself become an abstraction? What happens to the shared purpose and commitment of members if their fact-to-face interaction is reduced? Similarly, how should an "abstract" organization be managed?

If information technology is to live up to its promise for greater productivity, managers need to consider its consequences for human beings and the qualities of their work environments. The demands for a thoughtful and energetic management response go deeper than the need for a "friendly interface" or "user involvement." The underlying nature of this technology requires understanding; the habitual assumptions used in its design must surface. Managers' ability to meet these demands will be an important determinant of the quality of work in future organizations.

Note

1. "Social Effects of Automation," International Federation of Automated Control Newsletter, No. 6, September 1978.

THE EXECUTIVE
AND THE COMPUTER

AN OVERVIEW

Though everyone knows by now that computers are adding daily to our store of information, and many point to this effect as information overload, managers, especially top executives, still feel frustrated by the lack of the information they really need to run their company. To help executives obtain these data, John Rockart describes a method of developing critical success factors (CSF), which are areas in which results, if they are satisfactory, will ensure the organization's competitive success. Rockart says that the CSF concept reveals the weakness of traditional financial accounting systems as a support for executive decision making (though cost accounting data are useful in reporting on CSFs). By carefully attending to data on the performance of the particular CSFs that are appropriate for their companies, managers can not only keep tabs on their competitive position but also in the process become more aware of the significant areas that need their attention.

Some executives, however, may not be satisfied with developing and exploring their company's critical success factors. They may join the growing numbers of computer-literate corporate managers who use terminals in their own offices to monitor and plan business activities. Rockart and Michael Treacy describe these top-level managers in "The CEO Goes On-Line." Whether these executive information systems arise from increased availability of user-friendly facilities or from managers' need for more timely information, or both, these systems appear to share several characteristics: they supply the kind of access to information that only computers can provide; they have a common core of data on important business variables; they are used for status access to key variables; and they all depend on a high level of personal support to the executive user. The executive user's support person is perhaps the earliest form of a new type of administrative assistant who, though technologically trained, is separate from the regular data processing functions of the company.

Such involvement of top executives with computers can start on a small scale, both in dollar and in staff terms, and can grow, if that is deemed desirable, only as other persons and sections of the corporate office decide to "buy in." This was the incremental approach adopted by Continental Illinois Bank, which has seen its electronic support of top managers grow to become a model for many others. Starting from the same dissatisfaction with incomplete data for corporate executives, coupled with time-consuming tasks of the support staff who tried to fill the gap, the bank decided to build on the information systems it already had in an effort to improve the situation. In "Doing Your Office Over—Electronically," Louis Mertes describes how the system evolved. The basic premise was that location should have no bearing on the functions that would develop. Executives, and others, could do their work via computer hook-up wherever they happened to be. This geographic independence, plus the step-by-step pragmatic implementation, seems to have assured the usefulness and acceptability of this project, which, though it started small, has spread to include many of the bank's employees.

Though the computer seems ready to deliver one more blessing to the corporate world in freeing the executive from his desk-bound existence, again the coin has another side—the manager who gets away from his office now knows the office is only as far away as his telephone, for dictating and receiving his "electronic" mail, and his home terminal can serve as a constant reminder of his corporate duties. Mertes doesn't see the final outcome as negative, but he suggests that managers ought now to concern themselves with the best ways to deal with what he calls the "tools of remote work" in order to ensure an effective office in the future.

27
Chief Executives Define Their Own Data Needs

JOHN F. ROCKART

What are the real informational needs of the chief executive officer or any other top executive of a company? If presented in the form of computer printouts, often the reports submitted are what some subordinate thinks contain pertinent and useful information. Then again, if presented by word of mouth, the informal approach overlooks the kind of routine data (often computer-based) that should be supplied regularly to the top executive. This article examines the several methods now in use of providing information to top management, discusses the advantages and disadvantages of each, and offers a new approach that focuses on individual managers and their hard and soft informational needs. The discussion includes five illustrative examples from which the author draws some generalizations about the method and the chief executive's data needs.

He could have been the president of any one of a number of successful and growing medium-sized companies in the electronics industry. He had spent the previous day working to salt away the acquisition of a small company that fitted an important position in the product line strategy he had evolved for his organization. Most of this day had been spent discussing problems and opportunities with key managers. During both days he had lived up to his reputation of being an able, aggressive, action-oriented chief executive of a leading company in its segment of the electronics field.

Unfortunately, the president had chosen the late afternoon and early evening to work through the papers massed on his desk. His thoughts were not pleasant. His emotions ranged from amusement to anger as he plowed through the papers. "Why," he thought, "do I have to have dozens of reports a month and yet very little of the real information I need to manage this company? There must be a way to get the information I need to run this company!''

In effect, he was expressing the thoughts of many other general managers—and especially chief executives officers—whose needs for information are not as clearly determined as are those of many functional managers and first-line supervisors. Once one gets above the functional level, there is a wide variety of information that one might possibly need, and each functional specialty has an interest in "feeding" particular data to a general manager. As in this case, therefore, a massive information flow occurs. This syndrome is spelled out with differing emphases by the recent comments of two other chief executives:

> The first thing about information systems that strikes me is that one gets too much information. The information explosion crosses and criss-crosses executive desks with a great deal of data. Much of this is only partly digested and much of it is irrelevant. . . .[1]

> I think the problem with management information systems in the past in many companies has been that they're overwhelming as far as the executive is concerned. He has to go through reams of reports and try to determine for himself what are the most critical pieces of information contained in the reports so that he can take the necessary action and correct any problems that have arisen.[2]

It is clear that a problem exists with defining exactly what data the chief executive (or any other general manager) needs. My experience in working with executives for the past decade or more is that the problem is universally felt—with individual frustration levels varying, but most often high.

In this article, I will first discuss four current major approaches to defining managerial information needs. Next, I will discuss a new approach developed by a research team at MIT's Sloan School of Management. Termed the "critical success factor (CSF) method," this approach is being actively researched and applied today at the MIT center. Finally, I will describe in detail this method's use in one major case as well as provide summary descriptions of its use in four other cases.

Current Procedures

In effect, there are four main ways of determining executive information needs—the *by-product* technique, the *null* approach, the *key indicator* system, and the *total study* process. In this section of the article, I will offer a brief synopsis of each of these and discuss their relative strengths and weaknesses.

By-Product Technique
In this method, little attention is actually paid to the real informational needs of the chief executive. The organization's computer-based information pro-

cess is centered on the development of operational systems that perform the required paperwork processing for the company. Attention is focused, therefore, on systems that process payroll, accounts payable, billing, inventory, accounts receivable, and so on.

The information by-products of these transaction-processing systems are often made available to all interested executives, and some of the data (for example, summary sales reports and year-to-date budget reports) are passed on to top management. The by-products that reach the top are most often either heavily aggregated (for example, budgeted/actual for major divisions) or they are exception reports of significant interest (for example, certain jobs now critical by some preset standard). All reports, however, are essentially by-products of a particular system designed primarily to perform routine paperwork processing.

Where the information subsystem is not computer-based, the reports reaching the top are often typed versions of what a lower level feels is useful. Alternatively, they may be the ongoing, periodically forthcoming result of a previous one-time request for information concerning a particular matter initiated in the dim past by the chief executive.

Of the five methods discussed herein, the by-product approach is undoubtedly the predominant method. It leads to the welter of reports noted in the introductory paragraphs of this article. It has the paper-processing tail wagging the informational dog.

The approach is, however, understandable. Paperwork must be done and clerical savings can be made by focusing on automating paper-processing systems. It is necessary to develop this class of data processing system to handle day-to-day paperwork. However, other approaches are also necessary to provide more useful management information.

Null Approach

This method is characterized by statements that might be paraphrased in the following way: "Top executives' activities are dynamic and ever changing, so one cannot predetermine exactly what information will be needed to deal with changing events at any point in time. These executives, therefore, are and must be dependent on future-oriented, rapidly assembled, most often subjective, and informal information delivered by word of mouth from trusted advisers."

Proponents of this approach point to the uselessness of the reports developed under the by-product method just noted. Having seen (often only too clearly) that (1) the *existing* reports used by the chief executive are not very useful, and (2) he, therefore, relies very heavily on oral communication, advocates of this approach then conclude that all computer-based reports— no matter how they are developed—will be useless. They look at inadequately designed information systems and curse all computer-based systems.

Proponents of the null approach see managerial use of information as Henry Mintzberg does:

> . . . it is interesting to look at the content of managers' information, and
> at what they do with it. The evidence here is that a great deal of the
> manager's inputs are soft and speculative—impressions and feelings about
> other people, hearsay, gossip, and so on. Furthermore, the very ana-
> lytical inputs—reports, documents, and hard data in general—seem to
> be of relatively little importance to many managers. (After a steady diet
> of soft information, one chief executive came across the first piece of
> hard data he had seen all week—an accounting report—and put it aside
> with the comment, "I never look at this.")[3]

To some extent, this school of thought is correct. There is a great deal of
information used by top executives that must be dynamically gathered as
new situations arise. And, most certainly, there are data that affect top
management which are not computer-based and which must be communicated in informal, oral, and subjective conversations.

There are, however, also data that can and should be supplied regularly
to the chief executive through the computer system. More significantly, as
I will note later on, it is also important to clearly define what informal (*not*
computer-based) information should be supplied to a top executive on a
regular basis.

Key Indicator System

A clear contender today for the fastest growing school of thought concerning
the "best" approach to the provision of executive information is the key
indicator system. This procedure is based on three concepts, two of which
are necessary and the third of which provides the glamour (as well as a few
tangible benefits).

The first concept is the selection of a set of key indicators of the health
of the business. Information is collected on each of these indicators. The
second concept is exception reporting—that is, the ability to make available
to the manager, if desired, only those indicators where performance is significantly different (with significance levels necessarily pre-defined) from
expected results. The executive may thus peruse all the data available *or*
focus only on those areas where performance is significantly different from
planned.

The third concept is the expanding availability of better, cheaper, and
more flexible visual display techniques. These range from computer consoles
(often with color displays) to wall-size visual displays of computer-generated
digital or graphic material. A paradigm of these systems is the one developed
at Gould, Inc. under the direction of William T. Ylvisaker, chairman and
chief executive officer. As *Business Week* reports:

> Gould is combining the visual display board, which has now become a
> fixture in many boardrooms, with a computer information system. In-
> formation on everything from inventories to receivables will come di-
> rectly from the computer in an assortment of charts and tables that will
> make comparisons easy and lend instant perspective.

Starting this week Ylvisaker will be able to tap three-digit codes into a 12-button box resembling the keyboard of a telephone. SEX will get him sales figures. GIN will call up a balance sheet. MUD is the keyword for inventory.

About 75 such categories will be available, and the details will be displayed for the company as a whole, for divisions, for product lines, and for other breakdowns, which will also be specified by simple digital codes.''[4]

At Gould, this information is displayed on a large screen in the boardroom, and is also available at computer terminals. The data are available in full, by exception, and graphically if desired.

As in most similar key indicator systems I have seen, the emphasis at Gould is on financial data. Daniel T. Carroll, reporting on Gould's system in mid-1976, described the system's "core report."[5] The report, available for each of Gould's 37 divisions, provides data on more than 40 operating factors. For each factor, current data are compared with budget and prior-year figures on a monthly and year-to-date basis. The report, as noted by Carroll, is ever changing, but its orientation toward "profit and loss" and "balance sheet" data, as well as ratios drawn from these financial data, is evident.

Total Study Process

In this fourth approach to informational needs, a widespread sample of managers are queried about their total information needs, and the results are compared with the existing information systems. The subsystems necessary to provide the information currently unavailable are identified and assigned priorities. This approach, clearly, is a reaction to two decades of data processing during which single systems have been developed for particular uses in relative isolation from each other and with little attention to management informational needs. In effect, this approach was developed by IBM and others to counter the by-product method previously noted.

The most widely used formal procedure to accomplish the total study is IBM's Business Systems Planning (BSP) methodology. BSP is aimed at a top-down analysis of the information needs of an organization. In a two-phase approach, many managers (usually from 40 to 100) are interviewed to determine their environment, objectives, key decisions, and informational needs. Several IBM-suggested network design methods and matrix notations are used to present the results in an easily visualized manner.

The objectives of the process are to develop an overall understanding of the business, the information necessary to manage the business, and the existing information systems. Gaps between information systems that are needed and those currently in place are noted. A plan for implementing new systems to fill the observed gaps is then developed.

The total understanding process is expensive in terms of manpower and all-inclusive in terms of scope. The amount of data and opinions gathered is staggering. Analysis of all this input is a high art form. It is difficult, at best, to determine the correct level of aggregation of decision making, data gathering, and analysis at which to work.

Yet the top-down process tends to be highly useful in most cases. The exact focus of the results, however, can be biased either toward top management information and functional management information or toward paperwork processing, depending on the bias of the study team. I have not seen a BSP study that gives priority to top executive information in the study's output. The design, cleaning up, and extension of the paper-processing information network is too often the focus of the study team.

Each of the four current procedures just discussed has its advantages and disadvantages. The by-product technique focuses on getting paperwork processed inexpensively, but it is far less useful with regard to managerial information. It too often results in a manager's considering data from a single paperwork function (e.g., payroll) in isolation from other meaningful data (e.g., factory output versus payroll dollars).

The null approach, with its emphasis on the changeability, diversity, and soft environmental information needs of a top executive, has probably saved many organizations from building useless information systems. It, however, places too much stress on the executive's strategic and person-to-person roles. It overlooks the management control role of the chief executive, which can be, at least partially, served by means of routine, often computer-based, reporting.[6]

The key indicator system provides a significant amount of useful information. By itself, however, this method often results in many undifferentiated financial variables being presented to a management team. It tends to be financially all-inclusive rather than on-target to a particular executive's specific needs. The information provided is objective, quantifiable, and computer stored. Thus in the key indicator approach the perspective of the informational needs of the executive is a partial one—oriented toward hard data needs alone. More significantly, in its "cafeteria" approach to presenting an extensive information base, it fails to provide assistance to executives in thinking through their real informational needs.

The total study process is comprehensive and can pinpoint missing systems. However, it suffers, as noted, from all of the problems of total approaches. There are problems concerning expense, the huge amount of data collected (making it difficult to differentiate the forest from the trees), designer bias, and difficulty in devising reporting systems that serve any individual manager well.

New CSF Method

The MIT research team's experience in the past two years with the critical success factors (CSF) approach suggests that it is highly effective in helping executives to define their significant information needs. Equally important, it has proved efficient in terms of the interview time needed (from three to six hours) to explain the method and to focus attention on informational needs. Most important, executive response to this new method has been excellent in terms of both the process and its outcome.

The actual CSF interviews are usually conducted in two or three separate sessions. In the first, the executive's goals are initially recorded and the CSFs that underlie the goals are discussed. The interrelationships of the CSFs and the goals are then talked about for further clarification and for determination of which recorded CSFs should be combined, eliminated, or restated. An initial cut at measures is also taken in this first interview.

The second session is used to review the results of the first, after the analyst has had a chance to think about them and to suggest "sharpening up" some factors. In addition, measures and possible reports are discussed in depth. Sometimes, a third session may be necessary to obtain final agreement on the CSF measures-and-reporting sequence.

Conceptual Antecedents

In an attempt to overcome some of the shortcomings of the four major approaches discussed earlier, the CSF method focuses on *individual managers* and on each manager's *current information needs*—both hard and soft. It provides for identifying managerial information needs in a clear and meaningful way. Moreover, it takes into consideration the fact that information needs will vary from manager to manager and that these needs will change with time for a particular manager.

The approach is based on the concept of the "success factors" first discussed in the management literature in 1961 by D. Ronald Daniel, now managing director of McKinsey & Company.[7] Although a powerful concept in itself for other than information systems' thinking, it has been heavily obscured in the outpouring of managerial wisdom in the past two decades. It has been focused on and clarified to the best of my knowledge only in the published work of Robert N. Anthony, John Dearden, and Richard F. Vancil.[8]

Daniel, in introducing the concept, cited three examples of major corporations whose information systems produced an extensive amount of information. Very little of the information, however, appeared useful in assisting managers to better perform their jobs.

To draw attention to the type of information actually needed to support managerial activities, Daniel turned to the concept of critical success factors. He stated,

> . . . a company's information system must be discriminating and selective. It should focus on "success factors." In most industries there are usually three to six factors that determine success; these key jobs must be done exceedingly well for a company to be successful. Here are some examples from several major industries:
>
> ☐   In the automobile industry, styling, an efficient dealer organization, and tight control of manufacturing cost are paramount.

☐   In food processing, new product development, good distribution, and effective advertising are the major success factors.

☐   In life insurance, the development of agency management personnel, effective control of clerical personnel, and innovation in creating new types of policies spell the difference.[9]

Critical success factors thus are, for any business, the limited number of areas in which results, if they are satisfactory, will ensure successful competitive performance for the organization. They are the few key areas where "things must go right" for the business to flourish. If results in these areas are not adequate, the organization's efforts for the period will be less than desired.

As a result, the critical success factors are areas of activity that should receive constant and careful attention from management. The current status of performance in each area should be continually measured, and that information should be made available.

As Exhibit 1 notes, critical success factors support the attainment of organizational goals. Goals represent the end points that an organization hopes to reach. Critical success factors, however, are the areas in which good performance is necessary to ensure attainment of those goals.

Daniel focused on those critical success factors that are relevant for

Exhibit 1.   How Attainment of Organizational Goals is Supported by CSFs

Example	Goals	Critical Success Factors

For-profit concern	Earnings per share
	Return on investment
	Market share
	New product success
		Automotive industry
		  Styling
		  Quality dealer system
		  cost control
		  Meeting energy standards
		Supermarket industry
		  Product mix
		  Inventory
		  Sales promotion
		  Price

Nonprofit concern	Excellence of health care
	Meeting needs of future health care environment
		Government hospital
		  Regional integration of health care with other hospitals
		  Efficient use of scarce medical resources
		  Improved cost accounting

any company in a particular industry. Exhibit 1 updates Daniel's automobile industry CSFs and provides another set of CSFs—from the supermarket industry and a nonprofit hospital.

As this exhibit shows, supermarkets have four industry-based CSFs. These are having the right product mix available in each local store, having it on the shelves, having it advertised effectively to pull shoppers into the store, and having it priced correctly—since profit margins are low in this industry. Supermarkets must pay attention to many other things, but these four areas are the underpinnings of successful operation.

Writing a decade later, Anthony and his colleagues picked up Daniel's seminal contribution and expanded it in their work on the design of management control systems. They emphasized three "musts" of any such system:

> The control system *must* be tailored to the specific industry in which the company operates and to the specific strategies that it has adopted; it *must* identify the 'critical success factors' that should receive careful and continuous management attention if the company is to be successful; and it *must* highlight performance with respect to these key variables in reports to all levels of management.[10]

While continuing to recognize industry-based CSFs, Anthony et al. thus went a step further. They placed additional emphasis on the need to tailor management planning and control systems to both a company's particular strategic objectives and its particular managers. That is, the control system must report on those success factors that are perceived by the managers as appropriate to a particular job in a particular company. In short, CSFs differ from company to company and from manager to manager.

Prime Sources of CSFs

In the discussion so far, we have seen that CSFs are applicable to any company operating in a particular *industry*. Yet Anthony et al. emphasized that a management control system also must be tailored to a particular *company*. This must suggest that there are other sources of CSFs than the industry alone. And, indeed, there are. The MIT team has isolated four prime sources of critical success factors:

1. *Structure of the particular industry.*   As noted, each industry by its very nature has a set of critical success factors that are determined by the characteristics of the industry itself. Each company in the industry must pay attention to these factors. For example, the manager of *any* supermarket will ignore at his peril the critical success factors that appear in Exhibit 1.

2. *Competitive strategy, industry position, and geographic location.*   Each company in an industry is in an individual situation determined by its history and current competitive strategy. For smaller organizations within an industry dominated by one or two large companies, the actions of the major companies will often produce new and significant problems for

the smaller companies. The competitive strategy for the latter may mean establishing a new market niche, getting out of a product line completely, or merely redistributing resources among various product lines.

Thus for small companies a competitor's strategy is often a CSF. For example, IBM's competitive approach to the marketing of small, inexpensive computers is, in itself, a CSF for all minicomputer manufacturers.

Just as differences in industry position can dictate CSFs, differences in geographic location and in strategies can lead to differing CSFs from one company to another in an industry.

3. *Environmental factors.* As the gross national product and the economy fluctuate, as political factors change, and as the population waxes and wanes, critical success factors can also change for various institutions. At the beginning of 1973, virtually no chief executive in the United States would have listed "energy supply availability" as a critical success factor. Following the oil embargo, however, for a considerable period of time this factor was monitored closely by many executives—since adequate energy was problematical and vital to organizational bottom-line performance.

4. *Temporal factors.* Internal organizational considerations often lead to temporal critical success factors. These are areas of activity that are significant for the success of an organization for a particular period of time because they are below the threshold of acceptability at that time (although in general they are "in good shape" and do not merit special attention). As an example, for any organization the loss of a major group of executives in a plane crash obviously would make the "rebuilding of the executive group" a critical success factor for the organization for the period of time until this was accomplished. Similarly, while inventory control is rarely a CSF for the chief executive officer, a very unusual situation (either far too much or far too little stock) might, in fact, become a high-level CSF.

Like Organizations, Differing CSFs

Any organization's situation will change from time to time, and factors that are dealt with by executives as commonplace at one time may become critical success factors at another time. The key here is for the executive to clearly define at any one moment exactly those factors that are crucial to the success of his particular organization in the period for which he is planning.

One would expect, therefore, that organizations in the same industry would exhibit different CSFs as a result of differences in geographic location, strategies, and other factors. A study by Gladys G. Mooradian of the critical success factors of three similar medical group practices bears this out.[11] The medical group practices of the participating physicians were heterogeneous with regard to many of these factors. Each group, however, was well managed with a dynamic and successful administrator in charge.

Mooradian defined the CSFs through open-ended interviews with the administrator of each group practice. She then asked the managers to define their critical success factors and to rank them from most important to least

Exhibit 2.   Critical Success Factors for Three Medical Group Practices

	Clinic #1	Clinic #2	Clinic #3
Most important	Government regulation	Quality and comprehensive care	Efficiency of operations
	Efficiency of operations	Federal funding	Staffing mix
	Patients' view of practice	Government regulation	Government regulation
	Relation to hospital	Efficiency of operations	Patients' view of practice
	Malpractice insurance effects	Patients' view of practice	Relation to community
	Relation to community	Satellites versus patient service	Relation to hospital
		Other providers in community	
Least important		Relation to hospital	

important. Finally, to verify the factors selected, she obtained the opinions of others in the organization.

Exhibit 2 shows the administrators' key variables for the three group practices, ranked in order as perceived by the managers of each institution. It is interesting to note that several of the same variables appear on each list. Several variables, however, are unique to each institution. One can explain the difference in the CSFs chosen by noting the stages of growth, location, and strategies of each clinic:

☐   The first medical group is a mature clinic that has been in existence for several years, has a sound organization structure, and has an assured patient population. It is most heavily concerned with government regulation and environmental changes (such as rapidly increasing costs for malpractice insurance), which are the only factors that might upset its highly favorable status quo.

☐   The second group is located in a rural part of a relatively poor state. It is dependent on federal funding and also on its ability to offer a type of medical care not available from private practitioners. Its number one CSF, therefore, is its ability to develop a distinctive competitive image for the delivery of comprehensive, quality care.

☐   The third clinic is a rapidly growing, new group practice, which was—at that point in time—heavily dependent for its near-term success on its ability to "set up" an efficient operation and bring on board the correct mix of staff to serve its rapidly growing patient population.

In looking at these three lists, it is noticeable that the first four factors on the mature clinic's list also appear on the other two lists. These, it can be suggested, are the all-encompassing industry-based factors. The remaining considerations, which are particular to one or the other of the practices but not to all, are generated by differences in environmental situation, temporal factors, geographic location, or strategic situation.

CSFs at General Manager Level

To this point, I have discussed CSFs strictly from the viewpoint of the top executive of an organization. Indeed, that is the major focus of the MIT research team's current work. It is, however, clear from studies now going on that CSFs, as might be expected, can be useful at each level of general management (managers to whom multiple functions report). There are significant benefits of taking the necessary time to think through—and to record—the critical success factors for each general manager in an organization. Consider:

☐ The process helps the manager to determine those factors on which he or she should focus management attention. It also helps to ensure that those significant factors will receive careful and continuous management scrutiny.

☐ The process forces the manager to develop good measures for those factors and to seek reports on each of the measures.

☐ The identification of CSFs allows a clear definition of the amount of information that must be collected by the organization and limits the costly collection of more data than necessary.

☐ The identification of CSFs moves an organization away from the trap of building its reporting and information system primarily around data that are "easy to collect." Rather, it focuses attention on those data that might otherwise not be collected but are significant for the success of the particular management level involved.

☐ The process acknowledges that some factors are temporal and that CSFs are manager specific. This suggests that the information system should be in constant flux with new reports being developed as needed to accommodate changes in the organization's strategy, environment, or organization structure. Rather than changes in an information system being looked on as an indication of "inadequate design," they must be viewed as an inevitable and productive part of information systems development.

☐ The CSF concept itself is useful for more than information systems design. Current studies suggest several additional areas of assistance to the management process. For example, an area that can be improved through the use of CSFs is the planning process. CSFs can be arrayed hierarchically and used as an important vehicle of communication for management, either as an informal planning aid or as a part of the formal planning process.

Let me stress that the CSF approach does not attempt to deal with information needs for strategic planning. Data needs for this management role are almost impossible to preplan. The CSF method centers, rather, on information, needs for management control where data needed to monitor and improve existing areas of business can be more readily defined.

Illustrative CSF Example

Let us now turn to an example of the use of this approach. The president referred to at the start of this article is real. He is Larry Gould, former president of Microwave Associates, a $60-million sales organization serving several aspects of the microwave communication industry.[12] When he first looked carefully at the "information" he was receiving, Gould found that some 97 "reports" crossed his desk in a typical month. Almost all were originally designed by someone else who felt that he "should be receiving this vital data."

However, the reports provided him with virtually nothing *he* could use. A few gave him some "scorekeeping data," such as the monthly profit statement. One or two others provided him with bits and pieces of data he wanted, but even these left major things unsaid. The data were either unrelated to other key facts or related in a way that was not meaningful to him.

The concept of critical success factors sounded to him like one way out of this dilemma. He therefore, with the MIT research analyst, invested two two-and-a-half-hour periods in working through his goals, critical success factors, and measures, First, he noted the objectives of the company and the current year's goals. Then, he went to work to assess what factors were critical to accomplish these objectives.

Factors & Measures

The seven critical success factors Gould developed are shown in Exhibit 3, along with from one to three prime measures for each factor (although he also developed some additional measures). The reader should note that this specific set of CSFs emerged only after intensive analysis and discussion. At the end of the first meeting, nine factors were on Gould's list. By the end of the second meeting, two had been combined into one, and one had been dropped as not being significant enough to command ongoing close attention.

Most of the second interview session centered on a discussion of the measures for each factor. Where hard data were perceived to be available, the discussion was short. Where softer measures were necessary, however,

Exhibit 3.   CSFs Developed to Meet Microwave Associates' Organizational Goals

Critical success factors	Prime measures
1. Image in financial markets	Price/earnings ratio
2. Technological reputation with customers	Orders/bid ratio
	Customer "perception" interview results
3. Market success	Change in market share (each product)
	Growth rates of company markets
4. Risk recognition in major bids and contracts	Company's years of experience with similar products
	"New" or "old" customer
	Prior customer relationship
5. Profit margin on jobs	Bid profit margin as ratio of profit on similar jobs in this product line
6. Company morale	Turnover, absenteeism, etc.
	Informal feedback
7. Performance to budget on major jobs	Job cost budgeted/actual

lengthy discussions of the type of information needed and the difficulty and/ or cost of acquiring it often ensued. Yet convergence on the required "evidence" about the state of each CSF occurred with responsible speed and clarity in each case. Some discussion concerning each CSF and its measures is perhaps worthwhile. Consider:

1. *Image in financial markets.*   Microwave Associates is growing and making acquisitions as it seeks to gain a growth segment of the electronics industry. Much of the company's growth is coming from acquisitions. Clearly, the better the image on Wall Street, the higher the price-earnings ratio. The measure of success here is clear: the company's multiple vis-à-vis others in its industry segment.

2. *Technological reputation with customers.*   Although Microwave Associates has some standard products, the majority of its work is done on a tailor-made, one-shot basis. A significant number of these jobs are state-of-the-art pieces of work that lead to follow-on production contracts. To a very large extent, buying decisions in the field are made on the customer's confidence in Microwave's technical ability. Sample measures were developed for this CSF. The two measures shown in this exhibit are at the opposite extremes of hard and soft data. The ratio of total orders to total bids can be easily measured. While this hard measure is indicative of customers' perception of the company's technical ability, it also has other factors such as "sales aggressiveness" in it.

The most direct measure possible is person-to-person interviews. Although this measure is soft, the company decided to initiate a measuring process through field interviews by its top executives. (Other measures of this CSF included field interviews by sales personnel, assessment of the rise or fall of the percentage of each major customer's business being obtained, and so forth.)

3. *Market success.* On the surface, this CSF is straightforward. But, as shown by the measures, it includes attention to *current* market success, as well as the company's progress with regard to significant *new* market opportunities (for example, the relative rate of growth of each market segment, opportunities provided by new technology, and relative—not just absolute—competitive performance).

4. *Risk recognition in major bids and contracts.* Because many of the jobs accepted are near or at the state of the art, controlling the company's risk profile is critical. As noted in the exhibit, a variety of factors contribute to risk. The measurement process designed involves a computer algorithm to consider these factors and to highlight particularly risky situations.

5. *Profit margin on jobs.* When profit center managers have low backlogs, they are often tempted to bid low to obtain additional business. While this procedure is not necessarily bad, it is critical for corporate management to understand the expected profit profile and, at times, to counter lower-level tendencies to accept low-profit business.

6. *Company morale.* Because of its high-technology strategy, the company is clearly heavily dependent on the esprit of its key scientists and engineers. It must also be able to attract and keep a skilled work force. Thus morale is a critical success factor. Measures of morale range from hard data (for example, turnover, absenteeism, and tradiness) to informal feedback (for example, management discussion sessions with employees).

7. *Performance to budget on major jobs.* This final CSF reflects the need to control major projects and to ensure that they are completed on time and near budget. Adverse results with regard to timeliness can severely affect CSF No. 2 (technological perception), and significant cost overruns can similarly affect CSF No. 1 (financial market perception). In general, no single job is crucially important. Rather, it is the *profile* of performance across major jobs that is significant.

Reports & Subsystems

Given the foregoing CSFs and measures, the next step was to design a set of report formats. This step required examination of both existing information systems and data sources.

For the soft, informal, subjective measures, this process was straightforward. Forms to record facts and impressions were designed so as to scale (where possible) perception and highlight significant soft factors.

For some of the hard computer-based measures, existing information systems and data bases supplied most of the necessary data. However, in

every case—even where *all* data were available—existing report forms were
inadequate and new reports had to be designed.

Most important, however, two completely new information subsystems
were needed to support the president's CSFs. These were a "bidding"
system and a vastly different automated "project budgeting and control"
system. (Significantly, each of these subsystems had been requested many
times by lower-level personnel, who needed them for more detailed planning
and control of job bidding and monitoring at the product-line manager and
manufacturing levels.) Subsequently, these subsystems were placed at the
top of the priority list for data processing.

In summarizing the Microwave case, it is clear that the exercise of
discovering information needs through examination of the chief executive's
critical success factors had a number of specific benefits. All of the seven
general advantages of the CSF method for information systems development
previously noted applied to some extent. However, the importance of each
of these varies from organization to organization. At Microwave, the most
striking advantages were:

☐ The conscious listing (or bringing to the surface) of the most significant areas on which attention needed to be focused. The process
of making these areas *explicit* provided insights not only into information needs, but also into several other aspects of the company's
managerial systems.

☐ The design of a useful set of *reports* to provide the information
needed for monitoring ongoing operations at the executive level. (There
clearly were other data needed—that is, for developing strategy, dealing with special situations, and so on.) The CSF route, however, focused on the data needed for the ongoing "management control"
process, and this need was significant at Microwave.

☐ The development of *priorities* for information systems development. It was clear that information needed for control purposes by the
chief executive should have some priority. (It also highlighted priorities
for other management levels.)

☐ The provision of a means of hierarchical *communication* among
executives as to what the critical factors were for the success of the
company. (Too often, only goals provide a major communication link
to enhance shared understanding of the company and its environment
among management levels.) This hierarchical approach provided another—and we believe more pragamatic and action-oriented—means
of communication. At Microwave, there is a current project aimed at
developing and sharing CSFs at the top four management levels.

Other Case Examples

The critical success factors developed in four other cases provide useful
additional background for drawing some generalizations about the method
and executive information needs. These CSFs are arrayed in Exhibit 4.

Exhibit 4. CSFs in Four Cases

Chief Executive of a Major Oil Company	President of a Store Furnishings Manufacturer	Director of a Government Hospital	Division Chief Executive of an Electronics Company
1. Decentralize organization.	1. Expand foreign sales for product lines B and C.	1. Devise method for obtaining valid data on current status of hospital operations.	1. Support field sales force.
2. Improve liquidity position.	2. Improve market understanding of product line A.	2. Devise method for resource allocation.	2. Strengthen customer relations.
3. Improve government/business relationships.	3. Redesign sales compensation structure in three-product lines.	3. Manage external relationships.	3. Improve productivity.
4. Create better societal image.	4. Improve production scheduling.	4. Get acceptance of concept of regionalization by all hospital directors.	4. Obtain government R&D support.
5. Develop new ventures.	5. Mechanize production facilities.	5. Develop method for managing regionalization in government hospital group.	5. Develop new products.
	6. Strengthen management team.	6. Strengthen management support, capability, and capacity.	6. Acquire new technological capability.
		7. Improve relationship with government department central office.	7. Improve facilities.
		8. Meet budgetary constraints.	

485

Major Oil Company. The chief executive of this centralized organization responded quickly and unhesitatingly concerning his critical success factors. His goal structure was oriented toward such traditional measures as increasing return on investment, increasing earnings per share, and so forth. Yet he felt there were two major keys to profitability in the future. One was to improve relationships with society as a whole and with the federal government in particular. The other was the urgent need to provide a broader base of earnings assets in petroleum-shy future decades.

As a result of this view of the world, the CEO had initiated major programs to develop new ventures and to decentralize the organization. To facilitate the acquisition process, emphasis was placed on cash flow (liquidity) as opposed to reported earnings. In addition, prime attention was given to understanding and improving external relationships.

All of these efforts are reflected in the company's critical success factors shown in Exhibit 4. Progress in each of these areas is monitored weekly. CSFs Nos. 1, 3, and 4 are reported on with regard to both actions taken and the appropriate executive's subjective assessment of results attained. Liquidity measures are provided by computer output. New venture success is now assessed by a combination of hard and soft measures.

Store Furnishings Manufacturer. This midwestern company has three major product lines. The largest of these is a well-accepted but relatively stable, traditional line on which the company's reputation was made (product line A). In addition, there are two relatively new but fast-growing lines (B and C). The president's preexisting information system was a combination of monthly financial accounting reports and several sales analysis reports.

The president's critical success factors directly reflected the changing fortunes of his product lines. There was a need to concentrate on immediate foreign penetration (to build market share) in the two "hot" lines. At the same time, he saw the need to reassess the now barely growing line on which the company was built three decades ago.

Equally significant, whereas direct selling had been the only feasible mode for the traditional line, the new lines appeared to respond heavily to trade advertising to generate both leads and, in some cases, direct-from-the-factory sales. Because margins are relatively tight in this competitive industry, one factor critical to the company's success with this new product structure, therefore, was a redesign of the sales compensation structure to reflect the evidently diminished effort needed to make sales in the new lines.

A similar need for cost-consciousness also dictated attention to the CSFs of production scheduling efficiency and productivity improvements through the increasing mechanization of production facilities. Finally, strengthening the management team to take advantage of the opportunities presented by the new product lines was felt to be critical by this president.

The analysis of CSFs in this case indicated a need for two major changes in formal information flow to the president. Subsequently, a far more meaningful production reporting system was developed (to support CSF No. 4), and a vastly different sales reporting system emphasizing CSFs Nos. 2 and 3 was established.

Government Hospital.   The CSFs for the director of a government hospital reflect his belief in the need for his organization to radically restructure itself to adapt to a future health care environment perceived as vastly different. He believes that his hospital and his sister government agency hospitals must provide specialized, cost-conscious, comprehensive health care for a carefully defined patient population. Moreover, this care will have to be integrated with that provided by other government hospitals and private hospitals within the region of the country in which his hospital exists.

The director's critical success factors are thus, as shown in Exhibit 4, concerned primarily with building external links and managing cooperation and resource sharing within the set of eight government agency hospitals in his region. The director is also concerned with the development of adequate data systems and methods to manage effective and efficient use of scarce medical resources.

The organization currently has only minimal management information—drawn in bits and pieces from what is essentially a financial accounting system designed primarily to assure the safeguarding and legal use of government funds. The director's desire to get involved in a CSF-oriented investigation of management information needs grew from his despair of being able to manage in the future environment with existing information.

The MIT research team is currently conducting a study involving CSF-based interviews with the top three levels of key managers and department heads in the hospital. Their information needs are heavily oriented toward external data and vastly improved cost accounting.

Major Electronics Division.   This decentralized electronics company places return-on-investment responsibility on the top executive of a major division. His first two CSFs indicate his view of the need for an increasing emphasis on marketing in his traditionally engineering-oriented organization. As Exhibit 4 shows, his CSFs Nos. 3, 6, and 7 are oriented toward the need for more cost-effective production facilities.

Equally important is his attention to new product development (CSF No. 5) in a fast-moving market-place. In conjunction with this, CSF No. 4 reflects his view that a healthy portfolio of government R&D contracts will allow a much larger amount of research to be performed, thereby increasing the expected yield of new ideas and new products. Thus he spends a significant share of his time involved in the process of assuring that government research contracts are being avidly pursued (although they add relatively little to his near-term bottom line).

Efforts to improve the information provided to this division manager have revolved primarily around making more explicit the methods of measuring process in each of these CSF areas. More quantitative indexes have proved to be useful in some areas. In others, however, they have not improved what must be essentially "subjective feel" judgments.

Supportive CSF Information

Previously, I discussed the advantages (both general and specific to one case) of using the CSF process for information systems design. Additionally, some important attributes of the types of information necessary to support the top executive's CSFs can be drawn from the five examples. Consider:

☐ Perhaps most obvious, but worth stating, is the fact that traditional financial accounting systems rarely provide the type of data necessary to monitor critical success factors. Financial accounting systems are aimed at providing historical information to outsiders (e.g., stockholders and others). Only very occasionally is there much overlap between financial accounting data and the type of data needed to track CSFs. In only one of the companies studied was financial accounting data the major source of information for a CSF, and there for only one factor. However, the need for improved *cost* accounting data to report on CSFs was often evident.

☐ Many critical success factors require information external to the organization—information concerned with market structure, customer perceptions, or future trends. Approximately a third of the 33 CSFs in the five examples fit this description. The data to support these CSFs are not only unavailable from the financial accounting system but, in the majority of cases, are also unavailable as a by-product of the organization's other usual day-to-day transaction-processing systems (e.g., order entry, billing, and payroll). The information system must therefore be designed, and the external information consciously collected from the proper sources. It will not flow naturally to the CEO.

☐ Many other CSFs require coordinating pieces of information from multiple data sets that are widely dispersed throughout the company. This is perhaps best noted in the Microwave case, but it is a recurrent feature in all companies. This situation argues heavily for computer implementation of data-base systems that facilitate accessing multiple data sets.

☐ A small but significant part of the information concerning the status of CSFs requires subjective assessment on the part of others in the organization, rather than being neatly quantifiable. About a fifth of the status measures at the companies studied require subjective assessment. This is significant managerial data, and top executives are used to these soft but useful status measures.

(However, it should be noted, many more of the measures at first devised were subjective. It takes considerable work to find objective measures, but in more instances than originally perceived, suitable objective measures are available and can be developed.)

☐ Critical success factors can be categorized as either the "monitoring" or the "building" type. The more competitive pressure for current performance that the chief executive feels, the more his CSFs tend toward monitoring current results. The more that the organization is insulated from economic pressures (as the government hospital was) or decentralized (as the oil company was becoming), the more CSFs become oriented toward building for the future through major change programs aimed at adapting the organization to a perceived new environment.

In all cases that I have seen thus far, however, there is a mixture of the two types. Every chief executive appears to have, at some level, both monitoring and building (or adapting) responsibilities. Thus a great deal of the information needed will not continue to be desired year after year. Rather, it is relatively short-term "project status" information that is needed only during the project's lifetime. Periodic review of CSFs will therefore bring to light the need to discontinue some reports and initiate others.

Notes

1. Interview with Anthony J.F. O'Reilly, president of H.J. Heinz Co., *M.I.S. Quarterly*, March 1977, p. 7.

2. Interview with William Dougherty, president of North Carolina Bank Corporation, *M.I.S. Quarterly*, March 1977, p. 1.

3. See Henry Mintzberg, "Planning on the Left Side and Managing on the Right," *HBR*, July–August 1976, p. 54

4. "Corporate 'War Rooms' Plug into the Computer," *Business Week*, August 23, 1976, p. 65.

5. Daniel T. Carroll, "How the President Satisfies His Information Systems Requirements," published in *Society for Management Information Systems Proceedings*, 1976.

6. Management control is the process of (a) long-range planning of the activities of the organization, (b) short-term planning (usually one year), and (c) monitoring activities to ensure the accomplishment of the desired results. The management control process thus follows the development of major strategic directions that are set in the strategic planning process. This definition roughly follows the framework of Robert N. Anthony, *Planning and Control: A Framework for Analysis* (Boston: Division of Research, Harvard Business School, 1965).

7. See D. Ronald Daniel, "Management Information Crisis," *HBR*, September–October 1961, p. 111.

8.   See Robert N. Anthony, John Dearden, and Richard F. Vancil, ''Key Economic Variables,'' in *Management Controls Systems* (Homewood, Ill.: Irwin, 1972), p. 147.

9.   Daniel, ''Management Information Crisis,'' p. 116.

10.   Anthony, Dearden, and Vancil, ''Key Economic Variables,'' p. 148.

11.   Gladys G. Mooradian, ''The Key Variables in Planning and Control in Medical Group Practices,'' unpublished master's thesis (Cambridge, Mass.: MIT, Sloan School of Management, 1976).

12.   Since this was originally written, Gould has assumed the position of chairman of the board at M/A-COM, Inc., a holding company of which Microwave Associates is a subsidiary.

28

The CEO Goes On-Line

JOHN F. ROCKART and MICHAEL E. TREACY

Senior executives of large corporations have customarily relied on functional staff for the information on which to base key decisions. The task of gathering data and preparing analyses has been simply too time-consuming, too cumbersome to be left to the executives themselves. Today, however, improved computer technology, coupled with a heightened analytical orientation among top managers, is beginning to change the pattern by which a company funnels information to the apex of its organizational pyramid. In fact, in some companies the responsibility for using such data-based support has moved into the executive office itself and, perhaps more important, the top managers of these companies have become active participants in the process, not just final consumers of its output. Though still few in number, these companies offer an intriguing glimpse of tomorrow's executive information systems.

Computer terminals are no strangers to corporate offices. Clerks have had them for years. Middle managers are increasingly using them. So are key staff personnel. But the thought that the CEO and other top officers of a billion-dollar company might regularly spend time at their own terminals usually elicits an amused smile and a shake of the head. Somehow, the image of top executives hard at work at a keyboard just doesn't seem right.

After all, their day is supposed to be filled with meetings with key divisional officers, briefings, telephone conversations, conferences, speeches, negotiations. What is more, the classic research on what executives actually do shows them to be verbally oriented, with little use for "hard" information. According to Henry Mintzberg, "A great deal of the manager's inputs are soft and speculative—impressions and feelings about other people, hearsay, gossip, and so on. Furthermore, the very analytic inputs—reports, documents, and hard data in general—seem to be of relatively little importance."[1]

But consider:

☐ Ben W. Heineman, president and chief executive of Northwest Industries, spends a few hours almost every day at a computer terminal in his office. Heineman accesses reports on each of his nine operating

491

companies and carries out original analyses using a vast store of data and an easy-to-use computer language. The terminal has become his most important tool for monitoring and planning activities.

☐   Roger E. Birk, president of Merrill Lynch, and Gregory Fitzgerald, chief financial officer, have access via computer terminals in their offices to a large number of continually updated reports on the company's worldwide operations. The system, to which a graphics capability has recently been added, was initiated by former president of Merrill Lynch and now Secretary of the Treasury Donald T. Regan as a vehicle for quickly generating information on the latest financial developments.

☐   John A. Schoneman, chairman of the board and CEO of Wausau Insurance Companies, and Gerald D. Viste, president and chief operating officer, use an on-line data base of information about their own business and those of competitors. At their terminals they develop numerical and graphic analyses that help determine the company's strategic direction.

☐   George N. Hatsopoulos, president of Thermo Electron, writes programs in the APL language to format data contained in several of his company's data bases. As a result, he can quickly study information about company, market, and economic conditions whenever he desires.

Although these examples do not yet represent common practice for senior corporate officers, they do suggest a trend toward greatly increased computer use in top-executive suites. In fact, during the past two years we have studied some 16 companies in which at least one of the three top officers, most often the CEO, directly accesses and uses computer-based information on a regular basis. In the pages that follow we present a status report on this rapidly growing phenomenon.

An Information System for Executives

Top managers' use of computers is spreading for three primary reasons: user-oriented terminal facilities are now available at an acceptable price; executives are better informed of the availability and capabilities of these new technologies; and, predictably, today's volatile competitive conditions heighten the desire among top executives for ever more timely information and analysis.

Whatever its specific causes, this trend is indisputably a measured response to a widely perceived need or set of needs. Our study indicates that the actual patterns of executive computer use represent variations on only a few basic themes. Though these patterns evolved independently and may appear quite different, their similarities are striking—so striking in fact that they suggest the emergence in a number of companies of a new kind of executive information support (EIS) system.

From our observations, we can generalize a simple model of EIS structure and development into which fit all the individual systems we have seen. This model helps illuminate both the process of executive information support and the factors that determine its success.

All EIS systems share . . .

. . . A Central Purpose

Obviously, the top executives who personally use computers do so as part of the planning and control processes in their organizations. The provision of information to senior management for such purposes is certainly nothing new; the reason for EIS systems is to support a more effective use of this information. Those managers with terminals of their own have decided that they need a better understanding of the workings of their corporations. To achieve this, they have sought out the individually tailored access to the broader, more detailed sweep of data that only computers can provide.

. . . A Common Core of Data

Although no two EIS systems are identical, each contains what we call a "data cube" (see Exhibit 1)—that is, data on important *business variables* (for example, the major general ledger accounting variables and, equally important, the nonfinancial substantive figures—such as unit sales by product line—that underlie and explain the accounting numbers) through *time* (budgeted, actual, and revised data on key variables is kept on a month-by-month basis for a number of past years, usually five, and is available in the form of projections for several years into the future) and by *business unit* (whatever the nature of those units—geographic, divisional, or functional).

What sets this data cube apart from information traditionally gathered by staff members and included in reports to top management is the sheer breadth of its cross-functional sources and the depth of its detail. With such inclusive information at their fingertips, executives can of course work through traditional accounting comparisons of "actual," "last year," and "budget" for a single business unit. But they can also look at a few variables, such as working capital and its major components, across time for a single subsidiary or at a single variable—say, a product line's performance in physical units as well as dollars—across all subsidiaries.

Further, a number of companies have extended these axes of data to include information, however incomplete, on major competitors, key customers, and important industry segments.[2] Much of this information can be purchased today in the form of any of the several thousand machine-processable data bases sold by information vendors. For competitive financial data, for example, one common source is Standard & Poor's Compustat tape, which provides 10 years of data on 130 business variables for more than 3,500 companies.

Operating data from a growing number of industries are readily available from industry associations or other published sources. Some of these

Exhibit 1.   The Data Cube

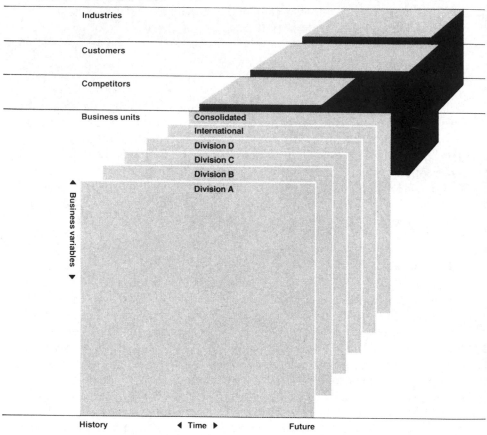

sources—customer surveys, market sampling, and the like—are fairly "soft," but they are accurate enough for managerial planning and control purposes.

. . . Two Principal Methods of Use

The EIS systems in our study are used in two quite different ways by executives: (1) for access to the current status and projected trends of the business and (2) for personalized analyses of the available data. Let us look briefly at these two modes of use.

Status Access.   When executives have "read only" access to the latest data or reports on the status of key variables, they can peruse the information requested but can do very little, if any, data manipulation. In industries where market conditions change rapidly, where there are many factors to watch, or where hour-to-hour operational tracking is important, the status access of this sort can be of great use. This is indeed the case at Merrill Lynch and at several other financial companies.

The status access approach also provides an easy, low-cost, and low-risk means to help an executive become comfortable with a computer terminal. At Owens-Illinois, for example, the first stage in the development of an EIS system will—for just these reasons—provide only status access for the CEO and other senior executives. Moreover, taking this approach can send a clear signal throughout an organization that top management intends to put more emphasis than it had in the past on quantitative analysis in the planning and control process. As one CEO put it, "The terminal on my desk is a message to the organization."

Personalized Analysis. Executives can, of course, use the computer not only for status access but also as an analytic tool. At Northwest Industries, Wausau, and Thermo Electron, senior managers have chosen the contents of the data bases available to them and have learned to do some programming themselves. Instead of merely having access to the data, they are able to do creative analyses of their own.

The type of analysis performed differs from manager to manager. Some merely compute new ratios or extrapolate current trends into the future. Some graph trends of particular interest to gain an added visual perspective. Some work with elaborate simulation models to determine where capital investments will be most productive. All, however, enjoy a heightened ability to look at, change, extend, and manipulate data in personally meaningful ways. But to make this approach effective, executives must be willing to invest much of their own time and energy in defining the needed data and in learning what the computer can do.

. . . A Support Organization

Finally, all the systems we observed depend on the provision of a high level of personal support to their executive users. This support is essential if those systems are to have a fair chance to demonstrate their full potential. Users require at least some initial training and ongoing assistance with computer languages. And they need help in establishing and updating data bases as well as in conceptualizing, designing, and improving their systems and their analyses.

In the organizations we observed, a group of EIS "coaches," often former consultants, gives EIS users continuing assistance. Their primary role is "to help" rather than "to do." Because such EIS coaches must be a different breed of expert from data processing analysts and because they need to be shielded from involvement in the normal run of EDP fire-fighting activities, the companies we studied have separated them organizationally from their regular data processing operations.

Northwest Industries: An Example

Perhaps the most impressive example of an EIS system, both in design and use, is that at Northwest Industries (1980 sales: $2.9 billion). The development of this system began in 1976 when Heineman decided that he needed a specially tailored data base to aid him in monitoring, projecting, and planning the progress of his nine operating companies. A great believer in the advantages of "not being the captive of any particular source of information," Heineman wanted to be able to analyze various aspects of the business himself but saw little opportunity to do so without a computer-based system to reduce data-handling chores.

In January 1977, the six top executives at Northwest were given access to an experimental system through which they could retrieve more than 70 reports and perform such limited analyses as compound growth calculations, variance analysis, and trend projections. By February, Heineman had reached the limits of the system's capabilities and was demanding more.

Additional capabilities came in the form of a new access and analysis language, EXPRESS, which facilitated not only simple file handling and data aggregation but also extensive modeling and statistical analyses of data series. To complement these improved capabilities, Northwest has since added to its executive data base:

☐   350 financial and operational items of data on planned, budgeted, forecasted, and actual monthly results for each operating company for the past eight and the next four years.

☐   45 economic and key ratio time series.

☐   Several externally subscribed data bases, including Standard & Poor's Compustat and DRI services.

Northwest's EIS system with its extensive and continually growing data base is now used by almost all managers and executives at corporate headquarters to perform their monitoring and analytic functions. But the driving force behind the system and its most significant user remains Heineman. Working with the system is an everyday thing for him, a natural part of his job. With his special knowledge of the business and with his newly acquired ability to write his own programs, Heineman sees great value in working at a terminal himself rather than handing all assignments to staff personnel.

"There is a huge advantage to the CEO to get his hands dirty in the data," he says, because "the answers to many significant questions are found in the detail. The system provides me with an improved ability to ask the right questions and to know the wrong answers." What is more, he finds a comparable advantage in having instant access to the data base to try out an idea he might have. In fact, he has a computer terminal at home and takes another with him on vacations.

Supporting Heineman and other Northwest executives are a few information systems people who function as EIS coaches. They train and assist users in determining whether needed data are already available and whether any additional data can be obtained. They also help get new information into the data base, train users in access methods, and teach them to recognize the analytic routines best fitted to different types of analyses. Only for major modeling applications do these coaches actually take part in the system design and programming process.

The Promise of EIS Systems

Most of America's top managers still have no terminal-based access whatsoever. They find the idea of working at a terminal a violation of their managerial styles and their view of their roles. They are perfectly comfortable asking staff to provide both manual and computer-generated analyses as needed. What is more, EIS systems provide no clear, easily defined cost savings. In fact, we know of no system that a traditional cost-benefit study would justify in straight labor-saving terms. Why, then, are managers implementing them in growing numbers?

Three principal reasons suggest themselves. Most significant is the assistance EIS systems offer analytically oriented top executives in their search for a deeper understanding of their companies and industries. We believe that many top managers are basically analytic and that they are now both aware of the new tools offered by EIS and finding them to their liking. (For some of their specific comments, see the ruled insert.)

Second, EIS systems can be structured to accommodate the information needs of the individual manager. Although the Merrill Lynch system, for example, is principally geared for status access, Gregory Fitzgerald, the chief financial officer, often writes his own programs to carry out personally tailored analyses.

Finally, the systems can start small (less than $100,000), providing support to a single data-oriented member of the corporate office. In fact, an EIS system can begin either at a line-executive level or as a system for the sole use of a particular functional staff, such as finance or marketing (see Exhibit 2). It can then evolve as others become interested, adding the data sets and access methods appropriate to each new user. This pattern of growth marks a logical progression since the executives, personal assistants, and key functional staffs in the corporate office form, in effect, an "executive information support organization" *jointly* responsible for preparing and analyzing the data needed at the corporate level. EIS support of an individual user enhances the information-processing capability of the entire corporate office, for the data needed by different members of the office tend to overlap.

But EIS systems have the added advantage that they need grow and develop only as additional individuals "buy in." Unlike the huge, one-shot, multimillion-dollar projects necessary for such classic data processing systems as order entry or manufacturing control, EIS systems can evolve by increments in precise step with the distinct needs of each corporate office.

Not all senior managers, of course, will find an EIS system to their taste, but enough user-friendly technology now exists to accommodate the needs of those who wish to master a more data-intensive approach to their jobs.

Exhibit 2.   A Conceptual Model of Executive Information Support

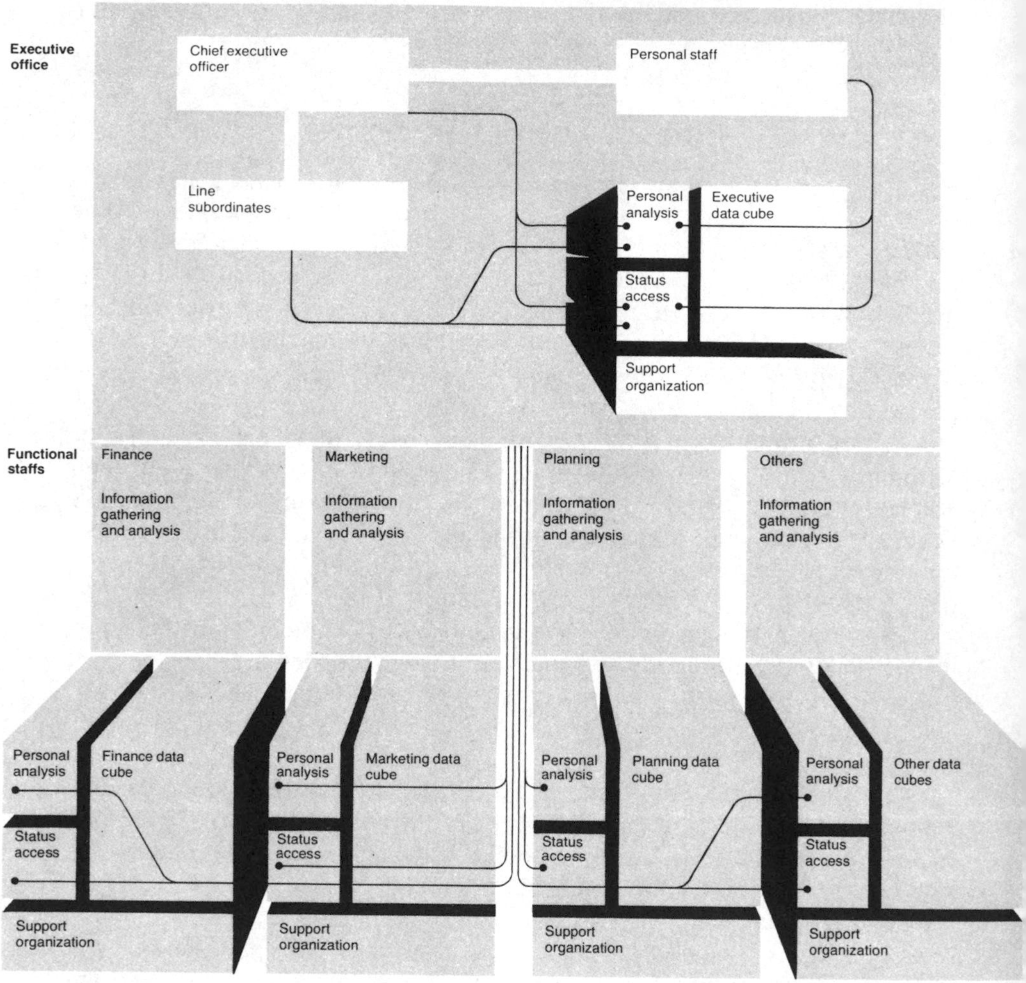

Notes

1. See Henry Mintzberg, "Planning on the Left Side and Managing on the Right," *HBR,* July–August 1976, p. 49.

2. For one method of defining those variables that should be included, see John F. Rockart, "Chief Executives Define Their Own Data Needs," Chapter 27, this book.

Appendix: What Top Managers Are Saying About EIS Systems

"The system has been of infinite help in allowing me to improve my mental model of the company and the industry we're in. I feel much more confident that I am on top of the operations of our company and its future path."

"Your staff really can't help you think. The problem with giving a question to the staff is that they provide you with the answer. You learn the nature of the real question you should have asked when you muck around in the data."

"It saves a great deal of the time spent in communicating with functional staff personnel. Today, for an increasing number of problems, I can locate the data I want, and I can develop it in the form I want, faster than I could describe my needs to the appropriate staffer."

"Some of my best ideas come at fallow times between five in the evening and seven the next morning. Access to the relevant data to check out something right then is very important. My home terminal lets me perform the analysis while it's at the forefront of my mind."

"Comparing various aspects of our company with the competition is a very fast way of defining the areas in which I should place most of my attention. The system allows me to do exactly that."

"I think graphically. It's so nice to be able to easily graph out the data in which I'm interested. . . . And it's especially nice to be able to adjust the display to see the data in the exact perspective that best tells the story."

"I've always felt that the answers were in the detail. Now, at last, I can pore through some of that detail. That's my style. It used to mean long nights and plenty of staff and lots of frustration. Now it's somewhat easier. And frankly, it also saves me a great deal of staff time that was formerly spent on routine charting and graphing."

"I bring a lot of knowledge to the party. Just scanning the current status of our operations enables me to see some things that those with less time in the company would not see as important. Although the resulting telephone calls undoubtedly shake up some of my subordinates, I think in the long run this is helpful to them, too."

"The system provides me with a somewhat independent source for checking on the analyses and opinions presented both by my line subordinates and by my functional staffs. There is a great deal of comfort in being relatively independent of the analyses done by others."

"By working with the data I originally thought I needed, I've been able to zero in on the data I actually need. We've expanded our data base significantly, but each step has led to better understanding of our company and its environment."

"Frankly, a secondary, but very real, advantage of the use of the system by me is the signal it gives to the rest of the company that I desire more quantitatively oriented management of the organization. I want my subordinates to think more analytically, and they are. I feel we're on the way to becoming a significantly better-managed company."

29
Doing Your Office Over
– Electronically

LOUIS H. MERTES

Using existing technology, Continental Illinois Bank, seventh largest U.S. bank, has made the "office of the future" a reality. Building on a network of interactive small-scale computers and a large central processing unit, Continental developed a central library containing the bank's vast data base. So that bank managers could have a link to the office at home, at the airport, or in a hotel room, remote telephone dictating facilities were linked to the bank's word processing machines. An electronic mail system now allows managers to communicate without paper memorandums, and the messages are stored in an electronic filing cabinet. The author points out that Continental executives now have an office wherever there is a telephone, and he discusses some of the present and possible future effects of this flexible arrangement.

Computers have always been associated with counting—lots of counting and at very high speeds. They perform, with greater efficiency and higher productivity, many of the tasks once done by people. If computer technology were taken higher into the corporate structure, right into the manager's office, would the same degree of increased productivity result? Could other, related technologies also contribute to the higher productivity of an "office of the future"? Consider these illustrations:

☐ You call a colleague, but he's not in. Later, he returns your call, but now you're not in. You call him back, and again he's not in. This game is a kind of telephone tag, and it wears constantly on the patience and productivity of every business executive.

☐ You draft a memorandum to your superior. Your secretary types the memo on official corporate stationery. She hands it back for your review and signature. If you find no errors, you sign it and hand it back for her to duplicate for your own files. An envelope is addressed, the memo is inserted, and the message is whisked out of your office and into your boss's office. And it only took 3½ days! The memo was not sent overseas. It only had to go across the street to the other building where your boss works. Too many people spent time on its creation, reproduction, and delivery.

☐ Let's say you're a commodities lender. You pick up the phone and hear one of your customers request $500,000. The customer needs confirmation of the loan within the next 30 minutes. Naturally, he tells you his credit is good. But can you risk approving a loan without doing research on the customer to obtain up-to-date financial information?

This article discusses how the so-called office of the future technology has become a reality at Continental Illinois Bank, minimizing many of the routine, time-consuming chores. In the first section, I shall outline characteristics of the corporation's data processing system to illustrate how we moved toward an office of the future. The second section traces the evolution of some key projects, and the third discusses further efforts by Continental to integrate product lines. Finally, I explore some social and organizational implications that surfaced as we implemented these new technologies.

Underlying Philosophy

Until 1977, data and text processing had developed at Continental Bank as it had in most large organizations. With data processing, we had automated the highly labour-intensive functions of the bank. These included check processing, bookkeeping, and other high-volume arithmetic functions. As technologies improved, we applied them to word processing—another labor-intensive, high-volume growth segment of the banking industry.

However, before 1977 none of our advances in data and text processing directly involved managers or the administrative areas. Managers who tried to use the reports produced by data processing found that none really satisfied their needs because the data involved only raw numbers from which they could establish no relationship to other data. Yet these were the very people who had been consuming the most time searching for information, communicating it, following up on it, and traveling to and from meetings to discuss it. To meet their needs, managerial support staffs often had to perform many time-consuming tasks as well.

Business executives historically have lost valuable time to "nickel and dime" activities. Envision, for example, a manager calling one of his staff for a status report on a project. If this person is away from his desk when the manager calls, the two might not connect until later that day or perhaps the next day. Meanwhile, both continue to waste time trying to make contact. If an administrative assistant is brought into the picture to provide supporting data, more calls are made and more time is spent discussing what kinds of data are needed and how to set up and type the status report.

Then more time is spent as a staff member types the report and puts it through an editing sequence that includes correction of typing and substantive mistakes as well as more review. If the manager is presenting the report at a different location, other personnel become involved with scheduling, transportation, and other seemingly small but important details. When he finally gives the report, someone may discover that a critical piece of information has been overlooked, making the entire report ineffective. Thus, the entire data-gathering and delivery effort proves fruitless.

This rather grim scenario is typical at most large companies. At Continental, we became increasingly aware of what was happening. In late 1977, we launched a program designed to end this unwelcome circus.

By mid-1977, demand for an integrated information source at Continental was growing. We had tried to satisfy ad hoc requests for information with our quick response system, which allowed users to retrieve from the computer a limited amount of information based on a primary account characteristic, such as account number, account name, and so forth. The average time between request and delivery was about one week. While the design of this system approached some developmental goals, it did not satisfy Continental's needs in terms of response time, cost, and range of content.

Meanwhile, to keep up with growing demand for information, data and information-processing companies that had been one-product manufacturers started merging different technologies. We felt that a major revolution in office equipment would result. The greatest hope for our installation, however, was that our many computer processing systems could be integrated so that one terminal could be used to access all forms of information, much like the setup for a telephone conference call.

We were certain that communications and data processing products produced in the future would be different from today's. But with much of the technological and equipment development providing confusing signals about the future, we decided to begin making our own changes using existing technology.

We already had some experience with systems integration from our own development of intercomputer communication. A few years earlier, we had established a working link between our interactive small-scale computer and our large-scale information processing computers. In effect, these different units were "talking" to each other. We decided to capitalize on that capability.

What we developed is known as the central library, a computerized stronghold of virtually every byte of information that had been captured and stored. We did not put the microcomputer, or "mini," into use at Continental, because its makeup fragments information on the basis of use and user location and thus would have defeated everything we had gained in our centralization of information and data.

The central library is much like a traditional library. Information, regardless of origin, is captured and stored by an indexing scheme that involves filing under various headings: names, account numbers, dollar amounts, check serial numbers, or transaction dates.

How the System Evolved

Once the central library was established to support all forms of information storage, capture, and retrieval, we defined strategic goals to bring us closer to our conception of the office of the future.

We began by subdividing principal office work patterns into three categories: text preparation and communication, acquisition of information, and voice communication. Tools were designed to fit each of these categories according to a basic philosophy that an employee's physical location in relation to his or her job should have no bearing on the configuration of the office functions we would develop.

To date, four products have been created and are being used by Continental employees. These include word processing and remote dictation, electronic mail, what we call the instantaneous retrieval information system, and audio mail. Each product is designed to accommodate a large user group to achieve maximum utilization.

Word Processing & Remote Dictation

Wherever a "work center" had enough volume and could reduce its clerical staff to justify the expense, we introduced the most basic forms of word processing. Initially, the primary function of these centers was to copy-type a variety of materials. Later, however, we introduced transcription and dictation capabilities, making the WP centers a new means of increasing productivity.

Although overall productivity increased, the dictation aspect faced a major constraint—the managers' proximity to the word processing center was vital to the turnaround of text preparation. To address this problem, we established remote telephone dictation facilities so that managers could use their telephones as dictation machines. They could pick up a phone at their desk, airports, or even in hotel rooms thousands of miles away from the word processing centers. Thus, we shortened the turnaround time of text preparation and eliminated the geographic constraints.

Remote dictation requires only the availability of a telephone because the instrument's technology permits the user to key or dial various commands, such as record, play back, or rewind. In a way, remote dictation involves a microphone (telephone) on an extremely long cord (telephone line).

Once we had remote dictation in place and had established our electronic mail system as a text-delivery mechanism (described later in this section), we had an answer to the other half of our text-transport problem. Mail users (approximately 25% of bank employees) can now create, review, edit, and communicate text without ever being near an office. Furthermore, we found that we could create "satellite" word processing centers since the centers' locations no longer had to be in close proximity to their users.

Continental currently operates a word processing satellite about 25 miles from downtown Chicago and the bank. Located at a community college, the satellite center is used to teach students how to operate the various pieces of word processing machinery. During nonteaching periods, some of the students work for Continental using the word processing skills they have acquired.

The satellite project is an experiment to test whether this expensive equipment can be used for more than one work shift and to observe its performance over periods of up to 16 hours a day. A similar test with less expensive word processing equipment involves home installations. In this experiment, the equipment is used only eight hours a day by typist-level operators who for various reasons do not wish to commute to a central word processing center in one of Continental's buildings.

In both experiments, we are beginning to realize that, again, location and proximity of a major support function are not the issue. What is important is finding skilled personnel who may not be able or willing to travel into the central business district of a large metropolitan area. A program such as this—which can be set up in the home—can bring employment to the physically handicapped, who in general tend to be highly capable and dependable employees but who are physically unable to leave their homes, or to parents of young children. Because the dictation is recorded and the finished work is held in computer memory banks, a strict nine-to-five workday is no longer critical except in cases involving high-priority work.

It is important to remember that our experiment at Continental concerns itself chiefly with the equipment and an overall technological test of the system. Obviously, working at home suits some but not others; however, at this stage of the program we are not actively trying to determine how people adapt to a home work environment.

Electronic Mail

Late in 1977, we decided to build a prototype of an electronic mail system to give users computer communication with each other. Supporting the system was the central library, which offered users a single depository for their memorandums. The prototype, more sophisticated than the basic text-communication media, would offer users a limited text-editing function that they could use before sending an item to other system participants. We also built into the prototype a multiple addressing capability, among other features.

We initiated a pilot program to help Continental systems personnel understand the concept of electronic mail and the functions such a system would require. The pilot was conducted within the bank's systems division and involved a group selected on the basis of varying job descriptions and task requirements. We wanted to learn how people at all organizational levels would use the system, including secretaries creating text.

The earliest indication of a developing market for electronic mail within the pilot program group came from participants who were in different buildings. For example, two of the bank's senior systems people were located in the bank's main building about two miles away from their staffs, who were working in Continental's data processing center. Electronic mail quickly proved itself a highly effective means of communication for the pilot's participants because it eliminated delays in transmitting paper-based memorandums, which otherwise took one business day on the average to reach their destination.

Another market segment that emerged during the pilot was the employee group separated from other groups by time. Shift managers in our data processing center provide a classic example. These managers, who work an 8-hour shift in the center's 24-hour operation, have limited opportunities to exchange information expeditiously. Electronic mail provided them with a means of communication that was both timely and secure.

Our European systems personnel who participated in the pilot also proved the system to be an excellent transatlantic communications tool because it broke down distance and time-zone barriers. This element is significant since the bank has a work force of nearly 2,000 people in some 100 different foreign locations.

A senior project manager from the bank's properties development division made especially good use of this tool. Recently he was given a two-year assignment at the bank's European headquarters in London. Normally assignments of this duration require the relocation of the employee and his or her family. In this case, however, the employee's wife did not want to leave behind a business she had founded and was running by herself. Electronic mail provided the couple with a way of easing the two-year separation.

One mail terminal was installed at the employee's home in the United States for his wife to use. Another was located in his London office. Twice a day throughout each week, electronic mail provided a link between the employee and his wife. Through this easy communication device they were able to discuss and reach agreement on the sale of his car, for example, and to handle other daily problems that can constitute a burden for widely separated spouses.

A third market segment evolved from the need of managers to communicate quickly with a large group of people. We had already learned that audio mail was an excellent vehicle for person-to-person communications because it did not require that the caller actually establish a conversation with the called party. However, when a person wanted to communicate the same message to a number of others, he or she had to make either several calls or a ''mass distribution'' mailing of paper memorandums. With electronic mail, however, we could overcome the multiple-recipient problem by creating lists, based on a single entry on the electronic mail terminal, of persons who were to receive the memorandum.

This convenience is achieved by creating a list that has an identifying name like "senior managers." The names of all senior executives are entered on the list and kept on file. Then, when a memorandum must go to each of these people, the user need only address his or her message to "senior managers." The computer duplicates the message as many times as there are names on the list and automatically files a copy of the message in each recipient's "electronic filing cabinet" in the mail system.

Further development of the electronic mail system permitted pilot-program participants to "archive" documents electronically in the electronic filing cabinet. This single addition to the system eliminated any further need for filing paper copies of memorandums. A built-in tickler feature also allows assignment of follow-up dates. We added an electronic margin-notation capability as well to allow users to respond to mail without repeating or reentering the original memorandum.

For the bank officer, being out of town on business no longer means being out of touch with the bank. He or she needs only a portable terminal and a telephone in the hotel room to continue a varied line of communications with other Continental people in Chicago or with most other Continental bank facilities around the United States and abroad.

Our market research, educational efforts, and additional selective functions have led the electronic mail system from the pilot stage to a bankwide system with about 3,000 users, roughly one-fourth of Continental's staff. By making access to electronic mail possible for authorized users from any terminal they choose, we have successfully continued to apply our philosophy of making employee location irrelevant to the timely and efficient completion of work. A growing number of our employees have an office wherever the nearest phone is.

Downtime on a system of this magnitude can be terribly disabling and can alienate the user. Continental's electronic mail system has maintained a high level of operating performance, with downtime amounting to only 1% to 2%, or 5 to 10 minutes, per day. A system with a poorer performance rate becomes ineffective; its users find they cannot depend on it and will tend not to accept it as a primary communication medium.

The IRIS Data Base

Following our philosophy of using a general-purpose function to provide information to authorized bank users, we assigned two members of our systems development staff to the task of establishing our instantaneous information retrieval system (IRIS). We needed a search function that would give an IRIS user a simple means of drawing on vast amounts of data and text. A good deal of flexibility already existed for drawing on the data we had held in traditional data processing files. However, we did not have a general-purpose text and data file that could handle requests in plain English. Within a month, however, the first IRIS data base had been established.

A week later, we demonstrated the system to all of the bank's off-shore managers who had come to Chicago for a conference. During the week of preparation for the demonstration, we created a data base containing more than 140,000 names and addresses plus information related to our general banking services area. The data base—drawn from the bank's demand-deposit accounting system, the commercial lending system, the international lending system, and the European bookkeeping system—was demonstrated to the conferees. The managers saw for the first time in the history of the organization a complete composite, stored in one central location, of all the bank's data concerning customers. In addition, they observed that any of the information stored in the data base was retrievable through the most general of search queries.

Encouraged by the success of the off-shore managers' conference, we began looking at other ways we could use IRIS. One obvious need was in the bank's check-processing facility, where a search through customer files to determine whether a particular check had been presented for payment often required 40 minutes or more. We had estimated that 24 man-months would be needed to develop the program to give check processing personnel on-line capabilities. To our surprise, the project required only one man-month to reach implementation stage and one additional month to build the file to full size, involving 19 million checks.

Once a data base for the check-processing search had been created for IRIS, we established a systems marketing group and gave this group the responsibility of demonstrating the value of IRIS to others in the bank. Marketing group representatives, who each handled an area of the bank as though it were a sales account, also worked to identify new information needs that would require the creation of other IRIS data bases.

As a result of the marketing effort, we now have 2,200 authorized IRIS users, or 22% of Continental employees. More than 120 data bases are available to authorized users, with over 20 billion characters of information on file in the central library. The users operate more than 800 IRIS terminals, located throughout Continental's worldwide organization.

We have learned a great deal from the IRIS effort, particularly about the behavior of the IRIS users. As we increased the number of terminals and improved our ability to offer information to our administrative or front office personnel, who traditionally have not been computer users, we found that education was the key to facilitating the system's use. We also learned a lot about how a general-purpose information retrieval product like IRIS can be used to our benefit.

By taking a general-purpose approach to on-line retrieval, we significantly reduced the time required to build each new IRIS data base. In the case of the check processing data base, we realized an 11 to 1 reduction in the time spent on its development and were able to provide customers on-line access to "check paid" files, for example.

With such advancements, we can justify the cost of providing on-line access to IRIS for users of some of the bank's batch processing systems.

For example, our mortgage servicing personnel have a batch processing system to which transactions are entered each night. Reports produced from nightly batch runs are delivered to the users on the following morning. Queries about mortgage status formerly involved labor-intensive searches, but when mortgage servicing personnel were given on-line access to their master file, the time-consuming process ended. What's more, we were able to establish the on-line mortgage servicing system quickly and inexpensively.

IRIS cut out a lot of paperwork. For the mortgage servicing area, for example, on-line access eliminated the need for printing, transporting, and storing bulky and expensive paper printouts. By replacing paper storage with electronic storage in the form of disk drives—which have been decreasing steadily in cost over the years in terms of cost per character stored—and by using IRIS as a filing and retrieving facility, we reduced the total cost of producing, disseminating, filing, and retrieving information.

IRIS also has proved extremely useful as a quasi-broadcast facility. The bank's bond and money market services department, which keys quotations directly into IRIS for negotiable instruments such as bankers' acceptances, certificates of deposit, and treasury bills, establishes through IRIS a ready source of broadcast data used frequently by personnel in the bank's commercial lending department. Formerly these quotations were printed on paper and were distributed to persons on a large mailing list, usually a day later. The volatility of the quotations meant that the quotation sheets often became obsolete while they were being printed. With IRIS these quotations are kept current and therefore remain useful.

When a Continental commercial banker visits an out-of-town client, he or she may carry along a small computer terminal that is the key to the wealth of information and data stored in the bank's central library in Chicago. With this ready access to information, the commercial banker has available all the tools he or she needs for a productive and decisive business meeting.

Audio Mail

In any large organization, much important information is transmitted by telephone, especially when messages are urgent. But studies by large companies have revealed that the telephone is only 50% effective for intraoffice calls. The reason is the well-known and frustrating game I call telephone tag.

Even when a secretary or receptionist is available to take a caller's message, the chances of connecting on a return call remain the same, about 50%. Conceivably, two people in the bank might spend more time trying to reach each other by telephone than if they had written each other memorandums. We decided to focus our efforts on what became known as audio mail. An immediate search of available equipment for the storage and forwarding of audio mail turned up a lot of potentially useful devices that were on suppliers' drawing boards but that would not be available to the public for several years. Rather than wait, we decided to exploit the existing audio technology.

In 1978, we installed ordinary telephone answering devices in the offices of Continental personnel who received many calls each day. These answering devices, which have been in production for nearly 15 years, were not altered in any way for the Continental pilot program.

We began the pilot with 35 answering devices. In the early days, we found that many callers disliked talking to a machine. We explained that the idea was not to talk to the machine but rather to dictate a message into it.

Those who had the machines were instructed to record a greeting and to ask the caller to leave his or her name, phone number, and a message of any length. Emphasis was placed on "any length" messages to encourage responses beyond, "This is Mr. Doe. Please call me." A more detailed summary of the purpose of the call gives the recipient of the message enough information to return the call effectively. When a call was directed to a person who also had an answering device, it was even possible for two people to complete a transaction without ever speaking directly to each other.

We found that among pilot participants' calls, the machine intercepted 65% in the recipient's absence, while the recipient handled the other 35%. Our immediate reaction to the test data was concern that those who had machines were answering so few calls in person. Later, however, we found that the test results of 35% coincided almost perfectly with the amount of time an employee actually has on average for handling calls personally.

At first, bank employees confronted with a recorded message often felt inclined to hang up. As time went on, however, an increasing number began leaving short messages, and finally they left longer, more complete messages. It generally took only the completion of one business transaction via the system to win over those employees who had been skeptical.

Today more than 300 of the telephone answering devices are being used at Continental. Since the pilot program, the only change has been the addition of a remote, pocket-size signaling device that permits the user to call his or her answering machine to get messages that have come into the office. This additional feature is again in keeping with our general philosophy of maintaining a high level of communications without respect to the geography of work stations.

Integrating the System

Inside the bank, an employee can use electronic mail to create a variety of interoffice correspondence, while IRIS serves as a near-infinite storage facility for indefinite retention of electronic mail files. Outside the bank, in the accountant's office of one of Continental's corporate customers, IRIS can determine for the accountant whether a check has cleared the corporation's account at Continental for payment. If the accountant has reason to order a stop payment on the check and finds that it has not yet cleared, he or she can use the same terminal plus electronic mail to execute the stop payment order.

A typist working for the bank at home uses electronic mail as the transmittal medium once he or she has transcribed dictation onto his or her word processor. The information, often in the form of a letter, is directed back to the bank via electronic mail, after which the information is fed to a mechanical printer for reproduction on a bank officer's letterhead.

As basic communications systems grow, it becomes quite natural to expand systems product lines to include analytic features. Data held in IRIS, for example, can be further summarized and analyzed and subsequently transmitted to other persons by electronic mail. The user can employ each of these features while working at one terminal.

Taking the system a step beyond the analytic function, we established a computer graphics capability, whereby the data, after analysis, can be displayed in the form of a chart. For example, the graphics may appear on a black-and-white or color video screen, which also has a paper printer. The displayed data can be transmitted to other terminals for video display, using electronic mail and its central library.

We have worked toward this integration of systems to provide users a straightforward means of office support. We believe a person should be able to go to a single source of information to get the job done on time in a comfortable working environment.

Social & Organizational Implications

The energy problem in the United States has led many organizations to look for new ways to cope, including possible changes in work habits. In particular, it has forced them to focus attention on moving ideas, work messages, and other data from place to place rather than transporting people. It is clear that the time is coming when an office worker will not need to leave home to do the kind of work that has always been conducted in the conventional office setting.

The communications and data processing technology that exists today can be used in such a way that all a worker needs is a telephone and an inexpensive computer terminal in the home to conduct even the most traditional forms of office transactions. Using the central library tools discussed in this article, many of our employees can be just as effective working in their homes as in their offices in Chicago's central business district. The technological capability to establish remote work stations is no longer in question.

We now feel we have gained enough experience in each of the office areas to begin drawing some tentative conclusions about the effect on human behavior.

Electronic mail, for example, may be labeled by some as a workaholic's dream. We believe, however, that a computer terminal in an executive's home does not need to promote the symptomatic nonstop work pattern associated with the workaholic but serves only as a substitute for the paper medium once carried to and from the office in the workaholic's attaché case. When paper was the exclusive medium, the boss never knew whether a memorandum was drafted in the office, aboard a commuter train, or at the kitchen table after the late, late show. Electronic mail's capacity to log time and date does pinpoint that information and it is subject to abuse by over-zealous middle managers, who might view the technology as a means of scoring points with their superiors. Such managers could also use it as a form of "electronic intimidation" of subordinates, who might believe that the separation of home and office is sacred.

The social implications of permanent home work stations will be many; however, we know only a few at this time. Depending on the level of responsibility and the task performed, some workers view a trip to the office each day as an escape from their domestic environment. Others consider the same trip tiring, time consuming, costly, and even unnecessary.

Not everyone views the home work environment as desirable because not everyone holds the same values for work, travel, and leisure time. What's more, some workers thrive on interaction with coworkers while others do not; and some feel the need of a structured work situation.

One question as yet unanswered is whether managers will be less effective or will feel less effective if they cannot come out from the confines of their offices to see their subordinates performing assigned tasks at assigned work stations.

Managers who do concern themselves with this kind of structure and view it as a necessity may well be the kind of managers whose paper-shuffling skills will be replaced with office automation. Indeed, when managers' offices have all been automated, two groups will surface. One, made up of the traditional paper shufflers, will struggle with an unfilled gap in each workday; the other will use the added time to be more creative and more effective.

As the costs of moving people from place to place increase, along with the costs of paper and office space, remote working arrangements and other organizational changes will evolve, especially as the expense of the required technology decreases.

How can the tools of remote work best be implemented? How can corporations achieve the highest levels of productivity in ways that will benefit employees as well as the company? These are the questions top managers should consider today to ensure an effective office in the future.

Although our development of information systems technology at Continental is only a few years old, we have gone well beyond the point of no return. Our eagerness to enter the arena at the earliest possible stage was based on a belief that late entry would imprison us in a catch-up position. If we have it to do again, nothing of the essentials would be changed. We felt that our methodology was especially successful. The systems we have developed thus far represent a mere sampling of the high technology that will be an integral part of all of our daily lives, both inside and outside the office.

About the Authors

Brandt Allen is the James C. Wheat, Jr., Professor of Business Administration at the Graduate Business School of the University of Virginia where he teaches courses in controllership and computer systems management. Mr. Allen holds a BS and MBA from the University of Washington and a doctorate from Harvard University. Before joining the Virginia faculty in 1970 he was an assistant professor for three years at the Harvard Business School. His industrial experience includes four years of service with the Boeing Company. Mr. Allen is a member of the Financial Executive's Institute, the American Accounting Association, the Society for Management Information Systems, and the Advisory Board of the Computer Security Institute. He is the author of numerous articles, monographs, and books and is a frequent lecturer in both the United States and Europe.

Jack R. Buchanan is director of the Division of Innovations and Systems Development at the Federal Judiciary Center.

Martin D. J. Buss is the director of planning for Philip Morris International. Previously, he was a senior consultant with Arthur D. Little, Inc., in Cambridge, Massachusetts, where he worked internationally on a broad range of organizational, strategic, and planning issues of concern to top management. He has particular experience in information processing gained through many years as a practitioner in the field in various countries in Europe. Before joining Arthur D. Little, Inc., Mr. Buss was responsible for organization and planning in a Spanish bank and was the chief executive of the bank's data processing subsidiary. He was educated in England and is a professionally qualified Chartered Company Secretary.

Cyrus F. Gibson is a vice president of Index Systems, Inc. and is the officer responsible for the Education Services and Organizational Change Management Group. He consults to senior and information systems management on the strategic assessment of information systems, the design and change of organizational structure and control systems, planning for management information and decision support systems implementation, and policy-set-

ting with respect to personnel management. Before joining Index, Mr. Gib-
son was an associate professor at the Harvard Business School. He holds
a BE from Yale University, an MBA from the Harvard Business School, and
a PhD from M.I.T.'s Sloan School for Management. Among his publications
are Managing Organizational Behavior.

Robert C. Goldstein *is an associate professor of management information*
systems in the Faculty of Commerce and Business Administration at the
University of British Columbia in Vancouver, Canada. He holds a BS from
the Massachusetts Institute of Technology and a PhD from the Harvard
Business School. Mr. Goldstein's research has generally been in the areas
of data base systems and computer-privacy issues. He has developed a series
of models for estimating the impact, financial and otherwise, of altering
computerized information systems to protect personal privacy. Two books,
The Cost of Privacy *and* Modeling Privacy Costs, *have been published out*
of this work. In the late 1960s, Mr. Goldstein was one of the developers of
what is generally considered to be the first complete relational data base
management system. He continues to be active in that area of research,
and is especially interested in techniques for increasing the efficiency of
data base systems while maintaining the integrity of the stored data.

Harold J. Leavitt *is Walter Kenneth Kilpatrick Professor of Organizational*
Behavior and Psychology at the Graduate School of Business, Stanford
University. Mr. Leavitt has been a vice president of the Institute for Man-
agement Sciences, adviser to the National Training Labs, consultant for
the European Productivity Agency, Paris, and the Ford Foundation, and a
member of the editorial boards of such publications as the Journal of Applied
Behavioral Science *and the* Journal of Experimental Social Psychology. *He*
is the author of numerous articles and publications, among them Managerial
Psychology, *now in its fourth edition and fourteenth language. Mr. Leavitt*
has served as director of the Stanford Executive Program and co-director
of a new executive program in Asia sponsored jointly by Stanford and the
National University of Singapore.

Richard G. Linowes *is a researcher and consultant in the area of organization*
effectiveness with special interests in devising creative organizational forms
made possible through the use of the new information technologies. His
professional experience includes several years at the Washington, D.C.,
office of Arthur Andersen & Co. and a short period with Matsushita Electric
Industrial Co. in Osaka, Japan. He has been involved in consulting projects
for numerous firms from the manufacturing industries and retailing financial
services. He holds a DBA from Harvard Business School, an MS from the
University of Michigan, and an AB from Princeton.

Fred R. McFadden *is professor of information systems at the University of*
Colorado, Colorado Springs. He received his MBA from UCLA and his PhD
from Stanford. Mr. McFadden is co-author of the textbooks First Course

in Data Processing *and* Introduction to Computer Based Information Systems. *He is also the author of numerous journal articles on information systems and his text on data base management will be published shortly.*

---

*F. **Warren McFarlan** received the AB degree from Harvard College and the MBA and DBA degrees from Harvard Graduate School of Business Administration. He has been a member of the Harvard Business School Faculty since 1964, teaching courses on management control and management information systems. He taught in Harvard's International Senior Managers Program in Lausanne, Switzerland during 1973 and 1974. On his return to this country, he became Faculty Chairman of the Advanced Management Program. He was Chairman of the Business School's Executive Education Program from 1977 through June 1980. Mr. McFarlan is a director of several U.S. companies and has worked with a number of U.S. and foreign organizations on a consulting basis. He is the co-author of* Information Systems Administration, Managing Computer Based Systems, *and* Corporate Information Systems Management: The Issues Facing Senior Management *and co-editor of* Data Processing Manager's Handbook.

***James L. McKenney** is a professor at the Harvard Business School.*

***Louis H. Mertes** is senior vice president of The Continental Illinois Bank and Trust Company. He was a contributor to the book* Communications in the Twenty-First Century *and has published in the* Harvard Business Review. *Mr. Mertes has an MBA from the University of Chicago.*

***Richard L. Nolan** is chairman and co-founder of Nolan, Norton & Company, a leading international organization of counselors to management focusing on the effective management of computer-based technologies. Mr. Nolan is responsible for the strategy and direction setting activities of the firm. The author of seven books and more than 100 articles on data processing management, he has consulted with dozens of organizations worldwide including DuPont, IBM, and Digital. He is the originator of the Stages Theory for analyzing data processing growth, a theory he researched and developed while an associate professor at Harvard Business School. Before joining Harvard Business School, Mr. Nolan was a member of the U.S. Department of Defense. Using sophisticated computer modeling methodologies he was responsible for analysis of the country's defense requirements to maintain strategic mobility capability. Prior to that, he was an assistant professor at the University of Illinois, and was the financial systems manager at Boeing. Mr. Nolan has a BA in production and operations research, an MBA in organization, and a PhD in business administration from the University of Washington.*

***Harvey L. Poppel** is a senior vice president of Booz Allen & Hamilton Inc., and director of its information industry practice. Mr. Poppel consults with both leading information industry suppliers and large business users. He* *has published extensively in such periodicals as the* Harvard Business Review *and* Forbes. *He is a Certified Management Consultant and a member of the Institute of Management Consultants. Mr. Poppel has served on Booz Allen's Board of directors.*

Philip Pyburn *is assistant professor of management information systems, director of the Information Systems Research Center, and senior research associate of the Asian Management Center at the Boston University School of Management.*

John F. Rockart, *director, Center for Information Systems Research, and senior lecturer of management science, Sloan School of Management, M.I.T., has taught and conducted research within the areas of management planning and control systems and the use and management of computer-based information systems. He presently manages the research portfolio of the center, which is supported by 20 major corporations, and directs several CISR research projects. Before joining the Sloan School in 1966, Mr. Rockart spent four years with IBM. His most recent research interests are the "Critical Success Factor" concept, top managerial information use, and the management of end-user computing. He is co-author of* Computers and the Learning Process *(with Michael Scott Morton).*

Lynn M. Salerno *is an associate editor of the* Harvard Business Review. *Prior to her appointment at HBR Ms. Salerno was an editor at the Harvard University Press and director of publications for the American Bar Foundation of the American Bar Association. She has a PhD from the University of Chicago and is currently writing a book called* Manager's Guide to The Information Age.

Allan H. Schmidt *has served as director of the Harvard Laboratory for Computer Graphics and Spatial Analysis from 1965 to 1982. During that time he was responsible for the development, demonstration, and dissemination of numerous computer mapping software packages which are currently used worldwide. He also has organized and conducted six international conferences concerned with the theory and application of computer graphics. He is the co-author of* Computer Images. *He is also head of a private consulting firm, Allan H. Schmidt Associates.*

Paul A. Strassmann *is vice president of strategic planning for the Information Products Group of the Xerox Corporation. Prior to this appointment he served for 20 years in progressively increasing responsibilities for information resource management in the Xerox Corporation, Kraft, and General Foods. As general manager of the information services division of Xerox he had direct responsibility for data centers, telecommunications networks, management services, and administrative systems.*

James D. Suver *is a professor at the University of Colorado. He is co-author* *of "Where Does Zero Based Budgeting Work?," which appeared in the* Harvard Business Review.

Hirotaka Takeuchi *is a professor at the Harvard Business School.*

Michael E. Treacy, *assistant professor of management science, Sloan School of Management, M.I.T., focuses his teaching and research on decision support systems, information requirements for senior managers, and the role of staff in supporting executive management processes. He has special interests in the design and use of organization-wide support systems that provide common data and analytic tools to both staff and managers. In addition, he is tracking and forecasting developments in decision support system generators. Mr. Treacy received his doctorate in MIS from the Sloan School. He consults and lectures for several corporations, primarily in the areas of information support systems and the future of end user computing.*

Frederic G. Withington *is a vice president of Arthur D. Little, Inc. Mr. Withington has performed some 200 studies of virtually every aspect of information technology for many users and vendors. Since 1964 he has directed Arthur D. Little's data processing industry analysis and forecasting activities, which has led to a variety of expert witness assignments. He has written four books and over 30 articles and papers, which have been translated and published in most parts of the world. His numerous professional activities have included a visiting professorship at the Harvard Business School. Before joining Arthur D. Little, Mr. Withington was Eastern Regional Manager of Technical Services for the Burroughs Corporation, and before that he managed a programming group at the National Security Agency. He has a BA in physics from Williams College.*

Shoshanah Zuboff *is assistant professor of organizational behavior and human resource management at the Harvard Business School. Ms. Zuboff received her PhD in psychology from Harvard University. Formerly a research associate with the Sloan School of Management and the Center for Information Systems Research at M.I.T., Ms. Zuboff has consulted widely with a variety of business and nonprofit organizations. She is currently conducting research on the social and psychological implications of computer technology in the workplace. She has also published articles in* Office: Technology and People *and* Dissent.

Author Index

Subject Index